MW00562530

THE APOSTLE PAUL

THE APOSTLE PAUL

His Life, Thought, and Letters

Stanley E. Porter

WILLIAM B. EERDMANS PUBLISHING COMPANY
GRAND RAPIDS, MICHIGAN

Wm. B. Eerdmans Publishing Co.
2140 Oak Industrial Drive N.E., Grand Rapids, Michigan 49505
www.eerdmans.com

© 2016 Stanley E. Porter
All rights reserved
Published 2016

Library of Congress Cataloging-in-Publication Data

Names: Porter, Stanley E., 1956- author.
Title: The Apostle Paul: his life, thought, and letters / Stanley E. Porter.
Description: Grand Rapids: Eerdmans Publishing Company, 2016.
Includes bibliographical references and indexes.
Identifiers: LCCN 2016013133 | ISBN 9780802841148 (pbk.: alk. paper)
Subjects: LCSH: Bible. Epistles of Paul—Criticism, interpretation, etc. | Paul, the Apostle, Saint.
Classification: LCC BS2650.52 .P67 2016 | DDC 225.9/2 [B]—dc23
LC record available at https://lccn.loc.gov/2016013133

Contents

Abbreviations

AB	Anchor Bible
ABD	*Anchor Bible Dictionary* (ed. D. N. Freedman; 6 vols.; New York: Doubleday, 1992)
ASBT	Acadia Studies in Bible and Theology
BAFCS	Book of Acts in Its First Century Setting
BBR	*Bulletin for Biblical Research*
BECNT	Baker Exegetical Commentary on the New Testament
BNTC	Black's New Testament Commentaries
BS	Biblical Seminar
DPL	*Dictionary of Paul and His Letters* (ed. G. F. Hawthorne and R. P. Martin; Downers Grove, IL: InterVarsity, 1993)
ECHC	Early Christianity in Its Hellenistic Context
FFNT	Foundations and Facets: New Testament
HUT	Hermeneutische Untersuchungen zur Theologie
ICC	International Critical Commentary
JBL	*Journal of Biblical Literature*
JSNT	*Journal for the Study of the New Testament*
JSNTSup	Journal for the Study of the New Testament Supplement Series
LBS	Linguistic Biblical Studies
LCL	Loeb Classical Library
LEC	Library of Early Christianity
LNTS	Library of New Testament Studies
NCB	New Century Bible
NewDocs	*New Documents Illustrating Early Christianity* (ed. G. H. R. Horsley et al.; 10 vols. to date; North Ryde, NSW, Australia: Ancient History Documentary Research Centre, Macquarie University, 1981–)
NICNT	New International Commentary on the New Testament

NIGTC	New International Greek Testament Commentary
NIV	New International Version (1978 unless otherwise indicated)
NovT	*Novum Testamentum*
NovTSup	Novum Testamentum Supplement
NRSV	New Revised Standard Version
NTG	New Testament Guides
NTL	New Testament Library
NTM	New Testament Monographs
NTS	*New Testament Studies*
NTT	New Testament Theology
NTTS	New Testament Tools and Studies
PAST	Pauline Studies
PNTC	Pillar New Testament Commentary
RILP	Roehampton Institute London Papers
SBLDS	Society of Biblical Literature Dissertation Series
SBLSBS	Society of Biblical Literature Sources for Biblical Studies
SNTSMS	Society for New Testament Studies Monograph Series
TENT	Texts and Editions for New Testament Study
TNTC	Tyndale New Testament Commentary
WBC	Word Biblical Commentary
WUNT	Wissenschaftliche Untersuchungen zum Neuen Testament

Preface

There are many introductions to the life, thought, and letters of Paul the apostle. Some concentrate upon his life,[1] while others focus upon his thought,[2] and still others on his letters.[3] A few of them, like this book, try to integrate all three of them—including on occasion material from the book of Acts[4]—into a useful portrait of the man and what he said and thought as revealed through his letters. This book represents my best efforts to provide a comprehensive treatment of the life, thought, and letters of one of the first, and arguably the greatest, Christian theologians.

He emerged out of an unusual background, first as an overt antagonist of the very movement that he eventually embraced—or, rather, that almost literally embraced him in a most unexpected way as he was traveling with the

---

1. See F. F. Bruce, *Paul: Apostle of the Heart Set Free* (Grand Rapids: Eerdmans, 1977); and E. Lohse, *Paulus: Ein Biographie* (Munich: Beck, 1996).

2. This is typically found in Pauline theologies. Some of the most important of these are H. Ridderbos, *Paul: An Outline of His Theology* (trans. J. R. De Witt; Grand Rapids: Eerdmans, 1975); J. D. G. Dunn, *The Theology of Paul the Apostle* (Grand Rapids: Eerdmans, 1998); and T. R. Schreiner, *Paul, Apostle of God's Glory in Christ: A Pauline Theology* (Downers Grove, IL: InterVarsity, 2001). See also Michael Wolter, *Paul: An Outline of His Theology* (trans. Robert L. Brawley; Waco, TX: Baylor University Press, 2015).

3. See C. J. Roetzel, *The Letters of Paul: Conversations in Context* (5th ed.; Louisville: Westminster John Knox, 2009); and J. A. Harrill, *Paul the Apostle: His Life and Legacy in Their Roman Context* (Cambridge: Cambridge University Press, 2012).

4. There is much discussion among scholars regarding the relationship of the book of Acts to the study of Paul. This is not the place to enter into that discussion, except to say that I believe that Acts, though not a primary source in the same way as Paul's letters are for the study of Paul, is an important source regarding early Christianity. On this topic, see S. E. Porter, *The Paul of Acts: Essays in Literary Criticism, Rhetoric, and Theology* (WUNT 115; Tübingen: Mohr-Siebeck, 1999).

express purpose of destroying the movement whose founder he may well have heard teach. He used the unusual convention of writing occasional letters to churches and to some of his closest associates as the particular vehicle of conveying his immediate and deepest thoughts about God, Jesus the Christ, and other matters that he believed were of importance for his readers. He did so in the middle of pursuing an active teaching ministry that involved several major journeys throughout the wider Mediterranean world. Modern scholarship tends to disfavor use of the term "missionary journey" to describe these three major ventures, but I can think of no better term to use to describe these major efforts that catapulted early Christianity from a nascent movement within Judaism into what quickly became—I would contend, during Paul's lifetime—a movement that was increasingly and sooner rather than later separate from Judaism—at least as it was perceived by many of those who looked on with wonder and amazement and certainly suspicion. He affected not least the Romans themselves, into whose territory his message of good news, which involved God's love, redemption, and hope, through the death and resurrection of Jesus Christ, increasingly permeated until it reached the very heart of the empire.

He was at the center of this movement both as a person and through the letters that he wrote. He wrote more than the letters we have in our New Testament, although we are not certain how many letters he actually wrote. Much critical scholarship says that he wrote possibly four or more to the Corinthians, possibly two to the Romans and one to the Ephesians (besides the letter we call Ephesians), probably two or more to the Philippians, one probably to the Laodiceans, and no doubt not all of the ones that are ascribed to him in the New Testament, although others argue that he wrote at least the thirteen attributed to him even if the others were not incorporated into the final and authoritative Pauline letter canon. Through his profound letter-writing, Paul has come to be recognized, along with the ancient land manager Zenon, Cicero the statesman, and Seneca the philosopher, along with pseudo-Plato and pseudo-Demosthenes, as one of the greatest letter writers of ancient times.

As can be seen from the brief summary of some of the ideas developed further and in different ways in this volume, this book is not simply a chronicle of the opinions of others, even if I try to make a reasonable attempt to survey major positions on many if not most of the important issues in contemporary Pauline scholarship. There are a number of areas in which I endorse and even further support traditional views of Pauline scholarship. These include the number of authentic Pauline letters, the major contours of Paul's thought, essentially rejecting the so-called New Perspective on Paul, the unity of the individual Pauline letters, Rome as the place of Paul's major letter-writing imprisonment, Galatians as the first letter to be written, to name just a few.

However, there are also a number of areas in which I chart new territory in Pauline thought. I do not hesitate, even in a volume that I recognize might be used as a general introduction to Paul and even possibly as a textbook for either beginning or even advanced students of Paul, to venture out on my own. Those interested in the unique contribution to Pauline scholarship found in this volume—even if some of these areas are developed more fully in other places—will want to note my views on Paul's life and the possibility that he had at least seen and heard Jesus during the course of Jesus's earthly ministry, which made his conversion more understandable as well as profound. I also believe that Paul, not one of his closest followers or a later associate, had a major role to play in the initial gathering of the Pauline letter collection, on the basis of copies of his letters that he retained in his possession, and that the collection that we have in our Bibles roughly reflects this ordering by decreasing length within the ecclesial and personal letters. I also believe that there is significant evidence to show that pseudepigraphal authorship was not widely accepted in the ancient world and that authors then, as today, disliked others claiming authorship of their work. I take some differing views on Pauline chronology that make it easier to understand how and when Paul wrote all of the letters attributed to him. I further emphasize Paul's Greco-Roman background, while at the same time fully recognizing his Jewish heritage, and attempt to bring these together in a unique way. I also believe that there is greater continuity between the Paul we observe in and through his letters and the Paul depicted in the book of Acts.[5] The writer of Acts was not a disciple of Paul, but he certainly provides a reinforcing portrait of the work of Paul in the course of his missionary endeavors. Lastly, while recognizing the contextual and occasional nature of Paul's letters, I also wish to differentiate two major levels of his theological thought—the assumptions that he brings to his thought and the developed thoughts that elaborate his major ideas.

At one time, I had the no doubt mistaken notion that this volume would serve as a useful and up-to-date replacement for F. F. Bruce's *Paul: Apostle of the Heart Set Free*. The more I develop my own thought and the more I return to Bruce's now forty-year-old volume, the more I realize what a gem Bruce's book is. I used this book myself when I was in seminary. At the time, I found it somewhat frustrating, because Bruce essentially follows the chronology of

---

5. Helpful in the relationship between the two are T. E. Phillips, *Paul, His Letters, and Acts* (Peabody, MA: Hendrickson, 2009); and S. E. Porter, "The Portrait of Paul in Acts," in *The Blackwell Companion to Paul* (ed. S. Westerholm; West Sussex, UK: Wiley-Blackwell, 2011), 124–38. For a standard view that minimizes their relationship, see J. Knox, *Chapters in a Life of Paul* (New York: Abingdon, 1950; 2nd ed., Macon, GA: Mercer University Press, 1987); and D. A. Campbell, *Framing Paul: An Epistolary Biography* (Grand Rapids: Eerdmans, 2014).

Paul's life and comments on other issues and the letters as they fit within this chronological framework. I was used to less chronologically sensitive and more theologically and historically regimented approaches to New Testament studies, including the Pauline letters. Over the years, however, I have come to appreciate that Paul's major calling in life was as the apostle of the Gentiles who needed to travel the Mediterranean area in pursuit of spreading the good news regarding Jesus the Christ, and that this metaphor of life or journey provides an excellent way to structure discussion of Paul's letters and thought as well. However, when I undertook to write a book to challenge Bruce's effort, I found that I ended up with a different type of book and one that can never be considered a replacement of it. As a result, the basic material of this volume first appeared as two substantial chapters in another book that I coauthored with Lee Martin McDonald, *Early Christianity and Its Sacred Literature*.[6] This book was relatively short-lived (although I must admit that it sold quite a few copies), even though I strongly believe that, to this day, it is still the best introduction to the New Testament to appear possibly since James Moffatt's introduction in the late 1910s. *Early Christianity* has now long been out of print and unavailable even in print-on-demand format. I have taken and reworked this material, adding substantially in places where I think that critical discussion of Pauline thought can be usefully updated. This has led to both a general editing, including the updating of bibliography throughout, and especially the addition of a number of sizeable discussions treating recent issues in new and, I trust, provocative ways. These have been fully integrated into the texture of this volume. I have also included relatively full summaries of each of Paul's letters. One of the criticisms of the earlier iteration of this material was that there was a lack of discussion of the content of the individual letters themselves. This has now been remedied. The result, I believe, is a volume that should provide a substantial general introduction to Paul and his life, thought, and letters, but more than that, a volume that introduces and explicates some new areas in Pauline studies for a wider audience than simply scholars (though certainly including them). At the end of each chapter, I also include a stratified bibliography of sources for further reading, many but not all of which are referred to at some point in each chapter. Throughout this volume, I concentrate upon English-language sources. However, at a few (very few) points I include works in other languages (in particular, German) for those who wish to explore such sources in more detail.

I wish to thank six people or groups of people in particular for the appearance of this volume. The first is Lee Martin McDonald, my coauthor in

---

6. L. M. McDonald and S. E. Porter, *Early Christianity and Its Sacred Literature* (Peabody, MA: Hendrickson, 2000).

the initial iteration of this material, for his agreeing to work together with me on this volume, which has now developed into a separate monograph on the apostle Paul. The second is James Ernest, then of Hendrickson Publishing, now of Eerdmans, who was the initial editor of the volume, and whose editorial improvements are still to be found in this further revised volume. The third is my colleague Christopher Land, who made many very helpful comments on the manuscript, but also agreed to use a draft of this manuscript as a required text in his doctoral seminar, Pauline Studies, so that his students could read through it and offer helpful suggestions. He even devoted a portion of one class session for us to discuss the volume. The fourth is all of the students of that course on Pauline Studies at McMaster Divinity College, in particular Cynthia Chau, Parimal Christian, Caroline Schleier Cutler, Jason Jung, Seokhoon Jung, Tat Yu Lam, Ben Montoya, and Chris Stevens, along with others. I appreciate all their efforts to read critically and instructively so that the final version of this volume is much better and more useful than the earlier versions. Finally, I wish to thank two of my graduate assistants. Karl Armstrong (who was also in the Pauline Studies course) performed a thorough reading of the near-final manuscript and provided many helpful comments and suggestions. Last and most strongly, I wish to thank another graduate assistant, David Yoon, who through this process has become more of a colleague than an assistant. This manuscript would probably never have reached completion without the work on it by Dave, who performed heroic efforts of every sort to get this manuscript in shape for publication. Besides general copyediting, widespread editorial assistance, and updating and creation of bibliographical material, he utilized many of my own publications and incorporated them in various ways so as to represent my latest thought on the individual topics. Dave also added a number of passages in various places to develop the arguments as they needed to be made, as well as providing the necessary cohesive editorial glue to create a unified manuscript. Dave is also responsible for the initial drafts of the summaries of the individual letters based upon my outlines and views on the major interpretive issues—for the writing of these summaries and all else, I am greatly appreciative and thankful. I cannot, Dave, thank you enough.

I finally wish to end this preface with not just traditional and customary thanks, but heartfelt and sincere thanks for the support and encouragement of my dear wife, Wendy. Right after her encouragement of my finishing a commentary on Romans (which I did, through no small feat of her tireless efforts, the encouraging help of others, and God's grace and presence) has been her gentle prodding to finish this book on Paul. Throughout all of these ventures and adventures, she has been the greatest companion, friend, and encourager. Thank you again!

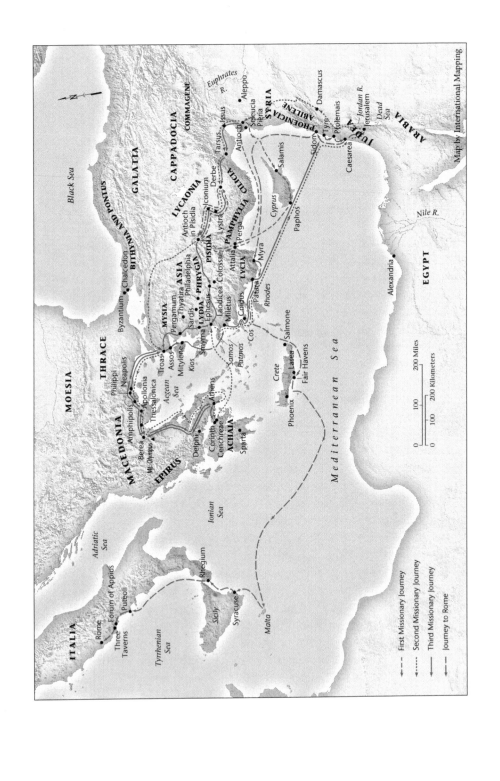

Map by International Mapping

ITALIA
Rome
Forum of Appius
Three Taverns
Puteoli
Tyrrhenian Sea
Rhegium
Sicily
Syracuse
Malta

MOESIA
THRACE
Byzantium
Chalcedon
BITHYNIA AND PONTUS
GALATIA
Black Sea

MACEDONIA
Philippi
Neapolis
Amphipolis
Apollonia
Thessalonica
Berea
Mt. Olympus
EPIRUS
Delphi
ACHAIA
Corinth
Cenchreae
Athens
Sparta
Ionian Sea
Adriatic Sea

Aegean Sea
Troas
Assos
Mitylene
Kios
MYSIA
Pergamum
Thyatira
ASIA
Sardis
Smyrna
LYDIA
Ephesus
Miletus
PHRYGIA
Laodicea
Colossae
PISIDIA
Antioch in Pisidia
LYCAONIA
Iconium
Lystra
Derbe
CAPPADOCIA
COMMAGENE
Euphrates R.
Aleppo
Tarsus
CILICIA
Issus
Antioch
Seleucia Pieria
SYRIA
Damascus
ABILENE
PHOENICIA
Sidon
Tyre
Ptolemais
Caesarea
JUDEA
Jerusalem
Jordan R.
Dead Sea
ARABIA

Samos
Patmos
Cos
Cnidus
Rhodes
LYCIA
Patara
Myra
Attalia
PAMPHYLIA
Perga
Salamis
Cyprus
Paphos

Crete
Phoenix
Lasea
Salmone
Fair Havens

Mediterranean Sea

Nile R.
Alexandria
EGYPT

200 Miles
100
0
200 Kilometers
100
0

First Missionary Journey
Second Missionary Journey
Third Missionary Journey
Journey to Rome

PART 1

The Pauline Tradition

1

Paul the Person

1. Introduction

What transformed a Jew who persecuted Christians (Phil 3:6; Acts 8:1; 9:1–2; 22:4–5; 26:9–12) into perhaps the single most important follower of Jesus Christ of his (or any) time—as theologian, writer, missionary, preacher, and church planter? No study of the early church can neglect Paul and his writings. In fact, any such study must put Paul near the center of its account, right after Jesus himself as the most important figure in the development and spread of Christianity from an initially regionally located sect of Judaism into a movement that came to be recognized, even by the Romans themselves, as a distinctive religious movement. The story of Paul's life and ministry is intriguing and enigmatic, and it continues to be so as scholars vigorously debate many of the important issues related to him, such as the most significant influences on his pre-Christian life and on his turning to belief in Jesus as the Christ, and especially the meaning and value of his letters.[1] This first chapter discusses the person of Paul, as an initial attempt to ground further discussion of his thought and writings in the realia of his life. This chapter, therefore, discusses Paul's place within the early church, his physical appearance, his upbringing and education, his relationship to the Roman Empire, his occupation, his religious and ethnic background, his conversion, his relationship to Jesus, and, finally, the relationship between the book of Acts and Paul. These various topics are

---

1. For an overview of Paul's world, or perhaps better worlds, see R. Wallace and W. Williams, *The Three Worlds of Paul of Tarsus* (London: Routledge, 1998); J. P. Sampley, ed., *Paul in the Greco-Roman World: A Handbook* (Harrisburg, PA: Trinity, 2003); and S. E. Porter, ed., *Paul's World* (PAST 3; Leiden: Brill, 2008). Each of these books addresses the complex socio-religious environment in which Paul lived and ministered.

all discussed in order to help situate Paul within his world of the first century. At points, fairly extensive footnotes are provided in order to provide guidance to subjects that are of current importance in Pauline studies.

2. The Value of Paul for the Early Church

Paul's value for the study of the New Testament can be summarized in three major points. First, Paul is probably the earliest writer of the New Testament. Some might put the book of James prior to Paul's letters.[2] Even if Paul was not the earliest, however, he certainly made the most sizable contribution at an early date. Paul is therefore the writer closest to early Christianity in terms of its most significant early events, such as the death and resurrection of Jesus Christ, which had a crucial role in the formulation of his theology. At times, Paul is concerned to make sure that his readers know that the message he proclaims, his gospel or good news regarding Jesus as the crucified and resurrected Christ, is his own and was not simply derived from others.[3] As he says in Gal 1:16–17, "I did not consult any person, nor did I go up to Jerusalem to see those who were apostles before I was" (NIV slightly altered). However, he also makes it clear that his gospel is in continuity with that of the other apostles (e.g., Gal 2:1–10, where he goes to Jerusalem to consult with the apostles; and 1 Cor 15:3–11, where he passes on tradition that he received) (see below on Paul's status as an apostle). Earliest Christianity—that is, the Christian belief and practice most closely tied to Jesus Christ and Christianity's formative events—has always occupied a privileged place in Christian history and belief, and Paul has pride of place in this hierarchy.[4]

Second, Paul is rightly known as the apostle to the Gentiles (Rom 11:13; cf. 1:5, 13; 15:16, 18; Gal 1:15–16; Acts 26:17–18).[5] He was instrumental in carving out a Gentile Christianity free from the strictures of Judaism, including obedience to the Old Testament law, especially as it was manifested in circumcision,

---

2. E.g., S. McKnight, *The Letter of James* (NICNT; Grand Rapids: Eerdmans, 2011), 37–38.

3. On the gospel or good news of Paul, see J. D. G. Dunn, "The Gospel according to St. Paul," in *The Blackwell Companion to Paul* (ed. S. Westerholm; West Sussex, UK: Wiley-Blackwell, 2011), 139–53.

4. The only other early church figure to rival Paul is Peter, and we know much more about Paul than we do about Peter, through both the book of Acts and their early writings (we have thirteen letters attributed to Paul but only two to Peter).

5. See S. F. Winter, "Paul's Attitudes to the Gentiles," in *Attitudes to Gentiles in Ancient Judaism and Early Christianity* (ed. D. C. Sim and J. S. McLaren; LNTS 499; London: Bloomsbury, 2013), 138–53.

Jewish forms of worship, the practice of food laws, and the celebration of certain feasts (see chapter 4 §3A). Christians today still live in light of Paul's thinking on such a vital issue as the relation of Christian belief to its roots in Judaism. Paul was able to carve out this Gentile ministry through the course of a number of highly interactive missionary ventures that took him well beyond Palestine, across Asia Minor, and into Europe (Macedonia and Achaia in what we now call Greece, then Italy, and possibly even Spain).[6] These ambitious adventures were instrumental in establishing and maintaining a foothold for Christianity in Europe and afforded an opportunity for Paul to compose a number of letters that, although not written primarily as works of timeless theology, are still seen to be relevant in addressing issues in contemporary Christianity.[7]

Third, Paul was the first and perhaps the greatest Christian theologian. He has often been called the second founder of Christianity,[8] a comment indicative of the crucial role that his thinking and writing played in forming early Christianity as a movement. In some senses, this statement is wrong, as Paul did not found Christianity but expanded the scope of its message. In another sense, however, it is exactly right. Paul was not the only one involved in early Christian missionary endeavors (at the commencement of his first missionary journey he was apparently under the authority of Barnabas, according to Acts 13:1–3; cf. Acts 10 and Peter's evangelization of Cornelius), but he was certainly the most successful and is now the best known. He played a sizable role in transforming Christianity from a regional religious sect of Judaism, confined to certain areas of Palestine, into a genuine world religion, and this all within his own lifetime. It is not an understatement to say that Christianity today is essentially Pauline Christianity, at least in the West.

The importance of such an individual would lead us to believe that there should be an abundance of primary material about him available for assessment. But this is simply not the case. There are two primary sources of evidence for Paul's life and ministry—his letters and the book of Acts (although many would

---

6. We do not know if Paul successfully traveled to Spain. He clearly wished to go, as Rom 15:24 and 15:28 make clear and as some early church writers believed (*1 Clement* 5.7; Muratorian fragment line 39). See R. Brown and J. P. Meier, *Antioch and Rome: New Testament Cradles of Catholic Christianity* (London: Chapman, 1983), 98n202, for defense of the likelihood of this trip.

7. See J. M. Scott, *Paul and the Nations: The Old Testament and Jewish Background of Paul's Mission to the Nations with Special Reference to the Destination of Galatians* (WUNT 84; Tübingen: Mohr-Siebeck, 1995), esp. 1–180, where he defines Paul's concept of "nations" in relation to fulfillment of the Abrahamic promise (Gen 12:3).

8. See W. Wrede, *Paul* (London: Longman Green, 1907), 179, who labeled Paul as Christianity's second founder.

minimize the importance of Acts; see §10)—though some other later sources from church history are also important. Among his letters, certainly his major letters are important sources of information about him and his thinking, but it must be remembered that they were written to specific church situations and people, and so must be interpreted before they can be used for historical reconstruction. Within any particular context, there is no compelling reason why Paul should have revealed everything about himself or the totality of what he thought about a given topic or issue. One would only expect him to state what he thought was appropriate for the situation.[9] There is the further issue, to be discussed below, of how authorship of the letters is to be evaluated. Whereas thirteen letters are attributed to Paul in the New Testament, many scholars doubt the authenticity of many of them, to the point where a number of scholars believe that only seven of them are authentic (Romans, 1–2 Corinthians, Galatians, Philippians, 1 Thessalonians, and Philemon). The second source of information regarding Paul, the book of Acts, has been evaluated in a number of ways, from a radical (and sometimes rather simpleminded) skepticism that doubts the author's integrity at every turn, to an almost naive acceptance of everything that it says. The first view dates back to the rise of higher criticism of the New Testament in the early nineteenth century, and the latter has become prominent in some circles that eschew critical study of the Bible. The discussion in this chapter places primary emphasis on Paul's letters, but I will also refer to Acts where appropriate as an important secondary source on the mission of Paul.[10]

3. Paul's Physical Appearance

On the basis of his New Testament image and abiding importance in the church, one would expect Paul to cut a dashing and impressive figure. Little is actually known, however, about what Paul looked like, even though there has been some speculation.[11] On the one hand, he is described as a "young man"

---

9. On methodology in reading the Pauline letters, see N. T. Wright, *The Climax of the Covenant: Christ and the Law in Pauline Theology* (Edinburgh: T&T Clark, 1991), esp. 4–13; cf. V. P. Furnish, "On Putting Paul in His Place," *JBL* 113 (1994): 3–17.

10. I believe that Acts was written sufficiently early so as to constitute a pertinent source for consideration. See S. E. Porter, "Was Paulinism a Thing When Luke–Acts Was Written?" in *Reception of Paulinism in Acts* (ed. D. Marguerat; Bibliotheca Ephemeridum Theologicarum Lovaniensium 229; Leuven: Peeters, 2009), 1–13, esp. 9–12.

11. A. J. Malherbe, *Paul and the Popular Philosophers* (Minneapolis: Fortress, 1989), 165–70. Cf. A. Deissmann, *St. Paul: A Study in Social and Religious History* (2nd ed.; trans. W. E. Wilson; 1927; repr. New York: Harper, 1957), 55–57.

at the death of Stephen (Acts 7:58), probably somewhere between eighteen and thirty years old. On the other hand, he refers to himself as an "old man" in Phlm 9, probably between forty and sixty (since Philemon was written by Paul a few decades after the first "appearance" of Paul in Acts 7, these two statements cohere).[12] In either case, these figures are compatible with Paul being born sometime early in the first century (AD 5–15), probably in the first decade. This would mean that he was only a slightly younger contemporary of Jesus himself (see §9).

An early noncanonical Christian text, the *Acts of Paul* (second century), refers to Paul as a small man, bald, bowlegged, ruddy in complexion, knit-browed, with a slightly long nose (§3; the text also says that sometimes he appeared as a man but at other times he had the face of an angel).[13] This text is a fairly late one for providing a "snapshot" of Paul (it claims, however, to be based on a description by Titus), but there is perhaps some confirmatory biblical evidence that Paul was not the most imposing of physical figures. In Acts 14:8–18, after performing a healing at Lystra, Paul and Barnabas are worshiped by the crowd—Barnabas as Zeus and Paul as Hermes. Zeus, the primary god of the Greek pantheon, had lightning and thunder at his disposal and would have been seen as an awe-inspiring and authoritative figure. Hermes, on the other hand, was the messenger god. There was apparently genuine respect for Hermes in this area of Asia Minor, and Paul, as spokesman, was probably rightly seen as the messenger of the group; nevertheless, Hermes was not as elegant or magnificent a god as Zeus. He was also known as the god of the rock pile, an "earthy" god not of the first rank but, rather, of the second rank of Greek gods.[14] This Lystran scene *perhaps* indicates, not only by function but also by personal appearance, that Paul was the less physically imposing of the two early Christian missionaries.

---

12. As P. van der Horst, *Ancient Jewish Epitaphs: An Introductory Survey of a Millennium of Jewish Funerary Epigraphy (300 BCE–700 CE)* (Kampen, Netherlands: Kok Pharos, 1991), 73–84, indicates on the basis of grave inscriptions in Palestine, the average age of demise of a Palestinian Jewish man in the first century AD was about twenty-nine. Therefore, anyone over thirty would have been considered old. Cf. J. D. G. Dunn, *Beginning from Jerusalem* (Christianity in the Making 2; Grand Rapids: Eerdmans, 2009), 510. There is some debate whether Phlm 9 should be understood as "old man" or "elder."

13. For the original text, see R. A. Lipsius and M. Bonnet, *Acta Apostolorum Apocrypha* (Leipzig: Mendelssohn, 1891), 237. For an English translation, see J. Bollók, "The Description of Paul in the Acta Pauli," in *The Apocryphal Acts of Paul and Thecla* (ed. J. Bremmer; Kampen, Netherlands: Kok Pharos, 1996), 1–15 at 1.

14. See W. Burkert, *Greek Religion* (trans. J. Raffan; Cambridge, MA: Harvard University Press, 1985), 156–59; cf. W. K. C. Guthrie, *The Greeks and Their Gods* (Boston: Beacon, 1950), 87–94.

Evidence from Paul's letters also implies that he cut a less than over-whelmingly impressive physical figure. In 2 Cor 10:10, Paul cites his adversaries as depicting him as a good writer but as physically unimpressive and not a good speaker: "His letters are weighty and forceful, but in person he is unimpressive and his speaking amounts to nothing" (NIV). There may be some rhetorically strategic reasons why Paul characterizes himself in such a dichotomous way, but his troubles at Corinth with adversaries and his initial failure to win the Corinthians over to his way of thinking may give evidence that, in person, he was not as impressive as he would have liked to be or as many expected him to be as a public speaker—certainly on the strength of his letters. Furthermore, in Gal 4:13–14, Paul refers twice to a physical ailment. Scholars have long debated what this ailment was, especially in light of 2 Cor 12:7–9, which refers to Paul's thorn in the flesh.[15] Most seem to accept J. B. Lightfoot's theory that Paul's thorn in 2 Cor 12 was a physical ailment, but this affliction may have been some form of spiritual disability, since Paul refers to it as a messenger of Satan that torments him.[16] In Gal 4:15, however, Paul refers to the Galatians as at one time willing to tear their eyes out for him, perhaps indicating that Paul's physical disability was bad eyesight.[17] That Paul wrote with big letters at the end of Galatians (6:11 and possibly other verses) may be an indication of poor eyesight as well.[18] In any case, Paul was apparently plagued by physical problems from fairly early on in his ministry, since Galatians is probably one of his earliest letters. These physical ailments came in conjunction with a number of other afflictions that Paul was made to suffer. In 2 Cor 11:23–28, Paul recounts a litany of abuses he suffered in the course of his ministry. Injuries seem to have been a constant feature of his ministry. These include imprisonment, beatings, exposure to death, being whipped, beatings with rods, stoning, shipwreck, subjection to physical dangers, fearing robbery, attack on ethnic grounds, general danger, betrayal, lack of sleep and food, and exposure. Since he concludes by mentioning his concern for the

---

15. J. B. Lightfoot, *St. Paul's Epistle to the Galatians: A Revised Text with Introduction, Notes, and Dissertations* (2nd rev. ed.; London: Macmillan, 1866), 183–89.

16. Cf. D. I. Yoon, "Paul's Thorn and His Gnosis: Epistemic Considerations," in *Paul and Gnosis* (ed. S. E. Porter and D. I. Yoon; PAST 9; Leiden: Brill, 2016), 23–43. Some might also consider this a mental disability, but this seems unlikely.

17. G. Harrop, *The Strange Saints of Corinth* (Hantsport, NS: Lancelot, 1992), 62–63. However, this language may reflect an ancient idiom regarding giving someone one's eyes. See D. J. Moo, *Galatians* (BECNT; Grand Rapids: Baker, 2013), 286.

18. Moo, *Galatians*, 282–83, 392. I agree with Moo that it is unlikely that Paul writes in large letters because he is angry. It is more likely that he writes in this way because of his eyesight, as well as not being trained as a scribe.

churches and since this is in a context of creating a counterboast to his Corinthian opponents, there may well be some rhetorical embellishments here. The kinds of things he recounts, however, are compatible with what is known from Paul's other letters and especially from Acts. Such experiences as receiving thirty-nine lashes, being stoned and shipwrecked, and being imprisoned all must have taken a terrible physical toll on him over the years. When Paul tells the Galatians that he bears the marks of Jesus (Gal 6:17), he is probably referring to the numerous beatings he received during his ministry, and this would inevitably have taken a toll on his body.

4. Paul's Upbringing and Education

Paul first appears in Acts at the stoning of Stephen, where Acts says that "the witnesses laid their clothes at the feet of a young man named Saul" (7:58 NIV) and that "Saul [Paul] was there, giving approval to his death" (8:1 NIV). We see that Paul is already an adult (even if a young man), and his letters are the products of his ministry after his conversion. Paul, however, had a life before reaching adulthood, even if there seems to be scant evidence of his upbringing and education. Paul does not mention his past very much or in specific detail in his letters, but a number of retrospective statements in his letters, as well as Acts, can be drawn upon to give some idea of his background.

Few scholars doubt that Paul was born in Tarsus, a significant city in the region of Cilicia (Acts 21:39; 22:3; cf. Strabo, *Geography* 14.5.13), although the fourth-century church father Jerome posited that Paul was actually born in the town of Gischala in Galilee and that Paul's parents moved the family to Tarsus when he was very young.[19] (If true, this would have some important implications for Paul's purported Roman citizenship; see §5; it may also have been suggested to reinforce Paul's Hebraic or Jewish roots.) Jerome gives no ostensible reason or evidence (except for an unknown source) as to why he would claim Paul's origin in Galilee instead of Tarsus, although those who side with Jerome presume he had good reasons for asserting as he did. Some scholars question Paul's Tarsian birth because of there being no other attestation to it outside of Acts, even in his own letters, and claim that the reason

---

19. Jerome (*De Virus Illustribus* [Patrologia Latina 23.646]), however, does not provide convincing reasons why he would contradict the accounts in Acts. He is followed by J. Murphy-O'Connor, *Paul: His Story* (Oxford: Oxford University Press, 2003), 2; and J. D. Tabor, *Paul and Jesus: How the Apostle Transformed Christianity* (New York: Simon & Schuster, 2012), 233, but they simply accept Jerome's statement at face value over Luke's accounts in Acts.

why Acts has Tarsus as his birthplace, and hence makes Paul to be a Roman citizen, is so that its Roman readers would see Paul as a noble figure worthy of their attention.[20]

In any case, Tarsus, a city with a long history, probably was founded sometime in the late third or early second millennium BC.[21] It was saved by Alexander the Great from destruction by the retreating Persians in 333 BC. The Romans gave it increased privileges, including political self-rule, and it had established itself as an important cultural center. Its population at the time of Paul's birth was probably around half a million. Tarsus was a university town just slightly behind the class of such cities as Alexandria and Athens as centers of learning. It was especially flourishing at the time of Paul's youth, although it apparently declined later in the century. Well-known rhetoricians and philosophers made their way to Tarsus, but we do not know if Paul ever heard any of them speak.

As a Greco-Roman city, Tarsus would have had a Greco-Roman educational system. This probably consisted of two tracks, organized on social lines. The first track consisted of elementary school and was for those of the lower social orders, including slaves. The second track consisted of grammar school and rhetorical training and was for those of status or the upper class. The latter received their elementary education either at home or in the initial stages of their grammatical education. Elementary education taught students how to read, write (including some basic letter-writing), and do basic mathematics. The second track of education began with the *grammaticus*, or grammar teacher, and, once basic reading and writing were mastered, consisted of reading and memorizing the major classical authors, especially Homer and Euripides. At this stage the student would learn grammar and how to compose essays and letters, besides studying other subjects, such as geometry and music. The second stage of elite education took place in the gymnasium, where the student studied rhetoric under the guidance of philosopher-teachers, for the purpose of becoming a good citizen.[22]

---

20. S. E. Porter, "The Portrait of Paul in Acts," in *The Blackwell Companion to Paul* (ed. S. Westerholm; West Sussex, UK: Wiley-Blackwell, 2011), 124–38, esp. 128. Cf. also S. E. Porter, *The Paul of Acts: Essays in Literary Criticism, Rhetoric, and Theology* (WUNT 115; Tübingen: Mohr-Siebeck, 1999), 98–101, 189–206.

21. J. McRay, *Paul: His Life and Teaching* (Grand Rapids: Baker, 2003), 21–25. See also M. Hengel with R. Deines, *The Pre-Christian Paul* (trans. J. Bowden; London: SCM, 1991), 4–6; and U. Schnelle, *Apostle Paul: His Life and Theology* (trans. M. E. Boring; Grand Rapids: Eerdmans, 2005 [2003]), 58–60.

22. Greco-Roman education is a subject of great discussion in current New Testament scholarship. For important treatments representing the most recent thought, see A. D. Booth,

It is difficult to know the extent of Paul's exposure to this educational system. Scholars argue everything from Paul having left Tarsus before participating in any of the Greek educational system to Paul having completed the entire course of education all the way through to the gymnasium and formal rhetorical training. There is evidence that Paul had some education in Greek thought, but it is also possible that he received this in Jerusalem, since Palestine was a part of the larger Greco-Roman world and had access to Greek thinking even if it did not have the same formal educational system (it was only in the second century AD and beyond that Judaism renounced connections with Greek culture and language).[23] The rabbinic rules concerning education correspond surprisingly well with the Greek system. In light of the precedence of the Greek sources and the Hellenistic influence on Palestine before the development of even the antecedents of rabbinic Judaism, it is possible that the prescribed system of Jewish education took its formative influence from the Greek system.[24]

"The Schooling of Slaves in First-Century Rome," *Transactions of the American Philological Association* 109 (1979): 11–19; R. A. Kaster, "Notes on 'Primary' and 'Secondary' Schools in Late Antiquity," *Transactions of the American Philological Association* 113 (1983): 323–46; R. Cribiore, *Gymnastics of the Mind: Greek Education in Hellenistic and Roman Egypt* (Princeton: Princeton University Press, 2001); A. W. Pitts, "Hellenistic Schools in Jerusalem and Paul's Rhetorical Education," in *Paul's World* (ed. S. E. Porter; PAST 4; Leiden: Brill, 2008), 19–50; S. E. Porter, "Paul and His Bible: His Education and Access to the Scriptures of Israel," in *As It Is Written: Studying Paul's Use of Scripture* (ed. S. E. Porter and C. D. Stanley; Society of Biblical Literature Symposium 50; Atlanta: SBL, 2008), 97–124; and S. E. Porter and A. W. Pitts, "Paul's Bible, His Education, and His Access to the Scriptures of Israel," *Journal of Greco-Roman Christianity and Judaism* 5 (2008): 9–41. This is opposed to the traditional view of a tripartite educational system as described in H. I. Marrou, *A History of Education in Antiquity* (trans. G. Lamb; London: Sheed & Ward, 1956), 186–205, 242–54; D. L. Clark, *Rhetoric in Greco-Roman Education* (New York: Columbia University Press, 1957), 59–66; S. F. Bonner, *Education in Ancient Rome: From the Elder Cato to the Younger Pliny* (London: Methuen, 1977); W. V. Harris, *Ancient Literacy* (Cambridge, MA: Harvard University Press, 1989), 233–48; and R. F. Hock, "Paul and Greco-Roman Education," in *Paul in the Greco-Roman World: A Handbook* (ed. J. P. Sampley; Harrisburg, PA: Trinity, 2003), 198–227.

23. See M. Hengel, *Judaism and Hellenism: Studies in Their Encounter in Palestine during the Early Hellenistic Period* (trans. J. Bowden; Philadelphia: Fortress, 1974), the classic work on this topic; supplemented by Hengel's *Jews, Greeks, and Barbarians: Aspects of the Hellenization of Judaism in the Pre-Christian Period* (trans. J. Bowden; London: SCM, 1980); and *The "Hellenization" of Judaea in the First Century after Christ* (trans. J. Bowden; London: SCM, 1989). On Paul as a Diaspora Jew (although perhaps not as accurate regarding Paul's acculturation and accommodation to Hellenization), see J. M. G. Barclay, "Paul among Diaspora Jews: Anomaly or Apostate?" *JSNT* 60 (1995): 89–120.

24. In a related area, rhetoric, D. Daube, "Rabbinic Methods of Interpretation and Hellenistic Rhetoric," *Hebrew Union College Annual* 22 (1940): 239–64, shows that rabbinic methods of interpretation derived from Hellenistic rhetoric.

The Jewish educational system also consisted of two major stages. From ages five to twelve the student began the study of Scripture and then of the legal traditions (Mishnah, tractate 'Abot 5.21). Josephus notes that the law and the traditions were taught in every city to Jewish boys "from our first consciousness" (*Against Apion* 2.18 LCL), as does Philo (*On the Embassy to Gaius* 210). At age thirteen, the boy became a bar mitzvah, or "son of the commandment," and took upon himself the full obligation of the law. The youths with more educational promise would have needed to be sent to Jerusalem to study under more advanced teachers, since there is no textual or archeological evidence of availability of any advanced instruction equivalent to what became the rabbinic school in any city except for Jerusalem before AD 70. That Paul may have been educated in such a way is posited on the basis of Paul's argument in Rom 7, where he speaks of an age of innocence (7:9), followed by one of knowledge (7:9–11), and then one of responsibility (7:15–21), corresponding to the periods outlined above.[25] It is difficult to substantiate from this passage, however, that Paul was educated in this way. Many who emphasize Paul's Jewish education, however, believe that it may have been at the age of thirteen that Paul went to Jerusalem to continue his education under Gamaliel, possibly living with his own married sister there (Acts 23:16).[26]

The question of where Paul was educated is raised directly in Acts 22:3. How this verse is rendered, however, drastically influences how this question is answered. There are three ways in which this verse has been interpreted and hence translated, depending upon how one understands the word "this" and the word "and" or "but" at the beginning of the second clause. The first interpretation has Paul saying he is a Jew, "born in Tarsus of Cilicia, brought up in this city, educated at the feet of Gamaliel," with three separate clauses, the second of which is left ambiguous (is "this city" referring to Tarsus or Jerusalem?). This solution does not answer the question. The author of Acts may intentionally have left the passage ambiguous because he did not know where or when Paul was educated, but this is not the most likely way that he would have communicated this. The second interpretation has Paul saying he is a Jew, "born in Tarsus of Cilicia, but brought up in this city [Jerusalem], educated at the feet of Gamaliel," with perhaps Paul physically pointing to his surroundings, Jerusalem, where he made the utterance. This is the most com-

25. See W. D. Davies, *Paul and Rabbinic Judaism: A Comparison of Patterns of Belief* (4th ed.; Philadelphia: Fortress, 1980), 23–31; assessed by S. E. Porter, "The Pauline Concept of Original Sin, in Light of Rabbinic Background," *Tyndale Bulletin* 41.1 (1990): 9–13.

26. On Paul's pre-Christian past, see Hengel with Deines, *Pre-Christian Paul*, esp. 59–66, including discussion of Acts 22:3.

mon understanding, reflected in the NIV, NRSV, and other translations. The third interprets the sentence to have Paul saying he is a Jew, "born in Tarsus of Cilicia and brought up in this city [Tarsus], educated at the feet of Gamaliel."

Is either of the last two interpretations more likely? Most scholars think that Paul probably grew up in Jerusalem, although the exact age of his arrival in the city is unknown.[27] The arguments for this position are several. The first is that the grammar of Acts 22:3 seems to indicate this, with the second interpretation seen by most scholars to be the most convincing. The second is that Paul's speech here in Acts is delivered in a context where a conscious effort is being made to identify Paul with Jerusalem. He has just been taken into Roman custody but has been allowed to address the crowd, which has accused him of taking a Gentile, Trophimus, into the temple. It is in Paul's best interests to make sure that the Jerusalem rioters see him as identified with Jerusalem, so it is understandable that, in this speech, there is a downplaying of his ties with Tarsus and the possible corrupting influence of Gentile culture. Despite these reasons, I think that the more likely interpretation is the third. The conjunction between the first and second clauses, translated above as "but" in the second interpretation and "and" in the third, indicates a shift in condition, but not necessarily a strongly adversative relationship. As a result, Paul does not need to be shifting cities, as in option two, but merely indicating a shift from his childhood to his schooling in Tarsus (a parallel use of the same conjunction is found in Acts 16:12).[28] If this is correct, then Paul was born in Tarsus and received his grammatical education there, before moving to Jerusalem, possibly around the age of thirteen to fifteen, to receive his rabbinical education under Gamaliel.

Some may question, however, the consistency of the depiction in Acts of Paul as educated at the feet of Gamaliel in Jerusalem—how is it that Paul had apparently such a different approach to religiosity than did Gamaliel, his teacher in Jerusalem? Acts 22:3 is the only place in the New Testament where Paul is said to have been a student of Gamaliel; Paul's clear Pharisaic ties (Phil 3:5–6), however, make his association with Gamaliel highly likely.[29] Unfortunately, not much more is known of Gamaliel from biblical or extrabiblical sources. What is known indicates that, early in the rise of the Christian movement, Gamaliel was quite tolerant of it. Acts 5:38–39 reveals Gamaliel, a member of the Sanhedrin, taking a conciliatory position, apparently in keeping with the

---

27. E.g., E. J. Schnabel, *Paul the Missionary: Realities, Strategies, and Methods* (Downers Grove, IL: InterVarsity, 2008), 43.

28. Cf. Pitts, "Hellenistic Schools in Jerusalem," esp. 27–33.

29. See K. Lake and H. J. Cadbury, "English Translation and Commentary," in *The Acts of the Apostles*, part 1 of *The Beginnings of Christianity* (ed. F. J. Foakes-Jackson and K. Lake; 5 vols.; London: Macmillan, 1920–33), 4.278–79.

Pharisaic doctrine that God triumphs over human actions (Mishnah, tractate 'Abot 4.14; 3.19; cf. Josephus, *Jewish Antiquities* 13.172; 18.13). He recommends a tolerant attitude, because—so his reasoning goes—if this new movement is of God, one would not want to stand against it and hence against God himself. If it is not of God, it will fail anyway. This is a very different attitude from that of Paul, his pupil, who became an active persecutor of early Christians.[30]

Several factors must be considered regarding Paul's relation to Gamaliel. The first is simply the difference in temperament or insight between the two men. It is entirely possible that Paul, perhaps because of his youthful enthusiasm or a natural zealousness, believed that he saw the situation more clearly than his older, more mature, and, at least in his eyes, overly cautious teacher.[31] The second factor is whether Paul's persecution was directed at the same group that Gamaliel is addressing in Acts 5. Gamaliel's attitude concerns Palestinian-Jewish Christians such as Peter and the other apostles. But there is good evidence that Paul directed his persecution against Hellenistic Jewish Christians, as indicated by his role in the stoning of Stephen in Acts 8:1 and by his traveling outside Jerusalem to Damascus to persecute followers of "the Way" in Acts 9. Perhaps Paul retrospectively saw them as like those Diaspora Jews he had left behind when he came to Jerusalem to study under Gamaliel, believing that their form of Judaism was tainted and corrupt (he was probably a graduate of their educational system). After all, Paul presents himself as a legalist before his conversion (Phil 3:6), one who wanted to keep the law in its totality and not be seen in any way as accommodating to those who would do otherwise. The third factor to consider is whether Gamaliel and other Jewish leaders underwent a change of heart regarding the early Christian movement.[32] When Gamaliel made his pronouncement in Acts 5, Christianity was a new movement still essentially confined to Jerusalem. By the time of Paul's persecution of believers, however, the movement had already shown signs of spreading, perhaps resulting in a change of attitude among the Jewish hierarchy.

The evidence for Paul's having had a Jewish education is minimal; nevertheless, there is some evidence for Paul's having at least some Greco-Roman

---

30. There is a later rabbinic tradition of an unnamed pupil of Gamaliel who disputed with him. Some think that this was Paul, but there is no way of knowing who it was (Babylonian Talmud, tractate *Shabbat* 30b). For an attempt to reconstruct Gamaliel's teaching in relation to Paul's, see B. Chilton and J. Neusner, "Paul and Gamaliel," in *Historical Knowledge in Biblical Antiquity* (ed. J. Neusner, B. D. Chilton, and W. S. Green; Blandford Forum: Deo, 2007), 329–73.

31. See T. R. Glover, *Paul of Tarsus* (London: SCM, 1925), 57.

32. See R. N. Longenecker, "Acts," in *The Expositor's Bible Commentary* (ed. F. E. Gaebelein; 12 vols.; Grand Rapids: Zondervan, 1981), 9.100.

education.[33] A couple of fairly obvious and important examples include his use of the Greek letter form (see chapter 5 §1) and his clear knowledge of the Septuagint.[34] This is not clear evidence of formal training in a Greek school system, however, since the letter form was widely known and used by many who never attended school, and amanuenses or scribes were frequently employed in the production of letters.[35] Paul took full advantage of this as well (see, e.g., Rom 16:22, where Tertius mentions himself by name), so he himself would not have required formal training beyond the grammar school level. A second type of evidence would be his quotation of extrabiblical authors.[36] Here there is a surprising lack of widespread primary evidence from Paul's letters. Paul is quoted as citing the fourth-century BC poet Aratus in Acts 17:28 (*Phaenomena* 5; cf. Cleanthes, *Hymn to Zeus*, line 4) and the sixth-century BC poet Epimenides in Titus 1:12. The only quotation in a major Pauline letter, however, is from the play *Thais* by the third-century BC dramatist Menander, cited at 1 Cor 15:32: "Let us eat and drink, for tomorrow we die" (NIV). But this quotation is generally thought to have been part of the shared common knowledge of the time, much like "To be or not to be"—from Shakespeare's *Hamlet*—which many people might quote without having studied (or even read) any of Shakespeare's plays. Or it may have been one of many individual quotations contained within a quotation book used in grammar school education.[37]

A third piece of evidence for Paul's Greek education might be his use of forms of classical rhetoric.[38] This is a topic of widespread discussion in New

33. Schnelle, *Apostle Paul*, 63–69. Citing K. Haacker, "Zum Werdegang des Apostels Paulus," *Aufstieg und Niedergang der römischen Welt* 26.2:824–26, Schnelle states that Paul must have had at least some exposure to Latin education as well, since in Rom 13:1–7 and Phil 3:20 he thinks in the categories of the Roman political system (cf. Hengel with Deines, *Pre-Christian Paul*, 10, who thinks Paul knew some Latin as well). See chapter 10 §2D1 and chapter 11 §2A.

34. Schnelle, *Apostle Paul*, 108–11. For more detail, see C. D. Stanley, *Paul and the Language of Scripture: Citation Technique in the Pauline Epistles and Contemporary Literature* (SNTSMS 74; Cambridge: Cambridge University Press, 1992).

35. See E. R. Richards, *The Secretary in the Letters of Paul* (WUNT 2/42; Tübingen: Mohr-Siebeck, 1991); J. Murphy-O'Connor, *Paul the Letter-Writer: His World, His Options, His Skills* (Collegeville, MN: Liturgical, 1995), 1–6; and H.-J. Klauck, *Ancient Letters and the New Testament* (Waco, TX: Baylor University Press, 2006), 55–60.

36. See, e.g., E. B. Howells, "St. Paul and the Greek World," *Greece and Rome* 11 (1964): 7–29, who deals with explicit and implicit quotations, among other evidence of Paul's Greek education.

37. These quotation books are known from copies of exercises that we have on papyrus and from references by authors, such as Quintilian.

38. For important definitions of terms, see L. M. McDonald and S. E. Porter, *Early Christianity and Its Sacred Literature* (Peabody, MA: Hendrickson, 2000), 30–32; cf. D. L. Stamps, "Rhetorical Criticism of the New Testament: Ancient and Modern Evaluations of Argumen-

Testament scholarship over the last few decades. A number of scholars argue that Paul avails himself of the full range of tools available to a rhetorician of the time, so that his letter to the Galatians, as an example, is a form of either deliberative or judicial rhetoric, like a speech delivered by an ancient rhetorician, such as Demosthenes (fourth century BC). Two questions, however, can and must be raised regarding the rhetorical hypothesis. The first is whether this kind of rhetorical analysis of letters was something that was even known to the ancients. There is good evidence that the categories of rhetoric were used not for the analysis and examination of speeches or any writings, including letters, but only for the creation, formulation, and presentation or performance of speeches. The second question is how accessible this knowledge was to those who did not reach the higher level of the educational system, the study of rhetoric in the gymnasium. Paul does make use of several rhetorical conventions, including especially the diatribe style (e.g., Rom 1–14; 2 Cor 10-13), but this was probably not due to formal rhetorical training but because this was the way in which teachers and philosophers created arguments and carried on discussion in the ancient world.[39]

In all, the evidence of Paul progressing very far in the Greco-Roman educational system is lacking. He almost assuredly received an elementary education and may well have attended grammar school, but Paul was not trained as a rhetorician, and to examine his letters as if they are instances of ancient rhetoric is probably misguided. Nevertheless, he may well have acquired the basics of a grammar school education (in Tarsus), including a highly functional use of the Greek language, before proceeding to formal religious training.

5. Paul and the Roman Empire

Throughout the course of his missionary journeys in Acts, as well as within a number of his letters, Paul is either depicted as having or demonstrating

---

tation," in *Approaches to New Testament Study* (ed. S. E. Porter and D. Tombs; JSNTSup 120; Sheffield: Sheffield Academic, 1995), 129–69.

39. On Paul and ancient rhetoric, and why Paul's letters should not be examined as orations, see S. E. Porter, "Paul of Tarsus and His Letters," in *Handbook of Classical Rhetoric in the Hellenistic Period, 330 B.C.–A.D. 400* (ed. S. E. Porter; Leiden: Brill, 1997), 533–85; Porter, "The Theoretical Justification for Application of Rhetorical Categories to Pauline Epistolary Literature," in *Rhetoric and the New Testament: Essays from the 1992 Heidelberg Conference* (ed. S. E. Porter and T. H. Olbricht; JSNTSup 90; Sheffield: Sheffield Academic, 1993), 100–122; J. T. Reed, "Using Ancient Rhetorical Categories to Interpret Paul's Letters: A Question of Genre," in *Rhetoric and the New Testament*, 292–324; and P. H. Kern, *Rhetoric and Galatians: Assessing an Approach to Paul's Epistle* (SNTSMS 101; Cambridge: Cambridge University Press, 1998).

knowledge of the Roman Empire. Two issues regarding the relationship between Paul and the Roman Empire are prominent: the nature of his citizenship
and his response to the ubiquitous emperor cult. The question of whether Paul
was a Roman citizen is complicated by two considerations.[40] The first is how
one defines citizenship. The other is that explicit claims to Roman citizenship
by Paul appear in only Acts, never in his letters.

There were several different levels of citizenship in the Roman Empire:
one could, for example, be a citizen of the Roman state, a citizen of a particular city, or a member of one of the orders or "tribes" of citizens. The word
Paul uses to describe his being a citizen of Tarsus in Acts 21:39 could refer to
any one of these levels. In Acts 16:38 and 22:25, Paul makes the explicit claim
to being a Roman citizen. Some scholarship on Acts argues that it is not a
historically based account but, rather, a literary creation (perhaps like an
ancient romance), designed to create an image of Paul as a hero of the early
church.[41] As a result, many have come to doubt Paul's citizenship of Tarsus
and his Roman citizenship. For example, John Lentz concludes that Acts is
designed to depict Paul as the ideal Greco-Roman man.[42] In a more detailed
survey of the ancient evidence, Brian Rapske shows the plausibility of a person being a citizen of a city such as Tarsus, a citizen of Rome, and a devout
Jew all at the same time. What he cannot prove absolutely is that Paul was
in fact such a person, although the probabilities weigh clearly in that direction.[43] It is perhaps surprising that in Paul's letters, even with his ministry to

40. On Roman law in general, see B. Nicholas, *An Introduction to Roman Law* (Oxford:
Clarendon, 1962); A. Watson, *The Law of the Ancient Romans* (Dallas: Southern Methodist
University Press, 1970); on the social context, see J. E. Stambaugh and D. L. Balch, *The New
Testament in Its Social Environment* (Philadelphia: Westminster, 1986). On Roman citizenship,
see A. N. Sherwin-White, *The Roman Citizenship* (2nd ed.; Oxford: Clarendon, 1973).

41. See R. Bauckham, "The Acts of Paul as a Sequel to Acts," in *The Book of Acts in Its
Ancient Literary Setting* (ed. B. W. Winter and A. D. Clarke; BAFCS 1; Grand Rapids: Eerdmans,
1993), 105–52, responding to work such as R. Pervo, *Profit with Delight: The Literary Genre
of the Acts of the Apostles* (Philadelphia: Fortress, 1987). More recent work along a similar,
though still unconvincing, line is M. P. Bonz, *The Past as Legacy: Luke–Acts and Ancient Epic*
(Minneapolis: Fortress, 2000).

42. J. C. Lentz Jr., *Luke's Portrait of Paul* (SNTSMS 77; Cambridge: Cambridge University
Press, 1993).

43. B. Rapske, *Paul in Roman Custody* (BAFCS 3; Grand Rapids: Eerdmans, 1994), 72–90.
Many Roman historians have little trouble believing that Paul was a Roman citizen. See, e.g.,
E. T. Salmon, *A History of the Roman World from 30 B.C. to A.D. 138* (6th ed.; London: Routledge, 1968), 196n1; R. Wallace and W. Williams, *The Acts of the Apostles* (London: Duckworth,
1993), 10; and the classic and still valuable studies by A. N. Sherwin-White, *Roman Society and
Roman Law in the New Testament* (Oxford: Clarendon, 1963), 144–93, and *Roman Citizenship*,
273, who provides much documentation on this issue.

the Gentile world, he does not mention his origin in Tarsus, his citizenship of Tarsus, or his Roman citizenship. This may be because, for Paul, his most important citizenship was "in heaven" (Phil 3:20). But the argument that Paul was neither a Roman citizen nor born in Tarsus because he does not mention it in his letters is, finally, an argument from silence and does not hold much weight. It seems probable, then, especially in light of the way this evidence is used in Acts, that he was a full citizen of Tarsus and of Rome on the basis of his family origins.[44]

How was it that Paul's family secured Roman citizenship? The two most illustrative passages in Acts regarding Paul's citizenship are 16:37-39 and 22:25-29. In the first, after being imprisoned overnight in Philippi and then released, Paul raises the question whether his treatment has been legal for a Roman citizen. As he says in 16:37: "They beat us publicly without a trial, even though we are Roman citizens" (NIV), at which point the Philippian penal hierarchy gets very concerned. In the second, after Paul has been taken into Roman custody in Jerusalem and the commander has ordered that he be beaten, Paul raises the question whether it is legal for a Roman citizen to be treated in such a way: "As they stretched him out to flog him, Paul said to the centurion standing there, 'Is it legal for you to flog a Roman citizen who hasn't even been found guilty?'" (22:25 NIV). The centurion immediately reports this to his superior. When the commander arrives to sort out this potential difficulty, he tells Paul that his citizenship was purchased at a great price, while Paul responds by stating that he inherited his (22:28).

At the time of these episodes, there had been a general expansion of Roman citizenship. By the middle of the first century BC, the entire population of the Italian peninsula had been made Roman citizens. By the middle of the first century AD, there was a sizable number of citizens throughout the empire, and in 212 an edict was issued that made all free inhabitants of the empire citizens.[45] In the course of this expansion, there were several ways in which Roman citizenship could be acquired: it could be given to slaves who were manumitted, be bestowed for various reasons, including performing valuable services to the empire either in the military or otherwise, be purchased for a large sum, or be inherited from a father who was a citizen.[46] Least likely

---

44. See S. A. Adams, "Paul the Roman Citizen: Roman Citizenship in the Ancient World and Its Importance for Understanding Acts 22:22-29," in *Paul: Jew, Greek, and Roman* (ed. S. E. Porter; PAST 5; Leiden: Brill, 2008), 309-26.

45. See Wallace and Williams, *Acts of the Apostles*, 25; and Watson, *Law of the Ancient Romans*, 29.

46. The money did not actually go toward the purchase of citizenship but to paying off various officials in the process. The amount of five hundred drachmas apparently was common

of these possibilities is that Paul acquired citizenship through his ancestors' military service.[47] Instead, some think that, being in the tent-making business, Paul's father or grandfather may have performed valuable service to the Roman Empire and been awarded citizenship that Paul inherited; others speculate that one of Paul's relatives had purchased citizenship. It simply cannot be said for certain how Paul's citizenship was secured, although he possessed it from birth and did not himself acquire it.[48]

Simply invoking his citizenship, however, did not necessarily mean that Paul would immediately receive special treatment. It was more difficult in the ancient world to carry substantial proof of citizenship, especially when a person was away from a place where he or she may have been known or where family archives were kept. Paul may have carried some form of passport that citizens possessed, perhaps the kind of document that would have been found among Paul's scrolls. Citizens often carried small tablets that specified their status. As can be imagined, documentation indicating Roman citizenship would have been valuable in the Roman world, so there were many incidents of forgery, with severe penalties if discovered. A wise commander would not have necessarily accepted the documentation at face value but would probably have tried to secure some proof that the documents were genuine by, for example, intensively interrogating Paul. During a public scuffle as seen in several of Paul's arrests and events leading up to his arrests, this type of intense and detailed questioning was probably not possible for the tribune. Some claim that Paul's not stopping multiple beatings (e.g., 2 Cor 11:24–25) by invoking his citizenship proves that he was not a legitimate citizen of Rome. It should be noted, however, that some of these beatings were at the hands of his fellow Jews, who probably did not give his Roman citizenship any recognition, and that, though citizens were protected from receiving that type of punishment, this was not always observed, and there are cases where that part of the law was simply ignored.[49] Being a Roman citizen entailed

---

according to some later sources, roughly the equivalent of two years' wages for an average day laborer (Dio Chrysostom 34.21–23). Cf. Hengel with Deines, *Pre-Christian Paul*, 5; Schnelle, *Apostle Paul*, 60; and H. Omerzu, *Der Prozess des Paulus: Eine exegetische und rechtshistorische Untersuchung der Apostelgeschichte* (Beihefte zur Zeitschrift für die neutestamentliche Wissenschaft 115; Berlin: de Gruyter, 2002), 28–39.

47. Josephus notes that, in the first century BC, many Jews acquired Roman citizenship and also received exemption from military service by the consul Lucius Lentulus (*Jewish Antiquities* 14.228–40; cf. also Hengel with Deines, *Pre-Christian Paul*, 11).

48. See Rapske, *Paul in Roman Custody*, 72–90.

49. Just because the law existed does not mean that everyone followed it; cf. Schnelle, *Apostle Paul*, 61; and Hengel with Deines, *Pre-Christian Paul*, 7, who note the following examples: Josephus (*Jewish War* 2.308), who notes that the procurator Gessius Florus scourged

a number of privileges, including the right to a public accusation and trial, exemption from certain kinds of punishment—in most instances including crucifixion—and protection against summary execution. A Roman citizen had the right of appeal, although in times of civil unrest this right may have been abrogated. It does not appear that a citizen necessarily had the right to appeal to Caesar to have his case heard. In any event, an appeal probably would not have been heard by Caesar but, rather, by some judicial official appointed by him.[50]

The Roman citizenship of Paul's family raises the question whether his family performed Roman religious rites, such as worship of the emperor as a god. Would this account for Paul's leaving Tarsus? Several factors must be considered here. First, one must recognize that Diaspora Judaism was a complex and diverse phenomenon, in many ways integrated into the surrounding religio-cultural milieu, even if not fully acculturated. This does not mean that the Jews were not in many instances respected for their high moral standards and their belief in God, as the existence of Godfearers in Acts bears witness (10:2, 22, 35; 13:16, 26, 43, 50; 16:14; 17:4, 17; 18:7),[51] but Judaism in the larger Greco-Roman world was merely one of a number of religious and cultural minorities, with various levels of acculturation and assimilation.[52] Second, the institutionalization of Roman emperor worship as something that was compelled of citizens did not occur until the second century. Augustus was cautious in his tolerance of the emperor cult, allowing those in the East to

---

and crucified Jerusalem Jews who had the same status as Roman knights (*equites*); Suetonius (*Galba* 9), who tells of Galba, a governor of the province of Hispania Tarraconensis, crucifying a Roman citizen; and Cicero (*In Verrem* 2.5.161–67), who tells of spurning Verres for whipping and crucifying Roman citizens.

50. See F. F. Bruce, *Paul: Apostle of the Heart Set Free* (Grand Rapids: Eerdmans, 1977), 363–67, for documentation of the above statements. In fact, Nero had made it clear that he would not himself hear cases (Tacitus, *Annals* 13.4.2).

51. Some scholars doubt the veracity of Acts regarding the existence of Godfearers. However, their credibility is shown by I. Levinskaya, *The Book of Acts in Its Diaspora Setting* (BAFCS 5; Grand Rapids: Eerdmans, 1996), esp. 51–126; cf. J. Reynolds and R. Tannenbaum, *Jews and Godfearers at Aphrodisias* (Cambridge: Cambridge Philological Society, 1987).

52. See J. M. G. Barclay, *Jews in the Mediterranean Diaspora: From Alexander to Trajan (323 BCE–117 CE)* (Edinburgh: T&T Clark, 1996), for a thorough and detailed study. He notes (p. 10) that there are only five locations of Diaspora Judaism with sufficient evidence for detailed study: Egypt, Cyrenaica, the province of Syria, the province of Asia, and Rome. Although he notes some very telling religious phenomena, such as apparent worship of Pan by Jews at El-Kanais in Egypt (pp. 99–100), there is further evidence worth considering, including praise to "the gods" in a Jewish papyrus from Egypt (C.Pap.Jud. I 4 = P.Cair.Zen. I 59076 [257 BC], reprinted in J. L. White, *Light from Ancient Letters* [FFNT; Philadelphia: Fortress, 1986], no. 16, pp. 39–40). See also a Dacian bilingual curse tablet (*NewDocs* 2.12).

engage in it more freely than those in the West, where Romans would have been less willing to proclaim the deity of the emperor. At the time of Jesus Christ's birth, this kind of worship would probably have been, at most, optional, so there would have been no compelling reason for the Jews to have performed these kinds of rituals. In any event, Jews had previously served foreign military leaders on several occasions. During the period of Seleucid rule, they were hired on a few occasions as mercenaries, and Jewish officers had served various rulers. Third, the Jews in Greco-Roman cities may have been separated into their own order or tribe (the citizenry of a Greco-Roman city were divided into orders for management of the city's affairs). This would have meant that they had a degree of autonomy and self-government that allowed them to follow some of their own religious practices. Despite the last two considerations, Paul might have perceived moral and religious laxity among Jews in Tarsus, and this may have been a factor compelling him to go to Jerusalem to train to be a Pharisee under Gamaliel. Since Jerusalem was the religious center of Judaism, he might have viewed it as free from the perceived corruption of the Diaspora.

A connected question scholars try to answer, in relation to Paul and the Roman Empire, is how significant the empire was to Paul and how much it influenced the writing of his letters. This question is discussed by scholars such as Richard Horsley, John Barclay, John Harrison, and N. T. Wright, among others.[53] Another way to ask this question might be: What was Paul's relationship to Roman imperialism, especially the emperor cult?[54] Most notably, Wright and Barclay take opposing viewpoints in answer to this question.[55] Wright proposes that the empire was indeed significant for Paul on the basis of Paul's quite frequently using imperial terminology (though Wright calls them "key words") in his letters, words like "lord" (κύριος), "savior" (σωτήρ), "coming"

---

53. R. A. Horsley, ed., *Paul and Empire: Religion and Power in Roman Society* (Harrisburg, PA: Trinity, 1997); J. M. G. Barclay, *Pauline Churches and Diaspora Jews* (WUNT 275; Tübingen: Mohr-Siebeck, 2011), 363–88; J. R. Harrison, *Paul and the Imperial Authorities at Thessalonica and Rome: A Study in the Conflict of Ideology* (WUNT 273; Tübingen: Mohr-Siebeck, 2011); N. T. Wright, *Paul: In Fresh Perspective* (Minneapolis: Fortress, 2005), 50–79; "Paul and Empire," in *The Blackwell Companion to Paul* (ed. S. Westerholm; West Sussex, UK: Wiley-Blackwell, 2011), 285–97; and *Paul and the Faithfulness of God* (2 vols.; Christian Origins and the Question of God 4; Minneapolis: Fortress, 2013), 2.1271–1319. For a good recent history of scholarship on Paul and Empire, see Barclay, *Pauline Churches*, 364–67.

54. For a more detailed outworking of this question, see S. E. Porter, "Paul Confronts Caesar with the Good News," in *Empire in the New Testament* (ed. S. E. Porter and C. L. Westfall; McMaster New Testament Studies; Eugene, OR: Wipf & Stock, 2011), 164–96.

55. Others have contributed to this discussion, but I will interact primarily with these two in this section. A helpful collection of essays is found in Horsley, ed., *Paul and Empire*.

(παρουσία), "good news" (εὐαγγέλιον), and "righteousness" (δικαιοσύνη),[56] used according to Richard Hays's categories of allusion and echo.[57] Wright then turns to individual texts, beginning with Phil 3:20–21, which is probably one of the "obvious points" at which to begin, and shows how this so-called imperial vocabulary is evident. Paul tells the Philippian believers that their citizenship is in heaven and uses words like "savior" and "lord," which are "classic Caesar-titles" that readers would have immediately associated with the empire.[58] Wright then turns to 1 Thess 4 and sees words like "coming meeting" (παρουσία ἀπαντήσις) as Paul again using imperial vocabulary. In 1 Cor 15, Paul talks about the resurrection of Jesus "as inaugurating that period of history which is characterized by the sovereign rule of Jesus which will end with the destruction of all enemies, putting all things under his feet—echoing the same psalms to which Paul alludes in Philippians 3.21."[59] Wright surveys Galatians, Ephesians, and Romans and finds that these letters, too, share imperial language. A major problem, however, is that Wright seems to exaggerate the effects of the use of imperial vocabulary.[60] Furthermore, to call those words—"lord," "savior," "coming," "gospel," and "righteousness"—imperial, for example, seems to be overreaching, as these words appear frequently in the documentary papyri as mundane words.[61] Barclay, on the other hand, argues that the empire was not significant for Paul (see the earlier comment on Phil 3:20). His critique of Wright's claim that Paul used imperial language is to the point: "The notion that Paul found it necessary to write in code is without historical foundation; and since the text itself gives no indication of any such thing, we may dismiss the suggestion as a fantasy."[62] Rather, Barclay states that, for Paul, the empire was insignificant; in the scope of the "drama of history," the Roman Empire would not play the role of a significant actor. For Paul,

56. Wright, *Paul: In Fresh Perspective*, 70–71. Cf. also Wright, *Paul and the Faithfulness of God*, 2.1294.

57. R. B. Hays, *Echoes of Scripture in the Letters of Paul* (New Haven: Yale University Press, 1989). Reiterated in Hays, *The Conversion of the Imagination: Paul as Interpreter of Israel's Scripture* (Grand Rapids: Eerdmans, 2005).

58. Wright, *Paul: In Fresh Perspective*, 71.

59. Wright, *Paul: In Fresh Perspective*, 75.

60. Barclay, *Pauline Churches*, 370.

61. As James Barr said earlier, "The linguistic bearer of the theological statement is usually the sentence and the still larger literary complex and not the word or the morphological and syntactical mechanisms"; *The Semantics of Biblical Language* (Oxford: Oxford University Press, 1961), 269. There is also the possibility that Wright is committing the fallacy that Barr labels illegitimate totality transfer, in which Wright is illegitimately transferring the total (anti-imperial) meaning he sees in these words on each of Paul's uses.

62. Barclay, *Pauline Churches*, 382.

Rome was not new, not different, not epoch making; Rome did not rule the world, the God of Jesus Christ did.[63] When Paul talks about the powers and rulers of this world, he is not simply referring to Caesar or Rome, but to all individual, social, political, and cosmic powers that exist.[64] Paul, as a faithful Jew, would have been expected not to worship at the feet of Caesar, and this he makes explicit and clear in his letters, not implicitly through allusion and echo.

A mediating position seems to capture Paul's attitude toward the Roman Empire as revealed in his writings. While Paul was not preoccupied with Rome as the sovereign power of the day, he did acknowledge and live within the empire, which was pervasive in its culture and social backdrop to the developing Christian movement. There are various passages in Paul's letters for analysis, but the main ones that directly reveal his attitude are in Rom 13:1–7; 1 Cor 7; and 2 Cor 8. The first, Rom 13:1–7, is concerned with obedience to the state, in which Paul commands obedience only to just authorities, not to all authorities in an unqualified way.[65] This might well include obedience to a Rome that was still relatively stable and just, before Nero's later insanity set in. First Cor 7 is concerned with regulations concerning marriage and divorce of Christians within the Roman legal system. Second Cor 8 suggests a divine hierarchy instead of the Roman institutional hierarchy.[66] In these passages, Paul does not advocate a rejection of hierarchy, but does endorse the proper kind of hierarchy. Paul engages in empirical replacement, whereby the imperial cult that originated with the patronage and beneficence of the emperor and was translated down through the authority structures to the common people was not eliminated, but was replaced by a divine hierarchy. The divine hierarchy originates with the one true God, whose son the Lord Jesus Christ commanded and worked through Paul to the church at Corinth and through them to other saints. Paul was not necessarily a "counterimperial" theologian,[67] nor did he completely deny the empire; he recognized that while the empire was an earthly authority of some power, the true authority over him and his fellow believers was the God of Jesus Christ, and their allegiance was to be toward him, not Caesar.

---

63. Barclay, *Pauline Churches*, 386.

64. Barclay, *Pauline Churches*, 383.

65. See S. E. Porter, "Romans 13:1–7 as Pauline Political Rhetoric," *Filología Neotestamentaria* 3.6 (1990): 115–39; cf. Porter, *The Letter to the Romans: A Linguistic and Literary Commentary* (NTM 37; Sheffield: Sheffield Phoenix, 2015), 243–50.

66. Porter, "Paul Confronts Caesar." The rest of this paragraph is taken from p. 192 of this essay.

67. Wright, *Paul and the Faithfulness of God*, 2.1306. See R. Saunders, "Paul and the Imperial Cult," in *Paul and His Opponents* (ed. S. E. Porter; PAST 2; Leiden: Brill, 2005), 227–38, who also takes somewhat of a mediating view.

6. Paul's Occupation and Early Christian Social Status

There is abundant evidence that Paul worked as some form of craftsman or leather worker (Acts 18:3; 1 Cor 4:12; cf. 1 Thess 2:9; 2 Cor 12:14).[68] This has traditionally been taken to mean that he was a tentmaker, but this may be too restrictive. Someone of his trade probably worked with all sorts of materials, making not only tents but sails for boats, canopies for theaters, and various forms of military equipment. A person in this line of work was probably considered to be skilled and hence above the social level of the general populace, which was engaged in menial or physical labor on the land, although there is much debate on whether a tentmaker was considered to be a lower-level occupation or lower/middle-class worker or artisan.[69] Some scholars suggest that Paul worked as a craftsman because he was a Pharisee and every Pharisee was required to have a usable trade, but the evidence for such a Pharisaic practice is not strong (cf. Mishnah, tractate 'Abot 2.2; Tosefta, tractate *Qiddushin* 1.22). A more likely explanation is that learning a skill was typical of both Jews and others throughout the Greco-Roman world. People would spend time learning a skilled trade for two or three years as an apprentice, then continue it throughout their adult lives. A skill was not only useful to Paul for providing for his material needs; it served a useful function in his missionary strategy. Paul would travel from city to city using his trade as a way of maintaining himself in his travels (as did other craftsmen and even other itinerant teachers) and of establishing and maintaining his apostolic credibility. He would often stay in the home of a convert (Acts 16:15, 40; 17:5–7; Phlm 22), working there or in a local shop (Acts 18:3, 11). Rather than be a financial burden on a local church and be mistaken for one of those disreputable itinerant teachers in the ancient world who would exploit their listeners for financial gain and then leave (cf. Lucian, *Passing of Peregrinus* 11–14; *Salaried Posts in Great Houses* 20, 37), Paul was able to point to his working with his hands instead of being a burden on the local congregation

---

68. See R. F. Hock, *The Social Context of Paul's Ministry: Tentmaking and Apostleship* (Philadelphia: Fortress, 1980), esp. 11–25.

69. R. F. Hock, "The Problem of Paul's Social Class: Further Reflections," in *Paul's World* (ed. S. E. Porter; PAST 4; Leiden: Brill, 2008), 7–18; also Hock, "Paul's Tentmaking and the Problem of His Social Class," *JBL* 97 (1978): 555–64. Hock argues that Paul saw his own craftsmanship from an aristocratic upbringing, contra T. D. Still, "Did Paul Loathe Manual Labor? Revisiting the Work of Ronald F. Hock on the Apostle's Tentmaking and Social Class," *JBL* 125 (2006): 781–95. Cf. Hengel with Deines, *Pre-Christian Paul*, 15–17, who argue that due to the many benefits of such a career in craftsmanship, it should not be considered to be a lower-class occupation.

(1 Thess 2:9). He was an early practitioner of a form of lifestyle evangelism in which he was able to inspire his listeners with his own willingness to work in his own support (4:10–12). With this flexibility of time and place in view, it is not surprising that Paul chose tentmaking as a means of supporting himself while pursuing his ministry and missionary travels.

The question of Paul's occupation raises the larger question of the socio-economic status and standing of the early Christian movement as a whole. This question continues to be debated and is directly linked to the question of the nature of early Christian social organization. Wayne Meeks was one of the first to offer a thorough social description of early Christianity.[70] In the course of his research, he noted the urban setting of early Pauline Christianity. Not only was Paul a "city person," but Pauline Christianity was a city movement. As a result, Meeks finds evidence for Christianity as reflecting the kind of social stratification found within urban environments of the first-century Roman Empire. Following the work of E. A. Judge and Abraham Malherbe,[71] as opposed to the work of Adolf Deissmann,[72] Meeks concludes that early Christianity tended to mirror the social stratification of the empire. This would mean that Christians followed what has come to be characterized as a pyramid of socioeconomic hierarchy. A very small percentage of wealthy people sit at the top; the largest group of the poor, many without even enough to provide for daily living, at the bottom; and in between various intermediate levels, such as artisans or others who we might call a middle class (though recognizing that they are not the equivalent of the modern middle class). Meeks recognizes that the New Testament evidence is occasional and ad hoc in nature. Nevertheless, by examining what is said about a number of people in the New Testament (e.g., some of those mentioned by Paul in Rom 16:1–23, such as Phoebe, Prisca and Aquila, Erastus, and Gaius; Chloe's people in 1 Cor 1:11; and Apollos in 1 Cor 1:12 and 3:1–4:6; among others), Meeks is able to posit a rough idea of the social distribution of some of those within the Pauline churches. Meeks's findings have been refined in later work, including

70. W. A. Meeks, *The First Urban Christians: The Social World of the Apostle Paul* (New Haven: Yale University Press, 1983), esp. 9–73. For a recent summary, see G. Theissen, "The Social Setting of Pauline Communities," in *The Blackwell Companion to Paul* (ed. S. Westerholm; West Sussex, UK: Wiley-Blackwell, 2011), 248–67. Related to the question of the socioeconomic status of Christians is the nature of early Christian groups, called churches. Meeks discusses this (*First Urban Christians*, 74–110). See also chapter 4 §3H.

71. See E. A. Judge, *The Social Pattern of Christian Groups in the First Century* (London: Tyndale, 1960); and A. J. Malherbe, *Social Aspects of Early Christianity* (Baton Rouge: Louisiana State University Press, 1977).

72. See Deissmann, *Paul*, 29–52.

recent discussion of his major work twenty-five years later. In this further discussion, many of Meeks's conclusions were upheld, even if some of the particular findings were disputed. One of the major results was reassessment of the distribution of those within the pyramid of socioeconomic hierarchy.[73] Not all accept these findings.

For example, Justin Meggitt argues that Christianity instead was basically a movement of the poor.[74] The major difference between Meeks and Meggitt revolves around their view of the ancient economy. Meggitt describes this as the difference between the "primitivist" and the "modernist" approaches to ancient economy.[75] In some ways, this ends up as an opposition between minimalists and maximalists. The primitivists emphasize the agrarian and preindustrial nature of the ancient economy, in which the very few landowners constituted the wealthy, and most of the others struggled with poverty.[76] The modernists find correlations between the ancient and modern economies, with the tendency to find similar patterns between modern categories and ancient functions.[77] As a result, Meggitt claims that even people who, for example, owned slaves were not necessarily wealthy, but virtually all were struggling to develop survival strategies. Most scholarship tends to find the view reflected by Meeks to be a more accurate account of the ancient Roman economy, and with it the social stratification of early Christianity.[78] It was not a movement of the wealthy, to be sure, but there were at least some within the so-called middle classes who were part of the movement. Paul as a tentmaker would

73. See especially B. W. Longenecker, "Socio-Economic Profiling of the First Urban Christians," in *After the First Urban Christians: The Social-Scientific Study of Pauline Christianity Twenty-Five Years Later* (ed. T. D. Still and D. G. Horrell; London: T&T Clark, 2009), 36–59, as well as other essays in this volume. Longenecker extends his argument regarding the socioeconomic composition of early Christianity to contend that Paul was concerned with the poor in general; *Remember the Poor: Paul, Poverty, and the Greco-Roman World* (Grand Rapids: Eerdmans, 2010). I believe that Longenecker overextends here on the basis of questionable exegesis and that Paul's vision of social justice was confined to the church. See S. E. Porter, "Reframing Social Justice in the Pauline Letters," in *The Bible and Social Justice: Old Testament and New Testament Foundations for the Church's Urgent Call* (ed. C. L. Westfall and B. R. Dyer; McMaster New Testament Studies; Eugene, OR: Wipf & Stock, 2015), 125–51.

74. J. J. Meggitt, *Paul, Poverty and Survival* (Studies of the New Testament and Its World; Edinburgh: T&T Clark, 1998), esp. 41–178.

75. Meggitt, *Paul, Poverty and Survival*, 41–42.

76. The primitivist position is represented by M. I. Finley, *The Ancient Economy* (London: Chattto & Windus, 1973).

77. The modernist position is represented by M. Rostovtzeff, *Social and Economic History of the Roman Empire* (2 vols.; Oxford: Oxford University Press, 1957).

78. For a reasonably balanced description, see P. Garnsey and R. Saller, *The Roman Empire: Economy, Society, and Culture* (Berkeley: University of California Press, 1987).

have been within this group, as were a number of those who traveled with him and to whom and from whom he wrote.

7. Paul's Religious and Ethnic Background

At several places in his letters, Paul chronicles his ethnic and religious background in Judaism. Philippians 3:5–6 states that Paul was "circumcised on the eighth day, of the people of Israel, of the tribe of Benjamin, a Hebrew of Hebrews; in regard to the law, a Pharisee; as for zeal, persecuting the church; as for legalistic righteousness, faultless" (NIV). Similarly, 2 Cor 11:22 rhetorically asks, "Are they Hebrews? So am I. Are they Israelites? So am I. Are they Abraham's descendants? So am I" (NIV). In Gal 1:13–14, Paul states that his readers "have heard of my previous way of life in Judaism, how intensely I persecuted the church of God and tried to destroy it. I was advancing in Judaism beyond many Jews of my own age and was extremely zealous for the traditions of my fathers" (NIV). Finally, in Rom 11:1, Paul declares that "I am an Israelite myself, a descendant of Abraham, from the tribe of Benjamin" (NIV). Seeing how Paul conceived himself helps us to understand better his conversion and his subsequent Christian experience.

With Phil 3:5–6 as a framework,[79] the following elements of his past are worth recounting. First, Paul says that he was circumcised on the eighth day, the day that was prescribed by Jewish law (Gen 17:12; Lev 12:3). Hence, Paul clearly lays claim to having been Jewish by birth and by outward sign.

Second, he says that he was of the race of Israel—that is, a physical descendant from the line that led directly back to the patriarchs.

Third, and more specifically, he claims to have been of the tribe of Benjamin, a troublesome tribe to be sure, but considered part of Judah since the division of the two kingdoms, the tribe within whose ancestral territory Jerusalem was located. Because of the Babylonian captivity, Jews in Paul's time, especially those of the Diaspora, were not all able to trace their genealogy to establish their tribal descent (Neh 11:7–9, 31–36). Not all scholars are convinced of Paul's genealogy; many note that Paul was named after the most famous member of the tribe of Benjamin, King Saul. Saul would have been Paul's Jewish name or alternative name (*supernomen*), with Paul being his *cognomen*, or personal name, a common one that had the sense of "small," whether used

---

79. See P. T. O'Brien, *The Epistle to the Philippians* (NIGTC; Grand Rapids: Eerdmans, 1991), 368–81; and S. Kim, *The Origin of Paul's Gospel* (WUNT 2/4; Tübingen: Mohr-Siebeck, 1981; repr. Grand Rapids: Eerdmans, 1982), 32–50.

pejoratively for size or as a term of affection. (Most Romans had three names, including not only a *cognomen* but also a *praenomen*, or family name, and *nomen*, or surname. Paul's other two names are unknown, a phenomenon not unique to Paul, for this is the case even when it comes to well-known people of the ancient world.)[80]

Fourth, Paul is said to be a Hebrew of Hebrews. References to Israel and the tribe of Benjamin provide racial and ethnic distinctions, but Paul's specification of himself as a Hebrew of Hebrews is probably a linguistic distinction, meaning more than simply being Jewish.[81] In Acts 6:1, a distinction is made between Hellenists and Hebrews, probably differentiating between Palestinian Jews who spoke Greek and those who spoke a Semitic language—probably Aramaic—as their native language and could worship in this language or Hebrew. (Philo, in *On Dreams* 2.250 and *On the Life of Abraham* 28, makes a similar distinction.)[82] Paul here identifies with the Aramaic-speaking branch of the Jewish people, making the claim that even though he may be a Diaspora Jew, he is a native speaker of Aramaic, as probably were his parents. This would have distinguished him from the vast majority of Diaspora Jews, who did not know Aramaic or Hebrew and were thus obligated to attend Greek-speaking synagogues and use the Septuagint as their Bible. Paul is depicted as using Aramaic on several occasions (Acts 21:40; 22:2; 26:14). Of course, this does not mean that Paul did not have native competence in Greek as well; he did, as is clearly evidenced in the ease with which he moved in the Greco-Roman world, along with the facility he demonstrates in his letters and the familiarity he shows with the Septuagint.

Fifth, Paul identifies himself with the Pharisees (cf. Acts 26:5, where Paul says that he "lived as a Pharisee"; NIV). The Pharisees were characterized by a theology that mixed determinism and free will, with an emphasis on application of the law to daily life.[83] In 23:6, Paul reportedly calls himself "a Pharisee,

---

80. See C. J. Hemer, "The Name of Paul," *Tyndale Bulletin* 36 (1985): 179–83. No Roman in the New Testament is addressed by their three names. The transition from Paul's Jewish *supernomen* to his Roman *cognomen* at Acts 13:9 raises the question of the relation of Paul's name to that of the Roman proconsul, Sergius Paulus (13:7), here addressed by *nomen* and *cognomen*. However, Paul would have received his Roman name at birth.

81. Hengel with Deines, *Pre-Christian Paul*, 68.

82. See H. A. Brehm, "The Meaning of Ἑλληνιστής in Acts in Light of a Diachronic Analysis of ἑλληνίζειν," in *Discourse Analysis and Other Topics in Biblical Greek* (ed. S. E. Porter and D. A. Carson; JSNTSup 113; Sheffield: Sheffield Academic, 1995), 180–99.

83. On the Pharisees, see G. Porton, "Diversity in Postbiblical Judaism," in *Early Judaism and Its Modern Interpreters* (ed. R. A. Kraft and G. W. E. Nickelsburg; Philadelphia: Fortress, 1986), 69–72, with bibliography; and J. Neusner and B. D. Chilton, eds., *In Quest of the Historical Pharisees* (Waco, TX: Baylor University Press, 2007).

the son of a Pharisee" (NIV), which may mean that his father was a Pharisee, although it is more likely that this means that he had a Pharisee in his family line or that he had been the student of a Pharisee (i.e., Gamaliel).

Sixth, Paul refers to his zeal being evidenced in persecuting the church (cf. Gal 1:13–14). It is difficult to substantiate where exactly such persecution took place, since the only direct accounts of Paul's participation in persecution seem to be his relatively minor role in the stoning of Stephen and his trip to Damascus with the intention of persecuting Christians there. In Acts 26:10, he is cited as referring to persecuting in Jerusalem and casting his vote against those who were put to death. Since the apostles seem to have been relatively unaffected by such persecution even though they were in and around Jerusalem (or perhaps chose to remain in spite of it), Paul's persecution was probably not of Palestinian-Jewish but of Hellenistic-Jewish Christians, such as Stephen and his group.[84] Immediately after his conversion, when Paul arrived in Damascus and proclaimed Jesus in the synagogues there, the crowds were amazed because they had heard of his reputation as being a persecutor, and in fact knew of his original purpose in coming to their city (9:21). It was while Paul was going to Damascus, probably for the first time to pursue Hellenistic-Jewish Christians, that he had his "conversion" experience. He was otherwise unknown to those in Damascus.[85] He was also known by those in Jerusalem as a persecutor, as they reacted with fear toward him even after his conversion (9:26), although the fear was not great enough for them to leave town.

Seventh, Paul says that as to legalistic righteousness, he was faultless. This verse is variously interpreted. Earlier in the last century it was not uncommon for scholars to see Paul as being psychologically ill at ease with being a Jew, which contributed to the formulation of his theology as a Christian.[86] But there is no evidence here of Paul's being troubled by guilt, stress, doubt, or depression over his failure to keep the law.[87] This verse does not state that Paul considered himself "righteous" on the basis of keeping the law or even that he kept all of the law (and he later writes in Rom 7:17–25, from the perspective of

---

84. Dunn, *Beginning from Jerusalem*, 274–78.

85. See Hengel with Deines, *Pre-Christian Paul*, 65–79.

86. E.g., Deissmann, *Paul*, 92–96. In Acts 26:14, when the Lord is quoted as saying, "It hurts you to kick against the goads" (NRSV), this does not imply Paul's living in a state of rebellion but is an aphoristic statement forbidding opposition to God. See L. T. Johnson, *The Acts of the Apostles* (Sacra Pagina 5; Collegeville, MN: Liturgical, 1992), 435.

87. Cf. K. Stendahl, "The Apostle Paul and the Introspective Conscience of the West," *Harvard Theological Review* 56 (1963): 199–215; repr. in Stendahl, *Paul among Jews and Gentiles and Other Essays* (Philadelphia: Fortress, 1976), 78–96.

a Christian, of his own failure to keep the law). He is stating instead that, so far as the demands of the law were concerned (a righteousness based on legalism), he did what the law demanded and was faultless so far as this requirement could be met—he actively tried to obey the law.

8. Paul's Conversion

The commencement of the persecution of Hellenistic-Jewish Christians (Acts 8:1) led to their fleeing to areas outside Judea.[88] There may have been some sort of extradition policy in effect, whereby breakers of the law, even though they broke the law outside Palestine, could be returned to Jerusalem to be punished under Jewish law. Such a policy was apparently originally instituted in 142 BC but had been redefined by Julius Caesar in 47 BC. In his persecuting zeal, Paul undertook his journey to Damascus to bring back Christians to Jerusalem. If the document Paul carried with him did not go so far as to give him legal authority, apparently it would at least have implored the cooperation of the synagogue leaders there.[89] This implies that there were already Christians in Damascus only a few years after Jesus's death. It also provides further evidence that Paul was persecuting primarily Hellenistic-Jewish Christians who had had some direct or indirect contact with Jerusalem.

Paul's conversion is mentioned three times in Acts (9:3–6; 22:6–11; 26:12–18; the first time a recounting of events in narrative sequence and the other two times descriptions in Pauline apologetic sections), once explicitly in Gal 1:15–16, and less directly in 1 Cor 15:8 (see §9 on 1 Cor 9:1, as referring to Paul seeing Jesus).[90] Some scholars, especially those who want to harmonize these accounts on every particular detail, debate about the precise events involved in Paul's conversion experience, since the three passages seem to differ in some details.[91] For example, only in the Acts 26 testimony does Paul cite

---

88. This persecution by ca. 44 was aimed also at non-Hellenistic Jews. See Acts 12:1–5.

89. For the evidence of this, see Bruce, *Paul*, 72–73. Cf. also J. L. White, "Ancient Greek Letters," in *Greco-Roman Literature and the New Testament* (ed. D. E. Aune; SBLSBS 21; Atlanta: Scholars, 1988), 85–106.

90. See A. D. Nock, *Conversion: The Old and the New in Religion from Alexander the Great to Augustine of Hippo* (Oxford: Oxford University Press, 1933); and A. F. Segal, *Paul the Convert: The Apostolate and Apostasy of Saul the Pharisee* (New Haven: Yale University Press, 1990), 72–114.

91. McRay, *Paul*, 53–55; cf. also C. W. Hedrick, "Paul's Conversion/Call: A Comparative Analysis of the Three Reports in Acts," *JBL* 100 (1981): 415–32; C. K. Barrett, *A Critical and Exegetical Commentary on the Acts of the Apostles* (2 vols.; ICC; Edinburgh: T&T Clark, 1994–98), 1.439–40; and J. D. G. Dunn, *Jesus Remembered* (Christianity in the Making 1; Grand Rapids: Eerdmans, 2003), 210–12. See also Porter, "Portrait of Paul in Acts," 128.

Jesus as saying, "It hurts you to kick against the goads" (26:14 NRSV), while Acts 9 and 22 leave this statement out. A typical explanation, however, for these variations is that Luke uses a literary technique to complement each one of these episodes[92] or, going further, that Luke had access to three different sources (Paul himself, the church in Jerusalem, and the church in Antioch) and reduplicates the versions of these sources in each of these three accounts.[93] The most probable explanation, however, is that, in each of these recountings, Paul (and/or Luke) was addressing himself to a specific goal and audience, and the differences can be accounted for by these different purposes. One suggestion that explains the different emphases in these three accounts might be that the first account (Acts 9) summarizes what happened on the road to Damascus, the second account (Acts 22) emphasizes Paul's Jewish identity when he speaks to the Jewish crowd, and the third (Acts 26) sees continuity between Judaism and Paul's mission.[94] Furthermore, it seems that on many occasions far too much is made of the differences among these three Damascus road accounts.

Recent discussion questions whether this singular and significant event in Paul's life ought to be referred to as a "conversion," since the term "conversion" seems to imply a change from no religion to religion, or a change from one religion to another. In either case, Paul had been a religious person before his conversion and continued to be one after, viewing his conversion as something that developed naturally from—and was in many essential ways in harmony with—his previous belief. As a result, some want to refer to Paul's experience as a calling akin to that of some Old Testament prophets (e.g., Isaiah or Jeremiah; see Isa 6; Jer 1:4–19),[95] others as a visionary or ecstatic experience similar to those in other religious traditions, and still others as a revelatory event.[96]

As Alan Segal shows, however, regardless of the other elements that may have been present in Paul's Damascus road experience (including a vision similar to that of an Old Testament prophet), "conversion" is entirely appropriate to describe what happened to Paul, since his experience had affinities with conversion experiences in Judaism of the time. The characteristics of conversion that Segal cites are three: the identification by the convert of a lacking in his previous existence that is remedied by the new group (Phil 3:7-8), a restructuring of the convert's reality according to the presuppositions of the

92. Hedrick, "Paul's Conversion/Call," 427–32.

93. McRay, *Paul*, 54.

94. See Dunn, *Jesus Remembered*, 212.

95. J. Munck, *Paul and the Salvation of Mankind* (Atlanta: John Knox, 1959), 24–35.

96. See Kim, *Origin*, 55–56.

new group, and a resulting integration of the convert's old perspective in the new.[97] Although Paul saw himself in continuity with essential Judaism after this crucial event and used it as the basis of his thought (see chapter 3 §3), he came to see that the work of Christ superseded Jewish practice and belief. A distinct element in at least some contemporary Judaism endorsed works as a means of entering and retaining one's covenantal status, but Paul placed his emphasis on the justifying work of God through Christ. Whereas Jews thought of themselves as obligated to keep the law with the hope of attaining and maintaining righteousness before God,[98] Paul saw the law as totally ineffective in this quest and hence as having already accomplished its purpose. Judaism had rejected Jesus as Christ or the Messiah, but for Paul, Jesus was the Christ and the fulfillment of the Old Testament prophecies. In this respect, Paul's experience may well be characterized as conversion.

Paul's experience on the Damascus road nevertheless included a series of events similar to the calls of the prophets Isaiah and Jeremiah, in which God singled out these specific individuals and called them to fulfill his intended purpose. When these prophets were called, they were given a specific message to preach. It is not clear that Paul realized his entire message at the time of his conversion,[99] but what is clear is that by the time he wrote Gal 1:15–16 (a retrospective view compatible with conversion), he saw that an essential part of his calling was wrapped up with being the apostle to the Gentiles.[100] So far as actual physical signs are concerned, both sight and sound attended his call. In his letters, Paul mentions that he saw Jesus (1 Cor 15:8; Gal 1:16). That Paul believed that he received his commissioning as apostle to the Gentiles at this time gives credence to the idea that he heard a voice, as is recorded in all three accounts in Acts (9:4–6; 22:7–8; 26:14–18), as well as seeing the risen Lord. It is, however, possible that references to the content of the voice are Luke's extrapolations from what is said in the Pauline letters (such as Gal 1:15–16). As for Paul, he treats the appearance as an actual and valid revelation of Jesus Christ, one that conveyed authority for his missionary endeavors.

---

97. Segal, *Paul*, 75, 117–49.

98. This is, of course, the traditional understanding of the religion of New Testament Judaism, contra the New Perspective on Paul; see chapter 4 §3B.

99. Kim, *Origin*, 67–74 and passim. However, as much of his argumentation is based upon a questionable understanding of the function of the Greek aorist tense form (Kim interprets it as punctiliar, referring to a singular past event; see, e.g., pp. 11, 13, 25), this calls into question his understanding.

100. See R. Y. K. Fung, "Revelation and Tradition: The Origins of Paul's Gospel," *Evangelical Quarterly* 57 (1985): 25–34; cf. M. Winger, "Tradition, Revelation, and Gospel: A Study in Galatians," *JSNT* 53 (1994): 65–86; cf. also Dunn, *Beginning from Jerusalem*, 519–20.

9. Paul and Jesus

We know from the account of Paul's conversion in Acts, along with Paul's letters, that the risen Lord appeared to him.[101] Scholarship is relatively quiet, however, when it comes to the idea that Paul may ever have come into personal contact with Jesus during his earthly ministry.[102] Whenever the two, Paul and Jesus, are mentioned in the same sentence, the dominant topic of conversation has been the debate between continuity and discontinuity between their teachings. Ever since Ferdinand Christian Baur aired the idea that Paul's Hellenistic doctrine was developed in opposition to the earliest Jewish Christianity and proposed the Pauline theology versus Petrine theology dichotomy, the distinction between Paul and Jesus has been a crucial topic.[103] While I do not think this dichotomy is necessary, or even an accurate account of what went on in the early church, an important factor in the discussion is whether Paul actually met, and even conversed with, Jesus. For those scholars who do address this issue, the scholarly consensus is that Paul did not meet Jesus, and some further claim that he did not even think twice about him before his conversion.[104] While it is probably not the place to develop a full-fledged argument for my theory, there are two main reasons why it is certainly plausible that Paul met Jesus during his earthly ministry.

First, most scholars simply assume that Jesus and Paul never met before Jesus's death and ascension. However, one reason to think that they did in fact cross paths is their similar and even intertwined parallel lives.[105] Jesus was

---

101. This section is based on S. E. Porter, *When Paul Met Jesus: How an Idea Got Lost in History* (Cambridge: Cambridge University Press, 2016). Some of this section is taken verbatim from this volume.

102. Most scholars who address the issue of Paul and Jesus address it from the perspective of their teachings, rather than the possibility of any personal encounters. For example, in A. J. M. Wedderburn, ed., *Paul and Jesus: Collected Essays* (JSNTSup 37; Sheffield: JSOT Press, 1989), the essays focus on the various teachings of these two influential figures of Christianity, but the authors do not really address the issue of whether they actually engaged one another in person, though occasionally mentioned in passing. This is understandable, given that the primary focus was whether the teachings of Jesus and Paul have continuity or discontinuity. The other question, whether they actually met and engaged with each other, also has some interesting implications for this discussion.

103. For a survey of research on this topic, see V. P. Furnish, "The Jesus-Paul Debate: From Baur to Bultmann," in *Paul and Jesus: Collected Essays* (ed. A. J. M. Wedderburn; JSNTSup 37; Sheffield: JSOT Press, 1989), 17–50.

104. E.g., J. Murphy-O'Connor, *Paul: A Critical Life* (Oxford: Oxford University Press, 1997), 15–16.

105. See J. Murphy-O'Connor, *Jesus and Paul: Parallel Lives* (Collegeville, MN: Liturgical, 2007).

born in Palestine and lived his entire life there, much of it in Galilee, but with several probable trips to Jerusalem and other surrounding areas, including an attention-drawing final week in the central city of Judaism, Jerusalem. Paul, though not born in Palestine, moved there probably in his midteen years in order to be educated by the leading rabbi of the time, Gamaliel, and hence moved in the circles of the Pharisaic leaders in Jerusalem. This would have placed Paul at the center of much activity within Pharisaic circles of the time, and even involved him in travel outside of Jerusalem—providing further occasions for him to incidentally encounter Jesus if not intentionally seek him out. Such a scenario seems not only possible, but even plausible, as was argued by several scholars before me (though now some time ago).[106]

The second major reason is statements in Paul's letters where he seems to indicate, or at least imply, that he knew Jesus. In fact, I will go further and suggest that these passages indicate that Paul makes an overt claim to having known Jesus while he was in his earthly, preresurrection body. First is the conversion account found in three different forms in Acts, already discussed above. The key to understanding this episode is the dialogue between Paul and the risen Jesus. Paul hears a voice that addresses him: "Saul, Saul, why are you persecuting me?" Paul answers: "Who are you, Lord?" (26:14–15 NRSV). There are three immediate issues in this exchange to address. The first is the sense of the word "Lord." It appears that the semantic range for the respectful word "Lord" (κύριος) in the New Testament is wide, one of the meanings (and the most common within ancient Greek literature) being a respectful "sir," another the recognition of a superior "master," and the third being a referent to a supernatural being.[107] The respectful "sir," however, even if common, is much too tame a response for a man who has just seen a light flash around him, been knocked to the ground, and been directly addressed by name by the very risen Jesus whom he recognizes. As indicated by the question asked of him, the context shows that Paul already knows that he is addressing the Lord Jesus.

The second issue is the nature of the question, "Why are you persecuting me?" The question does not ask Paul why he is persecuting Christians or fol-

---

106. E.g., W. M. Ramsay, "Historical Commentary on the Epistles to the Corinthians," *Expositor* 6th series 3 (1901): 343–60, esp. 356–60; J. Weiss, *Paulus und Jesus* (Berlin: Reuther & Reichard, 1909); translated as *Paul and Jesus* (trans. H. J. Chaytor; London: Harper & Brothers, 1909); Weiss, *Jesus im Glauben des Urchristentums* (Tübingen: Mohr-Siebeck, 1910), 42; and J. H. Moulton, "The Gospel according to Paul," *Expositor* 8th series 2 (1911): 16–28.

107. J. P. Louw and E. A. Nida, *Greek-English Lexicon of the New Testament Based on Semantic Domains* (New York: United Bible Societies, 1988), list κύριος within four semantic domains (12.9; 57.12; 37.51; and 87.53).

lowers of Christ or the like, but it asks, "Why are you persecuting *me*?" with "me" placed before the verb in Greek to make it salient within the question structure.[108] The voice seems to have been accompanied by an actual appearance of Jesus, which makes the use of "me" completely understandable. At this point, we do not know that Jesus appeared to Paul, but later in the account Luke states that Paul's traveling companions heard something but saw nothing (9:7). This implies that Paul did see something—which is repeated in the words of Ananias in 22:14 ("to see the righteous one and to hear a voice") and the report in Jerusalem in 9:27 ("he saw the Lord"). This is not a disembodied voice that Paul hears but a voice spoken by the risen Jesus himself, who now stands before him. The question itself both asks and answers the question regarding who is speaking and who is the focus of attention: the "me" is the risen Jesus.

The third issue is the meaning of the question, "Who are you?" asked by Paul. This may seem like a question regarding identification of the speaker— who is this person speaking before me? It seems so to many commentators.[109] However, as we have already seen, it is highly unlikely that Paul does not know to whom he is speaking. He recognized the voice and the appearance of the one whose followers he is persecuting. Paul is not asking after the identity of the speaker—that he already apparently knows—but he wants to know how one gets from the person he once encountered to the person who has just addressed him.

The second passage is 1 Cor 9:1: "Have I not seen Jesus our Lord" (NIV). Paul rhetorically asks, expecting a positive answer, whether he has seen the Lord Jesus. Many commentators take this as referring to the Damascus road experience, sometimes by sheer assumption.[110] Three particular features in this verse, however, might help to clarify whether Paul means that he had

---

108. The sense of the verb as "persecute" rather than simply "pursue" (if such a distinction is warranted) is seen in the nature of Paul's entire pursuit as recorded in Acts 9 and that the risen Lord addresses his question directly to Paul. The indication is not that Paul is simply pursuing Jesus (as if he were inadvertently seeking to follow after him), but that he is persecuting him by persecuting his followers.

109. For example, F. F. Bruce, *The Acts of the Apostles: Greek Text with Introduction and Commentary* (3rd ed.; Grand Rapids: Eerdmans, 1990), 235; and Barrett, *Acts of the Apostles*, 1.450, even though they recognize that Paul has had a supernatural or divine encounter. See also C. T. Wood, *The Life, Letters, and Religion of St. Paul* (Edinburgh: T&T Clark, 1925), 12.

110. For example, see Wright, *Paul and the Faithfulness of God*, 2.1421, who simply assumes without discussion that 1 Cor 9:1 refers to seeing the risen Jesus. A pleasant exception is C. N. Johnston, *St. Paul and His Mission to the Roman Empire* (London: A&C Black, 1911), 16 and n2, who takes 1 Cor 9:1 as the "possible exception" to the view that all proposed verses refer to the risen Christ.

seen Jesus on the Damascus road or whether he possibly means that he had seen Jesus in his earthly existence. The first feature is the logic of the exegetical argument. The usual logic of the argument begins with the premise that Paul had not seen Jesus during his earthly life. However, what if that premise is not correct? What if we eliminate that premise and assess this verse on the basis of the logic of its argument without that premise? The statement that Paul has seen Jesus occurs in his discussion regarding his apostleship. There seems to have been the belief, at least within some circles of the early church, that apostleship required that the person had been with Jesus during his ministry and witnessed the resurrection (and that Paul was sometimes criticized for claiming to be an apostle, because he did not fulfill these criteria). It is true, and Paul never denies it, that he had not been with Jesus throughout the course of his ministry. That does not mean, however, that he had not at least had a glimpse of him. On that basis, therefore, he may have been at least minimally qualified as an apostle. I think that that is exactly what Paul is saying here. The logic fits the case. Paul is free and does not need to exercise his various rights. He is an apostle. And if at least part of what it means to be an apostle is to have seen Jesus, then he claims to have seen Jesus.

The second consideration in this verse is the verb "see" (ὁράω), used in the perfect tense. This Greek verb is related to a number of other verbs for seeing, all of them in various ways concerned with physical seeing.[111] This verb too is used of perception by sight, but also has various figurative modulations, such as pay attention to, understand, visit, and experience.[112] The use of the verb in this context cannot specify whether this is a literal or figurative seeing. However, sound lexical analysis demands that we begin with the broad sense and then modulate to more specific meanings by means of context.

The third issue to consider is the object of the verb "see": "Jesus, our Lord." The object of Paul's seeing is not Christ, Jesus Christ, Christ Jesus, Lord, or any other similar combination, but simply Jesus (though modified as "our Lord"). It is significant that Paul refers to him as Jesus here. In his letters, Paul uses "Jesus" mostly in contexts where he is referring to the earthly figure, especially his life and death and being raised from death. For example, Rom 8:11 speaks of the spirit raising Jesus from the dead; 1 Cor 12:3 speaks of cursing Jesus; 2 Cor 4:10–11 speaks of the life and death of Jesus; 2 Cor 4:14 speaks of our being raised

111. Louw and Nida, *Greek-English Lexicon of the New Testament,* place it in semantic domain 24, within the subcategory of "see," along with other verbs such as βλέπω and θεωρέω. See also Ramsay, "Historical Commentary," 356n.

112. These are some of the categories used by Louw and Nida, *Greek-English Lexicon of the New Testament.* See also J. Kremer, "Ὁράω," in *Exegetical Dictionary of the New Testament* (ed. H. Balz and G. Schneider; 3 vols.; Grand Rapids: Eerdmans, 1990–93), 2.526–29, esp. 527.

with Jesus; 2 Cor 11:4 seems to refer to false teaching regarding Jesus as a person; Gal 6:17 refers to the stigmata of Jesus; Eph 4:21 grounds the truth of Christ in Jesus, presumably the man Jesus; and 1 Thess 4:14 speaks of Jesus dying (2 Cor 4:5 may be an exception, unless "Jesus" is used so as not to repeat "Jesus Christ Lord" from earlier in the verse; i.e., for stylistic reasons). The presumption is that if Paul writes "Jesus," he is referring to Jesus, the earthly figure. The reference here may possibly be to the risen Jesus whom Paul saw on the road to Damascus, but even there, that passage makes better sense if Paul had previously seen him (besides, Paul addresses him as Lord there, not Jesus). Perhaps 1 Cor 9:1 refers to the risen Jesus, but even so, if my analysis is correct, that vision entailed recognition of the risen Jesus on the basis of previously having seen the earthly Jesus. I especially think that 9:1 makes better sense if Paul is referring to seeing the earthly Jesus in light of his appositional modification, "Jesus the Lord."

Finally, there is 2 Cor 5:16, a notoriously controversial passage.[113] Despite the controversy and continuing confusion, I believe that a probable interpretation is that Paul had seen the physical Jesus but that a believer's new relationship with Christ is not based on knowing him in this physical way. I realize that this passage is highly problematic, but offer the following literalistic translation, with Greek words and phrases interposed, as a means of instigating further discussion: "(a) Therefore (ὥστε), from now on (ἀπὸ τοῦ νῦν) we (ἡμεῖς) know (οἴδαμεν) no one (οὐδένα) according to flesh (κατὰ σάρκα). (b) If indeed (εἰ καὶ) we know (ἐγνώκαμεν) according to flesh (κατὰ σάρκα), Christ (Χριστόν), (c) but (ἀλλὰ) now (νῦν) we no longer know (οὐκέτι γινώσκομεν)." An interpretation of this, by clause, would look something like this: (a) states "(from now on) we know, or are in a state of knowing (on the basis of experience), in a human way no one," (b) that "we know, or are in a state of knowing (whether on the basis of experience or not), Christ," and (c) "we are (no longer) in the process of knowing (whether on the basis of experience or not)." Paul uses a first-class conditional in clause b, which makes an assertion for the sake of argument.[114] It appears that Paul is putting

113. This passage has been treated repeatedly in the past. For bibliography up to Rudolf Bultmann, see Furnish, "Jesus-Paul Debate," 29n44; J. W. Fraser, "Paul's Knowledge of Jesus: II Corinthians v.16 Once More," *NTS* 17 (1970–71): 293–313; and Fraser, *Jesus and Paul: Paul as Interpreter of Jesus from Harnack to Kümmel* (Appleford: Marcham, 1974), 46–62; and for more recent bibliography, see C. Wolff, "True Apostolic Knowledge of Christ: Exegetical Reflections on 2 Corinthians 5.14ff.," in *Paul and Jesus: Collected Essays* (ed. A. J. M. Wedderburn; JSNTSup 37; Sheffield: JSOT Press, 1989), 81–98 (although Wolff, I believe, is not exegetically sound on a number of points, often simply repeating previous views).

114. S. E. Porter, *Idioms of the Greek New Testament* (2nd ed.; Biblical Languages: Greek 2; Sheffield: Sheffield Academic, 1994), 254–67.

forward for consideration whether he has known Christ. One might translate the conditional sentence as: "if indeed/also we knew in a human way Christ, but now we no longer know [him]," or "although we knew in a human way, Christ, but now we no longer know [him]."[115] This may seem like a relatively tenuous way to make the statement that Paul had seen Christ, but we need to consider that he is making the statement within an argument in which he wishes to minimize its contemporary relevance. That time of knowing Christ is in the past, insofar as knowing him as a human is concerned for Paul, and what is important now is that, though we no longer know him as he was, we know him now in a new and spiritual way.[116]

Although I do not think I have said the final word on this matter, I think that, combining the plausibility that Jesus and Paul had similar parallel lives and the various statements Paul makes in his letters, it seems likely that Paul had met Jesus during his earthly ministry. Even if each of these sets of passages is a slender thread, their combined strength results in a cord of greater strength.

10. The Book of Acts and the Apostle Paul

It is not often recognized how much of what is tacitly assumed to be reliable knowledge of Paul is dependent upon the book of Acts.[117] For example, a clear statement of Paul's conversion experience on the Damascus road (as noted in the recounting above), the itinerary of his several missionary journeys, the Hellenistic side of his background and experience, including his coming from Tarsus and his Roman citizenship—all of these are found primarily, if not exclusively, in Acts, not in the Pauline letters. Consequently, critical scholarship often raises questions about whether these are accurate depictions of Paul. A number of other items related to Paul's life and experience are known only

---

115. Weiss, *Paul and Jesus*, 51, takes the concessive. Some commentators make more of the use of "but" (ἀλλά) here than is probably warranted, drawing upon classical usage. See M. J. Harris, *Second Epistle of Paul to the Corinthians: A Commentary on the Greek Text* (NIGTC; Grand Rapids: Eerdmans, 2005), 428, following F. Blass and A. Debrunner, *A Greek Grammar of the New Testament and Other Early Christian Literature* (trans. R. W. Funk; Chicago: University of Chicago Press, 1961), §448(5) (pp. 232–33). In any case, the strong adversative conjunction marks a contrast between the protasis and the apodosis.

116. For a more detailed and thorough line of argument for this view, see Porter, *When Paul Met Jesus*.

117. For a fuller treatment on various topics related to Paul and Acts, see Porter, *Paul of Acts*; and Porter, "Portrait of Paul in Acts"; cf. T. E. Phillips, *Paul, His Letters, and Acts* (Library of Pauline Studies; Peabody, MA: Hendrickson, 2009).

from Acts, and critical scholarship doubts them even more seriously, such as his numerous public speeches—for example, at Athens (Acts 17:22–31). This raises several important questions regarding the relationship between the Paul of Acts and the Paul of his letters.[118]

The traditional view of the authorship of Acts is that it is the second of two volumes composed by a traveling companion of Paul, Luke the physician. This authorship is attested since the second century in church tradition.[119] This tradition is reasonably early, but it must be recognized that the Gospels and Acts are formally anonymous, and so certainty regarding authorship cannot be established. Scholars debate the evidence for and against the traditional view, recognizing various amounts of credibility in Paul's references to Luke among Paul's faithful companions (Col 4:14; 2 Tim 4:11; Phlm 24).[120] Nevertheless, a good number of scholars probably give more credibility to the traditional view of Lukan authorship. Further support for Lukan authorship is often found in the "we" passages of Acts (16:10–17; 20:5–15; 21:1–18; 27:1–29; 28:1–16).[121]

Critical scholarship of the last hundred or so years, however, called this traditional authorial attribution into question. The thought that the author of Luke–Acts was a physician can no longer be definitively supported from the text itself, since the so-called medical language found in Luke–Acts is apparently typical of Luke's level and style of writing, and the majority of references to Luke as Paul's traveling companion are found in what are frequently called deutero-Pauline books, that is, books that were not necessarily written by Paul but, quite possibly, significantly later (these books often include 1–2 Timothy and Titus [the so-called Pastoral Epistles], Ephesians, Colossians, and 2 Thessalonians; see chapter 6 §2 and the chapters on the individual letters). Furthermore, there are a number of ways of explaining the use of the "we" passages, and the firsthand account is only one of them. These passages have been viewed in a number of ways: as a diary or literary source, either from the author himself but more likely from another writer (i.e., source solution); as a form of redacted document, reflecting the author's editorial manipulation for his purposes (i.e., redaction solution); or as a fictional device to tell of a sea

---

118. For a comprehensive survey of scholarship on Pauline chronology and Acts, see R. Riesner, *Paul's Early Period: Chronology, Mission Strategy, Theology* (trans. D. Scott; Grand Rapids: Eerdmans, 1998), 1–28.

119. McDonald and Porter, *Early Christianity and Its Sacred Literature*, 294–97.

120. For a more complete overview of the relationship between Luke and Paul, see S. E. Porter, "Luke: Companion or Disciple of Paul?" in *Paul and the Gospels: Christologies, Conflicts, and Convergencies* (ed. M. F. Bird and J. Willitts; LNTS 411; New York: T&T Clark, 2011), 146–68.

121. Porter, *Paul of Acts*, 99; cf. 10–46, 47–66.

voyage or as an indication of the redactional activity of the author, pointing to the incorporation of a source document or the author's own firsthand account (i.e., literary solution).[122] Even if the "we" passages are thought to represent a firsthand account (the language does not necessarily mean an eyewitness), the most that can be argued is that another source is being used. It does not resolve the issue of authorship.[123]

Important for the relation of Paul to Acts are a number of questions regarding the accuracy and reliability of Acts in relation to what is known about Paul through his letters. A number of elements seem to some scholars to be so at odds with the picture of Paul gained through his own letters as to raise the question whether the person who wrote Acts could possibly have been a firsthand witness or close acquaintance:

1. Paul's literary contribution to the New Testament is only as a letter writer, but the author of Acts never depicts Paul as a letter writer. Nowhere in Acts is Paul seen carrying on the kind of ministry depicted in his letters, that is, maintaining and guarding his relationships with his churches through his epistolary correspondence. Paul certainly is depicted in Acts as being pastorally concerned for his churches (e.g., 15:36, 41), but this does not include the sending of letters. Furthermore, scholars are divided on whether and how the author of Acts, regardless of his possible knowledge of Paul's writing activities, uses the letters. This argument from silence is probably overused. A number of topics not discussed in Acts, or even in some of Paul's letters, are known to be important to Paul's ministry. Further, I believe that there are indications that the author of Acts does know the Pauline letters, as indicated, for example, by the similarities found in Acts 20:18-35 and 1 Thessalonians.[124]

2. In the letters, Paul never explicitly mentions his missionary strategy as including visiting synagogues, but in Acts Paul clearly begins many of his

122. Porter, *Paul of Acts*, 10. For summaries of issues, see S. M. Praeder, "The Problem of First Person Narration in Acts," *NovT* 29 (1987): 193-218; C. J. Hemer, *The Book of Acts in the Setting of Hellenistic History* (ed. C. Gempf; WUNT 49; Tübingen: Mohr-Siebeck, 1989; repr. Winona Lake, IN: Eisenbrauns, 1990), 308-34; C.-J. Thornton, *Der Zeuge des Zeugen: Lukas als Historiker der Paulusreisen* (WUNT 56; Tübingen: Mohr-Siebeck, 1991), 93-119; and W. S. Campbell, *The "We" Passages in the Acts of the Apostles: The Narrator as Narrative Character* (Atlanta: SBL, 2007), 1-9; among others.

123. Issues related to Acts are conveniently discussed in Foakes-Jackson and Lake, *Acts of the Apostles*; and Winter and Clarke, *Book of Acts in Its Ancient Literary Setting*.

124. See, e.g., S. Walton, *Leadership and Lifestyle: The Portrait of Paul in the Miletus Speech and 1 Thessalonians* (SNTSMS 108; Cambridge: Cambridge University Press, 2000).

preaching ministries in cities by attending the synagogue (e.g., Salamis in 13:5, Pisidian Antioch in 13:14, Iconium in 14:1, Thessalonica in 17:1–2, Berea in 17:10, Athens in 17:17, Corinth in 18:4, and Ephesus in 18:19). Paul's statement that he was flogged five times (2 Cor 11:24) indicates that during this time he placed himself under the rules of the synagogue (or at least was punished in such a way). However, one must not overlook Paul's explicitly stating in Romans that his ministry was to the Jews first, then to the Greeks (1:16).

3. According to his own words in his letters, Paul apparently was not able to convince his audiences with his speeches on several occasions (e.g., 2 Cor 10:10, but with due care in interpreting this passage), even though in Acts Paul is portrayed as a highly convincing rhetorician (13:9–11, 16–41; 14:15–17; 17:22–31; 22:1–21; 24:10–21; 26:2–27), whose speeches have elicited analysis from a rhetorical perspective.[125] However, we must be careful not to overemphasize Paul's success in Acts. He also encountered a number of difficulties, despite his evident rhetorical abilities (e.g., 13:50–51; 14:5–6, 19; 18:6–7; 22:22; cf. 19:30, where he is forbidden to try to use his rhetoric).

4. Paul never mentions his Roman citizenship in the letters, but in Acts his citizenship is a crucial item of information that he cites at several significant junctures, especially when his safety is being threatened by what he sees as unjust charges (e.g., at Philippi in 16:37, at Jerusalem in 22:25, and at Caesarea in 25:11).

5. One would not be able to gather from Acts that Paul jealously guarded his apostleship with regard to the Corinthian church, warranting the kind of epistolary exchange that we find in the letters themselves (e.g., 1 Cor 9:1–18; Gal 1:1; 1:11–2:10).

First of all, these kinds of contrasts can be overdrawn, however. In Acts, we see Paul, for example, establishing the churches in Asia Minor on the outward portion of his first missionary journey and then visiting these same churches on the return journey (13:13–14:25). The second missionary journey is said in Acts to have come about from a desire by Paul to revisit the churches he had founded earlier (15:36). Acts does not depict the nature of the conflict at Corinth, but Acts does depict Paul in conflict at times—for instance, at Ephesus (Acts 19). And since Acts was written, by all accounts, after the conflict

---

125. See M. L. Soards, *The Speeches in Acts: Their Content, Context, and Concerns* (Louisville: Westminster John Knox, 1994); cf. S. E. Porter, "Hellenistic Oratory and Paul of Tarsus," in *Hellenistic Oratory: Continuity and Change* (ed. C. Kremmydas and K. Tempest; Oxford: Oxford University Press, 2013), 319–60, esp. 344–59.

with the Corinthian church had been resolved sufficiently for Paul to write Romans from there, in all likelihood, only a year later, perhaps the author—who admittedly emphasizes Paul's triumphs—thought it unnecessary to retain this disappointing memory. This tendency to idealization perhaps accounts for the difference in depicting Paul's rhetorical skills—the author of Acts sees Paul's ultimate triumphs, whereas Paul himself, in the middle of his conflicts, or perhaps even for rhetorical reasons, downplays his abilities (e.g., 2 Cor 10:10).[126] It is probably fair to say that Acts emphasizes the Hellenistic side of Paul more than the letters do, which in many ways, at least regarding personal details of his life, emphasize the Jewish and Christian side. The Paul of Acts is a missionary on the forefront of the Christian movement, whereas in his letters Paul appears in a much more pastoral light as he writes to various churches and congregations.

Second, the emphases of Acts and Paul's letters are different. For example, in Acts Paul has frequent contact with Romans, so it is appropriate to discuss his citizenship in the context of his arrest and their safeguarding him. In several of his letters, Paul is keen to emphasize his role as an apostle to groups of Christians. For example, his conflicts with the Judaizers of Galatia and with the opponents at Corinth revolve around his calling as an apostle. Paul clearly sees himself as an apostle in his letters and uses that term (e.g., Rom 1:1; 11:13; 1 Cor 1:1; 4:9; 9:1–2; 15:9; 2 Cor 1:1; 11:5; 12:11–12; Gal 1:1). This is not an emphasis in Acts, although Acts does not deny his apostolic calling (13:4; 14:4, 14). It is noted by some that in Acts the depictions of Paul's conversion are all different from each other in some essential details—for example, concerning what his traveling companions saw or heard, or the lack of an emphasis on Paul's seeing Christ, items found in his letters (1 Cor 9:1; 15:8; Gal 1:15–16).[127] The problem of whether Acts is internally consistent is, of course, not directly a problem of the Pauline letters. Regarding these depictions in Acts, one must clarify what it means when they say that Paul saw a light and whether it was not possible for this experience to have been interpreted by him as his vision of Christ. It seems very likely that it was (see discussion above).

Third, not only are there different emphases between Acts and Paul's letters, but there appear to be several differences in theological emphasis as well. For example, it is noted that in Acts Paul uses arguments from natural theology

126. See D. Litfin, *St. Paul's Theology of Proclamation: 1 Corinthians 1–4 and Greco-Roman Rhetoric* (SNTSMS 79; Cambridge: Cambridge University Press, 1994), who emphasizes Paul's proclamation over his rhetoric.

127. See I. Jolivet Jr., "The Lukan Account of Paul's Conversion and Hermagorean Stasis Theory," in *The Rhetorical Interpretation of Scripture: Essays from the 1996 Malibu Conference* (ed. S. E. Porter and D. L. Stamps; JSNTSup 180; Sheffield: Sheffield Academic, 1999), 210–20.

on several occasions, as in his speeches to the philosophers on the Areopagus (17:22–31) and to the people of Lystra, who wanted to worship Paul and Barnabas as gods (14:15–17). Another example is the lack of emphasis in Acts on Jesus's death, which is a major theological emphasis in the Pauline letters. Paul makes Jesus's death foundational for his theology, but it does not appear to be one of his major emphases in Acts. In his letters, Paul sees a relationship between the law and sin (Gal 3:19; Rom 4:13–16; 5:20; 1 Cor 15:26; 2 Cor 3:6), but in Acts, Paul is seen as performing some legalistic rituals—circumcising Timothy (16:1–3; but cf. Gal 5:2), taking a vow and cutting off his hair (Acts 18:18), and performing acts of purification in the temple (21:26). These differences in emphasis, however, do not necessarily mean that Acts contradicts the Pauline letters. Luke's theology may simply have been different from Paul's. Or, more likely, Paul's audiences in Acts were usually different than Paul's audiences in his letters, so we should expect a difference in the content and subject matter to match what his overall perspective was in each of these contexts. In addition, Paul does use a naturalistic argument in Rom 1:18–32, where he depicts the general depravity of humanity, and this argument is foundational to the entire discussion in Romans, so there is some overlap in foci between Acts and Paul's letters. Finally, references to the death of Jesus Christ, though few in Acts, are not unknown; 20:28, for instance, refers to the blood of Christ. From the outset of Acts, the death and resurrection of Jesus seem to be assumed.

Fourth, it seems that the major difficulties between Acts and Paul's letters revolve around the chronological and historical details, which do not easily seem to match up.[128] For example, there is no "painful visit" (2 Cor 2:1) from Ephesus to Corinth recorded in Acts during Paul's lengthy stay in Ephesus (Acts 19). Paul's stay in Arabia (Gal 1:15–17) is not developed in Acts. Galatians (1:18; 2:1) mentions only two visits to Jerusalem after his conversion, whereas Acts records three (9:26; 11:30 with 12:25; 15:2–30). It is highly debated how the Jerusalem Council of Acts 15 fits in with the events recorded in Gal 2. Some argue that the visit of Gal 2 is the one recorded in Acts 15, while others contend that it is the visit of 11:30 and 12:25. Paul mentions that he suffered (2 Cor 1:8; 11:23–28) in ways that the book of Acts does not mention. Acts closes with Paul concluding a two-year imprisonment, apparently looking forward to release. This and his imprisonment for two years in Caesarea (Acts 23–26), together with a night in a Philippian jail (16:22–39), are his only imprisonments recorded in Acts. This raises the question of how to fit the so-called Prison Epistles into this chronology. Five of Paul's letters can be categorized

---

128. Recent discussions of Paul's letters and Acts, however, are not contentious as they used to be; cf. Porter, "Portrait of Paul in Acts," 124–38.

as imprisonment letters—Colossians, Philemon, Ephesians, Philippians, and 2 Timothy—although even by a traditional view of authorship and chronology they are not all apparently from the same imprisonment. A traditional position is that Colossians, Philemon, Ephesians, and probably Philippians were written from a Roman imprisonment. (The view that Paul was imprisoned in Ephesus, the next most likely, does not have an explicit episode to point to in the account in Acts.) This leaves the question of where in the chronology to place the Pastoral Epistles, as 2 Timothy is also apparently an imprisonment epistle. This suggests a second imprisonment theory, according to which Paul was released from his Roman imprisonment after Acts ends (after Acts was written?) and then began another itinerant ministry before a second Roman imprisonment and execution under Nero (after 64) (Eusebius, *Ecclesiastical History* 2.22.1–8). In another historical difference between Acts and Paul's letters, Paul's stay in Arabia (Gal 1:15–17) is not mentioned in Acts, but it must be said that this is not an important detail in the letters either. Perhaps of greater interest is the extended account of numerous various sufferings in 2 Cor 11:23–28, which find only incidental correlatives in Acts (e.g., 16:22; 21:32).

Many of these individual items are of curiosity where it would be desirable to have more details, but they do not necessarily bring Acts into contradiction with the Pauline letters.[129] They provide a challenge to the interpreter to weigh the evidence fairly from the several sources and to construct a reasonable chronology. The next chapter deals precisely with the chronology of Paul and how the evidence in his letters and Acts can be used to reconstruct a fairly coherent chronology of Paul's life and ministry.

11. Conclusion

We often think of Paul only in relation to his letters, even though much of our actual knowledge of him is strongly influenced by what is also recounted in the book of Acts. This chapter provides much essential information regarding Paul, attempting to ground the letters in an actual human being, but also raises numerous questions about him. For many of the topics of discussion, whereas the Pauline letters provide some scattered incidents of information, they do not provide the kind of chronological framework so necessary to organize the missionary ventures of Paul. As a result, I draw freely upon Acts where nec-

---

129. Cf. G. Lüdemann, *Paul: The Founder of Christianity* (Amherst, NY: Prometheus, 2002), 22–64, who takes the view that Acts is to be taken as a theological document and places priority on the Pauline letters for a historical reconstruction of Paul's life.

essary, while also recognizing the state of scholarly discussion. Nevertheless, a distinct portrait of an individual emerges from this examination. Without repeating the details noted above, we see when and where he was born, and a variety of facts that enter into understanding his letters. Along the way, we have also discussed a number of controversial issues that must be noted at the outset of study of Paul. I presented some new perspectives on some of these issues, which include my view of Paul's relationship to the Roman Empire, his firsthand knowledge of Jesus, and the relationship of Paul's letters to the book of Acts. In the chapters that follow, I will address more specific topics that continue to arouse important debates among scholars of Paul.

Sources for Further Study

Basic Sources

Hengel, M., with R. Deines. *The Pre-Christian Paul*. Translated by John Bowden. Philadelphia: Trinity, 1991.

Hengel, M., and A. M. Schwemer. *Paul between Damascus and Antioch: The Unknown Years*. Translated by J. Bowden. Louisville: Westminster John Knox, 1997.

Jewett, R. *Dating Paul's Life*. London: SCM, 1979.

Longenecker, R. N. *The Ministry and Message of Paul*. Grand Rapids: Zondervan, 1971.

McDonald, L. M., and S. E. Porter. *Early Christianity and Its Sacred Literature*. Peabody, MA: Hendrickson, 2000.

Murphy-O'Connor, J. *Paul: His Story*. Oxford: Oxford University Press, 2003.

Sampley, J. P., ed. *Paul in the Greco-Roman World: A Handbook*. Harrisburg, PA: Trinity, 2003.

Thiselton, A. C. *The Living Paul: An Introduction to the Apostle's Life and Thought*. Downers Grove, IL: InterVarsity, 2011.

Wallace, R., and W. Williams. *The Three Worlds of Paul of Tarsus*. London: Routledge, 1998.

Westerholm, S., ed. *The Blackwell Companion to Paul*. West Sussex, UK: Wiley-Blackwell, 2011.

Advanced Sources

Hagner, D. A., and M. J. Harris, eds. *Pauline Studies: Essays Presented to F. F. Bruce*. Grand Rapids: Eerdmans, 1980.

Harrison, J. R. *Paul and the Imperial Authorities at Thessalonica and Rome: A Study in the Conflict of Ideology*. WUNT 273. Tübingen: Mohr-Siebeck, 2011.

Hock, R. F. *The Social Context of Paul's Ministry: Tentmaking and Apostleship*. Philadelphia: Fortress, 1980.

Horsley, R. A., ed. *Paul and Empire: Religion and Power in Roman Society*. Harrisburg, PA: Trinity, 1997.

Meeks, W. A. *The First Urban Christians: The Social World of the Apostle Paul*. New Haven: Yale University Press, 1983.

Porter, S. E. *The Paul of Acts: Essays in Literary Criticism, Rhetoric and Theology*. WUNT 115. Tübingen: Mohr-Siebeck, 1999.

———, ed. *Paul's World*. PAST 4. Leiden: Brill, 2008.

Porter, S. E., and C. D. Land, eds. *Paul and His Social Relations*. PAST 7. Leiden: Brill, 2013.

Schnabel, E. J. *Paul the Missionary: Realities, Strategies, and Methods*. Downers Grove, IL: InterVarsity, 2008.

Schnelle, U. *Apostle Paul: His Life and Theology*. Translated by M. E. Boring. Grand Rapids: Eerdmans, 2005 (2003).

Wright, N. T. *Paul and the Faithfulness of God*. 2 vols. Christian Origins and the Question of God 4. Minneapolis: Fortress, 2013.

2

The Chronology of Paul's Ministry
and His Imprisonments

1. Introduction

This chapter first examines the chronology of Paul's missionary ventures and then discusses the possible places of his imprisonments. Any reconstruction of Paul's missionary ministry must be extrapolated from the available literary texts, even when the book of Acts is used as one of the sources in this reconstruction. But even if Acts is considered to be a source for constructing the missionary journeys of Paul, nowhere in this book does it label Paul's travels as "missionary" journeys, and it is even disputed whether there were three, as is conventionally thought. As the chronologies below try to illustrate, there are a number of ways to construe the evidence regarding Paul's travels, and anywhere from three to five missionary journeys can be counted (some even combine what we have called the second and third journeys into a single endeavor to make it a total of two)—assuming that they are even to be given such a label. Paul's missionary journeys are often understood as well-planned, organized, and sponsored ventures, but this is perhaps not the best way to think of them. They seem in many ways much more spontaneous, under the guidance of the Holy Spirit and circumstances.

As for organization, the church at Antioch seems to have been central in planning and supporting several of the ventures (Acts 13:1–3; 15:1–2; 15:35–16:1). But even this is shrouded in some mystery: even though Paul seems to have begun from Antioch on several occasions, very little is known about what role the church played apart from its commissioning Paul and Barnabas (or, better, Barnabas and Paul; see 13:1–3) for the first venture into Asia Minor. Some argue that after Paul's confrontation with Peter, mentioned in Gal 2:11–21, Paul was no longer welcome in Antioch.[1] In fact, it is not proper, according to the

---

1. See N. Taylor, *Paul, Antioch, and Jerusalem: A Study in Relationships and Authority in*

account in Acts, to speak of Paul and Barnabas on a first *missionary journey*, since the indication in Acts is that this first expedition, on which John Mark also went, was led by Barnabas, at least in its early stages (13:1). Nor did the journeys always return to Antioch; one of these journeys concluded in Jerusalem, though through no fault of Paul's (21:17). At least Paul's third trip to Jerusalem—during which he was apparently falsely accused and arrested[2]—was his own idea, instigated by his desire to bring the collection from the Gentile churches to Jerusalem (it is unknown how large the collection was or whether it got to Jerusalem and into the proper hands, since it is not mentioned in the account in Acts 21).[3] There are other factors to consider in plotting the Pauline chronology as well. One is how to describe Paul's ministry before he appears to take a prominent part in Acts and before he began his letter-writing. Another is how to characterize his ministry on the way to Rome, at Rome, and possibly (see the chronology below) after his release from imprisonment in Rome (if in fact he was released before being rearrested and killed under Nero). All of these questions merit some comment as I reconstruct the Pauline chronology and try to gain some insight into the strategy of Paul's mission.

2. Paul's Mission and Ministry

Scholars continue to debate the merits and validity of using Acts in the reconstruction of a Pauline chronology. Ferdinand Christian Baur was the first to contend that Acts was a document written much later than the events described within it, as a second-century apologetic argument to show the unity of early Christianity. In light of this goal, Baur claims that the author of Acts decidedly omitted certain conflicts within the early church, namely between "Pauline" Christianity and "Petrine" Christianity, and, in this vein, he holds

---

Earliest Christianity (JSNTSup 66; Sheffield: JSOT Press, 1992), 123–39. Cf. J. D. G. Dunn, "The Incident at Antioch (Gal. 2:11–18)," *JSNT* 18 (1983): 3–57, soundly critiqued by J. L. Houlden, "A Response to J. D. G. Dunn," *JSNT* 18 (1983): 58–67; and D. Cohn-Sherbok, "Some Reflections on James Dunn's: 'The Incident at Antioch (Gal. 2:11–18),'" *JSNT* 18 (1983): 68–74.

2. The narrative in Acts 21 leaves open the strong possibility that Paul was treated duplicitously by the leaders of the Jerusalem church. Their asking Paul to participate in the purification ritual seems like an unnecessary test, and they had to know that Paul might have caused some stir in the temple. See S. E. Porter, *The Paul of Acts: Essays in Literary Criticism, Rhetoric, and Theology* (WUNT 115; Tübingen: Mohr-Siebeck, 1999), 172–86.

3. On the collection, see D. Georgi, *Remembering the Poor: The History of Paul's Collection for Jerusalem* (Nashville: Abingdon, 1992); and D. J. Downs, *The Offering of the Gentiles: Paul's Collection for Jerusalem in Its Chronological, Cultural, and Cultic Contexts* (WUNT 2/248; Tübingen: Mohr-Siebeck, 2008).

that Gal 1–2 more accurately reflects the relationship and status of Paul to the others.[4] Another significant scholar, however, who ended up doubting Baur's contentions and asserted the reliability of Acts as a reflection of Pauline chronology is the Scottish archeologist William Ramsay, who was originally a follower of Baur's line of thought. Ramsay's travels throughout Turkey among other factors convinced him of the veracity of the events in Acts.[5] I think that Baur was wrong and Ramsay was much closer to being correct.[6] As a result, the chronology offered below relies heavily upon what is offered in Acts and considers its contribution to constitute an important and indispensable body of material that ultimately complements what is revealed sometimes in only sketchy form in Paul's letters.[7] Besides legitimate dispute over the ordering of the chronology itself, there is also much discussion about the exact dates

4. F. C. Baur, *Paul the Apostle of Jesus Christ: His Life and Work, His Epistles and His Doctrine* (2 vols.; London: Williams & Norgate, 1873–75; repr. Peabody, MA: Hendrickson, 2003). This theory of the origins of Christianity has been revived in M. D. Goulder, *A Tale of Two Missions* (London: SCM, 1994).

5. E.g., W. M. Ramsay, *St. Paul the Traveller and the Roman Citizen* (London: Hodder & Stoughton, 1896); *The Cities of St. Paul: Their Influence on His Life and Thought* (London: Hodder & Stoughton, 1907); *The Bearing of Recent Discovery on the Trustworthiness of the New Testament* (London: Hodder & Stoughton, 1915); among others.

6. Even those who contend that they are reconstructing Paul's life apart from the book of Acts often end up with surprising overlap with the traditional view, as admitted in J. C. Hurd Jr., "Pauline Chronology and Pauline Theology," in *Christian History and Interpretation: Studies Presented to John Knox* (ed. W. R. Farmer, C. F. D. Moule, and R. R. Niebuhr; Cambridge: Cambridge University Press, 1967), 225–48, esp. 244. One of the major figures in such an attempt was John Knox (*Chapters in a Life of Paul* [New York: Abingdon, 1950; 2nd ed., Macon, GA: Mercer University Press, 1987]); the latest (and most fulsome) attempt is D. A. Campbell, *Framing Paul: An Epistolary Biography* (Grand Rapids: Eerdmans, 2014). His fundamental distinctions regarding primary and secondary sources must be reexamined. At the end of the day, even by using just Paul's letters, many prior and extratextual judgments must be made. The result appears to have some inconsistencies (e.g., regarding authorship, the Pastorals, letter unity, etc.).

7. The following discussion is similar in approach to that of C. J. Hemer, "Observations on Pauline Chronology," in *Pauline Studies: Essays Presented to F. F. Bruce* (ed. D. A. Hagner and M. J. Harris; Grand Rapids: Eerdmans, 1980), 3–18; cf. also G. Ogg, *The Chronology of the Life of Paul* (London: Epworth, 1968); J. C. Hurd Jr., *The Origin of 1 Corinthians* (New York: Seabury, 1965), esp. 3–42; K. P. Donfried, "Chronology: New Testament," *ABD* 1.1016–22; L. C. A. Alexander, "Chronology of Paul," *DPL* 115–23; D. A. Carson, D. J. Moo, and L. Morris, *An Introduction to the New Testament* (Grand Rapids: Zondervan, 1992), 223–31; R. Riesner, *Paul's Early Period: Chronology, Mission Strategy, Theology* (trans. D. Stott; Grand Rapids: Eerdmans, 1998), esp. 3–32; S. E. Porter, "The Portrait of Paul in Acts," *The Blackwell Companion to Paul* (ed. S. Westerholm; West Sussex, UK: Wiley-Blackwell, 2011), 124–38; and Porter, "Pauline Chronology and the Question of Pseudonymity of the Pastoral Epistles," in *Paul and Pseudepigraphy* (ed. S. E. Porter and G. P. Fewster; PAST 8; Leiden: Brill, 2013), 56–88.

of these events and about how the dates of composition of the Pauline letters fit within this chronology. Thus, the following chronology is offered with the recognition that much of the dating is tentative, even though I have attempted to make it as accurate as possible (see the map on page xiv for reference to the places mentioned).

A. Paul's Conversion and Early Ministry Years (ca. 33–47)

1. Conversion (Gal 1:15–16; Acts 9:3–7; cf. 22:3–16; 26:12–18) (33–34)

There are small, apparent discrepancies between the accounts in Acts of Paul's conversion (e.g., over whether and what his traveling companions saw or heard),[8] but the basic events of his encounter on the road to Damascus when he was on his way to persecute the church are highly consistent.[9] By all reckonings, this was a crucial moment in Paul's life and resulted in his subsequent ministry.

2. Damascus (Acts 9:8–22)

Paul spent several days in Damascus after his conversion, proclaiming the message of Christ, apparently before being compelled to leave because of a plot to kill him (9:23; 2 Cor 11:32–33).

3. Arabia (Nabatea) and Damascus (Gal 1:17–18) (33–37)

Recorded in Galatians, though not in Acts, are Paul's three-year stay in the Arabian desert and his return to Damascus. It is uncertain whether the attempt to kill him took place in his first or second visit to Damascus, although the date for the rule of the ethnarch King Aretas is probably around 37, thereby indicating the second visit (Acts 9:23; 2 Cor 11:32–33).[10]

8. I address these in S. E. Porter, *When Paul Met Jesus: How an Idea Got Lost in History* (Cambridge: Cambridge University Press, 2016), 75–94, along with other issues concerning Paul and Jesus.

9. For an argument regarding the continuity of Paul's testimonies, see J. D. G. Dunn, *Jesus Remembered* (Christianity in the Making 1; Grand Rapids; Eerdmans, 2003), 210–12.

10. See the recent discussion of Aretas in D. A. Campbell, "An Anchor for Pauline Chronology: Paul's Flight from 'The Ethnarch of King Aretas' (2 Corinthians 11:32–33)," *JBL* 121 (2002): 279–302, who thinks that the date of King Aretas's power is 36/37 and that this provides a firm anchor for Pauline chronology.

4. Jerusalem (Gal 1:18–20; Acts 9:26–29) (37)

This was Paul's first visit to Jerusalem, where he stayed for at least fifteen days, speaking with the apostles and debating with the Greek Jews until they tried to kill him.

5. Syria and Cilicia (Gal 1:21; Acts 9:30) (37–47)

Paul apparently spent ten years in the Tarsus area of Syria. Nothing else is known about his stay here, although we might well speculate that he engaged in some form of Christian teaching, at least enough so as to become known to Barnabas and sought out as a teacher.

6. Antioch (Acts 11:25–26) (47)

Barnabas sought Paul out and brought him to Syrian Antioch, where they met with the church and taught together.

7. Jerusalem (Gal 2:1–10; Acts 11:27–30; 12:25) (47)

This was probably Paul's second visit to Jerusalem, the so-called famine visit to bring aid to the church in Judea. It apparently occurred fourteen years (less likely seventeen years) after Paul's conversion, referred to in Gal 1:23. Many disagree, however, that these passages are referring to the same meeting, instead thinking that this was the visit to Jerusalem in Acts 15:2–29 (see chapter 7 §2C).

B. First Missionary Journey (Acts 13–14) (47–49)

1. Antioch (Acts 13:1–3)

Barnabas and Saul were sent on the first missionary journey[11] from the church at Syrian Antioch. They departed from the port at Seleucia for the first leg of their journey to Cyprus.

---

11. Although I stated above my reservations in using the term "missionary journey" to describe Paul's travels, I will use this term to reflect the conventional way of identifying these trips by Paul and his companions.

2. Cyprus (Acts 13:4-12)

a. Salamis (Acts 13:5)

Barnabas and Paul preached in the synagogue and were accompanied by John Mark.

b. Paphos (Acts 13:6-12)

At Paphos, Elymas the false prophet was blinded, and, as a result, the Roman proconsul, Sergius Paulus, believed.[12]

3. Asia Minor (Acts 13:13-14:26)

a. Perga (Acts 13:13)

Paul and his companions sailed to Perga in Pamphylia, where John Mark left them.

b. Pisidian Antioch (Acts 13:14-50)

Paul preached in the synagogue at Pisidian Antioch in Phrygia, but the Jews stirred up the people so that Paul and Barnabas were forced to leave the city.

c. Iconium (Acts 13:51-14:6)

Paul and Barnabas went to the synagogue and preached with success in Iconium in Phrygia, but unbelieving Jews again stirred up the people against them, and they had to flee.

---

12. D. A. Campbell believes that a highly fragmentary inscription dates the proconsulship of Sergius Paulus to before the death of the emperor Tiberius in 37, and hence Paul's first missionary journey was right after Paul's conversion and ten years earlier than usually thought (and before the Aretas incident). See Campbell, "Possible Inscriptional Attestation to Sergius Paul[l]us (Acts 13:6-12), and the Implications for Pauline Chronology," *Journal of Theological Studies* n.s. 56 (2005): 1-29. The reconstruction of the emperor and of Sergius Paulus are tentative and subject to question.

d. Lystra (Acts 14:6–20)

After performing a healing, Paul and Barnabas were mistaken by those in Lystra in Lycaonia for the gods Hermes and Zeus (see chapter 1 §3). When agitators from Iconium and Antioch arrived, Paul was stoned and left for dead.

e. Derbe (Acts 14:20–21)

Paul and Barnabas preached in Derbe in Lycaonia and then returned to those they had previously evangelized by way of Lystra, Iconium, and Pisidian Antioch, strengthening the churches and appointing elders as they went (14:21–23).

f. Perga (Acts 14:24–25)

In the region of Pamphylia, they preached in the city of Perga.

g. Attalia (Acts 14:25–26)

From the port of Attalia in Pamphylia, Paul and Barnabas sailed back to Syrian Antioch.

4. Syrian Antioch (Acts 14:26–28)

At Antioch, Paul and Barnabas gave a report of all that God had done and stayed with the disciples.

Galatians? (49). Some, if not most scholars, place the composition of the letter to the Galatians much later (see chapter 7 §2B2), but on the basis of the lack of reference to the Jerusalem Council (Acts 15), the equation of Gal 2:1 with Acts 11:27–30, and the Roman regional nomenclature at the time, I believe that it is most likely that Galatians was sent to the churches in Pisidian Antioch, Iconium, Lystra, and Derbe, that is, the southern Phrygian Galatian region, evangelized on Paul's first missionary trip, soon after he visited them (see chapter 7 §2B1).

5. Jerusalem (Acts 15:1–35) (49)

According to Acts, Paul and Barnabas represented the position of the Antioch church at a meeting in Jerusalem. Many critical scholars doubt that such a meeting took place. Others think that Paul's mentioning of going to Jerusalem in Gal 2:1–10 is a reference to this meeting (see chapter 7 §2C).

C. Second Missionary Journey (Acts 15:36–18:22) (50–52)

1. Antioch (Acts 15:36–40)

After a split with Barnabas over John Mark, who had left the pair at Perga in Pamphylia, Paul took Silas and departed on his second missionary journey.

2. Syrian Cilicia (Acts 15:41)

Paul traveled through the region of Cilicia in the province of Syria, strengthening the churches there.

3. Phrygian Galatia—Derbe and Lystra (Acts 16:1–6)

After being kept by the Spirit from preaching in the province of Asia, Paul preached in the area of Phrygian Galatia (and possibly sent emissaries to Colossae, if he did not visit there himself; see chapter 11 §3), circumcising Timothy in Lystra, whose father was a Greek but whose mother was a Jewess. Paul and his companions were forbidden by the Spirit from entering Bithynia (Acts 16:7–8).
Galatians? (50–52). Galatians may have been written sometime around this time, that is, after the Jerusalem Council of Acts 15 and during the second missionary journey, which would coincide with either the southern or the northern hypothesis discussed in chapter 7 §2B. Galatians could have been written from any of the places visited during this missionary journey, with Phrygian Galatia being the first major stop on this journey and possibly within the territory itself that he addressed.

4. Troas (Acts 16:8–10)

In Troas in Asia, Paul had a vision of a man from Macedonia calling him and his companions to Macedonia. They traveled from Troas to Samothrace, to Macedonian Neapolis, and then to Philippi (16:11).

5. Philippi (Acts 16:12–40)

In Philippi, the leading city of the district of Macedonia, Lydia was converted, and Paul and Silas were imprisoned for exorcising a slave girl and depriving her owners of their means of profit (her owners were paid for her prophecies). An earthquake released them from prison, leading to their jailer's conversion. Here Paul called upon his Roman citizenship.

6. Thessalonica (Acts 17:1–9)

After passing through Amphipolis and Apollonia, Paul and his companions arrived in Thessalonica in Macedonia, where Paul preached in the synagogue. As a result, there was an attack on his host, Jason.

7. Berea (Acts 17:10–14)

After preaching in the synagogue, Jews from Thessalonica stirred up the crowd in Macedonian Berea against Paul, who was then forced to leave.

8. Athens (Acts 17:15–34)

While Paul was waiting for Silas and Timothy (who perhaps made an unrecorded trip to Macedonia before going to Corinth; see chapter 8 §2D), he engaged in dialogue in the synagogue and addressed the philosophers in a speech on Mars Hill in Athens, which is located in Achaia.

9. Corinth (Acts 18:1–18) (Autumn 50–Spring 52)

During his one-and-a-half-year stay in Corinth, Paul appeared before Gallio, the Roman proconsul of Achaia. There he met Priscilla and Aquila, who had fled from Rome in response to Claudius's edict of 49;[13] later, after being opposed in the synagogue, he taught in the house of Titius Justus.

1–2 Thessalonians (50–52). It is generally agreed that 1 Thessalonians and 2 Thessalonians (if the latter is authentically Pauline; see chapter 8 §3A, B)[14] were written during Paul's stay in Corinth; see 1 Thess 3:1.

10. Ephesus (Acts 18:19–21)

This was Paul's first visit to Ephesus in Asia, where he left Priscilla and Aquila. He began his ministry here by preaching in the synagogue. Paul then left Ephesus to return by ship to Palestine.

13. There is much debate whether the edict of Claudius took place in 49 or 41. See G. Lüdemann, *Paul, Apostle to the Gentiles: Studies in Chronology* (trans. F. S. Jones; Philadelphia: Fortress, 1984), esp. 164–70. The 49 date is probably correct. See P. Lampe, *From Paul to Valentinus: Christians at Rome in the First Two Centuries* (trans. M. Steinhauser; Minneapolis: Fortress, 2003), 11–18.

14. A major proponent for the pseudonymity of 2 Thessalonians is G. S. Holland, *The Tradition That You Received from Us: 2 Thessalonians in the Pauline Tradition* (HUT 24; Tübingen: Mohr-Siebeck, 1988). See also chapter 8 §3A.

Philippians? (52/53). Those who hold to an Ephesian imprisonment think that Philippians may have been written during this short stay, requiring a short imprisonment (see chapter 11 §2).

11. Caesarea and Jerusalem (Acts 18:22)

Acts says that Paul landed at Caesarea and went up and greeted the church; this probably refers to going up to Jerusalem to meet with the church and its leaders there.

12. Antioch (Acts 18:22)

Paul closed this missionary journey by returning to Antioch.

D. *Third Missionary Journey (Acts 18:23–21:17) (53–57)*

1. Antioch (Acts 18:23)

Paul began his third missionary journey from Antioch, just as he did the previous two.

2. Galatia and Phrygia (Acts 18:23)

Paul is said to have visited Galatia and Phrygia, which, as in Acts 16:6, probably refers to the Phrygian region of the Galatian province and would have included the cities of Pisidian Antioch and Iconium.

3. Ephesus (Acts 19) (Spring or Autumn 53–55/56)

After recounting the arrival of Apollos, a Jew from Alexandria, in Ephesus, Acts says that while Apollos was in Corinth, Paul arrived at Ephesus. Sometime either before arriving in Ephesus or early in his stay, Paul probably wrote his first letter to the Corinthians (now lost, unless 2 Cor 6:14–7:1 is part of it; see chapter 9 §2D). Here he baptized the Ephesians into the name of the Lord Jesus, and they received the Holy Spirit. Paul stayed in Ephesus for two years and three months. During this time, Paul spoke in the synagogue for three months before opposition forced him to preach in a room owned by a certain Tyrannus. He also performed miracles (Acts 19:11). Apparently at the end of the period, the silversmith Demetrius caused a riot because the trade in idols of

Artemis had diminished as a result of the success of Paul's preaching. During this time Paul also probably made what is known as the "painful visit" to Corinth, traveling by boat across the Aegean Sea (2 Cor 2:1).

Galatians? (spring or autumn 53–summer 55). Galatians may have been written during Paul's stay in Ephesus (if my above contention is not correct regarding an earlier date), which would coincide best with a North Galatia hypothesis (see chapter 7 §2B).

1 Corinthians. (spring 55). It is generally agreed that Paul wrote from Ephesus his second letter to the Corinthians (what we call 1 Corinthians; see 1 Cor 16:8), and then, after his "painful visit" to them, his third, the "severe letter" (also probably lost, although some think fragments in 2 Corinthians [actually the fourth letter], such as 2 Cor 10–13, might be part of it; see chapter 9 §3B2).[15]

Philippians? (55). For those suggesting an early date for Philippians, this would be the most likely time of composition (see chapter 11 §2).

4. Troas (2 Cor 2:12–13)

Upon leaving Ephesus, Paul traveled to Troas, where he waited to no avail for Timothy's word on how the Corinthians received his "severe letter." When Timothy did not meet him there, he proceeded to Macedonia.

5. Macedonia (Acts 20:1–2)

Paul traveled through the area, probably visiting Philippi and Thessalonica (perhaps Berea) and possibly getting as far as Illyricum in Dalmatia (Rom 15:19–20). This traveling may have taken up to a year.

2 Corinthians (56). Second Corinthians (or at least 2 Cor 1–9; see chapter 9 §3B1), the fourth and final letter to the Corinthian church, was probably written during this time, probably from Philippi.

6. Greece (Acts 20:2–3) (56 or 57)

Paul stayed three months in Greece, almost certainly in Corinth. Because of a plot by the Jews, he did not sail for Syria.

Galatians? (56 or 57). Galatians may have been written at this time because

---

15. For a helpful analysis regarding the unity of 2 Corinthians, see C. D. Land, *Is There a Text in These Meanings? The Integrity of 2 Corinthians from a Linguistic Perspective* (NTM 36; Sheffield: Sheffield Phoenix, 2015). Land, however, argues that 1 Corinthians may have been the severe letter and that there was no intermediary visit.

of its similarities to Romans, according to a different version of the North Galatia hypothesis (see chapter 7 §2B).

Romans (spring 56 or 57). Romans was probably written from Corinth during this time (Rom 15:14–29).

1 Timothy? (56 or 57). It is suggested that 1 Timothy, if it is authentic, and many scholars do not believe that it is, and if it were written during the course of Paul's ministry (not post-Acts 28), would have been written by Paul from Corinth or possibly Troas (20:6–12).[16]

Titus? (57). It is suggested that Titus was written after Paul had written Romans, but before he made his way back through Macedonia to Asia Minor and on to Jerusalem.

7. Macedonia, including Philippi (Acts 20:3–6) (Passover 57)

Accompanied by many traveling companions, Paul made his way back to the east through Macedonia, including Philippi.

8. Troas (Acts 20:6–12)

During Paul's seven days in Troas, he preached the sermon during which Eutychus dropped off to sleep and fell three floors to the ground.

9. Miletus (Acts 20:13–38)

Traveling by way of Assos and other cities on the coast of Asia, Paul and his companions arrived at Miletus, where he spoke to the elders of the Ephesian church, who tried to talk him out of going to Jerusalem because of his prediction of danger.

10. Tyre (Acts 21:3–7)

Passing through several ports, Paul and his companions arrived on the coast at Tyre. He met with disciples who tried to dissuade him from going to Jerusalem and then sailed on to the port of Ptolemais, from which they proceeded to Caesarea.

---

16. The various alternatives for 1 Timothy and Titus are discussed in Porter, "Pauline Chronology," esp. 77–84. See also chapter 12 §3C.

11. Caesarea (Acts 21:8–14)

In Caesarea, a prophet named Agabus came from Judea and attempted to dissuade Paul from going to Jerusalem.

12. Jerusalem (Acts 21:15–23:32) (Pentecost 57)

Paul agreed to perform a vow to demonstrate that he had not abandoned the law. While in the temple area, a number of Jews from Asia (possibly Ephesus) stirred up the crowd to accuse Paul of opposing the law of Moses (antinomianism) and bringing Greeks into the temple area. When a riot ensued, he was taken into the custody of the Romans, although he was allowed to address the crowd. Paul was interrogated, kept in protective custody, and appeared before the Sanhedrin. When a plot against his life was uncovered, he was transferred to Caesarea.

E. Paul in Roman Custody (57–62)

1. Paul's Caesarean Imprisonment (Acts 23:33–26:32) (57–60)

Paul was in Roman custody in Caesarea under two Roman procurators, Felix and Festus. He also made a defense before Agrippa before having his case referred to Rome to be heard by the emperor.

2 Timothy? (57–60). A few scholars think that 2 Timothy was written during Paul's Caesarean imprisonment. A few scholars also think that all of the so-called Prison Epistles were written from a Caesarean imprisonment (see §3 below).

2. Paul's Travels to Rome (Acts 27:1–28:15) (Autumn 60–Spring 61)

Paul sailed to Rome under the custody of a centurion named Julius. Passing by Cyprus, Cilicia, and Pamphylia, the ship landed at Myra in Lycia. There they boarded an Alexandrian ship for Rome. While they were sailing by Crete (with a stop in the harbor at Fair Havens), a storm came up that finally shipwrecked them on Malta (they were sailing late in the sailing year and so were susceptible to storms; Acts 27:9 says they were sailing long after Yom Kippur, so possibly in October or November). After three months and the passing of winter, they again set sail and arrived at Puteoli (the primary western Roman seaport in the Bay of Naples), on the western Italian coast.

3. Paul's Roman Imprisonment (Acts 28:16–31) (61–62)

Paul was imprisoned in Rome for two years in a private house. He may have died in prison during this imprisonment.

Philippians, Colossians, Philemon, and Ephesians (61–62). If these letters were written from a Roman imprisonment and they are all genuinely Pauline (see chapter 6 §2 and chapter 11 on the individual letters), they would have been written during this time. Establishing the order of their writing is difficult; some put Philippians at the beginning of this period, and others put it at the end. Other views of the imprisonment would put the letters earlier (see §3 for further discussion).

2 Timothy? (61–62). A few scholars think that 2 Timothy was written during Paul's Roman imprisonment, along with the other prison letters.

F. Paul's Possible Release from Prison and Later Reimprisonment (62–65)

Since Acts does not record the closing period of Paul's life, the following is a possible scenario of what happened after his release, if he was in fact released.

1. Paul's Travels in the Mediterranean Area

Acts apparently does not record these travels to such places as Macedonia and possibly Ephesus (1 Tim 1:3), probably Crete (Titus 1:5), Nicopolis (3:12), Troas (2 Tim 4:13), and Miletus (4:20).

1 Timothy and Titus (64–65). These two letters, if they are authentically Pauline, and many scholars do not believe that they are, would most likely have been written during this period of freedom (see chapter 12 §3C).[17]

2. Pauline Reimprisonment (2 Tim 1:16–17; 4:6) (64–65)

Paul, according to this view, was reimprisoned and died during the Christian persecutions by Nero (possibly as late as 67).

2 Timothy (64–65). If this letter is authentically Pauline, and many scholars do not believe that it is, it would most likely have been written during this final imprisonment of Paul (see chapter 12 §3C).

---

17. See my discussion in S. E. Porter, "Pauline Authorship and the Pastoral Epistles: Implications for Canon," *BBR* 5 (1995): 105–23.

3. Paul's Imprisonments

That Paul was imprisoned is not a matter of dispute. The question is not even how many times he was imprisoned, although that is up for debate. What is important is that it appears that during one of his imprisonments he wrote at least two letters (Philippians and Philemon) and possibly more (Colossians and Ephesians, and possibly 2 Timothy).[18] Traditionally Philippians, Colossians, Philemon, and Ephesians are attributed to the same imprisonment, while 2 Timothy is attributed to a later imprisonment. What is the evidence regarding these various imprisonments, and what bearing do these facts have upon discussion of the Prison Epistles? The evidence is inconclusive, but as Craig Wansink shows, it is important to understand Paul's imprisonments in terms of both the physical conditions that he would have been subject to and the influence these may have had upon how he developed various themes in his letters. I do not have space to develop the influence of imprisonment upon Paul's writings. It is, nevertheless, worth recounting the evidence for the various imprisonments.[19]

A. Paul the Prisoner

That Paul was imprisoned is attested in several different ways. First, numerous references in his letters witness to his imprisonment: Phil 1:14; Col 4:10; Eph 6:20; Phlm 1, 23; 2 Cor 11:23; and 2 Tim 1:8. Second, there are references to Paul's imprisonments elsewhere in the New Testament, particularly in Acts: 16:23–26, in Philippi for one night; Acts 23–26, in Caesarea for roughly two years; and 28:30–31, in Rome for two years. Third, there are references in extrabiblical sources, the most noteworthy being Eusebius (*Ecclesiastical History* 2.22), who reports that Paul was imprisoned for two years in Rome before

---

18. I think a good case can be made for Pauline authorship of all thirteen of the letters attributed to him. See especially chapters 6 and 12 of this book, and for a fuller argument for this position, see S. E. Porter, "Paul and the Pauline Letter Collection," in *Paul and the Second Century* (ed. M. F. Bird and J. R. Dodson; LNTS 412; London: T&T Clark, 2011), 19–36; also Porter, "Paul and the Process of Canonization," in *Exploring the Origins of the Bible: Canon Formation in Historical, Literary, and Theological Perspective* (ed. C. A. Evans and E. Tov; ASBT; Grand Rapids: Baker, 2008), 173–202.

19. See C. S. Wansink, *Chained in Christ: The Experience and Rhetoric of Paul's Imprisonments* (JSNTSup 130; Sheffield: Sheffield Academic, 1996), esp. 27–95, on the conditions of imprisonment. Cf. also B. Rapske, *Paul in Roman Custody* (BAFCS 3; Grand Rapids: Eerdmans, 1994), esp. 195–422, for Paul's imprisonments in Acts.

being released, later reimprisoned, and killed during this last imprisonment (the major evidence for Paul's second Roman imprisonment). The evidence is conclusive and decisive—Paul was in prison on several occasions. But where might he have been in prison when he wrote the so-called Prison Epistles (Ephesians, Philippians, Colossians, and Philemon, and possibly 2 Timothy)? The answer to this question is explored below.

B. Places of Imprisonment

Four major locations are suggested for the imprisonment during which Paul wrote the Prison Epistles (the number of letters may be fewer, depending upon one's view of the Pauline authorship of several of the letters). J. A. T. Robinson and Bo Reicke make commendable attempts to place the Pastoral Epistles into what is known of the Pauline chronology from Acts (and is reflected above in the chronology), but their similar schemes are generally rejected by scholars.[20] They raise some important issues, but generally the differences in the Pastoral Letters—granted, many of these have been overdrawn—seem to require (so most scholars) that they be treated on their own, either as pseudonymous compositions or, more likely to my mind, as products of a period of writing that extends beyond the end of Acts (a period suggested by Eusebius). This leaves us with the remaining so-called Prison Epistles. The four major places of imprisonment during which writing of these letters could have occurred are, in decreasing order of probability, Rome, Ephesus, Caesarea, and Corinth.[21]

1. Rome

The Roman imprisonment is the traditional and still the majority view regarding the place of Paul's imprisonment during the composition of the Prison

20. See J. A. T. Robinson, *Redating the New Testament* (Philadelphia: Westminster, 1976), 31–85, esp. 84; and B. Reicke, *Re-examining Paul's Letters: The History of the Pauline Correspondence* (ed. D. P. Moessner and I. Reicke; Harrisburg, PA: Trinity, 2001); cf. also W. Metzger, *Die letzte Reise des Apostels Paulus: Beobachtungen und Erwägungen zu seinem Itinerar nach den Pastoralbriefen* (Stuttgart: Calwer, 1976), esp. 29–59; and J. van Bruggen, *Die geschichtliche Einordnung der Pastoralbriefe* (Wuppertal: Brockhaus, 1981), who differs in his reconstruction, but offers one of the most thorough treatments. For assessment of these theories, see Porter, "Pauline Chronology," 77–87, and discussion in chapter 12 §3C.

21. See Hurd, *1 Corinthians*, 14, 330, for representatives of the various positions. See also J. D. G. Dunn, *The Epistles to the Colossians and to Philemon: A Commentary on the Greek Text* (NIGTC; Grand Rapids: Eerdmans, 1996), 308–9, for an overview of the arguments for the Roman and Ephesian origins.

Epistles. As noted above, Eusebius says that Paul was brought to Rome and that with him was Aristarchus, whom he calls a fellow prisoner in Col 4:10 (cf. also Acts 27:2, where Aristarchus is said to be accompanying Paul). Paul's imprisonment at Rome was "without restraint" (so says Eusebius), which is compatible with the kind of freedom mentioned at the end of Acts (28:30) and consistent with—and even necessary for—the kind of ministry, including writing and receiving people, that seems to occur in the Prison Epistles. For example, Timothy is said to be the coauthor or cosender of all of the Prison Letters, and, in all of these letters, Paul mentions people who have come to him, including Epaphroditus, Epaphras, and Onesimus, to name only a few (e.g., Phil 2:25; Col 4:10–12, 14). It is likely, according to this view, that Onesimus fled (or traveled) to the capital of the empire in order to escape detection. Rome was a city of probably around one million people at this time, fully half of them slaves. It is understandable that an escaped slave wishing to go undetected would have selected Rome as a city in which he could live unnoticed.

When the Roman imprisonment is compared with other possible places mentioned in the sources cited above, it appears to be the only viable option. So far as hard evidence is concerned, the half-night imprisonment at Philippi is clearly inadequate; and even the Caesarean imprisonment, though it lasted for two years (Acts 24:27), seems to have involved a different situation, in which Paul's movements and the possibility even of receiving people and writing letters would have been more restricted, especially if there were fears of a plot against his life (23:16). The last piece of evidence for the Roman imprisonment is the thought reflected in the Prison Letters. The great theological themes of the major letters, such as justification apart from works, do not seem to be emphasized in these letters. While this might point to a period earlier than the time of composition of the main letters, this is not a serious option, and hence would seem to indicate a later date. This later date is supported by discussion in these letters of several topics in which there is a more developed theology in terms of the church as the body of Christ, and by the orderliness that had become more predominant in these churches (compare the Corinthian letters with Phil 1:1 and the household codes [German *Haustafeln*], which specify mutual submission between members of the household, in Colossians and Ephesians).[22]

Even though there is strong evidence for the Roman imprisonment, not all are convinced. There are two major objections to the Roman hypothesis. The

---

22. The differences in treatment of these issues become a problem only if one assumes that churches in different cities had similar organizational structure and development. This is an assumption that many New Testament scholars seem to make (perhaps because of their Anglican or German Lutheran affiliations), but it may not have been the case.

first concerns the Pauline chronology as established by Acts. If it is thought desirable to fit all of the Pauline letters into this chronology, it appears very difficult to do so, apart from Robinson's and Reicke's schemes mentioned above (which is definitely worth considering). The second concerns the distance between Rome and the cities involved in the prison correspondence. The distance between Colossae and Rome was approximately a thousand miles. If it is assumed that Onesimus ran away from Philemon in Colossae, he would have been required to travel a considerable distance both by land and by boat. The increased danger of traveling by boat lay in the fact that, had he been detected, there was no way to escape short of attempting to swim the Mediterranean! Furthermore, other trips of visitors are involved in this scenario. Besides Onesimus, Epaphras and Epaphroditus came to Paul, although the latter traveled a shorter distance from Philippi. Then Tychicus and Onesimus returned to Colossae with the two letters to the Colossians and Philemon. Such long journeys seem to be treated in a rather casual way in the letters, considering the distances involved. Nevertheless, this is not atypical for documentary papyrus letters in general, in which safety is more important than distance (cf. Phil 2:25–29 regarding Epaphroditus). Finally, the reference that Paul makes in Phlm 22 to his intention to visit Colossae and to have a bed prepared for him may seem a bit difficult to understand in light of both his intention to travel to the west from Rome (Rom 15:24, 28) and the distance involved.

2. Ephesus

There is no record of an Ephesian imprisonment in Acts or Paul's letters, but there is explicit mention in the apocryphal *Acts of Paul* 6. Consequently, an argument for Ephesian imprisonment would depend on inference and late evidence, but a plausible case is made for it, nonetheless. According to this position, first argued by Adolf Deissmann, who was followed by a significant number of other scholars,[23] Paul was imprisoned in Ephesus during one of his two trips to the city, perhaps during his first visit on his second missionary

23. A. Deissmann, *Paul: A Study in Social and Religious History* (2nd ed.; trans. W. E. Wilson; 1927; repr. New York: Harper, 1957), 17n1; G. S. Duncan, *St. Paul's Ephesian Ministry: A Reconstruction with Special Reference to the Ephesian Origin of the Imprisonment Epistles* (London: Hodder & Stoughton, 1929); cf. F. J. Badcock, *The Pauline Epistles and the Epistle to the Hebrews in Their Historical Setting* (London: SPCK, 1937), 54–71; C. R. Bowen, "Are Paul's Prison Epistles from Ephesus?" *American Journal of Theology* 24 (1920): 112–35; F. Watson, *Paul, Judaism, and the Gentiles: Beyond the New Perspective* (rev. and exp. ed.; Grand Rapids: Eerdmans, 2007), 141. Watson affirms Pauline authorship of only Philippians and Philemon, which affects his view of the location of the letters.

journey (Acts 18:19–21) or, more likely, during his third missionary journey after the incident with Demetrius, who convinced his fellow idol makers that Paul was hurting their business (19:23–41). He then wrote Philippians, Colossians, and Philemon; the composition of Ephesians was reserved for a later period (if it was written by Paul at all). There is no direct reference to this imprisonment, but there are several lines of indirect evidence, including the plausible scenario just outlined. Included in this evidence is Paul's testifying in 2 Cor 11:23 that he was imprisoned many times and that he had troubles in Asia, including fighting with wild beasts in Ephesus (1 Cor 15:32), having severe trials (2 Cor 1:8), and Priscilla and Aquila risking their lives for him (Rom 16:3–4). The Marcionite prologue for Colossians, one of a set of later Latin prologues attached to Paul's letters, lists Ephesus as the place of origin of the letter to the Colossians.[24] Ephesus was situated only a hundred miles from Colossae, a short distance for Onesimus to travel after fleeing Colossae. Ephesus was known to have a slave underground into which Onesimus could have hoped to be integrated. This location seems to make better sense of Paul's reference in Phlm 22 to prepare for his visit.

In spite of the case made for an Ephesian imprisonment, it still fails to displace the Roman imprisonment theory. There are several possible reasons for this. First, though there are references in Paul's letters to various troubles in Asia, in particular Ephesus, including his fighting with beasts (1 Cor 15:32),[25] none of these references is clearly a reference to an imprisonment. Few, if any, would take the reference to fighting with wild beasts as something that happened during an imprisonment, for the simple reason that Paul would almost assuredly not have been left alive to recount this event if it had literally happened (and was not a metaphorical reference to conflict with humans). Furthermore, there is no evidence that such punishment was used on Christians at this early of a date. Even though 2 Cor 11:23 refers to other imprisonments, it does not specify an Ephesian imprisonment. It is doubtful that so significant an imprisonment would be completely overlooked by the author of Acts, especially since he mentions Paul's being in Ephesus on several occasions, as well as

24. See B. M. Metzger, *The Canon of the New Testament: Its Origin, Development, and Significance* (Oxford: Clarendon, 1987), 97–99. The Marcionite prologues are brief introductions found in a number of Latin manuscripts, such as the sixth-century Codex Fuldensis. Many think that they go back to Marcion. They are published in A. Souter, *The Text and Canon of the New Testament* (rev. C. S. C. Williams; London: Duckworth, 1954), 188–91.

25. See A. J. Malherbe, "The Beasts at Ephesus," in Malherbe's *Paul and the Popular Philosophers* (Minneapolis: Fortress, 1989), 79–89; and H. Koester, "Ephesos in Early Christian Literature," in *Ephesos: Metropolis of Asia* (ed. H. Koester; Valley Forge, PA: Trinity, 1995), 120–24, esp. 120.

the trouble that he had with Demetrius. It is not impossible that Onesimus fled to Ephesus, but the distance is perhaps too close for an escaped slave to expect to be able to blend in, especially since his master probably would have started his search in that very city. Furthermore, there is no evidence that a pretorian guard, which is mentioned in Phil 1:13, was located in a senatorial province.[26] Finally, the significance of Phlm 22 and Paul mentioning the preparation of a room for him is probably missed. It is not that Paul would have been likely to drop in but, rather, that Paul is making use of the convention of the "apostolic presence," in which he would use his authority as a way of creating leverage for his requests.

3. Caesarea

The Caesarean imprisonment theory, although Acts refers to an imprisonment there, has never been a particularly strong position to maintain or defend.[27] It is argued that Aristarchus's sharing of Paul's imprisonment (Col 4:10) can be harmonized with Paul's imprisonment in Caesarea (Acts 24:23) and Tychicus's going on to Colossae (Col 4:8) just as easily as with the Roman imprisonment. Indeed, it is claimed, in light of the distances of Rome and Ephesus from Colossae, the one being too far and the other too close, Caesarea is the most likely place for Onesimus to have gone, especially since he would have had to travel only by land, not by sea. The request for accommodation in Phlm 22 came more likely, this position maintains, from Caesarea, before Paul appealed to Caesar, when there was still hope that he would be freed from there. His heading from Caesarea to Colossae would have been part of his westward movement, which was anticipated when he wrote Romans (15:24).

Even though what is said of Caesarea may be compatible with the evidence in Acts and Colossians, it is highly unlikely that Paul's Prison Epistles were written there. Caesarea was a very Roman city of approximately fifty thousand inhabitants with the headquarters of the Roman procurator, so it is highly unlikely that Onesimus could have hoped to blend in there as an escaped slave or that so much missionary activity could have gone on there as required (see Col 4:3–4, 11).

---

26. See M. Silva, *Philippians* (2nd ed.; BECNT; Grand Rapids: Baker, 2005), 7.

27. See Robinson, *Redating the New Testament*, 57–80. Dunn (*Colossians and Philemon*, 307) agrees that it has not gained much popularity, in spite of efforts by German scholars Martin Dibelius and Ernst Lohmeyer, who wrote influential commentaries on Colossians and Philemon.

4. Corinth

It is also suggested that Paul was imprisoned in Corinth,[28] probably when he appeared before Gallio after the Jews made accusations against the Christians regarding worshiping in illegal ways (Acts 18:12–17). The polemic, for example, of Phil 3:1–11 is said to be consistent with other Pauline writings of this time (e.g., 2 Corinthians), and the distance would have been suitable for communication with those in Asia. Although this position is based upon inference, the argument is that there was a period of imprisonment after the charges were brought against Paul and before his case was heard before Gallio, even though it was immediately dismissed. The time would have been sufficient for production of the Prison Epistles, since Paul was in Corinth during this stay for over a year. This would move the composition of letters written during this imprisonment to around 50–52.

This view has little to commend it. Not only does it require an imprisonment that is not mentioned in Acts, Paul's letters, or any other source even though it would have been literarily important; it also requires a complete rethinking of the theological development of Paul's letters. That some of Paul's great doctrines, such as justification, are not major topics in the Prison Epistles is not the chief problem. The problem is that Paul appears to have a more developed view of the church as body in several of the Prison Epistles than he does in the major epistles (compare Eph 4:15–16 and 5:29–32 with 1 Cor 12:12–31; Philippians may not show the same degree of development, perhaps suggesting a date different from the other Prison Letters). This kind of development does not make sense. It is understandable that Paul would choose not to emphasize certain beliefs in subsequent letters, but it is difficult to account for an underdevelopment of ideas compared to the Prison Letters. Furthermore, the atmosphere reflected in the Prison Epistles does not seem to be the same as that of the Corinthian situation, where Paul is surrounded by friends engaged in active ministry.

5. Summary

It is clear that the Roman imprisonment still has the most to commend itself, even if one cannot be dogmatic about this conclusion. Although the distances involved are great, they are not insurmountable in light of what we know of travel in the Greco-Roman world. If the conditions were favorable, it was

---

28. See R. P. Martin, *Philippians* (NCB; Grand Rapids: Eerdmans, 1976), 44–45, for an assessment of this position.

possible for a person to make a trip from Rome to a place on the eastern Mediterranean in about four to seven weeks.[29] There is the further possibility that Onesimus may have been sent on a trip by his master, a trip that may have taken him to the vicinity of Paul, even Rome itself. Rightly understood as the invocation of apostolic authority that it is, Phlm 22 presents no difficulty to this position. Nor does Paul's possible decision after his release to travel around the eastern Mediterranean rather than head to Spain present a difficulty (such travels do not preclude a trip to Spain). Paul's statements in Romans describing his intended program are not determinative.

4. Conclusion

Much remains highly speculative regarding the life and ministry of Paul. Attempts to reconstruct his life apart from the use of Acts, though they have been tried, end up looking surprisingly similar to the one recorded in Acts. By using the book of Acts, we can help to narrow down a number of the possibilities, especially regarding such issues as the place of Paul's imprisonments and where he wrote the Prison Epistles. The chronology also helps us to trace and appreciate the patterns of the development in Paul's thought, as well as aiding in discerning more and less plausible scenarios according to Paul's thought. Even if we are not able to find a suitable alternative descriptive terminology of Paul's "missionary journeys" or settle on adequate descriptive labels for the other periods in Paul's life, we can at least appreciate the overall patterns of his work and ministry. As will be discussed further when we examine each of the individual letters, there remains much speculation regarding authorship and chronology issues of the individual letters, including consideration being given to those who believe that all of Paul's letters can be accounted for with a single Roman imprisonment. Nevertheless, this chronology provides a useful framework for considering the overall contours of his life and thought.

Sources for Further Study

Basic Sources

Bruce, F. F. *Paul: Apostle of the Heart Set Free*. Grand Rapids: Eerdmans, 1977.
Hemer, C. J. "Observations on Pauline Chronology." Pages 3–18 in *Pauline Studies:*

---

29. See Silva, *Philippians*, 5–6n5.

Essays Presented to F. F. Bruce. Edited by D. A. Hagner and M. J. Harris. Grand Rapids: Eerdmans, 1980.

Lüdemann, G. *Paul, Apostle to the Gentiles: Studies in Chronology.* Translated by F. S. Jones. Philadelphia: Fortress, 1984.

Ogg, G. *The Chronology of the Life of Paul.* London: Epworth, 1968.

Ramsay, W. M. *St. Paul the Traveller and the Roman Citizen.* London: Hodder & Stoughton, 1896.

Reicke, B. *Re-examining Paul's Letters: The History of the Pauline Correspondence.* Edited by D. P. Moessner and I. Reicke. Harrisburg, PA: Trinity, 2001.

Advanced Sources

Dunn, J. D. G. *Beginning from Jerusalem.* Christianity in the Making 2. Grand Rapids: Eerdmans, 2009.

Lampe, P. *From Paul to Valentinus: Christians at Rome in the First Two Centuries.* Translated by M. Steinhauser. Minneapolis: Fortress, 2003.

Phillips, T. E. *Paul, His Letters, and Acts.* Peabody, MA: Hendrickson, 2009.

Porter, S. E. *The Paul of Acts: Essays in Literary Criticism, Rhetoric, and Theology.* WUNT 115. Tübingen: Mohr-Siebeck, 1999.

Porter, S. E., and G. P. Fewster, eds. *Paul and Pseudepigraphy.* PAST 8. Leiden: Brill, 2013.

Riesner, R. *Paul's Early Period: Chronology, Mission Strategy, Theology.* Translated by D. Scott. Grand Rapids: Eerdmans, 1998.

Robinson, J. A. T. *Redating the New Testament.* Philadelphia: Westminster, 1976.

Taylor, N. *Paul, Antioch, and Jerusalem: A Study in Relationships and Authority in Earliest Christianity.* JSNTSup 66. Sheffield: JSOT Press, 1992.

Wansink, C. S. *Chained in Christ: The Experience and Rhetoric of Paul's Imprisonments.* JSNTSup 130. Sheffield: Sheffield Academic, 1996.

3

Background to Paul's Thought

1. Introduction

In this chapter, I examine the sources of Paul's thought. In considering the formative influences on Paul's thought, the complex nature of the ancient Greco-Roman world must be considered. This world was not one in which Judaic and Greco-Roman cultures stood side by side as equals.[1] It was a huge world, primarily as a result of Alexander's conquests, with surprisingly dense communication and trade holding it together. Alexander the Great had been instrumental in establishing Greek as the *lingua franca*, or common language of trade and commerce, of the Hellenistic world through his ambitious program of conquest, which extended from Greece proper down to Egypt and east toward India. Where the language of the conquerors went, so did their social institutions and culture, since language is the single most important tool in the establishment of society and the spread of culture. Even though he was not able to consolidate his rule after his spectacular conquests and his empire was divided among four generals soon after his death at the relatively young age of thirty-three (323 BC), Alexander's love of Greek culture (Aristotle had been his teacher) had a lasting effect. Wherever he went, Greek culture and influence followed, and they had a pervasive influence on the conquered as

---

1. For a seminal article including an overview of the issue of the languages used in ancient Palestine, see J. A. Fitzmyer, "The Languages of Palestine in the First Century A.D.," *Catholic Biblical Quarterly* 32 (1970): 501–31; repr. in *The Language of the New Testament: Classic Essays* (ed. S. E. Porter; JSNTSup 60; Sheffield: JSOT Press, 1991), 126–62. Although he specifically argues in this article for Aramaic influence upon the Greek of the New Testament, the summary of issues is very helpful. For a recent discussion of many of the issues, see S. E. Porter and A. W. Pitts, eds., *The Language of the New Testament: Context, History, and Development* (ECHC 3/LBS 6; Leiden: Brill, 2013).

the indigenous people strove to establish useful relationships with the conquerors. In linguistic terms, Greek was the "prestige" language, spoken by soldiers, merchants, traders, and anyone who wanted to profitably coexist or even thrive with them.[2] Jews were involved in most avenues of Hellenistic life; they even served as mercenaries in the armies of the Hellenistic world (1 Macc 11:41–51; cf. 10:36), besides being actively engaged in various forms of business. Not only did Alexander leave the legacy of Greek language to these disparate peoples; he left a strong cultural heritage, including the organization of cities and government.[3]

The Hellenistic world was one of great accomplishments in many areas. For example, important philosophical schools developed, such as Stoicism; a huge amount of literature was written; genuine literary scholarship was practiced in Alexandria, centered upon its tremendous library; and theoretical science developed such things as geometry, whereby the circumference of the earth was calculated (the calculation was in error but only because one of the factors was inaccurate). The Greek educational system was emulated throughout the Hellenistic world. A gymnasium was built near the temple in Jerusalem in the second century BC. To give some idea of the influence of Greek culture even upon the Jews, since exercise in the gymnasium was done naked and since the Greeks and Romans considered circumcision to be a form of bodily mutilation, some Jews reportedly attempted to have their circumcision surgically masked (called epispasm; cf. 1 Macc 1:14–15). The Hasmoneans had been, essentially, local Hellenistic rulers, and this acceptance of Greek culture by the bulk of the Jewish population continued for several centuries, including under the Herodian rulers who ruled during the lifetimes of Jesus and Paul. It was only after the Bar Kokhba revolt of AD 132–35 that Judaism turned decisively away from Hellenism.

The ancient world before the time of Alexander had been, for the most part, less well unified; now people could conceivably be citizens of the world, not simply citizens of a particular city. But this expansiveness also brought a

2. Regarding prestige language and the language(s) of the New Testament, see S. E. Porter, "The Greek Language of the New Testament," in *Handbook to Exegesis of the New Testament* (ed. S. E. Porter; Leiden: Brill, 1997), 99–130; Porter, "Did Jesus Ever Teach in Greek?" *Tyndale Bulletin* 44 (1993): 199–235; and Porter, "The Functional Distribution of Koine Greek in First-Century Palestine," in *Diglossia and Other Topics in New Testament Linguistics* (JSNTSup 193/ Studies in New Testament Greek 6; Sheffield: Sheffield Academic, 2000), 53–78.

3. See W. Tarn and G. T. Griffith, *Hellenistic Civilisation* (3rd ed.; London: Edward Arnold, 1952), esp. 210–38. There are many fine treatments of Alexander the Great. For one worth considering, see P. Green, *Alexander of Macedon, 356–323 B.C.: A Historical Biography* (Berkeley: University of California Press, 1991).

backlash in the form of an emphasis upon the individual, as many people felt alienated and insignificant in such a vast and incomprehensible world. Partly as a result, the Greco-Roman world was dominated by superstition and syncretism, in which numerous kinds and ways of belief were often indiscriminately joined together by people as they sought spiritual meaning. It was within this larger context, dominated by Greek and Roman culture and religion, that Judaism existed as just one form of belief among many. In many ways, Jews were respected by others for their system of belief, and hence there were those who wished to emulate Jewish morality and theology. This did not keep the Jews above suspicion, however, not only in Palestine, where the Romans and the Greeks before them had always had trouble with rebellion and insurrection, but in other places in the empire as well, such as Rome, where the Jews were expelled en masse probably in AD 49 by an edict of the Emperor Claudius, and Alexandria, where similar conflicts arose. As a result, it is unfair to evaluate Paul's thinking in terms of a simple either/or regarding Hellenistic and Jewish elements. Indeed, the more the topic is explored, the more it must be recognized that the Judaism of the turn of the eras was Hellenistic Judaism, even the forms practiced in Palestine. When we turn to Paul's writings, such a syncretistic balance is certainly found.[4]

4. On the above history and development, see C. G. Starr, *A History of the Ancient World* (3rd ed.; New York: Oxford University Press, 1983), 359–625; M. Hengel, *Judaism and Hellenism: Studies in Their Encounter in Palestine during the Early Hellenistic Period* (2 vols.; trans. J. Bowden; Philadelphia: Fortress, 1974); Hengel, *The "Hellenization" of Judaea in the First Century after Christ* (trans. J. Bowden; London: SCM, 1989); F. Millar, *The Roman Near East, 31 B.C.–A.D. 337* (Cambridge, MA: Harvard University Press, 1993), 27–79, 337–86. For further discussion of the range of topics and information, see, among others, T. R. Glover, *Paul of Tarsus* (London: SCM, 1925); F. C. Grant, *Roman Hellenism and the New Testament* (Edinburgh: Oliver & Boyd, 1962); M. Grant, *Herod the Great* (London: Weidenfeld & Nicolson, 1971); A. A. Long, *Hellenistic Philosophy: Stoics, Epicureans, Sceptics* (2nd ed.; London: Duckworth, 1986); M. E. Stone and D. Satran, eds., *Emerging Judaism: Studies on the Fourth and Third Centuries B.C.E.* (Minneapolis: Fortress, 1989); J. D. Newsome, *Greeks, Romans, Jews: Currents of Culture and Belief in the New Testament World* (Philadelphia: Trinity, 1993); T. Engberg-Pedersen, ed., *Paul in His Hellenistic Context* (Edinburgh: T&T Clark, 1994); W. E. Helleman, ed., *Hellenization Revisited: Shaping a Christian Response within the Greco-Roman World* (Lanham, MD: University Press of America, 1994); E. S. Gruen, *Heritage and Hellenism: The Reinvention of Jewish Tradition* (Berkeley: University of California Press, 1998); H.-J. Klauck, *The Religious Context of Early Christianity: A Guide to Graeco-Roman Religions* (trans. B. McNeil; Edinburgh: T&T Clark, 2000 [1995/96]); J. J. Collins and G. E. Sterling, eds., *Hellenism in the Land of Israel* (Notre Dame, IN: University of Notre Dame Press, 2001); A. Tripolitis, *Religions of the Hellenistic-Roman Age* (Grand Rapids: Eerdmans, 2002); S. E. Porter, ed., *Paul: Jew, Greek, and Roman* (PAST 5; Leiden: Brill, 2008); S. E. Porter and A. W. Pitts, eds., *Christian Origins and Greco-Roman Culture: Social and Literary Contexts for the New Testament* (ECHC 1/TENT 9;

2. Greco-Roman Elements in Paul

The influence of the Greco-Roman context and culture upon earliest Christianity, including Paul, has not received as much attention in recent years, due to the heavy interest in Jewish backgrounds of the New Testament. The way the discussion is often bifurcated into two parts, as if they were two equal forces, distorts the issues involved. The Greco-Roman world was one dominated by Rome, which had inherited the cultural legacy of Greece and then melded together in varying and sometimes competing ways various local cultural elements into what we know as Rome. This section, however, will show that both Greco-Roman and Jewish influences pervaded Paul's thought and theology, with perhaps the Greco-Roman context—in particular the Hellenistic elements within that culture—being more influential than is usually given credit. The first obvious Greco-Roman influence upon Paul is the Greek language.

A. Greek Language

Greek was one of Paul's first languages (the other was Aramaic). He probably spoke Greek not only at home but also in his dealings outside his own home while he lived in Tarsus. After all, Greek was the language of communication of even Diaspora Judaism during the Hellenistic period. The translation of the Hebrew Bible into what became known as the Septuagint (LXX) was begun in Egypt during the third century BC out of recognition that most of the Jews living there were linguistically incapable of understanding, or meaningfully worshiping in, their religious language, Hebrew. So the largest and most ambitious translation project of the Greek and Roman world was begun, extending over the next two centuries; the entire translation was completed probably sometime in the first century BC.[5] Some Diaspora Jews may have been able to worship in Hebrew or Aramaic, but the vast majority also worshiped in Greek. Even though more Aramaic was spoken in Palestine by Jews than elsewhere, it is estimated by Martin Hengel that, of the Jewish

---

Leiden: Brill, 2013); and S. E. Porter and A. W. Pitts, eds., *Christian Origins and Hellenistic Judaism: Social and Literary Contexts for the New Testament* (ECHC 2/TENT 10; Leiden: Brill, 2013).

5. On the Septuagint, see S. P. Brock, "The Phenomenon of the Septuagint," in *The Witness of Tradition* (ed. A. S. van der Woude; Oudtestamentische Studien 17; Leiden: Brill, 1972), 11–36; N. F. Marcos, *The Septuagint in Context: Introduction to the Greek Version of the Bible* (trans. W. G. E. Watson; Leiden: Brill, 2000), esp. 305–19; T. M. Law, *When God Spoke Greek: The Septuagint and the Making of the Christian Bible* (Oxford: Oxford University Press, 2013); and K. H. Jobes and M. Silva, *Invitation to the Septuagint* (2nd ed.; Grand Rapids: Baker, 2015), 13–33.

population of Jerusalem itself, a minimum of 10 to 20 percent spoke Greek as their first language (this says nothing of the non-Jewish population, which would have almost certainly spoken Greek),[6] and many more than this would have had a secondary bilingual capacity, acquired in order to conduct business and commerce within the dominant surrounding Greco-Roman culture. In other regions of Palestine, such as the Decapolis or many of the truly Hellenistic cities, such as Caesarea, Tiberias, or Sepphoris in Galilee, Greek would have been predominant, even for Jews.[7] Other areas of the Roman East, such as Arabia, witnessed significant usage of Greek. Jewish funerary inscriptions give substantial evidence of the influence of Greek language upon the Jewish population worldwide. Fully 75 percent of the extant Jewish tombs in Rome from the first century BC to the fourth century AD use Greek for their epitaphs. In Palestine, 55 to 60 percent of the extant tomb inscriptions, from mostly the first to fifth centuries AD, are written in Greek; roughly 40 percent of those in Jerusalem itself are in Greek.[8]

Paul was born and reared in this Greco-Roman world. It is therefore not surprising that all of Paul's writings are in Greek. Since Greek was the *lingua franca*, Paul had the reasonable expectation that, wherever he wrote in the world of his time, he could communicate if he wrote in Greek. Perhaps a similar expectation is even found in a letter written by an associate of the Jewish rebel Bar Kokhba to several of his deputies regarding supplies. He writes in lines 11–15 that "[the letter] is written how[ever] in Greek because th[e de]sir[e *or* th[e oppo]rtuni[ty(?) was not to be f[ou]nd in Hebrew to w[rit]e."[9] This rebel of the Jewish cause against Rome wrote here in Greek rather than Hebrew, implying that it was more effort, or there were fewer people available, to write in Hebrew. The writer had every expectation that the readers would be able to understand his letter. Even though Jewish literature was not read extensively outside their own circles, Jewish writers often wrote in Greek, even for their religious literature. Ben Sira reputedly translated his grandfather's

6. Hengel, *Hellenization*, 10. I think that there is reasonable evidence that the percentage may have been higher.

7. Hengel, *Hellenization*, 14–15.

8. See P. van der Horst, *Ancient Jewish Epitaphs: An Introductory Survey of a Millennium of Jewish Funerary Epigraphy (300 BCE–700 CE)* (Kampen, Netherlands: Kok Pharos, 1991).

9. To be clear, the quotation is either "the desire" *or* "the opportunity"; textual mutilations make it difficult to discern the original Greek reading. The complete text with translation is found in S. E. Porter, "The Greek Papyri of the Judaean Desert and the World of the Roman East," in *The Scrolls and the Scriptures: Qumran Fifty Years After* (ed. S. E. Porter and C. A. Evans; Journal for the Study of the Pseudepigrapha Supplement 26/RILP 3; Sheffield: Sheffield Academic, 1997), 293–316 (text on 315–16, discussion on 298–308); cf. Fitzmyer, "Languages of Palestine," in *Language of the New Testament*, 142.

work from a Semitic language into Greek in Egypt; parts of the Testaments of the Twelve Patriarchs were composed in Greek; in Palestine, additions to Daniel and Esther were made in Greek; and 1 Esdras and 2 Maccabees are thought to have been originally composed there in Greek. A number of Jewish works, including 2 Esdras and Judith, have survived predominantly in Greek, although they were probably originally composed in Hebrew.[10]

B. Epistolary Form and Style

Besides writing in Greek, Paul utilizes one of the common literary forms exploited by the Greco-Roman world: the letter. The Greco-Roman letter, like the letter of today, had established forms, consisting of various sections and formulas. Paul qualifies as one of the great masters of the Greco-Roman letter form, adapting the set form to his particular purposes. He wrote personal letters (e.g., to Philemon), but he also apparently originated and developed the ecclesiastical letter, the letter to a church or possibly a group of churches. Although there were standard forms of address, Paul developed his own opening formula, which theologizes the standard letter opening—"grace and peace." He also used two other sections of the letter—the thanksgiving and the paraenesis (= admonitory material)—as a way of emphasizing Christian ethical standards (see chapter 5 §3B, D).

Within the letter form, Paul also makes use of several other well-known literary conventions of the time. Two in particular are worth noting: the diatribe, and vice and virtue lists.

The diatribe is a communication technique, or possibly even a literary genre, developed by Cynic and Stoic philosophers during the Hellenistic period.[11] It is a dialogical form in which a teacher and student(s) engage in a verbal question-and-answer exchange in order to learn more about the subject being discussed. Along with this basic dialogical format, there are a number of other linguistic features, such as hortatory forms ("let us . . .") to create

---

10. The above evidence is discussed in S. E. Porter, "Jesus and the Use of Greek in Galilee," in *Studying the Historical Jesus: Evaluations of the State of Current Research* (ed. B. D. Chilton and C. A. Evans; NTTS 19; Leiden: Brill, 1994), 123–54 at 123–47.

11. The nature of diatribe is discussed in S. K. Stowers, *The Diatribe and Paul's Letter to the Romans* (SBLDS 57; Chico, CA: Scholars Press, 1981); Stowers, "The Diatribe," in *Greco-Roman Literature and the New Testament* (ed. D. E. Aune; SBLSBS 21; Atlanta: Scholars Press, 1988), 71–83; A. J. Malherbe, *Paul and the Popular Philosophers* (Minneapolis: Fortress, 1989), 25–33; and C. Song, *Reading Romans as a Diatribe* (Studies in Biblical Literature 59; New York: Peter Lang, 2004).

pleas to action; particular connective words, including strong contrastive ones
("but"); antithetical and parallel statements; rhetorical questions; and words
of direct address. A number of ancient authors used the diatribe, the most
famous perhaps being the ex-slave and philosopher Epictetus.[12] His diatribes
have obviously been put into literary form in his writings (perhaps by Arrian,
who wrote his teaching down), but they appear to reflect, at several points,
actual conversations. The form probably originated in philosophical literature,
indicating a classroom or instructional environment, and then was taken over
in the synagogue for pedagogical purposes.

Paul has several sustained sections of diatribe, in particular Rom 1–11
and sections in 1–2 Corinthians. In his writings, the discussion may reflect
genuine questions being asked by those in the churches to which he wrote,
but his diatribes are not transcriptions of actual conversations. Paul in effect
creates his opponent, who raises crucial questions and objections to which his
narrative voice profitably responds. Paul often addresses this literary creation
as "person" or "you," with the single individual often standing for a group that
thinks or acts similarly. As an example, here is Rom 3:1–8 laid out in diatribe
fashion (Q = Paul's dialogical partner; P = Paul's narrative response):[13]

Q. What therefore is the advantage of being a Jew, or what is the advantage
of circumcision?

P. Much in every way! First, they have been entrusted with the words of
God.

Q. But what if some do not have faith? Their lack of faith won't nullify God's
faithfulness, will it?

P. Indeed not! Let God be true and every person a liar—as it is written: "So
that you may be justified in your words and will prevail in your judging."

Q. But if our unrighteousness establishes God's righteousness, what shall
we say? The God who brings his wrath is not unjust, is he? (I am using
a human argument.)

P. Indeed not! How will God then judge the world? "If the truth of God by
my falsehood multiplies into his glory, why am I still condemned as a
sinner?" Why not—as we are being slandered and as some claim that we
say—"Let us do evil things so that good things may come about"? Their
condemnation is deserved.

12. His works are conveniently found in *Epictetus* (trans. W. A. Oldfather; 2 vols.; LCL;
Cambridge, MA: Harvard University Press, 1925–28).

13. My translation; cf. S. K. Stowers, "Paul's Dialogue with a Fellow Jew in Romans 3:1–9,"
Catholic Biblical Quarterly 46 (1984): 707–22, for a different arrangement of the dialogue.

The form of the diatribe is well illustrated by this reconstructed dialogue, all written by Paul himself.

Paul also makes use of vice and virtue lists. Such lists were especially used by Stoic philosophers in moral exhortation to catalogue or inventory personal vices and virtues.[14] They were not meant to be comprehensive lists of all of the instances of a particular category, but give representative examples as a means of focusing on the particular subject. Sometimes the lists are of character traits; other times they are personified. In either case, the effect is designed to be the same. Their use by Paul is in keeping with Stoic philosophy, by which the world is seen to function according to rational principles and the goal of human life is to align oneself with the divine rational spirit. Instances of virtue lists in the letters attributed to Paul are found in 2 Cor 6:6–7; Phil 4:6–9; and Eph 4:2–3. Examples of vice lists are found in Rom 1:29–31; 13:13; 1 Cor 5:10–11; Eph 4:31–32; 5:3–5; 1 Tim 1:9–10; 6:4–5; and Titus 1:7–10. A good example of the use of a vice list and a virtue list together is in Gal 5:19–23:

> The acts of the sinful nature are obvious: sexual immorality, impurity and debauchery; idolatry and witchcraft; hatred, discord, jealousy, fits of rage, selfish ambition, dissensions, factions and envy; drunkenness, orgies, and the like. I warn you, as I did before, that those who live like this will not inherit the kingdom of God. But the fruit of the Spirit is love, joy, peace, patience, kindness, goodness, faithfulness, gentleness and self-control. Against such things there is no law. (NIV)

C. Hellenistic Thought and Philosophy

Paul not only uses Greco-Roman literary forms and conventions; his thought also well illustrates some of the principles of Hellenistic thought. In the early twentieth century, emphasis was placed on how Paul's thinking was similar to that of a variety of Greco-Roman mystery religions.[15] Mystery religions are

---

14. See D. E. Aune, *The New Testament and Its Literary Environment* (LEC; Philadelphia: Westminster, 1987), 194–96; A. J. Malherbe, *Moral Exhortation: A Greco-Roman Sourcebook* (LEC; Philadelphia: Westminster, 1986), 138–41, with examples; and J. Thompson, *Moral Formation according to Paul: The Context and Coherence of Paul's Ethics* (Grand Rapids: Baker, 2013), esp. 87–110.

15. The classic study from this perspective is W. Bousset, *Kyrios Christos: A History of the Belief in Christ from the Beginnings of Christianity to Irenaeus* (trans. J. E. Steely; Nashville: Abingdon, 1970). More balanced is the conclusion of G. H. C. MacGregor and A. C. Purdy, *Jew and Greek: Tutors unto Christ; the Jewish and Hellenistic Background of the New Testament*

not well understood because, by definition, they were private religious cults that apparently practiced secretive initiation procedures in which the initiates became in some way intimately involved with the god, often through a ritual that may have included some sort of a baptism-like practice. Our best-known source is the Hermetic Corpus, but this was written much later than the New Testament and was probably influenced by the New Testament rather than the other way around. There is little basis for claiming that Paul was in any way influenced by these religious practices, although some of the writings attributed to Paul may reflect a direct response to them. For example, in Eph 5:18, Paul (or the author) implores his readers not to be drunk with wine but to be filled with the Holy Spirit. The author of Ephesians may merely be countering a tendency in the Ephesian church to engage in indulgent practices. This language, however, is similar in several ways to that in Euripides's *Bacchae* (line 281, but cf. 278–301; cf. Plutarch, *De defectu oraculorum* 40.432E) about Dionysus, the god of wine, one of the most widely read texts of the Greco-Roman world and instrumental in several religious cults.[16] There is a good chance that Paul was opposing indulgence in Bacchanalian practices in Ephesus.

More can be made of parallels in thought between the Stoics and Paul. This is not because Pauline thought is Stoic in orientation but because Paul and Stoic (and other) philosophers were concerned with similar kinds of issues. If the account in Acts 17 of Paul appearing before the Areopagus on Mars Hill in Athens is historical (and there is good reason to think that it is),[17] then there is direct evidence that Paul engaged in philosophico-religious discussion with philosophers of the day, including Stoics and Epicureans, and that

---

(London: Nicholson & Watson, 1936), 273–91: "Striking resemblances there admittedly are, but they are in vocabulary and outward form rather than in essential thought and content" (289). Besides the sources already noted above, see also T. R. Glover, *The Conflict of Religions in the Early Roman Empire* (2nd ed.; London: Methuen, 1909); F. Cumont, *Oriental Religions in Roman Paganism* (repr. New York: Dover, 1956 [1911]); G. Murray, *Five Stages of Greek Religion* (London: Watts, 1935); F. C. Grant, ed., *Hellenistic Religions: The Age of Syncretism* (New York: Liberal Arts, 1953), with selections; and L. H. Martin, *Hellenistic Religions: An Introduction* (Oxford: Oxford University Press, 1987).

16. For further detail on this proposal, see S. E. Porter, "Ephesians 5.18–19 and Its Dionysian Background," in *Testimony and Interpretation: Early Christology in Its Judeo-Hellenistic Milieu: Studies in Honour of Petr Pokorný* (ed. J. Mrázek and J. Roskovec; JSNTSup 272; London: Continuum, 2004), 68–80; cf. C. A. Evans, "Ephesians 5:18–19 and Religious Intoxication in the World of Paul," in *Paul's World* (ed. S. E. Porter; PAST 4; Leiden: Brill, 2008), 181–200. On the Dionysian cult, besides other works cited above, see M. Nilsson, *The Dionysiac Mysteries of the Hellenistic and Roman Age* (Lund: Gleerup, 1957).

17. The reasons for this include the way Paul is depicted and his form of naturalistic argumentation, fundamental to Rom 1:18–32.

many—though not all—of his concerns would have found a sympathetic ear. Paul's speech in Acts 17 is crafted in such a way that it begins from the kind of argument that would have found general apologetic acceptance with these philosophers. It is only when resurrection is mentioned that objections are raised.[18] As mentioned above, Stoic thought was concerned with how one lived a life aligned with the pervasive divine rational force. In Stoic thought there is also a tension between divine necessity and human responsibility, well captured in Cleanthes's *Hymn to Zeus*, which speaks both of God being the ultimate cause who rules by immutable laws and of humans who exercise their own wills and end up doing evil and foolish things. These are the kinds of topics that any religious system must come to terms with, and as did the Stoics, so did Paul.

There are several examples of similarities in Pauline and Stoic thought. For example, in Rom 7:15 Paul struggles aloud with the dilemma of fighting against one's own will: "I do not understand what I do. For what I want to do I do not do, but what I hate I do" (NIV). The Stoic Epictetus (*Dissertationes* 2.26.4) speaks of a similar human dilemma: "What he wants he does not do and what he does not want he does." In 1 Cor 14:25, Paul speaks of God being within or among human beings. Seneca reflects similar thought when he says, "God is near you, he is with you, he is in you" (*Epistle* 41.1); and, "A holy spirit resides within us" (*Epistle* 41.2). In Rom 9:1, Paul speaks of the human conscience confirming the truth of what he is saying: "I speak the truth in Christ—I am not lying, my conscience confirms it in the Holy Spirit" (NIV). Again, Seneca says, "Nor can I consent to such things with a clear conscience" (*Epistle* 117.1).[19]

With such philosophical thinking being prevalent, it is not surprising to

---

18. See S. E. Porter, *The Paul of Acts: Essays in Literary Criticism, Rhetoric, and Theology* (WUNT 115; Tübingen: Mohr-Siebeck, 1999), 141–59.

19. A convenient summary of Stoic and Pauline parallels is found in E. D. Freed, *The New Testament: A Critical Introduction* (Belmont, CA: Wadsworth, 1991), 232–34, used here; and D. A. deSilva, "Paul and the Stoa: A Comparison," *Journal of the Evangelical Theological Society* 38 (1995): 549–64. For discussions of the influence of Stoic thought on a number of individual passages, see, e.g., J. W. Martens, "Romans 2.14–16: A Stoic Reading," *NTS* 40 (1994): 55–67; T. Engberg-Pedersen, "Stoicism in Philippians," in *Paul in His Hellenistic Context*, 256–90; Engberg-Pedersen, *Paul and the Stoics* (Edinburgh: T&T Clark, 2000), on parallels in Philippians, Romans, and Galatians; W. Deming, *Paul on Marriage and Celibacy: The Hellenistic Background of 1 Corinthians 7* (SNTSMS 83; Cambridge: Cambridge University Press, 1995); M. V. Lee, *Paul, the Stoics, and the Body of Christ* (SNTSMS 137; Cambridge: Cambridge University Press, 2006), specifically in relation to 1 Cor 12–14; and R. M. Thorsteinsson, "Stoicism as a Key to Pauline Ethics in Romans," and N. Huttunen, "Stoic Law in Paul?" both in *Stoicism in Early Christianity* (ed. T. Rasimus, T. Engberg-Pedersen, and I. Dunderberg; Grand Rapids: Baker, 2010), 15–38 and 39–58. On the influence of popular philosophy on Paul, see Malherbe, *Paul and the Popular Philosophers*.

see reflections about what constitutes the virtuous person. In Greek thought, and later in Roman, there was persistent speculation about what virtues (ἀρεταί) characterized the virtuous person. These virtues gave grounds for boasting. Paul appears to have been influenced by such debate, but he transformed it into its negative form, downgrading the convention of boasting in one's virtues and emphasizing what would have been looked down upon in contemporary society as virtueless. For example, in 2 Cor 10–13 (see also Phil 3:4–6), Paul turns traditional claims to fame on their heads when he begins by characterizing himself as meek and gentle (2 Cor 10:1). Paul defends his apostolic ministry by recounting what distinguishes his ministry, including his litany of abuses in 11:22–29. He begins in 11:21 by rhetorically stating, "What anyone else dares to boast about—I am speaking as a fool—I also dare to boast about" (NIV). And he concludes in 11:30 by declaring, "If I must boast, I will boast of the things that show my weakness" (NIV). Similarly, in Rom 5:3–5, Paul states a progressive and climactic series of Christian virtues that distinguish the believer: "We also boast in our sufferings, because we know that suffering produces perseverance; perseverance, character; and character, hope. And hope does not disappoint us, because God has poured out his love into our hearts by the Holy Spirit, whom he has given us" (NIV altered).[20]

Paul's logic and means of argumentation are also full of Greco-Roman features (e.g., the diatribe mentioned in §2B). Two of these are selected here for special mention: his literary style and his literary imagery. As mentioned in chapter 1 §4, there is varied opinion among scholars regarding the influence of classical rhetoric upon Paul. Some scholars come very close to arguing that Paul was in essence a Greek rhetorician or speechwriter who committed his work to paper,[21] but this is not the best explanation of his letters. It is certainly true that Paul's letters are persuasive, because he simply knew how to create a convincing argument that utilized the logical capacity of language rather than because he used rhetoricians' genres or forms of organization or development.[22]

20. See W. Meeks, *The Moral World of the First Christians* (LEC; Philadelphia: Westminster, 1986).

21. E.g., B. Witherington III, *New Testament Rhetoric: An Introductory Guide to the Art of Persuasion in and of the New Testament* (Eugene, OR: Cascade, 2009), 94–157. In response to his arguments, see S. E. Porter and B. R. Dyer, "Oral Texts? A Reassessment of the Oral and Rhetorical Nature of Paul's Letters in Light of Recent Studies," *Journal of the Evangelical Theological Society* 55.2 (2012): 323–41. See also chapter 1 §4.

22. See D. L. Stamps, "Rhetorical Criticism of the New Testament: Ancient and Modern Evaluations of Argumentation," in *Approaches to New Testament Study* (ed. S. E. Porter and D. Tombs; JSNTSup 120; Sheffield: Sheffield Academic, 1995), 129–69. See also chapter 1 §4.

For example, the outline of the argument of the book of Romans gives good evidence of how Paul's mind worked. Within the body of the letter he begins by describing the human predicament that requires God's response (1:18–3:20)—a treatment divided into three sections, progressing from a general indictment of humanity, to an implication of the moral person, and finally even to condemnation of the Jew. Then Paul presents the solution to a person's legal problem of incurring the wrath of God (3:21–4:25). Paul moves from there to dealing with a person's legal and personal relationship with God, which he characterizes as reconciliation and which brings a person full circle by overcoming the legal and personally alienating effects of Adam's sin through Christ's work on the cross (5:1–21). Paul then discusses the implications of this changed status by discussing more fully what it means to participate in a personal relationship with God, characterized as life in the Spirit (6:1–8:39).[23] He concludes the body of the letter by selecting one crucial example, that of Israel, to illustrate the faithfulness of God to his promises of election. This logical pattern provides what many have found to be a compelling argument, but the pattern does not conform to any of the established patterns of classical rhetoric, even though it makes significant use of a number of features of persuasive discourse, including the exemplum or paradigm (4:1–25 on Abraham; 5:12–21 on Adam) and the diatribe (Rom 1–11).[24]

Paul also utilizes various stylistic features: parallelism (e.g., Rom 3:21–26); metaphor and simile (1 Cor 12:12–16; 2 Tim 4:6); synecdoche and metonymy, where a part or related item stands for the whole (Rom 5:9, where Paul uses "by his blood" as a metonym for death; and 2 Cor 3:15, where Moses stands for the entire Pentateuch); antonomasia, where a substitute name is used (Rom 5:14, where "the one who was to come" describes Christ); irony (Phlm 9); litotes, a form of understatement (Rom 1:16); apostrophe, or direct address (7:1); and many others.[25] This is not to deny that Paul also uses some of the other means seen in the rhetoricians for creating and structuring an argument. But he does not do so in a systematic way that would distinguish him as a classical rhetorician, any more than any other persuasive writer of

23. See S. E. Porter, "A Newer Perspective on Paul: Romans 1–8 through the Eyes of Literary Analysis," in *The Bible in Human Society: Essays in Honour of John Rogerson* (ed. M. Daniel Carroll R., D. J. A. Clines, and P. R. Davies; Journal for the Study of the Old Testament Supplement 200; Sheffield: Sheffield Academic, 1995), 366–92.

24. For this argument developed from a linguistic standpoint, see S. E. Porter, *The Letter to the Romans: A Linguistic and Literary Commentary* (NTM 37; Sheffield: Sheffield Phoenix, 2015).

25. See S. E. Porter, "Paul of Tarsus and His Letters," in *Handbook of Classical Rhetoric in the Hellenistic Period, 330 B.C.–A.D. 400* (ed. S. E. Porter; Leiden: Brill, 1997), 533–85 at 576–84.

the time.[26] For example, as a means of proving his argument, Paul appeals to his character (ἦθος), as in Philemon, especially verses 8–9. Paul also appeals to emotion (πάθος) when the occasion warrants it, as in Gal 1:6–9. Of course, he also uses reason or logic (λόγος)—for instance, in the exemplum, or example (Rom 4:1–25; 5:12–21); the syllogism, a form of argument with major and minor premises (1 Thess 4); and various forms of definition.[27]

To substantiate the various elements of his argumentation throughout his writings, Paul frequently appeals to various institutions of the Greco-Roman world, showing his connection to the culture around him and illustrating the relevance of what he is saying to the world in which the churches he addresses live. Without going into significant detail, we can mention a few of these images from the Greco-Roman world: political terminology (Phil 1:27; 3:20; Eph 2:19), sportsmanship (Phil 2:16; 3:14; 1 Cor 9:24–27; 2 Cor 4:8–9; 2 Tim 4:7), commercial terminology (Phlm 18; Col 2:14), legal terminology (Gal 3:15; 4:1–2; Rom 7:1–3; 13:6), the slave trade (1 Cor 7:22; Rom 7:14), and celebrations and processions in honor of the emperor (2 Cor 2:15–16; 1 Thess 2:19; Col 2:15; cf. Josephus, *Jewish War* 7.132–33, 148–57).

All of these elements together show how significant the broader Greco-Roman world was to Paul in his relationship with earliest Christianity. But that does not mean that he neglected his Jewish context as well. To that, I now turn my attention.

3. Jewish Elements in Paul

As much as Paul was influenced by the Greco-Roman world that surrounded him, Paul was also, as mentioned above and in chapter 1 §7, a Jew. He was, more specifically, a Diaspora Jew, and so several of the characteristics of his approach to theological matters may almost seem as much Greco-Roman as they do Jewish.[28] Although many scholars probably overemphasize the "Jewishness" of

26. See S. E. Porter, "The Theoretical Justification for Application of Rhetorical Categories to Pauline Epistolary Literature," in *Rhetoric and the New Testament: Essays from the 1992 Heidelberg Conference* (ed. S. E. Porter and T. H. Olbricht; JSNTSup 90; Sheffield: Sheffield Academic, 1993), 100–122; and Porter, "Ancient Rhetorical Analysis and Discourse Analysis of the Pauline Corpus," in *The Rhetorical Analysis of Scripture: Essays from the 1995 London Conference* (ed. S. E. Porter and T. H. Olbricht; JSNTSup 146; Sheffield: Sheffield Academic, 1997), 249–74.

27. See F. Young, "The Pastoral Epistles and the Ethics of Reading," *JSNT* 45 (1992): 115.

28. The relationship of Judaism to its wider world is discussed in J. J. Collins, *Between Athens and Jerusalem: Jewish Identity in the Hellenistic Diaspora* (2nd ed.; Grand Rapids: Eerd-

Paul in recent times,[29] it is nevertheless worth noting a number of features of Paul's thinking that seem to reflect specifically Jewish thought and influence.

The Jewish world of the first century surrounded the Mediterranean, with Jewish communities to be found from Egypt to Rome and beyond.[30] Despite the widespread influence of Greco-Roman culture upon them, they also had their own distinctive religious, literary, and cultural traditions. These together formed the basis of what is referred to as Judaism, so that it constitutes a complex of traditions, beliefs, and practices.[31] Some of these were maintained through the centuries, while others developed within the context of their changing and developing communal lives. As a result, we find a range of Jewish literature that confronts contemporary Jewish life through theological reflection.[32] As with other Jews, the foundation and basis for Paul's thought,

---

mans, 2000); and M. Goodman, *Judaism in the Roman World: Collected Essays* (Ancient Judaism and Early Christianity 66; Leiden: Brill, 2007).

29. See J. C. Paget, *Jews, Christians, and Jewish-Christians in Antiquity* (WUNT 251; Tübingen: Mohr-Siebeck, 2010), for a helpful collection of essays regarding Jewish influences upon Christianity; cf. also R. Bauckham, *The Jewish World around the New Testament: Collected Essays* (WUNT 233; Tübingen: Mohr-Siebeck, 2008), 1, who notes "the obvious influence of the non-Jewish Greco-Roman world in which the New Testament writings also belong, but that influence was felt right across the Jewish world in varying ways and to varying degrees."

30. For some historical sketches of the development of Jewish thought and practice among its people, see W. Foerster, *From the Exile to Christ: Historical Introduction to Palestinian Judaism* (trans. G. E. Harris; Philadelphia: Fortress, 1964 [1959]); H. Jagersma, *A History of Israel to Bar Kochba* (trans. J. Bowden; London: SCM, 1982–85 [1979–85]); and, most recently, F. J. Murphy, *Early Judaism: The Exile to the Time of Jesus* (Grand Rapids: Baker, 2002).

31. For treatments of these various factors, see the accounts in A. Edersheim, *Sketches of Jewish Social Life* (updated ed.; repr. Peabody, MA: Hendrickson, 1994 [1877]); M. McNamara, *Palestinian Judaism and the New Testament* (Wilmington, DE: Glazier, 1983); A. R. C. Leaney, *The Jewish and Christian World 200 B.C. to A.D. 200* (Cambridge: Cambridge University Press, 1984); A. J. Saldarini, *Pharisees, Scribes and Sadducees in Palestinian Society* (repr. Grand Rapids: Eerdmans, 2001 [1988]); E. P. Sanders, *Judaism: Practice and Belief 63 B.C.E.–66 C.E.* (London: SCM, 1992); L. L. Grabbe, *Judaism from Cyrus to Hadrian* (London: SCM, 1992); and Grabbe, *An Introduction to Second Temple Judaism: History and Religion of the Jews in the Time of Nehemiah, the Maccabees, Hillel, and Jesus* (London: T&T Clark, 2010). See also E. P. Sanders, *Jewish Law from Jesus to the Mishnah: Five Studies* (London: SCM, 1990).

32. See G. W. E. Nickelsburg, *Jewish Literature between the Bible and the Mishnah: A Historical and Literary Introduction* (2nd ed.; Minneapolis: Fortress, 2005). The major collection of such writings, many of which may have been in existence during Paul's time, are the Jewish Pseudepigrapha. These include a wide range of literature, including testamentary literature often ascribed to significant Jewish figures (e.g., some of the patriarchs), and various types of wisdom literature. See J. H. Charlesworth, ed., *The Old Testament Pseudepigrapha* (2 vols.; Garden City, NY: Doubleday, 1985). The Qumran scrolls also have some importance for Pauline studies. See W. S. LaSor, *The Dead Sea Scrolls and the New Testament* (Grand Rapids: Eerdmans, 1972), esp. 168–78; K. Stendahl with J. H. Charlesworth, eds., *The Scrolls and the*

theological and otherwise, was his monotheistic belief in the one true God, who was the God of Abraham, Isaac, and Jacob,[33] and the father of Jesus the Christ, whom he raised from the dead. These beliefs are reflected, however, in other important Jewish influences upon Paul.

A. Jewish Scriptures

The single most noticeable Jewish influence upon Paul's thinking and writing is clearly the Scriptures of his people Israel, the Old Testament.[34] There are two major ways in which the Old Testament informs Paul's thinking. The first is through direct quotation,[35] and the second is through allusion and indirect quotation, in which the Old Testament becomes a part of the framework of Paul's thinking.[36] He directly quotes the Old Testament numerous times, including eighty-eight direct quotations in Romans, 1–2 Corinthians, and Galatians alone. Romans has fifty-three direct quotations.

There are two important factors to consider with regard to Paul's quotation of the Old Testament. The first is that Paul does not hesitate to quote the

---

New Testament (New York: Crossroad, 1992), esp. 157–82; and J. VanderKam and P. Flint, *The Meaning of the Dead Sea Scrolls: Their Significance for Understanding the Bible, Judaism, Jesus, and Christianity* (San Francisco: HarperSanFrancisco, 2002), esp. 350–57. The scrolls are translated in F. García Martínez and E. J. C. Tigchelaar, *The Dead Sea Scrolls* (2 vols.; Grand Rapids: Eerdmans, 1997–98).

33. U. Schnelle, *The Apostle Paul: His Life and Theology* (trans. M. E. Boring; Grand Rapids: Baker, 2003), 70–75.

34. For a useful overview, see S. Moyise, *Paul and Scripture* (London: SPCK, 2010).

35. See C. D. Stanley, *Paul and the Language of Scripture: Citation Technique in the Pauline Epistles and Contemporary Literature* (SNTSMS 74; Cambridge: Cambridge University Press, 1992).

36. For a chart of indirect quotations, see the UBS Greek New Testament (2nd ed.), 897–920. The issue of indirect quotations or allusions is one that has not been fully resolved in Pauline scholarly research. See R. B. Hays, *Echoes of Scripture in the Letters of Paul* (New Haven: Yale University Press, 1983), 29–32; M. B. Thompson, *Clothed with Christ: The Example and Teaching of Jesus in Romans 12.1–15.13* (JSNTSup 59; Sheffield: JSOT Press, 1991), 28–36; and many later works that are dependent upon them. For my own formulations regarding the New Testament use of the Old Testament and related terminology, see S. E. Porter, "Further Comments on the Use of the Old Testament in the New Testament," in *The Intertextuality of the Epistles: Explorations of Theory and Practice* (ed. T. L. Brodie, D. R. MacDonald, and S. E. Porter; NTM 16; Sheffield: Sheffield Phoenix, 2006), 98–110, esp. 106–10; Porter, "Allusions and Echoes," in *As It Is Written: Studying Paul's Use of Scripture* (ed. S. E. Porter and C. D. Stanley; Society of Biblical Literature Symposium 50; Atlanta: SBL, 2008), 29–40; and now Porter, *Sacred Tradition in the New Testament: Tracing Old Testament Themes in the Gospels and Epistles* (Grand Rapids: Baker, 2016), 1–47.

Old Testament even when he is writing to churches that are predominantly or even perhaps almost exclusively Gentile in composition (such as to the Romans). It is true that there probably were some Jews in virtually all of the Pauline churches, except perhaps the one at Philippi (Acts 16:13 may indicate, however, the presence of a synagogue in that city), but it is still significant that the use of the Old Testament figures large in his thinking. There are several possible explanations for this. Some scholars think that there was perhaps more Jewish presence in some of these churches than has been traditionally thought. There is significant discussion, for example, concerning the composition of the church in Rome (see chapter 10 §2C2). But when it is considered that the major sections citing or alluding to the Old Testament are almost indisputably addressed to what appears to be the Gentile faction (Rom 9–11; 14:1–15:13), this explanation seems insufficient. A second explanation is that the Jewish Scriptures were so influential even in the non-Jewish world that Paul could count on the Gentile population's familiarity with them. This explanation would make better sense if it could be shown that most of Paul's Gentile converts were members of the group called the Godfearers, those Gentiles who had respect for Jewish moral and theological life but were unwilling to commit themselves to full membership as proselytes (which required circumcision). There were almost assuredly some Godfearers among the converts, but the evidence (or lack of it) from the Pauline letters leaves this explanation short of substantiation. Perhaps the most likely explanation has less to do with Paul's audience than it does with Paul himself. Paul's mind and theological attitude were so suffused with biblical thinking—since much of what we now call the Old Testament was the Bible of both Judaism and Christianity at this time—that he often simply could not construct an argument without exploring its theological and hence biblical basis and implications. For just one small example of many that could be offered, when it comes to defining God's mercy, even though Paul is addressing primarily Gentiles whom he had not met (and therefore whose biblical literacy he did not know; see chapter 10 §2C), Paul cites the Old Testament—Isa 10:22–23; 1:9; Hos 2:23; 1:10—as the proof of what he is stating in Rom 9:25–29. Paul relies upon the Old Testament to substantiate what he is arguing, even if the text would have been unfamiliar to his readers, because it is the basis and foundation of Paul's own thought.

The second major factor to consider is that the version of the Old Testament that Paul seems to cite the most is the Old Greek version originally translated in Egypt, which we usually call the Septuagint (LXX). In some instances, it is admittedly difficult to know which version Paul may be citing, since he apparently felt free to adapt the text to his particular context or may have been using another version entirely; generally speaking, however, the Greek version is the basis of his citations. A good example of the potential difficulty in sorting out Paul's use of the Old Testament is found at 1 Cor 15:54–55, where Paul combines versions of Isa 25:8 and Hos 13:14. For the most part, the citation is a composite of the Greek Septuagint and the Hebrew version of the Old Testament, except for the word "victory," which Paul seems to have introduced if it was not from a source now unknown to us. Paul apparently felt free to provide his interpretation of the text in a nonrigid way, creating one continuous, well-structured quotation.[37] In this use of the Old Testament, Paul is unlike a number of his contemporary Jewish interpreters of Scripture, who tended to base their interpretation upon specific wording or phrasing, sometimes in a quite literalistic way (as is often found in Qumran pesher exegesis), and he is more like a number of secular Greco-Roman writers of the time, who felt free to embellish and alter their citations of classical sources.

Among scholars, one of the most intriguing and yet still unsettled issues in New Testament study focuses upon the use of the Old Testament in the New, now often referred to as intertextuality, that is, understood as the way in which various texts are related and speak to each other.[38] In Pauline studies, this difficulty is as prevalent as it is with any other writer. There are at least five major means of Old Testament interpretation used by Paul:[39]

1. In the typological use of the Old Testament, Paul draws an explicit correlation between a person or event in the Old Testament (the type) and its correlative in the work of Jesus Christ (the antitype). The emphasis is not on any preconceived idea in the mind of the original author how this person or event might find some kind of fulfillment in the work or ministry of Jesus; this correlation is explicitly drawn by Paul. A good example is

37. See Stanley, *Paul and the Language of Scripture*, 209–15.

38. The term was first used for Pauline studies apparently by Hays, *Echoes of Scripture*. For some criticisms of the use of this term in biblical studies, or at least the way in which it is used, see S. E. Porter, "The Use of the Old Testament in the New Testament: A Brief Comment on Method and Terminology," in *Early Christian Interpretation in the Scriptures of Israel: Investigations and Proposals* (ed. C. A. Evans and J. A. Sanders; Studies in Scripture in Early Judaism and Christianity 5/JSNTSup 148; Sheffield: Sheffield Academic, 1997), 79–96; Porter, *Sacred Tradition in the New Testament*, 3–25; and D. I. Yoon, "The Ideological Inception of Intertextuality and Its Dissonance in Current Biblical Studies," *Currents in Biblical Research* 13 (2013): 58–76.

39. See J. D. G. Dunn, *Unity and Diversity in the New Testament: An Inquiry into the Character of Earliest Christianity* (Philadelphia: Westminster, 1977; repr. Valley Forge, PA: Trinity, 1990), 81–102, on whom this discussion depends. Many other treatments of this subject are worth examining.

Paul's use of Ps 112:9 in 2 Cor 9:9, where he finds in the image of scattering abroad a model of generosity to be emulated by Christians at Corinth.[40]

2. Pesher interpretation is named after the kind of Old Testament interpretation practiced at Qumran, in which what was spoken of in the Old Testament is seen to be fulfilled in the contemporary circumstances of the faith community. In a number of passages, Paul makes a similar equation, seeing what was foretold in the Old Testament as specifically fulfilled in the New Testament era. For example, in 2 Cor 6:2, Paul sees the day of salvation referred to in his quotation of Isa 49:8 as having arrived in God's gracious work in Christ.[41]

3. Allegorical interpretation resembles typological interpretation in that Paul finds explicit points of correlation between the Old Testament antecedent and its New Testament fulfillment, with the difference that the points of comparison are more numerous and extended. The classic example is the use of Sarah and Hagar in Gal 4:21–31, with reference to Gen 16:15 and 21:2. Paul helps the reader to see what he is doing by labeling this as allegorical interpretation.[42] In an extended comparison, Hagar represents the current Jerusalem bound or enslaved to the law of Mount Sinai, and Sarah represents the new Jerusalem from above, free from enslavement to the law. In several ways, Paul's use of the allegorical method resembles the kind of interpretation found in the contemporary Hellenistic Jewish philosopher Philo of Alexandria. Scholars are divided on how closely Paul conforms to Philo's allegorical method, although it is fair to say that there is more than passing resemblance, especially in his treatment of such figures as Abraham.[43]

---

40. For more on typological interpretation, see L. Goppelt, *Typos: The Typological Interpretation of the Old Testament in the New* (trans. D. H. Madvig; Grand Rapids: Eerdmans, 1982). Cf. also R. T. France, *Jesus and the Old Testament* (London: Tyndale, 1971; repr. Vancouver, BC: Regent College Publishing, 1998), 38–79; and D. Baker, "Typology and the Christian Use of the Old Testament," in *The Right Doctrine from the Wrong Texts? Essays on the Use of the Old Testament in the New* (ed. G. K. Beale; Grand Rapids: Baker, 1994), 313–30.

41. For more on pesher, or Qumran exegesis, see R. N. Longenecker, *Biblical Exegesis in the Apostolic Period* (2nd ed.; Grand Rapids: Eerdmans, 1999), 24–29; and S. Berrin, "Qumran Pesharim," in *Biblical Interpretation at Qumran: Studies in the Dead Sea Scrolls and Other Related Literature* (ed. M. Henze; Grand Rapids: Eerdmans, 2005), 110–33.

42. In apparent backlash against the convoluted allegorism of medieval interpretation, some modern interpreters wish to resist allegorical interpretation in the New Testament at almost any cost, even by ignoring the text.

43. For more on allegorical interpretation, see Longenecker, *Biblical Exegesis*, 30–32; and R. P. C. Hanson, *Allegory and Event: A Study of the Sources and Significance of Origen's Interpretation of Scripture* (repr. Louisville: Westminster John Knox, 1959).

4. In a running commentary, another means of interpretation, a number of passages may be cited and briefly commented on as the author develops his theme. An excellent example of this technique is in Rom 9–11, where Paul is developing his theme of God's faithfulness despite Israel's rejection. Paul marshals scriptural texts from throughout the Old Testament in order to develop the various stages in his argument, which includes, for example, an elucidation of God's justice and election by citing a number of texts from Exodus and the Prophets; a substantiation of Israel's guilt and rejection by citing numerous passages from Deuteronomy and the Prophets; and a concluding description of God's faithfulness by citing a few passages from Deuteronomy and Psalms.[44]

5. A fifth means of interpretation is midrash. Sometimes midrash is used as the generic label to describe any form of interpretation of the Old Testament, but here it is distinguished as a means of interpretation commonly found among Paul's Jewish contemporaries. This method is difficult to characterize but is typified by the quotation of a passage and then a detailed commentary upon it, often including specific treatment of individual words. Paul avails himself of midrash on several occasions. He seems to make use of this technique in Gal 3:16, where he cites the specific use of the singular "seed" in Gen 12:7; 13:15; and 24:7 to point to Christ.[45]

If these methods of interpretation are valid as applied to Paul, one cannot limit his use of the Old Testament to a single model or category. He displays the kind of creative flexibility that takes a given text and sees the full possibilities of it for his argument, not bound by any one model or method.

Besides Paul's explicit use of the Old Testament, mention should be made of his allusions or indirect references to Scripture, sometimes called *allusions* or *echoes*.[46] It is difficult to define an allusion or indirect quotation; nevertheless, it is hard to deny that they exist.[47] These take a variety of forms in

44. Scholarly comment on Paul's use of the Old Testament in Rom 9–11 is abundant and growing. A useful treatment, though confined to use of Isaiah, is J. R. Wagner, *Heralds of the Good News: Isaiah and Paul "In Concert" in the Letter to the Romans* (NovTSup 101; Leiden: Brill, 2002).

45. For more on midrash, see Longenecker, *Biblical Exegesis*, 18–23; and M. P. Fernández, "Midrash and the New Testament: A Methodology for the Study of Gospel Midrash," in *The New Testament and Rabbinic Literature* (ed. Reimund Bieringer et al.; Journal for the Study of Judaism Supplement 136; Leiden: Brill, 2010), 367–86.

46. Cf. Hays, *Echoes of Scripture*; sometimes indirect references are called *intertextual echoes*. Again, refer to my analysis of this term in Porter, "Further Comments," 106–10; Porter, "Allusions and Echoes," 29–40; and Porter, *Sacred Tradition in the New Testament*, 27–47.

47. See Porter, "Use of the Old Testament in the New Testament"; and Porter, *Sacred Tradition in the New Testament*, 3–25.

Paul, but the most common is probably his citation of Old Testament figures. Frequently, as in the Gal 3 or Rom 4 discussions of Abraham,[48] these occur in conjunction with Old Testament quotations (see discussion above). But at other times, Paul simply mentions the figure, apparently with the expectation that his readers either know something of the person or can glean enough from the context to make the allusion useful. A number of Old Testament figures were generally known in the Greco-Roman world.

Moses, probably the best known in the Greco-Roman world, was thought of as a native or Jewish inhabitant of Egypt who was a lawgiver of an inferior law.[49] In 2 Cor 3:7–18, to draw a contrast with believers who are able to look directly at the radiance of the Spirit, Paul appeals to the incident recorded in Exod 34:29–35, where Moses covered his face with a veil after being in God's presence and the Israelites were not able to look on him. This well illustrates Paul's interpretive freedom in using the Old Testament, because he moves from the veil to the unbelief of the Israelites, saying that this emblem of lack of spiritual perception remains to the current day.

Paul also uses the figure of Adam, especially in 1 Cor 15 and Rom 5.[50] In Rom 5:12–21, he draws a series of contrasts between what Adam accomplished through his singular sin and the surpassing accomplishments of Christ. Although knowledge of Adam's sin enhances appreciation of the contrast, Paul includes sufficient information in the context for even a person uninformed about the specifics of Adam's sin to make sense of what Paul says regarding the greatness of Christ's work on the cross.

In another form of indirect quotation or allusion, Paul refers to Old Testament passages or even words of Jesus. He explicitly cites words of Jesus on only a few occasions (e.g., 1 Cor 7:10; 9:14), which raises questions in a number of scholars' minds. What is frequently overlooked, however, is how much Paul appears to allude to the words of Jesus, in addition to the essential facts of his life, death, and resurrection. As David Wenham points out, there is extensive verbal and thematic allusion in Paul's letters to the thoughts and ideas of Jesus. For example, in Rom 13:8–10 Paul apparently alludes to Jesus's words about loving one's neighbor (Mark 12:31 and par-

48. On Abraham, see Stowers, *Diatribe*, 171–73; G. W. Hansen, *Abraham in Galatians: Epistolary and Rhetorical Contexts* (JSNTSup 29; Sheffield: JSOT Press, 1989); and N. Calvert-Koyzis, *Paul, Monotheism and the People of God: The Significance of Abraham Traditions for Early Judaism and Christianity* (JSNTSup 273; London: T&T Clark, 2004).

49. See J. G. Gager, *Moses in Greco-Roman Paganism* (Society of Biblical Literature Monograph Series 16; Nashville: Abingdon, 1972).

50. On Adam, see J. R. Levison, *Portraits of Adam in Early Judaism* (Journal for the Study of the Pseudepigrapha Supplement 1; Sheffield: JSOT Press, 1988).

allels).[51] The usual explanations of Paul's use of this tradition are that he learned it from Christians who were more direct followers of Jesus or that it was specially revealed to him. Another explanation, and one that I think is worth strong consideration, is that Paul acquired at least some of this tradition directly by hearing Jesus speak on occasion during the course of his earthly ministry.[52]

B. Rabbinic Argumentation and Logic

Another Jewish influence on Paul is revealed in his use of forms of rabbinic argumentation and logic that were used in the first century. Talmudic tractate *Sanhedrin* 7.11 lists these as *Qal wa-homer* ("light and heavy"), *Gezera shawa* ("an equivalent regulation"), *Binyan 'ab mikkatub 'ehad* ("constructing a father from one," that is a principle from one reference), *Banyan 'ab mishshene ketubim* ("constructing a father from two"), *Kelal uperat uperat ukelal* ("general and particular, and particular and general"), *Kayotze bo mi-maqom 'aher* ("to which something [is] similar in another place"), and *Dabar halamed me'inyano* ("word of instruction from the context").[53] Contemporary rhetoricians debate the origin and development of these principles, since most of the so-called rabbinic forms of argumentation seem to have been derived from Greek sources on rhetoric as well.[54] It is not entirely clear when the rabbinic principles of interpretation became formulated, but even if they were later than the writing of Paul's letters, there is evidence that the principles themselves may well have been used earlier than their written codification, since they are found in Jesus's teaching also. In two of the most common of these principles used in Paul there is a logical movement from the greater to the lesser or from the lesser to the greater instances (*Qal wa-homer*). For example, in Rom 5:10, Paul says, "For if, when we were God's enemies, we

51. See D. Wenham, *Paul: Follower of Jesus or Founder of Christianity?* (Grand Rapids: Eerdmans, 1995); cf. A. J. M. Wedderburn, ed., *Paul and Jesus: Collected Essays* (JSNTSup 37; Sheffield: JSOT Press, 1989); and F. Neirynck, "The Sayings of Jesus in 1 Corinthians," in *The Corinthian Correspondence* (ed. R. Bieringer; Bibliotheca Ephemeridum Theologicarum Lovaniensium 125; Leuven: Leuven University Press/Peeters, 1996), 141–76.

52. See S. E. Porter, *When Paul Met Jesus: How an Idea Got Lost in History* (Cambridge: Cambridge University Press, 2016), 122–77, and chapter 1 §9 above.

53. See C. A. Evans, *Ancient Texts for New Testament Studies: A Guide to the Background Literature* (Peabody, MA: Hendrickson, 2005), 219–20, who provides the translations and examples.

54. See D. Daube, "Rabbinic Methods of Interpretation and Hellenistic Rhetoric," *Hebrew Union College Annual* 22 (1949): 239–64.

were reconciled to him through the death of his Son, how much more, having been reconciled, shall we be saved through his life!" (NIV). The implication is that, if humans could be made to be at peace with God while they were completely at odds with him, then once they have been brought into relation with him, it is a relatively easy thing to think of their salvation. Paul uses the opposite kind of logic as well. In 1 Cor 9:9–11, he cites the example of not muzzling an ox while it is treading grain (Deut 25:4), using this relatively trivial example as proof that, if this kind of rule holds in an insignificant case, then how much more can we expect in the significant case of a preacher such as Paul getting his due.

C. Synagogue

The last influence on Paul worth mentioning here is the synagogue. The history of the synagogue is difficult to reconstruct, and a great portion of the evidence for its physical plan and layout is found only in later archeological remains.[55] From this information, we can gather that the synagogue was an important Jewish institution, utilized "for prayer, for reading Torah and for carrying out community business."[56] Nevertheless, the synagogue had an important function in Paul's ministry, at least according to the book of Acts.

A crucial part of Paul's missionary strategy was apparently to take advantage of the presence of a Jewish synagogue in the cities he visited on his missionary journeys.[57] It is unfortunate that Paul does not mention his synagogal preaching in his letters, since a comparison could then be made with what

55. See J. Gutmann, ed., *Ancient Synagogues: The State of Research* (Brown Judaic Studies 22; Chico, CA: Scholars Press, 1981); and M. J. S. Chiat, *Handbook of Synagogue Architecture* (Brown Judaic Studies 29; Chico, CA: Scholars Press, 1982). Cf. A. Runesson, *The Origins of the Synagogue: A Socio-Historical Study* (Coniectanea Biblica: New Testament Series 37; Stockholm: Almqvist & Wiksell, 2001); and B. Olsson and M. Zetterholm, eds., *The Ancient Synagogue: From Its Origins until 200 C.E.* (Coniectanea Biblica: New Testament Series 39; Stockholm: Almqvist & Wiksell, 2004).

56. H. A. McKay, *Sabbath and Synagogue: The Question of Sabbath Worship in Ancient Judaism* (Leiden: Brill, 1994), 5. She rightly notes that the actual building follows from the gathering of (usually) men. In Paul's cases, the references appear to be to the physical place of gathering, though of course with such people present.

57. That is, unless the book of Hebrews is an instance of at least Paul's preaching to Jewish Christians. On such issues, without necessarily endorsing their conclusions, see A. W. Pitts and J. Walker, "The Authorship of Hebrews: A Further Development in the Luke–Paul Relationship," in *Paul and His Social Relations* (ed. S. E. Porter and C. D. Land; PAST 7; Leiden: Brill, 2013), 143–84.

he is recorded as saying in Acts—for example, 13:16-41, when he preached in Pisidian Antioch. This omission is somewhat surprising in light of how many Jewish references there are in Paul's letters, especially regarding his personal background. Nevertheless, Paul does make clear in his letters, such as Rom 1:16, that his evangelistic ministry was addressed first to the Jews and then to the Greeks, with this kind of statement perhaps intimating his overall missionary strategy.

On the other hand, perhaps he fails to mention preaching in the synagogue not because he did not preach in this place of Jewish gathering but because, for the most part, his practice was of short duration and/or often ended in disaster. Even after a first successful sermon in Pisidian Antioch, by the next week the Jews were talking abusively against Paul (Acts 13:45). Several of the most disappointing episodes occurred in Iconium (14:1-7), Thessalonica (17:1-9), and Corinth (18:1-6). Indeed, Paul's sizable successes in the synagogue were few. Consequently, when Paul wrote to a church founded in a city where he is recorded in Acts as having first preached in the synagogue, he may have thought that the productive result of his ministry had little to do directly with this contact. Still, it seems that Paul liked to enter a city in this way and establish at least a connection with the Jews who worshiped there.

4. Conclusion

Reconstructing the complex background to Paul's thought is not an easy task. The history of such discussion frequently swang from one extreme to the other, sometimes emphasizing the Greco-Roman influences at the expense of the Jewish and other times swinging to the other extreme. Rather than play one off against the other, I believe that the Greco-Roman world was a complex environment that included Judaism as one of its many and varied components. My brief survey shows that we can identify both Greco-Roman and Jewish elements that were influential upon Paul's thought and writing. While some interpreters may overemphasize his Jewish background to the neglect of any Greco-Roman influences (or even the other way around), I show that both his writings and his actions as seen in Acts demonstrate a significant number of Greco-Roman points of comparison and influence. This understanding is helpful in order to understand Paul as the apostle to the Gentiles and why Paul was in many ways qualified to fit such a role.

Sources for Further Study

Basic Sources

Engberg-Pedersen, T., ed. *Paul beyond the Judaism/Hellenism Divide.* Louisville: Westminster John Knox, 2011.

Glover, T. R. *Paul of Tarsus.* London: SCM, 1925.

Grabbe, L. L. *Judaism from Cyrus to Hadrian.* London: SCM, 1992.

Jobes, K. H., and M. Silva. *Invitation to the Septuagint.* 2nd ed. Grand Rapids: Baker, 2015.

Malherbe, A. J. *Paul and the Popular Philosophers.* Minneapolis: Fortress, 1989.

Millar, F. *The Roman Near East, 31 B.C.–A.D. 337.* Cambridge, MA: Harvard University Press, 1993.

Moyise, S. *Paul and Scripture.* London: SPCK, 2010.

Murphy, F. J. *Early Judaism: The Exile to the Time of Jesus.* Grand Rapids: Baker, 2002.

Nickelsburg, G. W. E. *Jewish Literature between the Bible and the Mishnah: A Historical and Literary Introduction.* 2nd ed. Minneapolis: Fortress, 2005.

Sanders, E. P. *Judaism: Practice and Belief, 63 B.C.E.–66 C.E.* London: SCM, 1992.

Starr, C. G. *A History of the Ancient World.* 3rd ed. New York: Oxford University Press, 1983.

Thompson, J. W. *Moral Formation according to Paul: The Context and Coherence of Pauline Ethics.* Grand Rapids: Baker, 2011.

VanderKam, J., and P. Flint. *The Meaning of the Dead Sea Scrolls: Their Significance for Understanding the Bible, Judaism, Jesus, and Christianity.* San Francisco: HarperSanFrancisco, 2002.

Advanced Sources

Collins, J. J. *Between Athens and Jerusalem: Jewish Identity in the Hellenistic Diaspora.* 2nd ed. Grand Rapids: Eerdmans, 2000.

Engberg-Pedersen, T., ed. *Paul in His Hellenistic Context.* Edinburgh: T&T Clark, 1994.

Goodman, M. *Judaism in the Roman World: Collected Essays.* Ancient Judaism and Early Christianity 66. Leiden: Brill, 2007.

Goppelt, L. *Typos: The Typological Interpretation of the Old Testament in the New.* Translated by D. H. Madvig. Grand Rapids: Eerdmans, 1982.

Gutmann, J., ed. *Ancient Synagogues: The State of Research.* Brown Judaic Studies 22. Chico, CA: Scholars Press, 1981.

Hengel, M. *The "Hellenization" of Judaea in the First Century after Christ*. Translated by J. Bowden. London: SCM, 1989.

————. *Judaism and Hellenism: Studies in Their Encounter in Palestine during the Early Hellenistic Period*. 2 vols. Translated by J. Bowden. Philadelphia: Fortress, 1974.

Longenecker, R. N. *Biblical Exegesis in the Apostolic Period*. 2nd ed. Grand Rapids: Eerdmans, 1999.

Marcos, N. F. *The Septuagint in Context: Introduction to the Greek Version of the Bible*. Translated by W. G. E. Watson. Leiden: Brill, 2000.

Paget, J. C. *Jews, Christians, and Jewish-Christians in Antiquity*. WUNT 251. Tübingen: Mohr-Siebeck, 2010.

Porter, S. E., ed. *Paul: Jew, Greek, and Roman*. PAST 5. Leiden: Brill, 2008.

Porter, S. E., and A. W. Pitts, eds. *Christian Origins and Greco-Roman Culture: Social and Literary Contexts for the New Testament*. ECHC 1/TENT 9. Leiden: Brill, 2013.

————. *Christian Origins and Hellenistic Judaism: Social and Literary Contexts for the New Testament*. ECHC 2/TENT 10. Leiden: Brill, 2013.

————. *The Language of the New Testament: Context, History, and Development*. ECHC 3/LBS 6. Leiden: Brill, 2013.

Rasimus, T., T. Engberg-Pedersen, and I. Dunderberg, eds. *Stoicism in Early Christianity*. Grand Rapids: Baker, 2010.

Stanley, C. D. *Paul and the Language of Scripture: Citation Technique in the Pauline Epistles and Contemporary Literature*. SNTSMS 74. Cambridge: Cambridge University Press, 1992.

Stowers, S. K. *The Diatribe and Paul's Letter to the Romans*. SBLDS 57. Chico, CA: Scholars Press, 1981.

4

Major Themes of Paul's Thought and Writings

1. Introduction

There have been many attempts to write compendia of Paul's beliefs, usually called Pauline theologies (see bibliography at the end of this chapter). In a sense, this chapter is such an effort, even if on a smaller scale and presented in a different configuration. Pauline theological beliefs—his major theological ideas—are usually discussed as positioned on the same conceptual level, as if they were all equally prominent. This is not the way, however, that Paul's major theological beliefs are represented in his letters. For example, as the letter structure makes clear (see chapter 5 §§1, 3), material is presented in the letter form in varying places in the ancient papyri, and these places help to determine the nature of the assertions being made. Something similar appears to be going on in Paul's mind when he thinks theologically. On the one hand, Paul holds a number of essential beliefs, and he does not spend much time or epistolary space justifying them. Consequently, when he deals with ideas related to these, he merely invokes these concepts and does not argue for their existence. On the other hand, there are also a number of beliefs that Paul does not hold as foundational but that he clearly believes are worth arguing for. For the most part, these are beliefs that, so far as can be determined from the biblical evidence, are primarily Pauline in orientation and development. The fundamental beliefs probably would have been held by a number of Christian believers, and some of them by any person who may have had any sort of religious orientation. But Paul seems to think that the developed beliefs need to be argued for, often at some length.

In the treatment that follows, the beliefs are divided into these two major conceptual, differentiating categories. This distinction helps to address the matter of the contingency and unity of Paul's letters. That is, in examining Paul's thought we are extrapolating generalities from letters that were occasional in nature, but yet reveal the common interests of the author.[1] As part of this exercise, I will attempt to determine the origin or conceptual background of these beliefs. The purpose of this chapter is not to delve deeply into any particular area and provide a detailed analysis of each topic (monographs can be, and have been, written on each of these topics), but my goal is to offer an overview of the various beliefs of Paul as revealed in his letters.

A number of developed beliefs originated in Greco-Roman (or sometimes called Hellenistic) thought, and a number originated in Jewish thought (see previous chapter). There are others whose origin it is difficult to determine. Identification of the origin of these beliefs may well have a bearing on how they are understood and interpreted, but for the most part Paul gives sufficient explication so that interpreters have at least a basic understanding of what he is asserting.[2]

2. Fundamental Beliefs

Paul's theological and expositional method consists of applying the implications of his theologically fundamental beliefs to various situations. The following are some of the most important of Paul's fundamental beliefs.

A. God

The concept of God is seen by at least one New Testament theologian as the center of Paul's thought.[3] Despite Paul's close ties to the Greco-Roman world

---

1. On the contingent element of Paul's letters, see J. C. Beker, *Paul the Apostle: The Triumph of God in Life and Thought* (Philadelphia: Fortress, 1980), 23-36, a distinction that is followed by most Pauline scholars.

2. I approach Paul's letters, the thirteen that are traditionally attributed to him, as the primary source of information about the theology of Paul. I am less concerned to argue for a theology of the Pauline letters, as if this could exist apart from the person of Paul. Hence, I do not find it plausible to argue for a genuinely Pauline theology on the basis of pseudepigraphal letters; see S. E. Porter, "Is There a Center to Paul's Theology? An Introduction to the Study of Paul and His Theology," in *Paul and His Theology* (ed. S. E. Porter; PAST 5; Leiden: Brill, 2006), 1-19, esp. 14-16. On some of these issues, see J. D. G. Dunn, "Prolegomena to a Theology of Paul," *NTS* 40 (1994): 407-32; also H. Ridderbos, *Paul: An Outline of His Theology* (trans. J. R. D. Witt; Grand Rapids: Eerdmans, 1975 [1966]); Dunn, *The Theology of Paul the Apostle* (Grand Rapids: Eerdmans, 1998); Porter, ed., *Paul and His Theology*; and F. J. Matera, *God's Saving Grace: A Pauline Theology* (Grand Rapids: Eerdmans, 2012).

3. L. L. Morris, *New Testament Theology* (Grand Rapids: Zondervan, 1986), chap. 1. This

and Hellenistic thought, as described above, Paul never wavers in his monotheistic belief in the God of the Old Testament.[4] Thus he cites the Shema (Deut 6:4) in 1 Cor 8:6 as a Christian affirmation (Paul's language is very similar to that of the Septuagint). He assumes that the God of Judaism and of the Old Testament, that is, the God of Abraham (Rom 4:3 and passim), is also the God of the New Testament, the Father of the Lord Jesus Christ (2 Cor 1:3) and the Father of a new people of God (Rom 9:6–9). For Paul, it is God who stands behind all of the important salvific and soteriological actions of the New Testament. Thus God demonstrates his love for humanity in Christ's death (5:8), predestines, calls, justifies, glorifies (8:29–30), and judges (2:16). Paul uses the word translated "God" (θεός) approximately 550 times, fully 40 percent of all the uses of this word in the New Testament, more than his corpus would warrant. It is difficult to specify all that Paul attaches to this word, which is not the only indicator in Paul's thinking about God. Nevertheless, the statistics tend to indicate how foundational the belief was for Paul.

B. Jesus Christ

In the Old Testament there were many messiahs,[5] or many people appointed for particular divine purposes.[6] In other words, there was not just one conception of the Messiah. Messianic figures in the Old Testament include kings (1 Sam 16:6; 2 Sam 1:14), priests (Exod 30:30), prophets (1 Kgs 19:16), and even Cyrus the Persian king (Isa 45:1). During the Second Temple period, with the return from exile, the rule of the Greek kings—in particular the Seleucids—the Hasmonean revolt, and subsequent domination by Rome, a variety of messianic expectations formed and grew among the Jews. It was into this environment that Jesus the Christ was born. Several of these messianic expectations included a political figure who would free the Jews of Roman tyranny, while

---

volume is used throughout this section. Cf. N. Richardson, *Paul's Language about God* (JSNT-Sup 99; Sheffield: Sheffield Academic, 1994).

4. See L. W. Hurtado, *One God, One Lord: Early Christian Devotion and Ancient Jewish Monotheism* (London: SCM, 1988); further developed in Hurtado, *Lord Jesus Christ: Devotion to Jesus in Earliest Christianity* (Grand Rapids: Eerdmans, 2003), esp. 29–53.

5. See R. Hess, "Images of the Messiah in the Old Testament," in *Images of Christ: Ancient and Modern* (ed. S. E. Porter, M. A. Hayes, and D. Tombs; RILP 2; Sheffield: Sheffield Academic, 1997), 22–33.

6. Cf. L. M. McDonald and S. E. Porter, *Early Christianity and Its Sacred Literature* (Peabody, MA: Hendrickson, 2000), 63–65, for a discussion on apocalypses and messiahs in the first-century context of Judaism.

others were expecting more of a prophetic figure. In many ways, although Jesus was pressured to fulfill a variety of messianic expectations, he did not satisfy the demands of any particular group. Nevertheless, in light of his resurrection, Christianity came to accept Jesus as the Christ (Greek for *messiah*), or God's anointed one. The Pauline writings use the word "Christ" approximately 380 times, or over 70 percent of the times that it is used in the New Testament. In the vast majority of instances it appears in collocation with Jesus's personal name (i.e., Jesus, and hence as Jesus Christ). The question for biblical scholars is how Paul viewed these two names when used together. There are three options.

Some say that "Christ" has become, in Paul's mind, simply a part of who Jesus is, so that it becomes another proper name for him.[7] Others say that "Christ" retains at least some of its messianic sense whenever it is used by Paul (as at least an honorific, if not a title).[8] A third group might well argue that the word order is determinative for its meaning: when the order is "Christ Jesus," the messianic sense is paramount (as in Rom 1:1), whereas when the order is "Jesus Christ," the word is used as a name. It is difficult to solve this issue for every instance on the basis of a widespread generalization, except to say that, even if Paul probably does not make a strong theological claim every time he uses the wording "Jesus Christ," he clearly accepts that Jesus was God's anointed Messiah, as evidenced through his death, resurrection, and exaltation (Phil 2:6–11; 1 Cor 15:20–25). This is one of the unargued assumptions of his theological belief.[9]

Paul goes further, however, and depicts Jesus Christ in terminology that is clearly meant to ascribe to him divine actions and existence; that is, he is seen as God or the Son of God (Rom 1:4). This is apparent in two major ways. First, in a number of Pauline passages Jesus Christ is described as enacting divine characteristics. One of the most significant of these statements is Phil 2:6–11. Some wish to see in this passage an equation of Christ with Adam, but the force of the passage is to depict Christ as being in the very form of God but not retaining his equality with God.[10] Similarly, Col 1:15–20 depicts Christ in

---

7. Suggested by N. Dahl, "The Messiahship of Jesus in Paul," in his *The Crucified Messiah* (Minneapolis: Augsburg, 1974), 37–47.

8. Argued recently by M. V. Novenson, "Can the Messiahship of Jesus Be Read off Paul's Grammar? Nils Dahl's Criteria 50 Years Later," *NTS* 56 (2010): 396–412; cf. Novenson, *Christ among the Messiahs: Christ Language in Paul and Messiah Language in Ancient Judaism* (New York: Oxford University Press, 2012).

9. For the most thorough treatment of Paul's Christology, see G. D. Fee, *Pauline Christology: An Exegetical-Theological Study* (Peabody, MA: Hendrickson, 2007).

10. Cf. M. Silva, *Philippians* (2nd ed.; BECNT; Grand Rapids: Baker, 2005), 98–112, esp. 109.

terms of divine characteristics and actions, such as creation. The passage says that the universe was created in, through, and for him.[11] There are two even more explicit passages, where the very words "God" and "Christ" are explicitly, grammatically linked. The first, despite longstanding controversy, is Rom 9:5. The understanding of 9:5 depends upon the punctuation that one places in the passage. The question is whether this verse makes two separate statements: "To them belong the patriarchs, and from them, according to the flesh, comes the Messiah. May he who is God overall be blessed forever"; or one statement: "To them belong the patriarchs, and from them, according to the flesh, comes the Messiah, who is God overall, blessed forever" (NRSV, which provides these options in notes). Murray Harris and George Carraway in separate studies show that the best understanding of this verse is that Christ is being described as God blessed forever (one statement is made).[12] But even though this is the only explicit statement of its kind in the undisputed Pauline letters, in light of Jewish divine-enthronement language (as found in, for example, Ps 2 and Ps 110) and Greco-Roman emperor cult language that saw the emperor as divine son, it is highly plausible, especially in a book such as Romans, that in this passage Paul is depicting Christ as God. The second passage is similar, Titus 2:13, where Paul refers to "our great God and Savior Jesus Christ" or "the great God and our Savior" (NRSV, with the latter in a note).[13]

The second way in which Paul describes Jesus in divine terms is the citation of Old Testament passages that explicitly refer to God in the Old Testament but are used by Paul to refer to Jesus Christ. The term "Lord" (κύριος) is used consistently in the later Greek Old Testament manuscripts to render the name of God,[14] and this may well account for one of the earliest Christian confessions: "Jesus is Lord" (e.g., Rom 10:9; 1 Cor 12:3), as a confession of the divine nature of Jesus.[15] More than that, however, several Pauline passages

---

11. See S. E. Fowl, *The Story of Christ in the Ethics of Paul: Analysis of the Function of the Hymnic Material in the Pauline Corpus* (JSNTSup 36; Sheffield: JSOT Press, 1990), 49–154; contra J. D. G. Dunn, *Christology in the Making: A New Testament Inquiry into the Origins of the Doctrine of the Incarnation* (2nd ed.; Grand Rapids: Eerdmans, 1989), 98–128 on Phil 2:6–11, 163–212 on Col 1:15–20.

12. G. Carraway, *Christ Is God over All: Romans 9:5 in the Context of Romans 9–11* (LNTS 489; London: Bloomsbury, 2013); contra Fee, *Pauline Christology*, 272–77.

13. See M. J. Harris, *Jesus as God: The New Testament Use of Theos in Reference to Jesus* (Grand Rapids: Baker, 1992), 143–72 on Rom 9:5, 173–85 on Titus 2:13. Cf. M. Hengel, *The Son of God* (trans. J. Bowden; London: SCM, 1976); repr. in *The Cross of the Son of God* (London: SCM, 1986), esp. 7–15.

14. J. A. Fitzmyer, "Κύριος, etc.," in *Exegetical Dictionary of the New Testament* (3 vols.; ed. H. Balz and G. Schneider; Grand Rapids: Eerdmans, 1990–93), 2.328–30.

15. See, e.g., S. E. Porter, "Saints and Sinners: The Church in Paul's Letters," in *The Church,*

refer to Jesus Christ by quoting an Old Testament passage that uses "Lord." For example, in Rom 10:13, referring to Jesus Christ, Paul says, "Everyone who calls on the name of the *Lord* will be saved" (quoting Joel 2:32, italic added). In Rom 14:11, Paul writes that the Lord, probably meaning Christ, says that "everyone will bow before me and everyone will confess to God" (quoting Isa 45:23). Also, 1 Cor 1:31 and 2 Cor 10:17, citing Jer 9:24, speak of boasting in the Lord; and 1 Cor 2:16, quoting Isa 40:13, asks "who has known the mind of the Lord?" and then goes on to say that "we have the mind of Christ."[16] Thus, even though the equation "Jesus Christ = God" does not explicitly appear in Paul's letters in numerous places (though it does in a few), it is clear from Paul's language that he thought of him as God, and this forms one of his fundamental assumptions.

In conjunction with Paul's basic belief in Jesus as the Christ is his use of the phrase "in Christ" (or related phrases, such as "in him" or "in the Lord"). Paul uses the phrase "in Christ" 165 times to describe the foundational relationship that the believer has with Christ. Defining exactly how Paul saw this relationship, however, is more problematic, since Paul does not state outrightly what he means by a person being "in Christ." As a result, many different proposals are put forward. Two of the older but still persistent viewpoints take the language more or less literally. For example, German scholar Adolf Deissmann speaks of a "mystical union," in which Christ's work results in a spiritual union between Christ and the believer. Deissmann's focus on a Christian mystical element in Paul's belief is often neglected in contemporary thinking.[17] Nevertheless, while this view has an attractive emphasis upon the sense of unity between the believer and Christ, noting especially the reciprocal language in which Christ is said to be in the believer and the believer in Christ, it fails to explain how this relationship functions.

A second view, which has had great influence over the last fifty years or so, emphasizes the corporate unity between Christ and the believer. This unity verges on a physical unity in which Christ is said to indwell the believer.[18] Un-

---

Then and Now (ed. S. E. Porter and C. L. Westfall; Eugene, OR: Pickwick, 2013), 41–67, esp. 43–45.

16. See D. B. Capes, *Old Testament Yahweh Texts in Paul's Christology* (WUNT 2/47; Tübingen: Mohr-Siebeck, 1992), esp. 115–49; and Capes, "YHWH Texts and Monotheism in Paul's Christology," in *Early Jewish and Christian Monotheism* (ed. L. T. Stuckenbruck and W. E. S. North; JSNTSup 263; London: T&T Clark, 2004), 120–37; cf. L. Hurtado, "Lord," *DPL* 563–64; and S. E. Porter, "Images of Christ in Paul's Letters," in *Images of Christ: Ancient and Modern* (ed. S. E. Porter, M. A. Hayes, and D. Tombs; RILP 2; Sheffield: Sheffield Academic, 1997), 95–112, esp. 101–5.

17. See A. Deissmann, *St. Paul: A Study in Social and Religious History* (2nd ed.; trans. W. E. Wilson; 1927; repr. New York: Harper, 1957), 297–99.

18. See, e.g., C. F. D. Moule, *The Phenomenon of the New Testament* (London: SCM, 1964), 29–42.

fortunately, this perspective is fundamentally flawed in its reliance upon an inaccurate assessment of the concept of corporate personality in biblical thinking. It was once thought that Jews of the Old Testament and New Testament did not differentiate between the individual and the group and hence saw a corporate solidarity between believers and Christ. But the ancient Israelites, while believing in corporate responsibility (i.e., that an individual could be responsible for the group), did not have trouble differentiating individuals from the group.[19]

The most likely explanation of what Paul means by being "in Christ" is that one falls within the sphere, power, or control of Christ. In a recent study on this topic, Constantine Campbell agrees that a spatial understanding of the preposition "in" (ἐν) seems to be preferred, but later concludes that there actually is no definable meaning for the phrase by a single description.[20] As 1 Cor 15:22 and Gal 1:22 make clear, to be "in Christ" is to be in Christ's sphere of influence, especially when Paul differentiates between earthly existence, under the control of the Adamic nature, and redemptive existence, under the control of Christ. This understanding also helps to explain how this terminology becomes virtually synonymous with what it means to be called a Christian (Rom 16:7) and, in a possible instrumental sense (1 Cor 1:2), what it means to be controlled by Christ.[21]

C. Holy Spirit

The Holy Spirit plays a more significant role in Paul's teaching than many scholars recognize.[22] Part of the neglect is probably caused by the potential

19. On this topic, see S. E. Porter, "Two Myths: Corporate Personality and Language/Mentality Determinism," *Scottish Journal of Theology* 43 (1990): 289–307, esp. 289–99.

20. C. R. Campbell, *Union with Christ: An Exegetical and Theological Study* (Grand Rapids: Zondervan, 2012), 73, 198–99; also 21–30 on methodology. Campbell does initially seem to conclude that the phrase "in Christ" is related to sphere and that the preposition "in" (ἐν) has a wide semantic range, but his overall study of the topic is questionable because of the inclusion of the phrases "with (σύν) Christ" and "through (διά) Christ," without including possible other phrases that communicate union with Christ. In other words, if one wants to study the concept of *union with Christ*, one cannot limit oneself to just a few prepositional phrases, but must use a wider range of expressions.

21. S. E. Porter, *Idioms of the Greek New Testament* (2nd ed.; Biblical Languages: Greek 2; Sheffield: JSOT Press, 1994), 159, for a defense of the spherical solution. On "in Christ," see K. Grayston, *Dying, We Live: A New Enquiry into the Death of Christ in the New Testament* (London: Darton, Longman & Todd, 1990), 382–94, for a summary of the issues.

22. For a comprehensive treatment of the Holy Spirit, see G. D. Fee, *God's Empowering Presence: The Holy Spirit in the Letters of Paul* (Peabody, MA: Hendrickson, 1994); cf. also H. B.

ambiguity of the Greek word translated "spirit" (πνεῦμα), which can be used not only for the Holy Spirit but for any number of other spirits, thereby making some contexts ambiguous (e.g., Rom 1:9).[23] For example, it is difficult to know, when Paul speaks of the Philippians standing firm in "one spirit" (NIV), whether the spirit referred to in Phil 1:27 is a divine or a human spirit. There is also the further question whether the spirit of God and the spirit of Christ in Rom 8:9 (cf. 8:14) are meant to be treated synonymously, although it seems that they should be. For Paul, the Holy Spirit is God's means of communicating with believers since Jesus Christ left the earth (8:16, 26) and is the abiding presence of God that governs the life of the believer (8:1–17).

The doctrine of the Trinity was not formulated until long after the New Testament was written, but the question is frequently raised regarding what assumptions Paul made about the relationship among the members of the Godhead. In Paul, there are several passages where his treatment of the three members points to his belief that they function on a similar level, if not in exactly the same way. For example, in Rom 8:9, Paul first mentions the Spirit as an independent being and then as the spirit of God and the spirit of Christ, as if the spirit as an independent being is in some way an emissary for these other beings. In 1:1–4, Paul mentions the functions of the three again: this time God is the originator of the gospel, the Son is the subject of the gospel message, and the spirit of holiness (assuming that this is the Holy Spirit; this is debated by commentators)[24] is the one who declared the Son to be the Son of God with power. In 2 Cor 13:14, at the close of the letter, Paul gives the grace benediction, invoking different though parallel functions for the Lord Jesus Christ, God, and the Holy Spirit. We might well call these kinds of passages proto-Trinitarian, in that they indicate that Paul conceived of an early form of Trinitarian relationship among the three, God, Jesus Christ, and the Holy Spirit (cf. also Col 3:16; Eph 5:19).[25]

Swete, *The Holy Spirit in the New Testament: A Study of Primitive Christian Teaching* (London: Macmillan, 1920), 169–253, a classic work; J. D. G. Dunn, *Baptism in the Holy Spirit: A Re-examination of the New Testament Teaching on the Gift of the Spirit in Relation to Pentecostalism Today* (Philadelphia: Westminster, 1970); C. F. D. Moule, *The Holy Spirit* (London: Mowbray, 1978), esp. 22–42; D. Ewert, *The Holy Spirit in the New Testament* (Kitchener, ON: Herald, 1983); and now A. C. Thiselton, *The Holy Spirit—In Biblical Teaching, through the Centuries, and Today* (Grand Rapids: Eerdmans, 2013), esp. 70–94.

23. In English, it is easy to distinguish between the *(Holy) Spirit* and a *spirit* but not in Greek, where there is no capitalization.

24. See for example the brief discussion in D. J. Moo, *The Epistle to the Romans* (NICNT; Grand Rapids: Eerdmans, 1996), 49–50.

25. See S. E. Porter, "Hermeneutics, Biblical Interpretation, and Theology: Hunch, Holy Spirit, or Hard Work?" in I. H. Marshall, *Beyond the Bible: Moving from Scripture to Theology* (Downers Grove, IL: InterVarsity, 2004), 97–127, esp. 122n59. This terminology and approach is

D. Grace

In the Pauline letters, the word translated "grace," which in its noun (χάρις) and verb (χαρίζομαι) forms appears approximately a hundred times, refers to God's love or unmerited favor toward humanity.[26] The significance of grace is illustrated in Rom 1:5, where it is seen as something to be received through Jesus Christ our Lord, almost as if it is salvation itself. In Eph 2:8 (cf. 2:5), the single most noteworthy usage of the word captures well the sense in which Paul uses the term: "By grace you have been saved through faith" (NIV) (although some would say that this relies upon the formulation by an early Pauline interpreter). There has been much scholarly discussion within the past thirty-five or so years on the significance and meaning of grace in Paul's thought and how it relates to his idea of works and the law within the context of ancient Judaism and his view of salvation. Some more recent discussion surrounds the Hellenistic reciprocity system as evidenced in various contemporary inscriptions and papyri.[27] I am not convinced, however, of how much that Greco-Roman background would have affected Paul's audience, and how much of the reciprocity system Paul meant to indicate in using the word "grace." More will be said regarding Paul's thought on grace in §3A below, but it is important to note that the relationship between grace and works is a central topic in what has been called the New Perspective on Paul.[28]

The Pauline letters are also known to contain the phrase "grace and peace" (χάρις καὶ εἰρήνη) in the salutation. This phrase departs from the opening of the typical Hellenistic letter in that it includes a double wish and uses noun forms in verbless clauses rather than the infinitive. The typical documentary

---

endorsed and adopted by Fee, *Pauline Christology*, 63n98, who defines it as "designating those texts where Paul himself, rigorous monotheist though he was, joins Father, Son, and Spirit in ways that indicate the full identity of the Son and Spirit with the Father without losing that monotheism"; 269–70 on Rom 8:9–11; 591–92 on 2 Cor 13:14. He cites other examples.

26. See J. Moffatt, *Grace in the New Testament* (London: Hodder & Stoughton, 1931).

27. J. R. Harrison, "Paul, Theologian of Electing Grace," in Porter, ed., *Paul and His Theology*, 77–108; cf. Harrison, *Paul's Language of Grace in Its Graeco-Roman Context* (WUNT 172; Tübingen: Mohr-Siebeck, 2003); J. M. G. Barclay, *Paul and the Gift* (Grand Rapids: Eerdmans, 2015).

28. See the discussion in J. M. G. Barclay, "Grace and the Transformation of Agency in Christ," in *Redefining First-Century Jewish and Christian Identities: Essays in Honor of Ed Parish Sanders* (ed. F. E. Udoh, S. Heschel, M. Chancey, and G. Tatum; Christianity and Judaism in Antiquity Series 16; Notre Dame, IN: University of Notre Dame Press, 2008), 372–89. Barclay helpfully summarizes the discussion regarding grace and works, but is conspicuous in stating his essential agreement with E. P. Sanders on the issue—that one attains salvation by grace, but stays in and is justified by works. See §3B below for more on this.

papyrus letter of that time simply conveys "greetings" (χαίρειν, an infinitive verb form cognate with the noun Paul uses), but Paul makes the change in form and adds the word "peace." This leads to the question: What is the purpose behind Paul's version of this greeting? And what kind of theological weight should be given to such differences? Some scholars see the use of "peace" as reflecting Jewish influence (as if "peace" were a translation of *shalom*), but the evidence for Jewish letters beginning in this way is relatively slight and so this solution is improbable.[29] Philip Tite notes that the phrase "grace and peace" is probably not originally Pauline but a conventional phrase from the early Christian worship context.[30] It is simply a Christianized expression of blessing already known by Christians, so Paul uses it in place of the common "greetings" most often used. This is an interesting idea, but lacks evidence from earlier Christian letters to establish such a claim. The most probable explanation is that the "grace and peace" greeting was a Pauline innovation. In any case, too much weight should not be given to this feature of the letter, although the differences are worth noting, since the introductory wording is apparently formulaic for Paul in his letters. The Greek word χάρις ("grace") has several derived cognate forms as well, including χάρισμα (1 Cor 12:4–11), sometimes simply transliterated "charisma" or translated "grace gift." For Paul, this word indicates some kind of gracious beneficence, divine or otherwise[31]—a special endowment of the Holy Spirit for work in the church.

E. Faith

The distinction traditionally drawn between the Hebrew and the Greek concepts of faith elevates the Hebrew idea as a religious one, in which belief and trust are paramount, and denigrates the Greek as a nonreligious and more philosophical and rhetorical concept related to persuasion.[32] Like so many

---

29. See S. E. Porter, "Peace, Reconciliation," in *DPL* 695–99, esp. 699. See chapter 5 §3A.

30. P. L. Tite, "How to Begin, and Why? Diverse Functions of the Pauline Prescript within a Greco-Roman Context," in *Paul and the Ancient Letter Form* (ed. S. E. Porter and S. A. Adams; PAST 6; Leiden: Brill, 2010), 57–99, esp. 73–74.

31. It is sometimes mistakenly equated with a "spiritual gift." The idea of a spiritual gift is indicated by context, such as Rom 1:11, where Paul refers to the "grace gift" as a "spiritual" one. See H. Ong, "Is 'Spiritual Gift(s)' a Linguistically Fallacious Term? A Lexical Study of Χάρισμα, Πνευματικός, and Πνεῦμα," *Expository Times* 125.12 (2014): 583–92.

32. See J. L. Kinneavy, *Greek Rhetorical Origins of Christian Faith* (New York: Oxford University Press, 1987); cf. R. Bultmann, "Πιστεύω, κτλ," *Theological Dictionary of the New Testament* 6.217–19.

of such Greek-versus-Hebrew disjunctions, in light of further investigation this one is also shown to be in error.[33] It now appears that in Classical Greek there was an early religious use of words in this "faith" (πιστ-) group, especially verbs, to refer to belief in gods. The Septuagint, in rendering its Hebrew source, maintains a similar kind of meaning, one that is further developed in Hellenistic Greek. The New Testament writers, including Paul, use it in a technical sense to refer to one's proper orientation of putting trust or having faith in God. The major forms of the "faith" words—noun (πίστις), verb (πιστεύω), and adjective (πιστός)—appear over 225 times in Paul's letters, virtually always with the sense specified above, except in some of the disputed letters, where, especially in the Pastoral Epistles, the noun is arguably used to refer to "what is believed" (e.g., Titus 1:2; Eph 4:5) rather than belief itself. Some take the latter meaning as an indication of later development in the meaning of this word group, in which belief as an act came to represent the content of that belief as Christianity moved toward doctrinal development, and hence as support for the pseudepigraphal authorship of such letters.[34] But the similar use of "faith" in Phil 1:27 shows that Paul could use the word in this way in the undisputed letters (cf. also Col 2:7) (this sense can be accounted for within the semantic range of the verb and semantic shift).

In one of the most intense recent debates, scholars have debated whether Paul's use of the phrase "faith of Jesus Christ" (πίστις τοῦ Ἰησοῦ Χριστοῦ; e.g., Rom 3:22; Gal 2:16), or similar phrases, refers to faith or belief directed toward Jesus Christ (the so-called objective genitive in Greek), or to the faith or faithfulness of Jesus Christ (the so-called subjective genitive).[35] Without denying the faithfulness of Jesus Christ or the weight of the arguments for this interpretation,[36] I maintain that Paul appears to be referring to the faith or belief

33. J. Barr, *The Semantics of Biblical Language* (Oxford: Oxford University Press, 1961), esp. 8–20, extensively condemns this dichotomizing of Greek and Hebrew against one another, especially as it usually involves positing differences in the thought patterns of their language users.

34. See D. R. Lindsay, "The Roots and Development of the πιστ- Word Group as Faith Terminology," *JSNT* 49 (1993): 103–18.

35. Most notably R. B. Hays, *The Faith of Jesus Christ: The Narrative Substructure of Galatians 3:1–4:11* (SBLDS 56; repr. Grand Rapids: Eerdmans, 2002 [1983]), esp. 141–55.

36. Proponents of the so-called subjective genitive reading, hence, the "faith/faithfulness of Christ," include the following: K. Barth, *The Epistle to the Romans* (trans. E. C. Hoskyns; Oxford: Oxford University Press, 1933), 41, 96; H. J. Hjungman, *Pistis: A Study of Its Presuppositions and Its Meaning in Pauline Use* (Lund: Gleerup, 1964), 38–40; R. N. Longenecker, *Paul, Apostle of Liberty* (New York: Harper & Row, 1964), 149–52; Longenecker, *Galatians* (WBC 41; Dallas: Word, 1990), 87–88; G. Howard, *Paul: Crisis in Galatia* (SNTSMS 35; Cambridge: Cambridge University Press, 1979), 57–58; F. J. Matera, *Galatians* (Sacra Pagina 9; Collegeville,

that a believer directs toward Jesus Christ.[37] The genitive construction here is apparently shorthand for the Greek phrase "to believe in." This explanation seems to make the best sense of several factors in Paul's argumentation, including his use of the verbal phrase speaking of belief (Rom 3:22) and his general theological orientation.[38] The underlying linguistic support for this so-called objective reading is argued for in greater detail in a recent article. Andrew Pitts and I contend that, when considering the following factors—the role of lexical semantics in sense disambiguation, a (re)consideration of the Greek case system, and examination of the major occurrences of the construction preposition + πίστις Χριστοῦ—the meaning of this debated phrase almost always seems to be that Christ is the object of faith.[39] In other words, since

MN: Liturgical, 1983), 93–94; D. A. Campbell, *The Rhetoric of Righteousness in Romans 3.21–26* (JSNTSup 65; Sheffield: Sheffield Academic, 1992), 58–69; Campbell, *The Quest for Paul's Gospel: A Suggested Strategy* (JSNTSup 274; London: T&T Clark, 2005), 191; Campbell, *The Deliverance of God: An Apocalyptic Rereading of Justification in Paul* (Grand Rapids: Eerdmans, 2009), 869–74; S. K. Stowers, *A Rereading of Romans: Justice, Jews, and Gentiles* (New Haven: Yale University Press, 1994), 201; L. T. Johnson, *Reading Romans: A Literary and Theological Commentary* (New York: Crossroad, 1997), 58–61; and J. L. Martyn, *Galatians* (AB 33A; New Haven: Yale University Press, 1997), 251, 263–75.

37. Despite many recent scholars arguing for the so-called subjective genitive, other scholars remain unconvinced and argue for the traditional objective genitive ("faith in Christ"). These include, among many others, C. E. B. Cranfield, *A Critical and Exegetical Commentary on the Epistle to the Romans* (2 vols.; ICC; Edinburgh: T&T Clark, 1975–79), 1.203; H. D. Betz, *Galatians* (Hermeneia; Philadelphia: Fortress, 1979), 117–18; A. Hultgren, "*Pistis Christou* Formulation," *NovT* 22 (1980): 248–63; F. F. Bruce, *The Epistle to the Galatians* (NIGTC; Grand Rapids: Eerdmans, 1982), 138–39; J. D. G. Dunn, *Romans* (WBC 38A; Waco, TX: Word, 1988), 1.166–67; Dunn, *The Epistle to the Galatians* (BNTC; New York: Bloomsbury, 1993), 138–39; J. A. Fitzmyer, *Romans* (AB 33; New York: Doubleday, 1993), 345–46; R. A. Harrisville, "ΠΙΣΤΙΣ ΧΡΙΣΤΟΥ: Witness of the Fathers," *NovT* (1994): 233–41; D. J. Moo, *The Epistle to the Romans* (NICNT; Grand Rapids: Eerdmans, 1996), 224–25; T. Schreiner, *Romans* (BECNT; Grand Rapids: Baker, 1998), 181–86; R. B. Matlock, "Detheologizing the ΠΙΣΤΙΣ ΧΡΙΣΤΟΥ Debate: Cautionary Remarks from a Lexical Semantic Perspective," *NovT* 42 (2000): 1–23; and R. Jewett, *Romans* (Hermeneia; Minneapolis: Fortress, 2007), 276–78.

38. For a summary of the issues in light of recent debate, see the collection of essays in M. F. Bird and P. M. Sprinkle, eds., *The Faith of Jesus Christ: Exegetical, Biblical, and Theological Studies* (Peabody, MA: Hendrickson, 2009); see also J. D. G. Dunn, "Once More, ΠΙΣΤΙΣ ΧΡΙΣΤΟΥ," in *Pauline Theology*, vol. 4: *Looking Back, Pressing On* (ed. E. E. Johnson and D. M. Hay; Society of Biblical Literature Symposium 4; Atlanta: Scholars Press, 1997), 61–81, responding to R. B. Hays, "ΠΙΣΤΙΣ and Pauline Christology: What Is at Stake?" in the same volume, 35–60. Another helpful summary is M. C. Easter, "The Pistis Christou Debate: Main Arguments and Responses in Summary," *Currents in Biblical Research* 9 (2010): 33–47.

39. S. E. Porter and A. W. Pitts, "Πίστις with a Preposition and Genitive Modifier," in *The Faith of Jesus Christ: Exegetical, Biblical, and Theological Studies* (ed. M. F. Bird and P. M. Sprinkle; Peabody, MA: Hendrickson, 2009), 33–53.

the function of the genitive is simply restrictive[40] without comment as to any subject or object of an action (both "faith" and "Christ" are nouns in this construction), the phrase simply refers to a faith that is restricted by Christ.

These few sections cover most, if not all, of the essential Pauline beliefs that can be found anywhere in his letters, since they provide the basic framework for his view of the Christian life. Paul does not attempt to argue for these beliefs. Instead, he assumes them and seems to think that his readers will likewise. However, these relatively few beliefs are not all that Paul wishes to convey theologically. Indeed, a good number of Paul's beliefs count not among his essential beliefs, but among his developed beliefs.

3. Developed Beliefs

This subheading is not meant to imply that these beliefs in some way are less important than, or secondary to, Paul's fundamental or essential beliefs. To the contrary, these developed beliefs often preoccupy scholars more than the essential beliefs, not least because they are treated at relatively greater length in Paul's letters and present plenty of material to which to respond. Whether these elements constitute the theological center of Paul's belief is frequently debated. Discussion concerning them takes several different turns in recent scholarly publication. Early in the last century, it was common to posit what constituted Paul's theological center; however, recent discussion shuns the very concept of a theological center, choosing instead to emphasize the contingent nature of each of Paul's letters. This makes it difficult to conceive of a single idea, even if a complex one, constituting the center or essence of Paul's belief.[41] Most of the following beliefs merit attention, but it is probably fair to say that a single idea cannot be seen to stand at the center of Paul's thinking; rather, a number of these beliefs have great importance in his thinking. The following list is not meant to be exhaustive, nor is the discussion as detailed as it could be.

A. Justification

Since the time of the reformer Martin Luther, who saw the heart of the gospel expressed in this idea, justification by faith has been one of the most im-

---

40. Porter, *Idioms*, 92.

41. On the idea of a center to Paul's theology, see Porter, "Is There a Center to Paul's Theology?" 6–12.

portant theological categories for discussing Paul.[42] In this section, I do not discuss the larger systematic-theological notion of justification, but mostly confine my comments to justification within the biblical material, primarily the New Testament.[43] Despite recent efforts by some New Testament scholars to call into question the centrality of justification (see some of the proposals below, such as apocalyptic), the notion is still important in Paul's thought and letters.

On the basis of both Old Testament and Greek usage, justification language in the Bible is traditionally defined in legal or forensic terminology, the idea being that the sinner stands before God, the righteous judge, who renders a verdict concerning him or her. When evaluated against the righteous standards of God's character, every human being is found to be a sinner and inadequate (Rom 1:18). For Paul, law-centered religion cannot be a substitute for this required righteousness (Gal 5:3-6). On the basis of faith or belief in Jesus Christ (this phrase is an abbreviated way of referring to the death of Jesus Christ on the cross), the human can be justified by God.[44] Several modern interpreters, however, reject the legal terminology and opt for eschatological language instead, in which God's righteousness is equated with his power and sovereignty. What God does in justifying sinners is a divine, regal fiat, announcing a new day when past failures are put away, debts are canceled, and guilt is removed (Rom 1:17; 3:21, where revelatory or epiphanic language is used). God delivers the promise of a new world in

42. See, e.g., Luther's declaration, printed at the beginning of *A Commentary on St. Paul's Epistle to the Galatians* (ed. J. P. Fallowes; trans. E. Middleton; London: Harrison Trust, n.d.), xi–xvi. Some recent book-length treatments of justification in the New Testament include M. A. Seifrid, *Justification by Faith: The Origin and Development of a Central Pauline Theme* (NovTSup 68; Leiden: Brill, 1992); Seifrid, *Christ, Our Righteousness: Paul's Theology of Justification* (New Studies in Biblical Theology; Downers Grove, IL: InterVarsity, 2000); D. A Carson, P. T. O'Brien, and M. A. Seifrid, eds., *Justification and Variegated Nomism: A Fresh Appraisal of Paul and Second Temple Judaism* (2 vols.; WUNT 2/140; Tübingen: Mohr-Siebeck/Grand Rapids: Baker, 2001-4); G. P. Waters, *Justification and the New Perspectives on Paul: A Review and Response* (Philipsburg, NJ: P&R, 2004); and N. T. Wright, *Justification: God's Plan and Paul's Vision* (Downers Grove, IL: InterVarsity, 2009).

43. For some of these considerations, see M. Husbands and D. J. Treier, eds., *Justification: What's at Stake in the Current Debates?* (Downers Grove, IL: InterVarsity, 2004). One of the most important essays is D. A. Carson, "The Vindication of Imputation: On Fields of Discourse and Semantic Fields," 46–78.

44. See J. A. Ziesler, *The Meaning of Righteousness in Paul: A Linguistic and Theological Enquiry* (SNTSMS 20; Cambridge: Cambridge University Press, 1972); and Seifrid, *Justification by Faith*, who also surveys recent developments. See also M. T. Brauch, "Perspectives on 'God's Righteousness' in Recent German Discussion," in E. P. Sanders, *Paul and Palestinian Judaism* (Philadelphia: Fortress, 1977), 523–42.

which his power reaches out to capture the entire universe for his sovereignty (3:24–25).[45]

Several questions are raised by these analyses.[46] One is whether this righteousness (or justification; both words refer to the same Greek word δικαιοσύνη and a number of its cognates) refers to the inauguration of a new relationship with God or the restoration of an old relationship. Another concerns the time when this justification occurs in the life of the believer, which is related to its status or nature. Traditionally, justification speaks of the establishment of a new relationship with God. Recent analysis of Paul and this concept, however, tends toward seeing justification more in terms of God's relationship to his covenant community, Israel. In this sense, if the language is borrowed from Old Testament thinking, according to which God's people are expected to uphold God's righteous standards, then the thought about justification might have in mind the restoration of a previous relationship. But when Paul introduces justification in his two most significant writings on the topic, Galatians and Romans (but cf. 1 Cor 6:11; Phil 3:9), he does so in conjunction with the story of Abraham. He refers to Abraham believing in God and this being accounted to him as righteousness (Gen 15:6, cited in Rom 4:3, 22; Gal 3:6). The force of these discussions seems to speak of the institution of a new relationship between God and humanity, one that precedes any performance of righteousness or fulfillment of the law.

Even if this is the case, a number of important issues concerning justification still require further discussion. The question of when this justification occurs is one topic of significant debate. Some posit that, since Paul uses several different Greek verb tenses to speak of justification, he apparently thinks that it is something past, present, and future.[47] But since the verb tenses in Greek are not essentially time based,[48] this argument is of little value in answering the question, and such equations are better avoided (this is not to say that justification is not past, present, and future, only that such a statement cannot rely upon the Greek verb tenses to make it).

A further issue concerns the nature of this justification. In other words,

---

45. The best known proponent of this position is E. Käsemann, " 'The Righteousness of God' in Paul," in *New Testament Questions of Today* (trans. W. J. Montague; Philadelphia: Fortress, 1969), 168–82. See also §3F below.

46. This subject is also directly related to the discussion of the New Perspective on Paul. See §3B below for discussion of that topic.

47. Something like this equation of justification with particular Greek tense forms is found in G. B. Caird, *New Testament Theology* (ed. L. D. Hurst; Oxford: Clarendon, 1994), 118. He is not the only one to do this.

48. See Porter, *Idioms*, esp. 20–45, where the issue of time and tense form is discussed.

when justification is mentioned by Paul, what kind of righteous status does he see the sinner having? For those who adopt the legal perspective on justification, a choice is sometimes made between acquittal/exoneration language and amnesty/pardon language. The idea of acquittal or exoneration should be rejected in light of Paul's view of sin, since this seems to imply that the sinner might well not have committed the offense for which the charge of guilt is brought. There are no innocent defendants in Paul's assessment (Rom 4:5; cf. 3:24). The language of amnesty is better suited to the Pauline analysis, in which a divine pardon is offered to the undeserving.[49]

What then is the status of this pardon? This is a topic that verges on the categories of systematic theology. For several scholars earlier in the nineteenth century, to say that righteousness is in any way imparted to the sinner smacked of a "legal fiction," in which the sinner is viewed as righteous when it is known full well from human experience that the individual continues to sin. This also calls into question the value of the divine decree of the pardon, since it seems to be ineffectual. Others view righteousness in terms of a declared or imputed righteousness, in which righteous status is given in anticipation of actual righteousness in the age to come. One's status before God is treated as if it were true, even though it will not become so until the eschaton. Although this view might avoid the problem of God's divine decree of righteousness, it does not mitigate the problem of God's apparently pretending to treat as righteous those who still are not.

In light of recent discussion, some scholars argue that the best solution is to view justification in primarily relational terms.[50] God is seen to have established a right relationship with humanity, so that a new attitude of humanity toward God as well as of God toward humanity is established. Some scholars therefore prefer to use the invented word "rightwise" instead of "justify."[51] Human recovery and renewal are begun, and their ultimate goals are totally righteous behavior and eternal life with a righteous God. I think that this tendency probably reflects the Reformation agenda in which justification was placed at the center of Paul's thought and was required to absorb or subsume other major theological notions within its scope. In this configuration, I think that it extends the meaning of justification too far. Justification is instead seen as addressing the narrower question of humanity's legal status before God. The

49. See W. Sanday and A. C. Headlam, *A Critical and Exegetical Commentary on the Epistle to the Romans* (5th ed.; ICC; Edinburgh: T&T Clark, 1902), esp. 30.

50. Cf. A. C. Thiselton, *The Living Paul: An Introduction to the Apostle's Life and Thought* (Downers Grove, IL: InterVarsity, 2009), 92–100, who also makes the point that justification seems to go broader than just legal status but a restored relationship.

51. Thiselton, *Living Paul*, 92; and Wright, *Justification*, 89.

human is a lawbreaker who is in need of remedy before a righteous God. The solution is justification or a fixing of one's legal status as a sinner before God, in which forgiveness for sin is effected through the sacrificial death of Jesus Christ appropriated through faith. This is clearly seen in Rom 3:21–26, where justification is seen as the legal solution to human sinfulness, described as a consequence of the argument of 1:18–3:20 regarding universal sinful humanity and supported by 4:1–25 with the example of Abraham's justification through faith.

B. Law and Its Relation to God's Work in Christ

The law and its relation to salvation is probably the single most discussed topic in recent Pauline studies, since it has implications for understanding how Paul characterizes his own Jewish background and for the nature of the Judaism he defines and confronts in his epistles. As a result, this section is more heavily documented than some other sections, because the topic generates extensive scholarly discussion.

The traditional and still widely held view (sometimes called the "Lutheran" view, because it is often attributed to Martin Luther) is that Paul saw Christianity as a religion of faith but that Judaism was a religion of works, in which one attempted (wrongly in Paul's eyes) to establish a right relationship before God by keeping the law rather than by faith. For Paul this was impossible, so he opposed the works-righteousness of Judaism with faith in Jesus Christ. In especially the last thirty-five years, a number of scholars argue for a revision of the traditional view of Paul, and consequently what he was opposing, especially in Galatians and Romans. This has come to be known as the New Perspective on Paul, although by now it is far from new (and whether it is in fact an accurate perspective is another question altogether). This brief discussion attempts to outline the issues and indicate why the traditional view is still more tenable than this more recent "new" perspective.

In 1977 E. P. Sanders published his *Paul and Palestinian Judaism*, a discussion that was supplemented and expanded in *Paul, the Law, and the Jewish People* in 1983.[52] In these books, he proposes a reconsideration of the Judaism

---

52. See E. P. Sanders, *Paul and Palestinian Judaism*; and *Paul, the Law, and the Jewish People* (Philadelphia: Fortress, 1983). Several previous scholars anticipated Sanders's view, including G. F. Moore, *Judaism in the First Centuries of the Christian Era* (2 vols.; repr. Peabody, MA: Hendrickson, 1997 [1927]); K. Stendahl, "The Apostle Paul and the Introspective Conscience of the West," *Harvard Theological Review* 56 (1963): 199–215; repr. in Stendahl, *Paul among Jews and Gentiles and Other Essays* (Philadelphia: Fortress, 1976), 78–96; and Sanders's

of the first century and Paul's reaction to it. Sanders's work has in effect resulted in a thorough rethinking of the Judaism of the time and Christian response to it. He was followed by many others, the three most widely known probably being Heikki Räisänen, James D. G. Dunn, and N. T. Wright.[53] Their position, followed by many since, has come to be identified as the New Perspective on Paul. Some of the distinctives of the positions of these four merit examination before a response is proposed.[54]

Räisänen argues that the traditional view is exactly what Paul thought, that is, that Judaism saw salvation as a human achievement through works, but that Paul was wrong on this point, primarily because he is internally inconsistent in his thinking. For example, at times Paul sees the law functioning differently for Jews and Gentiles (Rom 2:12), but at other times he holds that all humans are held accountable by it (2:13–14). Sometimes Paul seems to believe that some Gentiles fulfilled the law (2:27), but this requires a narrow view of law not applied elsewhere, where all humans are seen to be violators of the law (3:20). Sometimes Paul seems to think that the law is valid, but at other times he sees its function as having ended. Sometimes he views sin as having been caused

---

own teacher, W. D. Davies, *Paul and Rabbinic Judaism: A Comparison of Patterns of Belief* (4th ed.; Philadelphia: Fortress, 1980). Cf. C. Van Langingham, *Judgment and Justification in Early Judaism and the Apostle Paul* (Peabody, MA: Hendrickson, 2006), who in some ways outdoes Sanders by contending for a Judaism of grace and a Paul of works.

53. H. Räisänen, *Paul and the Law* (WUNT 29; Tübingen: Mohr-Siebeck, 1983; repr. Philadelphia: Fortress, 1986); and *Jesus, Paul, and Torah: Collected Essays* (trans. D. E. Orton; JSNT-Sup 43; Sheffield: JSOT Press, 1992); J. D. G. Dunn, "The New Perspective on Paul," *Bulletin of the John Rylands University Library* 65 (1983): 95–122; repr. in *Jesus, Paul, and the Law: Studies in Mark and Galatians* (London: SPCK, 1990), 183–206, along with other essays; *Romans* (WBC 38AB; Dallas: Word, 1988), 1.lxiii–lxxii; *The Theology of Paul's Letter to the Galatians* (New Testament Theology; Cambridge: Cambridge University Press, 1993), esp. 75–92; *Theology of Paul the Apostle*, esp. 338–40, 354–66; and *The New Perspective on Paul: Collected Essays* (WUNT 185; Tübingen: Mohr-Siebeck, 2005); N. T. Wright, *The Climax of the Covenant: Christ and the Law in Pauline Theology* (Edinburgh: T&T Clark, 1991); *What Saint Paul Really Said: Was Paul of Tarsus the Real Founder of Christianity?* (Grand Rapids: Eerdmans, 1997); *Paul: In Fresh Perspective* (Minneapolis: Fortress, 2005); and *Paul and the Faithfulness of God* (2 vols.; Christian Origins and the Question of God 4; Minneapolis: Fortress, 2013).

54. Several others support a similar position: F. Watson, *Paul, Judaism and the Gentiles: A Sociological Approach* (SNTSMS 56; Cambridge: Cambridge University Press, 1986), but with a change of heart, or at least social positioning, in the revised and expanded *Paul, Judaism, and the Gentiles: Beyond the New Perspective* (Grand Rapids: Eerdmans, 2007), esp. 1–26; and P. Tomson, *Paul and the Jewish Law: Halakha in the Letters of the Apostle to the Gentiles* (Assen/Maastricht: Van Gorcum; Minneapolis: Fortress, 1990); and Tomson, "If This Be from Heaven . . .": *Jesus and the New Testament Authors in Their Relationship to Judaism* (Sheffield: Sheffield Academic, 2001). A summary that is biased toward their perspective is M. Zetterholm, *Approaches to Paul: A Student's Guide to Recent Scholarship* (Minneapolis: Fortress, 2009).

by the law (7:7–11), but at other times he views the law as God's response to sin (5:20; 7:14). Räisänen rightly brings to the interpreter's mind the complexity and tension of Paul's thought regarding the law (and he is probably right that Paul thought of Judaism as legalistic), and several of his analyses merit consideration. But his failure to appreciate the larger context of Paul's argument (e.g., differentiating several major functions of the law in Paul's thought) and his questionable juxtaposition of certain passages (e.g., verses in Rom 7) leave his reinterpretation of Paul unsatisfactory.[55] Most scholars do not, however, go so far as Räisänen, and his work is not followed as much in recent discussion.

Offering a more consistent program of interpretation, Sanders claims that "covenantal nomism"[56] provides the fundamental theological concept underlying the Jewish thinking of the first century. By covenantal nomism he means that an Israelite's place in God's plan is determined by God's gracious covenant, with obedience to the law as a response. Salvation, therefore, is not a strict weighing and evaluation of transgressions but depends, rather, upon divine mercy. The righteous Jew is not necessarily the one who can keep all of the commandments but one who accepts and remains within the covenant community. Thus, salvation is achieved by God's grace and faith in him; remaining in that covenantal relationship with him is achieved by works. This is the form of Judaism that Paul would have known, not one in which salvation was founded upon works. Indeed, according to Sanders, Paul's thinking as a Christian is not significantly different from Jewish thinking, except that he saw salvation as resident in Jesus Christ. The problem with Judaism for Paul, according to Sanders, was that it was not Christianity. Starting from the assumption that the work of Christ changed the basic human condition (rather than working from the human dilemma to the solution), Paul worked back to the human problem of sinfulness. For Paul, the problem with Judaism was its thinking that it had special privileges it alone was able to pursue, whereas Paul saw the same grace available to Jews and Gentiles.

Dunn begins with Sanders's thinking but believes that Sanders does not go far enough in his estimation of the Jewish law.[57] For the Jew, according to Dunn, the law was an identity or boundary marker, a badge, that became a part of Jewish national consciousness as a distinctive people. Circumcision,

---

55. On Räisänen's interpretation of the law in Paul, see J. A. D. Weima, "The Function of the Law in Relation to Sin: An Evaluation of the View of H. Räisänen," *NovT* 32 (1990): 219–35.

56. "Covenantal nomism" is defined by Sanders (*Paul and Palestinian Judaism*, 75) as "the view that one's place in God's plan is established on the basis of the covenant and that the covenant requires as the proper response of man his obedience to its commandments, while providing means of atonement for transgression."

57. Dunn, *New Perspective on Paul*, 15.

food laws, and Sabbath observance gave the Jews a sense of privilege at being chosen by God and favored with the law and covenants.[58] For Paul, then, for example in Rom 2 or Gal 2, "works of the law" refers to reliance upon these boundary markers, especially circumcision in Gal 2. Paul argues against the Jews' use of the law as a boundary marker for their nationalist zeal. It does not refer to traditional Reformation categories that "works of the law" refers to human efforts to win God's favor by obedience to the law, or something to that effect. Instead, for Dunn, this phrase does not refer to this type of legalism but to Paul's "denot[ing] those obligations prescribed by the law which show the individual concerned to belong to the law, which mark out the practitioner as a member of the people of the law, the covenant people, the Jewish nation."[59] The difference, for Dunn, is that the Jew was not concerned with adhering to the law in order to gain God's favor and be in good standing with him, but that he was interested in obedience to the law in order to mark himself out as a member of God's community.

Several other proposals regarding "works of the law" are also put forward.[60] For example, this phrase means "works that the law does" and emphasizes the law as the performer of the action.[61] But for Paul, human performance of the law is what is meant, as Rom 3–4 illustrates. It is also argued that "works of the law" refers to "legalism," a distortion of the Jewish law into an attempt to bribe God.[62] But at several points in Paul's writings, "works of the law" is treated synonymously with "law" (Gal 2:16, 21; Rom 3:20, 21, 28) and opposed to faith (4:1–6), and thus seen not as negative in and of itself, though not to be relied upon for right status with God. There are other views as well, which Jacqueline de Roo surveys and ably critiques.[63]

Wright generally accepts the views of Sanders, Dunn, and others and focuses his attention on the phrase "righteousness of God" and the concept of justification. Using the law court metaphor, Wright states that it is nonsensical to think that a judge bequeaths, transfers, or imparts his righteousness to a

---

58. Dunn, *New Perspective on Paul*, 98–101. This is affirmed in Dunn's most recent essay to date regarding this issue: "A New Perspective on the New Perspective on Paul," *Early Christianity* 4 (2013): 157–82.

59. Dunn, *Jesus, Paul, and the Law*, 219–20; cf. also Dunn, *New Perspective on Paul*, 101.

60. For some helpful works on this concept, see, e.g., Sanders, *Paul, the Law, and Jewish People*; R. K. Rapa, *The Meaning of "Works of the Law" in Galatians and Romans* (Studies in Biblical Literature 31; New York: Peter Lang, 2001), esp. 3–7, 15–51; and J. C. R. de Roo, "Works of the Law" at Qumran and in Paul (NTM 13; Sheffield: Sheffield Phoenix, 2007), esp. 42–71.

61. L. Gaston, *Paul and the Torah* (Vancouver: University of British Columbia Press, 1987).

62. E. D. W. Burton, *A Critical and Exegetical Commentary on the Epistle to the Galatians* (ICC; Edinburgh: T&T Clark, 1921), 120, cf. 443–60.

63. De Roo, "Works of the Law," 42–71.

defendant; in other words, he does not accept that God grants imputation.[64] He claims that righteousness is not a substance to be exchanged or given and that this type of thinking is a category mistake. This perspective is clear in his earlier writings, but in recent work he states that justification (and hence, righteousness) is a declaration of the defendant's status as favorable, which is a *legal* statement.[65] The "righteousness of God," then, is not God's transference of some substance, but "God's covenant faithfulness" to his people.[66]

Sanders's and Dunn's and others' new or revised perspective on Judaism, Paul, and the law meets with many supporters. This may be partially attributed to Wright's popularization of their ideas to many readers. At the least, their ideas have made all interpreters more sensitive to issues of Pauline interpretation and aware of some of the possible tensions within his writings, even though the New Perspective has not, at least to my mind, proved convincing. Nevertheless, even Sanders and Dunn do not necessarily agree on some fundamental issues in this discussion. For example, Dunn criticizes Sanders for taking "works of the law" as a synonym of "law," but this equation of the two is exactly what Paul seems to be making.[67] At several places, since Paul equates "works of the law" with "law," Paul cannot simply be talking about the law taken in its restrictive sense, as Dunn believes (Gal 2:16 versus 2:21; 3:11; 5:4; and Rom 3:20a, 28 versus 3:20b, 21). "Works of the law" has something to do with the Mosaic law in its origin, nature, and function, or so it seems to be treated by Paul, as Rom 3:20–28 illustrates, where the commandments referred to appear to be from the Decalogue, which is cited above at 2:21–22. Such specialization of meaning as Dunn requires is also unwarranted in light of Paul's discussion of Abraham and his "works" preceding the giving of the law. This calls into question Dunn's view of Paul as addressing Jewish "boundary markers" (the works of the law).

---

64. Wright, *Climax of the Covenant*, 96–99. On this topic, see B. Vickers, *Jesus' Blood and Righteousness: Paul's Theology of Imputation* (Wheaton, IL: Crossway, 2006).

65. Wright, *Justification*, 90–92. See also Wright, "A New Perspective on Käsemann? Apocalyptic, Covenant, and the Righteousness of God," in *Studies in the Pauline Epistles: Essays in Honor of Douglas J. Moo* (ed. M. S. Harmon and J. E. Smith; Grand Rapids: Zondervan, 2014), 243–58. Wright appears here to be engaging in what Barr (*Semantics of Biblical Language*, 218) called "illegitimate totality transfer," by transferring an entire theological construct onto the use of this simple phrase in many if not most of its occurrences.

66. See now Wright, *Paul and the Faithfulness of God*, 795–804, which volumes arrived too late for more extended comment and critique.

67. See C. E. B. Cranfield, " 'The Works of the Law' in the Epistle to the Romans," *JSNT* 43 (1991): 89–101; repr. in *On Romans and Other New Testament Essays* (Edinburgh: T&T Clark, 1998), 1–14, who shows that Dunn's interpretation of "works of the law" as having the specified sense he claims, rather than indicating "obedience to the law," is highly questionable.

Other fundamental problems, however, with the entire New Perspective on Paul merit attention. Several further lines of criticism could be pursued, but I will summarize what I consider to be the most important and telling.[68] First, there is a serious question whether the Jewish evidence is correctly interpreted by the New Perspective. Sanders and his supporters attempt to characterize a pattern of religious belief, but this pattern strikes many interpreters as being fairly selective. Barry Smith, for example, argues for a more moderated and less disjunctive approach to the evidence of ancient Judaism, when he shows that God both as righteous judge and as merciful figure are well illustrated side-by-side throughout the Old Testament, Qumran, and rabbinic evidence—without resolution.[69] For example, the Old Testament evidence itself is more works oriented than the New Perspective admits. Numerous passages, such as Lev 18:3–5 and Deut 4:1; 5:33; 6:24–25; 8:1; 11:26–28, equate keeping God's commandments with life, and disobedience with condemnation and death. As de Roo states, "Sanders is famous for his statement that within first-century Judaism '*works are the condition of remaining "in," but they do not*

68. For strong criticism of the New Perspective, besides Seifrid, *Justification by Faith* and *Christ, Our Righteousness*, see especially S. Westerholm, *Perspectives Old and New: The "Lutheran" Paul and His Critics* (Grand Rapids: Eerdmans, 2004), esp. 261–445, a revised and expanded version of Westerholm, *Israel's Law and the Church's Faith: Paul and His Recent Interpreters* (Grand Rapids: Eerdmans, 1988), esp. 105–97, that I have found extremely helpful. For other criticism of various types, cf. also H. Hübner, *Law in Paul's Thought* (Edinburgh: T&T Clark, 1984); T. R. Schreiner, *The Law and Its Fulfillment: A Pauline Theology of Law* (Grand Rapids: Baker, 1993); F. Thielman, *Paul and the Law: A Contextual Approach* (Downers Grove, IL: InterVarsity, 1994); P. Stuhlmacher with D. Hagner, *Revisiting Paul's Doctrine of Justification: A Challenge to the New Perspective* (Downers Grove, IL: InterVarsity, 2001); Carson, O'Brien, and Seifrid, eds., *Justification and Variegated Nomism*; S. Kim, *Paul and the New Perspective: Second Thoughts on the Origins of Paul's Gospel* (Tübingen: Mohr-Siebeck; Grand Rapids: Eerdmans, 2002); S. J. Gathercole, *Where Is Boasting? Early Jewish Soteriology and Paul's Response in Romans 1–5* (Grand Rapids: Eerdmans, 2002); Waters, *Justification and the New Perspectives*; F. Watson, *Paul and the Hermeneutics of Faith* (New York: T&T Clark, 2004); B. D. Smith, *What Must I Do to Be Saved? Paul Parts Company with His Jewish Heritage* (NTM 17; Sheffield: Sheffield Phoenix, 2007), who contrasts Judaism's synergistic soteriology involving God both as righteous judge and as merciful with Paul's nonsynergistic soteriology; P. M. Sprinkle, *Law and Life: The Interpretation of Leviticus 18:5 in Early Judaism and in Paul* (WUNT 2/241; Tübingen: Mohr-Siebeck, 2008); and Sprinkle, *Paul and Judaism Revisited: A Study of Divine and Human Agency in Salvation* (Downers Grove, IL: InterVarsity, 2013). Excellent overall assessments are found in M. A. Seifrid, "Blind Alleys in the Controversy over the Paul of History," *Tyndale Bulletin* 45.1 (1994): 73–95; and A. J. Hultgren, "Paul and the Law," in *The Blackwell Companion to Paul* (ed. S. Westerholm; West Sussex, UK: Wiley-Blackwell, 2011), 202–15.

69. B. D. Smith, *The Tension between God as Righteous Judge and as Merciful in Early Judaism* (Lanham, MD: University Press of America, 2005), with extensive examples from all three bodies of material.

earn salvation. Yet, remaining within the covenant was the way to be saved, and, therefore, good works, even though enabled by God in his people, were still instrumental for salvation."[70] Furthermore, the rabbinic evidence Sanders in particular cites is admittedly late (i.e., second century AD and later), and his attempts to argue for early traditions are not always convincing. There is also some special pleading when, to deny the value of evidence that seems to speak of works in the rabbinic sources, he claims that these references assume the covenantal context that he presupposes. For example, after examining an important passage regarding the belief of the rabbi Akiba, one scholar concludes, "Careful exegesis of *m. Aboth* 3:16–17 demonstrates that the traditional view of first-century rabbinic soteriology as based on works-righteousness is not completely based upon pseudo-scholarship as claimed by Sanders."[71]

Recent analysis also argues that in a number of texts roughly contemporary with the period of the New Testament a works-oriented scheme is clearly evident, such as *Psalms of Solomon* (e.g., 10:4) and 1 Macc 2:51–52: "Remember the deeds of the ancestors, which they did in their generations; and you will receive great honor and an everlasting name. Was not Abraham found faithful when tested, and it was reckoned to him as righteousness?" (NRSV). Several Qumran documents seem to attest to similar belief, such as the *Manual of Discipline* (e.g., 1QS 11.3, 12). Especially notable is the Qumran document *Miqsat Maaseh ha-Torah* (4QMMT), which probably dates to a little earlier than the time of the New Testament.[72] This text explicitly states that "works of the law" (a phrase apparently unparalleled in other extrabiblical Jewish literature, except for a possible disputed reading in 4Q174)[73] will be accounted as righteousness, probably citing Gen 15:6 with reference to Abraham, the very text that Paul cites in Rom 4 and Gal 3, when he says that Abraham's faith was counted to him as righteousness (less likely is Ps 106:30–31, with reference to Phinehas). *Miqsat Maaseh ha-Torah* states, "We have written to you of some of the works of the law . . . for your good and for [that] of your people. . . . And

---

70. De Roo, "*Works of the Law,*" 68, citing Sanders, *Paul and Palestinian Judaism*, 543.

71. C. L. Quarles, "The Soteriology of R. Akiba and E. P. Sanders' *Paul and Palestinian Judaism,*" *NTS* 42 (1996): 185–95 at 195.

72. This text is published in E. Qimron and J. Strugnell, *Qumran Cave 4*, vol. 5: *Miqsat Ma'ase ha-Torah* (Discoveries in the Judaean Desert 10; Oxford: Clarendon, 1994), 62–63, but better translated in R. Eisenman and M. Wise, *The Dead Sea Scrolls Uncovered* (Shaftesbury: Element, 1992), 200, which is the translation cited here. For discussion of this interesting Qumran text, see J. Kampen and M. J. Bernstein, eds., *Reading 4QMMT: New Perspectives on Qumran Law and History* (Society of Biblical Literature Symposium 2; Atlanta: Scholars Press, 1996).

73. See de Roo, "*Works of the Law,*" 4–25.

this will be accounted to you for righteousness, because you are doing what is right and good before him" (4Q398 2 II). The word for "works" is cognate to the verb "doing," and the wording regarding accounting righteousness is very similar to that of Gen 15:6 in the Hebrew Masoretic Text. *Miqsat Maaseh ha-Torah* therefore seems to establish that some Jews around the time of the first century thought of works as leading to righteousness, that is, these works of cultic and ethical behavior were instrumental in their salvation.[74] Thus, not only did Paul rightly understand this segment of Judaism; he uses the same Old Testament texts in support of his discussion of the law, but concludes exactly the opposite. *Miqsat Maaseh ha-Torah* equates doing "works of the law" (whether biblical only or biblical and other) with establishing righteousness before God, but Paul states that it is apart from "works of the law"—by faith—that one is made righteous before God. The traditional understanding of Paul's view of righteousness in Judaism is apparently vindicated.

Second, New Perspective readings of the Pauline texts are subject to severe scrutiny. Besides Sanders and his followers usually addressing Palestinian Judaism—and Diaspora Judaism may have been different—this New Perspective framework has a distinctly legalistic element to it, in which staying in the covenant is predicated upon works, as Sanders, Dunn, and others admit. Even if the evidence were to indicate that the Jews believed in covenantal nomism as Sanders and others define it (and this is debatable, as the evidence above shows), it appears that Paul did not envision such a combination of mercy and deeds but grace alone (e.g., Gal 5:4; Rom 9:30–31; 11:20–21, where faith, not works, is the issue). Paul did not think in terms similar to those of a covenantal nomism of Judaism, at least as characterized by the New Perspective. Sanders, for example, contends that Paul's complaint against Judaism was that it was not Christianity, that Paul believed that salvation was in Jesus Christ, and that he worked back from this conclusion to the problem (from solution to plight). But, as Sanders must admit, in Rom 1–3 Paul works from plight to solution.[75] Furthermore, in Sanders's and Dunn's reckoning, there is a role for the Old Testament law in salvation, but this does not seem to conform to Paul's view

---

74. De Roo, "Works of the Law," 26–41. See also C. A. Evans, *Ancient Texts for New Testament Studies: A Guide to the Background Literature* (Peabody, MA: Hendrickson, 2005), 152–53, with bibliography. I find unconvincing attempts by those of the New Perspective to appropriate this Qumran text for their own understanding. Some of these are surveyed in J. VanderKam and P. Flint, *The Meaning of the Dead Sea Scrolls: Their Significance for Understanding the Bible, Judaism, Jesus, and Christianity* (San Francisco: HarperSanFrancisco, 2002), 351–52 and notes.

75. On this terminology, see F. Thielman, *From Plight to Solution: A Jewish Framework for Understanding Paul's View of the Law in Romans and Galatians* (NovTSup 61; Leiden: Brill, 1989). See also Wright, *Climax of the Covenant*, 258–62.

when he categorically excludes the role of the law (e.g., Rom 4:13–16). For Paul, it is not the law of the Old Testament that Christians are to follow but a new law of love, or love of Christ (Gal 5:14, 22–23). At least in Paul's mind, this does not seem to be nomism, since Paul at several points explicitly contrasts his view of how one gets right with God by faith with a justification that comes about by law.

Furthermore, for Paul, one's relationship is not covenantal, at least as this is understood in terms of an entire community of people. For Paul, one's gracious standing before God on the basis of faith is highly personal and individual (e.g., Rom 3:26, 28, and the specific instance of Abraham). This is not to deny the element of grace in Judaism (this has perhaps been overemphasized in recent thought but should not therefore be completely denied) but only to suggest that, at least in Paul's eyes, Judaism would at best be characterized as a system that depended upon grace *and* works. For Paul, this was not good enough, since God's grace mediated through faith must constitute the sole basis for justification (Rom 4:13–16), even if good works (not necessarily doing the Old Testament law but following a new law of love/Christ) followed from this through the work of the Spirit (Rom 8:1–11; Gal 3:1–6).[76]

Paul rightly thought that at least some, if not most, of the Judaism of his time believed that salvation was intimately connected with works (doing the Old Testament law), and he firmly rejected this in affirming that salvation was only by God's grace through faith (Rom 10:3). Consequently, statements in the Pauline writings that reject the doing of the law and assertions that justification is on the basis of the death and resurrection of Christ (e.g., Gal 2:21) are not simply rejections of the markers that gave Israelites their identity and pride (as Dunn emphasizes), nor simply christological statements, but also descriptions of the futility of attempts to secure justification through human actions.[77]

As seen in the above discussion, one of the major points of contention concerns the concept of "law" in Paul's writings. Most of the discussion seems to assume—or at least assume for the sake of discussion—that when Paul uses

---

76. See M. Hooker, "Paul and 'Covenantal Nomism,'" in *Paul and Paulinism: Essays in Honour of C. K. Barrett* (ed. M. D. Hooker and S. G. Wilson; London: SPCK, 1982), 47–56. Cf. B. S. Rosner, *Paul and the Law: Keeping the Commandments of God* (Nottingham: Apollos, 2013).

77. This topic of divine and human agency continues to be a lively one for discussion, related both to the law issue and to the issue of grace (see above). See the variety of essays in J. M. G. Barclay and S. J. Gathercole, eds., *Divine and Human Agency in Paul and His Cultural Environment* (London: T&T Clark, 2006); and K. B. Wells, *Grace and Agency in Paul and Second Temple Judaism: Interpreting the Transformation of the Heart* (NovTSup 157; Leiden: Brill, 2015).

the Greek word translated "law" (νόμος) he means the Old Testament law, unless otherwise indicated. This is, I believe, a mistake in several regards. The first is that it mistakenly makes one of the possible specific senses of a word to speak for the entire range of its usage. A second is that it confuses the notion of lexical meaning, failing to regard the central meaning of a lexical item.[78] As a result, the presumption is that when Paul speaks of the law he must mean the Old Testament law. This must be proved rather than assumed. The difficulty in defining Paul's thinking regarding the notion of law—in large part caused by the misguided linguistic analysis mentioned above—has been remedied, at least in part, by the application of some principles of modern linguistics to the analysis of the terminology—though this work remains virtually ignored.[79] As mentioned above, the traditional approach began with the assumption that "law" means something specific (often on the basis of the noun appearing with the article) and often means one thing, or primarily one thing, the Old Testament law.[80] Thus Paul was usually seen to be referring to the Jewish law, or at least to one of its forms, such as the Mosaic law in its entirety or the law specifically in its demands or requirements that must be kept.

To be preferred is an approach that defines "law" first in its sense relations within the Greek language and then examines how this sense is modulated in the various Pauline contexts in which it is used to denote specific instances of law. The word νόμος (often translated "law") has the sense of any standard, guide, or control on behavior or conduct. It might, then, be used to denote a variety of natural and human laws, such as the laws of nature and the laws or customs of specific societies and organizations. Paul seems to use it to denote, in many instances, the Jewish law or various permutations of it (e.g., Romans and Galatians), but also other human laws (Rom 7:23), specific principles of conduct (2:14), the law seen generically (4:15), and even principles by which the world functions (3:27; 8:2). In other words, only the general sense of "law" as standards or guidelines is able to account for the variety of uses by Paul of

78. I am an advocate of what is called lexical monosemy, in which there is a broad central meaning of each lexeme, modulated by context. See S. E. Porter, "Greek Linguistics and Lexicography," in *Understanding the Times: New Testament Studies in the 21st Century. Essays in Honor of D. A. Carson on the Occasion of His 65th Birthday* (ed. A. J. Köstenberger and R. W. Yarbrough; Wheaton, IL: Crossway, 2011), 19–61, esp. 27–37.

79. See M. Winger, *By What Law? The Meaning of Νόμος in the Letters of Paul* (SBLDS 128; Atlanta: Scholars Press, 1992). This approach is utilized in S. E. Porter, *The Letter to the Romans: A Linguistic and Literary Commentary* (NTM 37; Sheffield: Sheffield Phoenix, 2015).

80. Cf. Porter, *Idioms*, 103–14; for an extended study on the Greek article, see R. D. Peters, *The Greek Article: A Functional Grammar of ὁ-Items in the Greek New Testament with Special Emphasis on the Greek Article* (LBS 9; Leiden: Brill, 2014).

this single term. However, these particular uses are all understandable in light of its general sense.[81]

C. Reconciliation

Traditionally justification has been seen as the center of Paul's theology; some recent interpreters, however, instead see reconciliation as the central idea.[82] Justification language appears frequently in the main Pauline letters, but the language of reconciliation (verb καταλλάσσω, noun καταλλαγή) or peace (εἰρήνη) occurs relatively infrequently. Justification language has ties to Old Testament language, but reconciliation language owes its origins almost exclusively to the Hellenistic world. Reconciliation language is treaty language, in which parties at enmity, including God and humanity, have their hostility overcome and peaceful relations restored. For Paul, this can occur only through the work of Christ.[83]

Four passages are important for understanding Paul's thought about reconciliation. The first is 2 Cor 5:18–21, in which Paul proclaims what God has done through Christ. Some think that this passage is supplemented by traditional material (sayings that were already in use in the early church), but this is unlikely, especially since there is little evidence for previous theological usage of reconciliation terminology, and no precedent for the way Paul uses it here. In 5:18–19, God is the one who effects reconciliation "through Christ." In a difficult phrase, probably best rendered "God was reconciling the world to himself through Christ," Paul, by using the active voice form of the verb, is the first extant author to speak of the offended party (i.e., God) initiating reconciliation. So it is God who reconciles "us" or "the world" to himself, through the work of Christ on the cross.

Similar thought is conveyed in Rom 5:8–11, in which Paul establishes a clear (though difficult to define) relationship between justification and reconciliation (note the parallel phrasing in 5:1 and 5:9–10). In 5:1, 10, peace with

81. Lexical monosemy provides such a lexical semantic framework.

82. See, e.g., R. P. Martin, *Reconciliation: A Study of Paul's Theology* (Atlanta: John Knox, 1981). To find a *center* of Paul's theology, however, seems to be a misguided enterprise, as if to assume Paul *had* a singular center to his thought. Having said that, I do agree that reconciliation is an important concept in Paul's theology.

83. See Porter, "Peace, Reconciliation," 695–99; Porter, *Καταλλάσσω in Ancient Greek Literature, with Reference to the Pauline Writings* (Estudios de Filología Neotestamentaria 5; Córdoba: Ediciones El Almendro, 1994), esp. 125–89; and C. Breytenbach, *Versöhnung: Eine Studie zur paulinischen Soteriologie* (Wissenschaftliche Monographien zum Alten und Neuen Testament 60; Neukirchen-Vluyn: Neukirchener, 1989).

God and reconciliation are explicitly equated. The sense is that of an objective well-being, in which harmonious relations are established between God and humanity, who are clearly said to be enemies. The means of reconciliation are emphasized in Rom 5, where "through our Lord Jesus Christ" (or similar phrasing) is used three times (5:1, 11, 21; cf. 5:10).

Reconciliation language is also found in Col 1:20–22 (twice using a prefixed form of the verb). Understanding of this passage is often linked with interpretation of the so-called hymn in 1:15–20 (it is difficult to prove the "hymn's" pre-Pauline existence).[84] In 1:20, 22, both God and Christ are apparently seen as the agents or initiators of reconciliation. This indicates a shift in Paul's thinking from seeing God as the sole initiator to seeing Christ as the coinstigator of reconciliation with him. Nevertheless, this pattern is consistent with the depiction of Christ in Col 1. As in the other reconciliation passages, in Col 1 the agent of reconciliation is Christ, or the work of Christ on the cross (1:20, 22), but the goal of reconciliation here is also Christ (the end for which reconciliation is accomplished), who is reconciling all things, including things upon the earth and things in heaven. This cosmic reconciliation has aroused significant discussion, since it leaves open a universalism not found elsewhere in Paul. What is probably meant here, however, is that God's reconciling activity is a general principle that encompasses the entire cosmos.

Ephesians 2:14–17 is the fourth and final major reconciliation passage (cf. 1:9–10). Colossians 1 introduces cosmic reconciliation (the idea that the entire cosmos is in some way reconciled), but Eph 2 addresses the relationship of Jews and Gentiles. Paul states that, through reconciliation, Jews and Gentiles are said to become "one new person," and the dividing wall of hostility between them is torn down.[85] Thus, reconciliation unites humanity and then reconciles

84. E.g., J. D. G. Dunn, *The Epistles to the Colossians and to Philemon* (NIGTC; Grand Rapids: Eerdmans, 1996), 83–87. Dunn states that it is generally agreed that this is a preformed hymn at the time of writing of Colossians, but concedes that it cannot be proven that preformed material comprises this "hymn." Cf. J. T. Sanders, *The New Testament Christological Hymns: Their Historical Religious Background* (SNTSMS 15; Cambridge: Cambridge University Press, 1971), 75–87; and M. E. Gordley, *The Colossian Hymn in Context: An Exegesis in Light of Jewish and Greco-Roman Hymnic and Epistolary Conventions* (WUNT 2/228; Tübingen: Mohr-Siebeck, 2007).

85. This almost assuredly refers to the wall that separated Gentiles from the Jewish precincts in the temple in Jerusalem. Inscriptions declaring the death penalty for infringement of this separation have been found. One reads: "Let no foreigner enter within the screen and enclosure surrounding the sanctuary. Whosoever is taken so doing will be the cause that death overtaketh him." See A. Deissmann, *Light from the Ancient East: The New Testament Illustrated by Recently Discovered Texts of the Graeco-Roman World* (trans. L. R. M. Strachan; 4th ed.; London: Hodder & Stoughton, 1927), 80 (his translation), for the inscription now

humanity to God. Christ is said to be the agent of this reconciliation, with God as its goal, again effected by the work of Christ on the cross.

D. Sanctification or Holiness

Paul uses a number of different words and phrases to describe sanctification or holiness. This is an important category for him because it includes both soteriological status and ethical and eschatological perfection.[86] In other words, this concept describes a condition of those who are followers of Christ, instructing them in the importance of the consequential actions of salvation, even insofar as their eternal destiny is concerned. Paul desires holy and pure behavior by followers of Christ, even though he realizes that complete attainment in this life is not possible.[87]

Like many of Paul's theological ideas, sanctification overlaps with some other categories of his thought (e.g., 1 Cor 6:11), and his letters are often concerned to define the differences and similarities. Two examples illustrate this overlapping thought. On the one hand, in 1 Thess 3–4, sanctification appears to be the consequence of justification. Having finished the body of his letter in 1 Thess 3, Paul turns to ethical instruction in 1 Thess 4. He says that God's will for the Thessalonians is their sanctification (4:3, 7), and he defines this as purity, especially with regard to sexual morality as an example.[88] However, to

---

housed in the Istanbul Archeological Museum, first discovered by C. S. Clermont-Ganneau in Jerusalem in 1871 (OGIS 598). A second inscription is now housed in the Rockefeller Museum in Jerusalem. See also Josephus, *Jewish War* 5.2; *Jewish Antiquities* 15.11.5; *Against Apion* 2.8; Philo, *On the Embassy to Gaius* 212.

86. See S. E. Porter, "Holiness, Sanctification," *DPL* 397–402. Cf. D. S. Metz, *Studies in Biblical Holiness* (Kansas City: Beacon Hill, 1971), esp. 132–35, for a traditional view of holiness as a theological category.

87. For a recent treatment on sanctification in Paul, and more specifically, progressive sanctification, see J. M. Howard, *Paul, the Community, and Progressive Sanctification: An Exploration into Community-Based Transformation within Pauline Theology* (Studies in Biblical Literature 90; New York: Peter Lang, 2007), esp. 11–40. See also a number of the individual essays in K. E. Brower and A. Johnson, eds., *Holiness and Ecclesiology in the New Testament* (Grand Rapids: Eerdmans, 2007).

88. For treatment within the argument of 1 Thessalonians, see I. H. Marshall, *New Testament Theology: Many Witnesses, One Gospel* (Downers Grove, IL: InterVarsity, 2004), 143–44. Cf. also T. R. Schreiner, *Paul, Apostle of God's Glory in Christ: A Pauline Theology* (Downers Grove, IL: InterVarsity, 2001), 219–22. For an emphasis upon the ethical position, see U. Schnelle, *Apostle Paul: His Life and Theology* (trans. M. E. Boring; Grand Rapids: Baker, 2005), 185–88; and F. J. Matera, *New Testament Theology: Exploring Diversity and Unity* (Louisville: Westminster John Knox, 2007), 109–10.

limit Paul's discussion of sanctification to an ethical imperative is to limit the notion within Paul's theological thought. Paul makes clear that there is much more to sanctification than simply ethical or behavioral purity. On the other hand, in Rom 6:19–23 (part of the body of the letter), sanctification appears to overlap with justification, but without being equated with it. The difference is that, in this instance, it appears that sanctification has more of a soteriological than an ethical dimension. In 6:19–23, in the context of Paul's theological argument of Rom 1–8, especially the theme of "life in the Spirit" (Rom 6–8), he speaks of sanctification as the goal of justification. If justification is the initiatory salvific experience, sanctification may include this initiation as well as look forward to the end of the entire process, eternal life.[89]

E. Salvation

Salvation in Paul's thinking, like several of the other theological concepts noted above, also overlaps with a number of other important Pauline beliefs.[90] Words with the idea of saving—including "salvation" (σωτηρία), "save" (σῴζω), and "savior" (σωτήρ)—are used approximately sixty times in Paul and can be used by him to refer to a number of divine acts with respect to the human.[91] For example, salvation terminology in Rom 5:9–10 seems to overlap with both justification and reconciliation.[92] Salvation for Paul includes being delivered from sin, from death, and from this age, with the goal of eternal life (8:23–24). Thus, salvation is seen to be in keeping with the "secular" concept of savior as benefactor, in which one has, in some sense, a personal or moral obligation to look out for and take care of an inferior, who depends upon the beneficence of the superior.[93] In several of the Pauline contexts, "salvation" is an inclusive

89. The development of this argument is found in Porter, *Romans*, 63–178, esp. 140–42.
90. See Morris, *New Testament Theology*, 32–35.
91. As with justification, there is a tendency of some scholars to identify salvation with past, present, and future on the basis of the Greek tense forms. See Schreiner, *Paul, Apostle of God's Glory in Christ*, 225–26; cf. Schreiner, *New Testament Theology: Magnifying God in Christ* (Grand Rapids: Baker, 2008), 362–63. As noted above, salvation may have such temporal dimensions to it, but it is not established simply on the basis of the Greek tense forms, but on larger contextual arguments that are often overlooked or not taken into account.
92. Some scholars take salvation as essentially overlapping with justification, even if in an expanded form to include its eschatological outworkings. See, e.g., Dunn, *Theology of Paul the Apostle*, 317–532.
93. A now classic study of benefaction and its language in regard to the New Testament is F. W. Danker, *Benefactor: Epigraphic Study of a Graeco-Roman and New Testament Semantic Field* (St. Louis: Clayton, 1982). The issue of benefaction, however, is probably overdone

term that spans the extent of God's saving activity—for example, in Phil 2:12, where Paul speaks of working out one's salvation with fear and trembling. In Eph 2:5, 8, salvation is the capstone for describing the process by which humanity is brought into right relationship with God. A final, important example, Rom 1:16–17, provides the theme for the entire book of Romans. In this statement, salvation is defined in three ways: (1) justification as an initiatory event, corresponding perhaps to salvation as deliverance from sin and death in other contexts (Rom 3–4); (2) reconciliation as a sustaining event, corresponding to God as benefactor (Rom 5); and (3) sanctification as a life preparatory for eternity (Rom 6–8).[94]

F. Triumph of God

Recent scholarly thought emphasizes Paul as an apocalyptic thinker.[95] By this is meant that Paul looked forward to certain end-time occurrences with cosmic, universal, and definitive implications, such as universal judgment, all of which is to be brought about as a result of the death, resurrection, and return of Christ. This thought is, at many points, consistent with contemporary Jewish apocalyptic thinking and characterized by God's vindication of his covenantal promises made to Israel and the nations (see Rom 9–11, one

---

in some New Testament study. See B. W. Winter, *Seek the Welfare of the City: Christians as Benefactors and Citizens* (Grand Rapids: Eerdmans, 1994).

94. See Porter, *Romans*, 86–178.

95. See the history of development of this view of Paul in the following works: A. Schweitzer, *The Mysticism of Paul the Apostle* (trans. W. Montgomery; London: A&C Black, 1931), esp. 52–100; G. Vos, *The Pauline Eschatology* (Princeton: Princeton University Press, 1930; repr. Grand Rapids: Baker, 1979); Käsemann, "Righteousness of God"; A. T. Lincoln, *Paradise Now and Not Yet: Studies in the Role of the Heavenly Dimension in Paul's Thought with Special Reference to His Eschatology* (SNTSMS 43; Cambridge: Cambridge University Press, 1981); J. C. Beker, *Paul the Apostle; Paul's Apocalyptic Gospel: The Coming Triumph of God* (Philadelphia: Fortress, 1982); L. J. Kreitzer, *Jesus and God in Paul's Eschatology* (JSNTSup 19; Sheffield: JSOT Press, 1987); M. C. de Boer, *The Defeat of Death: Apocalyptic Eschatology in 1 Corinthians 15 and Romans 5* (JSNTSup 22; Sheffield: JSOT Press, 1988); B. Witherington III, *Jesus, Paul and the End of the World* (Downers Grove, IL: InterVarsity, 1992); J. L. Martyn, *Theological Issues in the Letters of Paul* (Studies of the New Testament and Its World; Edinburgh: T&T Clark, 1997), esp. part 2; D. A. Campbell, *The Deliverance of God: An Apocalyptic Rereading of Justification in Paul* (Grand Rapids: Eerdmans, 2009); and B. R. Gaventa, ed., *Apocalyptic Paul: Cosmos and Anthropos in Romans 5–8* (Waco, TX: Baylor University Press, 2013). For a critique of understandings of apocalyptic language when speaking of Paul, see R. B. Matlock, *Unveiling the Apocalyptic Paul: Paul's Interpreters and the Rhetoric of Criticism* (JSNTSup 127; Sheffield: Sheffield Academic, 1996).

of the most important passages in this discussion).[96] This implies a type of universalism, in which universal salvation was held out as a hope by Paul for those who heard the gospel and responded in obedience and faith. Paul was not as dualistic a thinker, however, as were many of his Jewish contemporaries, in that he did not make a rigid distinction between this age and the age to come but, rather, saw a continuum between the two (8:29-30). Thus Paul's view of the triumph of God captures his own eschatological perspective.[97] In this continuum between the now and the not yet, Paul sees the church as living in this tension between the ages, between the first and second comings of Christ, as well as between the powers of life and death. For Paul, this end of time has an imminency to it, but an imminency increasingly tempered by the reality that Christ's return might not be in Paul's own lifetime. Even in 1 Thessalonians, Paul's depiction of an imminent return with nothing to impede it (see 1:9-10; 4:13-5:8) is tempered by the reality that he may or may not be among those remaining at the time of the event (4:17). When he writes the letter to the Romans (e.g., 1:17-18), Paul also sees "righteousness" and "wrath" as apocalyptic terms, using them in anticipation of Christ's return, in hope for what is not yet seen or fulfilled. By the time of writing Philippians (e.g., 1:21-24; 2:17), Paul fully embraces the possibility of his own death before Christ's return. Thus, Paul's apocalyptic expectation is fully embraced within the realities of his missionary outreach to the Gentiles.

G. Gospel

The gospel in Paul can be interpreted in several different ways. In one sense, the gospel may well encompass all that Paul envisions about God's relationship with humanity.[98] In another, and more specialized sense, the gospel entails a particular kind of good news. The term often translated "gospel" or "good

96. See E. E. Johnson, *The Function of Apocalyptic and Wisdom Traditions in Romans 9-11* (SBLDS 109; Atlanta: Scholars Press, 1989).

97. For particular treatments of Paul's eschatology, besides some of the works cited above, see C. M. Pate, *The End of the Age Has Come: The Theology of Paul* (Grand Rapids: Zondervan, 1995); and J. Plevnik, *Paul and the Parousia: An Exegetical and Theological Investigation* (Peabody, MA: Hendrickson, 1997).

98. This is the way that it appears to be taken, e.g., by J. D. G. Dunn, "The Gospel according to St. Paul," in *The Blackwell Companion to Paul* (ed. S. Westerholm; West Sussex, UK: Wiley-Blackwell, 2011), 139-53, including such things as justification and participation; but cf. D. A. Campbell, *The Quest for Paul's Gospel: A Suggested Strategy* (JSNTSup 274; London: T&T Clark, 2005).

news" is used approximately eighty times by Paul in its noun (εὐαγγέλιον) and verb (εὐαγγελίζομαι) forms. But there is ongoing debate on how much Paul knew about the earthly Jesus, since he does not cite many incidents from his earthly life (see chapter 1 §9).[99] The debate is important since the gospel is about Jesus's life and ministry. In common with other New Testament writers, especially those of the Gospels themselves (in particular Matthew and Luke), Paul shares the perception that Jesus's work on the cross constituted a turning point in humanity's relation to God.

In conjunction with this perspective, Paul uses this terminology of good news in at least three apparent ways.[100] In the first, he refers to the gospel as good news that runs contrary to competing secular good news. The same Greek terminology was often used to refer to a significant secular event, such as the birth of a son to the emperor or the celebration of the emperor's birthday (e.g., in the so-called Priene inscription dated to 9 BC, erected to celebrate the birth of Caesar Augustus). There cannot help but be more than a little irony in Paul's mind, for example, when he refers to himself in a letter addressed to the church in the capital of the Roman Empire as a servant of Christ Jesus, an apostle, and one set apart for God's good news (not the emperor's or any other human's; Rom 1:16–17). For Paul, God is the origin or source of this good news, not some secular authority.[101] Paul's good news directly confronts the Roman view of the emperor as savior or benefactor when he sees God at work in bringing the good news through the death and resurrection of his son (5:7). Second, Paul views the good news in its objective accomplishments. Jesus Christ's death on the cross and resurrection constitute the content of the gospel (Rom 1:3–4; cf. 1 Cor 15:3–4). Consequently, for Paul, the gospel then becomes

99. It is highly dubious to claim with R. Bultmann, *New Testament Theology* (trans. K. Grobel; 2 vols.; New York: Scribners, 1951–55), 1.292, on the basis of 1 Cor 2:2 (cf. 2 Cor 5:16), that Paul knew nothing about Jesus. See S. E. Porter, *When Paul Met Jesus: How an Idea Got Lost in History* (Cambridge: Cambridge University Press, 2016), esp. 122–77, for discussion of the implications of Paul's firsthand knowledge of Jesus.

100. Cf. D. E. Aune, *Jesus, Gospel Tradition and Paul in the Context of Jewish and Greco-Roman Antiquity: Collected Essays II* (WUNT 303; Tübingen: Mohr-Siebeck, 2013), 3–24; original publication as "The Meaning of Εὐαγγέλιον in the *Inscriptiones* of the Canonical Gospels," in *A Teacher for All Generations: Essays in Honor of James D. VanderKam* (ed. E. F. Mason, K. Coblentz Bautch, A. K. Harkins, and D. A. Machiela; vol. 2; Journal for the Study of Judaism Supplement 153; Leiden: Brill, 2012), 857–82.

101. See S. E. Porter, "Paul Confronts Caesar with the Good News," in *Empire in the New Testament* (ed. S. E. Porter and C. L. Westfall; McMaster New Testament Studies; Eugene, OR: Wipf & Stock, 2011), 164–96; cf. L. R. Taylor, *The Divinity of the Roman Emperor* (Middletown, CT: American Philological Association, 1931; repr. Atlanta: Scholars Press, n.d.), esp. 267–83, for the evidence from the inscriptions and papyri regarding the emperor cult.

shorthand for, or a statement of, essential Christian belief, that is, the belief that leads to life or condemnation and is to be obeyed (Gal 2:5, 14; Rom 2:16; 10:16).[102] Third, Paul views the good news as a personal motivational factor. For Paul, the gospel was integral with his calling as an apostle to the Gentiles, not only as the substance of his belief but as a very real part of who he was. Paul claims that he received his gospel from the risen Christ, not from any human source, and to be opposed to it is to be accursed (Gal 1–2; Rom 15:15–20).

H. Church

The church forms an important backdrop to Paul's thinking and in this sense constitutes one of the basic assumptions of his thinking and writing.[103] He specifically addresses several of his letters to the churches located in Corinth, Galatia, and Thessalonica (Paul, however, uses more than simply the Greek word ἐκκλησία to refer to this concept of "church," including terms related to "common," κοινός, such as "fellowship," and others treated below). Even though he does not address specific churches in some others of his letters, in these an ecclesiastical setting is still understood (e.g., Philemon, Romans, Ephesians, Colossians, and the Pastorals, where church order and structure are addressed). Consequently, there are numerous references in Paul's writings to a specific church or to specific churches—the group of believers that probably met together within house churches or other structures in a given city to worship (e.g., 1 Cor 11:18; 16:19; Gal 1:22).[104] Paul assumes the existence of these churches, quite frequently addressing his letters to issues that have obviously arisen in the conduct and administration of these local bodies of believers.

This is not all that Paul says regarding the church, however. He also uses

102. See, e.g., the recent book by M. F. Bird, *Evangelical Theology: A Biblical and Systematic Introduction* (Grand Rapids: Zondervan, 2013), where the underlying thesis governing the structure of the book is that the gospel is central to any attempt at systematic theology. This probably gives "gospel" an encompassing or central role, certainly for Paul and probably for the rest of the New Testament.

103. The church is one of the categories often given its own separate treatment within studies of Paul. For example, see, among others, H. Conzelmann, *An Outline of the Theology of the New Testament* (trans. J. Bowden; London: SCM, 1969), 254–65; Ridderbos, *Paul: An Outline of His Theology*, 429–86; D. Guthrie, *New Testament Theology* (Leicester: InterVarsity, 1981), 742–78; and G. Strecker, *Theology of the New Testament* (ed. F. W. Horn; trans. M. E. Boring; Berlin: de Gruyter, 2000), 178–209.

104. On the types of structures used for early Christian worship, including but not exclusively houses, see E. Adams, *The Earliest Christian Meeting Places: Almost Exclusively Houses?* (LNTS 450; London: Bloomsbury, 2013).

the term "church" in a more widespread sense to refer to the community of believers that exists without reference to the confines of a given city or local community.[105] When referring to believers joined by their common faith, Paul uses a number of different analogies or metaphors. The most important (and certainly the most widely debated) is the analogy of the body.[106] In 1 Cor 12:12–28, Paul speaks of believers as a body with numerous parts, some that are traditionally held to be more important or useful and some that are regarded as less important or even trivial. Paul's point is that, just as the body has many parts, some of which are more highly regarded than others but all of which are vitally necessary for constituting the body, so it is with the body of believers. This body of believers is called the body of Christ, with the implication that the church constitutes Christ's body or is to be equated with Christ in his spiritual existence. The apostles, prophets, teachers, miracle workers, and so forth form a hierarchy within this body.

Similar, though not identical, language is used in Eph 5:22–32, where the analogy of the body is also used. In this context, the church is equated with Christ's body, and Christ is depicted as the head of the church. There has been significant debate among scholars whether these analogies can be made to correlate. On the one hand, in the Corinthian analogy the entire church is equated with Christ, and no specific differentiation of the head is made, with the implication that the various positions of leadership within the church are to be equated with the head, the hands, and so on as valuable parts of the body. On the other hand, in the Ephesian analogy, the differentiation is explicitly between the church as the body and Christ as the head having a position of authority over it. Whatever one decides regarding Ephesian authorship (see chapter 11 §5B), it is clear that the basis of both passages is a Pauline vision of the church and its relation to Christ, whether Paul himself expanded or made more explicit the analogy with Christ as the head.

---

105. See S. E. Porter, "Saints and Sinners: The Church in Paul's Letters," in *The Church, Then and Now* (ed. S. E. Porter and C. L. Westfall; Eugene, OR: Pickwick, 2012), 41–67; and the essays on Paul in J. Harrison and J. D. Dvorak, eds., *The New Testament Church: The Challenge of Developing Ecclesiologies* (Eugene, OR: Pickwick, 2012). Cf. R. Banks, *Paul's Idea of Community: The Early House Churches in Their Cultural Setting* (rev. ed.; Peabody, MA: Hendrickson, 1994); and J. W. Thompson, *The Church according to Paul: Rediscovering the Community Conformed to Christ* (Grand Rapids: Baker, 2014), esp. 175–98, where Thompson emphasizes that, for Paul, the universal church is known through the fellowship of the local church.

106. See, e.g., J. D. G. Dunn, "'The Body of Christ' in Paul," in *Worship, Theology, and Ministry in the Early Church* (ed. M. J. Wilkins and T. Paige; JSNTSup 87; Sheffield: JSOT Press, 1992), 146–62; E. Best, *One Body in Christ: A Study in the Relationship of the Church to Christ in the Epistles of the Apostle Paul* (London: SPCK, 1955); and Y. S. Kim, *Christ's Body in Corinth: The Politics of a Metaphor* (Minneapolis: Fortress, 2008).

Paul also uses a number of other terms to speak of the church. These prove of less significance so far as scholarly discussion goes, but their appropriateness to the individual letters in which they are found has literary and epistolary significance.[107] For example, in Gal 6:10, Paul speaks of the church as a household or family. This is entirely appropriate in the context of the controversy in Galatia, in which there were Christians who threatened to disrupt the familial unity of the Galatian church. In Phil 3:20, Paul speaks of members of the church as enjoying a common citizenship in heaven. It is likely that the Philippian church, for the most part enjoying Paul's praise, in light of its privileged position as an independent city populated by Roman citizens, came to put undue pride in its political privileges and opportunities. Paul takes this occasion to remind them that their citizenship is not primarily earthly but, rather, one that they enjoy in a heavenly realm. In 1 Cor 1:9, Paul speaks of God having called the believers of Corinth into fellowship with his Son Jesus Christ. Again he uses an appropriate metaphor for the situation of his readers, as he is responding to a church that has found difficulty with unity, threatening to be divided and factionalized by various groups claiming to owe allegiance to various leaders or figures.

I. Jesus's Death and Resurrection

The last concept in this brief summary of Paul's major teachings concerns Christ's death and resurrection. It was mentioned above at several points (§3A and §3C) that Paul believes that the work of God through Christ for believers is predicated upon the death and resurrection of Jesus Christ. In this sense, Paul's belief in the death and resurrection of Jesus Christ is not something that he argues for but something that he assumes. He does, however, at several places treat Christ's death and resurrection within a theological framework

107. More important for some contemporary scholarly discussion is the similarity of the church to other social organizations within the Greco-Roman world, in particular the Roman household, voluntary associations, the synagogue, and philosophical or rhetorical schools (these are Meeks's categories). For discussion of some of the similarities, see W. A. Meeks, *The First Urban Christians: The Social World of the Apostle Paul* (New Haven: Yale University Press, 1983), 75-84. For further discussion of the most prominent of these (besides some of the works mentioned above), see J. H. Hellerman, *The Ancient Church as Family* (Minneapolis: Fortress, 2001); P. A. Harland, *Associations, Synagogues, and Congregations: Claiming a Place in Ancient Mediterranean Society* (Minneapolis: Fortress, 2003); Harland, *Dynamics of Identity in the World of the Early Christians: Associations, Judeans, and Cultural Minorities* (London: T&T Clark, 2009); and P. Trebilco, *Self-Designations and Group Identity in the New Testament* (Cambridge: Cambridge University Press, 2012).

that shows their special significance (e.g., 1 Cor 15:3–8; 1:18–25). This salvation-historical view of redemptive history is worth noting in Paul's thought. Paul was obviously not the first to link these two events or to see them as fundamental to Christian belief. For example, in 15:3–4, possibly citing a passage formulated early on in the church and used to encapsulate the essence of Christian confession, Paul says that he passed on to the Corinthians what he received as of first importance: that Christ died for (our) sins, was buried, and was raised on the third day. There are similar formulations elsewhere in the Pauline corpus (e.g., 1 Thess 4:14; 1 Tim 3:16).

There are at least two other noteworthy elements to Paul's view of Christ's death. First, he puts an emphasis upon the crucifixion or the cross of Christ. Eighteen times he refers to the cross or crucifixion in his letters, not as a heroic or commendable event but as one that was ignominious and disgraceful.[108] For example, in 1 Cor 1:18, he refers to the message of the cross as foolishness for those who are perishing (cf. 2:2), and in Gal 3:13, he cites Deut 21:23 and its reference to the curse upon anyone who is crucified. This ignominy, however, is a part of what Paul sees as a very important element of the progress of salvation history, one that Christ fulfilled in his death and resurrection. Second, Paul sees the death of Christ as sacrificial, involving the shedding of blood. There is repeated debate regarding how Paul depicts Christ as a "sacrifice of atonement" in Rom 3:25 (whether Christ is seen as the seat of mercy or simply the means by which sins or God's wrath is turned away, this reference involves Old Testament sacrificial imagery), where his blood is depicted as the means by which this process is conducted (also 5:9).[109] Third, Paul sees the resurrection as a necessary extension of Christ's death. In Paul's mind the death was crucial, but the resurrection was a confirmation of what God was seen to be doing in Christ (4:25). Paul says that the resurrection marks the point at which God's son was seen to be the Son of God with power (1:4) and that the resurrection is the confirmation of the validity of faith. Without the

---

108. See M. Hengel, *Crucifixion* (trans. J. Bowden; London: SCM, 1977); repr. in *The Cross of the Son of God* (London: SCM, 1986), 93–185.

109. See L. Morris, *The Apostolic Preaching of the Cross* (3rd rev. ed.; Grand Rapids: Eerdmans, 1965), esp. 144–78, but throughout. I still find Morris's explanation the most convincing, despite continuing discussion. Cf. D. Seeley, *The Noble Death: Graeco-Roman Martyrology and Paul's Concept of Salvation* (JSNTSup 28; Sheffield: JSOT Press, 1990); and B. H. McLean, *The Cursed Christ: Mediterranean Expulsion Rituals and Pauline Soteriology* (JSNTSup 126; Sheffield: Sheffield Academic, 1996), although McLean argues that an apotropaic function or the removal of human sin was not able to account for the means by which sin was removed. Cf. A. T. Hanson, *The Paradox of the Cross in the Thought of Paul* (JSNTSup 17; Sheffield: JSOT Press, 1987), 25–37.

resurrection to confirm the validity of Christ's death, humans remain in their sinful condition (1 Cor 15:17).[110]

These events are part of a larger framework that Paul seems to work from, one in which the plan of God is depicted as being redemptive, with Christ's death and resurrection the climactic events in God's dealings with humanity. First of all, Paul speaks of the electing or predestining purposes of God that find their fulfillment in the work of God in Christ. For example, in Rom 8:33, Paul asks who will bring a charge against one of God's elect, since Christ, the one who died and was raised, is seated at God's right hand interceding (also 9:11; cf. Eph 1:4–5, 9). Second, Paul at various places mentions significant individuals who formed a crucial part of God's redemptive plan. The first is Adam, who established the sinful human condition. It was his disobedience that required a suitable and corresponding response by God to redeem humans from their condition, having been constituted sinners after Adam (Rom 5:12–21; cf. 1 Cor 15:22; 1 Tim 2:13–14). Christ, as the last Adam, undid the effects of Adam's sin.[111] Next in Paul's chronology is apparently Abraham (see chapter 3 §3A), the father of Israel, who was justified or reckoned righteous before God not on the basis of works or any accomplishment (certainly not the fulfillment of the law, which did not come for over four hundred years) but through his faith. Paul shows that the means of redemption for humanity has always been the same, through faith (Rom 4; Gal 3). Another figure, one more enigmatic for Paul's progress of salvation history, is Moses (see chapter 3 §3A). Moses was revered as the one who brought God's law to the people of God (Paul may have believed that the law had been mediated by heavenly beings and did not come directly from God; this may help explain his sometimes negative view of it; see Gal 3:20) and was one of the few Jewish heroes respected or even known by non-Jews. In Paul's eyes, he too points toward the work of Jesus Christ. When Moses had been with God, he had a radiance that could not be looked upon by the Israelites, who were living under the old covenant. Those who live under the new covenant reflect the unmediated glory (2 Cor 3:7–8). In Christ, the mystery of God, that is, his redemptive work through Christ's death and resurrection, has been revealed. The term "mystery" is used slightly differently in its several instances in the Pauline writings, but it seems to center on what God has done in Christ,

110. See R. B. Gaffin Jr., *The Centrality of the Resurrection: A Study in Paul's Soteriology* (Grand Rapids: Baker, 1978); and M. J. Harris, *Raised Immortal: Resurrection and Immortality in the New Testament* (Grand Rapids: Eerdmans, 1983).

111. See C. K. Barrett, *From First Adam to Last: A Study in Pauline Theology* (London: A&C Black, 1962), the classic treatment of this topic. See also R. Scroggs, *The Last Adam: A Study in Pauline Anthropology* (Oxford: Blackwell, 1966).

whether it involves believers seen as a whole or Jews and Gentiles (1 Cor 2:7 and frequently; cf. Col 2:2; Eph 6:19).

4. Conclusion

Although other topics could well be introduced regarding Paul's teachings—and there are many, such as prophetic criticism, adoption, and various images of Christ[112]—those discussed above provide a sufficient introduction to his thought to enable the reader to grasp several of his major ideas and emphases, especially as these appear in the letters themselves. None of Paul's letters provides a systematic or complete treatment of any of these assumed or defined beliefs, even if some letters provide more on one concept than another. In any case, when one comes across one of these ideas, the reader can draw upon this summary of many if not most of Paul's major beliefs as a guide to how the corpus of Paul's letters as a whole addresses these topics. However, the reader of Paul's letters must also always keep in mind that the Pauline letters themselves take precedence in estimating Paul's thought. Paul was not concerned to offer systematic and complete analyses of all of the notions that he introduces in his letters—as if he were writing a thesis or dissertation on a topic. Instead, he is concerned to address his readers and draw upon the appropriate thoughts to develop their understanding of the good news of God in Jesus Christ.

Sources for Further Study

Basic Sources

Fitzmyer, J. A. *Paul and His Theology: A Brief Sketch.* 2nd ed. Englewood Cliffs, NJ: Prentice Hall, 1989.
Matera, F. J. *God's Saving Grace: A Pauline Theology.* Grand Rapids: Eerdmans, 2012.
Morris, L. L. *New Testament Theology.* Grand Rapids: Zondervan, 1986.
Ridderbos, H. *Paul: An Outline of His Theology.* Translated by J. R. D. Witt. Grand Rapids: Eerdmans, 1975 (1966).

---

112. See Porter, "Images of Christ in Paul's Letters," and now Porter, *Sacred Tradition in the New Testament: Tracing Old Testament Themes in the Gospels and Epistles* (Grand Rapids: Baker, 2016), 227–45, for a survey. Many of the New Testament and Pauline theologies mentioned above contain some of these discussions.

Schreiner, T. R. *Paul, Apostle of God's Glory in Christ: A Pauline Theology*. Downers Grove, IL: InterVarsity, 2001.

Seifrid, M. A. *Christ, Our Righteousness: Paul's Theology of Justification*. New Studies in Biblical Theology. Downers Grove, IL: InterVarsity, 2000.

Westerholm, S. *Israel's Law and the Church's Faith: Paul and His Recent Interpreters*. Grand Rapids: Eerdmans, 1988.

Advanced Sources

Barclay, J. M. G. *Paul and the Gift*. Grand Rapids: Eerdmans, 2015.

Beker, J. C. *Paul the Apostle: The Triumph of God in Life and Thought*. Philadelphia: Fortress, 1980.

Bird, M. F., and P. M. Sprinkle, eds. *The Faith of Jesus Christ: Exegetical, Biblical, and Theological Studies*. Peabody, MA: Hendrickson, 2009.

Carson, D. A., P. T. O'Brien, and M. A. Seifrid, eds. *Justification and Variegated Nomism: A Fresh Appraisal of Paul and Second Temple Judaism*. 2 vols. WUNT 2/140. Tübingen: Mohr-Siebeck/Grand Rapids: Baker, 2001–4.

de Roo, J. C. R. *"Works of the Law" at Qumran and in Paul*. NTM 13. Sheffield: Sheffield Phoenix, 2007.

Dunn, J. D. G. *The Theology of Paul the Apostle*. Grand Rapids: Eerdmans, 1998.

Fee, G. D. *God's Empowering Presence: The Holy Spirit in the Letters of Paul*. Peabody, MA: Hendrickson, 1994.

―――. *Pauline Christology: An Exegetical-Theological Study*. Peabody, MA: Hendrickson, 2007.

Morris, L. *The Apostolic Preaching of the Cross*. 3rd ed. Grand Rapids: Eerdmans, 1965.

Porter, S. E. *Καταλλάσσω in Ancient Greek Literature, with Reference to the Pauline Writings*. Estudios de Filología Neotestamentaria 5. Córdoba: Ediciones El Almendro, 1994.

―――, ed. *Paul and His Theology*. PAST 5. Leiden: Brill, 2006.

Räisänen, H. *Paul and the Law*. WUNT 29. Tübingen: Mohr-Siebeck, 1983. Reprinted Philadelphia: Fortress, 1986.

Rosner, B. S. *Paul and the Law: Keeping the Commandments of God*. Nottingham: Apollos, 2013.

Sanders, E. P. *Paul and Palestinian Judaism*. Philadelphia: Fortress, 1977.

―――. *Paul, the Law, and the Jewish People*. Philadelphia: Fortress, 1983.

Schnelle, U. *Apostle Paul: His Life and Theology*. Translated by M. E. Boring. Grand Rapids: Baker, 2005.

Seifrid, M. A. *Justification by Faith: The Origin and Development of a Central Pauline Theme*. NovTSup 68. Leiden: Brill, 1992.

Smith, B. D. *The Tension between God as Righteous Judge and as Merciful in Early Judaism*. Lanham, MD: University Press of America, 2005.

Watson, F. *Paul, Judaism, and the Gentiles: Beyond the New Perspective*. Grand Rapids: Eerdmans, 2007 (1986).

Westerholm, S. *Perspectives Old and New: The "Lutheran" Paul and His Critics*. Grand Rapids: Eerdmans, 2004.

Winger, M. *By What Law? The Meaning of Νόμος in the Letters of Paul*. SBLDS 128. Atlanta: Scholars Press, 1992.

Wolter, M. *Paul: An Outline of His Theology*. Translated by R. L. Brawley. Waco, TX: Baylor University Press, 2015.

Wright, N. T. *Climax of the Covenant: Christ and the Law in Pauline Theology*. Edinburgh: T&T Clark, 1991.

————. *Paul and the Faithfulness of God*. 2 vols. Christian Origins and the Question of God 4. Minneapolis: Fortress, 2013.

5

The Pauline Letter Form

1. The Greek Letter in the Greco-Roman World

The Hellenistic period was a letter-writing age, and Paul was a letter writer.[1] As the great British classical scholar Gilbert Murray says of Paul, "He is certainly one of the great figures in Greek literature"[2] because of the importance of his letters. The joining together of the world surrounding the Mediterranean, which began during the time of Alexander the Great, not only brought a sense of extended unity to the entire region but also created the need for communication between people who were sometimes removed by great distances from each other. As a result, the letter became a very important form of communication, both for providing information and for maintaining relationships as a substitute for personal presence. The postal system was for official letters, so the vast majority of correspondence was private, carried by any person who would agree to do so.[3]

---

1. This is certainly much more evident with the discovery and publication of the numerous Greek documentary papyri from Egypt. Cf. A. Deissmann, *Bible Studies* (trans. A. Grieve; Edinburgh: T&T Clark, 1901); and *Light from the Ancient East: The New Testament Illustrated by Recently Discovered Texts of the Graeco-Roman World* (trans. L. R. M. Strachan; 4th ed.; London: Hodder & Stoughton, 1927). For a fuller treatment of the Pauline letter form, see S. E. Porter, "Exegesis of the Pauline Letters, Including the Deutero-Pauline Letters," in *Handbook to Exegesis of the New Testament* (ed. S. E. Porter; NTTS 25; Leiden: Brill, 1997), 539–50, followed here. See also the collection of various essays in S. E. Porter and S. A. Adams, eds., *Paul and the Ancient Letter Form* (PAST 6; Leiden: Brill, 2010), noted below. A recent commentary that utilizes letter form in analysis is J. A. D. Weima, *1–2 Thessalonians* (BECNT; Grand Rapids: Baker, 2014).

2. G. Murray, *Five Stages of Greek Religion* (London: Watts, 1935), 164. For a similar comment by indisputably one of the greatest German classicists of all time, see U. Wilamowitz-Moellendorff, *Die griechische Literatur des Altertums* (Stuttgart: Teubner, 1912), 232–33.

3. See S. Llewelyn, "Sending Letters in the Ancient World: Paul and the Philippians," *Tyndale Bulletin* 46 (1995): 339–49.

Thousands upon thousands of Greek letters from the Greco-Roman period have been found among a huge quantity of papyrus documents from the ancient world.[4] Papyrus was essentially the paper of the Greco-Roman world, a writing material manufactured when the papyrus plant, split into lengths, was pressed together and dried into flat sheets. The vast majority of these papyrus documents have been found in Egypt, in such areas as the Fayyum region and near the ancient city of Oxyrhynchus. The major discoveries occurred in the mid-nineteenth and early twentieth centuries. As the well-known English Greek grammarian and papyrologist James Hope Moulton titled his book about the importance of these discoveries—*From Egyptian Rubbish-Heaps*[5]—they were literally discovered in the old city dumps of these cities. The favorable atmospheric conditions of Egypt and their use in the packing of various mummies ensured that thousands of these texts could one day be discovered. Some of them are relatively large sheets of writing in good condition, while many are simply small fragments. The kinds of documents found include the range of things that one might expect: wills; land surveys; reports; receipts for various financial transactions; contracts for especially agriculture and related services; personal letters; a variety of judicial, legal, and official documents and letters (census reports are some of the most important); and numerous literary and theological works.[6]

As a part of the Greco-Roman world, early Christianity was also a letter-writing religion. Of the twenty-seven books found in the New Testament, twenty-one are identified as letters of various forms: letters to individuals (such as Philemon), letters to various groups or churches (such as Romans and 1 Peter), letters meant to circulate to various groups (such as Galatians), and anonymous letters (such as Hebrews, if it is a letter).[7] Even the book of

4. Convenient introductions to the papyri and their uses in scholarship can be found in E. G. Turner, *Greek Papyri: An Introduction* (2nd ed.; Oxford: Clarendon, 1980); R. S. Bagnall, *Reading Papyri, Writing Ancient History* (London: Routledge, 1995); H.-J. Klauck, *Ancient Letters and the New Testament: A Guide to Context and Exegesis* (Waco, TX: Baylor University Press, 2006); T. J. Kraus, *Ad fontes: Original Manuscripts and Their Significance for Studying Early Christianity: Selected Essays* (TENT 3; Leiden: Brill, 2007); and J. Muir, *Life and Letters in the Ancient Greek World* (Routledge Monographs in Classical Studies; New York: Routledge, 2008).

5. J. H. Moulton, *From Egyptian Rubbish-Heaps* (London: Kelly, 1916). See also W. F. Howard, *The Romance of New Testament Scholarship* (London: Epworth, 1949), 111–37, for a discussion of the discovery of the papyri.

6. Convenient collections of these letters, with relevance to New Testament study, can be found in a variety of places. See especially *Select Papyri* (trans. A. S. Hunt and C. C. Edgar; 3 vols.; LCL; Cambridge, MA: Harvard University Press, 1932–34); *NewDocs*; and J. L. White, *Light from Ancient Letters* (FFNT; Philadelphia: Fortress, 1986).

7. See, e.g., the discussion on the genre of Hebrews in P. Ellingworth, *The Epistle to the Hebrews: A Commentary on the Greek Text* (NIGTC; Grand Rapids: Eerdmans, 1993), 59–62.

Revelation, if it is not itself a letter, contains letters (Rev 2–3).[8] The same pattern was continued by the apostolic fathers; twelve of the fifteen texts by the nine authors are letters, such as *1 Clement*.[9] In any case, Paul is attributed with thirteen of the letters in the New Testament.

At first, the discovery of the papyri did not have a significant influence upon New Testament scholarship. The German scholar Adolf Deissmann was one of the foremost pioneers in recognizing the importance of ancient Greek letters for understanding the New Testament. He tells how, during a chance trip through the Marburg University library, he noticed an unbound volume of papyri and, on one page, the words "son of god," which led to his excited investigation of their language.[10] To him, it resembled that of the New Testament, and he proceeded to undertake some of the most important lexical studies of the Greek of this period. He was followed by a number of other important scholars, including Moulton, who did both lexical and grammatical investigations.[11]

One of the most important of Deissmann's findings concerned the nature of the Christian letter, including the letters of Paul. Deissmann noted that the letters from Egypt tended to be short, ranging in length from only a few words to approximately 300, the average being around 275. The letters of the New Testament, however, are significantly longer than these letters, with the exception of Philemon, which, at 335 words, is slightly longer than the average Egyptian documentary letter. On the other hand, there are a number of letters by literary figures, including those attributed to Plato, Isocrates, Demosthenes, Cicero (who reputedly wrote 931 letters), and Seneca. As a result of his studies, in conjunction with his analysis of the sociological makeup of the early church, Deissmann distinguished the "true letters" of the papyri from "literary letters" or "epistles." His analysis concluded that Paul's letters were true letters (except for the Pastoral Epistles), since they were addressed to a specific situation and

8. The genre of Revelation is a highly debated topic in New Testament scholarship. For some helpful overviews on this, see G. R. Beasley-Murray, *Revelation* (NCB; Grand Rapids: Eerdmans, 1974), 12–29; D. E. Aune, "The Apocalypse of John and the Problem of Genre," *Semeia* 36 (1986): 65–96; R. Bauckham, *The Theology of the Book of Revelation* (NTT; Cambridge: Cambridge University Press, 1993), esp. 1–17; and D. A. deSilva, *Seeing Things John's Way: The Rhetoric of the Book of Revelation* (Louisville: Westminster John Knox, 2009).

9. These are conveniently found in *The Apostolic Fathers: Greek Texts and English Translations* (ed. and rev. M. W. Holmes; 3rd ed.; Grand Rapids: Baker, 2006).

10. See Deissmann, *Light from the Ancient East*, 346n4.

11. For more on the language of the New Testament, see the collected essays in S. E. Porter, ed., *The Language of the New Testament: Classic Essays* (JSNTSup 60; Sheffield: JSOT Press, 1991); and, for more recent studies, S. E. Porter and A. W. Pitts, eds., *The Language of the New Testament: Context, History, and Development* (ECHC 3/LBS 6; Leiden: Brill, 2013).

specific people, reflected Paul's genuine and unaffected thoughts and ideas, and were written in the language of the people of the day, rather than in some artificial literary style.[12] This was in keeping with Deissmann's conclusion regarding the nature of the early church, that it was essentially a group of people connected with the lower economic levels of the times, of which Paul was a part. Most, though not all, New Testament scholars who have investigated the issue see the early church as much more socioeconomically diverse than did Deissmann (as discussed in chapter 1 §6). The vast majority of Christians may have been from the lower socioeconomic strata of near-subsistence living, but there also appear to have been a number from higher levels, such as artisans and even some with connections to the elite.[13] In any case, most studies of the letters of the New Testament are responses to Deissmann's classifications, even when they strongly disagree with him.

The general conclusion of later studies is that a variety of factors must be considered, rather than simply studying the length and supposed genuineness of the Pauline letters. Better than seeing a disjunction between letter and epistle is the idea that there is a continuum, which depends on at least the following factors: language, whether the letters have a formal or informal style; content, whether their subject matter is one of business, personal recommendation, praise or blame, or instruction; and audience, including whether the letters are public or private, or to individuals or groups. There are also other factors to consider in analyzing Paul's letters. Unlike most true letters, his are not private in the conventional sense; at the same time, they are not for any and all who might be interested in reading them. They are for groups of followers of Christ, or churches, hence the frequent use of the second-person-plural form of address. His letters are significantly longer than the average papyrus letter, and they have some unique features of organization, discussed below. The body of the Pauline letter is recognizably that of the ancient personal letter, the major difference being that the topics are not usually personal commendations but, rather, instructions in the Christian faith. In many respects, Paul's style is that of the everyday language, but he was also a linguistic innovator. He used

12. See especially Deissmann, *Bible Studies*, 1–59. For a critique of Deissmann's hypothesis and a discussion of research in Greek epistolography, see S. K. Stowers, *Letter Writing in Greco-Roman Antiquity* (LEC; Philadelphia: Westminster, 1986), 17–26.

13. The most important book on this topic is still probably W. A. Meeks, *The First Urban Christians: The Social World of the Apostle Paul* (New Haven: Yale University Press, 1983), reevaluated twenty-five years later in T. D. Still and D. G. Horrell, eds., *After the First Urban Christians: The Social-Scientific Study of Pauline Christianity Twenty-Five Years Later* (London: T&T Clark, 2009). For a contrary position, see J. J. Meggitt, *Paul, Poverty, and Survival* (Studies of the New Testament and Its World; Edinburgh: T&T Clark, 1998).

certain words in ways that were previously unknown (e.g., the use of the verb "reconcile" [καταλλάσσω] in the active voice, with the offended party, God, as subject; see 2 Cor 5:18–19),[14] and he shaped his language to meet the needs of the churches he was addressing.

2. Purposes of Letters

Letters in the ancient world seem to have functioned very similarly to the way they do in the modern world. There were at least three major purposes of letters in the ancient world, all of which are exemplified in Paul's letters.[15] First, letters were used to establish and maintain relationships. They were seen as a means of bridging the distance between the correspondents. For example, a husband might write from Alexandria to his wife back in Oxyrhynchus, maintaining contact by informing her how his job in Alexandria is going and when he is expecting to return home (e.g., P.Oxy. 744, which records such an account). Or Paul writing to the Philippians includes thanks for their generosity (Phil 4:10–20). For a relationship that has not been recently maintained, or maintained as one party thinks it should have been, the letter could also be used to revive the relationship (e.g., P.Oxy. 119, where a peevish boy writes to his father, who has gone to Alexandria without him; BGU 3.846, a letter from a prodigal son wishing to return home). One of the challenges of letter-writing is that between the parties there is not only a physical but also a temporal distance, both of which must be overcome. As a result, the recipient of a letter is often written to as if present. In this sense, the letter is a substitute for the personal presence of the writer. This is a very important function of the Greco-Roman letter, but it is not the only function.

The second purpose of a letter in the ancient world was to provide a form of dialogical interchange. The letter formed one side of a conversation, perhaps conveying various types of information. This information could give instructions, for example, regarding some function to be performed by the recipient, such as buying or selling an animal, or to make requests, such as sending money (e.g., P.Tebt. 40 regarding land management). It could convey

14. See S. E. Porter, *Καταλλάσσω in Ancient Greek Literature, with Reference to the Pauline Writings* (Estudios de Filología Neotestamentaria 5; Córdoba: Ediciones El Almendro, 1994), esp. 143. See also chapter 4 §3C.

15. The classic study of the purpose of the Greco-Roman letter is H. Koskenniemi, *Studien zur Idee und Phraseologie des griechischen Briefes bis 400 n. Chr.* (Soumalaisen Tiedeakatermian Toimituksia; Annales Academiae Scientiarum Fennicae 102.2; Helsinki: Akateeminen Kirjakauppa, 1956). His conclusions are incorporated into later studies.

information—for instance, the condition of life of the one initiating the conversation. The content of the letter could vary depending upon the nature of the correspondence; Paul uses 1 Corinthians to respond to particular issues raised by those at Corinth.

The third purpose was to provide a permanent record of some form of interaction between the sender and receiver. This is often the case with the legal texts found in the papyri. Receipts and acknowledgments of legal and other transactions bear witness to the kinds of dealings these people had (e.g., P.Eleph. 1 is a marriage contract). The stating of it in a letter provides a record of this transaction for future reference. Paul's letter to Philemon provides a good example of this kind of letter. A number of official letters also bear witness to governmental correspondence and decrees. These letters were meant to promulgate the decrees and ensure that there was a record of the terms of the order. The letter to the Romans may well be categorized as recording a set of Paul's beliefs in similar fashion.

3. Form of the Pauline Letter

The ancient Greek letter[16] is traditionally said to have three formal parts: opening, body, and closing.[17] At the beginning of the body of the letter there is often a thanksgiving section, in which the writer gives thanks to a god or the gods for the health and safety of the recipient. It is this form that Paul seems to have adapted to his own purposes. Likewise, Paul's letters also have an often extended exhortative portion before the letter closing. As a result of these features, scholars are divided over whether Paul's letters fall into three, four, or five parts.[18] The question revolves around whether these two sections are to be

16. The letter form is traditionally analyzed by looking at the structure of the letter in relation to how many parts it has and what those parts are, but I think there are still other ways of investigating the letter form apart from this type of structural view. In a recent essay, I examine a way to analyze the letter form from a functionalist perspective, rather than formalist; see S. E. Porter, "A Functional Letter Perspective: Towards a Grammar of Epistolary Form," in *Paul and the Ancient Letter Form* (ed. S. E. Porter and S. A. Adams; PAST 6; Leiden: Brill, 2010), 9–32.

17. There is much scholarly debate on whether the New Testament letters revolve around a three-, four-, or five-part structure. See, for more discussion, J. L. White, *The Body of the Greek Letter* (SBLDS 2; Missoula, MT: SBL, 1972); and White, *The Form and Structure of the Official Petition* (SBLDS 5; Missoula, MT: SBL, 1972).

18. The three-part letter is ably defended by J. L. White, "Ancient Greek Letters," in *Greco-Roman Literature and the New Testament: Selected Forms and Genres* (ed. D. E. Aune; Atlanta: Scholars Press, 1988), 85–105, esp. 97; the four-part by J. A. D. Weima, *Neglected Endings: The Significance of the Pauline Letter Closings* (JSNTSup 101; Sheffield: JSOT Press, 1994), 11; and the

seen, on functional and structural grounds, to be separate and distinct units within the letter or whether these are subsumed in the opening or close of the body of the letter.[19] Without wishing to distance Paul's letters from those of the wider Greco-Roman world, especially in light of how Paul enhanced the letter form, I believe that it is appropriate to expand the traditional form-based three-part structure and, using functional categories as well, talk of five parts to the Pauline letter form: opening, thanksgiving, body, paraenesis, and closing.

There are several further observations regarding the limitations of the three-part letter form. The three-part letter form provides a useful set of distinctions for three obvious parts of the ancient Greek letter: opening, closing, and middle part. However, even three-part advocates admit that there are other parts of the letter, such as a thanksgiving section and a paraenetic or exhortative section, either before or after the main body section. They prefer to include these parts as subsections within the body, but I think that there is enough distinction to warrant labeling these sections as a different part than the body.[20] This is not, however, to say that each of the Pauline letters has all five of these parts. As the outlines of the letters in chapters 7–12 below indicate, in some there are only four or possibly three of these parts. Nevertheless, when one of these sections is missing, it is worth asking whether there is a reason for Paul's departure from his standard form—in other words, there is probably some sort of functional importance why certain of these parts are left out. The outlines in chapters 7–12 depart from the outlines usually found in commentaries and other introductions because they utilize the ancient epistolary form as the standard rather than the usual thematic, theological, or subject-oriented approach.

A. Opening

The usual (though certainly not unvarying) opening of a letter in the ancient world included three elements: the sender, the recipient, and a word of greeting, often in the form "A to B, greetings [χαίρειν]." This was the standard form

---

five-part by W. G. Doty, *Letters in Primitive Christianity* (Philadelphia: Fortress, 1973), 27–43, who is followed in the discussion below (note especially the chart on p. 43).

19. As L. Alexander observes, the opening and closing seem to be the most identifiable parts of the letter; "Hellenistic Letter-Forms and the Structure of Philippians," *JSNT* 12 (1989): 87–101. The dispute tends to be, however, whether we should lump the rest as simply the body, or whether there are distinctly identifiable differences in the nonopening and nonclosing part(s) to warrant identifying them as separate sections.

20. Cf. Porter, "Functional Letter Perspective," 19–20.

from the third century BC to the third century AD, although the form "To B from A, greetings" was also found.[21]

Paul includes all three elements in his standard opening, with several modifications.[22] Three are worth noting. The first is that Paul more times than not includes others as coauthors or cosenders of his letters. Only Romans, Ephesians, and the Pastoral Epistles do not include a cosender. First Corinthians also lists Sosthenes; 2 Corinthians, Timothy; Galatians, all the brothers (though not a specific designation); Philippians, Timothy; Colossians, Timothy; 1–2 Thessalonians, Silas and Timothy; and Philemon, Timothy. The question is why Paul does this. Are these people also authors? Should the corpus be known as the Pauline and other authors' letters (especially Timothy)? Since a distinctive Pauline voice comes through the Pauline letters, most scholars do not wish to see these people as coauthors on an equal footing with Paul. Instead, they may best be seen as cosenders. Paul, by including these colleagues, such as his long-standing companions Timothy and Silas, perhaps shows that his gospel is not his alone, that what he is saying comes from a Christian community to another Christian community. Since Timothy is also frequently seen as a letter carrier in Acts and the Pauline letters, the specification at the beginning of the letter probably helped to establish the authority of the letter carrier, who may well have been responsible for reading the letter to the audience. There were some who read to themselves, but for the most part reading was done out loud in the ancient world, so most reading had the character of a public activity (Col 4:16).[23] Since perhaps only 15 to 20 percent of the men were literate,[24] virtually all of the writings of the New Testament, including

---

21. The classic study of letter openings (as well as other parts) is F. X. J. Exler, *The Form of the Ancient Greek Letter of the Epistolary Papyri (3rd c. BC–3rd c. AD): A Study in Greek Epistolography* (repr. Chicago: Ares, 1976 [1923]), 23–68.

22. For a more detailed analysis of Paul's opening compared to other ancient Greek letters, see S. A. Adams, "Paul's Letter Opening and Greek Epistolography," and P. L. Tite, "How to Begin, and Why? Diverse Functions of the Pauline Prescript within a Greco-Roman Context," both in *Paul and the Ancient Letter Form* (ed. S. E. Porter and S. A. Adams; PAST 6; Leiden: Brill, 2010), 33–55 and 57–100.

23. On this issue, see S. E. Porter and A. W. Pitts, "Paul's Bible, His Education, and His Access to the Scriptures of Israel," *Journal of Greco-Roman Christianity and Judaism* 5 (2008): 9–40, esp. 31–34.

24. See W. V. Harris, *Ancient Literacy* (Cambridge, MA: Harvard University Press, 1989), 16–46. Harris's minimalist estimations have been revisited in light of the literate culture of the Greco-Roman world. See M. Beard, ed., *Literacy in the Roman World* (Journal of Roman Archaeology Supplement Series 3; Ann Arbor: University of Michigan, 1991), and the several essays in Beard's volume; A. Millard, *Reading and Writing in the Time of Jesus* (Sheffield: Sheffield Academic, 2000); and R. Bagnall, *Everyday Writing in the Graeco-Roman East* (Berke-

the letters, would have been read out loud to their churches. It is worth noting that Romans and Ephesians do not have cosenders, perhaps because these letters were sent under different circumstances than the other Pauline letters, the first to a church that Paul had never visited and that was located outside his immediate sphere of influence (Paul had perhaps not been to Colossae either, but it was within his sphere of influence), and the second perhaps to no specific church but to a number of churches in Asia. The Pastorals also include no cosender, but if they are authentic and if they were sent to Timothy and Titus, two of Paul's closest associates, they would have no need of a cosender.

The second feature of the Pauline opening is that he sometimes expands the specification of the sender or recipient. For example, in Rom 1:1–6 Paul expands the designation of the sender. His designation of himself as set apart for the gospel of God leads to a lengthy expansion on the nature of this gospel, focusing upon its relation to Jesus Christ. In 1 Cor 1:2, there is expansion of the designation of the recipient, defining the church of God in Corinth in terms of those who are sanctified and called to be holy. Whereas designation of the title or position of the sender or recipient in a letter was known in the ancient world, this kind of expansion is virtually unknown before the time of Paul.

The third feature of the Pauline opening is that Paul apparently modified the conventional word of greeting. All of Paul's letters include not the verb "greetings" (χαίρειν) but the words "grace" (χάρις) and "peace" (εἰρήνη), with the word "mercy" (ἐλεημοσύνη) added in 1–2 Timothy. There is persistent scholarly interest in why Paul adds the word "peace."[25] The word for "grace" is cognate to the word "greetings," so it is easy to see that Paul is playing upon the standard convention for greeting. Some suggest that Paul includes "peace" as a translation of the Hebrew word for peace, *shalom*, and that this reflects his integration of Greek and Jewish elements into his letter, thus reflecting the very nature of Paul's ministry as apostle to the Gentiles, bringing the message of the crucified and resurrected Christ. Since this greeting is not found in any other Jewish letters of the time in Greek (*shalom* is found in Hebrew but not "grace and peace"), it is doubtful that this is what Paul is doing. This is not to minimize that Paul theologized or Christianized the letter opening, however. Grace is God's beneficent favor upon sinners, and peace is the condition of sinners being reconciled to God (cf. Rom 1:1–7, as an example).[26] In any case,

ley: University of California Press, 2011). See also S. E. Porter and B. R. Dyer, "Oral Texts? A Reassessment of the Oral and Rhetorical Nature of Paul's Letters in Light of Recent Studies," *Journal of the Evangelical Theological Society* 55.2 (2012): 323–41.

25. See S. E. Porter, "Peace, Reconciliation," in *DPL* 695–99 at 699. See chapter 4 §2D.

26. See J. Moffatt, *Grace in the New Testament* (London: Hodder & Stoughton, 1931); Porter, Καταλλάσσω, 154.

the Pauline letter opening is distinct and provides an entry point into the thinking of the apostle.

B. *Thanksgiving*

After the opening, many Greco-Roman letters then proceed to the health wish, in which a prayer or word of thanks is offered for the well-being of the addressee. In the Egyptian papyri, this is often addressed specifically to one of the Egyptian gods, such as Serapis. As in these thanksgivings, Paul sometimes uses a formula in which a verb of thanksgiving (εὐχαριστέω) is addressed to God with a reason for Paul's thanks (e.g., Rom 1:8; 1 Cor 1:4; Eph 1:16; Phil 1:3; Col 1:3; 1 Thess 1:2; 2 Thess 1:3; Phlm 4).[27] Paul again takes the convention of the Greco-Roman letter form and adapts it to his purposes, further developing the thanksgiving section. He includes within a letter such things as a prayer formula, in which he states that intercession is being made for his recipients (Rom 1:9–10; Phil 1:9–11), or a memorial formula, in which he states that he is keeping his recipients in his memory (Phil 1:3; Phlm 4), but these should be considered a part of the thanksgiving section. In this section, Paul, instead of giving thanks to the gods, gives thanks to *the* God for his recipients and for the blessings that they have received and for the blessings that they are to him. The thanksgiving is present in all of the church letters of Paul except Galatians. The lack of a thanksgiving in Galatians provides a jarring transition from the opening to the body of the letter, in which Paul expresses his astonishment that they have so quickly deserted their calling.[28] By contrast, 1 Thessalonians

---

27. On the Pauline thanksgiving and other thanksgivings, see P. Schubert, *The Form and Function of the Pauline Thanksgivings* (Berlin: Töpelmann, 1939); P. T. O'Brien, *Introductory Thanksgivings in the Letters of Paul* (NovTSup 49; Leiden: Brill, 1977); J. T. Reed, "Are Paul's Thanksgivings 'Epistolary'?" *JSNT* 61 (1996): 87–99; P. Arzt, "The 'Epistolary Introductory Thanksgiving' in the Papyri and in Paul," *NovT* 36 (1994): 29–46, to whom Reed responds; D. W. Pao, *Thanksgiving: An Investigation of a Pauline Theme* (New Studies in Biblical Theology 13; Downers Grove, IL: InterVarsity, 2002), esp. 17–19; and Pao, "Gospel within the Constraints of an Epistolary Form: Pauline Introductory Thanksgivings and Paul's Theology of Thanksgiving," P. Arzt-Grabner, "Paul's Letter Thanksgiving," and R. F. Collins, "A Significant Decade: The Trajectory of the Hellenistic Epistolary Thanksgiving," all in *Paul and the Ancient Letter Form* (ed. S. E. Porter and S. A. Adams; PAST 6; Leiden: Brill, 2010), 101–27, 129–58, and 159–84; cf. G. P. Wiles, *Paul's Intercessory Prayer: The Significance of the Intercessory Prayer Passages in the Letters of Paul* (SNTSMS 24; Cambridge: Cambridge University Press, 1974), who analyzes prayers in the thanksgiving, as well as the other parts of the letter.

28. See R. E. van Voorst, "Why Is There No Thanksgiving Period in Galatians? An Assessment of an Exegetical Commonplace," *JBL* 129.1 (2010): 153–72, who contends that the Galatians

is full of thanksgiving by Paul for the Thessalonian Christians. Some scholars go so far as to say that 1 Thessalonians is one large thanksgiving, estimating that as much as three-fifths of the letter is thanksgiving (see chapter 8 §2E). It is not surprising that Paul utilizes formulas that express joy or rejoicing in this portion of his letters (e.g., Phil 1:3–6; 1 Thess 1:2–10).

Two features of the Pauline thanksgiving are worth mentioning here. The first is that many scholars believe that Paul not only takes and adapts the convention of the health wish to a Christian thanksgiving but also utilizes this portion of the letter for the very important purpose of forecasting the topics that are to be discussed in the letter. There is some truth in this analysis, but it has limitations as well. For example, taking 1 Thessalonians again, in the thanksgiving proper (1 Thess 1:2–10), Paul mentions, among other things, the Thessalonians' work and what it produced: they were imitators of him and the Lord, they became a model to all of Macedonia and Achaia, and they were waiting for the return of Christ. All of these ideas are developed in various ways in the rest of the letter: their work in 2:1–16, their being imitators in 3:6–10, their being models in 4:1–12, and the return of Christ in 5:1–11. On the other hand, 1 Cor 1:7 mentions spiritual gifts and eschatology, but these are only two of the many topics discussed in 1 Corinthians.[29] There is perhaps a rough correlation, but certainly not a complete matching, leaving some topics to be introduced within the body of the letter. It is probably more accurate to say that the thanksgiving provides a general orientation to the relationship between Paul and the particular church and that this relationship is then developed in the rest of the letter. The second feature of the Pauline thanksgiving is the shift from giving thanks for the gods and what they have done in preserving the health of the recipients to giving thanks to God for the faithfulness of the recipients (e.g., Phil 1:3–8). Intercession on behalf of the recipient church also tends to occur in the thanksgiving section (e.g., Col 1:3).

C. Body

The body of the Pauline letter has been the least studied part in its relation to the Greco-Roman letter form, perhaps because the Greco-Roman letter

would not have expected a thanksgiving. However, the transition is jarring nevertheless, and lacks the transitional elements of the typical letter, with or without the thanksgiving. See F. F. Bruce, *The Epistle to the Galatians* (NIGTC; Grand Rapids: Eerdmans, 1982), 79–80, for discussion of the transition.

29. See J. Bailey and L. D. Vander Broek, *Literary Forms in the New Testament* (London: SPCK, 1992), 24, who claim that Paul "telegraphs" his ideas in the thanksgiving.

body has also not been heavily studied.[30] Since the body of the letter could be called upon to perform a large number of purposes, it is perhaps inevitable that less has been done regarding its formal or functional features. For Paul, the body of the letter tends to concern one or both of two general subjects. The first is what might be called Christian doctrine. The bodies of such letters as Romans, Galatians, and 1 Corinthians tend to outline and develop important Pauline theological categories, such as the sinfulness of humanity, justification, reconciliation, Christian unity, and the roles of the law, faith, and grace. The second general subject, reflecting similarities to the friendship letter of the Greco-Roman world, is Paul's own situation, especially in relation to the church to which he is writing. Philippians provides a very good example of this kind of letter, as do 1–2 Corinthians. In Philippians, Paul discusses his own situation of imprisonment, how he views his personal ministry, especially in relation to his own personal background, and how the Philippians should react. This letter also develops important theological ideas (e.g., Phil 2:6–11), but by using Christ as a model to imitate, a model that Paul himself has been trying to exemplify (3:14).

The body of the Pauline letter, like other ancient letters, can be divided into three parts: body opening, body middle or body proper, and body closing. All of these portions concern the matter of the letter body, but they serve various functions in introducing and concluding this matter. Paul relies upon a number of formulas both to mark the various portions of the body and to draw attention to the significance of various ideas. In the body opening, for example, Paul often makes use of several formulas. One is the request or appeal formula, with a form of the verb "encourage" (παρακαλέω). Paul uses this verb in a formula nineteen times in his letters (e.g., 1 Cor 4:16; 16:15; Phlm 8, 10), often for a transition from the thanksgiving to the body of the letter (e.g., 1 Cor 1:10) but sometimes for other kinds of transitions.[31] Paul also uses disclosure formulas, found in other kinds of Hellenistic letters as well.[32] Disclosure formulas typically have phrasing such as "I want you to know" or "I don't want

---

30. For a helpful overview of issues concerning the Pauline letter body, see T. W. Martin, "Investigating the Pauline Letter Body: Issues, Methods, and Approaches," in *Paul and the Ancient Letter Form* (ed. S. E. Porter and S. A. Adams; PAST 6; Leiden: Brill, 2010), 185–212; see also Exler, *Form of the Ancient Greek Letter*, 101–32; and White, *Body of the Greek Letter*.

31. See Weima, *Neglected Endings*, 145–48.

32. For a more detailed discussion on the Pauline disclosure formula, especially from a linguistic standpoint, see S. E. Porter and A. W. Pitts, "The Disclosure Formula in the Epistolary Papyri and in the New Testament: Development, Form, Function, and Syntax," in *The Language of the New Testament: Context, History, and Development* (ed. S. E. Porter and A. W. Pitts; ECHC 3/LBS 6; Leiden: Brill, 2013), 421–38.

you to be ignorant," marking some idea that the sender believes the recipients should know. Often disclosure formulas occur near the beginning of the body of the letter (e.g., Rom 1:13; 2 Cor 1:8; 1 Thess 2:1; Phil 1:12; Gal 1:11). In addition, Paul sometimes uses expressions of astonishment (e.g., Gal 1:6). The disclosure formula indicates that the sender expects that the recipients already know the information to be stated, while the expression of astonishment indicates that the sender completely objects to what the recipients are doing or saying (usually in relation to what is being disclosed). Paul also utilizes compliance formulas, in which he restates something that places an obligation of action upon the recipients, "as I already said" (e.g., Gal 1:9, 13–14).

The body closing also has a number of formulas. Whereas those of the body opening are designed to introduce or reintroduce already known or assumed information, the body closing formulas are designed to help the sender tie the argument of the body together and to close this portion of the letter. For example, Paul frequently uses a confidence formula, in which he expresses confidence that his recipients will understand what he has said and will act appropriately upon it (e.g., Rom 15:14; 2 Cor 7:4, 16; 9:1–2; Gal 5:10; 2 Thess 3:4; Phlm 21). He also uses an eschatological conclusion, which places what Paul has been saying in a larger framework, in which all the actions of both sender and recipients are seen in light of the imminent return of Christ (e.g., Rom 8:31–39; 11:25–26; 1 Cor 4:6–13; Gal 6:7–10; Phil 2:14–18; 1 Thess 2:13–16). Paul appeals to early Christian belief in the imminent return of Christ as a serious motivation for proper Christian action and belief, because one would not want to be caught deviating from these at Christ's return. Paul also employs a travelogue near the close of the body portion of his letter (e.g., 1 Thess 2:17–3:13). This is characterized by Robert Funk as the "apostolic parousia" or apostolic presence.[33] Paul indicates his reason for writing or his intention to send an emissary or even pay a personal visit to his recipients. In effect, the letter is a temporary substitute for the apostle's (or his designated representative's) presence. This imposes a certain amount of subtle pressure upon the recipients to be concerned for their belief and behavior in light of an impending visit of the apostle himself or his representative. The travelogue outlining the plans of the apostle usually occurs near the end of the body or even the paraenesis

---

33. R. W. Funk, "The Apostolic Parousia: Form and Significance," in *Christian History and Interpretation: Studies Presented to John Knox* (ed. W. R. Farmer, C. F. D. Moule, and R. R. Niebuhr; Cambridge: Cambridge University Press, 1967), 249–68. Whereas Funk tries to identify a formal category, the apostolic presence is better seen as a functional convention. Cf. M. M. Mitchell, "New Testament Envoys in the Context of Greco-Roman Diplomatic and Epistolary Conventions: The Example of Timothy and Titus," *JBL* 111 (1992): 641–62, who questions some of Funk's conclusions.

(Rom 15:14–33; Phlm 21–22; 1 Cor 4:14–21; 1 Thess 2:17–3:13; 2 Cor 12:14–13:13; Gal 4:12–20; Phil 2:19–24), but it is not necessarily found only at the close (Rom 1:10; 1 Cor 4:21; Phil 2:24).

D. Paraenesis

The paraenetic section of the letter is perhaps the most difficult to define, because it does not appear to have the same kinds of distinguishing features as the other parts of the letter. The other parts typically have identifiable formal characteristics, as well as functional features, that enable them to be identified. The paraenesis relies less upon these formal features (although there sometimes are words of encouragement) and more upon its approach to its content and its position within the letter structure.[34] There admittedly are exhortatory sections throughout Paul's letters, but the paraenetic section occurs near the end (or at least after the body) of the letter, as a concentrated grouping of admonishments regarding Christian behavior. Whereas the body of the letter concerns dogma or doctrine or a discussion of the fortunes of the apostle himself, the paraenetic part of the Pauline letter concerns Christian behavior, sometimes even a series of relatively less well-connected admonitory statements. Although advocates of the three-part letter form include the paraenesis at the end of the body section, I maintain that this section is distinct enough and well enough developed to distinguish it from the letter body proper. The paraenesis, rather than relying upon formal indicators, often

---

34. Some try to equate the movement from the body to paraenesis in terms of indicative-imperative. The history of this attempt to find explicitly grammatical warrant for what is at best an ethical construct appears to take its greatest impetus from Rudolf Bultmann, "The Problem of Ethics in Paul," in *Understanding Paul's Ethics: Twentieth Century Approaches* (ed. B. S. Rosner; Grand Rapids: Eerdmans, 1995), 195–217, originally published in German in 1924), perhaps made best known in English-language circles by Victor Paul Furnish, *Theology and Ethics in Paul* (Nashville: Abingdon, 1968). The terminology, as well as much of what it represents, must be rejected as grammatically unwarranted and potentially conceptually misleading. This does not mean that Paul is not concerned with moving from theology to ethics—he is. It does mean, however, that the terminology of indicative-imperative is not the way to formulate it or describe it. For a reasonable recent statement of the issues, see V. Rabens, "'Indicative and Imperative' as the Substructure of Paul's Theology-and-Ethics in Galatians? A Discussion of Divine and Human Agency in Paul," in *Galatians and Christian Theology: Justification, the Gospel, and Ethics in Paul's Letter* (ed. M. W. Elliott et al.; Grand Rapids: Baker, 2014), 285–305, who surveys recent literature. For a recent attempt to make such a scheme work, with appropriate reservations, see D. G. Horrell, *Solidarity and Difference: A Contemporary Reading of Paul's Ethics* (London: T&T Clark, 2005).

draws upon models of behavioral exhortation known within the Greco-Roman world. The paraenesis often specifies what is proper Christian behavior, using various traditional forms of moral instruction, including moral maxims, vice and virtue lists, and household codes (e.g., Eph 5:21–6:9; Col 3:18–4:1).

One of the reasons for distinguishing the paraenesis from the body of the letter is the significance of paraenesis for Christianity as a new or developing religious movement. There were many questions, not only regarding doctrine, but practice as well, and letter-writing was a predominant way of communicating proper Christian conduct and life. Paul draws upon material from a variety of sources, including the Old Testament, contemporary Jewish thinking, Greco-Roman thought, and Hellenistic moral traditions.[35] His best-known paraenetic sections are Rom 12:1–15:13; 1 Cor 5:1–16:12; Gal 5:13–6:10; and 1 Thess 4:1–5:22.[36] One potentially problematic paraenetic section is found in 1 Thess 4:1–5:22 (this also provides a good example of how to understand the nature of Pauline paraenesis). In this section, Paul begins by noting that the Thessalonians have already received instruction from him on how to live and please God (referring either to the body of the letter, 1 Thess 2–3, or possibly to this and his personal instructions during his time in Thessalonica), and now he is going to urge them to act in this way. His first set of instructions concerns their need for holy living (sanctification; see chapter 4 §3D); the second set concerns how, on the basis of their knowing about the coming of the Lord, this provides a grounds for encouraging others and building them up; and the third and final set entails a group of various exhortations regarding how they generally treat each other. There may be some new instruction in what he says in 4:13–5:11, but whatever may be offered here by way of instruction is less for doctrinal or instructive purposes than it is for exhortative motives—the Thessalonian Christians are instructed to use this information to encourage each other (see chapter 8 §2E). By contrast, what appears to be somewhat similar information regarding the coming of the Lord in 2 Thess 2:1–12, though it no doubt has an exhortative result, has the primary purpose of providing information and instruction regarding the man of lawlessness (note that Paul does not give any exhortative comments as a result of this instruction). Thus, in 2:1–12, this section is found within the body of the letter. The recognition of

35. On the other hand, Paul should also be considered an innovator of sorts with regard to the paraenetic sections of his letters; cf. A. W. Pitts, "Philosophical and Epistolary Contexts for Pauline Paraenesis," in *Paul and the Ancient Letter Form* (ed. S. E. Porter and S. A. Adams; PAST 6; Leiden: Brill, 2010), 269–306.

36. For more on the Pauline paraenesis, see Y. C. Whang, "Paul's Letter Paraenesis," in *Paul and the Ancient Letter Form* (ed. S. E. Porter and S. A. Adams; PAST 6; Leiden: Brill, 2010), 253–68.

the importance of Pauline paraenesis is at the heart of understanding how Paul crafts his theological argument within his letters. He does not offer instruction without also offering encouragement to Christian behavior.

E. Closing

In the closing of the letter, Paul is perhaps less bound to the Greco-Roman letter form than he is anywhere else. The typical Hellenistic letter would express a health wish, often using a closing imperative, a word of farewell, and the word "good-bye" (ἔρρωσο or plural ἔρρωσθε).

The Pauline closing might consist of any number of the following elements. He typically greets a number of people or conveys greetings to the recipients from those who are with him. The longest list of greetings is found in Romans (16:3–23), but there are lists of greetings in many of his letters (1 Cor 16:19–21; 2 Cor 13:12–13; Phil 4:21–22; 1 Thess 5:26; Phlm 23–25). Paul also frequently includes a doxology at the end of his letter (one might be included earlier as well, as in Gal 1:5). These doxologies often contain exalted language of praise and glory to God (e.g., Rom 16:25–27; Phil 4:20; 1 Thess 5:23). Paul also includes a benediction, which can take several different forms, depending upon whether it is a grace or a peace benediction. In either case, it (1) begins by conveying grace or peace upon the recipients, (2) continues by attributing a blessing to God, and (3) concludes by directing the blessing to the recipients (Rom 15:33; 16:20; 1 Cor 16:23; 2 Cor 13:14; Gal 6:18; Phil 4:23; 1 Thess 5:28; Phlm 25). Paul also occasionally speaks of greeting each other with a holy kiss (Rom 16:16; 1 Cor 16:20; 2 Cor 13:12; 1 Thess 5:26).[37]

Some argue that, like the thanksgiving, the closing also contains a brief recapitulation of the major ideas of the letter. Whereas it is often true that some of the ideas presented in the letter are also summarized in the closing, this does not seem to be the best description of the function of the closing. The closing of the letter is simply a way of concluding the correspondence, often not by adding to or even recapitulating what has already been said but by providing suitable words of closing. These words are similar to those used in

---

37. On features of the Pauline letter closing, see H. Gamble Jr., *The Textual History of the Letter to the Romans: A Study in Textual and Literary Criticism* (Studies and Documents 42; Grand Rapids: Eerdmans, 1977), 56–83; and Weima, *Neglected Endings*, 78–152. Weima identifies six epistolary conventions that consistently appear in Paul's closings: the peace, benediction, hortatory section, greetings, autograph, and grace benediction; J. A. D. Weima, "Sincerely, Paul: The Significance of the Pauline Letter Closings," in *Paul and the Ancient Letter Form* (ed. S. E. Porter and S. A. Adams; PAST 6; Leiden: Brill, 2010), 307–45.

other Greco-Roman letters, but Paul has again theologized and Christianized the closing, leaving his recipients with a bidirectional closing: on the one hand, praise and glory are ascribed to God (Rom 16:25–27, but see chapter 10 §2E2 on textual difficulties with this closing); on the other, grace or peace is wished upon the recipients (2 Cor 13:14).

4. Paul's Use of the Amanuensis

Amanuenses, or scribes, were widely used in the ancient world for the writing of both public and private documents.[38] Their training and competence varied, one's ability to pay often dictating the quality of service received. Since a good many people simply were unable to write, some papyri have what is called an illiteracy formula attached: at the close of the papyrus, the scribe, who has written the letter, states, "X wrote because Y does not know letters."[39] There were, however, other reasons for using a scribe. The cost of writing materials (such as papyrus) made it highly desirable to have a scribe who could write carefully and use as little papyrus and ink as possible—even though papyrus was not exorbitantly expensive and readily available for use. The difficulty of writing on the uneven papyrus surface, which varied with the quality of the papyrus and depended on whether one was writing on the recto (with the grain running horizontally) or the verso (with the grain running vertically), made professional scribes very useful.

There are clear indications that Paul, like other writers in the ancient world, used a scribe.[40] Romans 16:22 contains an explicit reference to the scribe, Tertius, who sends his greetings to the Christians in Rome. Other passages have more indirect references to Paul's use of a scribe. Even though he used a scribe, Paul, who was literate, took the pen in his own hand as a way of authenticating that the letter was written and sent under his authority. Ga-

38. See E. R. Richards, *The Secretary in the Letters of Paul* (WUNT 2/42; Tübingen: Mohr-Siebeck, 1991), who supplies much of the evidence in the discussion below; cf. R. N. Longe-necker, "Ancient Amanuenses and the Pauline Epistles," in *New Dimensions in New Testament Study* (ed. R. N. Longenecker and M. C. Tenney; Grand Rapids: Zondervan, 1974), 281–97; J. Murphy-O'Connor, *Paul the Letter-Writer: His World, His Options, His Skills* (Wilmington, DE: Liturgical, 1995), 8–37; M. L. Stirewalt, *Paul: The Letter Writer* (Grand Rapids: Eerdmans, 2003); and E. R. Richards, *Paul and First-Century Letter Writing: Secretaries, Composition, and Collection* (Downers Grove, IL: InterVarsity, 2004), 59–93.

39. See Harris, *Ancient Literacy*, 141. As examples, see P.Tebt. 104.39–40; and P.Hamb. 4.14–15.

40. Richards, *Paul and First-Century Letter Writing*, 81–93; and Stirewalt, *Paul: The Letter Writer*, 10–11, among many others.

latians 6:11 seems to indicate that Paul used a scribe, though scholars differ about when the scribe handed the pen over to Paul. The verse draws attention to Paul's hand, that of an untrained writer or perhaps someone whose eyesight was failing, being much larger than that of the professional scribe (see also 1 Cor 16:21; 2 Thess 3:17; Col 4:18, and Phlm 19; cf. possibly Rom 16:17–23).[41]

What was the exact role of the scribe? There is evidence from the ancient world that scribes performed a number of functions. One function was to take dictation, virtually word for word. There is fairly strong evidence that a form of shorthand was developed in the Hellenistic world that would allow scribes to take down what was being said so that they could transcribe it later in longhand (see P.Oxy. 724, a contract for the apprenticeship of a shorthand writer). Second, scribes were also capable of editing a writer's work, by using a rough draft or taking down the sense of what the author wished to say and then working out the individual wording. This might be one explanation of the composition of Ephesians, a letter whose authorship in the Pauline corpus is highly disputed. Because of its similarities to Colossians, as well as a number of distinctive features, it is possible that a scribe was instructed by Paul to compose the letter following the pattern of Colossians but emphasizing particular themes (is 1 Pet 5:12 similar?). Third, the scribe might simply be instructed to write a letter, without being given the exact or full sense of what was to be said. The scribe then composed the actual wording and came up with the sense of the correspondence. An example is found in Cicero's instructions to Atticus to write letters to anyone he had forgotten (*Epistulae ad Atticum* 3.15.8). The one issuing the order is still the author, because he is responsible for the writing that goes out under his name, although this might be considered a form of coauthorship. In other words, the range of scribal functions was considerable, and it is difficult from the extant evidence to be more specific regarding what a scribe might or might not do, or in what contexts certain roles would be appropriate.

Even though we know that Paul used scribes, almost assuredly quite frequently, this still does not answer the question how much the scribe did in a particular situation. Most scholars recognize a distinctive Pauline voice running through the letters, at least the main letters. This militates against the scribe being given virtually free rein to compose the letter. Nevertheless, a number of scholars find considerable linguistic and even theological differences between the so-called disputed and undisputed letters. A possible explanation of these differences is that a scribe was employed whose language did not match that of the Pauline voice. The scribal hypothesis is a very attractive one to explain a number of the issues regarding Pauline authorship, but it

41. Weima, *Neglected Endings*, 123, 221.

cannot be used uncritically because of the lack of proof and the lack of means for verifying. From the evidence at hand, there is no way to prove the roles that scribes played in the composition of the Pauline letters. What is certain, however, is that, for any author, including Paul, once the letter was signed by the sender, the letter became the product and responsibility of the one who instituted the correspondence, regardless of whether the exact wording was his conscious choice.

5. Conclusion

Although Paul's letters are part of the larger corpus of letters from the Greco-Roman world, they are also distinct and merit examination in their own right. Paul's letters were less formulaic than those of his letter-writing contemporaries, with more freedom of expression and variation. The content is uniquely Paul's and is rich with theological meaning as he addresses complex relations among church members or personal correspondents with the common language of the day. He had dynamic and changing relations with his churches, and he took the opportunity to address their situations with his authority as a leader of the church. This sense of authority comes through in his letters. Paul's style is not that of the typical papyrus, nor the florid and polished language of the literary letter. His is a living language for contemporary church situations.

Sources for Further Study

Basic Sources

Bailey, J. L., and L. D. Vander Broek. *Literary Forms in the New Testament: A Handbook.* Louisville: Westminster John Knox, 1992.

Deissmann, A. *Bible Studies.* Translated by A. Grieve. Edinburgh: T&T Clark, 1901.

Klauck, H.-J. *Ancient Letters and the New Testament: A Guide to Context and Exegesis.* Waco, TX: Baylor University Press, 2006.

Murphy-O'Connor, J. *Paul the Letter-Writer: His World, His Options, His Skills.* Wilmington, DE: Liturgical, 1995.

Richards, E. R. *Paul and First-Century Letter Writing: Secretaries, Composition, and Collection.* Downers Grove, IL: InterVarsity, 2004.

Roetzel, C. J. *The Letters of Paul: Conversations in Context.* 5th ed. Louisville: Westminster John Knox, 2009.

Schreiner, T. R. *Interpreting the Pauline Epistles.* 2nd ed. Grand Rapids: Baker, 2011.

Advanced Sources

Aune, D. E., ed. *Greco-Roman Literature and the New Testament: Selected Forms and Genres*. Atlanta: Scholars Press, 1988.

Deissmann, A. *Light from the Ancient East: The New Testament Illustrated by Recently Discovered Texts of the Graeco-Roman World*. Translated by L. R. M. Strachan. 4th ed. London: Hodder & Stoughton, 1927.

Doty, W. G. *Letters in Primitive Christianity*. Philadelphia: Fortress, 1973.

Exler, F. X. J. *The Form of the Ancient Greek Letter of the Epistolary Papyri (3rd c. BC–3rd c. AD): A Study in Greek Epistolography*. Reprinted Chicago: Ares, 1976 (1923).

Gamble, H., Jr. *The Textual History of the Letter to the Romans: A Study in Textual and Literary Criticism*. Studies and Documents 42. Grand Rapids: Eerdmans, 1977.

Horrell, D. G. *Solidarity and Difference: A Contemporary Reading of Paul's Ethics*. London: T&T Clark, 2005.

Kraus, T. J. *Ad fontes: Original Manuscripts and their Significance for Studying Early Christianity: Selected Essays*. TENT 3. Leiden: Brill, 2007.

Muir, J. *Life and Letters in the Ancient Greek World*. Routledge Monographs in Classical Studies. New York: Routledge, 2008.

O'Brien, P. T. *Introductory Thanksgivings in the Letters of Paul*. NovTSup 49. Leiden: Brill, 1977.

Porter, S. E., and S. A. Adams, eds. *Paul and the Ancient Letter Form*. PAST 6. Leiden: Brill, 2010.

Richards, E. R. *The Secretary in the Letters of Paul*. WUNT 2/42. Tübingen: Mohr-Siebeck, 1991.

Rosner, B. S, ed. *Understanding Paul's Ethics: Twentieth Century Approaches*. Grand Rapids: Eerdmans, 1995.

Weima, J. A. D. *Neglected Endings: The Significance of the Pauline Letter Closings*. JSNTSup 101. Sheffield: JSOT Press, 1994.

White, J. L. *The Body of the Greek Letter*. SBLDS 2. Missoula, MT: SBL, 1972.

———. *Light from Ancient Letters*. FFNT. Philadelphia: Fortress, 1986.

6

Pseudonymity and the Formation
of the Pauline Canon

1. Introduction

No contemporary discussion of the Pauline letters can avoid discussing the issue of whether any of Paul's letters are pseudonymous.[1] This chapter is devoted
to discussion of this topic, even though, as will be explicitly seen in discussion
of the individual letters in Part 2 of this volume, I believe that Paul is the author
of all thirteen of the letters attributed to him in the New Testament. There are
a number of formally anonymous works in the New Testament, such as all
four Gospels, Acts, Hebrews, and the Johannine Epistles, but so far as pseudonymous works are concerned, only those with explicit claims to authorship
can be considered as possibly pseudonymous.[2] Within the New Testament,

1. This section draws upon several previous essays that I have written on this important
topic, in particular S. E. Porter, "Pauline Authorship and the Pastoral Epistles: Implications
for Canon," *BBR* 5 (1995): 105-23. Cf. also "Pauline Authorship and the Pastoral Epistles: A
Response to R. W. Wall's Response," *BBR* 6 (1996): 133-38; "Exegesis of the Pauline Letters,
Including the Deutero-Pauline Letters," in *Handbook to Exegesis of the New Testament* (ed. S. E.
Porter; NTTS 25; Leiden: Brill, 1997), 531-39; "The Implications of New Testament Pseudonymy for a Doctrine of Scripture," in *Interdisciplinary Perspectives on the Authority of Scripture:
Historical, Biblical, and Theoretical Perspectives* (ed. C. R. Bovell; Eugene, OR: Pickwick, 2011),
236-56; and "Pauline Chronology and the Question of Pseudonymity of the Pastoral Epistles,"
in *Paul and Pseudepigraphy* (ed. S. E. Porter and G. P. Fewster; PAST 8; Leiden: Brill, 2013),
65-88.

2. Here genuine authorship is taken to include writing by a scribe or by someone under
the direct authority of the ascribed author. Kurt Aland makes a virtue of pseudonymity by
arguing that it derives from anonymity. See his "The Problem of Anonymity and Pseudonymity
in Christian Literature of the First Two Centuries," *Journal of Theological Studies* 12 (1961):
39-49; repr. in *The Authorship and Integrity of the New Testament* (London: SPCK, 1965), 1-13.
That school exercises and even fiction were written under pseudonyms does not enter into the

these potentially include the Pauline letters (in particular among those widely discussed in contemporary New Testament scholarship: 2 Thessalonians, Colossians, Ephesians, and the Pastoral Epistles) and the Petrine letters.[3]

There is a tendency to look at the question of pseudonymity (and anonymity) as if it were a problem only of the biblical and related literature (e.g., apocalyptic literature such as *1 Enoch*), when it was actually an issue throughout the ancient world. In fact, this is such a large topic that a thorough analysis cannot be offered here.[4] Pseudonymous writings existed in the ancient world, and these included letters. The evidence for this can be seen in at least two ways: there are comments in the ancient writers, including those of the early church, regarding writings that are known to have false authorship; and there are a number of writings, especially of a literary type, such as the Platonic and Cynic letters, that have been determined to be pseudonymous.[5] The issue that I am concerned with here is whether any pseudonymous writings exist in the New Testament, in particular whether certain Pauline letters such as the Pastorals are pseudonymous.

Before addressing this question, it is worth noting how pseudepigraphal literature was handled in the ancient world and the early church.[6] Discus-

---

equation, since they were part of an accepted convention whereby readers understood what was being done. Nevertheless, they were part of an environment in which pseudepigrapha were written.

3. I will not discuss the Petrine letters further here. The books of James, Jude, and Revelation are not included here because, although they claim authorship by persons with their respective names, they do not make a claim to a particular person. For a survey of authorship issues for these books, see L. M. McDonald and S. E. Porter, *Early Christianity and Its Sacred Literature* (Peabody, MA: Hendrickson, 2000), 528–31, 542, 557–58, respectively.

4. Nevertheless, this chapter is more heavily documented than some others because of the importance of the topic and to provide access to important sources on it.

5. See L. R. Donelson, *Pseudepigraphy and Ethical Argument in the Pastoral Epistles* (HUT 22; Tübingen: Mohr-Siebeck, 1986), esp. 9–23, 23–42. It may be true that there is less evidence of Christian pseudepigraphal letters (see D. A. Carson, D. J. Moo, and L. Morris, *An Introduction to the New Testament* [Grand Rapids: Zondervan, 1992], 367–68), but as the argument below explores, that may only mean that there was less detection.

6. For some recent discussions of this issue, see, e.g., M. Davies, *The Pastoral Epistles* (NTG; Sheffield: Sheffield Academic, 1996), 113–17; E. E. Ellis, "Pseudonymity and Canonicity of New Testament Documents," in *Worship, Theology, and Ministry in the Early Church: Essays in Honor of Ralph P. Martin* (ed. M. J. Wilkins and T. Paige; JSNTSup 87; Sheffield: JSOT Press, 1992), 212–24; D. A. Carson, "Pseudonymity and Pseudepigraphy," in *Dictionary of New Testament Background* (ed. C. A. Evans and S. E. Porter; Downers Grove, IL: InterVarsity, 2000), 857–64 (expanded upon in D. A. Carson and D. J. Moo, *An Introduction to the New Testament* [2nd ed.; Grand Rapids: Zondervan, 2005], 337–53); and K. D. Clarke, "The Problem of Pseudonymity in Biblical Literature and Its Implications for Canon Formation," in *The Canon Debate* (ed. L. M. McDonald and J. A. Sanders; Peabody, MA: Hendrickson, 2002), 440–68.

sions of pseudonymity often note that ancient secular writers were aware that some of the writings they were dealing with were pseudonymous. For example, among nonbiblical writers, Suetonius described a letter of Horace as spurious; Galen took only thirteen of the sixty or eighty Hippocratic texts as genuine and was concerned that his own works were being infiltrated by those he did not write; Philostratus disputed a work by Dionysius; and Livy reported that, when discovered, pseudonymous books attributed to Numa were burned. One of the most complex questions in the ancient world was the corpus of Lysias's speeches. Over 420 were ascribed to him, but many ancients knew that many were not genuine, and they formulated various lists attempting to determine those that were genuine. For example, one list includes as many speeches as possible but questions the authenticity of a third of them.[7]

A similar situation apparently held in Christian circles. Ancient writers may have commented favorably upon the possibility of pseudonymous writings unknown to them, but these instances are certainly few, if any, and this was not the usual response. The general, if not invariable, pattern was that, if a work was discovered to be pseudonymous, it was excluded from any group of authoritative writings. For example, Tertullian (*Baptism* 17) in the early third century tells of the author of "3 Corinthians" (mid-second century) being removed from the office of presbyter.[8] Bishop Salonius rejected Salvian's pamphlet written to the church in Timothy's name.[9] The best-known example is the instance where Bishop Serapion of Antioch rejected the *Gospel of Peter* around 200. According to Eusebius, after Serapion discovered the *Gospel of Peter* being read, he wrote to the church at Rhossus in Cilicia, "We receive both Peter and the other apostles as Christ; but as experienced men we reject the writings falsely inscribed with their names, since we know that we did not receive such from our fathers" (*Ecclesiastical History* 6.12.1–6 LCL). Despite initial tolerance because of its seeming innocuousness, the *Gospel of Peter* was rejected through a complex process that involved espe-

7. See M. Kiley, *Colossians as Pseudepigraphy* (BS 4; Sheffield: JSOT Press, 1986), 18 and nn9–12; cf. pp. 17–23, for reference to, and citation of, primary sources for the above; B. M. Metzger, "Literary Forgeries and Canonical Pseudepigrapha," *JBL* 91 (1972): 3–24 at 6 and passim, who discusses many instances of exposed pseudepigrapha; and K. J. Dover, *Lysias and the Corpus Lysiacum* (Berkeley: University of California Press, 1968).

8. See Carson, Moo, and Morris, *Introduction*, 368–69, who also cite the example of the letter to the Laodiceans, which, according to the Muratorian Fragment, was clearly rejected by the early church along with a letter to the Alexandrians; see G. M. Hahneman, *The Muratorian Fragment and the Development of the Canon* (Oxford Theological Monographs; Oxford: Clarendon, 1992), 196–200.

9. Donelson, *Pseudepigraphy and Ethical Argument*, 20–22; and Ellis, "Pseudonymity and Canonicity of New Testament Documents," 218.

cially theological and ecclesiastical issues, not least recognition of its false attribution of authorship.

Admittedly, in the ancient world, including that of Christianity, the several means and reasons by which pseudepigrapha were exposed and excluded from authoritative collections are diverse. One of the common arguments cited in favor of including pseudepigraphal writings in any canon is the so-called noble lie—that it is in the best interests of the readers that they not know or are deceived regarding authorship by someone other than the purported author. Lewis Donelson points out the shortcomings of this approach: the noble lie is still a lie, with all of the attendant moral implications.[10] Mark Kiley rightly claims that this gives valuable insight into pseudepigraphers' motives (indeed, it does).[11] Nevertheless, when they were detected, their work was discredited, no matter how noble the motive. As Donelson further observes: "No one ever seems to have accepted a document as religiously and philosophically prescriptive which was known to be forged. I do not know a single example."[12] He includes both Christian and non-Christian documents in this assessment.

2. Pseudonymity and the Pauline Letters

Contrary to some recent discussions, it is not so simple to establish pseudonymous authorship of any of the letters of the Pauline corpus simply by appealing to the New Testament letters that are disputed or even highly doubted, such as the Pastoral Epistles, Ephesians, possibly 2 Thessalonians and Colossians, or even 2 Peter. Such an appeal simply introduces a circularity to the argumentation, which can be solved only by discovery of some sort of external criteria to adjudicate the issues. But this poses difficulties in several respects. There are apparently no known explicit statements from the early centuries of the Christian church that someone knew that any of the Pauline letters were pseudonymous, so this line of inquiry does not resolve the issue. Nor is it sufficient to cite non-canonical Jewish, or especially Christian, documents as examples of pseudon-

10. Donelson, *Pseudepigraphy and Ethical Argument*, 18–22. The noble lie refers to Plato's acceptance of a lie that is useful for the one to whom the lie is told (see *Republic* 2.376e–82b; 3.389b, 414ce). The question might well be raised whether the noble lie was involved in efforts for acceptance of Hebrews. That Hebrews is anonymous removes it from discussion here.

11. Kiley, *Colossians*, 21.

12. Donelson, *Pseudepigraphy and Ethical Argument*, 11. Donelson (p. 18) notes that *Apostolic Constitutions* 6.16 accuses certain books of being forgeries while itself being pseudepigraphal. But this fourth-century (or later) document had limited acceptance for only a short period of time. It may not have been known to be pseudepigraphal during this time.

ymous literature, as if this proves its existence in the New Testament.[13] That
these documents are noncanonical is apparent confirmation that documents
found to be pseudonymous did not ultimately find a place in the canon, even
if this process of "discovery" took some time.[14] If anything, it might constitute
a prima facie argument that, at least for the sake of discussion at the outset, all
of the Pauline letters should be considered authentic, since they all survived
scrutiny and now are in the New Testament canon. Since, in the discussion of
the biblical books, issues such as style, language, and theology are inconclusive
and highly contentious (despite the claims of some scholars), argumentation
must be utilized that does not appeal to the body of primary texts in dispute.[15]

David Meade puts forward a suggestion regarding pseudepigraphy that
is fairly widely accepted.[16] His supposition is that, within the Old Testament,
there is a tradition of pseudonymous literature, in which traditions were supplemented, interpreted, and expanded in the names of earlier authors. He gives
three major traditions: the prophetic, the wisdom, and the apocalyptic. The
only one with direct relevance to the New Testament is the prophetic tradition.[17] Particularly in Isaiah, Meade sees this tradition developed by anonymous writers whose later writings were attached to the earlier authentic Isaiah.
Hence, Second Isaiah is not by the historical Isaiah who is attested in First
Isaiah itself and elsewhere in the Old Testament, but it can still be understood
only in terms of First Isaiah.[18]

Several factors need to be considered further, however, before this pattern
can be applied to the New Testament. It is easy to think that Meade's argument
has a parallel in the Pauline letters, since there was a pattern of attributing

13. A. T. Lincoln, *Ephesians* (WBC 42; Dallas: Word, 1990), lxx–lxxi.

14. This includes the Jewish works 2 Esdras and *1–2 Enoch* and the Christian works *Didache, 2 Clement, Barnabas,* etc. Admittedly, some of these documents floated on the edges of
various corpora of authoritative writings for some time.

15. A strong argument against pseudonymity in the Pauline corpus was recently made,
however, by drawing upon the idea that literature, even by the same author, has different
stylistic characteristics depending upon the particular type of literature involved (i.e., the linguistic notion of register). See A. W. Pitts, "Style and Pseudonymity in Pauline Scholarship: A
Register-Based Configuration," in *Paul and Pseudepigraphy* (ed. S. E. Porter and G. P. Fewster;
PAST 8; Leiden: Brill, 2013), 113–52.

16. D. Meade, *Pseudonymity and Canon* (WUNT 39; Tübingen: Mohr-Siebeck, 1986), esp.
17–43. His position was accepted by, e.g., Lincoln, *Ephesians,* lxviii.

17. The wisdom tradition in the Old Testament is essentially confined to anonymous
literature, and the apocalyptic tradition is confined to Daniel, for whom there is no tradition
of being an illustrious hero.

18. For a discussion of the growth of the Isaiah tradition, see Meade, *Pseudonymity and
Canon,* 26–42.

writings to a recognized figure, possibly and even probably after the person's death, and that this practice was known to the audience. But this is only a superficial similarity. First, the type of literature is different. Isaiah is anonymous literature, better compared with, for example, the Gospels. The Pauline letters are directly attributed to a known author. Second, the process of literary production is different. In the Isaianic writings, the tradition was expanded and compiled and the document itself grew. In the Pauline letters, the argument would have to be that the tradition grew by adding new documents to the corpus, not merely by expanding those in the corpus. This would imply that the corpus had already been gathered together—something not sufficiently established to be used as evidence in this discussion—and that the theology of the added letters posed no problem when placed side by side with the authoritative Pauline letters.[19] If such a process truly occurred, inclusion must have been early, since attestation of many, if not most, of the now disputed Pauline letters in the church fathers ranges from possibly as early as *1 Clement* to the third quarter of the second century. Third and most problematic for his theory, Meade himself admits that one cannot use the tool that he devised for discovering the pseudonymous origins of a given piece of literature.[20] His schema, according to his own analysis, is devised to explain the possible development of the tradition once it is shown that the material is pseudonymous. In other words, his proposal does not solve the issue being considered here of how to determine whether a work is pseudonymous. To my knowledge, no proposed scheme circumvents the difficulties raised above.

Before drawing out the implications for the New Testament canon, it is important to discuss the issue of deception in pseudonymous literature. This is a particularly sensitive issue. Apart from Donelson and only a few others, few scholars apparently want to admit that deception may have had a role to play in canonical formation and acceptance of any of the books in the New Testament: "We are forced to admit that in Christian circles pseudonymity was considered a dishonorable device and, if discovered, the document was rejected and the author, if known, was excoriated."[21] There were, nevertheless, all sorts of encouragements for skillful pseudepigraphal writing in the ancient world, including pietistic motives prompting those in the church to speak for an earlier figure,[22] and self-serving motives, such as the money paid by libraries for manuscripts

---

19. On the assembling of the Pauline corpus, with Paul probably involved for most, if not all, of his extant letters, see §4 below.

20. Meade, *Pseudonymity and Canon*, esp. 16.

21. Donelson, *Pseudepigraphy and Ethical Argument*, 16.

22. It is questionable whether this motive can be considered an innocent one. See Donelson, *Pseudepigraphy and Ethical Argument*, 10.

by particular authors.[23] This all occurred in the context of the apparently guaranteed exclusion of any document from an author's corpus upon discovery of its pseudonymous nature. This forces Donelson to conclude that the only way to speak of the Pastoral Epistles, with which he is directly concerned, is that they were produced and consequently accepted into the canon in conjunction with deception.[24] The same would presumably apply to any of the other supposedly pseudonymous Pauline letters. Of course, he is assuming that these letters are not genuinely Pauline. He goes further, however, claiming that eighteen of the twenty-seven books of the New Testament are pseudepigraphal and were included under deceptive means.[25] He has apparently joined anonymity with pseudonymity at this point (and thus unfortunately confused the issue further).

Donelson's analysis, however, needs to be considered further. This can be conveniently done by considering the circumstances surrounding the production of the Pastoral Epistles, in particular their personal features and the original audience or receivers of the letters. Many scholars struggle with the difficulties in the circumstances of these letters if they are authentic. The same questions must arise, however, regarding pseudonymous authorship. As Meade recognizes, if they are pseudonymous, there is a "double pseudonymity" of both author and audience, that is, we do not know the author or the original audience.[26] What sort of situations were at play when these letters were received into the church? It is undecided, even by those who take the Pastoral Epistles as pseudonymous, when the letters were written and/or regarded as authoritative; dates of pseudonymous composition range from an early date of 80–90 to the last half of the second century. In any case, the original audience would almost assuredly have known that Paul was dead. Were the letters simply introduced as new letters from Paul, or at least inspired by situations such that Paul would have said these things had he been there? Many argue that these pseudonymous writings are transparent fictions that no one would have thought were actually written by Paul. This reasoning, however, encounters this problem: why were they acknowledged in the first instance in light of the apparently universal response by the early church to known pseudepigrapha, which, as I have demonstrated, were consistently rejected? Also, this theory does not account satisfactorily for three important features of the Pastoral

23. See also M. L. Stirewalt Jr., *Studies in Ancient Greek Epistolography* (Society of Biblical Literature Resources for Biblical Study 27; Atlanta: Scholars Press, 1993), 31–42.

24. Donelson, *Pseudepigraphy and Ethical Argument*, 54–66.

25. Donelson, *Pseudepigraphy and Ethical Argument*, 16, citing M. Rist, "Pseudepigraphy and the Early Christians," in *Studies in New Testament and Early Christian Literature: Essays in Honor of A. P. Wikgren* (ed. D. E. Aune; NovTSup 33; Leiden: Brill, 1972), 75–91 at 89.

26. Meade, *Pseudonymity in the New Testament*, 127.

Epistles that have parallels in most of the disputed Pauline letters: (1) the specific selection of Timothy and Titus as the recipients of the letters, two men who would also by then have been dead or who would have been themselves in some sense literary creations; (2) the need for inclusion of very personal and arguably unnecessary details, especially in 2 Timothy regarding Paul's own life; and (3) the acceptance and endorsement of their developed theology.

An explanation might be that perhaps the letters were not simply introduced as what Paul would have said but were in some way subtly integrated into a collection of Paul's letters or slipped undetected into a collection that was being put together, something like a skilled sleight-of-hand artist slipping a card or two into a deck of cards. What could have accounted for such an action? It is easy to say that only the best motives would have governed this behavior, in the sense that the person who wrote them was a follower of the great apostle, Paul, and thought that he had been inspired to pass on words that the apostle would have conveyed to a serious situation. The person—and ultimately we must speak of a person or, at the least, a very small group of confederates—must have known that to come forward and say that the letter was not by Paul would have meant its rejection (and ecclesiastical trouble for that person); otherwise the efforts taken for its acceptance would not have been necessary. To extend this further, the same person may not have slipped the document into the system but may have discovered the document one day in a pile of the Pauline letters and, upon reading it, realized that this was Paul's word to a particular situation. This hypothesis encounters three difficulties requiring explanation:

1. The endorsement of the recognizably developed theology of the Pastoral Epistles (as noted above) presents a problem (see chapter 12 §3B).
2. The time lag between writing and discovery must have been relatively short, since some of the letters appear to have been at least known and possibly acknowledged, if not accepted, fairly soon (see chapters 7–12 for discussion of individual letters). The pseudepigraphal letters would have needed to penetrate Pauline churches to trade on the force of pseudepigraphal authorship, and that we have Pauline letters attests to the early respect given to his writings. This means that the risk of detection must have been even greater, with less time elapsing between the time of the apostle's life and the writing of the pseudepigraphal letters.
3. This scenario simply pushes back the deception a little further; the deception must have been perpetrated by someone earlier than the one discovering the letters. In any case, deception becomes a part of the process. In this instance, it would be a successful deception, since the church apparently accepted the letters as genuine.

In his commentary on Ephesians, Andrew Lincoln recognizes—if only in passing—several of these issues. At the end of his discussion, however, he says that pseudonymity does not affect canonicity or detract from the validity or authority of the particular pseudonymous document as part of the New Testament canon. He argues that to worry about such a thing is committing what he calls the "authorial fallacy," which he defines as setting more store by who wrote a document than by what it says.[27] As a first response, this may be applicable to formally anonymous documents, such as the Gospels or Hebrews, but not pseudonymous documents that identify a particular author as their source. Lincoln's authorial fallacy, however, requires further scrutiny. It seems that the question of authorship actually does have serious implications, even if it may not (and this is a highly debatable point) affect our understanding of what a document says. First of all, each of the Pauline letters in the New Testament is ascribed to a particular author, one who is well known in the New Testament. These letters are not anonymous, without any line of definite connection. Why would a pseudepigrapher have selected "Paul" as his pseudonym if authorial ascription were not important?[28] The convention of pseudepigraphal writing seems to demand ascription to an important and illustrious figure.

Second, even if one may have some sense of how to read a letter but not know who the author is, for Ephesians—as well as any other disputed Pauline letter—authorship does make a difference. Authorship is important for determining whether the situation being addressed is one in the 50s or the 180s, whether one is reading a letter confronting problems at the beginning of the Christian movement or developed problems of, for example, church order of an already institutionalized church.[29]

Third, one evaluates whether any disputed Pauline letter is pseudonymous by comparing it with the undisputedly authentic Pauline letters; otherwise there would be no issue at all. If Lincoln really believes that authorship makes no difference, then perhaps even asking the question of authorship at all is unnecessary or committing the "authorial fallacy," for these as well as any other books of the New Testament.

Fourth, the Pauline authorial question has consequences regarding the

---

27. Lincoln, *Ephesians*, lxxiii.

28. Some reasons pseudepigrapha occurred may include gaining acceptance for a particular perspective that the writer otherwise would not have received, giving honor to an earlier hero of the faith, or simply deceiving in order to gain acceptance. Cf. McDonald and Porter, *Early Christianity and Its Sacred Literature*, 639–41.

29. A clear case in point is Hebrews. Since so little is known of such issues as authorship, date of composition, addressees, and situation, the range of proposals is very wide.

New Testament canon. Lincoln is probably not implying that the canon should still be open and that documents that say the right things, whoever wrote them and whenever, should be included. He seems to be saying that the documents being considered are part of the accepted canon of documents of the church and hence should not be deleted but, rather, continue to be interpreted within this group. What is missing, however, is a recognition of how the church's canon came to be, especially the collection of Pauline letters. It is doubtful that Lincoln would say that the canon was given directly by God one day and had no more historical process to it than that. He could say with others that canonical formation involved a complex process intertwining various authorial, historical, theological, and interpretive issues, some of which have been raised above.

More recently, Bart Ehrman argues that many of the New Testament writings are pseudepigraphal (he prefers the term "forgery"), including some letters in the Pauline corpus.[30] Though he takes an extreme view regarding which New Testament books are pseudonymous,[31] he acknowledges that ancient pseudonymous literature was considered deceptive (hence, he uses the negative term "forgery" instead of "pseudonymity" or "pseudepigraphy"), but that these "forgers" committed these forgeries in the name of carrying on the Christian tradition.[32] Ehrman contends that, in the case of these forgers, they believed that the means justified the end of communicating the Christian message, and that, much like telling a white lie in order to prevent an assassination, the greater good prevailed over the deception (the noble lie, which I have already addressed above). He writes that the "authors assumed false names for one chief end: to provide for their views an authority that otherwise would have proved difficult to obtain had they written anonymously or in their own names."[33] His support for this, however, should be scrutinized further. He begins by asserting that pseudonymity was a commonly accepted phenomenon in antiquity, which contention I have already assessed and disputed above. He also asserts that there was much doctrinal controversy in the early Christian

---

30. B. Ehrman, *Forgery and Counterforgery: The Use of Literary Deceit in Early Christian Polemics* (Oxford: Oxford University Press, 2013), 1, 29–32. I critique Ehrman elsewhere regarding other text-critical issues and his exaggerated and unfounded conclusions; cf. S. E. Porter, *How We Got the New Testament: Text, Transmission, Translation* (ASBT; Grand Rapids: Baker, 2013), 65–72.

31. He considers nearly half of the New Testament as forgeries: Acts, Ephesians, Colossians, 2 Thessalonians, 1 Timothy, 2 Timothy, Titus, Hebrews, James, 1 Peter, 2 Peter, 1 John, and Jude (Ehrman, *Forgeries and Counterforgeries*, 529).

32. Ehrman, *Forgeries and Counterforgeries*, 546–48.

33. Ehrman, *Forgeries and Counterforgeries*, 150.

movement, and that many would have tried to contend for their truth. This is a fair generalization with which many would not disagree, although it can be greatly exaggerated. Nevertheless, these assertions alone do not necessitate that any of the New Testament books are pseudonymous.

Ehrman provides some general criteria by which ancient works were apparently determined to be pseudonymous, including variations in style, anachronisms and other historical problems, internal inconsistencies and implausibilities, theological *Sachkritik* (content criticism), and established patterns of usage,[34] and he uses these criteria to evaluate the New Testament books in question. The problem with these criteria, however, is that most of them, if not all of them, are highly subjective and ultimately indecisive, so that what one may consider inconsistent may be considered by another entirely consistent.[35] For example, because Paul uses fewer conjunctions in one letter compared to some of his other letters, does this require a different author?[36] This is highly doubtful. Much of Ehrman's argumentation for the forgery of these New Testament books is subjective in nature and requires much more substantive evidence to support his contention. In fact, most of the arguments are long known; most of them are inconclusive; and his discussion does not advance our knowledge or the state of discussion further.

3. Pseudonymity and New Testament Canonicity

With regard to New Testament canonicity, a number of factors must be weighed concerning the authorship of the Pauline letters. The internal evidence on the authorship of the disputed Pauline letters is often so ambiguous

34. Ehrman, *Forgeries and Counterforgeries*, 137–45.

35. For a good essay from a robust linguistic perspective regarding style and pseudonymity, see Pitts, "Style and Pseudonymity in Pauline Scholarship."

36. Citing Bujard, Ehrman (*Forgeries and Counterforgeries*, 175–76) notes the total number of conjunctions among several Pauline letters: 33 in Galatians, 31 in Philippians, 31 in 1 Thessalonians, but only 21 in Colossians. But when subtracting from these totals the conjunctions that occur in all the letters in question, because they are common words, the numbers become more revealing: 24 in Galatians, 22 in Philippians, 22 in 1 Thessalonians, but only 12 in Colossians. Bujard is said to go even further, subtracting those that occur in all but one of the letters in question, resulting in 24 in Galatians, 22 in Philippians, 22 in 1 Thessalonians, but only 12 in Colossians. What Ehrman overlooks, without even addressing the fallacy of conjunction counting, is that there may be a whole host of other factors to explain the "lack" of conjunctions in Colossians, other than a different author. See W. Bujard, *Stilanalytische Untersuchungen zum Kolosserbrief als Beitrag zur Methodik von Sprachvergleichen* (Göttingen: Vandenhoeck & Ruprecht, 1973), whose method can be described as only primitive at best.

that the issue cannot be decided simply on the basis of these factors.[37] The only reasonably strong basis for doubting the authenticity of the disputed letters is the developed theology thought to be found in each (e.g., purported changes in eschatological perspective, developed church order, views of personal relationships) and seen by many to be out of harmony with the "authentic" Pauline letters. That theological issues are the most distinguishing features of these letters, and yet all of the letters were accepted without demur, as far as we know, prompts the thought that there must have been other important factors at play if any of the letters are not Pauline. If they are not authentically Pauline, one must face certain implications for these books as part of the New Testament canon. The question of implications regarding canonicity cannot simply be dismissed.

For some, an authoritative canon is completely outmoded. This does not mean that the questions raised in this section are unimportant, however. The process of canonical formation in the early church, regardless of our not knowing as much as we would like, is important for both historical and theological reasons.

For those who are concerned about an authoritative canon of the New Testament, other issues are brought into prominence if some of the Pauline letters are not by Paul. First, in light of theological development and possible pseudepigraphal authorship, the disputed or pseudonymous Pauline letters should not be used in describing Pauline theology.[38] Pauline theology is here a slippery term, but one that must be defined at least in part. For some, it may simply mean a theology of all of the letters attributed to Paul, whether genuine or not, because they are in the New Testament canon. The disputed letters would thereby constitute evidence for the diversity of early Pauline theology so defined. For those concerned with trying to establish a Pauline theology based on what Paul may have actually thought and written, pseudonymous letters, of course, cannot be used to create a Pauline theology in this sense. They are instead part of a record of how some people responded to Paul, how successors developed his thought, how some people applied his ideas to later situations, or even how some people wished Paul could have spoken—each such letter can never be more than only one interpretation among many others. That they were included in the canon has enhanced their authority and may mean

37. Cf. Pitts, "Style and Pseudonymity in Pauline Scholarship," who suggests some new ways forward in this regard.

38. See S. E. Porter, "Is There a Center to Paul's Theology? An Introduction to the Study of Paul and His Theology," in *Paul and His Theology* (ed. S. E. Porter; PAST 3; Leiden: Brill, 2006), 1–19, esp. 14–16.

that they represent the most influential or powerful followers of Paul, but it would not raise their level of authenticity. They still would not be authentically Pauline and thus should not be used to formulate a *Pauline* theology.[39]

Second, we must come to terms with the question of deception in the New Testament, in particular concerning the Pauline letters. Is it so difficult to believe that the early church was in some way fooled into accepting these letters? As Donelson says, "We are further forced to admit . . . that the disreputable practice [of pseudepigraphy] was extremely common in early Christianity."[40] If the letters are not authentic, this must be the answer, since there is no clear record of objection to their acceptance. It seems likely, if any of the letters are inauthentic, that someone tried to ensure their acceptance by various means, including use of the Pauline letter form, inclusion of personal details, imitation of the Pauline style, and, especially, direct attribution to Paul. The writers apparently went to such lengths to include these items in the disputed letters because these "faithful" disciples, knowing that exposure as a forger would have meant trouble for themselves and their writings, were using every means possible to create as plausible a deception as possible. Their motives for writing may well have been noble, including finding a way for Paul to speak to their communities, but deception it was nevertheless.

It may even be postulated that the early church rightly accepted some of these writings, even if it was for the wrong reasons and under the wrong circumstances. This raises a new set of questions. For example, have certain documents been excluded from the canon simply because they were exposed as pseudonymous, when their motives for being written may have been no worse (and in fact better) than those of others and their content may well have been perfectly orthodox, perhaps even more edifying than some others? Why should these documents have been excluded simply because they were unable to escape detection? Why should the successfully deceptive document be privileged over the others, simply because of tradition, lack of perception, historical precedent, or having the proper content? These and related issues must be given due consideration in light of recent scholarship on pseudepigraphy and the authorship of books in the New Testament. These tough questions do not necessarily advocate for inclusion of pseudonymous writings in the Pauline canon. To the contrary, the difficulty of answering these questions, combined with the evidence available, points to the Pauline letters being actually authentic.

---

39. This raises the issue of a canon within a canon. See E. Käsemann, "The Canon of the New Testament Church and the Unity of the Church," in *Essays on New Testament Themes* (trans. W. J. Montague; London: SCM, 1968), 95–107.

40. Donelson, *Pseudepigraphy and Ethical Argument*, 16.

The implications of such an analysis can be seen in the discussion in chapter 4 regarding the essence of Paul's theology. The major categories discussed rely most heavily upon the undisputed major letters. But many of the categories are also enhanced by reference to significant passages in Paul's other letters as well. A factor not as fully appreciated as it might be, especially by students first coming to terms with the message of Paul's letters, is the difference that the issue of authorship makes for determining Paul's theology. A similar situation is found in the individual treatment of Paul's letters, as illustrated in the following chapters. The character and description of the corpus is affected by authorship.

4. The Pauline Letter Collection and Canon

The issue of the Pauline canon raises the question of how the Pauline letter collection came to be.[41] Assuming that the current Pauline canon (regardless of whether Hebrews should be included) is in fact the right one (as I think that it is), in light of what has been affirmed above, it seems that fairly early on Paul's letters received recognition as being of special worth (2 Pet 3:16), even if we apparently do not have all of them (see Col 4:16 regarding the reading of the now unknown Laodicean letter [cf. chapter 11 §5D4], and note 1 Cor 5:9 and the several letters to the Corinthians). What kinds of efforts were taken to gather together Paul's letters, which had been sent to various places in the Mediterranean world? And when were they collected?

Two important benchmarks that are useful in the discussion of the Pauline letter collection include Paul's death, which was probably around 65, after which no authentic letter could be written, and 𝔓46, a papyrus of Paul's letters dated to around 200.[42] 𝔓46 is an important document for this discussion, since

41. This section draws from previous work I have done and some material is taken verbatim; cf. S. E. Porter, "When and How Was the Pauline Canon Compiled? An Assessment of Theories," in *The Pauline Canon* (ed. S. E. Porter; PAST 1; Leiden: Brill, 2004), 95–128; "Paul and the Process of Canonization," in *Exploring the Origins of the Bible: Canon Formation in Historical, Literary, and Theological Perspective* (ed. C. A. Evans and E. Tov; ASBT; Grand Rapids: Baker, 2008), 173–202; "Paul and the Pauline Letter Collection," in *Paul and the Second Century* (ed. M. F. Bird and J. R. Dodson; LNTS 412; London: T&T Clark, 2011), 19–36; and *How We Got the New Testament*, 111–20.

42. There is much debate surrounding the dating of 𝔓46, but the generally accepted date is around 200. See S. R. Pickering, "The Dating of the Chester Beatty-Michigan Codex of the Pauline Epistles (𝔓46)," in *Ancient History in a Modern University* (ed. T. W. Hillard, R. A. Kearsley, C. E. V. Nixon, and A. M. Nobbs; 2 vols.; New South Wales, Australia: Ancient History Documentary Research Centre Macquarie University; Grand Rapids: Eerdmans, 1998),

it is one of the earliest extant manuscripts of the New Testament, and it contains most of Paul's letters, except for the Pastorals and parts of 2 Thessalonians and Philemon (the end of the manuscript is missing seven leaves). There are various explanations of the "missing letters." Some think that they were not included because they were not yet written (e.g., the Pastoral Epistles), while others think that the codex itself was limited to ten of the letters or that there was insufficient space to include the other three.[43] Another interesting fact about 𝔓46 is that it places Hebrews after Romans and before 1 Corinthians. Some suggest that Hebrews was a later addition to the Pauline collection, but its presence in 𝔓46 requires further discussion on the status of Hebrews as a Pauline letter.[44] Two other second-century "documents" that are important for this discussion are Marcion's canon (however, since we do not have in our possession today any direct writing of his, it is based on others who wrote of him) and the Muratorian Fragment.

About six prevalent theories address the issue of the formation of the Pauline letter collection.[45] The first, and probably the most dominant, of the theories is what is called the "gradual collection" theory,[46] which contends that the letters were gradually collected as their enduring value was realized. The origination of this theory is credited to German scholars Theodor Zahn and Adolf Harnack.[47] The letters would have first circulated in the regions to which they were addressed (Asia Minor, Rome, Macedonia, Achaia/Greece), then these regional collections would have been joined together. While proponents

---

2.216–27; and P. W. Comfort and D. P. Barrett, *The Text of the Earliest New Testament Greek Manuscripts* (Wheaton, IL: Tyndale House, 2001), 204–6.

43. E.g., J. D. Quinn, "𝔓46—The Pauline Canon?" *Catholic Biblical Quarterly* 36 (1974): 379–85; and J. Duff, "𝔓46 and the Pastorals: A Misleading Consensus?" *NTS* 44 (1998): 578–90.

44. See G. Zuntz, *The Text of the Epistles: A Disquisition upon the Corpus Paulinum* (Schweich Lectures 1946; London: British Academy, 1953), 15–16; and D. Trobisch, *Paul's Letter Collection: Tracing the Origins* (Minneapolis: Fortress, 1994), 20.

45. This section is a summary of Porter, "Paul and the Pauline Letter Collection," esp. 22–35; Porter, "When and How Was the Pauline Canon Compiled?" esp. 99–121. See also A. G. Patzia, *The Making of the New Testament: Origin, Collection, Text, and Canon* (Downers Grove, IL: InterVarsity, 1995), 80–83.

46. The term "gradual collection theory" is found in H. Y. Gamble, *New Testament Canon: Its Making and Meaning* (Philadelphia: Fortress, 1985), 36. C. F. D. Moule (*The Birth of the New Testament* [3rd ed.; San Francisco: Harper & Row, 1982], 263) calls it the "snowball" theory.

47. Their theories are found in the following important (though untranslated) works: T. Zahn, *Geschichte des Neutestamentlichen Kanons* (2 vols.; Erlangen: Deichert, 1888–92), 1.811–39; Zahn, *Grundriss der Geschichte des Neutestamentlichen Kanons: Eine Ergänzung zu der Einleitung in das Neue Testament* (Leipzig: Deichert, 1904), esp. 35–37; and A. Harnack, *Die Briefsammlung des Apostels Paulus und die anderen vorkonstantinischen Briefsammlungen* (Leipzig: Hinrichs, 1926), 6–27.

of this theory differ on the exact details of how the collection actually took place and which letters were actually included in the collection, the general consensus that unites the view is that there was a relatively early collection of these letters by the early church for the purpose of using them in liturgical worship, based on the references to Paul's letters in writings from *1 Clement*, Polycarp, and Ignatius. Most proponents of this theory take the second century to be a significant period of either solidifying the Pauline canon or consolidating it from other sources. The evidence for this position, however, is slight, and the difficulties—such as what or who compelled the regional collections to be joined together—are great.

In the second theory, sometimes called the "lapsed interest" theory,[48] a number of scholars follow Edgar Goodspeed and his student John Knox in arguing that Paul's letters were collected around 90 when, after a lapse of interest, there was a revival of interest in Paul's letters after publication of Acts. Goodspeed's theory that Ephesians was written as a type of cover letter for this collection is less widely received. The basis for this theory is the prominence of Ephesus as the second most important center of Christianity, next to Syrian Antioch, and hence a major place for Christian writing (e.g., Revelation, the Gospel and Epistles of John, letters of Ignatius).[49] A main argument for this view is that the book of Acts does not contain any acknowledgment of Paul's letters, whereas Christian literature after Acts contains references to them. After Acts was composed and disseminated, due to its focus on Paul as a premier apostle of the Christian movement, interest in Paul's letters became widespread, and efforts were made to gather them into a single collection. The difficulty with Goodspeed's hypothesis is the lack of evidence that interest in Paul's letters lapsed. Another problem, however, is that evidence from the second century also provides material that calls this theory into question, especially the notion of Ephesians as a cover letter for the Pauline letter collection. Besides the lack of text-critical evidence supporting this notion, most of the second-century documents point to other letters at the head of the collection— Marcion seems to place Galatians at the head, the Muratorian Fragment refers to Corinthians first, and 𝔓46 has Romans in this place.

---

48. This label can be attributable to D. Guthrie, *New Testament Introduction* (4th ed.; Downers Grove, IL: InterVarsity, 1990), 990–96.

49. E. J. Goodspeed wrote on this topic many times. See *New Solutions of New Testament Problems* (Chicago: University of Chicago Press, 1927), 1–20; *The Meaning of Ephesians* (Chicago: University of Chicago Press, 1933); and *An Introduction to the New Testament* (Chicago: University of Chicago Press, 1937), 210–21; developed further by J. Knox, *Philemon among the Letters of Paul* (repr. London: Collins, 1960 [1935]); and C. L. Mitton, *The Formation of the Pauline Corpus of Letters* (London: Epworth, 1955).

A third proposal is what may be called the "composite antignostic" theory. Walter Schmithals, an advocate of Ferdinand Christian Baur's dialectic (or even evolutionary) hypothesis regarding the origins of early Christianity, proposes that the Pauline letters were collected as a response to some situation. The difference between Schmithals and Baur, however, is that the Pauline letters were not a response to Jewish lines of thought (as in Baur), but a response to the prevalent Gnosticism that threatened Christianity at the time.[50] Schmithals also argues that the Pauline letters are composite in nature—that they are themselves the product of compiling various earlier letters to various cities into the more organized canonical letters within the Pauline letter collection. He concludes that there were actually six Corinthians letters, four Thessalonian letters, three Philippian letters, two Roman letters, and one Galatian letter. These multiple letters were written in short periods of time during Paul's third missionary journey, and then later edited and assembled by someone else into the first collection of Paul's letters, sometime in the 80s and probably in Corinth. But even as Schmithals admits, this theory is highly speculative, depending upon a number of suppositions. One of them is that this theory is dependent upon an early development of Gnosticism, which many would not hold to today.[51] Although elements that came to be identified with Gnosticism are reflected in Hellenistic philosophy, the kind of full-blown Gnosticism required for this theory to hold does not appear until the second century, well after the Pauline letter collection had taken place. A second problem with this theory is Schmithals's fragmentary hypothesis, which is a fundamental presupposition. Even those who maintain that some of the Pauline letters have other Pauline fragments in them do not usually find nearly as many letter parts as does Schmithals. The evidence is simply scant for such an extreme fragmentary view of Paul's letters.

A fourth theory of the Pauline letter collection may be called the "personal involvement" theory, of which there are various versions. Although some other proposals posit a single person involved in the collection of Paul's letters (Marcion as first collector, Onesimus as letter gatherer, or some unnamed person), this is not a central feature of those proposals. Rather than seeing it

50. W. Schmithals, *Paul and the Gnostics* (trans. J. E. Steely; Nashville: Abingdon, 1972), 239–74; translation of "Zur Abfassung und ältesten Sammlung der paulinischen Hauptbriefe," *Zeitschrift für die neutestamentliche Wissenschaft* 51 (1960): 225–45.

51. Cf. E. M. Yamauchi, *Pre-Christian Gnosticism: A Survey of Proposed Evidence* (London: Tyndale, 1973); P. Perkins, *Gnosticism and the New Testament* (Minneapolis: Fortress, 1993), who attempts a mediating view; and K. L. King, *What Is Gnosticism?* (Cambridge, MA: Harvard University Press, 2003), who wishes to eliminate the term altogether in a reconsideration of issues of orthodoxy and heresy.

as an abstract process that is sometimes seen to be in effect in some of these proposals, some scholars argue that such a process of collection makes the best sense if a single individual was ultimately responsible for compiling the Pauline letter collection. There are at least three major versions of this theory. First, C. F. D. Moule argues that Luke was the person responsible for the Pauline letter collection.[52] According to him, although there is no mention of Paul's letters in Acts, Luke probably gathered the letters together after composing Acts and after Paul's death, when he revisited the major Pauline cities. This letter collection included the ten, without the Pastoral Epistles, as he believes the earliest references to Paul's letters indicate (e.g., $\mathfrak{P}$46), and, according to Moule, the number of similarities between Acts and the Pastoral Epistles, such as vocabulary, content, and overall perspective, indicate that Luke wrote the Pastoral Epistles. Donald Guthrie proposes a second version of the personal involvement theory; he argues that Timothy was the person responsible for the Pauline letter collection.[53] Contra the lapsed interest theory, Guthrie contends that interest in Paul strongly continued after his death, due to his close connections with the major churches as either their founder or contributor in other ways. Timothy's collection of Paul's letters after the composition of Acts accounts for the lack of mention of them in Acts, and his close association with Paul, especially during the latter part of Paul's ministry, makes Timothy a favorable candidate as the main collector of Paul's letters. A third version of this theory involves not just one particular individual but a number of collectors, or a so-called Pauline school theory.[54] This version includes not only Luke and Timothy, but possibly others associated with Paul. It contends that, following Paul's death, some of Paul's companions and followers gathered, and possibly edited, the Pauline tradition. This may have resulted in the continuing application of the Pauline tradition to new ecclesiastical situations and even composition of the pseudepigraphic deutero-Pauline letters. There is much merit in such personal involvement theories, since any gathering of Paul's letters involves actual individuals being a part of that process, whether singular or multiple, named or unnamed, recognized or anonymous. The question is whether there is any evidence for Luke or Timothy or someone else to have made the collection. As far as Luke goes, there is more evidence that Luke would have collected the Pauline letters, but the theory that he wrote the Pastoral Epistles has never been widely accepted due to its many problems. For example, the question of why Luke would have written Acts but not mention

---

52. Moule, *Birth of the New Testament*, 264–65.
53. Guthrie, *New Testament Introduction*, 999–1000.
54. Gamble, *New Testament Canon*, 39.

the Pauline letters, yet be involved in their collection, and then written the Pastorals subsequently is not easily answered according to this theory. The possibility of Timothy as the main collector does not fall prey to the same kinds of criticisms as Luke, but the major problem with Timothy is that it is based on Guthrie's narrow chronology of Paul's life. The problem with the Pauline school theory, which arose as a response to the problems with Luke or Timothy, is that it is unfalsifiable and too vague (who exactly were the members of this Pauline school, and how many of them were there?). Furthermore, the issue of pseudonymity still stands regarding the Pastoral Epistles.

A fifth proposal, what may be called the "Pauline involvement" theory, is that Paul himself may have been involved in collecting together his letters. On the basis of analysis of New Testament canonical lists, the letter collections that we have in the early papyri and codices, and other collections of writings by ancient authors, David Trobisch argues that Paul was responsible for, or at least instigated, collection of his letters, beginning with the first four—Romans, 1-2 Corinthians, and Galatians.[55] He states that it "is highly probable that this old collection was edited and prepared for publication by Paul himself."[56] The four-letter collection, in light of Paul's own editing activity, consists of Rom 16 as a cover letter for Romans and the Corinthians letters as compiled from seven different Pauline letters, with all of the letters written as Paul's Jerusalem defense for the collection and his missionary activities.[57] The entire corpus was gathered in three stages, according to Trobisch. The first stage was the aforementioned Romans to Galatians. Ephesians to 2 Thessalonians were gathered in the second stage (in this sense Trobisch's theory is similar to Goodspeed's, with Ephesians as the first letter, hence cover letter, of this collection). The third stage includes the Pastorals and Philemon, with Paul decreasingly involved in the course of the process. Trobisch notes that, although the letters are placed in order roughly according to length in words in our modern Bibles, Ephesians is actually longer than Galatians, and 1 Timothy longer than 1 or 2 Thessalonians. Trobisch notes that the order of Paul's letters according to length is actually reflected in 𝔓46 (with Ephesians preceding Galatians). These disjunctions indicate to him the literary seams formed in the assembling of the corpus. Along the lines of Trobisch, Jerome Murphy-O'Connor, without seeing Paul as the original collector but instead positing Timothy, also presents a tripartite formation of

---

55. Trobisch, *Paul's Letter Collection*, esp. 5–24. See also D. Trobisch, *The First Edition of the New Testament* (New York: Oxford University Press, 2000), esp. 38–41.

56. Trobisch, *Paul's Letter Collection*, 54.

57. Trobisch, *Paul's Letter Collection*, 71–86, 88–91.

the Pauline letter collection.[58] According to him, the first collection consisted of Romans, 1–2 Corinthians, and Galatians and originated at Corinth; the second consisted of letters from neighboring churches in Asia Minor and Greece; and the third collection consisted of personal letters that were added to the first two. He bases his analysis upon the inconsistencies in decreases in length from Galatians to Ephesians and from 2 Thessalonians to 1 Timothy to indicate these three different collections. Although there is some merit to Trobisch's view, especially the possibility that Paul was involved, at least in the early stages, in collecting his own corpus of letters, the partial return to Baur's hypothesis on the authentic four letters is untenable (see chapters 11–12). Very few today argue that Baur's hypothesis is correct, and even the most skeptical concede at least seven authentic letters of Paul, with many scholars arguing for a greater number than seven (some would even include Hebrews to make the total number fourteen!). But even if seven letters are authentically Pauline, then Trobisch's scheme falls apart, because the first two expansive stages collapse. At most, Trobisch's evidence points to Paul's possible involvement in the initial stages of gathering together the entire collection of what we call the Pauline letter corpus. Furthermore, Murphy O'Connor shows that Trobisch's theory does not necessitate Paul's early involvement in the letter collection.

The sixth, and final, proposal is a variation of the Pauline involvement theory that I advocate elsewhere.[59] This proposal argues that Paul was involved not only in the collection of the four letters that Trobisch claims but in the entire thirteen-letter corpus attributed to him. While I realize that, initially, there may be some disagreement as to the authenticity of all thirteen letters of Paul, I believe that a good case can be made for Paul's authorship of all of them.[60] In defense of my proposal regarding Paul's gathering the entire corpus of his letters, there are a number of points of consensus from all of the previous theories noted above. These include the recognition that there was personal involvement of someone close to Paul and interested in his letters, the lack of need for theories that depend upon fragmentary hypotheses and the need to assemble Paul's letters before compiling them, the probability of there being a single gathering place of the letters and hence a limitation to the number of

58. J. Murphy-O'Connor, *Paul the Letter-Writer: His World, His Options, His Skills* (Collegeville, MN: Liturgical, 1995), 120–30.

59. See Porter, "Paul and the Pauline Letter Collection," 32–35; "Paul and the Process of Canonization," 191–200; and "When and How Was the Pauline Canon Compiled?" 121–27.

60. Many will find this point alone to be a serious objection. This theory, however, is based upon the personal and Pauline involvement hypothesis and the structure of $\mathfrak{P}46$ as its primary support. Nevertheless, I believe that a case can in fact be made for authenticity of all thirteen letters in the Pauline letter collection.

Pauline letter collections from the start of the transmission process, and the importance of 𝔓46 as the earliest manuscript that evidences a Pauline letter collection. While there is much debate regarding 𝔓46, there seems to be good evidence that it included at one point 2 Thessalonians and Philemon, and possibly even the Pastoral Epistles as well.[61] This evidence includes what we know about Marcion from Tertullian, the structure and reconstructed length of the manuscript, and what we know about Pauline letter-collection manuscripts. As Trobisch says, there is "no manuscript evidence to prove that the letters of Paul ever existed in an edition containing only some of the thirteen letters."[62]

Besides the above points of consensus, there are also some further arguments to be made in support of the Pauline involvement theory for all thirteen letters. The first is that it is entirely possible for one person to have collected the entire Pauline corpus, as the geographical distribution of these letters is not that wide. All of the letters—including the Pastoral Epistles—are confined within a roughly 1,100-mile expanse that stretches from Galatia in the east to Rome in the west, with other cities such as Colossae, Ephesus, Philippi, Thessalonica, and Corinth in between. Additionally, most of the letters were sent to cities or people within 150 miles from the Aegean Sea. Second, and more importantly, is the common practice in the ancient world of letter writers retaining copies of letters that were sent, especially those that were deemed to be important. Murphy-O'Connor notes that "it was normal practice for a copy of a letter to be retained by the sender."[63] A number of papyri contain copies of another person's letter (P.Zenon 10, 43) or refer to copies of letters being made (P.Mich. inv. 855; 8.498). There is also evidence that letters being written by and to Cicero were copied (*Epistulae ad Atticum* 1.17; 3.9; 13.6.3; *Brutus* 1.16.1; *Epistulae ad familiares* 3.3.2; 7.25.1; 9.12.2; 9.26.1; 10.12.2; 10.32.5; 10.33.2; *Epistulae ad Quintum fratrem* 2.12.4), as well as reference being made to the general practice of copying (*Epistulae ad familiares* 7.18.2; cf. Plutarch, *Eumenes* 2.2–3), but Cicero also refers to gathering his own letters into a collection (*Epistulae ad Atticum* 13; 16.5.5).[64] This practice of letter copying, then, is what Paul may very well be referring to in 2 Tim 4:13.[65] Bo Reicke also notes that Paul trav-

---

61. See, e.g., the arguments in Porter, "Pauline Authorship and the Pastoral Epistles"; and Porter, "Pauline Chronology." See also Duff, "𝔓46 and the Pastorals."

62. Trobisch, *Paul's Letter Collection*, 22.

63. Murphy-O'Connor, *Paul the Letter-Writer*, 12.

64. These references are from E. R. Richards, *Paul and First-Century Letter Writing: Secretaries, Composition, and Collection* (Downers Grove, IL: InterVarsity, 2004), 15–16, 156–59; Murphy-O'Connor, *Paul the Letter-Writer*, 12–13; and Trobisch, *Paul's Letter Collection*, 55–56.

65. See E. R. Richards, *The Secretary in the Letters of Paul* (WUNT 2/42; Tübingen: Mohr-Siebeck, 1991), 164–65, 187–88.

eled with a literary team that aided him in his various writing tasks and that composition of all of the Pauline letters can be dated within the parameters of the narrative of Acts.[66] It is highly likely, then, that Paul kept at least a copy of each of the letters that he wrote to the various churches, especially if he knew the letters were going to be used in instructing and teaching members of the budding Christian movement.

Aside from the common ancient practice of keeping copies of letters, another support for the Pauline involvement in collection of all thirteen letters is the relatively fixed order of his letters in the various Pauline corpora. With the exception of a few letters, such as Ephesians, Galatians, and the question of whether Hebrews should be considered within the Pauline corpus,[67] most of the collections of Paul's letters (such as 𝔓46, Codex Claromontanus [D^P 06], and a fourteenth-century minuscule [5]) have the letters in relatively the same order. The differences can be accounted for by later organizers' rationale in switching some of the letters; for example, Ephesians is actually longer than Galatians, and this might be a reason why 𝔓46 has Ephesians before Galatians (and may reflect the original order; however, the ancients counted lines, and they were considered very close in length).[68] 𝔓46 also shows that the Pauline corpus is organized into two parts, with the church letters going from longest to shortest, and then the personal letters doing likewise.

According to this theory of gathering the thirteen-letter Pauline collection, Paul would have composed his letters to various destinations in a mixed order between ecclesial and personal (see chapter 2 §2, which includes my proposal of Paul's chronology, including when his letters were possibly written in the context of his travels). But he and his literary team would have kept copies of these letters as they continued their missionary travels. The collection of Paul's letters would not have been an afterthought or required a later effort

---

66. B. Reicke, *Re-examining Paul's Letters: The History of the Pauline Correspondence* (ed. D. P. Moessner and I. Reicke; Harrisburg, PA: Trinity, 2001), 39–102.

67. Some wish to include the book of Hebrews within the Pauline corpus. There is little doubt in my mind that Hebrews was in some way related to the Pauline corpus from fairly early in Christian church history (perhaps written by a companion), but it is not Pauline in the same sense as the other thirteen letters. Not least, it lacks direct attribution to Paul. The book of Hebrews appears in various places within the manuscript collections of the Pauline letters. Trobisch notes, for example, that Hebrews appears (in the Pauline corpus of thirteen letters generally in the same order as usually followed, although with a few variations insignificant for this discussion) after Romans and before 1 Corinthians in 𝔓46; after 2 Thessalonians and before the Pastoral Epistles and Philemon in Codices Sinaiticus (ℵ 01), Alexandrinus (A 02), Vaticanus (B 03), and Ephraemi Rescriptus (C 04); and after the entire thirteen letters in Codex Claromontanus (D 06) and the Byzantine tradition. See Trobisch, *Paul's Letter Collection*, 20.

68. See Porter, *How We Got the New Testament*, 118.

to visit the various destinations or people to gather the letters, but rather they were kept by Paul and his literary team. But there are admittedly letters that Paul wrote that have been lost or unaccounted for, such as the "severe" letter he wrote to the Corinthians, or possibly the letter to Laodicea (Col 4:16; if this is indeed not a reference to one of the thirteen). These "lost" letters would be explained by various means, including the failure to copy the letter or to retain a copy of the letter (e.g., loss in a shipwreck or some other disaster), or Paul's decision not to keep or copy these particular letters (e.g., perhaps his severe letter, which was written in haste and anger and he later thought better of retaining it). Paul's letter collection, then, may have been kept together, up to and past his death, and efforts were made by followers, although some disagreements may have existed through the second century, to preserve his letter collection.

5. Conclusion

Pseudepigraphy was extant in the ancient world, as evidenced by many of the documents classified as apocryphal or pseudonymous Christian literature today. The issue of whether some of Paul's letters are pseudepigraphal is an important one, because of the various implications that arise from their origins. All of the thirteen letters attributed to Paul contain formal designations that Paul is the author (or at least one of the authors). Because of the difficulties, some conclude that authorship is not important but that the message contained in the letter should take priority. Others point out that pseudonymous literature violates standards of truth and honesty by condoning deception, and therefore should not be welcomed. Those who claim that some of Paul's letters are pseudepigraphal seem to base their conclusions on internal criteria—that the content or theology contained within these letters differs drastically from the ones that are undoubtedly authentic. In this chapter, I have sought to lay out some of the previous discussions regarding Paul and pseudonymy, to identify various theories regarding the Pauline letter collection, including some problematic implications for holding to Pauline pseudonymy, and to provide my own theory of how Paul's letters came to be. In light of this discussion, I hope to have provided a way forward in determining whether Paul's disputed letters are authentically Pauline, or whether later writers used his name for their own purposes.

Sources for Further Study

Basic Sources

Kiley, M. *Colossians as Pseudepigraphy.* BS 4. Sheffield: JSOT Press, 1986.
Patzia, A. G. *The Making of the New Testament: Origin, Collection, Text, and Canon.* Downers Grove, IL: InterVarsity, 1995.
Porter, S. E. *How We Got the New Testament: Text, Transmission, Translation.* ASBT. Grand Rapids: Baker, 2013.
Reicke, B. *Re-examining Paul's Letters: The History of the Pauline Correspondence.* Edited by D. P. Moessner and I. Reicke. Harrisburg, PA: Trinity, 2001.
Trobisch, D. *Paul's Letter Collection: Tracing the Origins.* Minneapolis: Fortress, 1994.

Advanced Sources

Donelson, L. R. *Pseudepigraphy and Ethical Argument in the Pastoral Epistles.* HUT 22. Tübingen: Mohr-Siebeck, 1986.
Gamble, H. Y. *New Testament Canon: Its Making and Meaning.* Philadelphia: Fortress, 1985.
Goodspeed, E. J. *New Solutions of New Testament Problems.* Chicago: University of Chicago Press, 1927.
Knox, J. *Philemon among the Letters of Paul.* Reprinted London: Collins, 1960 (1935).
McDonald, L. M., and J. A. Sanders, eds. *The Canon Debate.* Peabody, MA: Hendrickson, 2002.
Meade, D. G. *Pseudonymity and Canon: An Investigation into the Relationship of Authorship and Authority in Jewish and Earliest Christian Tradition.* WUNT 39. Tübingen: Mohr-Siebeck, 1986.
Porter, S. E. "The Implications of New Testament Pseudonymy for a Doctrine of Scripture." Pages 235–56 in *Interdisciplinary Perspectives on the Authority of Scripture: Historical, Biblical, and Theoretical Perspectives.* Edited by C. R. Bovell. Eugene, OR: Pickwick, 2011.
———. "Paul and the Process of Canonization." Pages 173–202 in *Exploring the Origins of the Bible: Canon Formation in Historical, Literary, and Theological Perspective.* Edited by C. A. Evans and E. Tov. ASBT. Grand Rapids: Baker, 2008.
———, and G. P. Fewster, eds. *Paul and Pseudepigraphy.* PAST 8. Leiden: Brill, 2013.

PART 2

THE PAULINE LETTERS

There have been several major periods in the discussion of the Pauline letters. After the period during which the canonical group of Pauline letters was recognized (see chapter 6 §4), the first is the period of the full Pauline corpus of thirteen or fourteen letters. Acceptance of Hebrews as Pauline appears to have been early, as reflected in the important early papyrus 𝔓46, where the Pauline corpus is arranged generally according to length, with Hebrews following Romans and preceding the Corinthian letters. In several other early manuscripts, Hebrews is also found within the Pauline corpus, although after 2 Thessalonians and before 1 Timothy.[1] This acceptance persisted in the West until the time of the Reformation, when a number of scholars, including Martin Luther, finally decided against its Pauline authorship. The Pauline canon that resulted remained intact until the time of the Enlightenment.

During the nineteenth century, a number of biblical scholars undertook a virtually complete reassessment of the shape of the Pauline corpus. We can now see that an unwarranted radical skepticism was expressed toward a number of the Pauline letters, although many of the results of this reformulation are still with us. Led by Ferdinand Christian Baur and by others who undertook similar independent investigations in continental Europe, there was a reevaluation of the history of earliest Christianity.[2] Baur argued that there was far

---

1. See D. Trobisch, *Paul's Letter Collection: Tracing the Origins* (Minneapolis: Fortress, 1994), 6–27. These early manuscripts include Codices Sinaiticus (א 01), Alexandrinus (A 02), Vaticanus (B 03), and Ephraemi Rescriptus (C 04).

2. On the history of the discussion, See W. G. Kümmel, *The New Testament: The History of the Investigation of Its Problems* (trans. S. M. Gilmour and H. C. Kee; Nashville: Abingdon, 1972), esp. 133–37; S. Neill and T. Wright, *The Interpretation of the New Testament, 1861–1986* (2nd ed.; Oxford: Oxford University Press, 1988), 20–29; and W. Baird, *History of New Testament Research* (3 vols.; Minneapolis: Fortress, 1992–2013), 1.258–69 and passim.

more contention among rival factions in the early church than is revealed in the documents of earliest Christianity, particularly the book of Acts.[3] According to Baur, Acts was a second-century composition that attempted to rewrite the history of earliest Christianity so as to conceal the major unresolved conflict between the Pauline (or antinomian, that is, rejecting the Mosaic law) and Jerusalem (or legalistic) Christian factions. In the course of Baur's and others' subsequent investigations, the number of unquestionably authentic Pauline letters was narrowed down from the canonical thirteen to, finally, four main, or pillar, epistles (often called the *Hauptbriefe*, "main letters"): Romans, 1–2 Corinthians, and Galatians. Even so, this does not mean that these letters were considered by Baur and others to have been written as single letters, as discussion in subsequent chapters illustrates, only that they consist mostly of authentic Pauline material. The major criteria for this assessment, which will be summarized and evaluated later in the following chapters, focused primarily upon matters of theology, historical situation, and language.

These criteria continue to constitute the major criteria for evaluation of the Pauline letters. One criterion is whether the theological perspective of a given book is consistent with what is thought most plausibly to represent Paul's thought. Thus, when 1–2 Thessalonians discuss eschatology, it is asked what their perspectives are, whether these perspectives are consistent with the kind of Jewish eschatology current during this time, whether the eschatological perspectives are consistent with each other, whether the eschatology is consistent with that of Paul's undisputed letters (the four mentioned above), and whether the language used to express these thoughts is consistent with Paul's standard vocabulary. For a further example, when the Pastoral Epistles (1–2 Timothy and Titus) discuss various positions of church leadership, it is asked whether these positions are plausibly found in the churches of the 60s, where these letters would fit within the Pauline chronology, especially his imprisonments, and whether the vocabulary (e.g., how he uses words related to "faith" and "belief") and content (e.g., salvation and church order) are consistent with his usage elsewhere (see chapter 4 §§2, 3).

Since the nineteenth century, during the third period, there has been a steady reassessment of the conclusions of Baur, his contemporaries, and his successors, however always in light of his conclusions. Scholars differ on numerous details and even on some of the major points of evidence and how they are to be evaluated, but it appears that seven of the Pauline letters are

---

3. Cf. F. C. Baur, *Paul the Apostle of Jesus Christ: His Life and Work, His Epistles and His Doctrine* (2 vols.; London: Williams & Norgate, 1873–75; repr. Peabody, MA: Hendrickson, 2003).

often placed into the category of undisputed letters: Romans, 1–2 Corinthians, Galatians, Philippians, 1 Thessalonians, and Philemon. This does not mean that every scholar believes that these were written by Paul, or that he wrote them alone or in their entirety as they stand in the Pauline canon, but that, generally speaking, these books constitute the basic corpus of Paul's authentic writings in the New Testament. The other six letters can be categorized as the disputed or deutero-Pauline letters: Ephesians, Colossians, 2 Thessalonians, 1–2 Timothy, and Titus (some, especially German scholars, might even call the Pastoral Epistles trito-Pauline, to indicate how removed they are from the authentic Paul).[4] Again, this does not mean that every scholar believes that these were not written by Paul, or that they do not contain authentic Pauline material, or, certainly, that they were written under Paul's name to deceive an ancient audience. But generally speaking, it cannot be assumed in scholarly discussion that Paul is their author. In some circles, the authenticity of these books is still being debated. This is less true of the Pastoral Epistles, whose authenticity is so widely doubted that authenticity is often, especially in German New Testament scholarship, not even a subject of discussion. There is more debate about the authenticity of Colossians, Ephesians, and 2 Thessalonians.

In this second part, I discuss the Pauline letters according to the reconstructed Pauline chronology in chapter 2 §2. The treatments are, therefore, divided into six chapters. Chapters 7–10 discuss undisputed letters of Paul according to the differentiation made above (apart from 2 Thessalonians, which is discussed in direct relationship to 1 Thessalonians). Chapter 11 discusses the Prison Epistles, those letters that, apart from 2 Timothy, are thought to have been written during one of Paul's imprisonments (see chapter 2 §3). This group of letters includes both undisputed (Philippians and Philemon) and disputed or deutero-Pauline letters (Ephesians and Colossians). The final chapter, chapter 12, treats the Pastoral Epistles, disputed deutero- or even trito-Pauline letters. In these chapters, where appropriate, the evidence for and against a given letter's authenticity is presented, along with discussion of the possible historical and theological contexts in which they were written (besides presenting a summary of the content of each letter, following an epistolary outline; see chapter 5 §3).

Although I do take positions and draw conclusions, the purpose of chapters 7–12 is not so much to convince the reader of any one position as to present each reader with sufficient data to arrive at their own informed de-

---

4. See, e.g., O. Wischmeyer, ed., *Paul: Life, Setting, Work, Letters* (trans. H. S. Heron with D. T. Roth; London: T&T Clark, 2012), 309–38, in a chapter entitled "The Reception of Paul in the First Century: The Deutero- and Trito-Pauline Letters and the Image of Paul in Acts."

cision. Along with the evidence for authenticity will be presented a suitable and plausible scenario for how the letter fits within the Pauline chronology.[5] Along with the evidence against Pauline authorship will be presented suitable alternatives for the writing of the letter. Comments in these chapters on the circumstances and purpose of composition, along with discussion of Paul's opponents in the churches where relevant, should be combined with the dimensions of Pauline belief discussed in chapter 4 to determine the particular contextual and theological contribution of each of the letters. No attempt is made at being complete in every dimension. Pauline studies is one of the most fruitful and productive areas of biblical scholarship, and these issues continue to generate lively and informative discussion. A more thorough and complete analysis of each of the issues can be found in volumes devoted to these topics. The theories that seem to me to be the most potentially enlightening will be discussed.[6]

5. Reference will occasionally be made to my personal knowledge of the various cities to which Paul writes. A useful further guide is S. E. Johnson, *Paul the Apostle and His Cities* (Wilmington, DE: Glazier, 1987).

6. For a more complete discussion of the various views of the Pauline opponents, see J. J. Gunther, *St. Paul's Opponents and Their Background: A Study of Apocalyptic and Jewish Sectarian Teaching* (NovTSup 35; Leiden: Brill, 1973); E. E. Ellis, "Paul and His Opponents: Trends in the Research," in *Prophecy and Hermeneutic in Early Christianity: New Testament Essays* (WUNT 18; Tübingen: Mohr-Siebeck, 1978; repr. Grand Rapids: Eerdmans, 1978), 80–115; J. L. Sumney, *"Servants of Satan," "False Brothers," and Other Opponents of Paul* (JSNTSup 188; Sheffield: Sheffield Academic, 1999); S. E. Porter, ed., *Paul and His Opponents* (PAST 2; Leiden: Brill, 2005); I. J. Elmer, *Paul, Jerusalem, and the Judaizers: The Galatian Crisis in Its Broadest Historical Context* (WUNT 2/258; Tübingen: Mohr-Siebeck, 2009); and the methodological statements found in J. L. Sumney, *Identifying Paul's Opponents: The Question of Method in 2 Corinthians* (JSNTSup 40; Sheffield: JSOT Press, 1990), esp. 75–112; and J. M. G. Barclay, "Mirror-Reading a Polemical Letter: Galatians as a Test Case," *JSNT* 31 (1987): 73–93. Not all of the letters involve opponents in a combative sense.

7

Galatians

1. Introduction

"The Epistle to the Galatians is spiritual dynamite, and it is therefore almost impossible to handle it without explosions. It has often been so in the history of the Church," says R. A. Cole in his short commentary on Galatians.[1] The book has indeed caused numerous explosions, from its earliest times up to the present. Not only does it appear to have caused a number of debates within the early church; it has been an important book in recent discussion of the nature of Judaism and Paul's characterization of it. In this chapter, I discuss the major critical issues regarding Galatians, including authorship, the crucial topic of its destination and hence its date of composition, Paul's visits to Jerusalem in relation to Acts and Galatians, and then the occasion and purpose of Galatians, before offering an outline and then exposition of its content.

2. Major Critical Issues

Galatians is surrounded by discussion of a number of major critical issues. The most perplexing is perhaps that related to its destination and hence its date of composition.

---

1. R. A. Cole, *The Letter of Paul to the Galatians* (2nd ed.; TNTC; Grand Rapids: Eerdmans, 1989), 9, also cited in R. P. Martin, *New Testament Foundations: A Guide for Christian Students* (2 vols.; 2nd ed.; Grand Rapids: Eerdmans, 1986), 2.145 (who cites the first edition).

THE PAULINE LETTERS

A. Authorship of Galatians

The opinion of German scholar Werner Georg Kümmel reflects the consensus regarding authorship of Galatians: "That Galatians is a real, genuine letter is indisputable."[2] Apart from a very few eccentric critics through the ages,[3] Galatians has always been considered authentically Pauline. As mentioned in the introduction to Part 2, for Ferdinand Christian Baur, to whom we owe a good portion of our enduring critical discussion regarding such issues as authorship, Galatians, along with Romans and 1–2 Corinthians, is one of the four main or pillar epistles.[4] As with 2 Corinthians, Philippians, and even Romans, however, this does not mean that all believe that every portion of the letter was written by Paul, or even at the same time. John O'Neill questions the authenticity of portions of Galatians, arguing that there were later interpolations.[5] But his questioning of particular passages does not call into question the integrity and authorship of the bulk of the letter. In any case, he is not followed in his view by many if any scholars. One of the strongest cases for authentic Pauline authorship of Galatians, besides early recognition by the church, is the autobiographical section at the beginning of the letter (Gal 1:11–24) and the theological topics he covers in it.

An important issue regarding the authorship of Galatians arises at the end of the letter, where Paul writes, "See what large letters I use as I write to you with my own hand!" (6:11 NIV). Most interpreters take this as an indication that an amanuensis wrote most of Galatians with the exception of this statement (it is debated whether the rest of the letter is written by Paul or just this statement), which is written to authenticate what has been written thus far.[6] Paul's use of an amanuensis is not surprising, since in some other letters, such as Romans (16:22), 1 Corinthians (16:21), Colossians (4:18), and 2 Thessalonians (3:17), there are similar, if not stronger, indications that an

2. W. G. Kümmel, *Introduction to the New Testament* (trans. H. C. Kee; 17th ed.; Nashville: Abingdon, 1975), 304. See J. B. Lightfoot, *St. Paul's Epistle to the Galatians* (8th ed.; London: Macmillan, 1884), 57–62, for evidence of its use in the church.

3. E.g., the Dutch scholar W. C. van Manen, "A Wave of Hypercriticism," *Expository Times* 9 (1897–98): 205–11, 257–59, 314–19.

4. F. C. Baur, *Paul the Apostle of Jesus Christ: His Life and Work, His Epistles and His Doctrine* (2 vols.; London: Williams & Norgate, 1873–75; repr. Peabody, MA: Hendrickson, 2003), 1.260–67.

5. J. C. O'Neill, *The Recovery of Paul's Letter to the Galatians* (London: SPCK, 1972).

6. E.g., D. J. Moo, *Galatians* (BECNT; Grand Rapids: Baker, 2013), 1; cf. F. F. Bruce, *The Epistle to the Galatians* (NIGTC; Grand Rapids: Eerdmans, 1982), 268; and R. Y. K. Fung, *The Epistle to the Galatians* (NICNT; Grand Rapids: Eerdmans, 1988), 300–301.

amanuensis helped Paul with the physical writing of the letter.[7] In any case, this usually does not result in any serious discussion of pseudonymity in Galatians, as the use of amanuenses was quite common in the ancient world (see chapter 5 §4).[8]

B. Destination and Date of Galatians

While the authorship of Galatians is not seriously questioned, a number of other critical issues continue to be debated with regard to the letter. Two of the most important are its destination and its date of composition. The question of its destination revolves around whether Paul was writing to Christians in North or South Galatia.[9]

1. Destination: North or South Galatia?

One of the major debates over the last hundred or so years regarding Galatians is its audience. The major question is whether the letter was addressed to the North Galatians, that is, those living in the ancient ethnic area of the Galatians, or Gauls (from what is now roughly France), who settled in Asia Minor in the fourth century BC from Europe, or to the South Galatians, that is, those living in the southern part of the Roman province of Galatia. There are several implications for this discussion. If the destination was North Galatia, the epistle almost assuredly had to be written after Paul's second missionary journey, with Gal 2:1–10 regarding Paul's visit to Jerusalem being a Pauline account of the Jerusalem Council in Acts 15 (or, in the minds of some, possibly the source for writing or creating the account in Acts 15). If the destination was South Galatia, then the letter could have been written as early as the end of Paul's first missionary journey, before the meeting of the Jerusalem Council. This would

---

7. Cf. J. A. D. Weima, "Sincerely, Paul: The Significance of the Pauline Letter Closings," in *Paul and the Ancient Letter Form* (ed. S. E. Porter and S. A. Adams; PAST 6; Leiden: Brill, 2010), 307–45, esp. 337–40, who writes, "The phrase τῇ ἐμῇ χειρὶ (Παύλου) ('in/with my own hand [of Paul]') implies that Paul had to this point been using a secretary to write the letter, but now takes up the pen himself to write personally to his readers" (337).

8. See the extensive discussion on ancient secretaries, including Paul's, in E. R. Richards, *Paul and First-Century Letter Writing: Secretaries, Composition, and Collection* (Downers Grove, IL: InterVarsity, 2004), esp. 59–93.

9. On the territory, see S. Mitchell, "Galatia," *ABD* 2.870–72; cf. W. Tabbernee, "Asia Minor and Cyprus," in *Early Christianity in Contexts: An Exploration across Cultures and Continents* (ed. W. Tabbernee; Grand Rapids: Baker, 2014), 261–320, esp. 268–300, with Phrygia on pp. 268–76 and Galatia on pp. 290–300.

not preclude it from being written later, however. If the letter was written as early as the end of the first missionary journey, then Gal 2:1–10 could be Paul's account of the so-called famine visit to Jerusalem of Acts 11:27–30 and 12:25 or a private meeting not mentioned in Acts.

The history of discussion of this issue of destination is surprisingly fairly recent.[10] The early church, from the second century on, took the North Galatia, or ethnic, view, since the region of Lycaonia had apparently separated from the province of Galatia and united with Cilicia, thus putting several of the churches founded by Paul on his first missionary journey (e.g., Lystra and Derbe) in a separate province from Galatia. By the fourth century, the Roman province of Galatia had been reduced to its original, smaller size, thus eliminating evidence of the larger territory. The North Galatia view was generally accepted until the late nineteenth century, when archeologist William Ramsay, as a result of firsthand exploration of Turkey (ancient Asia Minor), concluded that the South Galatia, or provincial, view (first raised in the mid-eighteenth century) was more plausible.[11] Scholars have been divided on this issue ever since. The arguments for the two positions are worth recounting, even if only briefly. I will recount the best arguments for the North Galatia hypothesis, followed by what I consider to be the more convincing arguments for the South Galatia hypothesis.

a. North Galatia Hypothesis

The North Galatia view has been held by many important scholars, including renowned biblical historian J. B. Lightfoot (who wrote before Ramsay's discoveries and provides the classic discussion of the North Galatia view), James Moffatt, Kümmel, Hans Dieter Betz, J. Louis Martyn, and Martinus de Boer,

---

10. For a good summary of the arguments, see I. J. Elmer, *Paul, Jerusalem, and the Judaizers: The Galatian Crisis in Its Broadest Historical Context* (WUNT 2/258; Tübingen: Mohr-Siebeck, 2009), 118–31.

11. See W. M. Ramsay, *The Church in the Roman Empire before A.D. 170* (4th ed.; London: Hodder & Stoughton, 1895), 97–111; *A Historical Commentary on Galatians* (London: Hodder & Stoughton, 1899); and "Galatia," *Hastings Dictionary of the Bible* 2.81–89. Ramsay's view was strongly endorsed by Mitchell, "Galatia," 2.870–72, esp. 871; C. Breytenbach, *Paulus und Barnabas in der Provinz Galatien: Studien zu Apostelgeschichte 13f.; 16,6; 18,32 und den Adressaten des Galaterbriefes* (Arbeiten zur Geschichte des antiken Judentums und des Urchristentums 38; Leiden: Brill, 1996), 99–173, with excellent plates; and J. M. Scott, *Paul and the Nations: The Old Testament and Jewish Background of Paul's Mission to the Nations with Special Reference to the Destination of Galatians* (WUNT 84; Tübingen: Mohr-Siebeck, 1995), esp. 181–215, who shifts the debate to reflect an Old Testament understanding of who the Galatians were.

among others.[12] The main assertions and lines of argument for this position are summarized as follows.

1. The term "Galatia," from the Gauls or Celts (Γαλάται, Κέλται) who migrated from Europe into Asia Minor in the fourth century BC, refers not to the Roman political province of the first century but to the people in northern Asia Minor who were subdued by the Romans. Use of the term "Galatians" in Gal 3:1 in this ethnic or racial sense would seem to support this interpretation.
2. Mentions of Galatia in Acts 16:6 and 18:23 illustrate the geographical sense of the term "Galatia," since the author also mentions Phrygia, which was another territory in that area. The emphasis should be on the word "and" in both verses ("Phrygia and Galatia" or "Galatia and Phrygia").
3. In Acts 16:6, Paul and his companions "passed through" Phrygia and Galatia because they "had been forbidden" from preaching in the province of Asia. This implies that they went north to the Galatian region and avoided central Asia.
4. Luke does not refer to Galatia when he mentions Paul going to Lystra and Derbe during the first missionary journey (Acts 14:6, 20–21); he mentions instead Lycaonia, a different province, in which these cities were located.
5. In Gal 4:13, when Paul says "because of weakness of the flesh I proclaimed the gospel to you formerly," the use of "former" (πρότερος) implies two former or previous visits, those recorded in Acts 16:6 and 18:23. (This datum could, however, also be used to argue for a later date consistent with the South Galatia view.)
6. Since the style and subject matter of Galatians seem to be most compatible with Romans, the dates of their composition must have been very close to each other. It is difficult to take Galatians, with its discussion of law, as Paul's first letter, to be followed by the Thessalonian letters, which do not even mention the law. (This argument again supports only a later date of composition, not necessarily the North Galatia hypothesis.)
7. The temperament of the Galatian Christians seems to reflect racial ste-

---

12. See Lightfoot, *Galatians*, 18–35; J. Moffatt, *An Introduction to the Literature of the New Testament* (3rd ed.; Edinburgh: T&T Clark, 1918), 90–101; Kümmel, *Introduction to the New Testament*, 296–98; H. D. Betz, *Galatians: A Commentary on Paul's Letter to the Churches in Galatia* (Hermeneia; Philadelphia: Fortress, 1979), 3–5; J. L. Martyn, *Galatians* (AB 33A; New York: Doubleday, 1997), 15–17; and M. de Boer, *Galatians* (NTL; Louisville: Westminster John Knox, 2011), 3–11. A different form of the North Galatia hypothesis that transforms the letter into anti-imperialist ideology is found in B. Kahl, *Galatians Re-imagined: Reading with the Eyes of the Vanquished* (Minneapolis: Fortress, 2010).

reotypes of the period concerning the Galatians as a people—fickle, superstitious, and unsophisticated (Gal 3:1).

8. Paul's address to them as "Galatians" seems to indicate that they were
ethnic Galatians, and it would seem unlikely that he would call inhabitants
of Lycaonia and Pisidia (South Galatia) Galatians, even if some ethnic
Galatians were included.[13]

9. By this view, when in Gal 1:21 Paul says that he later went to Syria and
Cilicia, he is referring to the first missionary journey in Acts 13–14.

b. South Galatia Hypothesis

The South Galatia hypothesis has been held by an equally important list of
scholars, including Ramsay, Edward DeWitt Burton, F. F. Bruce, Ralph Martin, Richard Longenecker, Frank Matera, Douglas Moo, and probably Donald
Hagner, among others,[14] although all scholars who hold to this position do
not agree about the time of writing (see below). The major arguments for the
South Galatia hypothesis are as follows.

1. The phrase "Phrygia and Galatia" in Acts 16:6 and 18:23 (in reverse) contains the use of Phrygia in an adjectival sense, thus referring to Phrygian
Galatia, the area of the Galatian province that includes the region of Phrygia. Ramsay was not able to provide an exact parallel of this usage, but
he found similar kinds of modification that indicated this pattern was
acceptable usage.[15]

2. The North Galatia view requires an unnatural detour to the north in Acts
16, in which the normal trade routes along the borders of the province
of Asia would not have been followed. Paul tended to follow the main
roads and visit the centers of communication in Roman provinces (i.e.,
from Syria to Cilicia to Iconium and then to Ephesus). The southern side
of the Anatolian plateau, which consisted of low hills with an adequate
water supply, was far more important than the north, which was very
difficult to get to. It is true that two places Paul visited, Lystra and Derbe,

---

13. De Boer, *Galatians*, 4.

14. Ramsay, *Galatians*, 68–77; E. D. W. Burton, *A Critical and Exegetical Commentary on
the Epistle to the Galatians* (ICC; Edinburgh: T&T Clark, 1921), xxix–xliv; Bruce, *Galatians*,
3–18; Martin, *Foundations*, 2.148–52; R. N. Longenecker, *Galatians* (WBC 41; Dallas: Word,
1990), lxi–lxxii, who provides an excellent summary of the issues; F. J. Matera, *Galatians* (Sacra
Pagina 9; Collegeville, MN: Liturgical, 1992), 19–26; Moo, *Galatians*, 4–8; and D. A. Hagner,
The New Testament: A Historical and Theological Introduction (Grand Rapids: Baker, 2012), 437.

15. E.g., Ramsay, *Galatians*, 75–76.

were "backward" places, by Ramsay's own admission, but at least these cities were in the area in which Paul was traveling and so did not require a radical detour.[16]

3. Paul is not precise in every instance, but unlike Luke, he normally uses Roman provincial titles, especially for areas where churches are located. Hence he uses Achaia or Greece rather than Hellas, which Luke uses.[17]

4. In Acts 16:6, Luke says that they, Paul and his fellow missionaries, traveled through the region of Phrygia and Galatia (or Phrygian Galatia), being forbidden by the Holy Spirit to speak the word in Asia. The aorist participle translated "forbidden" (κωλυθέντες) is best taken as indicating that the forbidding took place not before Paul and his companions passed through Phrygia and Galatia but at the same time or after. Hence the verse is best translated, "they passed through Phrygian-Galatia, then were forbidden to speak the word in Asia," probably referring to Ephesus. In Greek, this sequence is determined by the word order (the participial clause follows the main verb) rather than by the tense form of the participle.[18]

5. Acts mentions only Paul's time in South Galatia, never recording a North Galatian ministry.

6. Acts 20:4 refers to people from South Galatia (Gaius of Derbe, Timothy of Lystra) as involved in the collection, but no one from the north. No one from Corinth is mentioned either, but this is a different kind of omission in light of Paul's travel itinerary.

7. The mention in Gal 2:1, 9, 13 of Barnabas is better explained if Paul founded on the first missionary journey the churches to which he refers, since this was the only missionary journey on which Barnabas went with Paul.

8. In light of the subject matter of Galatians, including debate over the Jewishness of Gentiles, it is difficult to believe that Paul would not mention the meeting in Jerusalem in Acts 15 if that meeting had already occurred (if it really did take place, as it no doubt did). As will be discussed below, however, though the South Galatia hypothesis does allow for greater flexibility regarding the date of composition of the letter, if the letter was written before the Jerusalem Council, it almost assuredly had to be written to the South Galatia churches.

---

16. Lystra and Derbe were apparently visited by Paul after being chased out of Iconium (Acts 14:6).

17. On this terminology, see T. Mommsen, *The Provinces of the Roman Empire from Caesar to Diocletian* (trans. W. P. Dickson; 2 vols.; London: Macmillan, 1909), 1.252–56.

18. See S. E. Porter, *Verbal Aspect in the Greek of the New Testament, with Reference to Tense and Mood* (Studies in Biblical Greek 1; New York: Peter Lang, 1989), 385–87.

9. There is the possibility that the references in Gal 4:14 and 6:17 to Paul being received as an "angel of God" by the Galatians or receiving the marks of Jesus coincide with the identification of Paul with Hermes and Barnabas with Zeus by the Lystrans in Acts 14:11–18 and with references to physical harm in 14:19.

Most of the arguments above seem to be centered on two key issues: the meaning of "Galatia/Galatians" and a reconstruction of Paul's travels.[19] There are many strong arguments for both sides, but it seems that the evidence for the South Galatia hypothesis has the greater strength in regard to these two key issues. During the first century, the province of Galatia was a large one that included many regions that brought together ethnic groups of all different sorts, including ethnic Galatians. One Latin inscription of the Roman period, recording the full title of a governor of Galatia, illustrates this diversity: he is described as governor "of Galatia, of Pisidia, of Phrygia, of Lycaonia, of Isauria, of Paphlogonia, of Pontus Galaticus, of Pontus Polemoniacus, of Armenia."[20] With the evidence that is at hand, it is more plausible to think that the letter called Galatians was addressed to the churches at Lystra, Derbe, Iconium, and Antioch—churches that we know Paul visited and that were located in an area known in Roman times as Galatia—rather than conjecture about a different destination far removed from these in location. In addition, the South Galatia hypothesis fits better with the descriptions of Paul's travels in Acts, whereas there is no mention of Paul's travels through North Galatia (unless Acts 16:6 is to be interpreted as North Galatia). As classical historians Richard Wallace and Wynne Williams add, "How could Paul have addressed the Christians in these four cities collectively except as Galatians?"[21]

2. Date of Composition

The date of composition of Galatians[22] is closely linked to the two major views regarding its destination, although there is more flexibility with the South Galatia hypothesis (see chapter 2 §2).

---

19. Moo, *Galatians*, 5.

20. R. Wallace and W. Williams, *The Acts of the Apostles* (London: Duckworth, 1993), 23, citing no. 1017 from H. Dessau, *Inscriptiones latinae selectae* (Leipzig: Weidmann, 1892–1916).

21. Wallace and Williams, *Acts of the Apostles*, 74–75.

22. On the dating of Galatians, see J. C. Hurd Jr., *The Origin of I Corinthians* (New York: Seabury, 1965), esp. 18 for a useful chart.

a. North Galatia

There are three possible dates for those who hold to the North Galatia hypothesis. The first is sometime after the first possible visit by Paul to North Galatia (Acts 16:6), sometime during his second missionary journey (i.e., 50–52). The second, held by Betz and others, is early in Paul's Ephesian ministry in Acts 19 (i.e., 53–55), taking the word "quickly" of Gal 1:6 ("I am astonished that you are so quickly deserting the one who called you"; NIV) literally with reference to the Galatians' abandoning the faith.[23] Paul had visited the churches of Galatia in Acts 16:6 and 18:23 and then gone to Ephesus, where, according to this view, he must have written to them upon hearing of immediate danger. The third possible date is sometime after leaving Ephesus (Acts 19), giving a little bit of time between Paul's visit and his need for writing. Lightfoot dates the letter after the Corinthian letters, since there is no reference to the problem with Judaizers in the Corinthian correspondence, but before Romans—perhaps written in Macedonia—because of the theological similarities but less developed thinking (i.e., ca. 56–57). With the North Galatia hypothesis it is difficult to pin down the date. However, if one accepts the North Galatia hypothesis, it is probably better to argue for a date significantly before Romans, and hence for either the first or second option.

b. South Galatia

For those who hold to the South Galatia hypothesis, there are two possible time frames for composition. The later time of composition correlates with any of the dates suggested by the North Galatia hypothesis.[24] In this case, the "quickly" of Gal 1:6 indicates the quickness of their turning away rather than the length of time from their conversion to their turning. The earlier date of composition posits that Paul wrote to the churches after his first missionary journey but before the Jerusalem Council of Acts 15 (i.e., 49?). In this case, Gal 4:13 refers to the two visits on his first missionary journey. I tend to believe that Galatians was written at the end of Paul's first missionary journey and before the Jerusalem Council. This would probably make it the first letter of Paul written. If it was not written then, it was probably written in 50–52, and certainly before the letter to the Romans.

23. Betz, *Galatians*, 9–12.
24. R. H. Fuller, *A Critical Introduction to the New Testament* (London: Duckworth, 1966), 26; and M. Silva, *Explorations in Exegetical Method: Galatians as a Test Case* (Grand Rapids: Baker, 1996), 129–39.

C. Paul's Visits to Jerusalem in Acts and Galatians

The discussion concerning the date of the composition of Galatians can be further clarified if reference is made to the visits to Jerusalem mentioned in Galatians and in Acts.[25] There are two major schemes for understanding the relationship between the Jerusalem visits of Paul according to Galatians and Acts. The following discussion assumes that the Jerusalem Council of Acts 15—or something like it in its essential subject matter—actually happened. Ever since Baur, there has probably been unnecessary skepticism over whether the council of Acts 15 took place. The oddness of the council's conclusions compromising Christian freedom (i.e., regarding food offered to idols)—which Paul seems to take fairly lightly in his subsequent ministry (e.g., 1 Cor 8)—are sufficient to make a plausible case for its historicity; there is little motivation for the author to introduce potentially divisive issues on no historical grounds. I begin with what I consider to be the less plausible view and then discuss the one that I believe is more likely.

One possible reconstruction of the events of Galatians and Acts follows, with the important point being that Gal 2:1-10 is to be equated with the Jerusalem Council in Acts 15:2-29.

Table 1. Paul's Visits to Jerusalem, Version I

Galatians			Acts	
1:18–20	Paul sees Cephas and James		9:26–29	Barnabas takes Paul to the apostles
1:21	Paul visits Syria and Cilicia		9:30	Paul departs for Tarsus
2:1–10	Paul and Barnabas, along with Titus, meet James, Peter, and John		15:2–29	Paul and Barnabas meet with the apostles and elders at the council

In this scheme, there are various explanations of Acts 11:27–30, the famine visit, which is not mentioned in Galatians.[26] Some argue that the episode in Acts 11 is not historical and that Paul therefore does not mention it. Others argue that the two accounts in Acts 11 and 15 are duplicates that the author of Luke–Acts perhaps found in two separate sources, not realizing it was the same story. A third explanation is that the meeting of Acts 11, which appears

---

25. On the issue of Pauline autobiography in Galatians, see G. Lyons, *Pauline Autobiography: Toward a New Understanding* (SBLDS 73; Atlanta: Scholars Press, 1985).

26. See D. Guthrie, *New Testament Introduction* (4th ed.; Downers Grove, IL: InterVarsity, 1990), 474–83, for discussion of these issues.

to be a private meeting in which the apostles are not mentioned, is passed over in Galatians, since the challenge to which Paul is responding in Galatians concerns his relationship to the apostles. In any case, this first reconstruction understands the events in Gal 2 to be the same as the Jerusalem Council in Acts 15.[27]

A second possible reconstruction of the events in Galatians and Acts follows, with the important points being that Gal 2:1–10 is equated with the famine visit in Acts 11:27–30 and 12:25 and that the Jerusalem Council is not mentioned in Galatians.

Table 2. Paul's Visits to Jerusalem, Version II

Galatians		Acts	
1:18–20	Paul sees Cephas and James	9:26–29	Barnabas takes Paul to the apostles
1:21	Paul visits Syria and Cilicia	9:30	Paul departs for Tarsus
2:1–10	Paul and Barnabas, along with Titus, meet James, Peter, and John	11:27–30; 12:25	Paul and Barnabas bring famine relief
	—	15:2–29	Paul and Barnabas meet with the apostles and elders at the council

I find this scheme more convincing. Nevertheless, there are still some difficulties with this second equation. Most notably, the apostles and Titus are not mentioned in Acts 11, and it seems that Paul receives confirmation of his message to the Gentiles, even though this precedes his first missionary journey, which would have been the first test of his message. Despite this, the second solution is still a more plausible one. First, there is a place for Acts 11 and 15, without resorting to discrediting Luke's account. Second, the meetings of Acts 11 and Gal 2:1–10 (esp. 2:2) both look like private meetings. Third, Paul appears to be giving a strict chronology, so it would be surprising if he left out an important incident, especially one such as the meeting in Acts 11. This also raises the question of when the incident of Gal 2:11–14, Paul's confrontation with Peter (probably at Antioch), would have occurred. Some scholars think that Paul emerged unsuccessful from this confrontation, though this is probably not correct.[28] Most likely this meeting occurred before the events of Acts 15; otherwise the results of the meeting would have been reported in Galatians.

27. See, e.g., Elmer, *Paul, Jerusalem, and the Judaizers*, 81–116.
28. See N. Taylor, *Paul, Antioch, and Jerusalem: A Study in Relationships and Authority in Earliest Christianity* (JSNTSup 66; Sheffield: JSOT Press, 1992), 139. Cf. the comments below on Gal 1:10–2:14.

D. Occasion and Purpose of Galatians

The occasion of a Pauline letter is best defined as the specific circumstance or circumstances in force at the time of writing—for example, the audience's composition as a church, the history of its contact with Paul, and any relevant details regarding positive accomplishments or problems surrounding this contact. The purpose of a letter, on the other hand, is the reason standing behind the composition of a letter, so far as this can be reconstructed from the letter itself. There is often not an easy or clear line of distinction between the occasion and the purpose of a letter.

1. Evidence

The evidence for Paul's opponents at Galatia includes the following internal features: people had visited this mission field (Gal 1:7; 5:10, 12), possibly coming from James in Jerusalem (2:12), bringing another teaching and questioning Paul's authority and apostleship (1:9–11). They are characterized as troublemakers (1:7; 5:10) or agitators (5:12) and are seen as imposing requirements of Jewish law, especially circumcision (5:3, 11) and the observance of special days (2:16; 3:2, 21b; 4:10; 4:21; 5:4).

2. Paul's Response

Paul's response to the threat in the Galatian churches is vitriolic, evidencing his passion for the gospel. He characterizes the opponents' teaching as a perversion of the gospel (1:7) that represents a turning from God (1:6; 5:8), a falling from grace (5:4), and a denial of the promise of the Spirit (3:2–5). They have substituted a false message for the true one (1:8–9), a message that Paul received through revelation and that was later approved by those in Jerusalem (1:12; 1:13–2:10), exposing the opponents to judgment (5:10).[29] In effect, their teaching is contrary to justification by faith (3:21), attempts to make the law a means of justification (3:11), and undermines Christ's death (2:21).

3. Identity of Paul's Opponents in Galatia

Much has been written regarding the identity of Paul's (various) opponents,[30] with some scholars believing that Paul's opponents in Galatia were the same

---

29. For more on Paul's opponents, see the collection of essays in S. E. Porter, ed., *Paul and His Opponents* (PAST 2; Leiden: Brill, 2005).

30. See Longenecker, *Galatians*, lxxxviii–c; and J. D. G. Dunn, *The Theology of Paul's Letter*

ones that he faced in the other cities and churches in which he ministered.[31] In any case, there are various views as to who these opponents were, but I begin with some preliminary observations regarding this group that can be ascertained from the letter itself.[32] Most notably, Paul's opponents in Galatia were advocates of circumcision for Gentile followers of Jesus and were themselves circumcised, probably because they were Jewish themselves. They were also followers of Jesus; that is, they identified themselves with the Christian movement that affirmed Jesus as the Christ. Paul was not contesting their Christology but their version of what it would look like to follow Christ. The opponents were also apostles, or at the least some in the group were acknowledged or self-proclaimed as apostles (see the dynamics of Gal 2:11–12). Their authority came from the Jerusalem church, which is probably why Paul uses them to assert his own authority as an apostle, although he sets himself apart by asserting that the gospel he received was directly from the Lord and not simply a secondhand witness derived from the other apostles. Considering these starting points, there seem to be roughly four major views on the identity of these opponents of Paul in Galatia (and some other, less likely ones besides).

a. A view held since the second century through Luther to the present, and probably still the majority view, is that the opponents in Galatians were Judaizers, a radical Jewish-Christian group of opponents of Paul from Jerusalem[33] (perhaps sent by the Jerusalem apostles, as Baur speculated; see Gal 2:12).[34] They penetrated the churches that Paul founded and attempted

---

to the Galatians (NTT; Cambridge: Cambridge University Press, 1993). Some might wish to call Paul's opponents something else (see Hagner, *New Testament*, 441n10 for some options), but at least in Paul's eyes they are opposing him and his teaching, and so "opponents" is still the right word. The literature on Paul's opponents is voluminous, but for a few examples specific to Galatians, see G. Howard, *Paul: Crisis in Galatia: A Study in Early Christian Theology* (2nd ed.; SNTSMS 35; Cambridge: Cambridge University Press, 1990 [1979]); M. D. Nanos, ed., *The Galatians Debate* (Peabody, MA: Hendrickson, 2002), especially the articles in part 3; and J. C. Hurd, "Reflections concerning Paul's 'Opponents' in Galatia," in *Paul and His Opponents* (ed. S. E. Porter; PAST 2; Leiden: Brill, 2005), 129–48.

31. E.g., Hurd, "Reflections concerning Paul's 'Opponents.'"

32. Cf. J. D. G. Dunn, *The Epistle to the Galatians* (BNTC; Peabody, MA: Hendrickson, 1993), 9–11; cf. also Hurd, "Reflections concerning Paul's 'Opponents,'" 144.

33. Most scholars seem to deny that these Judaizers were sent from Jerusalem; they prefer to see this group as an anomalous group of Jewish Christians who acted without the sanction of Jerusalem. There is, however, good reason to believe that these Judaizers were from Jerusalem. The extreme success they experienced (which is why Paul had to write to the Galatians) is best explained by their carrying with them the approval of Jerusalem. Cf. Elmer, *Paul, Jerusalem, and the Judaizers*, 131–34.

34. See M. Luther, *A Commentary on St. Paul's Epistle to the Galatians* (ed. J. P. Fallowes;

to persuade the Gentile Christians to accept circumcision and adopt the
Jewish law as a necessary part of their belief in Christ, probably referring
to Abraham's circumcision as his first great act of faith.[35] That they apparently came from outside the Galatian church is supported by Paul's use of
the third person to refer to them (cf. 1 Cor 5:1–2 and 2 Cor 7:2–4, where
the second person is used for insiders).[36] These legalists, however, may
also have some protognostic tendencies (Gal 4:9–10), in which their lack
of regard for the earthly sphere results in libertinism (6:1).[37] It is more
likely, however, that the references to freedom and indulgence (5:13, 16;
6:1, 8) can be explained as simply part of the message of the Judaizers, to
which Paul responds by saying that, though it may seem that they are free
to do these things (using an inversion of Paul's own message?), there is a
limit to their freedom.[38]

b. A modification of the first position argues that the opponents are Jewish
Christians who have accepted circumcision and want to convince others
to do the same.[39] The reason for this is that, supposedly, zealot activity
in Jerusalem increased and Jewish Christians were trying to persuade
Gentile Christians to accept circumcision so that the Jewish Christians

trans. E. Middleton; London: Harrison Trust, n.d.); Lightfoot, *Galatians*, 29–30; C. K. Barrett,
Paul: An Introduction to His Thought (London: Chapman, 1994), 26–33; Hagner, *New Testament*, 440–42; cf. J. Munck, *Paul and the Salvation of Mankind* (Atlanta: John Knox, 1959),
87–134, who contends that the problem was Gentile Judaizers. See also Howard, *Paul: Crisis in
Galatia*, 1–19, who argues that the Judaizers were not opposed to Paul, although he was to them.

35. See G. W. Hansen, *Abraham in Galatians: Epistolary and Rhetorical Contexts* (JSNT-
Sup 29; Sheffield: JSOT Press, 1989).

36. Cf. Bruce, *Galatians*, 24–25.

37. Cf. W. Schmithals, *Paul and the Gnostics* (trans. J. Steely; Nashville: Abingdon, 1972),
13–64, who concludes that Paul's opponents were Jewish-Christian gnostics. This position is
not widely accepted.

38. See J. M. G. Barclay, *Obeying the Truth: A Study of Paul's Ethics in Galatians* (Edinburgh: T&T Clark, 1988).

39. See R. Jewett, "The Agitators and the Gentile Congregation," *NTS* 17 (1970–71): 198–
212; accepted by Martin, *Foundations*, 2.154–56. A recent, but fairly radical, variation on this
position is held by Mark Nanos, who argues that "the teachers opposing Paul are not Jewish
believers but non-Christ-believing representatives of local synagogues seeking to persuade the
Gentile believers to become Jewish proselytes" (the summary is from S. Chester, "Paul and
the Galatian Believers," in *The Blackwell Companion to Paul* [ed. S. Westerholm; West Sussex,
UK: Wiley-Blackwell, 2011], 63–78, quoting 64). See M. D. Nanos, *The Irony of Galatians: Paul's
Letter in First-Century Context* (Minneapolis: Fortress, 2002), esp. 75–199; and "Intruding
'Spies' and 'Pseudo-Brethren': The Jewish Intra-Group Politics of Paul's Jerusalem Meeting
(Gal 2:1–10)," in *Paul and His Opponents* (ed. S. E. Porter; PAST 2; Leiden: Brill, 2005), 59–97.
As Chester rightly points out, the proof against Nanos's view is what Paul directly says about
those who teach other gospels (see below).

would avoid persecution for association with Gentiles, arguing that God required it of them. Since the language of the letter is concerned with strictly Jewish practices and beliefs such as the law (Gal 3), circumcision (5:6; 6:15), and the calendar (4:10), and the opponents are characterized in terms of those who are not true followers of Christ, this view is unlikely.

c. A third position is that there are possibly two opponents, the Judaizers (see above) and libertine pneumatics, or those emphasizing life in the Spirit (6:1), who were attacking Paul's claim to apostleship. But the libertine dimension to the opponents can be explained simply as a part of the teaching of the Judaizers under the Judaizer hypothesis above. Since Paul seems to address his opponents as one cohesive group, it is not necessary to posit two sets of opponents.

d. A fourth possible view, advocated by Emanuel Hirsch, is that the opponents were Gentile Christians from Antioch who were converted to the ways of the Judaizers, who then in turn attempted to convert the Galatian Christians to their Judaizing ways.[40] The problem with this solution is that it is without any positive evidence that the opponents were Gentiles who were soliciting Jewish customs. It also seems unlikely that Paul would defend so fervently against these Gentile Christians and yet not mention once in the letter that they have been duped themselves by the "original" Judaizers. It seems that Paul would have attacked not only the Gentile converts to Judaizing, but the very ones who converted these Gentiles Christians as well—or at least to have made mention of them.

There are other views as well, but these are the ones that continue to be discussed and at least gather some enduring support.[41] Considering the above options, I maintain that the first, majority view—that Paul's opponents in Galatia were Judaizers—is still the most likely option. There is some discussion regarding the nature of these Judaizers and their agenda. A. E. Harvey argues that their agenda was not at all theological, as many make it out to be, but prac-

40. E. Hirsch, "Zwei Fragen zu Gal 6," *Zeitschrift für die neutestamentliche Wissenschaft* 29 (1930): 192–97.

41. Two other recent views both try to situate Galatians within the religious or cultural world of the time. Susan Elliott argues that Paul is opposed to self-castration practiced by some religious cults in Asia Minor; *Cutting Too Close for Comfort: Paul's Letter to the Galatians in Its Anatolian Cultic Context* (JSNTSup 248; London: T&T Clark, 2003). Justin Hardin sees Galatians as Paul's response to those in Galatia wishing to avoid the rising emperor cult; *Galatians and the Imperial Cult* (WUNT 2/237; Tübingen: Mohr-Siebeck, 2008). For response to both of these, see Chester, "Paul and the Galatians Believers," 64–65.

tical.[42] In other words, he contends that Paul was not involved in a debate over proper Christian doctrine, but fighting against "a tendency to adopt Jewish observances under threat of persecution or discrimination."[43] This does not explain, however, Paul's seemingly heated response to them for the *gospel* of Christ, which is in essence theological in nature. Paul makes clear that the Galatians' retroversion to rites like circumcision was a threat, not just to Christian practice, but to the gospel itself. Furthermore, as seen in a majority of Paul's letters, Christian practice seems to stem from Christian doctrine, as seen in the usual Pauline letter form where the body (containing doctrine) is usually followed by a section of paraenesis (see chapter 5 §3). The Judaizers, then, were a group that not only advocated Jewish rites without any doctrinal basis but advocated their beliefs regarding salvation through practices like circumcision.

E. Outline of Galatians

A. Opening (1:1–5)
1. Sender (1:1–2a)
2. Addressee (1:2b)
3. Greeting (1:3–4)
4. Doxology (1:5)
(B. Thanksgiving—none)
C. Body: in defense of the apostle (1:6–5:12)
1. Body's opening: a contrary gospel (1:6–9)
2. Paul's authority (1:10–2:14)
3. Paul's defense (2:15–4:31)
4. Body's close on Christian freedom (5:1–12)
D. Paraenesis (5:13–6:10)[44]
1. Love fulfills the law (5:13–15)
2. The Spirit overcomes the flesh (5:16–26)
3. The law of Christ is to help one another (6:1–10)
E. Closing (6:11–18)
1. Pauline authority (6:11–17)
2. Benediction (6:18)

42. A. E. Harvey, "The Opposition to Paul," in *The Galatians Debate* (ed. M. D. Nanos; Peabody, MA: Hendrickson, 2002), 321–33.
43. Harvey, "The Opposition to Paul," 330.
44. See F. J. Matera, "The Culmination of Paul's Argument to the Galatians: Gal. 5.1–6.17," *JSNT* 32 (1988): 59–91.

F. *Content of Galatians*

Opening (1:1-5)

In the conventional Pauline (and ancient Greco-Roman) beginning of a letter, Paul identifies himself as the writer. The opening is standard, except for a lengthy explanation of Paul's apostleship: "not from people nor through a person" (οὐκ ἀπ᾽ ἀνθρώπων οὐδὲ δι᾽ ἀνθρώπου), but through Jesus Christ himself.

A major issue regarding the opening concerns the original audience of the letter, that is, to whom exactly Paul is writing; or, in other words, who exactly are the "churches of Galatia" (ταῖς ἐκκλησίαις τῆς Γαλατίας). I conclude above that, while evidence points to either of the North Galatia or South Galatia theories, it seems as if Paul was writing to those churches that occupied the southern Roman province of Galatia, which consisted of various ethnic groups not limited to ethnic Galatians.

Body: Body's Opening (1:6-9)

The next section in most of Paul's letters, after the initial opening/greeting that identifies the writer and recipient, is a thanksgiving section. The thanksgiving provides a few statements of varying lengths giving thanks to God for the recipients of his letter and whatever traits or characteristics they have displayed or thanks for what God has been doing in them (cf. Rom 1:8; 1 Cor 1:4; Eph 1:16; Phil 1:3; Col 1:3; 1 Thess 1:2; 2 Thess 1:3; 2 Tim 1:3; Phlm 4). There is some scholarly debate as to whether Paul takes a Greco-Roman epistolary convention of thanksgiving, which does not typically include thanks to God, and Christianizes it, or whether he is simply doing something different in his thanksgiving section.[45] Instead, Paul skips this section altogether and goes immediately to rebuke the Galatians.[46] This absence of a conventional Pauline epistolary section is widely observed, but it seems few really note the signifi-

---

45. See J. T. Reed, "Are Paul's Thanksgivings 'Epistolary'?" *JSNT* 61 (1996): 87-99. Cf. D. W. Pao, "Gospel within the Constraints of an Epistolary Form: Pauline Introductory Thanksgivings and Paul's Theology of Thanksgiving," in *Paul and the Ancient Letter Form* (ed. S. E. Porter and S. A. Adams; PAST 6; Leiden: Brill, 2010), 101-27. It seems that Paul, reflecting the Greco-Roman letter-writing convention, adapts the thanksgiving section to his own Christian perspective.

46. Bruce (*Galatians*, 80) states that the reason for this is because Paul was "impelled by a sense of overmastering urgency to come straight to the point." But I do not think "urgency" goes far enough to describe what Paul is doing here with this omission.

cance of this omission and its effect on the organization of the letter.[47] In the opening of the letter, Paul presents all of the participants of the letter together, in syntactical unity (with Paul in the Greek nominative case and the Galatians in the dative, the usual pattern), and then elaborates their relationship in terms of the work of God through Christ. Whereas the reader, including the recipients, might have expected a statement or two of thanksgiving, Paul instead provides a sharp rebuke regarding their departure from the Christ who called them. This omission heightens this juxtaposed organizational contrast between the common recognition of the work of Christ and the quick and deleterious departure from the gospel and the seeking of another.[48]

In this body opening section, then, Paul communicates his utter astonishment that the Galatian believers had already and so quickly laid aside what they had formerly been taught by Paul regarding the gospel to accept the "other gospel" that the Judaizers were advocating. This section contains hyperbole, where Paul says that they should reject "another gospel," even if an angel from heaven were to preach one other than the one he has preached to them. It is not that an angel from heaven would actually preach another gospel, but Paul speaks rhetorically to stress that they should not accept any other gospel that deviates from what he has preached to them. He also uses strong language to express his astonishment and displeasure at the Galatians, stating that these Judaizers (though they are not called that here) should be accursed (ἀνάθεμα).

Body: Paul's Authority (1:10–2:14)

The next portion of the body consists of an explanation of Paul's authority for the gospel, which he does with an autobiographical sketch or testimony of his post-conversion experiences. In recounting events that are not mentioned in Paul's other conversion testimonies (Acts 22 and 26), Paul includes his journeys to Jerusalem on a few occasions and the "unknown" years between his conversion and preaching ministry. The prominent feature of this testimony is that he had been called directly by God to preach the gospel.[49] He was not

47. Cf. R. E. van Voorst, "Why Is There No Thanksgiving Period in Galatians? An Assessment of an Exegetical Commonplace," *JBL* 129.1 (2010): 153–72, who claims the Galatians had no reason to expect a Pauline thanksgiving.

48. For more on what I term a functional-letter perspective (used here in my exposition of the opening of Galatians), see S. E. Porter, "A Functional Letter Perspective: Towards a Grammar of Epistolary Form," in *Paul and the Ancient Letter Form* (ed. S. E. Porter and S. A. Adams; PAST 6; Leiden: Brill, 2010), 9–32, esp. 24–26.

49. Cf. D. I. Yoon, "Prominence and Markedness in New Testament Discourse: Galatians

taught or trained by any of the other apostles, but the gospel was a product of direct revelation. He mentions in this early part of the letter the issue of circumcision and how Titus was not even circumcised for the sake of keeping the gospel clear. Paul recounts how, after he had been ministering, the "pillars," James, Peter, and John, approved of his ministry to the uncircumcised.

The portion ends with what is commonly called the Antioch incident, where Paul confronted Peter for his hypocrisy in avoiding table fellowship with the Gentiles.[50] Paul recounts that he opposed Peter to his face, because of the hypocrisy Peter had displayed. Peter had previously joined in table fellowship with the Gentiles in Antioch, but, due to certain representatives from James, Peter withdrew. Not only did Peter withdraw, but a number of other Jewish believers followed suit, including Barnabas, who was Paul's close partner in ministry. Paul does not tell his readers the outcome of that confrontation, which has resulted in interpreters wondering about Peter's response.[51]

Body: Paul's Defense (2:15–4:31)

Many interpreters and Bible translators conclude that Paul's speech ends here, with the rest of this section being a discourse on justification and works of the law for the recipients.[52] In this view, Paul's rebuke of Peter serves as a smooth transition to speaking of what was really at stake in the Galatians' shift in thought. The vast bulk of the letter is Paul's defense of the gospel he preached to them, which includes not only a (re)iteration of the gospel message itself but also a defense of that gospel.

Paul begins this section with the statement—a summary of the gospel message he fights for—that "a person is not justified by the works of the law,

---

1,11–2,10 as a Test Case," *Filología Neotestamentaria* 26 (2013): 37–55, who examines linguistic prominence to analyze this passage.

50. Cf. J. D. G. Dunn, "The Incident at Antioch (Gal 2:11–18)," *JSNT* 18 (1983): 3–57, reprinted in J. D. G. Dunn, *Jesus, Paul, and the Law: Studies in Mark and Galatians* (Louisville: Westminster John Knox, 1990), 129–82, with additional notes; see also D. I. Yoon, "The Antioch Incident and a Textual Variant: ἦλθον or ἦλθεν in Galatians 2:12," *Expository Times* 125 (2014): 432–39, who claims that a minority reading of 2:12 would imply that Peter premeditated his withdrawal from the Gentiles, instead of simply reacting poorly to James's representatives arriving in Antioch.

51. Dunn seems to think that Paul's rebuke was unsuccessful; cf. Dunn, *Jesus, Paul, and the Law*, 160. But depending on one's view of the relationship between Gal 2 and Acts 15, in the latter episode Peter is seen to advocate Gentile inclusion and discourage placing an unnecessary burden on them.

52. Cf. Bruce, *Galatians*, 136, who states that Paul's rebuke of Peter is summarized and the implications are developed further in the rest of the letter.

but by faith in Jesus Christ" (2:16 NIV 2011).[53] This statement alone contains two points of contention that Pauline scholars have debated for years: the meanings of "works of the law" and "faith of/in Jesus Christ" (see chapter 4 §3B and §2E). In fact, it may be fair to say that the rest of the body of this letter is an expansion of this statement, that justification of an individual occurs not by obedience to the law, but by faith in Jesus Christ.

After presenting his summary of the gospel, Paul sets out to argue for and defend it in the remainder of this body section. He calls the Galatians "foolish" (ἀνόητοι) for being duped by these opponents, who have given them a false gospel. After a series of rhetorical questions, Paul reiterates that offspring of Abraham are those who live by faith, quoting from the Jewish Scriptures to support his contention.[54] To illustrate this point, he uses the analogy of a human covenant, which cannot be annulled once it has been ratified, to compare with promises God made to Abraham. The promises are not kept because of obedience to the law, Paul says, but are kept because they were promised by God. He anticipates the objection that the promises and the law are contrary to each other according to this scheme, so he "responds" by affirming that in fact they are not contrary to each other but complementary, since the function of the law was to make people aware of their transgressions, until the appropriate time for God to send Jesus Christ, who is the object of faith. Those who put their faith in Christ, then, are called heirs to the promises that were given to Abraham, regardless of race, social status, or gender. Paul continues his discourse, going into greater detail about what it means to be an heir of the promises of God. This leads to another illustration, an analogy regarding Hagar and Sarah from the Genesis account that uses them as an allegory for the son of the slave (Hagar) and the son of the free woman (Sarah). The son of the slave is still under the law, but the son of the free woman is under the promise, and Paul identifies the Galatians with the son of the free woman. While it may be politically incorrect today to speak of slavery, Paul uses this language to illustrate the difference between living under the law and living under the promise.[55]

53. Cf. de Boer, *Galatians*, 139.

54. There is much discussion regarding how Paul uses the Old Testament in his argument here, especially because of the seemingly enigmatic way in which he uses these quotations. Cf. e.g., Hansen, *Abraham in Galatians*, 109–39; and P. M. Sprinkle, *Law and Life: The Interpretation of Leviticus 18:5 in Early Judaism and in Paul* (WUNT 2/241; Tübingen: Mohr-Siebeck, 2008), 133–64.

55. On the slavery metaphors in Galatians, see S. Tsang, *From Slaves to Sons: A New Rhetoric Analysis on Paul's Slave Metaphors in His Letter to the Galatians* (Studies in Biblical Literature 81; New York: Peter Lang, 2005).

Body: Body's Close on Christian Freedom (5:1–12)

In light of just having written about slavery, Paul ends the body section of his letter with discussion of Christian freedom.[56] After his explanation of the gospel that he once taught them concerning justification not by works of the law but by faith, Paul's attention turns back to those who persuaded the Galatians with a false gospel.[57] He concludes the body section with an equally strong statement as the body opening: that he wishes that those who unsettle the Galatians would emasculate themselves.

Paraenesis: Love Fulfills the Law (5:13–15)

After having expounded what justification by faith apart from works of the law means, Paul now exhorts his readers as to what it means practically for them that they are free in Christ. He exhorts the Galatians not to use their freedom to satisfy the flesh, but instead to love one another. Even after such a lengthy discourse against the law (or perhaps more accurately *works* of the law), Paul still states that the entire law is summed up in the command to "love your neighbor as yourself" (NIV). This may well be a way Paul conveys that he is not entirely against the law but against the reliance upon obedience to the law as a means of attaining favor with God (and against the New Perspective; see chapter 4 §3B).

Paraenesis: Spirit Overcomes Flesh (5:16–26)

Continuing on the topics of freedom and satisfying the desires of the flesh, Paul further exhorts his readers to "walk by the Spirit," and contrasts this with "works of the flesh." He pits them against each other and describes, first, what the works of the flesh entail—characteristics such as sexual immorality, impurity, sensuality, idolatry—and second, what the fruit of the Spirit is—love, joy, peace, patience, and so on. He concludes that those who are of Christ Jesus have crucified the flesh, along with its passions and desires.

---

56. Cf. L. Morris, *Galatians: Paul's Charter of Christian Freedom* (Downers Grove, IL: InterVarsity, 2003).

57. The question of whether Paul had earlier preached a gospel of circumcision (5:11) was raised again recently by D. A. Campbell, "Galatians 5.11: Evidence of an Early Law-Observant Mission by Paul?" *NTS* 57 (2011): 325–47. Campbell's arguments against previous proposals are more convincing than his modern analogies used in support of his claims.

Paraenesis: The Law of Christ Is to Help One Another (6:1–10)

The third and final portion of the paraenesis continues the idea of walking by the Spirit and focuses on three more specific situations. The first situation, concerning one who is caught in sin, states that those who are spiritual are to help that person in a gentle manner, but also to keep watch themselves, lest they fall into the same temptation. The second is to help others by bearing their burdens, a more general situation. Paul states a few lines further down that each will have to bear their own load. At first glance, this may seem contradictory, except that in the first, Paul commands them to bear each other's burdens, but in the end, they must realize that everyone is responsible for their own. The third situation is that the Galatians were to help one another by sharing good things with the one who has taught them. This may be a partial reference by Paul to himself or to the other leaders in the churches in Galatia, but he recognizes that leaders need help as well, and the Galatians were to contribute by sharing all good things with them, possibly even including financial goods (to be taken as a general command).

Closing (6:11–18)

Paul closes the letter by taking the pen from his amanuensis and writing a few lines himself.[58] This statement is supposed to provide proof for the Galatians that Paul himself had written the letter. His final words go back to the main thesis of the body, regarding his opponents who advocate circumcision. Paul affirms again that circumcision, and even noncircumcision, does not mean anything, but a new creation is what is at stake. He tells the Galatians that he bears the marks of Jesus—most likely a reference to his scars from numerous beatings—and wishes no more trouble. He closes the letter by referring to his readers as "brothers (and sisters)," which indicates that he still has hope for them to turn around and accept the gospel he preached to them.

---

58. Cf. J. A. D. Weima, "Gal 6:11–18: A Hermeneutical Key to the Galatian Letter," *Calvin Theological Journal* 28 (1993): 90–107.

Sources for Further Study

Commentaries

Betz, H. D. *Galatians: A Commentary on Paul's Letter to the Churches in Galatia*. Hermeneia. Philadelphia: Fortress, 1979.
Bruce, F. F. *The Epistle to the Galatians: A Commentary on the Greek Text*. NIGTC. Grand Rapids: Eerdmans, 1982.
Burton, E. D. W. *A Critical and Exegetical Commentary on the Epistle to the Galatians*. ICC. Edinburgh: T&T Clark, 1921.
de Boer, M. *Galatians*. NTL. Louisville: Westminster John Knox, 2011.
Dunn, J. D. G. *The Epistle to the Galatians*. BNTC. Peabody, MA: Hendrickson, 1993.
Fung, R. Y. K. *The Epistle to the Galatians*. NICNT. Grand Rapids: Eerdmans, 1988.
Lightfoot, J. B. *The Epistle of St. Paul to the Galatians*. 8th ed. London: Macmillan, 1884.
Longenecker, R. N. *Galatians*. WBC 41. Dallas: Word, 1990.
Lührmann, D. *Galatians: A Continental Commentary*. Translated by O. C. Dean Jr. Minneapolis: Fortress, 1992.
Martyn, J. L. *Galatians*. AB 33A. New York: Doubleday, 1997.
Matera, F. J. *Galatians*. Sacra Pagina 9. Collegeville, MN: Liturgical, 1992.
Moo, D. J. *Galatians*. BECNT. Grand Rapids: Baker, 2013.
Ramsay, W. M. *A Historical Commentary on St. Paul's Epistle to the Galatians*. London: Hodder & Stoughton, 1899.

Monographs and Books

Barclay, J. M. G. *Obeying the Truth: A Study of Paul's Ethics in Galatians*. Edinburgh: T&T Clark, 1988.
Dunn, J. D. G. *Jesus, Paul, and the Law: Studies in Mark and Galatians*. Louisville: Westminster John Knox, 1990.
Elliott, S. *Cutting Too Close for Comfort: Paul's Letter to the Galatians in Its Anatolian Cultic Context*. JSNTSup 248. London: T&T Clark, 2003.
Elmer, I. J. *Paul, Jerusalem, and the Judaizers: The Galatian Crisis in Its Broadest Historical Context*. WUNT 2/258. Tübingen: Mohr-Siebeck, 2009.
Hansen, G. W. *Abraham in Galatians: Epistolary and Rhetorical Contexts*. JSNTSup 29. Sheffield: JSOT Press, 1989.
Hardin, J. *Galatians and the Imperial Cult*. WUNT 2/237. Tübingen: Mohr-Siebeck, 2008.
Howard, G. *Paul: Crisis in Galatia: A Study in Early Christian Theology*. 2nd ed. SNTSMS 35. Cambridge: Cambridge University Press, 1990 (1979).

Lyons, G. *Pauline Autobiography: Toward a New Understanding*. SBLDS 73. Atlanta: Scholars Press, 1985.

Morris, L. *Galatians: Paul's Charter of Christian Freedom*. Downers Grove, IL: Inter-Varsity, 2003.

Nanos, M. D. *The Irony of Galatians: Paul's Letter in First-Century Context*. Minneapolis: Fortress, 2002.

―――, ed. *The Galatians Debate: Contemporary Issues in Rhetorical and Historical Interpretation*. Peabody, MA: Hendrickson, 2002.

O'Neill, J. C. *The Recovery of Paul's Letter to the Galatians*. London: SPCK, 1972.

Porter, S. E., ed. *Paul and His Opponents*. PAST 2. Leiden: Brill, 2005.

Silva, M. *Explorations in Exegetical Method: Galatians as a Test Case*. Grand Rapids: Baker, 1996.

Tsang, S. *From Slaves to Sons: A New Rhetoric Analysis on Paul's Slave Metaphors in His Letter to the Galatians*. Studies in Biblical Literature 81. New York: Peter Lang, 2005.

8

1-2 Thessalonians

1. Introduction

In this chapter, I treat the letters of 1-2 Thessalonians together.[1] Many find these letters offer intriguing and often inspiring accounts of the relationship of the church at Thessalonica to its apostle. The two letters have traditionally been treated together, not only because of their purported common audience and authorship, but because they also have overlapping content. Nevertheless, despite these common features, a number of critical discussions regarding one or both of these letters merit their individual treatment.

2. First Thessalonians

First Thessalonians is now placed among the undisputed letters, even if this has not always been the case among critical scholars. However, there are many interesting and unique features of this letter, in particular its continuing emphasis upon thanksgiving by Paul for the Thessalonian believers. I begin with a brief discussion of the city of Thessalonica before treating Paul's visit there; the matter of authorship, date of composition, and epistolary unity; its relationship to Acts; and finally its occasion and purpose, before presenting an outline and its content.

---

1. For a thorough annotated bibliography of work on Thessalonians, see J. A. D. Weima and S. E. Porter, *An Annotated Bibliography of 1 and 2 Thessalonians* (NTTS 26; Leiden: Brill, 1998).

A. City of Thessalonica

The city of Thessalonica was technically a part of the ancient kingdom of Macedonia, the home of Alexander the Great and his father, Philip.[2] But since that time (mid-fourth century BC), with the influence that Philip and Alexander exerted upon restructuring this portion of the world, Macedonia had been considered part of the wider sphere of Greek influence, and for all intents and purposes Thessalonica was considered a Greek city. For a time, this northern portion of Greek territory, extending well into Macedonia proper, had existed independently as one of the Diadochian kingdoms after the dissolution of Alexander's empire following his death in 323 BC, but with Roman expansion across the Adriatic Sea, it was inevitable that Macedonia would engage in conflict with Rome. After several wars, Macedonia was finally incorporated into the Roman Empire, first as four separate republics, with Thessalonica the leading city of the southernmost of these republics, and then finally as the one large province of Macedonia in 148 BC.

The city of Thessalonica itself was founded in 315 BC and soon became an important city, as it lay on what became a major thoroughfare (known in Roman times as the Via Egnatia, or Egnatian Way) from the Adriatic Sea to Philippi and on to Byzantium. After a hundred years of Roman provincial rule, in 42 BC Thessalonica became a free city: its citizens enjoyed self-governance, under the authority of a person with the title of politarch or under some other form of governor. The accuracy of the account in Acts 17:6 referring to a politarch in Thessalonica used to be questioned, since it was the only literary text to record the title "politarch." In the twentieth century, however, several inscriptions bearing witness to the title were discovered, even though the exact function of this official is not entirely clear.[3]

The city seemed to consist of a mixed population, not untypical of numerous cities of the Roman Empire. According to Acts 17:2, there was a Jewish community in the city, since they had a synagogue where they worshiped.[4] Christianity came to Thessalonica during Paul's travels in approximately 50–52, on what is sometimes referred to as his second missionary journey. He began his ministry in this city by preaching in the synagogue, and it is reasonable, on the basis of what we find in the letter itself, to conclude that the account in

2. See H. L. Hendrix, "Thessalonica," *ABD* 6.523–27.
3. See G. H. R. Horsley, "The Politarchs," in *The Book of Acts in Its Graeco-Roman Setting* (ed. D. W. J. Gill and C. Gempf; BAFCS 2; Grand Rapids: Eerdmans, 1994), 419–31; *NewDocs* 2.34–35.
4. V. P. Furnish, *1 & 2 Thessalonians* (Abingdon New Testament Commentaries; Nashville: Abingdon, 2007), 26.

Acts, which says that there were converts, is accurate. According to Acts, the converts were both Jews and Godfearers—Gentiles who respected the moral, ethical, and theological disposition of Judaism but resisted full proselytization, which would have involved circumcision.[5]

B. Paul in Thessalonica

The account in Acts 17:1–9 says that, on his second missionary journey, Paul went to the synagogue in Thessalonica for three Sabbaths before the Jews were aroused to jealousy, formed a mob, and started a riot that forced Paul to leave the city. In light of the nature of the correspondence with the Thessalonians, especially the way it evidently adds to teaching on a number of issues that Paul apparently discussed with them, many scholars inquire exactly how long Paul was in Thessalonica. A number conclude that he must have been in the city longer than Acts states. William Ramsay, for example, argues that Paul was in Thessalonica for approximately six months.[6] Some determine that it is possible to posit a significantly longer period of time in the city, with the reference to three Sabbath days perhaps only describing his initial discussion or the length of time he attended the synagogue before he had converts.[7] Of course, there is also the possibility that the Acts account here does not completely record all that happened in Thessalonica.

From Thessalonica, Paul went on to Berea, where he was followed by troublemakers from Thessalonica (17:13). He then went to Athens (17:16–33) and then to Corinth (18:1–18), where he stayed for one and a half years, according to Acts (chapter 2 §2). This occurred during the reign of the Roman governor Gallio and provides one of the reasonably certain dates for establishing the Pauline chronology. Paul was apparently in Corinth from approximately 50 to 52, and it was during this time that he probably wrote his letter to the Thessa-

5. On the Godfearers, see M. C. de Boer, "God-Fearers in Luke–Acts," in *Luke's Literary Achievement: Collected Essays* (ed. C. M. Tuckett; JSNTSup 116; Sheffield: Sheffield Academic, 1995), 50–71; I. Levinskaya, *The Book of Acts in Its Diaspora Setting* (BAFCS 5; Grand Rapids: Eerdmans, 1996), 51–126; J. A. Overman, "The God-Fearers: Some Neglected Features," in *New Testament Backgrounds: A Sheffield Reader* (ed. C. A. Evans and S. E. Porter; BS 43; Sheffield: Sheffield Academic, 1997), 253–62; and J. M. Lieu, *Neither Jew nor Greek? Constructing Early Christianity* (Studies of the New Testament and Its World; New York: T&T Clark, 2002), 31–68.

6. W. M. Ramsay, *St. Paul the Traveller and the Roman Citizen* (London: Hodder & Stoughton, 1895), 228.

7. See L. Morris, *The First and Second Epistles to the Thessalonians* (rev. ed.; NICNT; Grand Rapids: Eerdmans, 1991), 3.

Ionian church known as 1 Thessalonians (the authenticity of 2 Thessalonians is discussed below). If 2 Thessalonians is authentic as well, it was probably written soon after 1 Thessalonians from Corinth. Mention in 1 Thessalonians of Philippi (2:2), Macedonia and Achaia (1:7-8), and Athens (3:1) matches what Acts tells us of Paul's itinerary during this trip through Asia Minor, Macedonia, and Achaia (or Greece). This occasion to write seems to have arisen fairly soon after Paul left the city, when he followed up on a number of the issues that he had apparently initially discussed with them during his time there. Perhaps the time Paul spent in Thessalonica is not as long as some scholars think necessary; a number of the issues raised in the letter appear to be ones that Paul would have reasonably discussed with the Thessalonians if he had been with them for a significant amount of time, such as the destiny of Christians who have died before the return of Christ.

Did Paul ever revisit the city, for which he had so many good things to say? He may well have done so on what is called his third missionary journey, probably about five years later (ca. 56), as is recorded in Acts 19:21 and 20:1-3. On this journey, Paul went to and from Achaia (Greece) through Macedonia and may well have passed through Thessalonica, possibly on his outward journey. On the basis of Paul's statement in Rom 15:19 regarding the spread of the gospel from Jerusalem all the way to Illyricum, some speculate that Paul may have traveled west on the Via Egnatia into the territory of Illyricum. He may have had the intention of crossing over the Adriatic Sea to Rome, or even of traveling into a Latin-speaking territory in preparation for a future trip to Rome or Spain. This cannot be established with any certainty and in fact is probably unlikely, especially since the phrasing in Romans may well refer only to the spread of the gospel from Jerusalem as far as (or up to) Illyricum.

C. Authorship, Date of Composition, and Epistolary Unity of First Thessalonians

The authorship of 1 Thessalonians is generally not now disputed.[8] It is widely accepted as genuinely Pauline, except by a very small number of the most negative of critics, several of whom wrote during the nineteenth century during a particularly skeptical period of continental European criticism.[9] The exter-

8. See R. Jewett, *The Thessalonian Correspondence: Pauline Rhetoric and Millenarian Piety* (FFNT; Philadelphia: Fortress, 1986), 3.

9. E.g., K. Schrader, *Der Apostel Paulus* (Leipzig: Kollman, 1836); and F. C. Baur, *Paul*

nal testimony to Pauline authorship of 1 Thessalonians is well established and includes Marcion (Tertullian, *Against Marcion* 5.15; mid-second century) and the Muratorian Fragment. Irenaeus, in the third century, also quotes it directly (*Against Heresies* 5.6.1; 5.30.2).[10]

This external evidence is confirmatory of the scenario recounted in the section above regarding when Paul would have written the letter in relation to the chronology of Acts. According to this scenario, Paul probably wrote the letter to the Thessalonians relatively soon after he left them, quite possibly during his two-year stay in Corinth (50–52). The internal evidence of 1 Thessalonians is confirmatory of this early and Pauline authorship as well, since there are several distinctive markings of Paul as the letter's author. The first is the opening of the letter, which claims to have come from Paul, Silas (or Silvanus), and Timothy. (The discussion of pseudonymity and the Pauline letters in chapter 6 §1 suggests that epistolary pseudonymity was a more widespread phenomenon in the ancient world than many more conservative scholars wish to recognize. A plausible case for the pseudonymity of this letter cannot, however, be made in light of the other criteria for authenticity.) Although the three people are named at the beginning, and the plurality is to be taken seriously in considering the role of all three in authorship, it seems that Paul is the predominant author of the letter, as evident in the "lapses" into first-person singular (2:18; 3:5; 5:27) that show up in the course of the letter.[11] Silas and Timothy seem to be named along with Paul to acknowledge that they were partners with him in their ministry to Thessalonica and possibly to further support the contents in Paul's letter—if Silas and Timothy had credibility among the Thessalonian believers.

Second, there is internal evidence of an early date for 1 Thessalonians in 5:12, where Paul, referring to church organization, mentions "those who . . . have charge of you." This seems to imply that at this point there was not a formal title for those in positions of leadership within local congregations of believers. That such titles apparently were developed quite early is confirmed by Phil 1:1, but that letter was probably written ten years later. (Acts 14:23, which mentions the appointment of "elders" [πρεσβυτέρους] on Paul's so-called first missionary journey, indicates the establishment of positions of church leadership early on but does not necessarily contradict this, since the

the Apostle of Jesus Christ: His Life and Work, His Epistles and His Doctrine (2 vols.; London: Williams & Norgate, 1873–75; repr. Peabody, MA: Hendrickson, 2003), 2.85–97.

10. See J. Moffatt, *An Introduction to the Literature of the New Testament* (3rd ed.; Edinburgh: T&T Clark, 1918), 69–70.

11. Cf. G. D. Fee, *The First and Second Letters to the Thessalonians* (NICNT; Grand Rapids: Eerdmans, 2009), 4–5.

author of Luke–Acts may be retroactively ascribing titles developed by the time of his writing, if indeed these are titles.)[12]

Third and finally, also confirmatory of an early and Pauline date is the issue of the parousia, or return of Christ (1 Thess 4:13–5:11). The author may well have had the expectation—or at least was open to the possibility—of being alive at the time of the return of Christ (although reference in 4:17 to "we who are left" does not necessarily indicate that Paul expects to be among this group). This is in any case an unlikely stance for a later (and hence non-Pauline) author to take, especially if it were known that Paul was dead, and it introduces an unnecessary hypothesis in light of what is known about the early eschatology of the church, with its expectation regarding Christ's return. The evidence is sufficiently ambiguous even among the undisputed Pauline letters that it would be unwarranted to posit too strongly what Paul's definitive position on Christ's imminent return was. But it is fair to say that he was at least open to this possibility, even if it was not, in his mind, as strong a likelihood later on (as 2 Corinthians, esp. 5:1–10, and Philippians, esp. 1:21–24 and 2:17, both later letters, seem to confirm). The scene regarding expectation of the parousia painted in this letter is consistent with the portrait of Paul drawn in Acts and makes it entirely likely that Paul would have written a letter of this sort to the Thessalonian church.

In spite of this substantial evidence regarding Pauline authorship, there is still some debate over the integrity or unity of the letter. Two passages—1 Thess 2:13–16 and 5:1–11—are suggested to be later interpolations.[13] The first passage is questioned on the grounds that it appears to be anti-Semitic, stating that the Jews are the ones who killed Jesus.[14] This purportedly reflects not only an un-Pauline theological perspective (cf. Rom 11:25–26) but also events after the destruction of Jerusalem. Hence, according to this view, it may well be a post–70 interpolation reflecting later Jewish-Christian tensions. This proposal should be rejected on many fronts: (1) it fails to appreciate the early tensions between Jews and Christians, at least from the time of Paul; (2) the kind of hyperbole found in this passage is well within the parameters of Paul's argu-

---

12. Paul's reference to himself as a servant in 1 Cor 3:5 and 4:1 may also show a stage of development in this terminology, although the contexts of these passages are not parallel to the more technical uses in the examples above.

13. The question of how evidence is evaluated regarding interpolations is ably raised by W. O. Walker Jr., *Interpolations in the Pauline Letters* (JSNTSup 213; Sheffield: Sheffield Academic, 2001), 211–20; cf. Walker, "The Burden of Proof in Identifying Interpolations in Pauline Letters," *NTS* 33 (1987): 610–18; and G. Friedrich, "1. Thessalonischer 5,1–11, der apologetische Einschub eines Späteren," *Zeitschrift für die Theologie und Kirche* 70 (1973): 288–315.

14. E.g., B. A. Pearson, "1 Thessalonians 2:13–16: A Deutero-Pauline Interpolation," *Harvard Theological Review* 64 (1971): 79–94; and Walker, *Interpolations*, 210–20.

mentative style; and (3) there is no good reason for this interpolation.[15] The most convincing argument is that the passage is misunderstood, so that 2:14 and 2:15 should be connected without a comma (added by later editors in any case), hence making the modifying clause restrictive: Paul is condemning only Jews who killed Jesus, not all Jews.[16]

Arguments that 5:1–11 is non-Pauline stem from the premise that the author was correcting Paul's mistaken view of the parousia. Used in support of this premise are changes in wording (παρουσία ["coming"], used elsewhere in this letter, gives way here to "day of the Lord") and parallels with passages that do not express eschatological imminence. This position has found few supporters, since the kinds of contrasts that it depends upon do not seem justified.[17] Despite arguments that draw attention to problems in the text and features of the language, these theories do not convince most scholars, so that it is fair to say that the letter can be treated in its entirety as authentically Pauline. (Redactional and partition theories are discussed in §3 below.)

D. First Thessalonians and Acts

If we disregard this evidence for coherence between 1 Thessalonians and the picture of the early church in Acts, a number of apparent discrepancies between 1 Thessalonians and Acts are worth mentioning (in addition to how many Sabbaths Paul spent in Thessalonica; see §2B above). The first concerns the composition of the Thessalonian church. In the letter itself, the author appears to be addressing Gentiles, since he mentions that they turned from idols to serve God (1 Thess 1:9); they have suffered from their own countrymen, just as other churches suffered from the Jews (2:14); and they now are unlike the heathen (4:5). The problem for some scholars arises from the account in Acts, where no mention is made of converts from paganism. It must be kept in mind, however, that the perspective of Acts may well be different from that of the letter, especially since, in several brief accounts in Acts of Paul's visits to cities, a far from complete list of events is recorded. More to the point is Acts not

15. A thorough defense of the authenticity of 1 Thess 2:14–16 is C. J. Schlueter, *Filling up the Measure: Polemical Hyperbole in 1 Thessalonians 2.14–16* (JSNTSup 98; Sheffield: Sheffield Academic, 1994).

16. A response to the supposed anti-Semitism, including the issue of punctuation, is found in S. E. Porter, "Translation, Exegesis, and 1 Thessalonians 2:14–15: Could a Comma Have Changed the Course of History?" *Bible Translator* 64.1 (2013): 82–98.

17. See Jewett, *Thessalonian Correspondence*, 36–42; and I. H. Marshall, *1 and 2 Thessalonians* (NCB; Grand Rapids: Eerdmans, 1983), 11–13.

recording that Paul's converts included Jews and Godfearers. There is sustained controversy regarding the category of Godfearers. A number of scholars, most recently led by Thomas Kraabel, argues that this category is an invention by the author of Luke–Acts and has no factual basis to describe a group in the religious climate of the ancient world.[18] It appears that Acts understands these people as Gentiles who found the moral, ethical, and theological perspective of Judaism commendatory and commensurate with their own inclinations. More recent publications drawing upon inscriptions give credence to the Acts account.[19] Acts does not say what proportion of Christian converts came from each category, but it is not unreasonable to conclude that the majority may well have been Gentiles, with most of these Godfearers.

A second point of contention revolves around the coauthorship of Timothy and Silas in light of the evidence in Acts. Acts 18:5 says that these companions rejoined Paul at Corinth, while 1 Thess 3:1–2 says that Timothy was in Athens. How can these data be made to square with the coauthorship of 1 Thessalonians and what we know of Pauline chronology?[20] The solution may well be that there was a journey—not recorded in Acts—by Silas and Timothy from Athens to Macedonia and then to Corinth. The chronology would be that Silas and Timothy waited in Berea while Paul went to Athens (Acts 17:14), from which he traveled to Corinth (17:16). Silas and Timothy arrived in Athens, but they were sent off again by Paul to Macedonia and then arrived in Corinth. This may well have provided the source of information from the church in Thessalonica to Paul, its apostle, who had so recently departed, apparently in some hurry, and was unable to impart anything close to all the teaching that the church required or that he would have been able to give bit by bit as situations arose. After Silas and Timothy rejoined Paul at Corinth and conveyed information from the church to him, he began his correspondence with them (18:5). Admittedly, this reconstruction is speculative, but its reading of the evidence must be considered.

E. Occasion and Purpose of First Thessalonians

It is important to establish the occasion and purpose of 1 Thessalonians. Timothy apparently brought back a good report after his visit (posited in §2D above,

---

18. A. T. Kraabel, "The Disappearance of the 'God-Fearers,'" *Numen* 28 (1981): 113–26.

19. E.g., P. W. van der Horst, "A New Altar of a Godfearer?" in *Hellenism–Judaism–Christianity: Essays on Their Interaction* (2nd ed.; Leuven: Peeters, 1998), 65–71. See also de Boer, "God-Fearers in Luke–Acts."

20. See also T. E. Phillips, *Paul, His Letters, and Acts* (Library of Pauline Studies; Peabody, MA: Hendrickson, 2009), 181–82.

but not stated in Acts) regarding the faith and love of the church at Thessalonica (1 Thess 3:6). According to Acts, Paul apparently had to leave Thessalonica in a hurry once the Jews were aroused to jealousy; it is not known how long Paul was in Thessalonica (Acts mentions three Sabbaths), and it is even possible that he was there longer than Acts records, perhaps even as long as six months (see section §2B above). Since he probably did not bring a number of issues to a satisfying conclusion because of his apparently speedy departure, perhaps some made accusations against Paul regarding his character. They may have chosen to depict him in a light similar to that of other itinerant teachers and philosophers in the ancient world, who entered a city and spoke publicly so long as they were well received and well rewarded by the people but who took advantage of these same people and then fled when trouble began.[21]

Paul therefore wrote to the Thessalonians with apparently a twofold purpose. The first was to express his general satisfaction with the believers in Thessalonica, and the second was to answer the charge that his motives might be suspect. He ends up answering a number of questions that Timothy evidently brought with him and that were being asked by the Thessalonian Christians, but his placement of these in the paraenetic section of the letter suggests that these were not initially at the forefront of his thinking or his purpose in writing.

Paul expresses satisfaction over the progress of the Christian community, using the thanksgiving of the letter (1:2–10) to express his thanks to God for their response to his message. He singles out their faith, love, and hope (1:3)—note his use of a rhetorically forceful list of three, the same list used in 1 Cor 13:13—as qualities that have produced results.[22] God has chosen them because the gospel came not only in words but in power and in the Holy Spirit (1 Thess 1:5). The Holy Spirit was the one who brought the message that they had received, the verification of which is their having become imitators of Paul and the compatriots of both himself and the Lord despite severe suffering. This may constitute an incidental reference to the persecution that some of the Christians at Thessalonica received when the Jews became hostile toward Paul. Later in the letter, Paul again encourages their perseverance in the face of opposition, this time from their own countrymen, that is, Gentiles (2:13–16). This section, too, expresses Paul's thanksgiving regarding the Thessalonians.

21. See A. J. Malherbe, "'Gentle as a Nurse': The Cynic Background to 1 Thessalonians 2," in *Paul and the Popular Philosophers* (Minneapolis: Fortress, 1989), 35–48. On Paul's relation to the church in Thessalonica, see Malherbe, *Paul and the Thessalonians: The Philosophic Tradition of Pastoral Care* (Philadelphia: Fortress, 1987).
22. Cf. Fee, *Thessalonians*, 23–26; also S. E. Porter, *Idioms of the Greek New Testament* (2nd ed.; Biblical Languages: Greek 2; Sheffield: Sheffield Academic, 1994), 95.

The thankful tone is so pronounced and interspersed throughout the first part of the letter that some propose that 1 Thessalonians is less a letter following the Pauline structure and more an expanded thanksgiving running throughout most of the first two chapters, possibly to 3:13, if not further.[23] In any case, the Thessalonians have become a model to all the believers in Macedonia and Achaia (Greece), and their faith is known everywhere (1:8–10). We would expect thankful expressions in the thanksgiving part of the letter. But it is also clear that Paul does not hesitate to withhold thanksgiving and commendation where they are not warranted, as in the letter to the Galatians. Indeed, there are few letters in the Pauline corpus, if any, where heartfelt thanks are more readily and freely given than in these opening verses of 1 Thessalonians.

Regarding the second purpose of the letter, Paul answers at some length in the body of the letter (2:1–12; 2:17–3:5) the apparent charges against him that he was self-seeking, cowardly, and mercenary in his dealings with the Thessalonians, as confirmed by his failure to return to see them.[24] The body of this letter, like other Pauline letters, is devoted not only to spiritual concepts but to a defense of his own ministry to the church (see the Corinthian correspondence and Galatians). He points out that he is not unaccustomed to opposition and even suffering, having come from Philippi, where he also suffered. The reason for his defense, he says, is that his motives are not erroneous or impure and certainly not based upon trickery. He is not trying to please humans but, rather, God, who tests human hearts and stands as his witness. For further proof of his sincerity, he points out that whereas his position as an apostle might have warranted some form of financial entitlement provided by the church, this was not his or his followers' approach. Not only did they share the gospel with the Thessalonians; they shared in a common physical existence as well. For Paul, this means that he engaged in physical work to help support

23. See E. Best, *A Commentary on the First and Second Epistles to the Thessalonians* (2nd ed.; BNTC; London: A&C Black, 1977), 33–34, for a survey of the opinions; J. Lambrecht, "Thanksgivings in 1 Thessalonians 1–3," in *The Thessalonians Debate: Methodological Discord or Methodological Synthesis?* (ed. K. P. Donfried and J. Beutler; Grand Rapids: Eerdmans, 2000), 135–62, for an attempt to integrate the sections; and Furnish, *1 & 2 Thessalonians*, 25, who notes the issue regarding what exactly constitutes the body of the letter, especially considering the so-called second thanksgiving section in 2:13–16. See below.

24. A major discussion in Thessalonians studies is the role of this section, esp. 2:1–12, as an apologetic for Paul's ministry. This view is defended in J. A. D. Weima, *1–2 Thessalonians* (BECNT; Grand Rapids: Baker, 2014), 120–79 for 2:1–16; and opposed in K. P. Donfried, "The Epistolary and Rhetorical Context of 1 Thessalonians 2:1–10," in *The Thessalonians Debate: Methodological Discord or Methodological Synthesis?* (ed. K. P. Donfried and J. Beutler; Grand Rapids: Eerdmans, 2000), 31–60. See the other essays on this passage in *Thessalonians Debate*, 61–131.

himself (2:8–9; see chapter 1 §6). Paul does confine his statements to his own position of leadership, however. Seeing in these accusations a potentially larger implication about the leadership of the church, he tells the Thessalonians that they owe their current leaders the same kind of respect (5:12–13). As to the second prong of the attack on his character—why he had not returned to see the church again—Paul seems aware of the difficulty this might have caused; he admits that his first visit was curtailed but assures them that he had made efforts to visit them again. When he was not successful—he attributes it to Satan stopping him and his coworkers—he sent Timothy, who had brought back the good report.

More space and attention in 1 Thessalonians are devoted to the issue of the parousia (4:13–18) and the day of the Lord (5:1–11) than to any other topic. But regardless of the space given it in the letter and the important role it has played in certain contemporary circles that have become preoccupied with biblical eschatology, the issue is not of primary significance for the purpose of the letter. This becomes evident when one considers the structure of the letter. As the outline below indicates, the body of the letter (2:1–3:13) is concerned with Paul's relationship with the Thessalonian Christians. The purpose is clearly to commend the Thessalonians in their behavior and to provide a rationale for his behavior with them and since meeting them in person. The material on the parousia falls within the paraenetic section of the letter (4:1–5:22)[25] and is followed by words of exhortation regarding the necessity of work, suggesting that some had become so interested in Christ's return that they had forgotten about their obligations in the present. Although the comments on the parousia are important material (see below), the parousia is not as central to the purpose of the letter as other topics, but is included for other, exhortatory reasons.

Paul discusses a number of important theological issues in this letter, but certain ones stand out as unique and significant. Because of the contingent nature of the Pauline letters and because 1 Thessalonians expresses only a portion of a complex relationship between Paul and the Christians at Thessalonica, it is difficult to establish the proportional significance of the topics discussed. For example, throughout this letter, Paul assumes without argumentation the conceptual framework of several theological beliefs. Thus, Paul does not argue for, but rather supposes, the existence of the "living and true God" (1:9), who is the Father of his Son, Jesus Christ, whom he raised from the dead (1:10). To

---

25. See Weima, *1–2 Thessalonians*, 245; contra many other commentators, who attempt to make discussion of the parousia doctrinal, e.g., J. Lambrecht, "A Structural Analysis of 1 Thessalonians 4–5," in *The Thessalonians Debate: Methodological Discord or Methodological Synthesis?* (ed. K. P. Donfried and J. Beutler; Grand Rapids: Eerdmans, 2000), 163–78.

Christ himself is ascribed the exalted status of being present with God, having died for believers (1:1; 5:10). Likewise, the Holy Spirit is seen as empowering believers to proclaim the gospel (1:5), giving joy (1:6), and helping them to be holy (4:8).

In two other areas, however, Paul does offer significant discussion. These occur in the paraenetic section of the letter, probably indicating that the material is presented with the idea of being less doctrinal than exhortatory (although there is a distinctive exhortatory sense about the whole letter)[26] and that it is designed to enhance the quality of the believer's life rather than to establish its theological basis. The first topic concerns Christian living (4:1–12), sanctification. This has already been treated regarding Paul's primary teaching (see chapter 4 §3D), but the way he treats it in this letter warrants further discussion. Underlying Paul's discussion with the Thessalonians is the apparent assumption that believers, both Paul and the Thessalonians themselves, are to display or live out a life in harmony with the gospel. Paul commends the Thessalonians for displaying lives that are worthy of imitation by other Christians because they are imitators of Paul and of the Lord. Paul apparently addresses these words to a church that had experienced persecution from fellow Gentiles, just as Paul had experienced persecution from Jews when he was in Thessalonica. Love, honesty, and good works are to characterize the Christian life, even when one is enduring trials and persecution. The goal, Paul says, is to be holy at Christ's coming. This theme is excellent for illustrating how Paul links the body of the letter with the paraenesis. He closes the body of the letter, as he often does, with one of his travelogues (2:17–3:13), which comes to an eschatological climax (3:11–13), where, in a doxological format, he wishes that God might present the Thessalonians blameless and holy at Christ's return. Then, in the first paraenesis of the letter (4:1–12), Paul discusses the theme of living to please God, introduced by an exhortatory formula (παρακαλέω, "entreat"). After telling the Thessalonians of the ideal, he now instructs them how to live. What he desires for them is holiness or sanctification (4:3–8) in the area of sexual and personal ethics and that they exemplify brotherly love (4:9–12). Christian sexual ethics came into direct conflict with pagan sexual ethics. Sexual practices often played a part in the religious cults of the time, to say nothing of their role in the general culture, where sexual immorality was common. Perhaps Paul realized or had heard that for many of the Gentiles in the church at Thessalonica it was difficult to change earlier practices. Paul, however, clearly considers Christian morality to be categorically different from pagan morality (4:4 is a difficult verse, meaning either "to gain mastery over his

26. See A. J. Malherbe, "Exhortation in First Thessalonians," *NovT* 25 (1983): 238–56.

body" [New English Bible] or "to take a wife for himself" [Revised Standard Version]; each has merit).[27]

The second issue on which Paul spends time is the parousia, or coming of the Lord.[28] This is not the place to try to solve the many enigmas of this passage, but a few observations are warranted. Paul's comments here apparently follow up on instructions he gave when he was in Thessalonica regarding the return of Christ, but perhaps his premature departure curtailed his teaching. The singular difficulty appears to have concerned the fate of believers who died before the return of Christ. Notice, however, how much Paul seems to assume they already know—for example, the resurrection of the dead (since this is what those who have "fallen asleep" are thought to miss out on [4:14]), the living believers' being caught up to heaven (4:15), and the nearness of the end (4:16). To comfort those concerned about dead friends or relatives, Paul conveys a useful chronology in which the living have no advantage over the dead, since the same spectacular events are to occur to both groups. The sequence he describes is for the dead in Christ first, and then the living (4:16–17), to be caught up to a "meeting the Lord in the air." The term "meeting" (ἀπάντησις) is used elsewhere of a delegation going outside a city to meet an important dignitary.[29] In 5:1–11, the transition in 5:1 can indeed indicate a shift in topic, but here it appears to indicate a logical shift, from the comforting facts regarding the return of Christ to the question of when this is supposed to occur. Again, Paul indicates that he does not need to write to the Thessalonians because they know a sufficient amount already. He instead contrasts those who are awaiting Christ's return with those who are going to be caught unprepared. For the latter, it will come like a thief in the night, so he instructs the Thessalonians to be sons of light and sons of day, prepared so as not to suffer wrath but, rather, experience salvation. The imagery Paul uses in this section is apocalyptic. Apocalyptic imagery is characterized by the otherworldly intervention of God in a situation where his followers are persecuted and despair of society being transformed from within. As depicted in works of apocalyptic literature, the translation from this world to another through a heavenly journey is the kind of experience the redeemed can expect.

27. F. F. Bruce, *1 and 2 Thessalonians* (WBC 45; Waco, TX: Word, 1982), 83; and Fee, *Thessalonians*, 143–50.

28. On this passage, see J. Plevnik, *Paul and the Parousia: An Exegetical and Theological Investigation* (Peabody, MA: Hendrickson, 1997), 65–121.

29. Bruce, *Thessalonians*, 102–3. Cf. M. R. Cosby, "Hellenistic Formal Receptions and Paul's Use of *apanthsis* in 1 Thessalonians 4:17," *BBR* 4 (1994): 15–33; response by R. H. Gundry, "A Brief Note on 'Hellenistic Formal Receptions and Paul's Use of *apanthsis* in 1 Thessalonians 4:17,'" *BBR* 6 (1996): 39–41.

Many commentators take 4:15, 17, where Paul speaks of being alive at the parousia of the Lord, to indicate that he believed that the return of Christ would occur during his own lifetime. Others, however, believe that in light of such passages as 2 Cor 5:1–10 and Phil 1:20–24, Paul was not necessarily teaching this belief. Positions claiming that Paul develops in his thinking from one position to another are also argued. Scholarly opinion generally sees Paul as living with a tension between Christ's already being present (at least in his church) and his expected return.[30] While it is not entirely certain that Paul believed that he would be alive at that time, since he uses the first-person plural throughout 1 Thessalonians, apparently sometimes referring to himself (e.g., 3:1) and sometimes referring to other believers as well (e.g., 2:1), there is a sense of imminence conveyed in the letter. It comes through in this section in the similar treatment of both the dead and the living at Christ's coming. Paul could well have thought that a number of those alive at the time of his writing would still be alive at Christ's return (and he may have wanted to be one, even if he recognized he may not be). Otherwise he would have responded in a different way, instructing his readers that the resurrection of those asleep would be the fate of all; but this is not what he says. Elsewhere in the letter, the sense of imminence also comes through with the emphasis on right living in the expectation that Christ could return and catch someone failing to live a holy life. It is possible to conceive of Paul believing at the outset of his ministry in the imminent return of Christ but being forced to temper his optimism, possibly from the start but certainly in subsequent writings in light of the increasing evidence that he himself would die before Christ's return. In any event, the sense of imminence is evident, even if Paul did not necessarily think he would be alive at the return. (Comparison of the eschatological teaching of this letter with 2 Thessalonians leads many scholars to call into question the authenticity of 2 Thessalonians; see §3A below.)

F. Outline of First Thessalonians

A. Opening (1:1)
  1. Sender (1:1a)
  2. Addressee (1:1b)
  3. Greeting (1:1c)
B. Thanksgiving (1:2–10)

---

30. See P. T. O'Brien, *The Epistle to the Philippians* (NIGTC; Grand Rapids: Eerdmans, 1991), 135-37.

C. Body: Paul's relationship with the Thessalonians (2:1–3:13)
  1. Body's opening: Paul's defense (2:1–12)
  2. Further thanksgiving (2:13–16)
  3. Pauline travelogue: Paul's relationship with the Thessalonians
     (2:17–3:13)
D. Paraenesis (4:1–5:22)
  1. Living to please God (4:1–12)
  2. Coming of the Lord (4:13–5:11)
  3. Final exhortations (5:12–22)
E. Closing (5:23–28)
  1. Doxology (5:23–24)
  2. Prayer wish (5:25)
  3. Greetings (5:26–27)
  4. Benediction (5:28)

G. Content of First Thessalonians

Opening (1:1)

The opening of this letter is a short, standard Pauline opening, where he includes two of his companions, Silvanus (or Silas) and Timothy. These two were partners with him in his travels to and from Thessalonica (cf. Acts 17:4, 10; 18:5; 1 Thess 3:6). He writes to the church (note the singular) of the Thessalonians and concludes the opening with the usual Pauline "grace to you and peace."

Thanksgiving (1:2–10)

The next section is the thanksgiving section, where at some length Paul expresses his gratitude toward the Thessalonians. He tells them that he constantly prays for them, and that he remembers them in his prayers regarding their work of faith, labor of love, and steadfastness of hope. Many commentators write about this trifecta and see the meaning here to be a work produced by faith, a labor produced by love, and a steadfastness produced by hope.[31] The reason for Paul's remembrance of the Thessalonian Christians is that they were chosen by God, since the gospel Paul preached came not just in speech, but in power, the Holy Spirit, and full conviction. They imitated Paul and the Lord, and in turn, they became an example to the rest of the regions of Macedonia and Achaia. In fact, the example of the Thessalonians has been so positive that their reputation has

---

31. Cf. Porter, *Idioms*, 95, on the various functions and meanings of the genitive.

gone even beyond Macedonia and Achaia. Paul has heard from all over the region that the Thessalonians have turned to God from serving idols, a God who is living and true. Paul does not simply give a shallow and empty thanksgiving, but there are tangible reasons why Paul has such a positive remembrance of them.

Body: Paul's Defense (2:1–12)

The body of the letter begins with an apologetic for Paul's ministry. He reminds the Thessalonians that he came to them from Philippi after having suffered and being shamefully treated, and in spite of opposition, Paul and his coworkers did not shrink away from proclaiming the gospel of God to them. This should prove to them that Paul's motives did not spring from any error, impure intentions, or deceit, but from the desire to please God in faithfully proclaiming the gospel. Paul denies any accusations against him and his compatriots, but asserts instead that their attitude toward the Thessalonians was like that of a nursing mother. A text-critical issue appears here, whether Paul says "we were *gentle* among you," or "we were *infants* among you." Most commentators take the view that the original wording is probably "gentle" (ἤπιοι) instead of "infants" (νήπιοι), following internal criteria, although the external evidence seems to favor strongly the νήπιοι reading.[32] If Paul said "we were infants among you," with the metaphor of a nursing mother, this may mean that Paul, in defending his ministry as being from pure motives, is asserting his innocence, comparing himself with an infant.

Paul continues with his defense by reminding his readers of tangible evidences that his ministry was not out of impure motives, such as working another job in order not to be a financial burden on the Thessalonians. In general, their conduct was also holy and righteous before them, and Paul refers to another analogy, this time of a father with his children who instructs and encourages them to walk in a manner worthy of God.

Body: Further Thanksgiving (2:13–16)

Some scholars posit that this may be a separate section or a part of the extended thanksgiving section from 1:2–10,[33] or perhaps that this is an interpolation in-

32. Most interpreters seem to go along with the internal evidence in this case. However, see S. Fowl, "A Metaphor in Distress: A Reading of νήπιοι in 1 Thessalonians 2.7," *NTS* 36 (1990): 469–73; and J. A. D. Weima, "'But We Became Infants among You': The Case for νήπιοι in 1 Thess 2.7," *NTS* 46 (2000): 547–64; cf. Fee, *Thessalonians*, 68–73; and Furnish, *1 & 2 Thessalonians*, 56–62.

33. I contend, however, that a thanksgiving section is distinct in the Pauline letter form from the greeting and body (see chapter 5 §3B). It seems, however, that not too much should

serted by a later redactor.[34] But that there is a word of further thanksgiving in the body does not necessitate considering it a separate section. It seems that, taking into consideration my outline for the Pauline letter form (chapter 5 §3) as fivefold (opening, thanksgiving, body, paraenesis, and closing), this does not necessitate a strict compartmentalization of these categories; but these constitute a general pattern that can be seen in Paul's letters. Furthermore, there may be a specific function for a further note of thanksgiving appearing in the body section. In other words, the question must be proposed and answered: why does Paul include a word of thanksgiving in the body section? Using the functional letter perspective theory outlined in chapter 5 §3,[35] I believe that there is a specific function to be noted when Paul diverts from his conventional letter structure. Here, Paul may have wanted to emphasize or make salient his thanks to and for the Thessalonians.

While earlier in the letter Paul thanks God for the Thessalonians' great example in their communities and abroad, he is thankful to them for receiving the messengers' word, not as their own word but as the word of God. They practiced their faith in such a way that they even suffered at the hands of their own compatriots.

Body: Pauline Travelogue (2:17–3:13)

Paul transitions to a short section detailing his departure and subsequent interactions with the Thessalonians, as a further support for his authentic motives. He recounts how he and his coworkers were torn away from the Thessalonians, which matches the account in Acts where Paul and Silas went away at night in order to avoid persecution (Acts 17:10). But he reminds them that this was only physical absence, as his heart continued to be with them; he desired to see them again face to face. While Paul's colleagues were in Athens, he sent Timothy to them, to check on them and encourage them in their faith during their persecution. Paul reminds them that persecution is inevitable in the Christian life, as Paul had taught them previously while he was with them. However, his concern was so grave that he sent Timothy to make sure the tempter had not swayed them.

---

be made of the "problem" of 2:13–16 being thankful, since the premise of this problem is that Paul is limited to thanking his readers in only one section, not more. This is clearly not the case. See discussion above.

34. See Schlueter, *Filling up the Measure*; Porter, "Translation"; and discussion above.

35. See also S. E. Porter, "A Functional Letter Perspective: Towards a Grammar of Epistolary Form," in *Paul and the Ancient Letter Form* (ed. S. E. Porter and S. A. Adams; PAST 6; Leiden: Brill, 2010), 9–32.

Timothy's report back to Paul and his coworkers is positive and full of encouragement. They are continuing in their faith and love and had kindly remembered Paul and the others, sharing the desire to be reunited with them. This report results in immense joy for Paul, and his thanksgiving continues for the Thessalonians. At the end of this body section, Paul breaks into a short benediction, wishing his return to them and well-being and continued righteousness for them.

Paraenesis: Living to Please God (4:1–12)

In light of Timothy's report of their ongoing pursuit of holiness, Paul exhorts his readers, in keeping with the instructions he had taught them before, to continue their walking with and pleasing God. Paul states that the will of God is sanctification, namely in the area of sexual purity, so as to control themselves in holiness and honor, and to avoid acting like the Gentiles do in their lustful passion. By living in sexual impurity, they would be sinning against one another, and Paul warns them that God is an avenger in these things, as Paul had warned them before.

In the area of brotherly love, however, the Thessalonians did not need much instruction but encouragement to continue doing as they were. What they may have lacked in sexual purity, they had shown in love, gaining a reputation that spread throughout Macedonia. Paul encourages them to continue, as well as living quietly[36] and minding their own affairs, so that they would perpetuate their positive reputation with outsiders.

Paraenesis: Coming of the Lord (4:13–5:11)

Paul addresses what seems to be a concern of the Thessalonians, possibly a concern reported by Timothy while he had visited them. Due to possible persecution of some for their faith, or some natural deaths, the Thessalonians would have witnessed the deaths of family and friends, and this would have led to questions about what happens to them after their death and before the parousia of Christ. Paul reassures them that, as believers, they do not have to grieve as others do, but just as Jesus was resurrected, there will be a future time when those who have fallen asleep in the Lord will rise again and be reunited with them. While many theological discussions center on this passage regarding the eschatological details of the parousia, the main point Paul makes here is not chronologically to detail the precise events that will take place, but

---

36. See the discussion of the meaning of "live quietly" below as related to 2 Thess 3:12.

exhortatively to reassure the Thessalonians that those who have fallen asleep in the Lord will rise again in the future: they will not be left behind.

This view of the future resurrection leads Paul to exhort the Thessalonians not to live as if they are unaware, but to know that this day of the Lord will come at any moment, imminently. In light of this truth, they should live in light, rather than in darkness, and live sober lives of love and hope of salvation (a condensed "armor of God" is presented here by Paul; cf. Eph 6:10–20). Paul instructs them to continue to encourage themselves with this truth, as they already are doing.

Paraenesis: Final Exhortations (5:12–22)

Paul closes the paraenetic section of this letter by further individual exhortations of the Thessalonians. He asks them to respect those who labor among them and over them in the Lord, presumably those who worked at preaching and teaching the congregation in that city. That Paul does not use a specific title for those preachers or teachers points to this letter having been written early, before there were established leadership titles, such as elder or bishop. He asks them to esteem highly their leaders because of their work.

Paul commands his readers to be at peace among themselves and then presents a fourfold instruction on general behavior toward others: admonish the idle, encourage the fainthearted, help the weak, and be patient with all. This categorization of responses shows the Thessalonians (as well as modern readers) that certain types of people merit a certain type of response, based on the need. Those who are weak benefit little from being admonished but rather need help, while those who are fainthearted would benefit greatly from encouragement. Paul warns them about seeking revenge, since it is God who repays evil for evil. To close off this paraenetic section, Paul gives a series of short commands: rejoice always, pray without ceasing, give thanks in everything, do not quench the Spirit, do not despise prophecies but test everything, and abstain from every type of evil.

Closing (5:23–28)

Paul closes the letter with another benediction, this time regarding the Thessalonians' sanctification and blamelessness. He assures them that God will surely see to their sanctification. He requests that they pray for Paul and his coworkers, that they greet one another with a holy kiss, and that they accept the charge to read this letter publicly. He ends the letter in a conventional Pauline way, by wishing that the grace of the Lord Jesus Christ be with them.

3. Second Thessalonians

Many of the issues that pertain to 1 Thessalonians are also pertinent for 2 Thessalonians, especially if 2 Thessalonians was authentically written by Paul. The history of discussion of 2 Thessalonians often revolves around its relationship with 1 Thessalonians, and this influences such issues as authorship and authenticity. However, there is much more to 2 Thessalonians than simply these two issues. In this section, I begin with discussion of authorship and authenticity, attempt an explanation of the issues over authorship, treat the relationship of 2 Thessalonians to 1 Thessalonians, and briefly account for the occasion and purpose of 2 Thessalonians if it is authentic, before offering an outline and summary of its content.

A. Authorship and Authenticity of Second Thessalonians

Many scholars today seriously question the authenticity of 2 Thessalonians. There has been some question about Pauline authorship since the nineteenth century (due to Ferdinand Christian Baur), but this dispute has arisen most strongly within the last forty or so years, with the vast majority of scholars before 1970 arguing for authenticity.[37] If, at the end of the discussion below, the evidence seems to weigh in favor of Pauline authorship, then the situation in Thessalonica noted above and its probable correlation with the evidence presented in Acts will need to be consulted. If the evidence instead seems to weigh for pseudonymity, then the interpreter is faced with an instance of what has been called "double pseudonymity" (see chapter 6 §2),[38] that of not knowing either the author or the original audience. I believe that the arguments are clearly in favor of Pauline authenticity for 2 Thessalonians.

When arguments regarding the Pauline authorship of 2 Thessalonians are presented, the following seem to carry the most weight. There are two kinds of evidence, external and internal.

---

37. Some of the major proponents of non-Pauline authorship of 2 Thessalonians include Baur, *Paul the Apostle of Jesus Christ*, 2.85-97; W. Wrede, *Die Echtheit des Zweiten Thessalonicherbriefs* (Texte und Untersuchungen; Leipzig: Hinrichs, 1903); B. Rigaux, *Saint Paul: Les épitres aux Thessaloniciens* (Études bibliques; Paris: LeCoffre/Gembloux: Duculot, 1956), 124-32; and W. Trilling, *Untersuchungen zum 2. Thessalonicherbrief* (Erfurter Theologische Studien 27; Leipzig: St. Benno, 1972), 11-45. Cf. G. S. Holland, *The Tradition That You Received from Us: 2 Thessalonians in the Pauline Tradition* (HUT 24; Tübingen: Mohr-Siebeck, 1988), 1-5, 129-58, who is a major recent proponent of non-Pauline authorship.

38. D. Meade, *Pseudonymity and Canon* (WUNT 39; Tübingen: Mohr-Siebeck, 1986), 127.

1. External Evidence

Although external evidence from the church father Justin is not decisive (*Dialogue with Trypho* 32, 110, 116), 2 Thessalonians is found in Marcion's collection and the Muratorian Fragment, is cited in Polycarp (*To the Philippians* 11.3 [1:4]; 11.4 [3:15]), Tertullian (*Antidote for the Scorpion's Sting* 13; *Resurrection of the Flesh* 24), Irenaeus (*Against Heresies* 3.7.2; 5.25.1), and Clement of Alexandria (*Stromata* 5.3), and is possibly referred to in Origen (*Against Celsus* 2.65). It may be cited in *Barnabas* as well (18.2 [2:6]; 4.9 [2:8]; 15.5 [2:8, 12]).[39] Thus the external evidence and attestation for 2 Thessalonians is stronger than that for 1 Thessalonians and for most of the other disputed epistles.

2. Internal Evidence

The most detailed argument against Pauline authorship of 2 Thessalonians was made in 1972 by Wolfgang Trilling. Trilling's work had widespread influence, but it also garnered severe criticism.[40] In what follows, an evaluation is made of the major arguments that Trilling and others make against Pauline authorship. The internal evidence can be evaluated in several different spheres: attestation of the letter itself, tone, apparent audience, similarities of circumstances to 1 Thessalonians, and teaching and theology.[41]

a. The attestation of the letter clearly points to Paul at least as the ostensible author. Like 1 Thessalonians, the letter purports to have been written by Paul, Silas (or Silvanus), and Timothy (2 Thess 1:1). Second Thessalonians does not refer directly to 1 Thessalonians, but it has an indirect reference to the author having previously corresponded with the recipients (2:15). This statement may be interpreted in conjunction with the implication

---

39. See Moffatt, *Introduction*, 82.

40. Trilling, *Thessalonicherbrief*, accepted by, e.g., H. Koester, *Introduction to the New Testament* (2 vols.; FFNT; Philadelphia: Fortress, 1982), 2.241–46; but rejected, e.g., by Marshall, *Thessalonians*, 29–45; Weima, *1–2 Thessalonians*, 46–54; and P. Foster, "Who Wrote 2 Thessalonians? A Fresh Look at an Old Problem," *JSNT* 35.2 (2012): 150–75. An excellent summary and evaluation is found in Jewett, *Thessalonian Correspondence*, 10–18. As Jewett clearly indicates, not all of the arguments are worth considering.

41. Cf. T. D. Still, *Conflict at Thessalonica: A Pauline Church and Its Neighbours* (JSNTSup 183; Sheffield: Sheffield Academic, 1999), 47–55. Christina Kreinecker introduces the relationship of 2 Thessalonians to the documentary papyri as a new factor in the argument; "The Imitation Hypothesis: Pseudepigraphic Remarks on 2 Thessalonians with Help from Documentary Papyri," in *Paul and Pseudepigraphy* (ed. S. E. Porter and G. P. Fewster; PAST 8; Leiden: Brill, 2013), 197–220.

suggested by 2 Thessalonians that it was sent in response to some other inauthentic letter (2:2; 3:17). The author also claims to be Paul in 3:17, where he purports to affix a final greeting in his own hand, something that distinguishes his letters. That Paul affixes his signature to this letter but not to 1 Thessalonians raises intriguing questions regarding authenticity; some speculate that this is an attempt by the pseudonymous author to convince the recipients that the letter is authentic. This issue is discussed below in §3C.

b. As noted above, it is virtually unanimously accepted that 1 Thessalonians was written with an almost overwhelming sense of thanksgiving to the Christians in Thessalonica, but many perceive a change of tone in 2 Thessalonians. The warm and friendly tone of 1 Thessalonians is, according to some, exchanged for a more formal and frigid tone in 2 Thessalonians.[42] Whereas 1 Thess 1:2 says that "we always give thanks," 2 Thess 1:3 and 2:13 state that "we must always give thanks," as if there is some impediment to the same kind of thanksgiving. By most accounts of those who argue for authenticity, 2 Thessalonians was written very soon after 1 Thessalonians, thus making this change in tone perplexing. This purported change, however, may not be as severe as some think. Paul refers in 2 Thessalonians to the readers as "brothers and sisters" (3:1), asks for prayer from them (3:1-2), and is polite in dealing with the problem of idleness, one already raised in 1 Thess 5:14. A possible change in circumstances for Paul or his readers—including a failure by the Thessalonians to take note of Paul's teaching—might make some change in tone warranted, especially if the Thessalonians still failed to understand his comments on eschatology. There is no reason why Paul must remain static in his attitude toward his readers.

c. While the audience of 1 Thessalonians appears to be of Gentile composition, it is argued that the readers of 2 Thessalonians appear to be Jewish, or at least know the thought of the Old Testament better than the audience of the first letter (See 2 Thess 1:6-10 on retribution) and are more familiar with the imagery often associated with Jewish apocalyptic writings (2:1-12). But the lack of direct quotations of the Old Testament in 2 Thessalonians raises the question whether there is any imagery or thinking in the letter that would not be readily understood in context. Furthermore, the composition of the church, as discussed in 1 Thessalonians, included a large number of Gentiles, but many of these Gentiles came apparently

---

42. R. F. Collins, *Letters That Paul Did Not Write* (Good News Studies 28; Wilmington, DE: Glazer, 1988), 222-23.

from the ranks of the Godfearers (see §2D above); they therefore probably would have been very familiar with the thought and even language of the Old Testament.

d. Another question often raised about the authenticity of 2 Thessalonians concerns the similarities between the two letters: why would Paul have written two letters so similar to each other within such a short space of time? First and 2 Thessalonians are linguistically and literarily the two most closely linked of the Pauline letters.[43] This can be illustrated not only by the use of particular vocabulary items but by repeated instances of parallel phrasing as well (2 Thess 1:1–2 and 1 Thess 1:1; 2 Thess 1:3 and 1 Thess 1:2; 2 Thess 1:11 and 1 Thess 1:3; 2 Thess 1:8 and 1 Thess 4:5; 2 Thess 2:14 and 1 Thess 5:9; 2 Thess 3:8 and 1 Thess 2:9; 2 Thess 3:10 and 1 Thess 3:4).[44] One must be careful with such an argument against authenticity, however. All sorts of situations can be suggested that might warrant such a procedure. For example, if the author believed that the situation warranted discussion of similar issues once more, would he not tend to use similar language? The short space in time could argue in favor of similar language, since it appears less likely that the author would undergo a radical shift in style in so short a time. This argument, in its present form, is simply untenable. One can envision a similar argument being made for non-Pauline authorship if the books were dissimilar in language. This raises the very important question of what constitutes differences and similarities in language and how such differences are weighed and how they bear on the issue of authorship. In other words, what are the various formal criteria that would determine whether two letters contain similar or dissimilar language? How is this usable as a test for authenticity?

e. The final issue often raised in discussion of authenticity concerns the teaching and theology of 2 Thessalonians, especially its eschatological teaching.[45] Eschatological teaching is part of Paul's paraenetic directives in 1 Thessalonians, but it constitutes the body of the letter of 2 Thessalonians. Perhaps even more noticeable, however, is the supposed change in eschatological perspective. First Thessalonians has a sense of imminence, but this appears to be far less intense in 2 Thessalonians, because the author states that certain events have to take place before the coming of the Lord can occur (2 Thess 2:1). The characterization of the man of lawlessness,

---

43. Holland, *Tradition That You Received*, 2–3.
44. See Best, *Thessalonians*, 51.
45. T. D. Still, "Paul and the Macedonian Believers," in *The Blackwell Companion to Paul* (ed. S. Westerholm; Chichester, West Sussex: Wiley-Blackwell, 2011), 30–45, esp. 36–38.

furthermore, appears to draw upon other New Testament writings or some form of apocalyptic thinking. The man of lawlessness, it is claimed, appears to be another way of describing the antichrist, quite possibly copied from Rev 13:1–9 (or even 1 John), making the letter obviously derivative and later than the time of Paul. Speculation regarding such a figure, especially in light of Paul's own life, also provokes thoughts about whether this is a depiction of the Nero myth. (There apparently grew up speculation in apocalyptic circles that Nero, the cruel persecutor, had not died but would return to resume once more his oppression.) Some scholars propose, however, that one need not look to the Nero myth for an explanation of the man of lawlessness, since the idea is found in Second Temple Jewish literature (e.g., *1 Enoch* 85–90; *Jubilees* 23:16–32; *Sibylline Oracles* 3:388–400) and might well be used to refer to a pseudomessianic figure.[46]

Other theological ideas are sometimes cited as not being as important in 2 Thessalonians as they are in 1 Thessalonians. For example, the Spirit (2 Thess 2:2, 8, 13), the death and resurrection of Christ (cf. 1 Thess 4:14), and God do not seem to be as significant to the author of 2 Thessalonians as they are to the author of 1 Thessalonians. It does appear that some of these ideas are not as extensively mentioned in 2 Thessalonians as they are in the other letter, but one must be careful how this evidence is handled. For example, the Spirit and God are two of the Pauline theological assumptions, ideas that he does not appear to believe he needs to justify, and seems simply to assume (see chapter 4 §2A and §2C). We must be cautious, therefore, how much weight we attach to theological ideas that even in Paul's undisputed letters he does not believe he must argue for. The failure to mention these ideas cannot constitute a sufficient argument to establish non-Pauline authorship. Nevertheless, it is noteworthy that both 1 Thessalonians and 2 Thessalonians equate Christ with God, with similar phrasing used in each (e.g., 2 Thess 2:13 and 1 Thess 1:4).

These are the five major internal arguments, along with a few other factors, that are often presented regarding the authorship of 2 Thessalonians. As I attempted to show, none of them is decisive to overcome the overwhelming and clear external evidence for Pauline authorship. In fact, many of the internal arguments provide little compelling evidence to doubt Pauline authorship of 2 Thessalonians, but instead provide confirmatory evidence for Paul as the author.

---

46. See Bruce, *Thessalonians*, 179–88; and G. C. Jenks, *The Origins and Early Development of the Antichrist Myth* (Beihefte zur Zeitschrift für die neutestamentliche Wissenschaft 59; Berlin: de Gruyter, 1991), for surveys of the positions.

B. Explaining Difficulties in Pauline Authorship of Second Thessalonians

Despite the evidence above, there are still those who find 2 Thessalonians to be non-Pauline. If a traditional estimation of Pauline authorship is rejected in spite of the evidence that 2 Thessalonians was sent to the entire church at Thessalonica—then how, why, and by whom was the letter composed? The number of scenarios has been significant, covering a full range of options.

Several explanations wish to retain the idea of Pauline authorship while still addressing the differences between the two letters.[47] For example, several proposals revolve around the intended audiences of the letters. Thus, the German scholar Adolf Harnack proposes a divided-church theory, according to which 1 Thessalonians was addressed to the Gentiles of the church and 2 Thessalonians was addressed to the Jewish Christians at Thessalonica.[48] This theory takes account of several features noted above regarding the sense gained from each of the letters (at least by some scholars) about the primary audience. Fellow German scholar Martin Dibelius proposes that 1 Thessalonians was addressed to the small group of leaders of the church while 2 Thessalonians was for public reading; conversely, Earle Ellis proposes that 2 Thessalonians was addressed to Paul's coworkers in the city to deal with the problem of idleness induced by eschatological thinking, whereas 1 Thessalonians was addressed to the church as a whole.[49] A number of problems with these solutions, however, make them seem unlikely to most scholars (besides the solutions' being, in some instances, contradictory). The evidence of a divided church is slender according to internal and external evidence. In 1 Thess 2:13–16, the Judean church is held up to the Thessalonians as an example to be followed—unlikely if the letter is addressing only the Gentiles of the Thessalonian church. The similarities of the letters in so many regards—both are addressed to the same church and both mention idleness—also argue against the kind of distinction that these theories require. The instruction of 1 Thess 5:27 that the letter be read aloud certainly argues against its being a private letter.

An idea first suggested in the nineteenth century and recently revived is that the material found in 1–2 Thessalonians is perhaps more than two letters.

---

47. See Marshall, *Thessalonians*, 26–27, who lists the following positions. Cf. also Fee, *Thessalonians*, 238–41.

48. A. Harnack, "Das Problem des zweiten Thessalonicherbriefes," *Sitzungsberichte der preussischen Akademie der Wissenschaften: Philosophisch-Historischen Klasse* 31 (1910): 560–78.

49. M. Dibelius, *An die Thessalonicher I II, an die Philipper* (3rd ed.; Handbuch zum Neuen Testament 11; Tübingen: Mohr-Siebeck, 1937), 57–58; and E. E. Ellis, *Prophecy and Hermeneutic in Early Christianity: New Testament Essays* (Grand Rapids: Eerdmans, 1978), 19–21.

Therefore, a number of partition theories are proposed. The most well-known, by Walter Schmithals, goes a long way toward providing a defense of Pauline authorship, taking note of several of the difficulties about the structure of 1–2 Thessalonians. These include the apparent second major thanksgiving in 1 Thessalonians, closing at 3:11. Schmithals proposes four letters—compiled into the canonical two letters—each epistle ending with a section introduced by "may the Lord/God" (2 Thess 3:16; 1 Thess 5:23; 2 Thess 2:16; 1 Thess 3:11): Thessalonians A = 2 Thess 1:1–12; 3:6–16; Thessalonians B = 1 Thess 1:1–2:12; 4:2–5:28; Thessalonians C = 2 Thess 2:13–14; 2:1–12; 2:15–3:3 (or 3:5); 3:17–18; and Thessalonians D = 1 Thess 2:13–4:1.[50] The unfortunate problem with this idea (and others like it), as creative and sensitive as it purports to be with handling the textual difficulties, is that there is no text-critical evidence that the letters were ever arranged in this way. There is no external evidence that the letters were ever circulated in anything other than the form in which they are found canonically. All of the textual changes must have been made before the writing of our extant New Testament manuscripts. This could have happened, but it cannot be proven from the evidence that we have. This theory is also dependent upon 2 Thessalonians being written before 1 Thessalonians, a theory that is far from proven (see below). The dilemma that haunts this and other partition theories is that, on the one hand, it is asserted that Paul's words were venerated in the early church and thus preserved, while, on the other hand, it must be admitted that sections of the original forms of these letters—such as the Pauline openings and closings, as well as possibly other major portions—were excised and lost.

It is also proposed that 2 Thessalonians was sent to another church in Macedonia—not the one at Thessalonica, which received 1 Thessalonians. The two letters were sent at about the same time. Some of the suggestions for the original destination of 2 Thessalonians include Berea and Philippi, cities with which Paul had significant contact during his second missionary trip (Acts 16:12–40; 17:10–15).[51] Berea is the city that he visited right after leaving Thessalonica in a hurry when jealous Jews reportedly rioted. Philippi is the most significant city visited before Thessalonica; there Paul had a successful ministry, not even excluding his night in jail. This theory certainly can account for the two letters being written close together and using similar language. It has difficulty, however, explaining

---

50. W. Schmithals, *Paul and the Gnostics* (trans. J. Steely; Nashville: Abingdon, 1972), 212–13, refuted by Best, *Thessalonians*, 45–50.

51. E. Schweizer, "Der zweite Thessalonicherbriefe ein Philipperbrief?" *Theologische Zeitschrift* 1 (1945): 90–105; and M. Goguel, "L'énigme de la seconde épitre aux Thessaloniciens," *Revue de l'histoire des religions* 71 (1915): 248–72.

the textual evidence—that no extant text of 2 Thessalonians bears witness to a destination other than Thessalonica. There are, furthermore, the supposed significant differences in theology, especially regarding eschatology. If the theologies are in conflict, it is unlikely that Paul was responsible for sending these letters with two different perspectives to these cities.

Another explanation has not been as seriously considered as it probably should be—that 2 Thessalonians departs from the standard Pauline letter because of coauthorship or the role of an amanuensis. According to this theory, 2 Thessalonians (or 1 Thessalonians) may have been composed by Timothy (who is mentioned in the opening salutation of six other Pauline letters) or Silvanus (Silas).[52] Reconstructing the exact circumstances that would have warranted this involvement from a coworker or even an unnamed scribe is nearly impossible, other than what we know of the obvious impediments to Paul himself writing: the need to make a living, difficult physical circumstances, or other commitments. Even if one or both of the cosenders or another person was involved, Paul's name was clearly attached to it in 2 Thess 1:1 and 3:17. This would be due to Paul's status in the Thessalonian community as its founding apostle and his active involvement in, and concern for, the church there, as illustrated by his first letter to it. This would warrant the second letter being called Pauline as well. Such a solution solves a number of problems, including the evident similarities of the letters and the shift in tone, but there are other problems it does not solve. For example, if the eschatology is different between 1 Thessalonians and 2 Thessalonians (however, it is not clear that it is), it is difficult to account for Paul's putting his name to both letters. There is the further problem of quantifying such a theory. Apart from the several names included in 2 Thess 1:1, there is no specific evidence for it.

The most plausible explanation for those who dispute Pauline authorship of 2 Thessalonians is that the letter is pseudonymous—that is, that it was written some time later than 1 Thessalonians by a sympathetic follower of Paul using his name. It is sometimes asked whether a church that had received one genuine letter would be willing to accept a second letter not by the same author. This presumes, however, that the pseudonymous letter was sent to the Thessalonian church during the time when the recipients of the first letter were still alive (or even sent there at all). Especially in light of the contents of the

---

52. See, e.g., K. P. Donfried on 2 Thessalonians in Donfried and I. H. Marshall, *The Theology of the Shorter Pauline Letters* (NTT; Cambridge: Cambridge University Press, 1993), 84–87; and Donfried, "Issues of Authorship in the Pauline Corpus: Rethinking the Relationship between 1 and 2 Thessalonians," in *2 Thessalonians and Pauline Eschatology: For Petr Pokorný on His 80th Birthday* (ed. C. Tuckett; Leuven: Peeters, 2013), 81–113.

first and the second letters, and the language of 2 Thessalonians regarding the second coming of Christ, the evidence points away from such an audience. The theories on the circumstances of this composition vary; some propose that the letter was written around the turn of the first and second centuries to a church experiencing a problem similar to that of the original Thessalonian church, perhaps a problem made even more acute by the still delayed return of Christ.[53] Why the author would have included a reference to Paul's signature at 2 Thess 3:17 can be answered in several ways—for instance, the literary convention of including realistic and evidentiary statements, not to deceive but to indicate the relationship of the letter to its apostolic precursor (although not all are convinced by such reasoning). Many significant problems remain with any theory of the pseudonymity of 2 Thessalonians, many more, I believe, than if it is accepted as authentic.

C. Order of Composition of First and Second Thessalonians

For those who believe that both epistles are Pauline and that they could have arrived in Thessalonica one soon after the other (any number of the proposals mentioned above could be compatible with this situation), there is still the question of which was sent first. The traditional view is that Paul wrote 1 Thessalonians first and then 2 Thessalonians soon afterward, probably within the same year. This position is questioned by a number of scholars (e.g., Charles Wanamaker, in an English-language commentary on the Greek text).[54]

I offer here some of the arguments employed to establish that 2 Thessalonians preceded 1 Thessalonians and is therefore the earlier of the two, with brief responses to each:

1. The traditional order is apparently based upon length (e.g., the early codex of the Pauline letters 𝔓46 has the individual letters arranged according to length), not chronological order, thus opening up at least the possibility that 2 Thessalonians was written first.[55] But does this indicate that 2 Thessalonians should be first or was sent first? The argument does not directly address that issue.

53. See B. Childs, *The New Testament as Canon: An Introduction* (Philadelphia: Fortress, 1985), 371.

54. C. A. Wanamaker, *The Epistles to the Thessalonians: A Commentary on the Greek Text* (NIGTC; Grand Rapids: Eerdmans, 1990), 37–45, who provides arguments for 2 Thessalonians being written before 1 Thessalonians.

55. Bruce, *Thessalonians*, xli.

2. Second Thessalonians 2:5 and 3:10 give reasons for a misunderstanding that Paul tries to solve, opening up the possibility that the more settled tone of 1 Thessalonians indicates that the problem is now resolved. This is a matter of judgment. These passages may just as easily indicate Paul's continuing frustration that the Thessalonians are still having difficulties despite his previous letter to them.

3. Some contend that the eschatology in 2 Thessalonians is more primitive and that 1 Thessalonians reflects Paul's later realization that Christ would not return as soon as he had thought. It is debatable that this is the way to read these two letters, since 2 Thess 2:7 talks of "the one who now restrains" and 1 Thess 4:17 talks of "we who are alive" (even if this does not necessarily indicate Paul's expectation of being alive).

4. It is argued that 2 Thessalonians indicates trials that are being endured or are still ahead (1:4–5), while 1 Thessalonians says that trials are over (2:14). There are several responses to this. First, one should not overstress the temporal values of the verb tenses in an English translation, since Greek tense forms are not time bound. Second, it is difficult to know the exact nature of the troubles in Thessalonica. Are there new troubles? Has Paul spoken with assurance to encourage the Thessalonians, even though they may be experiencing more troubles? This cannot be known.

5. Second Thessalonians 3:11–12 seems to speak of difficulties with idleness in the congregation as if this was a new development, but these difficulties seem familiar in 1 Thess 5:14. Similarly, it appears to some that 1 Thess 4:10–12 regarding loving fellow Christians and leading a quiet life needs 2 Thess 3:6–15 with its exhortations regarding idleness to be understood. But it could be argued in the opposite way that Paul's more general statements in 1 Thessalonians were not clear enough and needed fuller exposition in 2 Thessalonians for an abiding problem.

6. The same kind of logic appears in the argument that 1 Thess 5:1 regarding the times and dates of the day of the Lord is more understandable if 2 Thess 2:1–12 concerning the coming of the Lord is already known to the church. By this reckoning, however, 1 Thess 5:2 with its reference to the thief in the night should not be included; yet it is.

7. First Thessalonians 4:9 and 5:1, with "now concerning," seem to indicate the discussion of topics already broached, and it is posited that 2 Thess 3:6–15 with its exhortations regarding idleness and 2:1–12 on the coming of the Lord may be these topics. But they may also have been topics brought to Paul by Timothy, who is introduced before the "now concerning" passages (1 Thess 3:6).

8. Second Thessalonians 3:17 contains a personal reference to Paul's writing

in his own hand; it is argued that such a statement is important only in a first letter. But if spurious Pauline letters had been sent to the church, as 2 Thess 2:2 suggests, there might well be the need for an authentic sample of handwriting.

In all, these reasons are not convincing to establish that 2 Thessalonians was written before 1 Thessalonians, and the traditional order seems to be acceptable.

Besides this lack of convincing arguments against the priority of 1 Thessalonians, there are several reasons in support of it: (1) the problems of 1 Thessalonians seem to have deepened in 2 Thessalonians, especially concerning eschatological expectation and the accompanying tendencies toward idleness; (2) 2 Thess 2:2, 15 and 3:17 appear to refer to a previous letter, possibly (and probably) 1 Thessalonians; and (3) the personal references of 1 Thess 2:17–3:6 seem to precede 2 Thessalonians, where there are no personal greetings. These further reasons support 1 Thessalonians being written before 2 Thessalonians, even if one followed the other fairly quickly.

D. Occasion and Purpose of Second Thessalonians

The occasion and purpose of 2 Thessalonians are closely related to those of 1 Thessalonians. In light of the discussion above, that there is no convincing argument that 1 Thessalonians follows 2 Thessalonians, I work from the hypothesis that 2 Thessalonians was written after 1 Thessalonians when Paul learned that 1 Thessalonians had not been as effective as he had hoped that it might have been.[56] It is possible that there had also arrived at the church in Thessalonica a false letter arguing that the coming of Christ had occurred (2 Thess 2:2). If the church at Thessalonica had misunderstandings regarding the second coming, these misunderstandings may simply have been increased by the church's own thinking on the matter. In any case, Paul attempts to clarify the signs of the coming of Christ by specifying a number of events that indicate this has not occurred: since the apostasy or rebellion (2:3) and the coming of the man of lawlessness (2:3) have not yet happened, because they have been restrained (2:7), the day of the Lord has not yet come. Because of this misunderstanding about the impending coming of the Lord, it appears that some in the congregation may have given up work. Paul reprimands them (3:6, 11–12)

---

56. Perhaps Paul learned this when Timothy returned to Paul and Silas in Corinth; cf. Fee, *Thessalonians*, 241.

with the admonition that they should not be idle but should earn the bread that they eat, rather than depend upon others to support them.[57]

E. *Outline of Second Thessalonians*

A. Opening (1:1–2)
   1. Sender (1:1a)
   2. Addressee (1:1b)
   3. Greeting (1:2)
B. Thanksgiving (1:3–12)
   1. The Thessalonians' faith (1:3–4)
   2. God to judge their afflicters (1:5–10)
   3. Intercession formula (1:11–12)
C. Body: the parousia (2:1–12)
   1. The topic: the parousia and being gathered to him (2:1)
   2. Words of comfort (2:2–4)
   3. Signs to be seen (2:5–7)
   4. Christ's triumph (2:8–12)
D. Paraenesis (2:13–3:15)
   1. Thanksgiving for the Thessalonians (2:13–15)
   2. Doxology (2:16–17)
   3. Paul's request for prayer (3:1–5)
   4. Paul's instructions to follow his example (3:6–15)
E. Closing (3:16–18)
   1. Doxology (3:16)
   2. Personal signature (3:17)
   3. Benediction (3:18)

F. *Content of Second Thessalonians*

Opening (1:1–2)

The same three writers of the first letter, Paul, Silvanus (or Silas), and Timothy, are identified. The opening is fairly standard here, including identifying the

---

57. For a study that arrives at roughly similar conclusions on many if not most major points regarding 1–2 Thessalonians, see C. R. Nicholl, *From Hope to Despair in Thessalonica: Situating 1 and 2 Thessalonians* (SNTSMS 126; Cambridge: Cambridge University Press, 2004).

writers, naming the recipients, who are the church (singular) of the Thessalonians, and offering the standard Pauline greeting: grace to you and peace from God our Father and the Lord Jesus Christ.

Thanksgiving (1:3–12)

While this thanksgiving section is not as lengthy as in his first letter to the Thessalonians, Paul nevertheless says that he gives thanks to God for them always, because their faith was growing abundantly, and their love was increasing as well. His thanksgiving continues by acknowledging the afflictions they were receiving for their faith. He encourages them by reminding them of God's justice and retribution, especially when Jesus is revealed from heaven. Paul states that Jesus will exact vengeance on unbelievers through eternal destruction and will be marveled at by believers, including the Thessalonians. Because of this, Paul says that he prays for the Thessalonian believers, so that God would make them worthy of their calling and fulfill every good intention and every work of faith according to his power, so that God's name might be glorified in them.

Body: Parousia (2:1–12)

Whereas the subject of the parousia occupies the paraenetic section in 1 Thessalonians, it is the main subject here and occupies the body section. The Thessalonian believers apparently were deeply perplexed by some misconceptions about the coming of the Lord, so Paul tells them that the "day of the Lord" has not yet come and not to believe false testimonies that it had already come. Paul instructs them that there are a few precursors to the day of the Lord, including the rebellion and the man of lawlessness, who is also called the son of destruction, who exalts himself above every other so-called god or object of worship and proclaims himself as God. The mystery of lawlessness is already at work,[58] but the Lord Jesus will come and destroy the man of lawlessness, along with his false signs and wonders. Those who are deluded will believe in this man of lawlessness, because they loved unrighteousness instead of truth.

Paraenesis (2:13–3:15)

Paul gives the Thessalonian believers a brief word of thanksgiving again (as above, a separate section of thanksgiving is not necessary, but it is included in

---

58. On the restrainer that keeps the man of lawlessness in check, see the opinions debated in Nicholl, *From Hope to Despair*, 225–49.

the paraenetic section); however, this time he says with softer language that they *ought* to give thanks (ὀφείλομεν εὐχαριστεῖν), which may indicate that Paul's enthusiasm for the Thessalonians has decreased, at least a little, since the writing of 1 Thessalonians. Nevertheless, Paul gives thanks for them, for the reason that God has chosen them for salvation, through sanctification, which is why they were called. In light of this, he commands them to hold to the traditions that were passed on to them.

After praying for them, Paul requests for them to pray for him and his coworkers, that they would be protected against wicked and evil people. But as soon as he asks for prayer, Paul returns to encouraging the Thessalonians by saying that the Lord would establish and guard them, and he expresses his confidence in their obedience to his commands.

His final command to them is to keep away from a brother or sister who walks in idleness. Paul uses himself as an example of how he did not walk in idleness while he was with them, but he and his companions worked hard to support themselves so that they would not be a financial burden to them. Although Paul and his coworkers had a right to be supported by them, he did not use that right, so as to be an example for them to follow. Those who are idle are commanded to work with quietness and eat their own bread (a metaphor for earning their own living), instead of being dependent on others for daily needs.[59] Paul ends the paraenetic section with a stern warning: those who do not heed the words in the letter should be ousted, that such a person may be ashamed. This, however, does not mean this dissenter is an enemy, but he should be warned as a brother.

Closing (3:16–18)

Paul closes the letter with a short benediction, asking for peace for the Thessalonian believers. Then he states that he writes this greeting with his own handwriting to confirm its authenticity (cf. Gal 6:11; Col 4:18).

---

59. The meaning of working or living quietly (cf. 1 Thess 4:11) is debated among interpreters. Bruce Winter suggests that the client-patron relationship in the Greco-Roman world is what Paul is discouraging here for the Christian, where the client is at the beck and call of the patron, and to be engaged in political activism. He claims that this is Paul's call to political quietism for Christians; *Seek the Welfare of the City: Christians as Benefactors and Citizens* (Grand Rapids: Eerdmans, 1994), 41–60, esp. 49–51. This seems to be an unlikely interpretation and without any hint in the text of any sort of political involvement by the Thessalonians. Instead, the traditional view that the Thessalonians in anticipating the parousia were stopping their daily work seems to best fit the context. Cf. Fee, *Thessalonians*, 334.

Sources for Further Study

Commentaries

Best, E. *A Commentary on the First and Second Epistles to the Thessalonians*. BNTC. London: A&C Black, 1977.

Bruce, F. F. *1 and 2 Thessalonians*. WBC 45. Waco, TX: Word, 1982.

Fee, G. D. *The First and Second Letters to the Thessalonians*. NICNT. Grand Rapids: Eerdmans, 2009.

Frame, J. E. *A Critical and Exegetical Commentary on the Epistles of St. Paul to the Thessalonians*. ICC. Edinburgh: T&T Clark, 1912.

Furnish, V. P. *1 & 2 Thessalonians*. Abingdon New Testament Commentaries. Nashville: Abingdon, 2007.

Marshall, I. H. *1 and 2 Thessalonians*. NCB. Grand Rapids: Eerdmans, 1983.

Menken, M. J. J. *2 Thessalonians*. London: Routledge, 1994.

Morris, L. *The First and Second Epistles to the Thessalonians*. 2nd ed. NICNT. Grand Rapids: Eerdmans, 1991.

Richard, E. J. *First and Second Thessalonians*. Sacra Pagina 11. Collegeville, MN: Liturgical, 1995.

Wanamaker, C. A. *The Epistles to the Thessalonians: A Commentary on the Greek Text*. NIGTC. Grand Rapids: Eerdmans, 1990.

Weima, J. A. D. *1–2 Thessalonians*. BECNT. Grand Rapids: Baker, 2014.

Monographs and Books

Donfried, K. P., and I. H. Marshall. *The Theology of the Shorter Pauline Letters*. NTT. Cambridge: Cambridge University Press, 1993.

Donfried, K. P., and J. Beutler, eds. *The Thessalonians Debate: Methodological Discord or Methodological Synthesis?* Grand Rapids: Eerdmans, 2000.

Holland, G. S. *The Tradition That You Received from Us: 2 Thessalonians in the Pauline Tradition*. HUT 24. Tübingen: Mohr-Siebeck, 1988.

Jewett, R. *The Thessalonian Correspondence: Pauline Rhetoric and Millenarian Piety*. FFNT. Philadelphia: Fortress, 1986.

Malherbe, A. J. *Paul and the Thessalonians: The Philosophic Tradition of Pastoral Care*. Philadelphia: Fortress, 1987.

Nicholl, C. R. *From Hope to Despair in Thessalonica: Situating 1 and 2 Thessalonians*. SNTSMS 126. Cambridge: Cambridge University Press, 2004.

Schlueter, C. J. *Filling up the Measure: Polemical Hyperbole in 1 Thessalonians 2.14–16*. JSNTSup 98. Sheffield: Sheffield Academic, 1994.

Still, T. D. *Conflict at Thessalonica: A Pauline Church and Its Neighbours.* JSNTSup 183. Sheffield: Sheffield Academic, 1999.

Weima, J. A. D., and S. E. Porter. *An Annotated Bibliography of 1 and 2 Thessalonians.* NTTS 26. Leiden: Brill, 1998.

9

1–2 Corinthians

1. Introduction

As in the previous chapter on 1–2 Thessalonians, in this chapter I discuss both 1 Corinthians and 2 Corinthians, because they have traditionally been linked together by their common audience and authorship. At least as much as the Thessalonian letters, the two Corinthian letters have much in common, but they also have a number of important differences, along with a variety of individual features, that require that they be examined in separate detail. Even if Pauline authorship is not a major item of contention regarding these letters, one of the major issues is that these two letters seem to represent only part of Paul's correspondence with the Corinthian Christians, although the matter of their textual unity is also an object of dispute. All of these issues are treated in this chapter.

2. First Corinthians

First Corinthians, Paul's second longest letter after his letter to the Romans, has long held an important place within the Pauline letters, for a number of reasons. Some of these are theological but more of them are related to the paraenetic section of the letter. The letter also participates in a complex set of correspondence between Paul and the Corinthian church. I will first discuss authorship quickly before turning to the city of Corinth itself, the Corinthian church situation, the integrity of the letter, and its occasion and purpose, before outlining and summarizing its content.

A. Authorship of First Corinthians

German scholar Werner Georg Kümmel categorically states that "the genuineness of I Cor is not disputed."[1] First Corinthians constituted one of Ferdinand Christian Baur's four pillar epistles,[2] and its authorship continues to be undisputed among scholars, although some seriously question elements of its integrity and unity (see §2D).

B. City of Corinth

The city of Corinth during the Greco-Roman period is described by Gordon Fee as "the New York, Los Angeles and Las Vegas of the ancient world."[3] By this he probably means that it was a financial and commercial center, a city full of the upwardly mobile, and a center of religion and entertainment, much of it far from virtuous. This opinion can be substantiated from what is known of the city from the ancient records (Strabo, *Geography* 8.6.20–23 and Pausanias, *Description of Greece* 2).[4] The potential is great for overstatement about the city, however, since some of the records used to characterize Corinth probably refer to the time before 146 BC rather than Greco-Roman times.

Corinth was located at the land bridge between the Greek mainland and the Peloponnese. Because boats could be taken from one side of the land bridge to the other, it had two harbors, Cenchrea on the east and Lechaeum on the west. Thus, Corinth was strategically located to become a center of trade and travel and hence commerce of all sorts.

The ancient city of Corinth flourished in classical times until it was destroyed in 146 BC after joining with other cities of the area against the growing power of Rome. The city was rebuilt in 44 BC by Julius Caesar as a Roman colony, however, and then became capital of the Roman senatorial province of Achaia, so that those citizens living there enjoyed the rights

---

1. W. G. Kümmel, *Introduction to the New Testament* (trans. H. C. Kee; 17th ed.; Nashville: Abingdon, 1975), 275.

2. F. C. Baur, *Paul the Apostle of Jesus Christ: His Life and Work, His Epistles and His Doctrine* (2 vols.; London: Williams & Norgate, 1873–75; repr. Peabody, MA: Hendrickson, 2003), 1.268–320.

3. G. D. Fee, *The First Epistle to the Corinthians* (NICNT; Grand Rapids: Eerdmans, 1987; 2nd ed., 2014), 3.

4. These texts and others are cited in J. Murphy-O'Connor, *St. Paul's Corinth: Texts and Archaeology* (3rd ed.; Wilmington, DE: Glazier, 2002); cf. also his "Corinth," *ABD* 1.1134–39.

of citizens as if they lived in Rome. Since Corinth was partly populated by freedmen (as well as by Caesar's own veterans and urban trades persons and laborers), it tended toward a lower economic level, at least in the early Roman days.[5] But because of its prime location, there was an influx of people—both the wealthy and those who wished to be wealthy—who were involved in various forms of commerce and trading, and this development increased the city's material prosperity. By the time of the New Testament, however, many of these people, together with others attracted to the opportunities that it created, had attained significant wealth, so that a patronage or benefaction system seems to have been firmly in place. As a result, Corinth was arguably the most important city in the province of Achaia. The church probably reflected the mix of socioeconomic levels within the city, which perhaps led to many of the difficulties within the church, such as disputes over communion meals.[6] It is even posited that the Erastus of Rom 16:23, who is said to be "the city treasurer," may be the Erastus who is mentioned in a first-century Corinthian inscription as responsible for laying a pavement.[7] Although the identification of Erastus cannot be established, his title of city treasurer indicates that at least one person of high social standing was a member of the Corinthian church.

In natural resources, Corinth enjoyed many advantages. Because of its location, the city not only had the benefit of trade and travel by sea toward the east and the west; it also stood at the intersection of land travel between the Peloponnese and the Greek mainland. The city had an adequate water supply and natural defenses from Acrocorinth, a mountain of 1,857 feet overlooking a hill upon which was built a temple to the goddess Aphrodite. The city was host to the Isthmian Games, an athletic competition comparable to the rival Olympian Games. In light of Paul's use of athletic imagery (e.g.,

---

5. A. C. Thiselton, *The First Epistle to the Corinthians: A Commentary on the Greek Text* (NIGTC; Grand Rapids: Eerdmans, 2000), 3.

6. On the social structure of Corinth, especially concerning financial issues, see P. Marshall, *Enmity in Corinth: Social Conventions in Paul's Relations with the Corinthians* (WUNT 2/23; Tübingen: Mohr-Siebeck, 1987); J. K. Chow, *Patronage and Power: A Study of Social Networks in Corinth* (JSNTSup 75; Sheffield: JSOT Press, 1992); D. W. J. Gill, "In Search of the Social Élite in the Corinthian Church," *Tyndale Bulletin* 44.2 (1993): 323–37; and A. D. Clarke, *Secular and Christian Leadership in Corinth: A Socio-Historical and Exegetical Study of 1 Corinthians 1–6* (Arbeiten zur Geschichte des antiken Judentums und des Urchristentums 18; Leiden: Brill, 1993).

7. D. W. J. Gill, "Erastus the Aedile," *Tyndale Bulletin* 40.2 (1989): 293–301. This is disputed by S. J. Friesen, "The Wrong Erastus: Ideology, Archaeology, and Exegesis," in *Corinth in Context: Comparative Studies on Religion and Society* (ed. S. J. Friesen, D. N. Schowalter, and J. C. Walters; NovTSup 134; Leiden: Brill, 2010), 231–56.

1 Cor 9:24–27; Phil 3:12–16), it is possible that Paul may have even been in the city when the games were going on.[8] The structure of the surrounding area also lent itself to the natural acoustics of a large theater. This was appropriate for a city of perhaps a hundred thousand, the estimated population of Corinth.

There is widespread disagreement about what kinds of religious practices can be substantiated in Corinth during the Roman period. What is known is that the population included a mix of races and, with it, a mix of religions, virtually all of them pagan (except for the Jews and then later the Christians, as noted below). The temple of Aphrodite was only one of several religious institutions, for there were other temples as well; Pausanias describes twenty-six religious sites.[9] Aphrodite was the Greek goddess of love and life, and according to Strabo (*Geography* 8.6.20), the temple had a thousand cult prostitutes. This information is highly questionable in light of recent archeological discoveries from Corinth, which indicate that Strabo was either exaggerating or referring to pre–146 BC practices. There is no substantive evidence of cult prostitution during this time in Greece.[10] Associated with the reputation, if not the reality, of Corinthian religious and sexual life was its contribution to literary "culture." The verb "to Corinthize" (κορινθιάζεσθαι) was used by Aristophanes to mean "to fornicate" (fragment 354). Plays by Philetaerus and Poliochus were entitled *The Whoremonger* (Κορινθιαστής) (Athenaeus, *Deipnosophistae* 7.313C, 13.559A), and a "Corinthian girl" (Κορινθία κόρη) was a prostitute (Plato, *Republic* 404d). To be fair, reference was also made to "Corinthian style or workmanship," which referred to artistic (e.g., the Corinthian capitals on columns, with their ornate decoration) and literary accomplishments in Corinth. Despite exaggeration regarding religious practices in Corinth, we do know that the trade in idol meat was large and was responsible for the vast amount of meat available for sale. This meat was offered in idol sacrifice and then sold by the priests.[11]

There was a Jewish population in Corinth, attested by the stone remains of the lintel of a synagogue with an inscription.[12] The Jewish presence would be

---

8. See K. Quast, *The Corinthian Correspondence: An Introduction* (New York: Paulist, 1994), 20.

9. See Quast, *The Corinthian Correspondence*, 21, for descriptions of some of these.

10. H. Conzelmann, *1 Corinthians: A Commentary on the First Epistle to the Corinthians* (Hermeneia; Philadelphia: Fortress, 1972), 12.

11. See W. L. Willis, *Idol Meat in Corinth: The Pauline Argument in 1 Corinthians 8 and 10* (SBLDS 68; Chico, CA: Scholars Press, 1985); and P. D. Gooch, *Dangerous Food: 1 Corinthians 8–10 in Its Context* (Waterloo, ON: Wilfrid Laurier University Press, 1993).

12. A. Deissmann, *Light from the Ancient East: The New Testament Illustrated by Recently*

natural in such an accessible center, although Pausanias does not refer to the synagogue. Although all of the legal issues are not clear, it is possible that the Jews in Corinth had certain protected rights, including the right to assemble, permission to send the temple tax to Jerusalem, and exemption from certain kinds of activities on the Sabbath. According to Acts 18:4, Paul reasoned with the Jews every Sabbath in the synagogue.

The Roman proconsul would have held legal hearings in the city, since it became the capital of Achaia in 27 BC. Since the territories that they governed were often quite large (e.g., Galatia), the Roman proconsuls often made regular tours of their territory to hear cases and render judicial verdicts, as this was their main function. Gallio, according to what can be made of the Gallio inscription (see chapter 2 §2), was proconsul in 51/52, and it was before him that Paul appeared (Acts 18:12–17).[13] Gallio was probably hearing cases at this time, and according to Acts he considered the charges made against Paul to be a matter of Jewish law, not one that concerned him.

C. Corinthian Situation

A number of difficulties concerning the Corinthian situation revolve around such issues as how many letters Paul sent to the Corinthian church and how many of these we have in our New Testament, either in whole or in part. In other words, what is the relationship between the composition of the letters that we do have, 1–2 Corinthians, and the original letters that were sent to the Corinthians? How do the record of Acts and what is said in 1–2 Corinthians help to establish Paul's travel itinerary? These are difficult questions that have important implications for reading 1–2 Corinthians, so an attempt at reconstructing the surrounding events must be made.[14] The following is one possible scenario.[15]

Discovered Texts of the Graeco-Roman World (trans. L. R. N. Strachan; 4th ed.; London: Hodder & Stoughton, 1927), 16.

13. Cf. Thiselton, *First Corinthians*, 29–30.

14. Discussion of the issues regarding the Corinthian letters in an exegetical context is found in S. E. Porter, "Exegesis of the Pauline Letters, Including the Deutero-Pauline Letters," in *Handbook to Exegesis of the New Testament* (ed. S. E. Porter; NTTS 25; Leiden: Brill, 1997), 512–23, followed here.

15. For some other viewpoints, see Thiselton, *First Corinthians*, 29–41; and C. S. Keener, "Paul and the Corinthian Believers," in *The Blackwell Companion to Paul* (ed. S. Westerholm; West Sussex, UK: Wiley-Blackwell, 2011), 46–62.

1. Paul's Planting of a Church on His Second Missionary Journey (Acts 18:1–18) (Autumn 50–Spring 52)

Paul stayed in Corinth for a year and a half on this occasion, including his appearance before the proconsul Gallio, who dismissed the charges against him. Gallio probably either directly or through his verdict helped to guarantee Paul's safety in Corinth (1 Cor 2:1–8; 2 Cor 1:19). Paul began his ministry there by preaching in the synagogue. During his time in Corinth, he probably composed at least 1 Thessalonians, and 2 Thessalonians as well if it is considered authentically Pauline (as I think that it is; see chapter 8 §3A). When there was resistance to his teaching, Paul went to the house of Titius Justus. Upon leaving Corinth, Paul completed his second missionary journey by returning to Syrian Antioch by way of Ephesus, Caesarea, and Jerusalem.

2. Paul's Stay at Ephesus (Acts 19)

In the earlier part of his third missionary journey, sometime during spring 53–summer 55, Paul sent his first letter to the Corinthian church from Ephesus after "Chloe's people" informed him of problems in the church (1 Cor 1:11). Some scholars still think that 2 Cor 6:14–7:1 on being yoked to unbelievers is part of the lost letter. More recent work, however, plausibly shows that this is probably not the lost letter (see §2E below).[16] At nearly the same time, Paul apparently received a letter from the church asking for advice on a number of issues (see 1 Cor 5:1; 7:1). To this letter, Paul responded with 1 Corinthians, possibly delivered by Titus (2 Cor 12:18), who then returned to Paul (if Titus carried the "severe letter," discussed in §3B2, he probably did not deliver 1 Corinthians). Timothy was then sent on a special mission to Corinth (1 Cor 4:17; 16:10), where he discovered that there was a crisis, which included attacks being made on Paul's authority (2 Cor 2:5–11; 7:8–12). Timothy was unable to deal with the crisis and returned to Ephesus to tell Paul. Paul, upon hearing of these difficulties, visited Corinth briefly to deal with these issues in person, but he was rebuffed. This is later referred to by Paul as the "painful visit" (2 Cor 2:1; 12:14; 13:1–2), which is not recorded in Acts. After his visit, Paul sent a powerful letter in response, probably carried by Titus, to deal with this crisis concerning his apostleship. This letter is referred to as the "tearful" or "severe" letter (2 Cor 2:4; 7:8–12). Some

---

16. See M. E. Thrall, *A Critical and Exegetical Commentary on the Second Epistle to the Corinthians* (2 vols.; ICC; Edinburgh: T&T Clark, 1994), 1.25–36.

scholars maintain that 2 Cor 10–13 is a part of this letter.[17] The reasoning for this is based on, among other things, the use of the Greek verb tenses in the different sections. For example, in some pairs of verbs the so-called Greek present tense is found in 2 Cor 10–13 but a so-called past tense is found in 2 Cor 1–9, with the implication (at least in some scholars' minds) that the events described in the "past tense" occurred before those in the "present tense" (see 10:6 and 2:9; 13:2 and 1:23; 13:10 and 2:3). Unfortunately for this theory, as we have seen several times already, since the verbal tense forms in Greek do not primarily refer to time, they will not sustain such an argument.[18] For this and other reasons, most scholars probably would claim that this third letter to the Corinthians is now lost.[19] (For more on the unity of 2 Corinthians, see §2B.)

3. Macedonia and Philippi (Acts 20:1–2)

After writing this third letter to the Corinthians, Paul left Ephesus and went toward Macedonia (1 Cor 16:5–9). He was delayed along the way by a visit to Troas, where he waited for Titus but could not find him (2 Cor 2:12–13). He went on to Macedonia, where he met Titus, who said that the worst of the crisis in Corinth was over (7:6–16). Second Corinthians was written from Macedonia and sent by means of Titus and other "brothers" (9:3, 5); some think that 2 Cor 10–13 may have been sent separately from the rest of the letter—probably later if these chapters were separate (see §3B2).[20]

4. Corinth (Acts 20:3)

Paul traveled on to Corinth, from which, within a year, he wrote the letter to the Romans, apparently without any difficulties in Corinth. This indicates the likelihood that the Corinthian crisis was resolved in Paul's favor. Table 3 lays out what has been said above.

---

17. E.g., C. K. Barrett, *A Commentary on the Second Epistle to the Corinthians* (2nd ed.; London: A&C Black, 1990), 243–44. See, however, C. D. Land, *Is There a Text in These Meanings? The Integrity of 2 Corinthians from a Linguistic Perspective* (NTM 36; Sheffield: Sheffield Phoenix, 2015), who argues that 1 Corinthians may have been the severe letter and that there was no intermediary visit.

18. Cf. S. E. Porter, *Verbal Aspect in the Greek of the New Testament, with Reference to Tense and Mood* (Studies in Biblical Greek 1; New York: Peter Lang, 1989), esp. 75–108 and 163–239.

19. See Thrall, *Second Corinthians*, 1.5–18.

20. See Thrall, *Second Corinthians*, 1.18–20.

Table 3. Relationship of Events to Corinthian Letters

Events	Letters
Paul founds Corinthian church	
Paul stays at Ephesus	
Paul responds to information from Corinth	first letter to Corinth (2 Cor 6:14–7:1?)
Timothy visits Corinth	1 Corinthians
Paul's "painful visit" to Corinth	third letter to Corinth, so-called tearful or severe letter (2 Cor 10–13?)
Paul goes to Macedonia	
Titus reports that the crisis is over	2 Corinthians

D. Textual Integrity of First Corinthians

Even with the few issues noted above regarding reconstructing the Corinthian correspondence, the vast majority of scholars accept that 1 Corinthians is virtually intact; nevertheless, there are two textual issues to discuss. The first is the hypothesis of, for example, John Hurd and David Trobisch that 1 Corinthians is a composite document of various smaller Pauline units;[21] the second issue is that a number of passages may not be part of the original letter.

The major reason for the past speculation regarding the textual integrity of 1 Corinthians was the perception of differences in tone between passages that are restrictive in nature and those that are more lenient. Thus, passages such as 10:1–22 on food offered to idols, 6:12–20 on the avoidance of immorality, and 11:2–34 on the veiling of women and on conduct of the Lord's Supper were all placed together as taking a more restrictive tone than other passages in 1 Corinthians. These passages, together with 2 Cor 6:14–7:1 on being yoked to unbelievers and sometimes 1 Cor 9:24–27 on running the race for the prize, have been thought by some to constitute Paul's first letter to the Corinthians. The remainder of 1 Corinthians, except 1 Cor 1–4, was thought to be a second letter, and 1 Cor 1–4 was often suggested to be the third letter, the second and third letters being sent on separate occasions, though close in time. As even Hurd states, however, "Most scholars and the present writer, while recognizing the above points, do not believe that this evidence is strong enough to support the burden of proof which this kind

---

21. J. C. Hurd Jr., *The Origin of I Corinthians* (New York: Seabury, 1965), 43–47, with chart on 45; and D. Trobisch, *Paul's Letter Collection: Tracing the Origins* (Minneapolis: Fortress, 1994), 76–80.

of theory must always bear."[22] Scholars of previous generations often spent time discussing these hypotheses, but they do not merit significant discussion in most recent commentaries. The general thought is that tensions between these various passages, such as between 1 Cor 8 and 1 Cor 10 on food offered to idols, can be resolved when the character of the letter as responding to a number of different problems in the church is considered.[23] Research on the structure of the letter shows that patterns of argumentation may well account for the shape of the letter as we have it.[24]

The second issue concerns a few select passages that are often thought to be non-Pauline interpolations. The first is 1:2, where not only the church of God in Corinth is addressed but "all those everywhere who call on the name of our Lord Jesus Christ" (NIV). The argument is that this is too inclusive a statement for a letter addressed to a series of specific problems in the church at Corinth. But in light of how Paul saw himself as apostle to the Gentiles and not simply as apostle to the Corinthians, together with the problems in the Corinthian church, which may well have stemmed from the self-conceit of some Corinthians as categorically superior to others because they followed certain individuals, the opening of the letter is not inappropriate at all. Indeed, one might argue that this is just the kind of opening needed for a letter to a church with such problems. In this sense, Paul may have intended for this letter, like Colossians, to be read widely, and the introduction would have included that possibility. Also, there is no substantive textual evidence for the exclusion of this verse.[25]

The second textual problem is found at 14:33b–35. Fee summarizes the position for those who believe that these verses are non-Pauline: "Although these two verses are found in all known manuscripts, either here or at the end of the chapter, the two text-critical criteria of transcriptional and intrinsic probability combine to cast considerable doubt on their authenticity."[26] It is ironic that Fee dismisses Hans Conzelmann's desire to include 14:33b and 14:36 as Pauline by stating that it is "without textual warrant" for this theory when,

---

22. Hurd, *1 Corinthians*, 47.

23. See Gooch, *Dangerous Food*, 57–58.

24. See, e.g., A. C. Wire, *The Corinthian Women Prophets: A Reconstruction through Paul's Rhetoric* (Minneapolis: Fortress, 1990). See also R. E. Ciampa and B. S. Rosner, *The First Letter to the Corinthians* (PNTC; Grand Rapids: Eerdmans, 2010), 21–25, who argue that the tripartite categories of sexual immorality, greed, and idolatry are the main issues that Paul addresses to the Corinthians.

25. See Fee, *First Corinthians*, 33 (1st ed.), 29 (2nd ed.).

26. See Fee, *First Corinthians*, 699 (quotation) and n4 for evidence (discussion pp. 699–708, 1st ed.), but changed in placement and less detailed explanation in 2nd ed. (pp. 780–81). Cf. Conzelmann, *1 Corinthians*, 246.

as he admits, there is no textual warrant for his position either. The most that is at issue is whether the verses belong at their traditional place or after 14:40,[27] not whether they should be excised.

In light of these discussions, the integrity of 1 Corinthians is well established.

E. Occasion and Purpose of First Corinthians

There has been significant recent debate regarding the nature of the dispute in Corinth that brought forth the series of correspondences. The traditional view is fairly well established, but Fee calls this into question.

1. Disunity

The traditional view of the issue at Corinth is that it was about unity and disunity.[28] There are indications that the church was divided, possibly into a variety of factions, with various controversial issues or practices that warranted a series of comments from the apostle.

a. Inquiries about Issues

Assuming its literary unity, I believe it is clear that 1 Corinthians was not the first letter that Paul wrote to the church at Corinth (5:9). Since the first letter, Paul had apparently received two forms of communication from the church. Members of Chloe's household (1:11) had orally communicated to him, apparently about various quarrels and divisions within the church (1:10–17). He had also received written communication (7:1; probably 5:1), likely carried by Stephanas, Fortunatus, and Achaicus (16:16), about specific issues in the church that had divided it into various factions.

Many scholars commence their analysis of the major problems in the

---

27. See B. M. Metzger, ed., *A Textual Commentary on the Greek New Testament* (2nd ed.; Stuttgart: Deutsche Bibelgesellschaft, 1994), 499–500, for the options; and J. Shack, "A Text without 1 Corinthians 14:34–35? Not according to the Manuscript Evidence," *Journal of Greco-Roman Christianity and Judaism* 10 (2014): 90–112, for an argument against excising this passage.

28. Among recent scholars, see, e.g., R. E. Brown, *An Introduction to the New Testament* (New York: Doubleday, 1996), 526–28; D. E. Garland, *1 Corinthians* (BECNT; Grand Rapids: Baker, 2003), 13–14; and D. A. Hagner, *The New Testament: A Historical and Theological Introduction* (Grand Rapids: Baker, 2012), 480–82. Some commentators make no comment at this point.

church with 7:1, but 5:1 is probably a better place to begin. At this point, as the outline below indicates, Paul turns from the brief body of his letter, regarding the issue of unity in the church, to a lengthy paraenetic section in which he deals specifically with issues in the Corinthian church. He treats them in serial fashion, often giving an indication that he is switching topics by use of the phrase "now concerning" (περὶ δέ) (7:1, 25; 8:1; 12:1; 16:1), but this is not the only connective that he uses.[29] The following issues appear to be important. First, there seem to have been some questions regarding sexual purity. The church had tolerated a Christian man immorally engaged with his stepmother (1 Cor 5). The rationale for the church's tolerant behavior is not stated, but it appears that it reflected either accommodation to the surrounding sexual ethics of the city or a view of the human body that made self-indulgence tolerable because it was thought to have no consequences (perhaps similar to later gnostic ideas). There were also problems related to prostitutes (6:12–20). Some in the Corinthian church were apparently using Christian freedom as license to indulge their sexual appetites. The reason for this behavior is also not stated. Paul rejects such encounters on the basis that, unlike other sins, they constitute a sin against one's own body. A third dimension of the sexual difficulties at Corinth seems to have been problems with asceticism (7:1, 28).[30] Paul takes the occasion to address the issue of marriage in a Christian context. He is apparently directly responding to some within the Corinthian church who considered marriage to be sinful. In light of Paul's eschatology of imminence (7:29–31), he may agree that staying in one's present condition of singleness is preferable (7:24), but he does not take an ascetic's position.

A second major set of difficulties seems to have concerned pagan practices, especially food offered to idols. Only a small portion of an animal used in pagan sacrifice was burned, with the remaining amount usually being sold. This was the largest and cheapest supply of fresh meat for people to purchase. The majority of those who could afford such meat were of some financial wealth, indicating that the church included a range of people from various social and economic strata.[31] There seems to have been a controversy within

29. See M. M. Mitchell, "Concerning περὶ δέ in 1 Corinthians," *NovT* 31 (1989): 229–56. Paul also uses conditional structures (7:17; 13:1; 15:12), a knowledge formula (10:1), a strong adversative (15:35), and an emphatic cataphoric pronoun (11:17; 15:50).

30. See V. L. Wimbush, *Paul, the Worldly Ascetic: Response to the World and Self-Understanding according to 1 Corinthians 7* (Macon, GA: Mercer University Press, 1987); cf. W. Deming, *Paul on Marriage and Celibacy: The Hellenistic Background of 1 Corinthians 7* (2nd ed.; Grand Rapids: Eerdmans, 2004 [1995]).

31. See W. A. Meeks, *The First Urban Christians: The Social World of the Apostle Paul* (New Haven: Yale University Press, 1983), 98. For recent discussion, see S. J. Friesen, D. N.

the church between those who were scrupulous in not eating food that may have been offered to idols and those who held no scruple at eating this meat in places where it was known to be served (8:10; 10:27–28). Paul must tread a fine line between the argument that the pagan gods do not exist and there being in his mind an evil spirit world, and he must consider the believers who might stumble by seeing such behavior. This kind of contact with the institutions of the surrounding culture may also have accounted for Corinthian Christians' engagement in court cases with each other (6:1–11). Paul dismisses such involvement by saying that the church should appoint the lowliest of its members to judge these cases. The same kind of social division appears to have crept into the celebration of the Lord's Supper, where the wealthier members were taking advantage of the situation by turning what should have been a communal meal into an occasion for gluttony, so that the poorer members were not able to participate in the eating (11:17–34). Paul makes abuse of the ceremony a very serious matter: sinning against the body and blood of the Lord.

There also appears to have been some difficulty within the church about practices of worship, since there was a general spirit of disorder. For instance, apparently a number of women were particularly vocal during the service, and undue emphasis was put on the charismatic gifts, in particular speaking in divine or heavenly languages. Paul tells the women that they should show appropriate respect, including asking their husbands at home if they have questions about what is said in the service. And comparing the use of tongues with prophecy (1 Cor 12–14), Paul makes a general plea for order.

The last matter of concern for Paul is the issue of the resurrection (1 Cor 15). It is debated whether the Corinthian church held to a view that the resurrection of Christ had not occurred or whether it was experiencing a dispute over whether there would be a resurrection of believers, especially if some of the members believed that they had already entered the close of the age (the eschaton). In any case, Paul reestablishes the importance of Christ's resurrection as the guarantee of a future human resurrection, but as part of a larger scheme of Christ vanquishing death and ruling the world.

The question that emerges from this brief discussion of the various problems in the Corinthian church is, What may have provided the basis for this kind of tension within the community? In other words, what best accounts for the disunity within the community? The views are many and varied.[32] In a clas-

---

Schowalter, and J. C. Walters, eds., *Corinth in Context: Comparative Studies on Religion and Society* (NovTSup 134; Leiden: Brill, 2010), 151–323.

32. For a good survey, see J. D. G. Dunn, *1 Corinthians* (NTG; Sheffield: Sheffield Academic, 1995), 27–89.

sic essay (still untranslated into English), Baur expresses his belief that Paul's opponents were representatives of Jewish Christianity, the Petrine wing of the church.[33] This was based upon Baur's idea of a fundamental clash between Jewish and Gentile sections of the church in its earliest days. Evidence for a Petrine opposition in Corinth is further explored by Michael Goulder, who shows that what many think are random comments in the letter can be read as part of a structured opposition to a Petrine legalistic position (see 3:4-5, 22; 4:6).[34] There apparently was contact between the Corinthian church and Jerusalem (1:12; 3:22), but there does not seem to be an indication, at least in 1 Corinthians (cf. 2 Corinthians below), that the opposition is seen as coming from outside.[35]

b. Gnostics

A second hypothesis, one that tends to dominate discussion of 1 Corinthians, is that there were Jewish-Christian gnostics in the church.[36] Reflecting the kind of dualism that typifies gnostic thought, they disparaged the earthly and the fleshly and elevated esoteric knowledge (see references to "knowledge" in 1:18–2:16; 3:18–23) and the spiritual realm. The result may well have been over-indulgence (see, e.g., 1 Cor 5-6; 11:17-34). These Jewish-Christian gnostics were concerned to mediate the otherworldly to this world, but it raised some direct questions regarding their Christology, seen most clearly in Paul's response in 1 Cor 15. If Christ was God, how could he also be a man? Their position would have tended toward what became known as a docetic view, in which Christ's humanness would have been merely an appearance of being human.

---

33. F. C. Baur, "Die Christuspartei in der korinthischen Gemeinde, der Gegensatz des petrinischen und paulinischen Christentums in der ältesten Kirche, der Apostel Petrus in Rom," *Tübinger Zeitschrift für Theologie* 4 (1831): 61–206; repr. in Baur, *Historisch-kritische Untersuchungen zum Neuen Testament* (Stuttgart: Frommann, 1963), 1–146. See also F. C. Baur, *The Church History of the First Three Centuries* (trans. A. Menzies; 2 vols.; London: Williams & Norgate, 1878–79), esp. 1.44–52. For a recent proponent of Baur's theories on 1 Corinthians, see M. D. Goulder, *Paul and the Competing Mission in Corinth* (Library of Pauline Studies; Peabody, MA: Hendrickson, 2001).

34. B. J. Malina and M. Goulder, *Early Christian Conflict in Corinth: Paul and the Followers of Peter* (Peabody, MA: Hendrickson, 2001); also Goulder, *Paul and the Competing Mission in Corinth*, esp. 16–32.

35. See J. Painter, "Paul and the Πνευματικοί at Corinth," in *Paul and Paulinism: Essays in Honour of C. K. Barrett* (ed. M. D. Hooker and S. G. Wilson; London: SPCK, 1985), 237–50, esp. 239–40.

36. See, e.g., W. Schmithals, *Gnosticism in Corinth: An Investigation of the Letters to the Corinthians* (trans. J. E. Steely; Nashville: Abingdon, 1971).

Responses to the gnostic hypothesis are several. One is the recognition that there is a difference between protognostic tendencies and full-blown Gnosticism as it emerged in the second and third centuries with its myth of the heavenly redeemer, full of all sorts of emanations and manifestations. The most that can be argued is that there were at Corinth some protognostic tendencies in which heavenly knowledge had an exalted place over the earthly, but none of the gnostic Christology or worldview.[37] A second response to the gnostic hypothesis is that often what is cited as gnostic may reveal other influences, such as Jewish wisdom thought, rather than Gnosticism, for the primary reason that there is no evidence of gnostic or protognostic movements before the second and third centuries.[38]

c. Overrealized Eschatology

A somewhat related view is that the major problems at Corinth stemmed from an overrealized eschatology.[39] All the practices that those in the church were engaged in, such as baptism and the Lord's Supper, seem to have had, in the minds of the Corinthians, a mystical or magical element to them. Those practicing them thought quite highly of their spiritual status and depreciated earthly things; they thought of themselves as already having entered the eschaton, and lived accordingly. This kind of thinking may well have derived from some form of Hellenistic thought, including wisdom speculation. Many think that Hellenistic Judaism was responsible for these influences, but the focus must be on Hellenistic thought in general, of which Jewish thought was a component. The emphasis was upon general exaltation of esoteric knowledge, perhaps in conjunction with the kind of rhetorical teaching that was part of the Hellenistic Second Sophistic, a philosophical movement influenced by Platonic thought.[40] Besides the criticisms raised above regarding possible gnostic influences, it is questionable that the Corinthian church was so influenced by the normal categories of rhetoric associated with the Second Sophistic that

37. R. M. Wilson, "Gnosis at Corinth," in Hooker, ed., *Paul and Paulinism*, 102–14; cf. also Painter, "Paul," 240–46.

38. See B. A. Pearson, *The Pneumatikos-Psychikos Terminology* (SBLDS 12; Missoula, MT: Scholars Press, 1973); and S. J. Chester, *Conversion at Corinth: Perspectives on Conversion in Paul's Theology and the Corinthian Church* (Studies of the New Testament and Its World; London: A&C Black, 2005), 222–25.

39. See A. C. Thiselton, "Realized Eschatology at Corinth," *NTS* 24 (1977–78): 510–26; and Thiselton, *First Corinthians*, 40–41, for the standard discussion of this issue.

40. See G. W. Bowersock, ed., *Approaches to the Second Sophistic* (University Park, PA: American Philological Association, 1974).

one can claim that this was the background to the movement.[41] It is also precarious to try to create a divide between Hellenistic Judaism and Hellenism, since Judaism was thoroughly immersed in Hellenistic culture and thought.

d. Divisive Groups

Others argue that there was a wide variety of divisive groups in the Corinthian church, none of which was preeminent, even though some may have thought of themselves as such. For example, some were libertines (1 Cor 5; 6:12–20) who had misunderstood Christian freedom to have no concern for propriety or the thoughts of those Christians who may not have had the same view of Christian freedom; for them it became an excuse for excessive indulgence. Others were ascetics, who had opted for the opposite approach to Christian behavior, a very rigid one in which Christians were forbidden from engaging in such activities as marriage, because it was viewed as sinful (7:1–28). Still others were ecstatics who were allowing spiritual experience to lead to disorderly behavior in the church (1 Cor 14). Some of these may have had a realized eschatology, in which they thought that they had already attained the eschaton and that this justified their behavior. Each of these groups may have been associated with a particular individual or recognizable group in Corinth, or there may also have been, besides the groups named above, a number of people who sided with various individuals, including the Paul group, the Apollos group, the Cephas group, and the Christ group (1:12).[42]

2. Paul's Apostolic Authority

The traditional characterizations of the opponents at Corinth tend to emphasize the diverse internal struggles within the Corinthian church, but Fee argues that the major problem at Corinth was *"conflict between the church and its founder,"* Paul.[43] The crisis seems to have been over Paul's authority and the nature of the gospel. In 9:1–14, Paul engages in a rigorous defense of himself, rejecting the Corinthians' judgment of him and any perceived vacillation on his part. In response to their letter to him, in which they took exception to several of his positions in

41. Cf. D. Litfin, *St. Paul's Theology of Proclamation: 1 Corinthians 1–4 and Greco-Roman Rhetoric* (SNTSMS 79; Cambridge: Cambridge University Press, 1994), esp. 109–34.

42. C. K. Barrett, "Christianity at Corinth," in *Essays on Paul* (Philadelphia: Westminster, 1981), 1–27, esp. 3–6.

43. Fee, *First Corinthians*, 6 (1st/2nd ed.). This view is more recently supported by J. L. Sumney, *"Servants of Satan," "False Brothers," and Other Opponents of Paul* (JSNTSup 188; Sheffield: Sheffield Academic, 1999), 33–78.

his previous letter (5:9), Paul reasserts his authority (3:5–9; 4:1–5). Paul corrects the Corinthians regarding various problems as a whole church—hence his use of the second person—in three crucial passages (1:10–12; 3:4–5; 11:18–19). Contrary to most reconstructions of the situation, Fee thinks that there is no evidence of outside opposition having come into the church (so "opponents" may even be the wrong term); he believes instead that the problem stems from anti-Pauline sentiment in the church, probably started by a few who had eventually infected the whole church. These people considered themselves wise and thought that Paul's preaching was "milk" compared to their mature teaching (2:8; 3:1). His behavior was seen to be weak or vacillating on such issues as food offered to idols (8:1–11:1). When Paul emphasized that he was writing on spiritual things (14:37), it was in response to people who thought of themselves as "spiritual" and did not so consider Paul, since they had experiences to back their claims (1 Cor 12–14). Their spiritual endowment was related to their knowledge and wisdom (1 Cor 8–10). In fact, they went further, contending that they were already experiencing the Spirit in full measure; their number probably included some eschatologically inclined women who thought they had entered the new age (1 Cor 7, 11), contrary to the weak Paul, who had not.

Fee's position is to be commended, in that it provides a unified depiction of the problem and rightly focuses upon the apostle Paul and his defense of his apostleship (9:1–14); it has gained some, but not widespread, support from other Corinthians scholars. The predominant position seems to be one that sees Paul responding to fractious thinking in the Corinthian church that originates with influences from the surrounding Hellenistic world.

F. Outline of First Corinthians[44]

A. Opening (1:1–3)
  1. Senders (1:1)
  2. Addressee (1:2)
  3. Greeting (1:3)
B. Thanksgiving (1:4–9)
C. Body: church unity (1:10–4:21)
  1. Problem of disunity (1:10–17)
  2. The gospel contradicts human wisdom (1:18–2:5)

44. Cf. L. L. Belleville, "Continuity and Discontinuity: A Fresh Look at 1 Corinthians in the Light of First-Century Epistolary Forms and Conventions," *Evangelical Quarterly* 59 (1987): 15–37, esp. 23–24.

3. God's wisdom comes by the Spirit (2:6–16)
4. Divisiveness (3:1–23)
5. Paul as Christ's servant (4:1–21)
D. Paraenesis (5:1–16:12)
   1. Questions of morality (5:1–6:20)
   2. Questions of marriage (7:1–40)
   3. Questions of food sacrificed to idols (8:1–11:1)
   4. Questions of worship (11:2–34)
   5. Questions of spiritual gifts (12:1–14:40)
   6. Questions of the resurrection (15:1–58)
   7. The collection (16:1–12)
E. Closing (16:13–24)
   1. Admonitions (16:13–18)
   2. Greetings (16:19–20)
   3. Paul's signature (16:21)
   4. Curse on unbelievers (16:22)
   5. Benediction (16:23–24)

G. Content of First Corinthians

Opening (1:1–3)

Paul and Sosthenes are the cosenders of this letter, although an amanuensis probably helped them write a majority of it, perhaps Sosthenes himself.[45] They write to the "church of God in Corinth," which signifies that the church belongs to God, but is located in Corinth. They are called to be saints with all others who call on the Lord Jesus Christ. The opening ends with the familiar "grace to you and peace from God our Father and the Lord Jesus Christ."

Thanksgiving (1:4–9)

Paul (note change to first-person singular) gives thanks to God for the Corinthian believers because of the grace that was given to him that resulted in them being enriched in speech and knowledge. They are not lacking in any grace gift (χαρίσματι)[46] as they await the coming of the Lord. He encourages

---

45. Thiselton, *First Corinthians*, 1346–47.
46. Cf. H. T. Ong, "Is 'Spiritual Gift(s)' a Linguistically Fallacious Term? A Lexical Study of Χάρισμα, Πνευματικός, and Πνεῦμα," *Expository Times* 125 (2014): 583–92, who argues that

them by saying that God is faithful and the one who brings them into fellowship with him.

Body: Problem of Disunity (1:10–17)

Responding to a report by "Chloe's people" of the church's struggles with unity, Paul appeals to them to agree with one another and have no divisions within their group. The main source of division, it seems, is that they place too much emphasis on human messengers rather than on God himself. Some claim to be followers of Paul, others claim Apollos as their leader, and still others claim Cephas (Peter), or even Christ himself. Paul rhetorically asks, "Is Christ divided? Was Paul crucified for you?" (NIV) implying that they were not against each other but were all working together for the same cause. He confirms that his mission is to preach the gospel, but not in eloquence, so that the cross of Christ would not be emptied of its power.

Body: The Gospel Contradicts Human Wisdom (1:18–2:5)

Paul's mention of the gospel and cross leads him to expound on the message of the cross. He contrasts two responses to the cross—it is foolishness to the perishing, but to the saved it is the power of God. The world may have a different conception of what wisdom and power are, but the cross, which was a symbol of foolishness and weakness for both Jews and Gentiles, through the death of Christ became a symbol for wisdom and power.

Paul then tells the Corinthian believers to consider their calling, that they were not considered wise according to worldly standards—perhaps many of the members of the Corinthian assembly were of the lower-middle class citizens of the city[47]—but God chose them, the foolish and unwise according to the world, so that they would have no grounds to boast. On the same note, he reminds them that he had previously come to them, not with eloquent words and speech, but with much trembling, with the demonstration of the Spirit and of power, so that their faith would be in God, not in human wisdom.

---

the term often translated "spiritual gift" is a misconception, often taken from a list or catalogue in the New Testament, but that it includes more broadly any "gift" from God, including eternal life.

47. The socioeconomic level of the early Christians is a matter of continuing debate (see chapter 1 §6). Most follow Meeks, *First Urban Christians*, who sees the early church encompassing a range of socioeconomic levels. This is reassessed and both confirmed and modified by the essays in T. D. Still and D. G. Horrell, eds., *After the First Urban Christians: The Social-Scientific Study of Pauline Christianity Twenty-Five Years Later* (London: T&T Clark, 2009).

Body: God's Wisdom Comes by the Spirit (2:6–16)

Paul continues to draw the line between human wisdom and divine wisdom by stating that the Spirit of God is the one who reveals the secret things of God. He distinguishes between the natural person and the spiritual person, the former who does not understand the things of God compared to the latter who does understand because they are spiritually discerned.

Body: Divisiveness (3:1–23)

After distinguishing between natural people and spiritual people, Paul regrets to inform them that he could not address them as spiritual people, because of the jealousy and strife that they had among themselves. He had previously given them milk, a metaphor for basic teaching, instead of solid food, or advanced teaching, because they were not ready for it, and he claims they are still not ready because of the way they have been behaving. He addresses the issue of disunity due to their disagreement over who they are following, and tells them that neither he nor Apollos nor anyone else is significant, because God is the one who causes the growth. Paul, Apollos, and others were merely ones who planted and watered, with Paul using an agricultural metaphor. They all worked together for the same purpose, to build upon the same foundation that is Jesus Christ.

Building upon this architectural metaphor, Paul then rhetorically asks, "Do you (plural) not know that you (plural) are the temple of God?" Here, the issue is not related to sexual purity (that subject is taken up later in 6:19), but to the matter that, collectively, they were the temple of God and, by their unwarranted factions, they were in fact destroying this temple. Paul, Apollos, Cephas, and Christ all belong to the same body.

Body: Paul as Christ's Servant (4:1–21)

Addressing their dissension and advocacy of particular leaders over others, Paul states that they should regard all of them as servants of Christ and stewards of the mysteries of God. They have a greater judgment from God, but not from others. Paul informs them that he and Apollos have applied these things to themselves, and that they should not go beyond what is written, in order that they not distinguish one another on the basis of pride.

Paul then uses rhetorical irony, contrasting the apostles with the Corinthian believers. They were rich; the apostles were poor. They were kings; the apostles were last of all. The apostles were fools for Christ's sake; the Corinthians were wise. The apostles were weak; the Corinthians were strong. Paul then goes into further detail about the apostles' weaknesses, how they hunger and thirst, are poorly dressed and even homeless, and work with their hands as menial laborers. He calls himself and the apostles the refuse of all things. This section is filled with sarcasm and derisive statements, so that the Corinthians would be humbled and corrected.[48]

Paul reassures them, however, that his purpose is not to shame them, but to admonish them as his beloved children. While Paul does not condone factions, he does state that he considers himself a father among many guides in the faith. He urges them to imitate him and reminds them that this is the reason he sent Timothy to them so they would remember his example. He expresses his desire to come to them soon.

Paraenesis: Questions of Morality (5:1–6:20)

Paul begins first with the concern over sexual immorality (πορνεία) in the church; the immorality is so excessive that even pagans do not tolerate this type of behavior, where a man sexually sins with his stepmother. He asks them rhetorically, "Should you not rather mourn over this?" He firmly tells them to remove these two people from their group and rebukes their boasting about this situation. Using the metaphor of leaven, he warns them that a little evil will ruin the entire group by corrupting its genuineness and truth. Referring to a previous letter (see §2C above), he reiterates his command not to associate with sexually immoral people. This is not a reference to those in the world, but to those who claim to be followers of Christ, a brother or sister, but who practice sexual immorality, or even greed, idolatry, reviling, drunkenness, or swindling—they are not even to eat with them. Those in the world are expected to behave in these ways, but those in the church who behave in these ways are to be removed.

The second major issue that Paul addresses, after sexual immorality, is the subject of lawsuits. In another series of rhetorical questions, he wonders why they as believers would go to the secular courts to handle their disputes. Are they not competent enough to settle their own issues? It would be better for them to be wronged and defrauded than to go to court in order to settle a dispute. He then reminds them that the unrighteous do not inherit the kingdom of God, probably to inform them that these are the ones who are settling their disputes.

Paul then states the general principle that all things are permissible, but

---

48. Ciampa and Rosner, *First Letter to the Corinthians*, 178.

not all things are beneficial; he will not be enslaved by anything. Applying this to matters of sex, Paul reminds the Corinthians that their bodies belong to the Lord and are not meant for sexual immorality. Since they are members of Christ, they are not to join themselves to a prostitute (πόρνη), since they become "one," invoking a principle from Gen 2. In light of this, he commands them to flee from sexual immorality. Every other sin is outside of the body, but this sin is against one's own body, which is also the temple of the Holy Spirit. He reminds them of the redemption of Christ, so that they would glorify God with their body.

Paraenesis: Questions of Marriage (7:1–40)

Using the transition "now concerning" (περὶ δέ), Paul then addresses the opposite, extreme view related to sexuality: abstaining completely from it. Since the temptation to sexual immorality is great, Paul says that each man should have his own wife, and that each wife should have her own husband. They should not deprive one another of their sexual desires, except if it involves a short period of prayer and devotion, so that there is no temptation. He wishes that all were able like him to be celibate but realizes that not everyone has that ability.

Paul then gives three categorical commands. First, for the unmarried and widowed to remain single, or to marry if self-control is an issue; second, for married people to remain together; and third, for those with unbelieving spouses to remain together so that the unbelieving spouse would be made holy. As a general rule, Paul says that a person should live the life they were called to.

Paul then expounds on instructions for those who are virgins (παρθένος). Those who are single are better off remaining single, and those who are married should remain married. Paul reflects an eschatological mindset that considers the short-term nature of the present life, and he wants the Corinthians to have a similar mindset. He states that the single person has only to be concerned with pleasing the Lord, but the married person is divided in their attention. However, a single person marrying because of temptation is not a sin. Paul ends his discourse on marriage and singleness by stating that the marriage covenant remains until death severs it; then, the now single person is free to remarry, but he thinks remaining single is better.[49]

---

49. For a scholarly analysis on marriage, singleness, and divorce in 1 Cor 7, focusing on the Hellenistic context of the first century, see Deming, *Paul on Marriage and Celibacy*.

Paraenesis: Questions of Food Sacrificed to Idols (8:1–11:1)

Paul begins a new topic with the transition "now concerning" (περὶ δέ), regarding food sacrificed to idols. He contrasts knowledge and love by stating that love should be the motivation for the practice of eating foods that have been sacrificed to idols. Regarding knowledge, he admits that an idol is nothing and that the food has been created by God, so the one who eats this food eats with a clear conscience. But weaker believers, who may have participated in idolatry in the past, might witness that eating and stumble, so Paul advises the Corinthians that they should give up eating foods sacrificed to idols if it causes a weak believer to be made to stumble by it. Their freedom should not result in a lack of love for these weaker believers.[50]

In speaking of freedom, Paul turns to himself as an apostle as an example, and, through a series of rhetorical questions, states that he has chosen to give up his rights in order to benefit others. This includes the right to marriage (though other apostles did exercise that right) so that he could have a singular focus on the gospel, as well as the right to earn a living through the gospel so that the Corinthians would not feel burdened to provide for him. He broadens the application of restricting his freedom to all areas, and says that he relates to Jews as a Jew, and he relates to Gentiles as a Gentile. This is all for the sake of the gospel, and he urges the Corinthians to follow his example, using the metaphor of physical training.

Not only is he an example, but the fathers, the saints of the Old Testament, also are examples for them, although negative examples, since most of them failed. The Corinthians are not to be like them, idolaters, sexually immoral, testers of God, or grumblers. God has not given any temptation that they could not bear, but he provides a way for them to escape it. Going back to the subject of idolatry, Paul commands them to flee from it. They participate in the Lord's Supper, which is a participation in Christ's death, but in contrast the food of idols is nothing, so they should not worry about eating it, unless it is blatantly communicated that what they are served is idol food. The basic principle in all of this is to do all to the glory of God, whether eating, drinking, or whatever else. In this, Paul wants the Corinthians to imitate him.

---

50. For a detailed analysis of this passage, see C. D. Land, "'We Put No Stumbling Block in Anyone's Path, So That Our Ministry Will Not Be Discredited': Paul's Response to an Idol Food Inquiry in 1 Corinthians 8:1–13," in *Paul and His Social Relations* (ed. S. E. Porter and C. D. Land; PAST 7; Leiden: Brill, 2013), 229–83.

Paraenesis: Questions of Worship (11:2–34)

The next subject that Paul addresses involves corporate worship. As he had previously taught them, he states that the head of every man is Christ, the head of the woman is man, and the head of Christ is God.[51] Thus, a man should not cover his head, nor a woman uncover her head when prophesying, because of dishonor. Paul talks about the origins of man and woman, and their dependence upon one another in corporate gatherings.

Paul also does not commend the Corinthians when it comes to a specific activity in their corporate gatherings, the Lord's Supper. They apparently had no regard for one another when they met, and they would act selfishly when eating together. Some had an abundance of food while others did not, and others had an excess of drink to the point of drunkenness. The point of the Lord's Supper, Paul explains, is the significance of Christ's death on the cross and remembrance of it. Eating in an unworthy manner reflects selfishness and greed. The main principle they are to follow when gathering together for the Lord's Supper is to wait for one another to eat and drink.

Paraenesis: Questions of Spiritual Gifts (12:1–14:40)

Another transition occurs here with the connective "now concerning" (περὶ δέ), while Paul discusses the issue of spiritual gifts (πνευματικά; literally, "spiritual things"). He does not want them to be ignorant about them, so he spends three chapters expounding the nature of these gifts. While there is a variety of gifts, the purpose of these gifts is for the good of everyone and not for self-promotion. Some are given gifts of wisdom, knowledge, faith, healing, working of miracles, prophecy, discernment of spirits, tongues, and interpretation of tongues. All of these are given by the Spirit according to his will. All of these are given a special function in one body with many members, and each gift is as valuable as the other, to work together for the common good. In this light, God has appointed first apostles, then prophets, then teachers, and then miracles, healing, helping, administrating, and tongues, but not everyone is given all of these gifts.

Paul pauses at this point to show the manner in which these gifts are to be exhibited and administered. He gives three examples—tongues, prophecy, and knowledge—but without love, these gifts are nothing. Love is something that exhibits patience and kindness, does not envy or boast, and is not arrogant or rude. It is selfless and beneficent and rejoices with the truth. Love never

---

51. Various interpretive issues surround the meaning of "head" (κεφαλή). For a detailed summary of the various meanings, see Thiselton, *First Corinthians*, 812–23.

ends. On the other hand, prophecies, tongues, and knowledge, these "partial" things (τὸ ἐκ μέρους), will end when the "perfect" (τὸ τέλειον) comes, which is usually interpreted as the return of Christ.[52] Faith, hope, and love remain, but the greatest of these is love.

Paul then encourages the Corinthians to pursue love, but also the greater gifts, such as prophecy (the Corinthians seemed to have been preoccupied with tongues instead). The benefit of prophecy over tongues is that tongues is directed only to God, while prophecy benefits everyone else. This is not to say that tongues is prohibited; Paul wants them to speak in tongues. But the greater desire should be for the gift that benefits the entire group. But if someone does speak in a tongue, they should also pray for the ability to interpret whatever language is being spoken, so that others would be able to understand the utterance. The point of all of these gifts, Paul says, is that the group would be built up from the exercise of them. This means that there is to be order in the exercise of these gifts, where only two or three speak, and each in turn, and each exercise of these gifts is to have accountability to ensure authenticity.

Paraenesis: Questions of the Resurrection (15:1–58)

Paul makes a transition to another topic, the gospel and the resurrection, which he had passed on to them. The gospel is that Christ died for their sins in accordance with Scripture, was buried, and was raised on the third day, was seen by the disciples, and, at one point, by five hundred Christians at one time. Paul was the last to see the resurrected Jesus and says in effect that he is the least of the apostles, because of his former persecution. So because Christ was resurrected, Paul questions the Corinthians' belief that there is no resurrection of the dead. If there is no resurrection, then faith becomes meaningless, and they could live life however they desire. But in fact, Christ was raised from the dead, and so will they be raised, with resurrection bodies that are different from the earthly bodies they now inhabit. The dead will be raised in the twinkling of an eye, and they shall all be raised imperishable.

Paraenesis: The Collection (16:1–12)

With another transitional "now concerning" (περὶ δέ), Paul moves to the topic of the collection, in which he had also instructed the Galatian churches. Each

---

52. Much debate surrounds the meaning of the "perfect" (τὸ τέλειον) and the permanence or impermanence of these gifts. See Thiselton, *First Corinthians*, 1060–74; and D. A. Carson, *Showing the Spirit: A Theological Exposition of 1 Corinthians 12–14* (Grand Rapids: Baker, 1996), among many others.

person was to save up and lay aside a portion of their income during the week and give on the first day of the week. He tells them of his plans to travel through Macedonia before revisiting them again; he hopes to spend a good amount of time with them, possibly over the winter. He will send Timothy, and they are to receive him as well. Apollos will be visiting as well at the urging of Paul.

Closing (16:13–24)

The beginning of the closing of Paul's letter contains some short admonitions: to be alert and to stand firm in the faith, to be courageous and strong, and to do everything in love (cf. 1 Cor 13). The Corinthians are to support leaders such as Stephanas, who was one of the first converts in that area, and to give recognition to them (including Fortunatus and Achaicus). Paul tells them that the churches of Asia send them greetings, as well as Aquila and Prisca (Priscilla); in fact, all the brothers send them greetings. He ends the letter by stating that he writes the greeting in his own hand, thereby authenticating the contents of the letter.

3. Second Corinthians

Second Corinthians has proved almost as attractive to scholars as 1 Corinthians, generating continuing discussion of its many interesting critical and interpretive features. Even if the authorship of 2 Corinthians is not disputed, its unity and its relationship to 1 Corinthians continue to incite analysis and comment. Apart from these issues, 2 Corinthians provides insight into how the apostle Paul adjusted his perspective on a church that continually seemed to be involved in some type of controversy, even if we are not exactly certain of all that that controversy entailed. In this section, I quickly discuss the issue of authorship, and then treat at more length the unity of 2 Corinthians and then its occasion and purpose, before presenting an outline and its content.

A. Authorship of Second Corinthians

As with 1 Corinthians, Werner Georg Kümmel categorically states, "The authenticity of II Cor as a whole is uncontested."[53] Nevertheless, as we have seen,

---

53. Kümmel, *Introduction*, 287.

there is ongoing discussion of whether the entire book was written at the same time or whether it was later compiled from multiple letters. Although there are a number of strong advocates of a unified 2 Corinthians, many scholars argue that 2 Corinthians is in some sense a composite letter. In any case, the essential Pauline authenticity of the letter is not disputed.

B. Unity of Second Corinthians

Even if authorship is not disputed, the unity of 2 Corinthians continues to be widely discussed. The question of the unity of 2 Corinthians revolves around several significant passages.[54] They are not all equally disputed; nevertheless, they merit brief presentation, since many of the issues that they raise are among those recurring most often in discussions about the nature and shape of the Pauline letters.

1. Second Corinthians 6:14–7:1

The problems regarding this short passage (6:14–7:1) on being yoked to unbelievers in the body of the letter are three: (1) many see an abrupt change in tone from 6:13 to 6:14; (2) 6:13 seems to be a suitable introduction to 7:2, and when 6:14–7:1 is removed, the flow of the letter's argument is improved; and (3) the subject matter and style are seen to be inconsistent with the rest of the Corinthian correspondence.[55] For example, 1 Cor 5:9 says that one is "not to associate with sexually immoral people" (NIV), but 2 Cor 6:14–7:1, according to some interpreters, deals with the relations of believers and unbelievers; and 2 Corinthians is described as a letter of reconciliation (see esp. 5:18–21), but 6:14–7:1 seems to argue for exclusivism. Several major solutions are proposed for these difficulties.

---

54. See Thrall, *Second Corinthians*, 1.3–49, for a survey of opinions, with a tabulation on 47–49; also Goulder, *Paul and the Competing Mission in Corinth*, 240–48; F. J. Long, *Ancient Rhetoric and Paul's Apology: The Compositional Unity of 2 Corinthians* (SNTSMS 131; Cambridge: Cambridge University Press, 2004); Hagner, *New Testament*, 513–15; and Land, *Is There a Text in These Meanings?*, esp. 175–237.

55. Besides Thrall (*Second Corinthians*, 1.25–36), who surveys opinion, see the positions argued in J. A. Fitzmyer, "Qumran and the Interpolated Paragraph in 2 Cor. 6.14–7.1," *Catholic Biblical Quarterly* 23 (1961): 271–80; P. B. Duff, "The Mind of the Redactor: 2 Cor. 6:14–7:1 in Its Secondary Context," *NovT* 35 (1993): 160–80; W. J. Webb, *Returning Home: New Covenant and Second Exodus as the Context for 2 Corinthians 6.14–7.1* (JSNTSup 85; Sheffield: JSOT Press, 1993); and M. D. Goulder, "2 Cor. 6:14–7:1 as an Integral Part of 2 Corinthians," *NovT* 36 (1994): 47–57.

a. Interpolation Hypothesis

The first solution offered is that this small section is part of the first letter to the Corinthians (now lost), interpolated into 2 Corinthians.[56] It is possible, according to this view, that Paul's strong language of 6:14–7:1 favoring dissociation from the pagan world, sent as part of his first letter to the Corinthians, was misunderstood and interpreted to mean that there should be absolutely no contact whatsoever. Perhaps 1 Cor 5:10–11 then shows Paul clarifying his original statement, hence his correction that believers are "not to associate with sexually immoral people" (NIV).

This interpolation theory raises several questions, however. First, the shift in tone from 2 Cor 6:13 to 6:14 is not as severe as some postulate, especially if the language is seen as establishing degrees of exclusivism and association. For example, in 6:1–13, Paul makes common cause with the Corinthians as fellow workers and says that he has done nothing to discredit the ministry. After recounting a number of trials and triumphs, he repeats that, as he has been open to the Corinthians in all his affection, they, too, are to be open and generous in theirs. In 6:14–7:1, however, Paul addresses the relations of Christians and non-Christians, stating that they should not be mismatched—the Greek word for "being mismatched" (ἑτεροζυγέω) is a term for unevenly yoking animals to pull a plow. Paul supports this by several quotations of the Old Testament (Lev 26:12; 2 Sam 7:14; Isa 52:11; Hos 1:10), all of which support the idea that God's people are to separate from everything incompatible with his holiness. Second, composition over a space of time might well account for the shift in tone, even if gradual. Third, why would part of the lost first letter have been inserted at this place in 2 Corinthians, the fourth letter? Other places would have been just as likely, and there is apparently no evidence in the textual tradition of its absence in the earliest extant manuscripts. Many scholars at one time held that this passage was a fragment of the first letter, but this view is not widely held today.

b. Qumran Fragment

A second major solution proposed is that a non-Pauline fragment from Qumran was placed here. The reasons for this are several: (1) nine terms found in this passage are found nowhere else in Paul;[57] (2) the extreme exclusiveness is

---

56. E.g., W. O. Walker, *Interpolations in the Pauline Letters* (JSNTSup 213; Sheffield: Sheffield Academic, 2001), 199–209.

57. The *hapax legomena* are "mismatched, unequally yoked" (ἑτεροζυγέω), "partnership, share" (μετοχή), "fellowship, harmony" (συμφώνησις), "Beliar," "agreement" (συγκατάθεσις),

out of character for Paul; (3) there are similarities of thought with the Qumran community, such as its dualism and emphasis upon the temple; and (4) the words "flesh" and "spirit" are supposedly used in a non-Pauline way. These reasons indicate to some that 6:14–7:1 is non-Pauline and that the fragment may well have come from a group that reflected such exclusivity and emphasis upon the temple, that is, the Qumran covenanters.

In response to this suggestion, however, an argument based upon *hapax legomena* (terms used in a given corpus only one time) is not precise. This is especially true here, since many of the terms found in this "fragment" have cognates in Paul's letters (e.g., μετοχή, "partnership," is not found elsewhere in Paul but μετέχω, the verb for "share," is, e.g., in 1 Cor 9:10, 12; 10:17, 21, 30; similar comments can be made about ἐμπεριπατέω ["walk"] and περιπατέω ["walk"] or εἰσδέχομαι ["welcome, receive"] and δέχομαι ["receive"], as well as such words as ἕτερος and φωνή). Furthermore, 2 Cor 6:3–10 also has several unique words, but this passage is not suspected of being non-Pauline. Second, Pauline outbursts of various sorts often have unique words in them (e.g., 1 Cor 4:7–13 with six unique words, and 2 Cor 6:3–10 with four unique words), but they are not automatically suspected of being non-Pauline. Third, one must pay attention to what is Pauline and what is quoted from the Old Testament in this fragment. According to this position, the Old Testament quotations are largely responsible for the exclusivistic sense of the passage, not the surrounding Pauline material. Fourth, this supposed fragment is not at odds with established Pauline thought, and many of the ideas are found not only at Qumran but in other circles as well (e.g., Greek dualism).

c. Preformulated Material

A third proposal is that this passage may have been preformulated or borrowed in some way by Paul, who incorporated it into his account. This view attempts to accommodate the perceived change of tone and content and at the same time retain the integrity of the passage's Pauline composition. But as noted above, there is no external textual witness to a textual difficulty, certainly not that the passage was incorporated. It would need to have been incorporated very early, before the extant texts were widely copied, but such an occurrence is difficult to prove without any extant evidence. This view encounters a number of other problems. There may be a perceived shift in tone or content, but the passage can easily be seen to fit its context. If the subject of 2 Cor 6–7 is the

---

"walk" (ἐμπεριπατέω), "welcome, receive" (εἰσδέχομαι), "almighty" (παντοκράτωρ), and "defilement" (μολυσμός).

nature and degree of Christian relationships, 6:14–7:1 fits well as the second of its three sections. The first describes Paul and the Corinthians as fellow workers (6:1–13), emphasizing their common cause and mutual openness. But this openness does not imply compromise (6:14–7:1). Rather, it is predicated upon not taking advantage of each other (7:2–16). If Paul has used a preformulated or prewritten section, he has utilized it within his letter in such a way that he has made it his own.

The evidence cited above is hardly conclusive. As a result, most scholars today do not treat 6:14–7:1 as an interpolation.

2. Second Corinthians 10–13

a. Problems

Essentially five difficulties are identified with 2 Cor 10–13.[58] (1) Second Cor 1–9 is full of praise for the Corinthian believers, but 2 Cor 10–13 is characterized by condemnation, making it difficult to see how these two portions of the letter fit together in one integral composition. (2) The vocabulary regarding boasting and Paul's commending himself is used differently in the two major portions of the letter, implying that the letter is not a unity but a composition of at least two letters. The problem is seen most clearly in how a common word for boasting (καυχάομαι) is used positively in 2 Cor 1–9 but negatively in 2 Cor 10–13. For example, 5:12 implies that Paul has commended himself, while in 10:13 Paul says that he will not boast. (3) Scholars note a number of passages in 2 Cor 10–13 that appear to be forward looking while 2 Cor 1–9 appears to be looking backward. Some examples are 10:2 and 8:2 on confidence, 10:6 and 2:9 on obedience, 12:16 and 4:2 on trickery, 12:17 and 7:2 on fraud, 13:2 and 1:23 on sparing the Corinthians, and 13:10 and 2:3 on travel. On the basis of this evidence, 2 Cor 1–9 seems to be looking back at a situation that is now resolved, while 2 Cor 10–13 seems to be looking forward to resolution. (4) There appears to be a set of contradictions between 2 Cor 1–9 and 2 Cor 10–13. For example, in 1:24 Paul sees the Corinthians as "firm in the faith," while in 13:5 he admonishes them to see if they are "in the faith." Furthermore,

---

58. Besides Thrall (*Second Corinthians*, 1.5–20), who surveys opinion, see L. L. Welborn, "The Identification of 2 Corinthians 10–13 with the 'Letter of Tears,'" *NovT* 37 (1995): 138–53. There are various other taxonomies of the problems; cf. D. R. Hall, *The Unity of the Corinthian Correspondence* (JSNTSup 251; London: T&T Clark, 2003), 86–112; M. J. Harris, *The Second Epistle to the Corinthians: A Commentary on the Greek Text* (NIGTC; Grand Rapids: Eerdmans, 2005), 29–51; and I. Vegge, *2 Corinthians—A Letter about Reconciliation: A Psychogogical, Epistolographical, and Rhetorical Analysis* (WUNT 239; Tübingen: Mohr-Siebeck, 2008), 12–22.

in 7:16 he expresses confidence in them, while in 12:20–21 he is afraid for them. These attitudes seem to reflect different sets of circumstances at Corinth. (5) According to some scholars, Paul's reference to wanting to preach "beyond" Corinth (10:16) makes sense for Rome and Spain if 2 Cor 10–13 was written from Ephesus as the third Corinthian letter (since Rome and Spain are west of Ephesus and Corinth), but not from Macedonia as part of the fourth letter, since a southward geographical trajectory from Macedonia to Corinth would reach across the Mediterranean to Africa.

b. Solutions

Many solutions are proposed regarding the relationship of 2 Cor 1–9 and 2 Cor 10–13. They can be divided into essentially two possibilities: either the two individual sections represent two separate documents or they together constitute the same document.

i. Second Corinthians 10–13 Written and Sent Separately from 2 Corinthians 1–9   On the basis of the apparent discrepancies between the two portions, it is argued that this evidence points to the two portions being parts of separate letters. Many who argue for separate letters claim that 2 Cor 10–13 constitutes the "severe letter" sent by Paul as the third letter to the Corinthian church, soon after his disastrous visit to them. This would supposedly make sense of the general tenor of the differences noted above: 2 Cor 10–13 looks forward to resolution, and 2 Cor 1–9 reflects a later resolution; 2 Cor 10–13 treats boasting as a negative quality, probably reflecting Paul's antagonism to what he encountered in Corinth, but in 2 Cor 1–9, after resolution of the difficulties, he allows himself to boast of the Corinthians; in 2 Cor 10–13, Paul questions the faith of the Corinthians and reflects continuing fear of them, but in 2 Cor 1–9 he knows that they now have faith and he has confidence in them. In a variation on this, a small group of scholars argues that 2 Cor 1–9 and 2 Cor 10–13 were written and sent as separate letters, with 2 Cor 10–13 sent after 2 Cor 1–9, possibly even very soon after. The latter formulation apparently rests upon either seeing differences between the two sections (even though they are unavoidably close in content) or positing a new set of (now unknown) circumstances in the Corinthian church (after the apparent difficulties had been resolved). Because of obvious difficulties in making such distinctions, this variation has had far fewer adherents.

 In response to these alternatives, it is important to note that several of the apparent difficulties may not be quite as pressing as is sometimes claimed. For example, the apparent shift in tone may not be as great or severe as is sometimes thought.[59] The formulation is often made with 2 Cor 1–9 supposedly reflecting a settled situation and 2 Cor 10–13 reflecting uncertainty. It must be noted, however, that 2 Cor 1–9 refers to continuing opposition as well (e.g., 2:6, 17; 4:2–5; 5:11–13), even if the overall tone is more conciliatory. This may well indicate that even if the majority of the church at Corinth has been convinced by Paul's argument, there remains a minority that is still to be won over. Similarly, 2 Cor 10–13 does not categorically reflect opposition to Paul but only some opposition to his authority (e.g., 10:2, 7, 11–12; 11:5, 12–13, 18, 20; 12:11, 21; 13:2). Furthermore, the internal references within these two units may not necessarily reflect a relationship only between these two parts of the letter. There are several other possibilities. For example, the backward references in 2 Cor 1–9 could refer to the second letter, our canonical 1 Corinthians, instead of to 2 Cor 10–13. In another plausible scenario, Paul may have received word from Titus that there had been widespread positive response in the Corinthian church to his ministry but that it might not have been complete, especially if a new group of outsiders arrived (see below); thus, he still had grounds to hope for further necessary improvement. Consequently, Paul's comments in 2 Cor 10–13 might well reflect an appreciation for what had been done (2 Cor 1–9), together with a hope for further positive response (2 Cor 10–13).

It is fair to say that the vast majority of the supposed contradictions are, in fact, not formal contradictions but are merely discrepancies that can be relatively easily explained. For example, the reference to "beyond" in 10:16 is not a great difficulty when it is noted that, for Paul, "beyond" means beyond the confines of the eastern Mediterranean, and thus Rome and Spain, no matter from which direction he may be writing. Regarding commending himself in 3:1 and 5:12, Paul is referring to using letters of recommendation, and he compliments the Corinthian church as being his letter of recommendation. In 2 Cor 10–13, it is true that Paul disparages boasting, but he is addressing his opponents, not the Corinthians as a whole—he takes pride in the Corinthians (10:13–14; 11:16–21; cf. 1:12–14).

A further contradiction is actually introduced if 2 Cor 10–13 is taken as the "severe letter." In 12:18 there is reference to Titus, who delivered the "severe letter" and who now delivers 2 Corinthians (7:6–8; 8:6, 16–18). This could not be a reference to Titus as the deliverer of the "severe letter" if this is that letter, and the interrogative language of the passage indeed seems to be referring to the "severe letter." Thus, even if 2 Cor 10–13 was written at a different time than 2 Cor 1–9, it would not be the severe letter, unless the references were added later for some unaccountable reason.

59. Harris, *Second Epistle to the Corinthians*, 29–31.

Finally, there is no manuscript authority for dividing the letter into parts. This may seem to be a point not worth making, but there are some implications for the larger discussion. If two or more letters were contained in the one letter (see discussion of Philippians in chapter 11 §2C), it implies that the original openings and closings, as well as other portions, of the genuine letters were deleted. We may not understand the full situation, but this is different from such cases as the letter to the Laodiceans, where the entire letter is no longer extant (though this may be Ephesians itself; see chapter 11 §5D4). It is quite different to say that part of a letter was valued and retained but other portions of the same valued letter were excised and not retained. There seems to be an inherent contradiction between retention of Paul's writings as valuable and instructive, and expunging some portions. By today's standards we may think that openings and closings (and other portions now unknown to us?) are not as important, but this merely begs the question: can we say that they were not important for the early church, especially with the innovative Pauline opening, the occasionally theologically expanded description of the sender or addressee, and the benedictions and grace formulas? This is doubtful.

ii. Second Corinthians 10–13 as Part of Second Corinthians   The second solution is that, regardless of the difficulties above, 2 Cor 10–13 is part of the original letter. As noted, the shift in tone and other supposed contradictions, combined with the manuscript evidence, do not leave good grounds for clearly arguing for two or more letters. The responses to such arguments above, in fact, make a good case for a single, complete letter. Indeed, several other lines of evidence point away from separate letters and toward textual integrity. First, if 2 Cor 10–13 is a separate letter, these chapters do not seem to address the issue that was being confronted at Corinth. In 2:1–4 and 7:12, the reason for the severe letter was an individual who had in some way offended Paul. If this is the case, it is noteworthy that 2 Cor 10–13 makes no mention of this but addresses the Corinthians as a church. Paul's defense of himself in 2 Corinthians (e.g., 12:1, 11–15) is not focused upon individual difficulties but upon the situation in the church. This is, however, consistent with the rest of 2 Corinthians (as well as 1 Corinthians, e.g., 1 Cor 9:1–14, which focused on apostolic authority in relation to church difficulties). Second, the exhortation formula of 2 Cor 10:1 (with παρακαλέω) is consistent with the exhortative stance of the paraenetic section of a letter. The paraenetic section, by definition, implies a different tone than the body of the letter, although one need not overdraw this contrast. Nevertheless, a somewhat similar shift can be found in the relation of Rom 14 to the rest of Romans. Paul apparently does not hesitate to introduce strongly worded instruction even if he is concerned with his personal relationship with a church. Such instruction might be especially appropriate if new opposition to Paul was introduced into the Corinthian situation (see below).

There are other possible solutions to this supposed change of tone between 2 Cor 1–9 and 2 Cor 10–13. For example, some propose that Paul is deliberately using a literary device in this change of tone and that a major theme of reconciliation can be seen through the entire letter as a single work.[60] Further, the process of literary composition in the ancient world was quite different from the one used today, in which word processors are available to (ideally) ensure speed and consistency of content and presentation. The writing of a letter as lengthy as any of the major Pauline letters would have been a sizable undertaking, involving a scribe, the availability of writing materials, and a certain amount of time. Perhaps the letter or at least sections of the letter were written first in draft on a wax tablet before being copied onto the papyrus for sending. Reusable wax tablets used in the Greco-Roman world for such writing purposes have been found. In the course of this writing, editing, and copying, there would be plenty of opportunity for any number of developments, including a change of mind by Paul on what he wanted to express and how he wanted to say it, the receipt of new information regarding the Corinthian church, circumstances requiring that Paul be away from the letter for a period of time before returning to it in a different frame of mind, or even (Hans Lietzmann's now famous idea) that a night of insomnia after 2 Cor 9 would be enough to cause Paul's cranky attitude in 2 Cor 10 and subsequent chapters.[61] A number of plausible (and sometimes not so plausible) solutions can therefore account for the perceived change of tone, some of them requiring the supposition of separate letters and others not.

3. Second Corinthians 8–9

The questions regarding these two chapters[62] concern whether they were independent of 2 Cor 1–7, or whether one or more was separate, and if so, what

60. R. Bieringer, "Plädoyer für die Einheitlichkeit des 2. Korintherbriefes: Literarkritische und inhaltliche Argumente," in *Studies on 2 Corinthians* (ed. R. Bieringer and J. Lambrecht; Bibliotheca Ephemeridum Theologicarum Lovaniensium 112; Leuven: Leuven University Press, 1994), 131–79, esp. 133–42; Vegge, *2 Corinthians*, 34–37.

61. H. Lietzmann, *An die Korinther I–II* (3rd ed.; Handbuch zum Neuen Testament 9; Tübingen: Mohr-Siebeck, 1931), 139, also cited in R. P. Martin, *New Testament Foundations: A Guide for Christian Students* (2 vols.; 2nd ed.; Grand Rapids: Eerdmans, 1986), 2.182.

62. Besides Thrall, *Second Corinthians*, 2.36–43, who surveys opinion, see H. D. Betz, *2 Corinthians 8 and 9* (Hermeneia; Philadelphia: Fortress, 1988), 3–36; J. M. Gilchrist, "Paul and the Corinthians—The Sequence of Letters and Visits," *JSNT* 34 (1988): 47–69, esp. 50–51; V. D. Verbrugge, *Paul's Style of Church Leadership Illustrated by His Instructions to the Corinthians on the Collection* (San Francisco: Mellen Research University Press, 1992), esp. 100–104;

was the order in which they were sent. The arguments for the independence of 2 Cor 8–9 are essentially five: (1) 9:1 has a connective phrase that separates it from 2 Cor 8 and indicates the possibility of a new letter; (2) 2 Cor 8–9 duplicate information regarding the collection, emissaries, etc.; (3) 8:1–5 and 9:1–2 seem to be addressed to different groups, both out of character with the audience in 2 Cor 7; (4) 2 Cor 8 and 2 Cor 9 list different purposes for those Paul is sending, comments remarkably lacking from 2 Cor 7; and (5) there are contradictions in details from 2 Cor 8 to 2 Cor 9—for example, Paul introduces the collection in 9:1 as superfluous when he has already been discussing it (8:1–5). A sixth reason is sometimes given: the rhetorical structure found in each chapter supposedly points to unity and independence. This argument should not be given much credence for several reasons. The first is that rhetorical criticism is used in various ways, depending upon the interpreter, sometimes to prove unity of a letter and sometimes to prove unity of a subsection, thus making it difficult to show how it can be used to prove either. The second is that it has not been demonstrated (despite many strong assertions to the contrary) that the categories of ancient rhetoric, designed for the creation of speeches, are applicable to the analysis of ancient letters. All indications, in fact, are that they are not.[63] Nevertheless, on the basis of such reasoning as the five considerations above, several proposals are put forward. Some argue that 2 Cor 1–8 or 2 Cor 1–7 + 9 were units, with the remaining chapter sent separately. Others argue that 2 Cor 8 and 2 Cor 9 were independent of 2 Cor 1–7 and of each other, some claiming that 2 Cor 8 was sent first (probably to Corinth) and others that 2 Cor 9 was first (probably as a circular letter to a wider area of Achaia).

The reasons cited for positing one or more interpolations consisting of 2 Cor 8–9 raise important questions about the composition of 2 Corinthians but are far from conclusive proof that the letter is a composite of these once independent chapters. The first reason they are not conclusive is similar to 2 Cor 10–13, that there are no external text-critical indicators that the letter

---

S. K. Stowers, "Περὶ μὲν γάρ and the Integrity of 2 Cor. 8 and 9," *NovT* 32 (1990): 340–48; D. A. deSilva, "Measuring Penultimate against Ultimate Reality: An Investigation of the Integrity and Argumentation of 2 Corinthians," *JSNT* 52 (1993): 41–70; Hall, *Unity of the Corinthian Correspondence*, 100–102; and M. M. Mitchell, "The Corinthian Correspondence and the Birth of Pauline Hermeneutics," in *Paul and the Corinthians: Studies on a Community in Conflict; Essays in Honour of Margaret Thrall* (ed. T. J. Burke and J. K. Elliott; NovTSup 109; Leiden: Brill, 2003), 17–53, esp. 20–36.

63. See S. E. Porter, "The Theoretical Justification for Application of Rhetorical Categories to Pauline Epistolary Literature," in *Rhetoric and the New Testament: Essays from the 1992 Heidelberg Conference* (ed. S. E. Porter and T. H. Olbricht; JSNTSup 90; Sheffield: JSOT Press, 1993), 100–122. This applies to all of Paul's letters, not just 2 Corinthians.

ever was known or circulated in anything other than a single form. These textual alterations may have occurred, but they had to occur earlier than our text-critical evidence can support. This constitutes a poor use of an argument from silence. Second, the use in 9:1 of the connective phrase περὶ μὲν γάρ (often untranslated or just rendered with "for," as in the New American Standard Bible), rather than indicating separation of the chapter, indicates connection and continuation (cf. Acts 28:22). It is neither the equivalent of the transitional markers that Paul uses in 1 Corinthians (περὶ δέ) nor a formula to introduce new material. Third, one does not want to overemphasize the amount of duplication between the two chapters. Similar topics are raised, but they are treated in different ways, with 2 Cor 9 adding information not found in 2 Cor 8. Fourth, the argument that 8:1-5 refers to Macedonia as a model for the Corinthians but 9:2 refers to the Corinthians as a model for the Macedonians is not as contradictory as it first appears. Paul commends the Macedonians to the Corinthians in 2 Cor 8, but he uses the Macedonians as a witness to what the Corinthians should be doing in 2 Cor 9. Fifth, reference in 9:3, 5 to those Paul is sending is introduced in 8:16-24, the one clarifying the other. Sixth, concerning the seemingly superfluous mention of the collection in 9:1, perhaps the most difficult of the problems to explain, there are a number of possible explanations other than simply positing a separate letter. One is that the verse may be saying nothing more than that it is unnecessary for Paul to go on with the writing he is engaged in (so that "write" [τὸ γράφειν], with the Greek article and the present-tense infinitive, refers to what has already been said).

The tendency has been to separate either 2 Cor 8 or 2 Cor 9 or both from 2 Cor 1-7, but this is not necessary to make sense of these chapters. The connections of 2 Cor 8 with 2 Cor 1-7 are strong, and some of the information in 2 Cor 9, such as the identity of the "brothers" (9:3, 5), seems to require 2 Cor 8. All of this, as well as the lack of textual evidence, clearly points to the unity of the chapters with the rest of 2 Corinthians.

C. Occasion and Purpose of Second Corinthians

The problems addressed by 1 Corinthians seem to have been a variety of disunifying factors in the Corinthian church, but in the process of Paul's confrontation with the church, there seems to have been a development of the situation and the entry of new opponents. If the occasion that prompted the first couple of letters to the Corinthians was the possible fragmentation of the church, in 2 Corinthians it seems that the disunity has been largely overcome, at least to the point that apparently a minority of people were personally attacking Paul—

probably a new group of outsiders (from Jerusalem? 11:5, 13, 23; 12:11) questioning Paul's apostolic authority in a potentially persuasive way. Consequently, the opponents who elicited 2 Corinthians can be characterized by the nature of their attack. Paul vigorously opposed them, and it appears that the fourth letter to the Corinthians (no matter how much of it is found in our 2 Corinthians) dealt sufficiently with the problem so that Paul could consider the threat overcome. This reinforces the view that these opponents represent a minority position that was finally rejected by the church at Corinth. Nevertheless, there are several views regarding the situation to which 2 Corinthians is addressed.

1. Personal Attack against Paul

The nature of the attack against Paul seems to have consisted of a number of wide-ranging and not entirely fair accusations brought by these outsiders. These include accusations of his instability—as evidenced by a change of plans and vacillation (1:15–18)—lack of clarity in what he meant (1:13–14), ineffectiveness (10:10), tyrannical words (10:8), abandonment of the Corinthians (2:1; 13:2), failure to make his gospel clear (4:3), and pitiful speech (10:10; 11:6), probably indicating that he was not trained in rhetoric as some of them may have been.[64] Concerning his claim to being a representative of Christ or an apostle, Paul was apparently denigrated for a number of reasons: he had no formal letters of recommendation, as perhaps did other itinerant preachers and teachers (3:1; 4:2); his claims about belonging to Christ were apparently seen as unsupported, perhaps with the accusation that he had not actually seen Christ (10:7, with its emphasis on seeing); he arrived in Corinth without a clear mandate (10:13–14); and he was said to be inferior to the "superapostles." The latter were probably those who claimed authority from the church at Jerusalem (11:5; 12:11), a position that Paul himself may well have indirectly endorsed because he placed himself in a less exalted position by refusing financial support from the congregation (11:7–9). All of this may well have indicated to some that Paul was not even to be considered an apostle (12:12, 14) and that Christ was not speaking through him (13:3). More than this, Paul may well have been accused of having a deleterious effect upon the congregation because his behavior seemed to be offensive, including his praise of himself (3:1, 5; 4:5; 5:11–15; 6:3–5; 10:2, 8; 11:16–18; 12:1, 11). It was perhaps said that he was working duplicitously for gain (7:1; 12:17–18), even

---

64. Cf. S. E. Porter and A. W. Pitts, "Paul's Bible, His Education, and His Access to the Scriptures of Israel," *Journal of Greco-Roman Christianity and Judaism* 5 (2008): 9–41. Though Paul was probably exposed to basic rhetoric during his grammar school education (see chapter 1 §4), he was probably not a trained rhetor as some claim he was.

using the collection (8:20–21), that he was a coward (1:23; 8:2; 10:1, 10; 11:32–33), and that he ended up harming the Christian community by abandoning the Corinthians (2:1; 13:2) and exploiting the situation for his own benefit (7:2; 12:16).

2. Minority Accusations

To Paul's mind, at least as reflected in 2 Corinthians, the kinds of attacks made against him seem to have originated with a minority of people connected with the Christian community in Corinth, quite possibly Jewish Christians from Jerusalem, as already mentioned. Paul had to find a suitable tone in the letter and make his perspective clear. For example, he says that they were a minority (2 Cor 2:6; 10:2) who were paid—implying that they, as opposed to Paul, readily accepted financial compensation (2:17; 11:20), something he did not seek though he believed he was entitled to it (1 Cor 9:3–11)—and who had gained entrance into the church by letters of recommendation and self-commendation (2 Cor 3:1; 10:12, 18). They apparently did not hesitate to boast of their own excellence (5:12; 11:12, 18), to emphasize ecstatic experience that Paul counters with his own (5:13; 12:1–6), and to overtly claim both the apostolic office (11:5, 13; 12:11) and superiority to Moses (3:4–11), but without making known their own Jewish heritage (11:22). In response to such claims, Paul says that they in fact were preaching another gospel (11:4), had encroached on others' missionary territory (10:15–16), were immoral (12:21; 13:2), were boastful (10:12–13), and were led by a particular person (2:5; 7:12; 11:4). The result, to Paul's mind at least, was that they were Satan's servants (11:13–15). By contrast, Paul regarded himself as an apostle (1:1), and the proof of this lay in the Corinthians themselves (3:2–3), among whom he had done mighty things (12:12), reflecting his appointment from God (3:5–6; 4:7; besides his having seen Christ: 5:16; cf. 1 Cor 9:1).

Is it possible to characterize these false preachers more definitively?[65] Scholars engage in endless speculation, often focusing upon 2 Cor 11, especially 11:4. Some, such as Baur, C. K. Barrett, and John Gunther, characterize them as Judaizers (Gal 1:6–9), on the basis of their emphasis upon their Jewish heritage (2 Cor 3:4–7; 11:22).[66] But even though the problem in Corinth is serious,

65. See J. L. Sumney, *Identifying Paul's Opponents: The Question of Method in 2 Corinthians* (JSNTSup 40; Sheffield: JSOT Press, 1990), esp. 13–73 for a summary of the positions noted below, and 187–91 for his own conclusions. Cf. also Sumney, *"Servants of Satan,"* 79–133, but who divides the letter into 2 Cor 1–9 and 2 Cor 10–13; and the various essays contained in S. E. Porter, ed., *Paul and His Opponents* (PAST 2; Leiden: Brill, 2005), especially N. H. Taylor, "Apostolic Identity and the Conflicts in Corinth and Galatia," 99–128.

66. See Baur, "Die Christuspartei"; C. K. Barrett, "Paul's Opponents in 2 Corinthians" and "Ψευδαπόστολοι (2 Cor. 11.13)," both in his *Essays on Paul*, 60–86 and 87–107; and J. J. Gun-

Paul's response does not seem to be of the same kind as found in Galatians, hence making this perhaps not the best explanation. A second proposal comes from Rudolf Bultmann and Walter Schmithals, who claim that the opponents are "gnostics."[67] These scholars note the willingness to trade on ecstatic experience, but this position would require a fuller development of Gnosticism than is likely for the first century. This is not to say that there were not some gnostic tendencies, especially in their taking pride in the possession of "true knowledge," but a formalized Gnosticism does not seem to be the case. A third idea, by Dieter Georgi, is that these were Hellenistic Jews who were making claims regarding their miraculous powers.[68] This is the theory of the "divine man" (θεῖος ἀνήρ)—the man of God was expected to be some sort of miracle worker—for which there is not significant evidence before Christianity had taken firm root; consequently, the best parallels come from the third century and later. It is possible that these false preachers were followers of Apollos and reflected the Hellenistic Judaism of Alexandria.[69] They therefore may well have been educated and articulate spokesmen who were formidable opponents for Paul. There is merit in this suggestion, especially in light of 1 Corinthians (e.g., 1:12, 18–31; 2:1–5), but the ways in which Paul seems to handle the two situations are quite different: he is more conciliatory in 1 Corinthians but more confrontative in 2 Corinthians. This may well be because the situation had escalated, even though it is hard to form a hard line of connection between the two.

The most likely explanation of Paul's opponents is that this group of false preachers originated in Palestine, possibly as emissaries (whether legitimate or renegade) of the Jerusalem leaders or "superapostles," or as itinerant preachers who claimed to have been with Jesus, and who were unwittingly given as a result more due than they deserved at Corinth. This is not to say that the Jerusalem leaders necessarily were directly opposing Paul at Corinth, but one must not dismiss the degree of suspicion that apparently existed between the Jerusalem and Antiochian missionary efforts (see Acts 15:1–5; 21:20–21). The

---

ther, *St. Paul's Opponents and Their Background: A Study of Apocalyptic and Jewish Sectarian Teaching* (NovTSup 35; Leiden: Brill, 1973), 1–94.

67. R. Bultmann, *The Second Letter to the Corinthians* (ed. E. Dinkler; trans. R. A. Harrisville; Minneapolis: Augsburg, 1985); and Schmithals, *Gnosticism in Corinth*.

68. D. Georgi, *The Opponents of Paul in Second Corinthians* (Philadelphia: Fortress, 1986); contra C. Holladay, *Theios Aner in Hellenistic-Judaism: A Critique of the Use of This Category in New Testament Christology* (SBLDS 40; Missoula, MT: Scholars Press, 1977).

69. For a survey of opinion, see R. Pickett, *The Cross of Christ: The Social Significance of the Death of Jesus* (JSNTSup 143; Sheffield: Sheffield Academic, 1997), 39–74; cf. also F. Watson, *Paul, Judaism, and the Gentiles: Beyond the New Perspective* (rev. and exp. ed.; Grand Rapids: Eerdmans, 2007), 152–55, who posits that Apollos himself was also included in this group.

superapostles may have been the leaders in Jerusalem, and Paul's opponents in Corinth may have been claiming the authority of the Jerusalem church, whether they had it or not.[70] In response, Paul suggests that the Corinthians have been too quick to accept the false preachers' claims to have the authority and endorsement of the superapostles, whereas he asserts his equal standing and authority with any apostles, including those in Jerusalem. Anyone who says otherwise is a false apostle (2 Cor 11:5, 12–15).

D. Outline of Second Corinthians

A. Opening (1:1–2)
  1. Sender (1:1a)
  2. Addressee (1:1b)
  3. Greeting (1:2)
B. Thanksgiving (1:3–7)
C. Body: Paul's ministry to the Corinthians (1:8–9:15)
  1. Formal opening (1:8–11)
  2. Paul's explanation of his recent conduct (1:12–2:13)
  3. Paul's apostolic ministry (2:14–7:16)
  4. Collection for Jerusalem (8:1–9:15)
D. Paraenesis (10:1–13:10)
  1. Paul's personal appeal regarding his apostolic authority (10:1–12:10)
  2. Pauline travelogue (12:11–13:4)
  3. Final exhortation (13:5–10)
E. Closing (13:11–14)
  1. Call to unity (13:11)
  2. Greetings (13:12–13)
  3. Benediction (13:14)

E. Content of Second Corinthians

Opening (1:1–2)

Paul identifies himself and Timothy as the cosenders of this letter and identifies himself as an apostle of Christ Jesus by the will of God. He writes to the

---

70. Cf. R. P. Martin, "The Opponents of Paul in 2 Corinthians: An Old Issue Revisited," in *Tradition and Interpretation in the New Testament: Essays in Honor of E. Earle Ellis* (ed. G. F. Hawthorne with O. Betz; Grand Rapids: Eerdmans, 1987), 279–87.

church belonging to God at Corinth (as in 1 Corinthians) and extends the greeting to all the saints in Achaia.

Thanksgiving (1:3–7)

Though Paul does not directly give thanks to God for the Corinthians as he did in 1 Corinthians, this section is filled with a thankful attitude, including blessing to God (εὐλογητὸς ὁ θεός), who comforts his people in all of their afflictions. Those who are comforted, then, are able to comfort others who experience affliction with the same comfort they receive from God. The term "comfort" (παρακλήσις/παρακαλέω) is repeated ten times in this short section—it appears that Paul wants to emphasize the idea of comfort here.

Body: Formal Opening (1:8–11)

Referring to their afflictions, Paul does not want his suffering to be vague, but lets them know that he and his coworkers experienced extensive suffering in Asia, to the point of death. The point of this affliction, he says, is so that they would rely on God, who has the power to raise the dead. He asks them for continued prayer so that many will give thanks on behalf of them.

Body: Paul's Explanation of His Recent Conduct (1:12–2:13)

Paul communicates his pride in the Corinthians and hopes that they have as much pride in him as well. He wanted to visit them a second time, and the decision not to come was not based on indecision or wavering, but it was a difficult decision to make for their best interest. He recalls the previous letter that pained them and admits that it caused him pain as well, and that their joy would be his joy. His previous letter was difficult to write, because he did not want to cause them pain, but he wants them to know how much he loves them.

Not naming the offender who caused factions at Corinth, Paul urges his readers to forgive and comfort him. He apparently had repented of his divisiveness, and Paul had forgiven him as well. So he expects the Corinthians, at least those who support Paul, to forgive the offender also and to strive for unity. Paul then tells them that, when he went to Troas, he did not feel at peace because Titus was not there, so he went to Macedonia.

Body: Paul's Apostolic Ministry (2:14–7:16)

One of the accusations against Paul was that he was not a real apostle, and a majority of this letter is a defense against that accusation. He begins by saying that he and his coworkers are the aroma of Christ among those being saved. They are not like other peddlers of God's word but sincere and commissioned by God. But Paul did not have the types of commendations as others possibly did. He did not have letters of recommendation, because they themselves were his letter of recommendation, for all to see. This is the confidence that Paul and his companions have through Christ, that even though they are insufficient of themselves, their sufficiency comes from God.

Paul discusses the ministry that they have been entrusted with, contrasting it with the "ministry of death" that was in the Old Testament. That ministry resulted in the glory that Moses beheld, but the "ministry of the Spirit" is even greater. How much more glorious is the ministry with which they have been entrusted? With that in mind, they are to be bold, beholding the glory of God without a veil like Moses and being transformed. Knowing the gloriousness of this ministry, then, Paul insists that he does not need to proclaim this gospel in any underhanded or deceptive way, but he wants to let it be revealed for how great it is. He does not need to proclaim or promote himself but Jesus as Lord. Those who proclaim the gospel, however, are afflicted but not crushed, perplexed but not despairing, persecuted but not forsaken, struck down but not destroyed, to show that the power belongs to God and not themselves. So even though they experience hardships, they are not discouraged, knowing that there is an eternal glory waiting for them.

Paul continues to expound the glory to be seen, using an architectural metaphor of a tent and a house. The earthly body is the tent, wasting away, but Paul looks forward to the permanent house, the heavenly dwelling. He encourages them to think of being home with the Lord, instead of being home in the body. Paul's motivation for this is his love for the Corinthians—the love of Christ compels him, the same love that compelled Christ to die for others so they could live. In light of that, Paul does not regard anyone according to the flesh (as he once knew Christ), because those who are in Christ are a new creation. God reconciled us to himself through Christ and has given us the ministry of reconciliation. As ambassadors, we are to beseech others to be reconciled to God.

Paul warns the Corinthians not to receive the grace of God in vain, but to receive God's grace now. He does not put obstacles in anyone's way, but instead he as a servant of God is faced with all sorts of obstacles in his ministry, so that no fault could be found in him. He commands them not to be mismatched with unbelievers, since there is nothing in common between light and darkness, between Christ and an idol. They are to be separate from the world, to be cleansed from any sort of defilement.

He reiterates that they have not wronged anyone in any way and that he has great pride in them. Even in affliction, when Paul was in Macedonia, he struggled at every turn, on the outside fighting, but on the inside fearing. He recalls how Titus had come to comfort him, and he told Paul of their longing, mourning, and zeal for him. His previous letter grieved them, but it was grief in a godly way, since it led to repentance. Paul is proud of how they reacted to the letter and is comforted, not only by their reaction to it but by Titus being refreshed by them as well. Not only is Paul encouraged by the Corinthians; so is Titus. Paul ends this section by confessing his perfect confidence in them.

Body: Collection for Jerusalem (8:1–9:15)

Using a disclosure formula (i.e., "I/we want you to know"),[71] Paul lets the Corinthians know that, in spite of the affliction that the churches of Macedonia experienced, they overflowed with generosity, not only according to their means but beyond their means. He reports that their generosity was motivated by a desire to participate in the relief of the saints, so Titus was sent to encourage them in this matter. Just as Christ became poor so that they would become rich, they are to follow his example. Paul advocates that they all shared in the abundance and need that all of the saints experience.

Paul encourages the Corinthians by letting them know that the Macedonians (the province just north of them) have been encouraged by Paul's bragging about them. He wants them to be prepared, then, when the Macedonians come down to Corinth with Paul. But he also wants them to know that whatever they invest, they will get back the same amount in return; if they sow sparingly, they reap sparingly, but if they sow bountifully, they reap bountifully. They should not, however, give out of compulsion, but out of the generosity of their heart, because God loves a cheerful giver.

Paraenesis: Paul's Personal Appeal Regarding His Apostolic Authority (10:1–12:10)

Assuming the unity of the letter at this point (see §3B above), Paul reiterates that his ministry is authentic, and he confesses that while they think he is timid in person and bold only in writing, he is anything but timid. Some may accuse him of walking by the flesh, and that may be true in some ways, but he does not fight according to the flesh, for his weapons are spiritual, not physical. They break down arguments and every lofty thought against the knowledge of

---

71. S. E. Porter and A. W. Pitts, "The Disclosure Formula in the Epistolary Papyri and in the New Testament: Development, Form, Function, and Syntax," in *The Language of the New Testament: Context, History, and Development* (ed. S. E. Porter and A. W. Pitts; ECHC 3/LBS 6; Leiden: Brill, 2013), 421–38.

God and take every thought captive to obey Christ. Opponents accuse Paul of being aggressive only in his writing, but of being weak and frail in person. But he explains that what he says in his letters when he is absent, he does when present. Paul's boasting is not without limits, but in whatever area of influence to which God has assigned him. He reminds them that he was the one who first came to them and preached the gospel, and he hopes that the gospel will be spread to areas beyond them.

Paul requests permission to be a little foolish, as he feels a divine jealousy for them. Comparing them to Eve when the serpent deceived her, he states that they are easily led astray from a sincere and pure devotion to Christ. They seem to be easily swayed by others, but Paul affirms that he is not inferior to these other superapostles. In fact, while he may not be skilled in speaking, he is certainly knowledgeable, as he has already proven to them. They seem to have misunderstood his humility for weakness and taken for granted his financial independence, which was motivated by his love for them. He will continue to do this, so that these false, deceptive apostles will be undermined.

Paul continues his "foolishness" by continuing to boast, since they put up with such behavior. His boast is that he too is a Hebrew, an Israelite, a descendant of Abraham, and a servant of Christ. He has endured far more labors and imprisonments, including beatings, many them nearly killing him. On top of the physical afflictions he faced, he also had the mental and emotional concern for all the churches. But if he must boast, it will be about the things that show his weakness.

He continues to boast by referring to a man who, in a vision fourteen years prior to the letter, was caught up to the third heaven and was revealed things that are unutterable.[72] But because of these great revelations and the proclivity toward pride because of them, Paul was given a thorn in the flesh, a messenger of Satan, to torment him.[73] Paul pleaded with the Lord to have this removed, but the Lord responded by saying, "My grace is sufficient for you, for my power is made perfect in weakness" (NIV). So Paul concludes that he will boast all the more about his weaknesses, since his weakness proves God's strength.

72. Most commentators take this passage as Paul referring to himself in the third person; e.g., Barrett, *Second Epistle to the Corinthians*, 307–8; Harris, *Second Epistle to the Corinthians*, 835; and F. J. Matera, *II Corinthians* (NTL; Louisville: Westminster John Knox, 2003), 279–80. Some minority views take this as Paul referring to someone else; cf. Land, *Is There a Text in These Meanings?*

73. Most commentators take this to refer to a physical ailment, such as poor eyesight or an illness of some sort; cf. D. I. Yoon, "Paul's Thorn and His Gnosis: Epistemic Considerations," in *Paul and Gnosis* (ed. S. E. Porter and D. I. Yoon; PAST 9; Leiden: Brill, forthcoming), for a survey of proposals, but also the idea that this thorn was actually a spiritual tormenter.

Paraenesis: Pauline Travelogue (12:11–13:4)

Paul stops his boasting at this point and confesses his foolishness, but he also states that the Corinthians, in their lack of support for his prior ministry and abandonment of him, caused him to be this way. He affirms his status as a true apostle, no less than the others. He states his plans to join them for a third time, not being a burden but burdening himself for them, as parents do for their children. He will gladly spend himself and be spent for their souls, because of his love for them. But he states his fear that there will still be fighting, jealousy, anger, slander, gossip, and other such evil, and that he will mourn over those who have not repented of their sin. Upon this third visit, Paul warns them that he will not spare those who have not repented; this will be proof that Christ is speaking in him, since while Christ was crucified in weakness, he lives by the power of God.

Paraenesis: Final Exhortation (13:5–10)

As Paul nears the end of the letter, he tells the Corinthians to examine themselves, to see whether they are in the faith, whether Jesus Christ is in them. Paul also phrases this as a test of himself as an authentic apostle. In other words, if Christ is in them, then this is evidence of Paul's authenticity. Paul hopes that they will all pass the test, and not simply the appearance of it. He hopes that when he does come, he will not have to exert his apostolic authority except to build them up.

Closing (13:11–14)

Paul's letter ends with a series of brief exhortations, to rejoice and to strive for unity. He asks them to greet each other with a holy kiss. He ends with a benediction, that the grace of the Lord Jesus Christ, the love of God, and the fellowship of the Holy Spirit would be with them.

Sources for Further Study

Commentaries

Barnett, P. *The Second Epistle to the Corinthians*. NICNT. Grand Rapids: Eerdmans, 1997.

Barrett, C. K. *The First Epistle to the Corinthians*. BNTC. 2nd ed. London: A&C Black, 1971.

———. *The Second Epistle to the Corinthians.* 2nd ed. BNTC. London: A&C Black, 1990.

Betz, H. D. *2 Corinthians 8 and 9.* Hermeneia. Philadelphia: Fortress, 1988.

Bultmann, R. *The Second Letter to the Corinthians.* Edited by E. Dinkler. Translated by R. A. Harrisville. Minneapolis: Augsburg, 1985.

Conzelmann, H. *1 Corinthians: A Commentary on the First Epistle to the Corinthians.* Hermeneia. Philadelphia: Fortress, 1975.

Fee, G. D. *The First Epistle to the Corinthians.* 2nd ed. NICNT. Grand Rapids: Eerdmans, 2014 (1987).

Furnish, V. P. *II Corinthians.* AB 32A. Garden City, NY: Doubleday, 1984.

Garland, D. E. *1 Corinthians.* BECNT. Grand Rapids: Baker, 2003.

Harris, M. J. *The Second Epistle to the Corinthians: A Commentary on the Greek Text.* NIGTC. Grand Rapids: Eerdmans, 2005.

Hughes, P. E. *Paul's Second Epistle to the Corinthians.* NICNT. Grand Rapids: Eerdmans, 1962.

Martin, R. P. *2 Corinthians.* 2nd ed. WBC 40. Grand Rapids: Zondervan, 2014.

Plummer, A. *A Critical and Exegetical Commentary on the Second Epistle of St. Paul to the Corinthians.* ICC. Edinburgh: T&T Clark, 1915.

Quast, K. *Reading the Corinthian Correspondence.* New York: Paulist, 1994.

Robertson, A., and A. Plummer. *A Critical and Exegetical Commentary on the First Epistle of St. Paul to the Corinthians.* 2nd ed. ICC. Edinburgh: T&T Clark, 1911.

Seifrid, M. A. *The Second Letter to the Corinthians.* PNTC. Grand Rapids: Eerdmans, 2014.

Thiselton, A. C. *The First Epistle to the Corinthians: A Commentary on the Greek Text.* NIGTC. Grand Rapids: Eerdmans, 2000.

Thrall, M. E. *A Critical and Exegetical Commentary on the Second Epistle to the Corinthians.* 2 vols. ICC. Edinburgh: T&T Clark, 1994.

Monographs and Books

Bieringer, R., and J. Lambrecht, eds. *Studies on 2 Corinthians.* Bibliotheca Ephemeridum Theologicarum Lovaniensium 112. Leuven: Leuven University Press, 1994.

Burke, T. J., and J. K. Elliott, eds. *Paul and the Corinthians: Studies on a Community in Conflict; Essays in Honour of Margaret Thrall.* NovTSup 109. Leiden: Brill, 2003.

Chester, S. J. *Conversion at Corinth: Perspectives on Conversion in Paul's Theology and the Corinthian Church.* Studies of the New Testament and Its World. London: A&C Black, 2005.

Chow, J. K. *Patronage and Power: A Study of Social Networks in Corinth.* JSNTSup 75. Sheffield: JSOT Press, 1992.

Clarke, A. D. *Secular and Christian Leadership in Corinth: A Socio-Historical and Exegetical Study of 1 Corinthians 1–6*. Arbeiten zur Geschichte des antiken Judentums und des Urchristentums 18. Leiden: Brill, 1993.

Deming, W. *Paul on Marriage and Celibacy: The Hellenistic Background of 1 Corinthians 7*. 2nd ed. Grand Rapids: Eerdmans, 2004 (1995).

Dunn, J. D. G. *1 Corinthians*. NTG. Sheffield: Sheffield Academic, 1995.

Friesen, S. J., D. N. Schowalter, and J. C. Walters, eds. *Corinth in Context: Comparative Studies on Religion and Society*. NovTSup 134. Leiden: Brill, 2010.

Georgi, D. *The Opponents of Paul in Second Corinthians: Study of Religious Propaganda in Late Antiquity*. Philadelphia: Fortress, 1986.

Gooch, P. D. *Dangerous Food: 1 Corinthians 8–10 in Its Context*. Waterloo, ON: Wilfrid Laurier University Press, 1993.

Goulder, M. D. *Paul and the Competing Mission in Corinth*. Library of Pauline Studies. Peabody, MA: Hendrickson, 2001.

Hall, D. R. *The Unity of the Corinthian Correspondence*. JSNTSup 251. London: T&T Clark, 2003.

Hay, D. M., ed. *1 and 2 Corinthians*. Vol. 2 of *Pauline Theology*. Minneapolis: Fortress, 1993.

Land, C. D. *Is There a Text in These Meanings? The Integrity of 2 Corinthians from a Linguistic Perspective*. NTM 36. Sheffield: Sheffield Phoenix, 2015.

Litfin, D. *St. Paul's Theology of Proclamation: 1 Corinthians 1–4 and Greco-Roman Rhetoric*. SNTSMS 79. Cambridge: Cambridge University Press, 1994.

Long, F. J. *Ancient Rhetoric and Paul's Apology: The Compositional Unity of 2 Corinthians*. SNTSMS 131. Cambridge: Cambridge University Press, 2004.

Malina, B. J., and M. Goulder. *Early Christian Conflict in Corinth: Paul and the Followers of Peter*. Peabody, MA: Hendrickson, 2001.

Marshall, P. *Enmity in Corinth: Social Conventions in Paul's Relations with the Corinthians*. WUNT 2/23. Tübingen: Mohr-Siebeck, 1987.

Murphy-O'Connor, J. *St. Paul's Corinth: Texts and Archaeology*. 3rd ed. Wilmington, DE: Glazier, 2002.

Porter, S. E., ed. *Paul and His Opponents*. PAST 2. Leiden: Brill, 2005.

Schmithals, W. *Gnosticism in Corinth: An Investigation of the Letters to the Corinthians*. Translated by J. E. Steely. Nashville: Abingdon, 1971.

Sumney, J. L. *Identifying Paul's Opponents: The Question of Method in 2 Corinthians*. JSNTSup 40. Sheffield: JSOT Press, 1990.

———. *"Servants of Satan," "False Brothers," and Other Opponents of Paul*. JSNTSup 188. Sheffield: Sheffield Academic, 1999.

Vegge, I. *2 Corinthians—A Letter about Reconciliation: A Psychogogical, Epistolographical, and Rhetorical Analysis*. WUNT 239. Tübingen: Mohr-Siebeck, 2008.

Webb, W. J. *Returning Home: New Covenant and Second Exodus as the Context for 2 Corinthians 6.14–7.1.* JSNTSup 85. Sheffield: JSOT Press, 1993.

Willis, W. L. *Idol Meat in Corinth: The Pauline Argument in 1 Corinthians 8 and 10.* SBLDS 68. Chico, CA: Scholars Press, 1985.

Wimbush, V. L. *Paul, the Worldly Ascetic: Response to the World and Self-Understanding according to 1 Corinthians 7.* Macon, GA: Mercer University Press, 1987.

10

Romans

1. Introduction

"The principal and most excellent part of the New Testament . . . a light and a way in unto the whole scripture. . . . No man verily can read it too often or study it too well; for the more it is studied the easier it is; and the more it is chewed the pleasanter it is, and the more groundly it is searched the preciouser things are found in it, so great treasure of spiritual things lieth hid therein." Apart from the archaic form of the language, this passage could have been written by Martin Luther, John Wesley, Augustine, or even possibly Karl Barth, but it was actually penned by William Tyndale in his 1534 introduction to his translation of the New Testament.[1] The significance of the book of Romans, not only to the giants of the church mentioned above but to Christianity as a whole, is seen in the further observation by F. F. Bruce that Romans has been tied to every major Christian awakening.[2] Romans in fact merits much more attention than can be given to it even in a book such as this. In this chapter, I discuss the issues of authorship, date of composition, audience, occasion and purpose, and finally textual issues, before providing an outline and its content.

---

1. W. Tyndale, *Tyndale's New Testament* (1534 ed.; ed. D. Daniell; New Haven: Yale University Press, 1989), 207, from "A Prologue to the Epistle of Paul to the Romans," also cited in F. F. Bruce, *Romans* (rev. ed.; TNTC; Grand Rapids: Eerdmans, 1985), 9; cf. 56–58. See also J. R. Greenman and T. Larson, *Reading Romans through the Centuries: From the Early Church to Karl Barth* (Grand Rapids: Baker, 2005). The issues in this introduction are treated in more detail in S. E. Porter, *The Letter to the Romans: A Linguistic and Literary Commentary* (NTM 37; Sheffield: Sheffield Phoenix, 2015), esp. 1–23.

2. Bruce, *Romans*, 9. For an interpretation that questions this use of Romans, see S. K. Stowers, *A Rereading of Romans: Justice, Jews, and Gentiles* (New Haven: Yale University Press, 1994).

2. Interpretive Issues Regarding Romans

A. *Authorship of Romans*

Romans, one of Ferdinand Christian Baur's four pillar epistles, is yet another letter about which Werner Georg Kümmel expresses supreme confidence (at least for most of it): "The authenticity and homogeneity of Rom 1–15 are subject to no serious doubt."[3] I will address the question of Rom 16 below, but this statement concisely and accurately expresses the consensus that there is no serious critical doubt regarding Pauline authorship of at least the first fifteen chapters of this letter. Of late there have been two related discussions worth noting, however, if only because of their unusual and aberrant character. The first is the kind of criticism seen in the commentary on Romans by John O'Neill, who raises questions of authorship for certain sections and suggests that several of the most important passages and some of the most distinctively Pauline wording may not be authentic.[4] Nevertheless, he does not deny Pauline authorship of the letter, and only a few scholars follow his avenue of text-critical speculation.[5] A second analysis is that of Walter Schmithals, who divides the letter into two major letters plus some fragments. His claims regarding the two letters are not convincing, but even so, he does not deny Pauline authorship of the two letters and the fragments that he thinks went into the composition of the book.[6]

So far as the evidence from the early church is concerned, the external witness is unanimous. Writings and writers who bear witness to Romans are *1 Clement* 32.2 (Rom 9:4–5); 33.1 (Rom 6:1); 35.4–6 (Rom 1:29–32); 36.2 (Rom 1:21); 47.7 (Rom 2:24); 61.1 (Rom 13:1); Ignatius, *To the Ephesians* 9, 19.3; *To the Magnesians* 6.2, 9.1; *To the Trallians* 9.2; Marcion; Origen; and the Mura-

---

3. W. G. Kümmel, *Introduction to the New Testament* (trans. H. C. Kee; 17th ed.; Nashville: Abingdon, 1975), 314. Kümmel goes further in n30, however, saying that claims of "individual interpolated sections" such as 13:1–7 (he cites P. N. Harrison, C. H. Talbert, E. Barnikol, and J. Kallas; others could be cited as well) are unproved (some of these are discussed below). Cf. F. C. Baur, *Paul the Apostle of Jesus Christ: His Life and Work, His Epistles and His Doctrine* (2 vols.; London: Williams & Norgate, 1873–75; repr. Peabody, MA: Hendrickson, 2003), 1.321–81.

4. See J. C. O'Neill, *Paul's Letter to the Romans* (Harmondsworth, England: Penguin, 1975), 264–71, for the reconstructed letter.

5. Two examples are W. O. Walker Jr., *Interpolations in the Pauline Letters* (JSNTSup 213; London: Sheffield Academic, 2001), 166–89; and H. C. Waetjen, *The Letter to the Romans: Salvation as Justice and the Deconstruction of Law* (NTM 32; Sheffield: Sheffield Phoenix, 2011).

6. W. Schmithals, *Der Römerbrief als historisches Problem* (Studien zum Neuen Testament 9; Gütersloh: Mohn, 1975), esp. 180–211.

torian Fragment.[7] There are also many parallels to Galatians as confirmatory evidence.[8]

B. Date of Composition of Romans

The precise date of Romans is determined by what one does with Rom 16 (see §E below). If Rom 16 is seen as authentic to the letter, it allows for a fairly precise dating. If Rom 16 is not seen to be authentic, the dating can still be established within a one-year period.

On his third missionary journey, with his ministry in Ephesus ending after a stay of two years and three months, Paul decided to visit Macedonia and then Greece before going to Jerusalem to bring them the collection that he had been gathering (Acts 18:23–21:17, in particular 20:1–3 and 19:21; Rom 15:22–26, with reference to the collection being complete). If Rom 16 is original to the letter, then it is almost certain that Paul wrote the book of Romans to the Roman Christians while he was in Corinth on his third missionary journey (Acts 20:3). The evidence overwhelmingly points in this direction. The passage in Acts does not refer specifically to Corinth, but Rom 16:1 speaks of Phoebe, a deacon of the church at Cenchrea, the eastern port of Corinth, being commended to the church at Rome, with the probable indication that she is the one carrying the letter to the church.[9] Romans 16:23 mentions Gaius and Erastus. A Gaius who in Romans sends greetings is said to have been baptized by Paul in 1 Cor 1:14, and an Erastus who also sends greetings is said to have remained in Corinth in 2 Tim 4:20.[10] Even if Rom 16 is not original to the letter, it is still virtually certain that Paul wrote the letter to the Romans either during his travels throughout Macedonia (Acts 20:1–2) or, more likely, during his stay in Corinth.[11] This is

---

7. See J. Moffatt, *An Introduction to the Literature of the New Testament* (3rd ed.; Edinburgh: T&T Clark, 1918), 148–49.

8. For more on the discussion of the integrity of Romans, see R. N. Longenecker, *Introducing Romans: Critical Issues in Paul's Most Famous Letter* (Grand Rapids: Eerdmans, 2011), 15–42.

9. Cf. A. Chapple, "Getting *Romans* to the Right Romans: Phoebe and the Delivery of Paul's Letter," *Tyndale Bulletin* 62 (2011): 197–214. Contra S. Légasse, *L'Epître de Paul aux Romains* (Lectio divina commentaires; Paris: Cerf, 2002), 940, who takes a minority position that she was not the letter carrier.

10. Even if 2 Timothy is not authentically Pauline, it is possible that the Erastus mentioned is the same one and that the early church remembered where he lived.

11. In relating this letter to the church at Corinth, his troubles there seem to have waned considerably, and he was enjoying a peaceful time there while composing Romans; cf. G. R. Osborne, *Romans* (IVP New Testament Commentary Series; Downers Grove, IL: InterVarsity, 2004), 14–15.

established through the content of the letter, in which Paul states that he intends to visit Rome after he has delivered to the church at Jerusalem the collection that he has gathered in Macedonia and Greece (Rom 15:24–26). This closely matches his traveling itinerary in Acts 20.

Depending upon the date of the third missionary journey, the date of the composition of Romans is likely between 55 and 59, with a date around 56 or 57 very probable.

C. Audience of Romans

Establishing that Paul wrote the letter to the Romans and that he wrote it during his third missionary journey still does not solve the problem of his audience. He singles out the addressees of the letter with the words "to all God's beloved in Rome" (Rom 1:7 NRSV). This probably indicates that he has in mind all of the believers in that city—but who are those believers?

1. Rome during the Time of Paul

Rome of the first century was a large city, with probably somewhere around one million inhabitants.[12] Of these, perhaps forty thousand to fifty thousand of them were Jews, which was a fairly high concentration.[13] Jews first came to Rome apparently with the Roman general Pompey when he brought them back as slaves from his conquest of Palestine in 63 BC. Synagogues were formed; eleven to fifteen Jewish synagogues are known from sepulchral inscriptions to have been in Rome in the first century. One was called the synagogue of the olive tree (cf. Rom 11:17), and another the synagogue of the Hebrews, even though Aramaic would have been the language used by this Jewish population for worship (and Greek for daily life).[14]

In AD 41, the emperor Claudius (41–54) was crowned. Not a strong-willed

12. See J. S. Jeffers, *Conflict at Rome: Social Order and Hierarchy in Early Christianity* (Minneapolis: Fortress, 1991); cf. J. F. Hall, "Rome," *ABD* 5.830–34.

13. See D. Georgi, *The Opponents of Paul in Second Corinthians* (Philadelphia: Fortress, 1986), 83, who says that there were anywhere from four million to six million Jews in the Roman world, approximately one-seventh of the total population of the empire. Three times as many Jews lived in the Diaspora as lived in Palestine.

14. See H. J. Leon, *The Jews of Ancient Rome* (rev. ed.; Peabody, MA: Hendrickson, 1995), esp. 135–66; cf. W. Wiefel, "The Jewish Community in Ancient Rome and the Origins of Roman Christianity," in *The Romans Debate* (ed. K. P. Donfried; 2nd ed.; Peabody, MA: Hendrickson, 1991), 85–101.

man, he was governed by others, including his wives. He was apparently poisoned by one of his wives, Agrippina, who had persuaded him to appoint her son Nero (54–68) to succeed him (Suetonius, *Claudius* 44–45, admits that the poisoner was not precisely known). It was during Claudius's reign that the Jews were expelled from Rome. There are three controversial issues regarding this event: its cause, its precise date, and the date the expulsion order was lifted. The Roman historian Suetonius says that "since the Jews constantly made disturbances at the instigation of Chrestus, he expelled them from Rome" (*Claudius* 25.4 LCL). The majority of New Testament scholars interpret this to mean that there were a number of disputes among the Jews, probably Jewish Christians and non-Christian Jews, over the nature and identity of Jesus Christ.[15] "Chrestus," therefore, is taken as a variant or mistaken spelling of "Christ" by Suetonius. He appears to have thought that this Chrestus was a contemporary person who was stirring up the Jews in Rome. If this scenario is correct, it is more likely that the issue of the resurrection was causing an uproar among the Jewish population there. It is disputed by some New Testament scholars and classical scholars, however, that Suetonius is talking about such a scenario. It is perhaps more likely, according to this view, that there actually was a person named Chrestus who had caused the Jews to riot. With a slave population of approximately half the population of Rome, the Romans always feared uprisings. As Pliny states when one slave owner was attacked by his slaves, "No master can feel safe because he is kind and considerate; for it is their brutality, not their reasoning capacity, which leads slaves to murder masters" (*Epistle* 3.14 LCL).[16] During 139–133 BC in Sicily, slave revolts had been put down with great violence and bloodshed, and there was no wish to repeat them. So apparently Claudius issued an edict that forced the Jews to leave Rome, though it seems not to have resulted in the confiscation of their property (see Acts 18:1–3).

The second dispute concerns the date of Claudius's edict. The vast majority of scholars accept a date of 49, on the basis of the Christian writer Paulus Orosius (fifth century), who dates the event to the ninth year of Claudius's reign (*History against the Pagans* 7.6.15).[17] Some, however, argue that the date was 41

---

15. E.g., C. S. Keener, *Romans: A New Covenant Commentary* (New Covenant Commentary; Eugene, OR: Cascade, 2009), 11–12.

16. See K. R. Bradley, *Slaves and Masters in the Roman Empire: A Study in Social Control* (New York: Oxford University Press, 1987), 113n1, who cites other evidence as well: Tacitus, *Annals* 14.42–45; Pliny, *Epistle* 8.14.

17. See, e.g., R. Riesner, *Paul's Early Period: Chronology, Mission Strategy, Theology* (Grand Rapids: Eerdmans, 1998), 127–34; and P. Lampe, *From Paul to Valentinus: Christians at Rome in the First Two Centuries* (Minneapolis: Fortress, 2003), 11–16.

(or 43), on the basis of Dio Cassius's report of Claudius's edict forbidding Jews to meet (*Roman History* 60.6.6).[18] Claudius apparently was hostile toward Jews from the beginning of his principate (there are other edicts of his regarding the Jews, especially in Egypt; see P.Lond. 1912 [printed in *Select Papyri* 2.212]), perhaps resulting in his initially forbidding them to meet together. Nevertheless, the later date is probably still correct for the expulsion.

The third and last issue is when and how the edict would have expired. An edict such as this would have been decreed by the emperor to last in perpetuity, but in fact, such a decree would have been in force only so long as an emperor wished it. Consequently, if a new emperor came to power, he would have had the option of continuing to keep it in force or of allowing it to expire.[19] Apparently, Nero did not enforce the decree (if Claudius himself had in fact enforced it for so long), so that the Jews were allowed to return to Rome.

At first, Nero may have appeared to be an emperor concerned with justice and proper procedures, at least while he was still tempered by Seneca's influence, but by 65, Christians in Rome were being martyred by him.[20] He found the Christians easy victims to blame for a number of disasters and difficulties that he had in Rome, including a devastating fire in 64. As part of his "sport," Nero reportedly used Christians as human torches at his parties, all of which eventually led to sympathy for Christians (Tacitus, *Annals* 15.44.2–5, esp. 4).[21] It was likely during the persecution of Nero in 64/65 that Paul and perhaps Peter were martyred in Rome (*1 Clement* 5.4). Nero's reign came to an ignominious end when, insane, he died in a pathetic attempt at suicide. The scholar of Roman religion T. R. Glover reportedly said that little did the emperor suspect in his condemnation of Paul that "there would come a time when men would name their dogs Nero and their sons Paul."[22]

18. See G. Lüdemann, *Paul, Apostle to the Gentiles: Studies in Chronology* (trans. F. S. Jones; Philadelphia: Fortress, 1984), 164–71, among others.

19. Bruce, *Romans*, 17. Cf., however, H. Förster, "Die Aufenthalt von Priska und Aquila in Ephesus und die juristischen Rahmenbedingungen ihrer Rückkehr nach Rom," *Zeitschrift für die neutestamentliche Wissenschaft* 105.2 (2014): 189–227, who argues that the return may not have needed to await Claudius's death. He also examines the makeup of the Roman church.

20. See A. N. Sherwin-White, *Roman Society and Roman Law in the New Testament* (Oxford: Clarendon, 1963), 110–12; E. T. Salmon, *A History of the Roman World from 30 B.C. to A.D. 138* (6th ed.; London: Routledge, 1968), 175–82, part of a chapter on Nero; and Jeffers, *Conflict at Rome*, 16–17.

21. See B. Reicke, *The New Testament Era: The World of the Bible from 500 B.C. to A.D. 100* (Philadelphia: Fortress, 1968), 245–51.

22. As paraphrased in F. F. Bruce, *Paul: Apostle of the Heart Set Free* (Grand Rapids: Eerdmans, 1977), on the dedication page.

2. Christians at Rome

The founder of the Christian community at Rome is unknown. But by 49, when the Jews were expelled from Rome, there were apparently Jewish Christians among those who were compelled to leave (see Acts 18:2). How did those first Christians get to Rome? There is no record of any sort of apostolic visit, even by Peter or Paul, until long after there was a Christian presence in Rome. Eusebius (*Ecclesiastical History* 2.14.6) seems to think that Peter was the pioneer of the gospel in Rome, but this is merely an assertion, and it seems unlikely that neither Paul nor Luke would mention this in any of their writings.[23] This lack of knowledge of the Christian origins in Rome leads to widespread speculation regarding the early spread of Christianity, and several possible scenarios are worth considering. On the one hand, Rome was the center of the Roman Empire, and in literal and figurative senses, all roads led to Rome. So it is entirely possible that a Christian or a few Christians, in the course of their travels, would have come to Rome, perhaps to settle or at least to conduct business. During the course of their time there, they perhaps set up a Christian community. On the other hand, it is just as possible that Christianity made its way to Rome soon after the events at Pentecost. Acts 2:10 says that visitors from Rome were in Jerusalem on that day. Perhaps some of those converted were from Rome and returned there soon after, taking their newfound belief in the risen Christ with them and returning by way of Rome's main port, Puteoli (see Seneca, *Epistle* 77.1).[24] In any event, by the time Paul wrote to the Christians in Rome, Christianity could have been there for over a decade and become well established.[25]

If the church was well established in Rome, however, this does not mean that it was without problems and tensions. While Paul may not make direct statements in his letter to the Romans about his opponents, there is good reason to think that there was still some opposition to Paul, or at least his teachings, there.[26] Aside from possible opposition, however, some of the other

23. Cf. Longenecker, *Introducing Romans*, 60–75; also F. Watson, *Paul, Judaism, and the Gentiles: Beyond the New Perspective* (rev. and exp. ed.; Grand Rapids: Eerdmans, 2007), 167–74 (previously published as F. Watson, *Paul, Judaism, and the Gentiles: A Sociological Approach* [SNTSMS 56; Cambridge: Cambridge University Press, 1986], though with some rethinking of his original conclusions).

24. See Lampe, *From Paul to Valentinus*, 7–10.

25. Martin, *Foundations*, 2.34–35, 138–41.

26. See S. E. Porter, "Did Paul Have Opponents in Rome and What Were They Opposing?" in *Paul and His Opponents* (ed. S. E. Porter; PAST 2; Leiden: Brill, 2005), 149–68, for a fuller argument.

major problems would probably have been caused by the edict of Claudius and the subsequent return of the Jews after the edict expired under Nero.

There is widespread debate regarding the composition of the Christian community at Rome. The four major positions are that the church was predominantly Jewish Christian, predominantly Gentile Christian, a fairly evenly divided mixed group, or an aggregation of separate, independent churches. Paul Minear, Francis Watson (on different grounds and in different ways), and Peter Lampe (still further different grounds) argue for the last position, claiming that the Christian community at Rome consisted of multiple independent churches or what Lampe calls a fractionated church. In his reconstruction of the situation at Rome, Minear claims to have found five major church groups, each referred to by Paul in Romans and thus able to be characterized in a particular way.[27] In his assessment of Romans, Watson uses the specific references in 14:1–15:13 to the "weak" and "strong" to argue that there were two major church groups in Rome.[28] In his thorough archeological and textual study, Lampe looks at the social conditions of ancient Rome, with its varied population centers, as well as Paul's never referring to the "church" in Rome (even in 1:7), to conclude that the church was "fractionated," leading to great diversity and independence.[29] These views highlight the potential sociological conflicts in the Roman Christian community, but have not yet garnered widespread acceptance. The major problem with the kind of reconstruction of Minear and Watson is that it appears to be both too literalistic and too interpretive. Minear must differentiate these various groups on the basis of a number of incidental comments, but even so, he must do a fair amount of speculative synthesis. Why this number of groups and not more or less? Watson is almost certainly correct that there was some sort of difficulty in the Roman church(es), as is evidenced in 14:1–15:13, but to take these, at best, interpretively obscure references as clear indicators of two distinct churches is too literalistic and requires more extrapolation than is justified by the text. Lampe places surprising emphasis upon a few references in the book of Romans (e.g., 1:7; 16:4, 5, 10, 11, 15) and a historical reconstruction that works back from the fifth century to the first. Lampe has still not sufficiently explained Paul's writing a single letter to the Christians in Rome to justify such a fractured church or set of churches.

More likely the church was composed of both Jewish and Gentile Christians (hence one of the first three views, above), although it is difficult to know

---

27. P. S. Minear, *The Obedience of Faith: The Purpose of Paul in the Epistle to the Romans* (London: SCM, 1971).

28. Watson, *Paul, Judaism, and the Gentiles*, 175–82 (94–98 in previous edition).

29. Lampe, *From Paul to Valentinus*, 359–408.

what the mix was or how many churches there were.[30] A number of scholars argue that the church was composed of mostly Jewish Christians. The evidence often used for this position consists of passages that refer directly to the Jews or appear to allude to Jewish institutions and conventions. For example, in 2:17, Paul refers directly to those who bear the name "Jew"; in 3:1–2, he asks what advantage the Jew has over the Gentile; and in 16:3, 7, 11, he greets the Jewish coworkers Priscilla and Aquila and his "relatives." In Rom 4, using "Abraham, our ancestor" (4:1 NRSV) as an example of someone who was saved by faith, not by works, Paul relies upon an implicit Old Testament chronological argument in which the statement that he was reckoned righteous (Gen 15:6) preceded his circumcision (Gen 17). In Rom 9–11, there is a heavy reliance upon Old Testament quotations, often strung together and interwoven with Old Testament imagery (e.g., God as the potter and the people as the clay; Rom 9:20–23, citing Isa 29:16 and 45:9). Romans 15:7–12 seems to rely upon Old Testament quotations that are addressed specifically to the Jews, rather than to the Gentiles. One of the most important pieces of evidence in this reconstruction is the widespread use of the language of "law" (esp. Rom 3–4), which refers in most of these instances to the Jewish law, or Torah.

Nevertheless, this position, regardless of how popular it was in the past, is probably not the most likely scenario, for two reasons. The first is historical. If the Jews were expelled from Rome in 49 and had not begun to return until 54 at the death of Claudius or even somewhat before that, and if Romans was written around 56 or 57 (which is the scholarly consensus),[31] it would be difficult to suppose that a sufficient number of Jewish Christians had returned to become the dominant force in the church. The Gentile Christians, it must be kept in mind, would probably not have been expelled from Rome (except

---

30. See C. E. B. Cranfield, *A Critical and Exegetical Commentary on the Epistle to the Romans* (2 vols.; ICC; Edinburgh: T&T Clark, 1975–79), 1.17–22. Those connected with the predominantly Jewish view are—according to Cranfield—Baur, Zahn, and W. Manson, and those connected with the predominantly Gentile view are Sanday and Headlam, J. Denney, Barrett, and Kümmel. See also A. J. Guerra, *Romans and the Apologetic Tradition: The Purpose, Genre, and Audience of Paul's Letter* (SNTSMS 81; Cambridge: Cambridge University Press, 1995), 22–42, who argues for predominantly Jewish Christians, but because of the protreptic literary genre (see §D2e below); J. C. Walters, *Ethnic Issues in Paul's Letter to the Romans: Changing Self-Definitions in Earliest Roman Christianity* (Valley Forge, PA: Trinity, 1993), 56–66; and M. D. Nanos, *The Mystery of Romans: The Jewish Context of Paul's Letter* (Minneapolis: Fortress, 1996). For a predominantly Gentile Christian church, see Lampe, *From Paul to Valentinus*, 69–76, who notes that both Jews and Christians lived in the poor and overcrowded Trastavere area of Rome. For a strong argument for a clearly Gentile church, see A. Das, *Solving the Romans Debate* (Minneapolis: Fortress, 2007).
31. Contra Lüdemann, *Paul*, 262, who dates Romans to 51/52. See J. D. G. Dunn, *Romans* (WBC 38A–B; Waco, TX: Word, 1988), 1.xliii–xliv, for the consensus.

possibly those, if any, who followed the Jewish law and customs), and so they would have been responsible for maintaining the church during the intervening years. It seems most likely that they would have continued to be the predominant force at the time of Paul's writing to the Romans.

The second reason for disputing the Jewish-Christian hypothesis is the interpretation of the passages that are often cited in support of the position. For example, Rom 2:17 occurs in the middle of a section describing the sinfulness of all of humanity, not only of Jews. It is not clear that, even in 2:17 and following, the Jews emerge as the specifically addressed group. This could be said of most passages cited above, especially Rom 9–11. Although, because of their use of the Old Testament, these chapters may seem to have a distinctively Jewish feel about them, the references in this section make it clear that the exposition has Gentiles in mind. For example, 9:3–4 appears to have Paul speaking about a group other than his primary audience when speaking of the Jews. The same is true in 10:1–3 and even 11:1–2, other passages in which Paul expresses his concerns for the Jews. Most significant, perhaps, is 11:13, where Paul specifically states that he is speaking to those who are Gentiles, since he is the apostle to the Gentiles. And Paul's use of the Abraham story does not depend upon one's being Jewish to understand it—in fact, it may well be addressed to Gentiles.

Because of this, a second group argues for the predominantly Gentile composition of the church. The argument for this rests not only upon the historical scenario mentioned above—the expulsion and return of the Jewish Christians to Rome—but upon passages in Romans pointing to a Gentile audience. For example, in 11:13–32 Paul not only addresses the Gentiles directly (11:13) but, at the end of the section, speaks of the Jews being regrafted onto the olive tree, and he uses "you" to refer to the Gentiles in the course of his argument. Throughout Romans, Paul heralds his position as apostle to the Gentiles—for instance, in 1:5–6, chapters 9–11, and 15:15–16. If Rom 16 is part of the original letter and hence addressed to the church at Rome (see §2E1 for a defense of this position), it is worth noting that most of the names used in the greetings of 16:3–25 are Greek, not Jewish.[32] If there were many Jews in Rome, Paul apparently (according to this evidence) did not know them.

Nevertheless, this view perhaps also overlooks significant evidence: although the Jews may not have been predominant in the church at Rome, the framework of Paul's argument is predicated upon a Jewish understanding. It is possible that this is simply the way Paul thought and wrote; but it is at least

32. See P. Lampe, "The Roman Christians of Romans 16," in *The Romans Debate* (ed. K. P. Donfried; 2nd ed.; Peabody, MA: Hendrickson, 1991), 216–30; and Lampe, *From Paul to Valentinus*, 153–83.

as likely that Paul continued to use this way of structuring his argument—in a way that he does not use in his other letters—because of his knowledge of the significant Jewish population of the church at Rome (it is also worth noting that many Jews of this time had Greek names, making the argument from Rom 16 doubtful). First, the issue of law continues to be important throughout the letter. The only other Pauline letter where this issue looms so large is Galatians, where Paul is apparently confronting Judaizers, who argue that in order for Gentiles to become Christians, they must become Jews also. Paul is apparently not confronting Judaizers in Rome, but he at least appears to be arguing from a framework that the Jews would understand. Second, Paul relies heavily upon the Old Testament. Of the eighty or so direct Old Testament quotations in the Pauline letters, over fifty of these appear in Romans. It is perhaps not so striking that Paul, being a Jew, would choose to rely so heavily upon the Old Testament, certainly if he realized that there would be an audience that could appreciate his use of the Jewish Scriptures.

In conclusion, it is probably best to argue that the church at Rome was a mixed group, including both Jews and Gentiles.[33] This is the view of the majority of commentators on Romans. If one were to venture a guess as to the predominance of one group or another, there were probably more Gentiles in the church than Jews. It certainly appears that the Gentiles were the predominant force, since Paul seems to identify with them in Rom 15:1. A plausible scenario, based upon the above evidence, is that the Jews had returned to the church in Rome to find that their positions had been taken by Gentiles and that this had resulted in, if not overt conflict, some tension regarding the roles and relationships of the two groups (see 14:1–15:13). The Jews may have believed that they had a privileged position and that they were at least owed a greater role than they were currently exercising (2:17–24), and the Gentiles may have lost sight of certain Jewish distinguishing practices that needed to be shown respect (3:1; 14:13–23), even if they were not to dominate the church any longer. It was probably to such a church environment that Paul wrote.

D. Occasion and Purpose of Romans

Since Paul had not visited Rome when he wrote his letter to them, the occasion and purpose of the letter take on added and more complex significance.[34] In

---

33. Cf. the similar conclusion of Longenecker, *Introducing Romans*, 76–78, who identifies the influence of Baur on this discussion.

34. For these issues treated in an exegetical context, see S. E. Porter, "Exegesis of the

other words, the occasion is in many ways less closely related to the purpose. This results in widespread opinions regarding the purpose of Romans.

1. Occasion

The circumstances that elicited the letter to the Romans seem to be encapsulated in a number of important passages that occur at the beginning and the end of the letter. Paul states in 1:13–15 that he planned to come to Rome and that he is eager to preach the gospel to them, even though he has been prevented from doing so. In 15:22, he clarifies why he was prevented—he has been preaching in the eastern part of the Mediterranean. Now that he has preached from Jerusalem all the way to Illyricum (15:19) and has no place further to preach in the east (15:23), he sets his sights on Spain (15:24, 28). In conjunction with that journey, he intends to visit the church in Rome (15:23, 28–29), even though first he has to go to Jerusalem to deliver the collection that he gathered from the churches in Macedonia and Greece (15:26). There is speculation about whether Paul ever got to Spain. *First Clement* 5.7 is interpreted to imply that he did, but this is not certain, especially in light of what appears to have been his travels as represented in the Pastoral Epistles (see chapter 12 §4D3). There is the further question of whether Paul knew Latin, since the western part of the Roman Empire had become Latin speaking in the first century BC, a process apparently largely completed during the first century AD. Paul mentions that he had spread the gospel as far as Illyricum (the western Balkan region), but Illyricum was also a Latin-speaking area, so it is possible that Paul knew Latin and hence was fully prepared for a preaching mission to Spain, whether or not he ever got there.[35]

2. Purpose

The occasion of Paul's proposed visit to Rome was part of the westward expansion of his preaching mission. But the purpose or motivation for his writing

<hr/>

Pauline Letters, Including the Deutero-Pauline Letters," in *Handbook to Exegesis of the New Testament* (ed. S. E. Porter; NTTS 25; Leiden: Brill, 1997), 503–54, esp. 524–31.

35. On the spread of Latin, see M. Cary, *A History of Rome down to the Reign of Constantine* (2nd ed.; London: Macmillan, 1967), 463, 587; cf. S. E. Porter, "Latin Language," in *Dictionary of New Testament Background* (ed. C. A. Evans and S. E. Porter; Downers Grove, IL: InterVarsity, 2000), 630–31. W. M. Ramsay is followed by many in his hypothesis that Paul spoke Latin; *St. Paul the Traveller and the Roman Citizen* (London: Hodder & Stoughton, 1896), 225; e.g., S. E. Porter, "Did Paul Speak Latin?" in *Paul: Jew, Greek, and Roman* (ed. S. E. Porter; PAST 5; Leiden: Brill, 2008), 289–308; and H. T. Ong, "Can Linguistic Analysis in Historical Jesus Research Stand on Its Own? A Sociolinguistic Analysis of Matthew 26:36–27:26," *Biblical and Ancient Greek Linguistics* 2 (2013): 109–38, esp. 131.

the letter to the Romans is not so clear and has elicited an immense amount of debate.[36]

In recent discussion, the contingency of the Pauline letters has become important: Paul is a writer who is addressing in each letter a unique set of circumstances that warrants a response to that particular situation. J. Christiaan Beker emphasizes this contingency,[37] which is undeniable. When the Pauline letters are examined, however, it also becomes clear that a consistent personality stands behind Paul's letters (this is true of whatever corpus is accepted as genuine, usually by virtue of the criterion of consistency by which these corpora are defined). A transcontingent, or more universal, set of beliefs must also be considered when analyzing Paul's letters. Some wish to say that Paul is hopelessly contradictory, even within a given letter (and many of these comments refer to Romans), but such deconstructive criticism neither forms a sound interpretive model nor is borne out by the evidence at hand. It usually reflects a halfhearted effort to come to terms with the complexities with which Paul deals. In light of the ongoing discussion regarding Romans, however, at least eight proposals regarding purpose are worth mentioning.[38]

a. Compendium of the Christian Religion

The traditional view of Romans, summarized in Philip Melanchthon's phrase that Romans is a compendium of the Christian religion, is that the letter is as close to a systematic theology as is found in Paul's writings. The contention is that Paul has taken the occasion—writing to a church that he has not visited but that figures importantly in his future travel plans—to set out the major tenets of Christian belief, and he does so in a highly systematic and organized way, but within the letter form. This position tends to minimize the contingent elements of Paul's presentation, including the relevance of specific contextual factors, and emphasizes the major doctrines that constitute the Pauline gospel, including justification by faith, human sinfulness, the role of Adam and Christ, sanctification, reconciliation, the relations of Jews and Gentiles, and the role of the state. This position was virtually unchallenged until the work of Baur in

---

36. See the summary of various positions in A. J. M. Wedderburn, *The Reasons for Romans* (Edinburgh: T&T Clark, 1988); L. A. Jervis, *The Purpose of Romans: A Comparative Letter Structure Investigation* (JSNTSup 55; Sheffield: JSOT Press, 1991); and R. Morgan, *Romans* (NTG; Sheffield: Sheffield Academic, 1995), 60–77.

37. J. C. Beker, *Paul the Apostle: The Triumph of God in Life and Thought* (Philadelphia: Fortress, 1980), 23–36; "Paul's Theology: Consistent or Inconsistent?" *NTS* 34 (1988): 364–77.

38. Cf. Longenecker, *Introducing Romans*, 94–128, who presents roughly fourteen options; however, some of these can be amalgamated.

the early nineteenth century[39] and still has enduring currency. It is reflected in more recent writings such as Douglas Moo's commentary on Romans and in the work of N. T. Wright.[40] Wright combines it with Paul's missionary motive, in the sense that Paul's mission is founded on his theology—the two are seen to be inseparable.

There are two major objections to this position: (1) it appears to minimize the context or the circumstances to the point that it appears this letter could have been written to virtually any Christian community anywhere at any time; and (2) many of what some scholars would consider major Christian doctrines are lacking in Romans, making it at best an incomplete (and hence flawed?) compendium. Some of the subjects often cited as lacking are eschatology, Christology, the doctrine of the church, the Lord's Supper or Eucharist, and marriage. These two objections are not, however, strong. Romans has spoken to widely varying Christian communities throughout the last two millennia, probably more so than any other Pauline letter and even any other New Testament book. Besides, there is nothing inherently contradictory in saying that a work can be written with full consideration of a particular situation and, at the same time, with larger theological motives in mind. The second objection cannot be taken too seriously. One needs to look only at the list presented above to see that there are two major objections to it. The first is that it is not an accurate characterization of Romans. In what sense can it be said that Christology is not a major concern of the book?[41] It is clear from Paul's argumentative line that he predicates all of Christian existence—justification, reconciliation, and sanctification—upon the work of Christ (e.g., 1:3–4) and Christ's ongoing ministry through his Spirit (8:36–39). For example, in Rom 5, where Paul speaks of reconciliation, he states explicitly three times (5:1, 11, 21) that it was accomplished "through our Lord Jesus Christ" (or similar wording); these statements frame the entire chapter. The second objection is that the importance of many of these missing doctrines is a matter of dispute. The

39. F. C. Baur, "Über Zweck und Veranlassung des Römerbriefs und die damit zusammenhängenden Verhältnisse der römischen Gemeinde," *Tübinger Zeitschrift für Theologie* 3 (1836): 59–178; repr. in Baur, *Historisch-kritische Untersuchungen zum Neuen Testament* (Stuttgart: Frommann, 1963), 147–266, esp. 153–66. See also Baur, *Paul the Apostle of Jesus Christ: His Life and Work, His Epistles and His Doctrine* (2 vols.; London: Williams & Norgate, 1873–75; repr. Peabody, MA: Hendrickson, 2003), 1.331–65.

40. D. J. Moo, *The Epistle to the Romans* (NICNT; Grand Rapids: Eerdmans, 1996), esp. 22–24; and N. T. Wright, *The Climax of the Covenant: Christ and the Law in Pauline Theology* (Edinburgh: T&T Clark, 1991), 234.

41. For example, J. A. Fitzmyer, "The Christology of the Epistle to the Romans," in *The Future of Christology* (ed. A. J. Malherbe and W. A. Meeks; Minneapolis: Fortress, 1993), 81–90, shows that it clearly is a major concern.

lack of any particular doctrine in Romans may be significant, but this does not necessarily reveal a deficiency in Romans. Several of the doctrines mentioned above have only limited relevance in the other Pauline letters as well (e.g., the Lord's Supper, which is discussed in only 1 Corinthians).[42]

b. Manifesto of Paul's Deepest Convictions

In 1948, T. W. Manson argued a position that, in some ways, addresses one of the major objections to the first position, the letter as a compendium of the Christian religion. He claims that Romans was sent originally to the churches at both Rome (1:1–15:23 or 1:1–15:33) and Ephesus (Rom 1–16) and reflects not a full-blown compendium of all major Christian doctrine but, rather, the ideas that were deepest in Paul's thought.[43] Paul had to go to Jerusalem first, but he was also going to Rome on the way farther west. Unable to visit Ephesus, he sent this letter to both, in a larger form for the Ephesians. This would account for the names in Rom 16 that seem to be associated with Ephesus and for, in some manuscripts, the Roman destination being missing (see §2E). Thus, the letter is expanded in its scope from being a letter addressed to a single church to a type of circular letter.

The objections to this position are several, however. The first is that, in light of extant external textual evidence, a strong case cannot be made for the text circulating in a form that included only Rom 1–15. Besides, this would make for a somewhat abrupt and truncated close and an unnatural Pauline ending. The second objection questions why Paul would convey his deepest convictions to the church at Rome, instead of the other churches with which he had a closer relationship. It is understandable that a revised form would be sent to the church at Ephesus (the textual difficulties remain, however), but why Rome and not Corinth, or Antioch, or another church closely associated with him? Paul had never been to Rome, so why would he send a meditation upon his deepest convictions to a church other than one he had founded? It is more understandable that he would send a compendium of Christian belief to a church that he anticipated visiting, rather than an exposition of his deepest beliefs.

---

42. See A. J. B. Higgins, *The Lord's Supper in the New Testament* (Studies in Biblical Theology 6; London: SCM, 1952), 64–73.

43. T. W. Manson, "St. Paul's Letter to the Romans—and Others," in *The Romans Debate* (ed. K. P. Donfried; 2nd ed.; Peabody, MA: Hendrickson, 1991), 3–15. Possible support is now provided by D. Trobisch, *Paul's Letter Collection: Tracing the Origins* (Minneapolis: Fortress, 1994), 72–73. See also H. Koester, "Ephesos in Early Christian Literature," in *Ephesos: Metropolis of Asia: An Interdisciplinary Approach to Its Archaeology, Religion, and Culture* (ed. H. Koester; Valley Forge, PA: Trinity, 1995), 119–40, esp. 122–24.

c. Last Will and Testament

Günther Bornkamm argues that Paul was facing an unknown future on his contemplated journey to Jerusalem with the collection from the churches in Greece and Macedonia.[44] If the record in Acts 21:17–26 is to be trusted at this point (and it seems very likely that it is, since it creates a very plausible course of events in which the Jerusalem church is implicated in Paul's arrest), Paul had every reason to wonder about the reception that would await him in Jerusalem (Rom 15:31). His missionary ventures had been closely watched, and his proclamation of the gospel had aroused suspicion. For whatever reason, perhaps Paul had some sense or direct warning regarding the Jerusalem church; after all, he had been the center of controversy before (Acts 15:1–5; Gal 2:1–10). In anticipation of the troubles that may have been awaiting him, Paul took this occasion of writing to the Christian community at Rome to provide a permanent record of his message, as a forecast of the preaching and missionary ministry he wished to continue. Consequently, a balance maintained in the letter reflects one of his persistent battles and perhaps one of the issues to be faced in Jerusalem—legalism and antinomianism (opposition to the law). He had been accused of being an antinomian, but he was anxious to show that neither he nor the Christian faith was either antinomian or legalistic. There is insight to be gained from consideration of this view, especially in light of the circumstances that befell Paul.

Nevertheless, several objections must also be considered. First, in a similar objection to option b above, why did Paul choose to write this kind of a letter to Rome, a church that he had never visited? Bornkamm tries to make it clear that this is not the last will and testament of a person who anticipates he will not be able to carry on his ministry. If that is true, then in what sense is it a last will and testament? Furthermore, if it were to be his last, Paul may well have poured out his theological heart to his friends, certainly to one of the churches that could have been expected to maintain the Pauline mission. Second, does the kind of situation that Bornkamm posits appear in the letter? Does it reflect the unsettled state upon which this sort of view is predicated? To be sure, there are references to uncertainty regarding the church at Jerusalem (15:31), but these are offset by Paul's conviction that he is determined to make his way to Rome on his way to Spain after visiting Jerusalem (15:24). By comparison, Romans has none of the gloom found in passages such as 2 Cor 10–13 or especially 2 Tim 4:6–7 (which Bornkamm considers deutero-Pauline), where Paul seems genuinely exhausted and concerned regarding the future.

---

44. G. Bornkamm, "The Letter to the Romans as Paul's Last Will and Testament," in *The Romans Debate* (ed. K. P. Donfried; 2nd ed.; Peabody, MA: Hendrickson, 1991), 16–28.

d. Apology to Jerusalem

It is argued (though probably inaccurately) that the distinguishing mark of all of the genuine Pauline letters is mention of the collection (e.g., 1 Cor 16:1-4; 2 Cor 8-9).[45] This seems to be predicated upon a presumption about which letters are authentic. The point is still well taken that the collection is important in Paul's thinking. Consequently, it is posited that Romans, though addressed to the Roman churches and apparently formally directed toward them, is in fact a letter "addressed to Jerusalem."[46] That is, it was written with Jerusalem in mind, as if it were being overheard by that church, so that it would accept Paul's ministry along with his collection and so that he could overcome any possible objections it may have had to what he had been teaching on his missionary journeys. It is even possible that what he was writing in the letter was a dress rehearsal for the kind of speech that he would deliver to the leaders of the church in Jerusalem.

As seen above, Paul's concern regarding his reception in Jerusalem was valid; nevertheless, it is dubious that Romans is best seen as an apology to Jerusalem. There are three objections. First, this letter provides only an indirect way of offering an apology to the Jerusalem church for his belief and behavior, since it is sent in the completely opposite direction, that is, to Rome. Jerusalem is not mentioned in the letter in any way that would indicate that Paul is concerned that the letter he is sending to Rome might reach those in Jerusalem (the reference in 15:31 is completely insufficient to suggest that). Furthermore, some material in the letter would hardly appeal to Jews, especially an audience that Paul was trying to please (e.g., Rom 4, 11). Second, the collection, while it might provide a suitable occasion for writing the letter, hardly constitutes a sufficient purpose for writing such a lengthy and involved letter. This is clear when one notes that references to the collection are minimal. Third, it is unclear how this letter would help Paul achieve his apologetic purpose with Jerusalem, even if the letter were forwarded or served as a commendation on his behalf.

e. Letter of Self-Introduction

Perhaps a more realistic option is that Paul wrote this letter as a letter of self-introduction, possibly verging on an apologetic letter.[47] According to this theory,

---

45. M. Kiley, *Colossians as Pseudepigraphy* (BS 4; Sheffield: JSOT Press, 1986), 46.

46. J. Jervell, "The Letter to Jerusalem," in *The Romans Debate* (ed. K. P. Donfried; 2nd ed.; Peabody, MA: Hendrickson, 1991), 53-64.

47. F. F. Bruce, "The Romans Debate—Continued"; A. J. M. Wedderburn, "Purpose and

Paul wrote to the Roman Christians so that they would welcome him and speed him on his way to Spain (1:11–15; 15:24, 28). A certain amount of rapport was needed with members of that church so that they would be receptive to him and his gospel, since he might well be in need of financial support (prepared by his mention of the collection and his work on behalf of the church in Jerusalem). In the letter, Paul displays many of the features one would expect from a teacher or an apologist. For example, he uses the diatribe, a dialogical form of persuasion used by philosopher-teachers in the Hellenistic world (see chapter 3 §2B). In the epistolary convention, Paul of course writes both sides of the dialogue, but he raises issues, explains ideas, raises objections, and responds to them, all as a way of leading his audience through his argument. Whether one characterizes this as teaching the essentials of the Pauline gospel or as an attempt to provide an apologetic for Christian faith, Paul is seen as creating a useful platform for the continuation of his missionary work in the west. Just as Corinth, Ephesus, and Antioch had provided platforms for his work in the eastern Mediterranean, he envisioned Rome as his platform for moving farther west.

Appreciation of Paul's literary and philosophical techniques is crucial to understanding the way in which he promotes his gospel; nevertheless, there are some legitimate objections to this position. First, Paul seems to be engaging in too heavy a theology for just a simple attempt to say hello and introduce himself to the Romans. Would he not risk an adverse response by the Roman Christians if he touched on some disputed issue or if he, an outsider, delved into the issue of Jewish and Gentile relations? The counterargument is that it is not like Paul to change his approach or be overly concerned with offending his audience. This is one of his great points of consistency. Second, this kind of approach is not consistent with what Paul does elsewhere: he does not lay out his gospel for others to examine for approval. The church at Rome, however, was unique in Paul's experience. Even though he had possibly not visited the church at Colossae, he had at least been instrumental in its evangelization. And although he used other churches as bases, he had either been sent from them or been responsible for bringing the Christian message to them (e.g., Corinth and Ephesus). Now Paul was entering a new phase in his ministry, and perhaps it is a tribute to his abilities that he was able to adjust to the new situation. Third, it is difficult to believe that Paul was so unknown to the church at Rome that it warranted such an extended introduction, unless he had been misrepre-

---

Occasion of Romans Again"; and P. Stuhlmacher, "The Purpose of Romans"—all in *The Romans Debate* (ed. K. P. Donfried; 2nd ed.; Peabody, MA: Hendrickson, 1991), 175–93, 195–202, 231–42. On the apologetic or protreptic letter, see Guerra, *Romans and the Apologetic Tradition*, following D. E. Aune, "Romans as a *Logos Protreptikos*," in *Romans Debate*, 278–96.

sented to the Romans by others and felt a need to clarify his gospel. If he were that unknown, it seems likely that he would have needed more than simply the letter to the Romans to serve as an introduction. Fourth, the references to his visit to Rome are, at best, vague (1:11–13; 15:24, 28). Indeed, his plans seem to center more on Spain and less on Rome. Rome appears only incidental as a place that he would be visiting as he passed through to the west.

f. Providing the Roman Church with an Apostolic Grounding

Günter Klein argues that Paul wrote Romans as a letter to refound the church so that it would have an apostolic grounding to which it could point.[48] According to this position, Paul views some churches as full and complete, and others he does not. Paul says in 15:20 that he does not build upon another's foundation, but this can be reconciled with 1:15 and his eagerness to preach in Rome if it is seen that the church does not in fact have the kind of foundation that he sees as necessary for an apostolic church.

There are several substantive objections to this position, however. First, it is difficult to quantify what exactly the Roman church would lack by not having an apostolic foundation such as outlined by Klein. For example, Paul says in the letter that they are full of knowledge, capable, and proclaimers of the faith (1:6–16; 15:14–23). In fact, in 1:6, Paul characterizes the Romans as being "among" the Gentiles who have become obedient to the faith, making it unlikely that he is distinguishing them in any meaningful way. Second, even if it could be proven from Romans that Paul is forcefully asserting his apostolic authority (which he does not appear to be emphasizing; see 1:12), this would not necessarily mean that he is doing so to found or refound the church there. The evidence of such a refounding is absent. Third, no other situation similar to Klein's reconstruction—where a church has no apostolic founding and is seen to have some form of liability or detriment as a result—is found in the New Testament.

g. Gentile and Jewish Relations

Two major theories hold that the purpose of Romans is tied up with Gentile and Jewish relations.

i. The first depends upon the scenario suggested by Baur about the divide in early Christianity between Petrine, or Jewish, and Hellenistic, or Pauline,

---

48. G. Klein, "Paul's Purpose in Writing the Epistle to the Romans," in *The Romans Debate* (ed. K. P. Donfried; 2nd ed.; Peabody, MA: Hendrickson, 1991), 29–43.

elements.[49] This position argues that the letter was the earliest support for this great Gentile church in Rome, opposing the Jewish Christians there. According to this theory, Paul wanted to be able to deliver the picture of a unified Gentile Christianity when he presented his collection in Jerusalem, so this letter has nothing to do with Rome per se but with Rome as a church of Gentiles to which Paul can point as a noteworthy and significant success in support of his position as representative of the Hellenistic side of the equation.

As much truth as there may be to the conflict between Jewish and Hellenistic elements in the early church, there are limitations to this position. First, there are too many specific references in the letter for it to be unconcerned with the church at Rome (see, e.g., 1:8–15; 13:1–7; 14:1–15:33). Second, there are also too many references to the Jews, including lengthy discussion in Rom 9–11, for a letter that is merely designed to present a unified picture of Gentile Christianity. Third, no other letter does this, making it difficult to posit that Romans figures into a strategy for which it is the only evidence. Fourth, if the dispute in the early church is primarily an ethnic one, why is the issue not addressed in this way? Far too much is comprehensive in scope, including description of Jews and Gentiles in religious terms, to provide an argument that this letter is concerned only to promote the Hellenistic side of the argument.

ii. The second theory holding that Romans concerns Gentile and Jewish relations is represented by Minear and Watson and was discussed in §2C2 above. This position argues that divergent communities are being addressed, possibly the weak (Jewish) and the strong (Gentile), according to Watson, or groups differing in status, according to Minear. This theory takes seriously the conditional and contingent nature of the Pauline writings, and the specific references within the letter, especially those in the paraenetic section. According to this position, Paul perhaps gives something to each side in the dispute. For example, the Jews are allowed to retain pride in Abraham, while the Gentiles can see themselves as grafted onto the tree that Israel once solely occupied. The goal is to establish unity "in Christ," in that even though all are sinners, they share the same gospel.

There are two major objections to this reconstruction (besides those

49. Various forms of this view are held by R. Jewett, "Following the Argument of Romans," in *The Romans Debate* (ed. K. P. Donfried; 2nd ed.; Peabody, MA: Hendrickson, 1991), 265–77; W. S. Campbell, "Romans III as a Key to the Structure and Thought of Romans," in *Romans Debate*, 251–64, repr. in his *Paul's Gospel in an Intercultural Context* (Studies in the Intercultural History of Christianity 69; Frankfurt: Peter Lang, 1992), 25–42; and K. P. Donfried, "False Presuppositions in the Study of Romans," in *Romans Debate*, 102–24.

noted in §2C2). First, this theory does not seem to offer help in understanding the book of Romans until Rom 14–15. Interpreting the weak and the strong as referring to Jews and Gentiles leaves the vast bulk of the letter unexplained. Second, it is not clear that the weak and the strong are being addressed as divergent communities. The issue of what it means to be "in Christ" is addressed, but not enough is known of the composition of the church to make firm equations with particular groups.

h. Anti-Imperial Rhetoric

Many approaches to Romans draw upon ancient rhetoric as a means of analysis.[50] However, some recent scholarship argues that the letter to the Romans was a piece of anti-Roman rhetoric, that is, consciously constructed to persuade the Roman readers of the evils of Roman imperialism. N. T. Wright in fact heralds treatments of the imperial world out of which Paul's message arose as the "most exciting developments" in contemporary Pauline study.[51] Roman rule was about both power and symbols. The power was overtly demonstrated by the brutal army, but was symbolized by the city of Rome and the emperor. The emperor was both the political and the spiritual leader of the nation. In 9 BC, a number of cities in Asia Minor erected inscriptions commemorating the birth of Caesar Augustus. They commended his auspicious birth, addressed him as Lord, and gave thanks for the good news that accompanied announcement of his birth. In the letter to the Romans, Paul writes regarding the Lord Jesus Christ (1:4), who is seen to be both human (1:3) and the divine son of God (1:4, 7). This is the "good news" (1:1) of God that Paul wishes to bring to the Roman Christians. According to this position, Paul writes a letter to the heart of the Roman Empire in which he directly confronts the lordship of Caesar with the real son of God.[52]

There is much discussion regarding recent attempts to find primarily political purposes in writing the letter to the Romans, with scholars divided over the issue. This is part of a much larger discussion regarding the relationship of all of the writings of the New Testament to anti-imperialism. The specific objections regarding Romans are three. The first is that, whereas Paul may in the opening

50. E.g., B. Witherington, *Paul's Letter to the Romans: A Socio-Rhetorical Commentary* (with D. Hyatt; Grand Rapids: Eerdmans 2004); and R. Jewett, *Romans: A Commentary* (Hermeneia; Minneapolis: Fortress, 2007).

51. N. T. Wright, "Paul's Gospel and Caesar's Empire," in *Paul and Politics: Ekklesia, Israel, Imperium, Interpretation* (ed. R. A. Horsley; Harrisburg, PA: Trinity, 2000): 160–83, citing 160.

52. See S. E. Porter, "Paul Confronts Caesar with the Good News," in *Empire in the New Testament* (ed. S. E. Porter and C. L. Westfall; McMaster New Testament Studies; Eugene, OR: Pickwick, 2011), 164–96.

of Romans (and the major ideas noted above are all found in 1:1–7) address his letter to the heart of Rome by using terminology that would resonate with his audience, the rest of the letter focuses upon other, distinctly Christian issues. However one wishes to characterize these issues, they are related to Paul's message of the good news regarding justification, reconciliation, life in the Spirit, and other matters—not the Roman Empire. The second objection is that when Paul addresses matters that seem to be of concern to him regarding the Christians in Rome, he focuses not upon Rome but upon matters of Jewish–Gentile relations (14:1–15:13) and other, related issues. These are issues that had currency within the Roman context, but were not matters directly related to confronting Roman power. The third objection is that, if Paul was greatly concerned with Roman imperialism and the Roman Christians, then it is unclear why he places going to Jerusalem as a higher priority than visiting them, and why he wishes to use Rome—the seat of the enemy—as a support base, not to confront Rome, but to launch his further missionary ventures in Spain.

There is no consensus regarding the purpose of Paul's writing the letter to the Romans; nevertheless, several important points must be kept in mind. First, its status as a letter—a real letter written to a genuine Christian community—must be maintained. This is important for studying any of the letters, but Romans in particular, since so little is known of the relationship between the church and Paul. Second, one cannot avoid the confrontation with major theological categories in this letter. Not all of Paul's theology may be discussed in it, but much important theology is. Apparently, since the letter reflects beliefs that he considers very important, he structures his argument differently from any of his other letters. By doing so, he does come close to systematically presenting his theology. Nevertheless, there is also no harm in stating that there may be no *single* purpose of Paul in writing this letter but that his purpose is multifaceted; perhaps there were a number of reasons why Paul felt compelled to write this letter to them. This may explain why interpreters have various options that they debate; it may be that many of these purposes are true to varying degrees.[53]

E. Textual Issues in Romans

As noted in the above discussion, several major text-critical issues have direct bearing on understanding Romans. These merit at least brief mention, as they are directly related to the purpose of the letter.

---

53. Cf. Longenecker, *Introducing Romans*, 157–60, who provides a fivefold purpose of Paul in writing Romans.

1. Romans 15–16

Romans 15–16 is in nearly every manuscript of Romans, but the question still remains of whether these chapters belong there (e.g., a Latin summary of Codex Amiatinus does not describe 15:1–16:24; Tertullian's *Against Marcion* seems to imply that Marcion did not know Rom 15–16; and the descriptions of some other manuscripts seem to imply that Rom 16 was missing).[54] The difficulty is suggested by the placement of the doxology, which is usually found in 16:25–27 but is also sometimes found in other places in various manuscripts (e.g., after Rom 16 only; after both Rom 14 and Rom 16; after Rom 14 only, with and without Rom 16; and after Rom 15 only). Its movable placement suggests that there were different versions of the letter, to which other chapters may have been added. The textual debate concerns how to account for versions that may have had only Rom 1–14 or Rom 1–15, if in fact they ever existed.[55] (This textual issue is considered by some as the most complex in the entire New Testament.) Compounding the difficulty is the content of Rom 16, which includes a surprisingly large number of people to be greeted, especially since Paul had never been to the church at Rome. How would Paul know these people? Usually he does not greet those he does not know. Who are these people? There is speculation regarding a few of them, but for the most part, they are unknown, even though some of the names were popular in the Hellenistic world.[56] Paul had not been to Rome, but he had spent a long time in Ephesus (over two years according to Acts 19). Indeed, Priscilla and Aquila, mentioned in Rom 16:3, are last seen in Ephesus in Acts 18:19, and Paul calls Epaenetus in Rom 16:5 the "first convert in Asia" (Ephesus was capital of the Roman province of Asia). These points of connection suggest a relationship of Rom 16 to Ephesus (see the views of Manson and others in §2D2b).

The textual evidence in Romans suggests a number of possible forms of the original letter.[57]

a. *Romans 1–16 as the Entire Letter.* In a lengthy and informative treatment of the issues, Harry Gamble maintains that a consensus has been reached

54. See Moo, *Romans*, 6, who includes a chart of the major manuscripts; cf. Bruce, *Romans*, 26–27, who quotes the ending of Codex Amiatinus.

55. D. C. Parker, *An Introduction to the New Testament Manuscripts and Their Texts* (Cambridge: Cambridge University Press, 2008), 270–74; and Longenecker, *Introducing Romans*, 19–30.

56. See Lampe, "Roman Christians," 222–29; and *From Paul to Valentinus*, 153–83.

57. See H. Gamble Jr., *The Textual History of the Letter to the Romans* (Studies and Documents 42; Grand Rapids: Eerdmans, 1977), 127–42, esp. 141, who summarizes the various positions and their advocates.

that Rom 1–16 constitutes the letter to the Romans,[58] although some say that the doxology found at 16:25-27 was added later, perhaps by Marcion, to supply a suitable ending. This is the position that I find most convincing and from which my analysis is taken (believing that the doxology was original).

b. *Romans 1–16 Abbreviated to a Circular Letter of Romans 1–14 or Romans 1–15.* This view maintains the integrity of the original letter (Rom 1–16), as in the first position above, but argues that a later circular letter was created, which consisted of either Rom 1–14 or Rom 1–15.[59] This would account for the problems at 1:7 and 1:15 in a few late manuscripts, where "Rome" is omitted. The problem with this position is that it would mean possibly ending the letter at 14:23, in the middle of an argument that goes all the way to 15:13.[60] Another problem is that it overlooks specific references in 1:8–15 that are picked up near the end of Rom 15. Romans 15:33 is a somewhat better place to end the letter, but then there is no epistolary closing, which it would have been necessary to attach and for which there is no external textual evidence.

c. *Romans 1–14 as a Circular Letter.* It is argued that Rom 1–14 was originally written as a circular letter and then Rom 15 was added later when the letter was sent to Rome.[61] The support for this position supposedly comes from the general nature of the letter apart from Rom 1 and Rom 15–16. But the question is raised why this letter would consist of Rom 1–14, since the letter breaks off in the middle of an argument that goes to 15:13, as noted above about the second position. Furthermore, there is no alternative address to suggest any other recipients. In addition, there is the problem of Rom 16 and where it came from. Was it a letter addressed to Ephesus (see position d below)?

d. *Romans 1–15 as a Circular Letter.* This theory holds that Rom 1–15 was originally written as a circular letter, to which Rom 16, addressed to Ephesus, was attached. According to this position, there are two alternative scenarios. In the first, Rom 16 was the entire letter to the Ephesians, a

---

58. One example is J. A. Fitzmyer, *Romans* (AB 33; New York: Doubleday, 1993), 55–67, with bibliography.

59. J. B. Lightfoot, "The Structure and Destination of the Epistle to the Romans," in *Biblical Essays* (London: Macmillan, 1893), 285–374, esp. 287–320 (315–20) and 352–74; and, more recently, Gamble, *Textual History*, 115–24.

60. Keener, *Romans*, 170n1, states that Paul does not complete the thought in Rom 14 until 15:7 at the earliest.

61. See K. Lake, *The Earlier Epistles of St. Paul: Their Motive and Origin* (London: Rivingtons, 1911), 350–70, who includes a detailed discussion of alternative hypotheses.

small letter that accompanied and served as a cover letter for the larger Rom 1–15.[62] But is it possible that an entire Pauline letter was made up essentially of a list of greetings and other names? The second scenario—one with widespread appeal earlier in the last century—is that Rom 16 was part of a larger letter to the Ephesians and was later attached to Romans.[63] The problem with this theory is that there is no other reference to any other letter (as there is in Col 4:16 regarding the letter to the Laodiceans), and it would be extremely odd for only this part of an Ephesian letter to be kept. This position seems to work too hard to establish the Ephesian connection, on the basis of fairly slender evidence (and perhaps a desire to read the circular letter hypothesis of Ephesians into Romans). Paul had many acquaintances, and they were not necessarily confined to Ephesus (especially since similar names have been found in Rome). It is entirely possible that Priscilla and Aquila had returned from Ephesus to Rome, since they apparently traveled quite a bit (Acts 18:18). In addition, why would such extensive descriptions of the individuals have been provided in the posited letter to the Ephesians, whom Paul would have already known? The elaborate nature of the chapter seems to point away from an Ephesian reception. And again, there is the problem that Rom 15:33 is not the most natural close for a Pauline letter (see position b above).

e. *Romans 1–14 as a Marcionite Letter.* William Sanday and Arthur Cayley Headlam, followed by F. F. Bruce and others, argue that Marcion, the second-century Roman heretic excommunicated in 144, in arguing for a radical form of Christianity with a severe dichotomy between faith and law, may have edited the letter to the Romans.[64] The result of other Marcionite editing appears to have been the exclusion of significant portions of the New Testament that emphasized the Old Testament. The result was a corpus that consisted of an edited form of the Gospel of Luke and ten Pauline letters, excluding the Pastorals and Hebrews. Perhaps Marcion cut Rom 15 because it had too much Old Testament in it, besides objectionable passages (e.g., 15:4, 8, referring to the Old Testament and the Jews). As tempting as this theory is, there is simply too little knowledge of the situation to substantiate it thoroughly, even though Origen states that Marcion abridged Romans at 14:23 (*Commentary on Romans* 14:23

---

62. Manson, "St. Paul's Letter to the Romans," 5–14, followed by some more recent advocates, such as Martin, *Foundations*, 2.194–96.

63. E.g., Moffatt, *Introduction*, 135–39.

64. W. Sanday and A. C. Headlam, *A Critical and Exegetical Commentary on the Epistle to the Romans* (5th ed.; ICC; Edinburgh: T&T Clark, 1902), lxxxv–xcviii, esp. xcvi–xcviii; Bruce, *Romans*, 29; and Moo, *Romans*, 8.

[Patrologia Graeca 14.1290]). There are other texts with no Marcionite influence that have shorter readings. Nevertheless, since many of the early church fathers, such as Tertullian, do not cite Rom 15 and Rom 16, this has continued to be a very attractive explanation.[65]

f. *Romans 1–15 as Catholic Generalization.* This theory argues that the abbreviated form of the letter was a conscious revision done for legitimate purposes of catholic or universal instruction.[66] Because of the more specific Roman content of the final chapter, Rom 16, this theory holds that to use the letter in the wider church without losing valuable material, a shorter form was made for instructional purposes. There are two major problems with this position. The first is that there is little substantive proof that the letter was in fact used in this way. The second is that other Pauline letters with material specific to their intended audiences have not been abbreviated.

2. Doxology

The placement of the doxology (Rom 16:25–27) has proved very important in textual criticism of Romans. That the doxology appears in a variety of places in different manuscripts has given rise to speculation regarding the original integrity of the entire letter.[67] In many of the best and earliest manuscripts (including 𝔓61 and Codices Sinaiticus, Vaticanus, and Ephraemi Rescriptus, and many others), the doxology is found at the end of Rom 16. It is printed there in almost all English Bibles; in the rest, it is printed at the end of Rom 14. The text-critical evidence for its placement in the latter location is very weak, consisting of mostly late manuscripts (Codex Y and the Majority Text). A few manuscripts have it at the end of both Rom 14 and Rom 16 (Codices Alexandrinus and P and others). A third place for the doxology is at the end of Rom 15, as in the important 𝔓46 (ca. 200), the early Alexandrian papyrus. This is the earliest manuscript with the doxology, but it also includes 16:1–23 after the doxology; it is unclear what this indicates. The fourth alternative is for the doxology to be omitted altogether, but this apparently occurs only in a few late manuscripts (Codices F, G, and 629) and in what we know of Marcion's text from Origen's comments on 16:25–27 in his commentary on Romans.

65. See Cranfield, *Romans*, 1.6–7, who cites the church fathers. Tertullian does not appear to know these two chapters in any of his writings.

66. Bruce, *Romans*, 29–30.

67. See Gamble, *Textual History*, 131, for a chart of various manuscripts and the placement of the doxology; and Longenecker, *Introducing Romans*, 34–38.

F. Outline of Romans

A. Opening (1:1–7)
   1. Sender (1:1–6)
   2. Addressee (1:7a)
   3. Greeting (1:7b)
B. Thanksgiving (1:8–17)
   1. Paul's thoughts for the Roman church (1:8–15)
   2. Summary statement of the basis for thanksgiving: justification and sanctification (life) equal reconciliation (1:16–17)
C. Body (1:18–11:36)
   1. Human predicament revealed (1:18–3:20)
   2. Justification as the solution to the human sinful (legal) condition (3:21–4:25)
   3. Reconciliation as fulfillment of justification and anticipation of sanctification (5:1–21)
   4. Sanctification for the Christian believer (6:1–8:39)
   5. God's faithfulness despite Israel's rejection (9:1–11:36)
D. Paraenesis (12:1–15:33)
   1. Individual behavior (12:1–13:14)
   2. Group behavior (14:1–15:13)
   3. Apostolic presence (15:14–33)
E. Closing (16:1–27)
   1. Commendation and greetings (16:1–16)
   2. Closing warning (16:17–20)
   3. Personal greetings (16:21–23)
   4. Doxology (16:[24]–27)

G. Content of Romans

Opening (1:1–7)

One of the longest openings of Paul's letters appears in his letter to the Romans. Paul identifies himself as a servant of Christ Jesus, an apostle who has been called and set apart for the gospel. The rest of this opening introduces the gospel to them, that it was promised beforehand in the Scriptures, concerning his Son, a descendant of David, who displayed his power by his resurrection. It is through Christ that they have received grace and apostleship to bring about obedience to the faith. He writes to those in Rome who are loved by God and called to be saints.

Thanksgiving (1:8–17)

Paul gives thanks for the Romans because of the reputation of faith they had all over the world. He constantly makes mention of them in his prayers, hoping that he will be able to visit them one day. His desire to see them is due to his desire to impart some sort of spiritual gift to them in order to strengthen them, so they could be mutually encouraged. He had attempted to visit them before but was prevented, because he wanted to benefit from them as well as the rest of the Gentiles—this may be an indication that he was writing to at least a significant number of Gentiles in Rome. But he is also eager to preach the gospel to them, because he is unashamed of the gospel, since it is the power of God to save everyone who believes, to the Jews first but also to Greeks. In the theme statement of the letter, Paul offers a summary of the basis for thanksgiving, using a quotation from the Old Testament: the righteousness of God is revealed by faith to those who believe, and by such faith a righteous person can expect to live, what Paul means by reconciliation in relationship to God. Paul goes on, then, to expound this grand idea even further in the body of the letter.

Body: Human Predicament Revealed (1:18–3:20)

Paul begins the body of the letter by explaining the plight of humanity, that the wrath of God is revealed against the ungodliness and unrighteousness of humanity, who suppresses the truth. God has made himself evident to them in all of creation, but humanity has become futile in their thinking and traded the glory of the Creator for the lesser glory of created things. Because of this, God has allowed humanity to indulge in their sinfulness, including sexual immorality and all kinds of unrighteousness. They not only practice these things, but give approval to others who practice them.

Considering this truth, then, Paul tells the Romans that they have no excuse in judging others, since they themselves have formerly lived in that manner. God will judge everyone according to their works; those who seek (God's) glory, honor, and immortality will inherit eternal life, and those who seek self-approval and obey unrighteousness will obtain wrath and fury. Regardless of whether they have the law or whether they are a law to themselves, they are judged for what they do. He addresses the Jews in the group, those who teach others to obey the law, and asks them whether they themselves obey the law. Circumcision is of value, he says, but if that is the only law they obey while disregarding other laws, their circumcision means nothing.

In developing further his argument regarding the plight of humanity, Paul uses elements of the diatribe (see chapter 3 §2B; however, diatribe is characteristic all throughout the letter) and asks what advantage the Jew has, then, and what value circumcision is. He answers that there is actually much value, since the Jews were the first to receive the words of God. But their benefit does not mean they are exonerated in regard to their unrighteousness, since whether one is a Jew or a Gentile, all are under sin. Citing Ps 14 and Ps 53, Paul declares that no one is righteous, no one does good, and no one seeks after God. Even if someone should try to be justified by the law, it will not happen, since, through the law, one simply obtains knowledge of sin but is unable to fulfill that law.

Body: Justification as the Solution to the Human Sinful (Legal) Condition (3:21–4:25)

The solution to the plight of humanity is the righteousness of God obtained through faith in Jesus Christ.[68] While humanity is unable to be justified through obedience to the law—since all have sinned and lack the glory of God[69]—they are justified by faith in Christ, by the grace that is given to them through the redemption that is in him. This shows God's righteousness in being both the just and the justifier. This, then, gives no grounds for anyone to boast, because one is justified by faith, not by the law. This does not mean the law is excluded; on the contrary, the law is being upheld.

Continuing the diatribe, Paul asks what was gained by Abraham. Paul reminds his readers that the Scriptures say that Abraham believed in God, and that belief was counted to him as righteousness. Paul traces the relevance of circumcision in Abraham's faith and finds that his faith existed before his circumcision, since it was merely a later sign of what was fulfilled by him in faith. He was to be the father of all those who are not only outwardly circumcised,

68. The meaning of the Greek phrase "through faith of Jesus Christ" (διὰ πίστεως Ἰησοῦ Χριστοῦ) has been extensively debated in recent decades. The crux of the debate centers on the function of the genitive construction and its subsequent translation in English; that is, whether it should be considered a so-called subjective genitive (so Jesus is the subject of faith: "faith *of* Jesus Christ" or "faithfulness *of* Jesus Christ"), or whether it should be considered a so-called objective genitive (so Jesus is the object of faith: "faith *in* Jesus Christ"). The literature is abundant and growing, but see chapter 4 §2E for an introduction to the matter, and S. E. Porter and A. W. Pitts, "Πίστις with a Preposition and Genitive Modifier," in *The Faith of Jesus Christ: Exegetical, Biblical, and Theological Studies* (ed. M. F. Bird and P. M. Sprinkle; Peabody, MA: Hendrickson, 2009), 33–53, where we believe that we have linguistically solved the issue. We make the case that parallel instances involving the construction of preposition + "faith" + "Christ" (of course, in Greek), without an intervening article, always indicate the so-called objective relationship in the New Testament.

69. Cf. W. V. Cirafesi, "'To Fall Short' or 'To Lack'? Reconsidering the Meaning and Translation of Ὑστερέω in Romans 3:23," *Expository Times* 123 (2012): 429–34.

but those who walk in faith as he walked in faith. The promise to Abraham, that he would become the heir of the world, was given to him and his offspring not through the law but through faith. Abraham is the prime example of one who in faith obeyed God. He is the father of all, not only those who adhere to the law but those who have faith.

Body: Reconciliation as Fulfillment of Justification and Anticipation of Sanctification (5:1–21)

As a result of their justification by faith, they are to enjoy peace with God through Jesus Christ.[70] This justification results in access by faith into this grace, and they should boast in the glory of God. Not only that, but they should boast in their suffering, which produces endurance, which in turn produces character, which produces hope; and hope does not disappoint or bring them shame because God's love abounds. This love is seen in that while they were weak and sinful, Christ died for the ungodly, those who do not deserve it. Because of Christ's death, they have been saved from God's wrath (as mentioned in Rom 1) and have been reconciled to him.

In explicating Christ's reconciliation further, Paul explains how sin, and consequently death, entered into the world through the one man Adam, and how life is received by the one man Jesus Christ. Sin brought judgment and condemnation, but the one act of righteousness brought justification. One man's disobedience resulted in many being sinners, while one man's obedience made many righteous. Where sin abounds, because of the law, grace abounds even more.[71]

Body: Sanctification for the Christian Believer (6:1–8:39)

This, however, does not mean that the Roman Christians should continue in sin so that grace abounds even more. Paul rhetorically asks, how can one who died to sin still live in sin? Those who have been united with him in death are also

---

70. The significant discussion in this verse is the textual question of whether the original reading is the indicative ἔχομεν ("we have") or the subjunctive ἔχωμεν ("let us have"). Both the strong external manuscript evidence and the possibility of making sense of Paul's argument argue for the subjunctive reading; see S. E. Porter, "The Argument of Romans 5: Can a Rhetorical Question Make a Difference?" *JBL* 110 (1991): 655–77, esp. 662–65. This was recently endorsed by Jewett, *Romans*, 344.

71. It is argued that Rom 5 serves as the "peak" or the central part of Paul's argument in Rom 1–8; cf. J. H. Lee, *Paul's Gospel in Romans: A Discourse Analysis of Rom 1:16–8:39* (LBS 3; Leiden: Brill, 2010), 431–44.

united with him in life, and this means that those who are in Christ are no longer alive to sin, since they have been set free from sin. So Paul tells his readers not to let sin reign in them and not to obey its desires. Since they are under grace and no longer under law, sin should not have any rule over them. Continuing his diatribe, Paul asks if they should sin since they are no longer under law but under grace. Of course not, he says, because they are slaves to whomever they obey, and since they are slaves to righteousness and not sin, they should not obey sin any longer. They previously were slaves to sin, and they were not obligated by the law; but now they are slaves to righteousness and are no longer to obey sin.

Using the analogy of marriage to further his case, Paul states that the law binds a marriage only until one of the spouses dies; in that case, the living spouse is no longer under the law of marriage and is free to remarry. Similarly, those who have died to the law are now to belong to another, Jesus, who has defeated death, so that they would live in righteousness. The law is not sin, however, but through the law, they come to know sin, since the law specifies what sin is. The law showed what is holy, righteous, and good, but its effect upon them has been to create desires against it. The law does not produce death, but sin does. Paul speaks in the first person in this section to state the conflict between the good that is desired and the sin that is undesirable, and that committing sin seems to prevail over doing good.[72] He says, "For I do not do the good I want, but the evil I do not want is what I do" (7:19 NRSV). The conflict between "want" and "do" is evident in this passage.

Paul explains, however, that there is no condemnation for those in Christ Jesus, because the law of the Spirit of life has set them free from the law of sin and death. God has accomplished what the law could not do; he sent his Son to fulfill the requirements of the law for them so that those requirements would be fulfilled in them. Paul contrasts the flesh with the Spirit, stating that those who walk according to the flesh set their minds on things of the flesh, but those who walk according to the Spirit set their minds on things of the Spirit. Setting the mind on flesh leads to death, but setting the mind on the Spirit leads to life and peace. Those who set their mind on the flesh are hostile to God and cannot please God. But Paul reminds his readers that they are not of the flesh but of the Spirit, who dwells in them. And if the Spirit who raised Jesus from the dead is also in them, then the same Spirit will give them life as well.

As a result, they do not owe anything to the flesh, but are called sons of

---

72. Much debate surrounds the meaning of this passage, on the nature of the conflict that Paul presents here, whether he is referring to himself currently, his past conflict, himself as a representative figure, or some other option; cf. Moo, *Romans*, 455–67. I understand it as Paul speaking for himself, as a representative follower of Christ.

God. They have relinquished the spirit of slavery but have instead received the spirit of adoption, by which they call God "Abba Father." As adopted children, they are also heirs of God and fellow sufferers with Christ in order also to be glorified with him. These sufferings, Paul states, are not even comparable to the glory that is to be revealed to them. Creation groans and awaits eagerly for the revealing of who the sons of God are, and, along with creation, they wait eagerly to be fully redeemed, which is where their hope lies. The Spirit also helps them in their weaknesses; at times, when believers do not know what to pray for, the Spirit intercedes for them with groanings too deep for words. Paul assures them that all things work for the good of those who love God and are called according to his purpose. For those whom he foreknew, he also predestined, and those he predestined, he called; those he called, he justified; those he justified, he also glorified.

With that in mind, Paul breaks into doxology, asking, in diatribe form, if God is for them, who can be against them? If God gave his own Son for them, would he withhold anything else, but would he not give them all things? No one can accuse them; no one can condemn them; and neither can anyone separate them from the love of Christ, not even tribulation, hardship, persecution, famine, or anything else. But they are more than conquerors through Christ who loved them, and absolutely nothing else can separate them from the love of God in Christ Jesus.

Body: God's Faithfulness Despite Israel's Rejection (9:1–11:36)

While he rejoices at the benefits of being in Christ, Paul pauses here to consider his fellow compatriots, the Jews, and relays his great sorrow and unceasing anguish for them, since they are the ones who have been given adoption, glory, the covenants, the law, worship, and the promises. He reminds them that just because they descended from Abraham does not mean that they are really children of Abraham. When God promised offspring to Abraham, the promise was not made because of works but because of God; he will have mercy and compassion on whom he will. It does not depend on human effort but on God's mercy. Using a ceramic metaphor, Paul states that God is the potter and his people are clay. His purpose in molding clay is to show the riches of this glory. Whether Jew or Gentile, righteousness is obtained not by pursuing the law but by faith.

But Paul's desire and prayer is that his fellow Jews would be saved. He sees a zeal in them, yet this is a zeal that is not based on knowledge, since they seek to obtain righteousness through their own means rather than by submitting to God's righteousness. Rather than trying to obtain righteousness through the law, the righteousness by faith that results in salvation is obtained by confessing Jesus as Lord and believing that he was raised from the dead. There is no distinction here between Jew or Greek, for everyone who calls on the name of the Lord will be saved. And the way in which one can believe is if someone comes to them and proclaims the good news, the gospel, to them. This faith, then, comes from hearing the word of Christ. Unfortunately, Israel has heard, and yet they have remained a disobedient people.

In spite of this, Paul states that God has not rejected his people, and he cites himself as an example. He himself is a descendant of Abraham and of the tribe of Benjamin. He states that, at the time of his writing, a remnant has been chosen by grace. God has allowed Israel to be disobedient during this time, so that he would bring about the salvation of the Gentiles, and, in doing so, cause Israel to be jealous. Paul rhetorically asks, If Israel's trespass and failure mean riches for the rest of the world, how much more will their inclusion mean?

At this point, Paul addresses the Gentiles in the audience, and admits that, while he considers himself an apostle to the Gentiles, his mission also includes the hope that his fellow Jews will believe. Using another metaphor, this time from botany, Paul identifies some of the branches of Israel who have been cut off (due to their unbelief) and the Gentiles as wild olive shoots who have been grafted in to the olive tree. There is no boasting on these grounds, as they have been grafted in, and it is the root that supports them. But even if the branches who were cut off are grafted in again,[73] the boasting of the wild olive shoots may result in their being cut off as well, since God has the power to graft them in again. To warn his Gentile audience of becoming proud of their calling, he reveals this mystery, that a partial hardening has come upon Israel until the fullness of the Gentiles has come in. In this way, all of Israel will be saved. What God has promised beforehand is irrevocable, and this partial hardening does not mean that God's promises have been laid aside. Paul concludes this discourse on this mystery of God with a doxology, exclaiming how deep the riches and knowledge of God are and how unsearchable his judgments and inscrutable his ways.

Paraenesis: Individual Behavior (12:1–13:14)

Considering all of this, Paul commands his readers to offer their bodies as a living, holy and acceptable sacrifice to God; this is their reasonable (λογικός)

---

73. This may be a third class conditional (ἐάν [if] + subjunctive), which denotes a more probable, general condition; cf. S. E. Porter, *Idioms of the Greek New Testament* (2nd ed.; Biblical Languages: Greek 2; Sheffield: Sheffield Academic, 1994), 261–63.

worship. In other words, in light of all that has been said, the only reasonable response is to worship God by being a living sacrifice (as opposed to the sacrifices that were formerly offered). They were no longer to conform to the ways of the world but to be transformed by the renewing of their minds. They were not to think of themselves as better than they should, but to think with sober judgment. As the physical body contains many different parts that work in conjunction with each other, so the spiritual body contains many members that are of equal value and must work together in unity. Some exercise faith, some service, some exhortation, some teaching, and some other things. They are to have genuine love toward one another in their dealings with one another. This is especially shown in how they deal with being wronged; they are to bless rather than curse those who persecute them, not seeking revenge but trusting in the one who avenges the wronged. On the contrary, they are to do good to those who wrong them.

Paul encourages the Roman Christians to subject themselves to morally upright governing authorities, since they have been set in that position by God (see chapter 1 §5).[74] Since these authorities are representatives of God, they are to submit to them and do what is good. This includes the paying of taxes, revenue, respect, and honor to whom they owe these things. But they are also to owe nothing to anyone except to love one another, which is the sum of the commandments. The time has come for them to wake up and live in the light, no longer in pagan activities like orgies, drunkenness, sexual immorality, sensuality, or quarreling and jealousy, but to put on the Lord Jesus instead.

Paraenesis: Group Behavior (14:1–15:13)

Paul seems to transition here from individual behavior to group behavior, and he exhorts the Roman Christians to welcome the one who is weak in faith and not to quarrel about opinions on dietary and ceremonial issues.[75] If a weaker believer chooses to eat only vegetables or observes certain days over others, none should pass judgment on them but accept that they are serving their master in this way. If one who abstains, abstains to the Lord and one who partakes,

---

74. For defense of understanding these as morally upright authorities, see S. E. Porter, "Romans 13:1–7 as Pauline Political Rhetoric," *Filología Neotestamentaria* 3 (1990): 115–37. I also discuss the unlikelihood of 13:1–7 being a later interpolation, a position perhaps argued because interpreters fail to understand the passage correctly and hesitate to accept their incorrect interpretation (calling for absolute obedience).

75. For discussion of this passage and alternative views, see M. Reasoner, *The Strong and the Weak: Romans 14.1–15.13 in Context* (SNTSMS 103; Cambridge: Cambridge University Press, 1999).

partakes to the Lord, this is what is taken into account before God. Passing judgment on these matters becomes, then, a hindrance to the weaker believer, even though Paul knows that nothing is unclean if it is of the Lord. But if a fellow believer is grieved by their freedom to eat so-called unclean foods, one should not eat them, in order to love the weaker believer. The kingdom of God is not a matter of eating and drinking, but a matter of righteousness, peace, and joy in the Spirit, and these matters should not get in the way of pursuing these greater things.

Thus, Paul states that stronger believers have a duty to bear with the weaker believers in order to build them up. The greater purpose is to build up unity and harmony, so that, with one voice, they will glorify God together. Quoting the Jewish Scriptures, Paul gives them the example of Jesus, who became a servant to the circumcised in order to confirm the promises to the patriarchs so that the Gentiles might glorify God as well.

Paraenesis: Apostolic Presence (15:14–33)

In spite of these commands, Paul encourages his readers that he is satisfied with them and that they are full of goodness, knowledge, and ability to instruct one another. He explains that his boldness about some matters earlier in the letter was a simple reminder to them of his duty as a minister of the gospel of Christ. He speaks only what Christ has accomplished through him to bring the Gentiles to obedience, from Jerusalem as far as Illyricum. His goal is to preach Christ, not where he has already been proclaimed, but to those who have never heard.

Paul explains that this is what has prevented him from visiting Rome. However, since he does not have any more room to work in these regions, he is able to fulfill his desire to come see them on the way to Spain, hoping that they will also help him on his journey there. He is, however, going to visit Jerusalem first to help the saints there, as the churches in Macedonia and Achaia have contributed to their needs (referring to delivering the collection he mentions in the letters to the Galatians and Corinthians). Once he has fulfilled that need, he will make his way to Rome and then on to Spain. He asks for prayer at this time, that while in Judea and Jerusalem he would not be hindered by the unbelievers there and that his service in Jerusalem will be accepted without complications.

Closing (16:1–27)

This is a longer closing than in Paul's other letters (see §E1 above), and Paul begins it by commending to them Phoebe, a deacon (διάκονος) of the church at Cenchrea and the one who probably delivered this letter to Rome. They were also to greet many others, including Prisca (Priscilla) and Aquila, Paul's fellow workers, who risked their lives for him, as well as their home church. They were to greet Epaenetus (the first convert in Asia), Mary (who worked hard for them), Andronicus and Junia,[76] his kinspeople and fellows prisoners, among others. How Paul knew all of these people in Rome is a mystery, but it may be evidence of how many and how often people traveled in the ancient Roman world, and how Paul and his ministry were widely known.

Paul closes with a warning against those who cause division and hinder the doctrine that they were once taught. These people do not serve Christ but their own selfish motives, and although the obedience of the Romans was well known, he still wants them to be wise as to what is good, but innocent as to evil. He assures them God will quickly crush Satan under their feet.

He informs them that Timothy sends greetings, as well as Lucius, Jason, and Sospater. At this point, Tertius identifies himself as Paul's amanuensis and greets them, as do Gaius, Erastus, and Quartus. Paul ends this letter with a benediction: glory be forever to God, who is able to strengthen them with the gospel, according to the mystery that has now been revealed through the prophetic writings and now to all nations, so that all would be obedient in faith.

Sources for Further Study

Commentaries

Barrett, C. K. *A Commentary on the Epistle to the Romans*. BNTC. London: A&C Black, 1957.

Black, M. *Romans*. NCB. Grand Rapids: Eerdmans, 1973.

Bruce, F. F. *Romans*. Rev. ed. TNTC. Grand Rapids: Eerdmans, 1985.

Cranfield, C. E. B. *A Critical and Exegetical Commentary on the Epistle to the Romans*. 2 vols. ICC. Edinburgh: T&T Clark, 1975–79.

Dodd, C. H. *The Epistle of Paul to the Romans*. Moffatt New Testament Commentary. London: Hodder & Stoughton, 1932.

Dunn, J. D. G. *Romans*. 2 vols. WBC 38A–B. Dallas: Word, 1988.

Fitzmyer, J. A. *Romans*. AB 33. New York: Doubleday, 1993.

Jewett, R. *Romans: A Commentary*. Hermeneia. Minneapolis: Fortress, 2007.

---

76. Some textual issues here may have implications for who Junia/Junias really was; cf. E. J. Epp, *Junia: The First Woman Apostle* (Minneapolis: Fortress, 2005). She almost assuredly was a woman, despite the pleading of others.

Käsemann, E. *Commentary on Romans*. Translated by G. W. Bromiley. Grand Rapids: Eerdmans, 1980.

Keener, C. S. *Romans: A New Covenant Commentary*. New Covenant Commentary. Eugene, OR: Cascade, 2009.

Kruse, C. G. *Paul's Letter to the Romans*. PNTC. Grand Rapids: Eerdmans, 2012.

Leenhardt, F. J. *The Epistle to the Romans: A Commentary*. Translated by H. Knight. London: Lutterworth, 1961.

Moo, D. J. *The Epistle to the Romans*. NICNT. Grand Rapids: Eerdmans, 1996.

Morris, L. *The Epistle to the Romans*. PNTC. Grand Rapids: Eerdmans, 1988.

Murray, J. *The Epistle to the Romans*. 2 vols. in 1. NICNT. Grand Rapids: Eerdmans, 1968.

O'Neill, J. C. *Paul's Letter to the Romans*. Harmondsworth, England: Penguin, 1975.

Osborne, G. R. *Romans*. IVP New Testament Commentary Series. Downers Grove, IL: InterVarsity, 2004.

Porter, S. E. *The Letter to the Romans: A Linguistic and Literary Commentary*. NTM 37. Sheffield: Sheffield Phoenix, 2015.

Sanday, W., and A. C. Headlam. *A Critical and Exegetical Commentary on the Epistle to the Romans*. 5th ed. ICC. Edinburgh: T&T Clark, 1902.

Schlatter, A. *Romans: The Righteousness of God*. Translated by S. S. Schatzmann. Peabody, MA: Hendrickson, 1995.

Stuhlmacher, P. *Paul's Letter to the Romans: A Commentary*. Louisville: Westminster John Knox, 1994.

Waetjen, H. C. *The Letter to the Romans: Salvation as Justice and the Deconstruction of Law*. NTM 32. Sheffield: Sheffield Phoenix, 2011.

Witherington, B., with D. Hyatt. *Paul's Letter to the Romans: A Socio-Rhetorical Commentary*. Grand Rapids: Eerdmans 2004.

Ziesler, J. *Paul's Letter to the Romans*. London: SCM, 1989.

Monographs and Books

Donfried, K. P., ed. *The Romans Debate*. Rev. ed. Peabody, MA: Hendrickson, 1991.

Gamble, H., Jr. *The Textual History of the Letter to the Romans*. Studies and Documents 42. Grand Rapids: Eerdmans, 1977.

Guerra, A. J. *Romans and the Apologetic Tradition: The Purpose, Genre, and Audience of Paul's Letter*. SNTSMS 81. Cambridge: Cambridge University Press, 1995.

Haacker, K. *The Theology of Paul's Letter to the Romans*. NTT. Cambridge: Cambridge University Press, 1995.

Jeffers, J. S. *Conflict at Rome: Social Order and Hierarchy in Early Christianity*. Minneapolis: Fortress, 1991.

Jervis, L. A. *The Purpose of Romans: A Comparative Letter Structure Investigation.* JSNTSup 55. Sheffield: JSOT Press, 1991.

Lampe, P. *From Paul to Valentinus: Christians at Rome in the First Two Centuries.* Minneapolis: Fortress, 2003.

Lee, J. H. *Paul's Gospel in Romans: A Discourse Analysis of Rom 1:16–8:39.* LBS 3. Leiden: Brill, 2010.

Leon, H. J. *The Jews of Ancient Rome.* Rev. ed. Peabody, MA: Hendrickson, 1995.

Longenecker, R. N. *Introducing Romans: Critical Issues in Paul's Most Famous Letter.* Grand Rapids: Eerdmans, 2011.

Minear, P. S. *The Obedience of Faith: The Purpose of Paul in the Epistle to the Romans.* London: SCM, 1971.

Morgan, R. *Romans.* NTG. Sheffield: Sheffield Academic, 1995.

Nanos, M. D. *The Mystery of Romans: The Jewish Context of Paul's Letter.* Minneapolis: Fortress, 1996.

Reasoner, M. *The Strong and the Weak: Romans 14.1–15.13 in Context.* SNTSMS 103. Cambridge: Cambridge University Press, 1999.

Song, C. *Reading Romans as a Diatribe.* Studies in Biblical Literature 59. New York: Peter Lang, 2004.

Stowers, S. K. *A Rereading of Romans: Justice, Jews, and Gentiles.* New Haven: Yale University Press, 1994.

Walters, J. C. *Ethnic Issues in Paul's Letter to the Romans: Changing Self-Definitions in Earliest Roman Christianity.* Valley Forge, PA: Trinity, 1993.

Watson, F. *Paul, Judaism, and the Gentiles: Beyond the New Perspective.* Rev. and exp. ed. Grand Rapids: Eerdmans, 2007.

Wedderburn, A. J. M. *The Reasons for Romans.* Edinburgh: T&T Clark, 1988.

11

Prison Epistles: Philippians, Colossians, Philemon, and Ephesians

1. Introduction

This chapter discusses all of the letters (apart from 2 Timothy) that are usually called the Prison Epistles: Philippians, Colossians, Philemon, and Ephesians. The Prison Epistles (as discussed in chapter 2 §3) are letters that are placed together on the supposition that all of them were written while Paul was in prison. As is indicated in the discussion below, as well as previous discussion (e.g., in chapters 2 §2 and 6 §2), many scholars do not consider all of these letters to be authentically Pauline. Those often considered deutero-Pauline are Ephesians and Colossians. The further issue is whether one can speak of a single imprisonment, especially in light of perceived differences among the Prison Epistles (Philippians usually stands out from the others). The major issues are discussed below, taking all of the Prison Epistles as a group of authentic Pauline letters written from a single imprisonment, probably in Rome. I treat them in the order of Philippians, Colossians, Philemon, and Ephesians.

2. Philippians

Philippians is a well-loved Pauline letter, because of its Christ hymn (2:6–11). However, a number of critical issues regarding Philippians sometimes preoccupy scholars, rather than appreciating its positive and encouraging message from Paul to a beloved church. I first discuss the city of Philippi, and then treat authorship, literary integrity, the opponents, occasion, and purpose, and date and place of writing, before concluding with an outline and its content.

A. *City of Philippi*

The city of Philippi was located in the eastern part of the Roman province of Macedonia.[1] It was not, properly speaking, a Greek city (as Greece was in the Roman province of Achaia), but because Macedonia and Greece proper had been under common control since the time of Alexander the Great's father, Philip II of Macedon, it was seen as Greek.

The city was named after Alexander the Great's father, who began the campaigns that led to his son's massive conquests. It was built upon the site of a small market town called Krenides, which may mean "well" or "spring." In 356 BC Philip captured Krenides and renamed it after himself. This became a greatly expanding city on what became the Via Egnatia (the road that eventually stretched from the Adriatic Sea to Philippi to Byzantium), with gold mines forming the basis of a prosperous economy (Strabo, *Geography* 7 fragment 34). In 42 BC Antony and Octavian (who became Augustus Caesar in 27 BC) defeated Brutus and Cassius at Philippi, and from that time retired Roman soldiers were routinely settled there (Strabo, *Geography* 7 fragment 41).[2]

This settlement continued after Octavian defeated Antony and Cleopatra at the battle of Actium in 31 BC. The population of the city was composed of a mix of native Macedonians, Greeks, and Romans who emigrated to Philippi. As an Augustan colony (Acts 16:12), Philippi was one of the four most important in the region and by the third century was under the *jus italicum* (Italian law), the law that gave the colony the same rights as those in Italy. The strong Roman presence is indicated by 85 percent of the inscriptions found at Philippi from around the first century being in Latin and only 15 percent in Greek. This is unusual for a Greco-Roman city of the time, because Greek was the lingua franca in Philippi as elsewhere, at least in most of the eastern part of the empire (Greek inscriptions are better represented in Jerusalem than they are at Philippi!). This may indicate that Paul had some facility in Latin[3] before traveling to Illyricum

1. See D. W. J. Gill, "Macedonia," in *The Book of Acts in Its Graeco-Roman Setting* (ed. D. W. J. Gill and C. Gempf; BAFCS 2; Grand Rapids: Eerdmans, 1994), 397–417, esp. 411–13; R. P. Martin, *Philippians* (NCB; Grand Rapids: Eerdmans, 1976), 2–9; H. L. Hendrix, "Philippi," *ABD* 5.313–17; and, for a very important and thorough treatment, P. Pilhofer, *Philippi*, vol. 1: *Die erste christliche Gemeinde Europas* (WUNT 87; Tübingen: Mohr-Siebeck, 1995) and *Philipi*, vol. 2: *Katalog der Inschriften von Philippi* (WUNT 119; Tübingen: Mohr-Siebeck, 2000), especially on the inscriptional evidence.

2. On the army, see J. B. Campbell, *The Emperor and the Roman Army, 31 B.C.–A.D. 235* (Oxford: Clarendon, 1984).

3. On the Latin language, see S. E. Porter, "Latin Language," in *Dictionary of New Testament Background* (ed. C. A. Evans and S. E. Porter; Downers Grove, IL: InterVarsity, 2000), 630–31. On Paul's possible abilities with it, see S. E. Porter, "Did Paul Speak Latin?" in *Paul: Jew,*

(western Balkan region), a major Latin-speaking area of the empire (see Rom 15:19). Nevertheless, when writing to the Philippian Christians, Paul used Greek.

The religious climate of Philippi was syncretistic, as one might expect in a city that drew its population so widely from the surrounding Roman world. There is inscriptional and historical evidence for a variety of cults. These include those of the traditional Greek gods, various oriental cults such as Serapis and Isis, and the imperial cult.[4] The Acts account of Paul's visit to the city makes no mention of Paul beginning his missionary efforts by visiting a synagogue, although 16:13 refers to a "place of prayer" (προσευχή) where women congregated. There is widespread debate on whether to understand "place of prayer" as a synagogue. Some scholars argue that "place of prayer" was the way that Diaspora Judaism referred to its formal gatherings, while other scholars argue that the place was simply a place of prayer, possibly because there were insufficient men to convene a synagogue.[5] There is other evidence that there was a significant amount of henotheism in Philippi,[6] which may have made Paul's message more attractive to some of the city's inhabitants.[7] The incident in Acts with the fortunetelling slave girl (16:16–24) may give some indication of the kinds of superstitious beliefs present in the city.

The church at Philippi was founded on Paul's second missionary journey (16:11–40) as a result of his vision in which a man of Macedonia begged him to come to Macedonia to help its inhabitants (16:9). Paul's entry into Macedonia marked the beginning of his missionary endeavor in what we now call Europe. It is difficult to determine whether Paul and his companions were the first missionaries in Europe, but this may have been the case (see chapter 10 §2C2). In any event, this marked the beginning of Paul's efforts outside Asia Minor and was a significant turning point in the growth of the Christian movement

Greek, and Roman (ed. S. E. Porter; PAST 5; Leiden: Brill, 2008), 289–308; and H. T. Ong, "Can Linguistic Analysis in Historical Jesus Research Stand on Its Own? A Sociolinguistic Analysis of Matthew 26:36–27:26," *Biblical and Ancient Greek Linguistics* 2 (2013): 109–38, esp. 131.

4. See, e.g., an inscription from Neapolis, the seaport of Philippi (IGR 3.137), conveniently reprinted with other texts in L. R. Taylor, *The Divinity of the Roman Emperor* (Middletown, CT: American Philological Association, 1931; repr. Atlanta: Scholars Press, n.d.), 272.

5. See J. Gutmann, "Synagogue Origins: Theories and Facts," in *Ancient Synagogues: The State of Research* (Brown Judaic Studies 22; Atlanta: Scholars Press, 1981), 3; I. Levinskaya, *The Book of Acts in Its Diaspora Setting* (BAFCS 5; Grand Rapids: Eerdmans, 1996), 207–25. Some pertinent inscriptions are published in W. Horbury and D. Noy, eds., *Jewish Inscriptions of Graeco-Roman Egypt* (Cambridge: Cambridge University Press, 1992).

6. Henotheism is the worship of one god among possible other gods, as opposed to monotheism, which is the belief in the existence of only one god.

7. See C. J. Hemer, *The Book of Acts in Its Hellenistic Setting* (ed. C. Gempf; WUNT 49; Tübingen: Mohr-Siebeck, 1989; repr. Winona Lake, IN: Eisenbrauns, 1990), 231.

into a worldwide religion. On his first visit to Philippi, Paul saw results from his preaching, especially in the conversion of Lydia, originally from Thyatira in Asia Minor (16:11–15; cf. Rev 2:18–29). She is described as a seller of purple. Purple dye was in great demand as a color indicating success and status, and therefore it appears that she was a successful businesswoman. It is likely that Paul's missionary endeavor appealed to the business and professional element of society (see chapter 9 §2E).[8]

The evidence is uncertain, but Paul probably visited Philippi two more times on his travels, both on his third missionary journey. The second of the three times came as he traveled on the outward leg of his journey, which ended up in Greece, probably Corinth. Acts 20:1–2 does not state that Paul actually visited Philippi, but it does say that he traveled through Macedonia. Since Philippi was the major city he had previously visited in the area, it makes sense to think that he again went to Philippi, if only briefly, on this trip. The final time Paul visited Philippi was on the return leg of his third missionary journey. Acts 20:3 says that Paul decided to go back through Macedonia, and 20:6 indicates that he stopped off at Philippi.[9] Nothing more is said of Paul's second and third visits to Philippi, but evidence from the letter to the Philippians indicates that Paul's relationships with the church there continued to be warm and close, with the Philippian church taking an active concern in his ministry (see Phil 4:10–20 on its gift to Paul).

B. Authorship of Philippians

Although questioned in the nineteenth century by Ferdinand Christian Baur,[10] the authorship of Philippians is no longer widely disputed. Philippians is one of the seven current so-called undisputed letters of Paul. Its authenticity can be seen in the way the apostle describes himself (3:5–6); the way the letter conforms to what we know of Pauline chronology (Acts 16:11–40; 20:1–2, 6), Pauline style, and epistolary form; and the letter's conformity with Pauline thought.

---

8. See W. A. Meeks, *The First Urban Christians: The Social World of the Apostle Paul* (New Haven: Yale University Press, 1983); and T. D. Still and D. G. Horrell, eds., *After the First Urban Christians: The Social-Scientific Study of Pauline Christianity Twenty-Five Years Later* (London: T&T Clark, 2009).

9. The reference to the days of Unleavened Bread appears to be an indication of the time of year. It is too vague to provide evidence of Jews at Philippi.

10. F. C. Baur, *Paul the Apostle of Jesus Christ: His Life and Work, His Epistles and His Doctrine* (2 vols.; London: Williams & Norgate, 1873–75; repr. Peabody, MA: Hendrickson, 2003), 2.45–79.

Nevertheless, even for those who attribute the letter to Paul, not all agree that the entire letter was written by Paul to the Philippians at the same time.[11] Consequently, various interpolation and multiple-letter hypotheses are often suggested regarding the letter (see §2C below).

Besides these theories, however, many debate whether the so-called Philippian or Christ hymn at 2:6–11 is authentically Pauline or an early Christian tradition that Paul employed.[12] The supposed hymn, one of the most widely discussed New Testament passages, has a number of words that are unique in the Pauline or New Testament vocabulary, and its pronounced structure and style are not typically Pauline. Some theories posit that Paul incorporated a preformed hymn after adding several portions to conform its theology to his own, such as the reference to death on the cross (2:8).[13] The current debate is inconclusive. Unfortunately, debate over the hymn's origins diverts attention from the major issue: How does Paul use the hymn in Philippians?[14] This beautifully formulated passage contains what is called a tripartite or inverted pyramid formulation (not a two-part structure, as suggested by James Dunn).[15] The passage begins with the proclamation that Christ, though being in the form of God, did not consider equality with God as something to grasp onto. This statement places Christ within the heavenly realm as God's equal. The next stage is the descent of taking earthly form. This is spoken of as taking the form of a slave and becoming in human likeness to the point of the humility of death on a cross. Whether reference to death on the cross is original to the hymn or not, the contrast to his heavenly existence is stark and dramatic. In the third movement, God exalts Christ and gives him the name before which all other creatures bow, indicating a resumption of his initial state. Even for those who agree that there is a tripartite structure to this passage (and most scholars do), there is disagree-

11. W. G. Kümmel, *Introduction to the New Testament* (trans. H. C. Kee; 17th ed.; Nashville: Abingdon, 1975), 332.

12. Cf. J. T. Sanders, *The New Testament Christological Hymns: Their Historical Religious Background* (SNTSMS 15; Cambridge: Cambridge University Press, 1971), 58–74; and M. E. Gordley, *Teaching through Song in Antiquity: Didactic Hymnody among Greeks, Romans, Jews, and Christians* (WUNT 2/302; Tübingen: Mohr-Siebeck, 2011), 280–87.

13. See the survey and discussion in D. K. Williams, *Enemies of the Cross of Christ: The Terminology of the Cross and Conflict in Philippians* (JSNTSup 223; Sheffield: Sheffield Academic, 2002), 60–71.

14. For a survey of research, see R. P. Martin, *Carmen Christi: Philippians 2:5–11 in Recent Interpretation and in the Setting of Early Christian Worship* (rev ed.; Grand Rapids: Eerdmans, 1983), who argues for pre-Pauline origins; and G. D. Fee, "Philippians 2:5–11: Hymn or Exalted Pauline Prose?" *BBR* 2 (1992): 29–46, who defends Pauline composition.

15. J. D. G. Dunn, *Christology in the Making: A New Testament Inquiry into the Origins of the Doctrine of the Incarnation* (2nd ed.; Grand Rapids: Eerdmans, 1989), 114–21.

ment over whether the passage functions primarily theologically (broadly defined, sometimes soteriologically or christologically) or ethically. That is, in the middle of Paul's statements in Philippians, does this passage provide an intense "soteriological drama," or does it provide an ethical example that Paul presents to the Philippian believers?[16] The importance of this passage will be emphasized in the summary of the content of the letter to the Philippians below.

C. Literary Integrity of Philippians

A persistent issue in discussion of Philippians is its literary integrity. Despite being a single, relatively short letter, a few perceived breaks in the letter result in suspicion regarding whether the letter we now have was originally a single letter. As a result, there are numerous reconstructions of the letter or letters that now constitute Philippians,[17] some of which are outlined below (one author analyzes over twenty proposals regarding the multiple-letter hypothesis).[18] Commentaries and other introductions often refer to the longstanding debate (beginning as early as 1803) about integrity, but this is misleading, since writers in the early nineteenth century were not as quick to find divisions in the text as some modern scholars are. Since 1950, discussion has increased dramatically, and continues to the present.[19]

1. Evidence for Disunity

There are at least nine pieces of evidence to consider for possible disunity. Each of them merits brief examination.

16. See S. Fowl, *The Story of Christ in the Ethics of Paul: An Analysis of the Function of the Hymnic Material in the Pauline Corpus* (JSNTSup 36; Sheffield: JSOT Press, 1990), 83, as part of his summary of various views; cf. 49–76, for exegesis and history of research, including his emphasis on its ethical function over its compositional history. Cf. M. Bockmuehl, *The Epistle to the Philippians* (BCNT; Peabody, MA: Hendrickson, 1998), 125–48, who takes a christological position.

17. For a concise summary of the issues and an argument for unity of 1:1–4:9, see J. T. Reed, "Philippians 3:1 and the Epistolary Hesitation Formulas: The Literary Integrity of Philippians, Again," *JBL* 115 (1996): 63–90; cf. his *A Discourse Analysis of Philippians: Method and Rhetoric in the Debate over Literary Integrity* (JSNTSup 136; Sheffield: Sheffield Academic, 1997), 124–52, whose evidence is drawn on in this discussion.

18. D. E. Garland, "The Composition and Unity of Philippians: Some Neglected Literary Factors," *NovT* 37 (1985): 141–73, esp. 155n50.

19. See, e.g., J. Reumann, *Philippians* (Anchor Yale Bible 33B; New Haven: Yale University Press, 2008), 8–13, for bibliography and defense of three letters.

a. Philippians 1:27–28—"Whatever happens, conduct yourselves in a manner worthy of the gospel of Christ. Then, whether I come and see you or only hear about you in my absence, I will know that you stand firm in one spirit, contending as one person for the faith of the gospel" (NIV, altered)—seems to refer to an impending danger without apparent knowledge of a specific threat, but 3:2—"Watch out for those dogs, those people who do evil, those mutilators of the flesh" (NIV, altered)—seems to have a particular group in mind and so uses a stronger admonitory tone.

As discussed below, however, trying to determine the concerns and composition of the so-called opponents in the church at Philippi is not easy. The evidence is diverse, and it is difficult to characterize it in a straightforward description. As a result, many probably rightly decide that Paul is not responding to a threat to his apostleship but, rather, to various interests within the church that may well have threatened its unity. In light of this, it is difficult to posit literary divisions in the letter simply on the basis of statements that may imply various degrees of reality of a danger. Not much more can be drawn out of these two passages.

b. Philippians 4:10–19/20, in which Paul thanks the Philippians for money, is thought to be too late in the letter to be considered an expression of sincere and heartfelt thanks. Paul had apparently received a significant monetary gift from the Philippian church, a church that he had founded. The thought here is that the understated way in which he addresses the Philippians without actually saying "thank you" is inappropriate.

There are several responses to this argument: First, this word of thanks indicates that this is not the first or only communication of thanks by Paul. Paul could have sent oral thanks with Epaphroditus as the letter carrier, or he may have sent some earlier communication (e.g., 2:26). Second, Paul's word of thanks is not as brief as some posit and would not have been delayed if Epaphroditus had not fallen ill. But since he did fall ill, it is only now possible for Paul to respond to the gift of the Philippians. Third, Paul is in fact offering thanks to the Philippian church in a way generally consistent with social conventions for gratitude in the Greco-Roman world.[20]

20. See G. W. Peterman, "'Thankless Thanks': The Epistolary Social Convention in Philippians 4:10–20," *Tyndale Bulletin* 42.2 (1991): 261–70; and Peterman, *Paul's Gift from Philippi: Conventions of Gift Exchange and Christian Giving* (SNTSMS 92; Cambridge: Cambridge University Press, 1997), esp. 212–61; cf. also B. J. Capper, "Paul's Dispute with Philippi: Understanding Paul's Argument in Phil 1–2 from His Thanks in 4.10–20," *Theologische Zeitschrift* 49 (1993): 193–214; and K. L. Berry, "The Function of Friendship Language in Philippians 4:10–20," in *Friendship, Flattery, and Frankness of Speech: Studies on Friendship in the New Testament World* (ed. J. T. Fitzgerald; NovTSup 82; Leiden: Brill, 1996), 107–24.

One must be careful not to judge Paul by modern standards. There was a consistent disparagement of overt and bombastic verbal thanks among the ancients. The papyrus letters that address the issue of thanks attest that thanks between friends should be like for like, not simply in words. This evidence indicates not that Paul was neglecting his duty of thanking the church at Philippi but that the level of friendship was very close between the two parties, further evidenced by the amount of help that Paul offers in kind to them through his apostolic foundation and continued apostolic teaching and concern.

c. The use of "finally" (τὸ λοιπόν) in 3:1 and 4:8 is thought to be a clear indicator of division in the letter, implying that the material that comes next is the "final" word to be said. The spacing of these words of finality, especially in 3:1 combined with the word "rejoice," indicates to some that this is the conclusion to each of two letters (see schemas below).

It is not certain, however, that Paul or other ancient writers always used the word "finally" to close part of a letter (the papyri illustrate usage similar to Philippians).[21] For example, sometimes it appears that "finally" means no more than "then," other times "finally, so far as this point or topic is concerned" (e.g., 1 Thess 4:1; 2 Thess 3:1)—often considerably earlier than the letter's conclusion—and other times simply "from now on."[22]

d. There is an abrupt change of tone at Phil 3:2. Translations vary in how forcefully they render this verse, but most use strong words of warning about what is typically seen as possible opponents in the church. For example, the NIV renders 3:2 as "watch out for those dogs, those men who do evil, those mutilators of the flesh." This word of warning is seen to be particularly strong in contrast to the mild tone of 3:1.

There are several explanations of the strong transition at 3:2. First, some argue that the words themselves should not be so strongly rendered. G. D. Kilpatrick claims that the verb used should be rendered "consider."[23] While this may be true, there is still the problem of the way in which the opponents are characterized, in terms of dogs, evil-workers, and mutilators. By almost all accounts, these are unflattering and disparaging terms,

---

21. See, e.g., P.Oxy. 2149.5 (2nd–3rd century AD) and 1480.13 (AD 32), cited in Reed, "Philippians 3:1," 83n82.

22. Cf. M. E. Thrall, *Greek Particles in the New Testament: Linguistic and Exegetical Studies* (NTTS 3; Leiden: Brill, 1962), 25–30, whose grammatical analysis, however, is influenced by her epistolary analysis; and H. Gamble Jr., *The Textual History of the Letter to the Romans* (Studies and Documents 42; Grand Rapids: Eerdmans, 1977), 146.

23. G. D. Kilpatrick, "Βλέπετε, Philippians 3:2," in *In Memoriam Paul Kahle* (ed. M. Black and G. Fohrer; Berlin: Töpelmann, 1968), 146–48.

probably being used to characterize Jewish opponents. Second, J. B. Lightfoot thinks that a possible explanation for the transition is that there was some sort of break between 3:1 and 3:2.[24] But our standard chapter and verse divisions are often misleading and unhelpful; it is possible that if the chapter division took place between 3:1 and 3:2, the transition implied would not arouse the same kind of critical interest. Lightfoot's point, however, is that perhaps something Paul heard from a new messenger brought to his attention a more pressing situation at Philippi than he had at first envisioned. Perhaps this led to a change of mind on how to respond to the Philippians' situation. Third, there are similar abrupt transitions in other letters, but multiple-letter hypotheses are not suggested to explain them (e.g., Rom 16:17; 1 Cor 15:58; Gal 3:1; 4:21; 5:12). Furthermore, the supposed change in tone is not as long lasting as some have thought. Philippians 3:4 and following seem to return to the more relaxed tone of the earlier part of the letter. This also raises a further question: How could an editor have left such a rough seam if it is as abrupt as is often speculated? Finally, it is argued that 3:1b is stating that Paul is going to repeat the topics of 1:12–2:18 or even what he had previously told them in person; this would account for any duplication in Phil 3 of what is said earlier in the letter.[25]

e. Philippians 2:19–24 relates Paul's travel plans. It is sometimes argued that travel plans are usually and better kept for the end of Pauline letters. Since they occur at 2:19–24, they may well indicate that this is in fact near the end of the letter.

What is overlooked in this supposition is Paul's placing his travel plans in a variety of places in his letters. For the most part, they occur in the body of his letters, as does their mention in 2:19–24 (see the outline below), but this is not always the case. For example, in Romans, Paul unusually mentions his travel plans in the thanksgiving portion of his letter (1:11–15), besides at the end (15:23–29).

f. The word translated "rejoice" (χαίρετε) (Phil 3:1; 4:4) is used often at the beginning of papyri, but also at the conclusion in the sense of "farewell." The appearance of these words in 3:1 and 4:4 in conjunction with "finally"—arguably similar to the way that it is used in 2 Cor 13:11—supports the idea that the closings of two letters have been reached.

Forms of this word are used in the openings of papyrus letters, but there is relatively little evidence for their use in this way at the end of let-

24. J. B. Lightfoot, *St. Paul's Epistle to the Philippians* (London: Macmillan, 1891), 69–70, 143.
25. See T. Engberg-Pedersen, "Stoicism in Philippians," in *Paul in His Hellenistic Context* (ed. T. Engberg-Pedersen; Edinburgh: T&T Clark, 1994), 258n5.

ters. It is also a word that can be used in a variety of other ways as well. As will be seen below, one of the motifs of Philippians is joy and rejoicing. The use of this word is one way to express this idea, so it is not surprising to find it at various places throughout the letter. Its usage within Philippians is entirely idiomatic and consistent with this motif. Second Cor 13:11 is also better explained as use of the word in its more usual sense of "rejoice."

g. One scholar argues that the letter to the Laodiceans confirms that there were at one time independent Pauline letters to the church at Philippi.[26] It is not argued that the Laodicean letter that we have is actually a Pauline letter but that it reflects knowledge of the earlier textual tradition. The letter to the Laodiceans is a fourth-century Latin letter, quite clearly derivative from passages especially in Philippians, but also in Galatians. The letter supposedly quotes canonical Philippians in order, but in its citations, according to one reconstruction of the multiple-letter hypothesis, it cites only one of the letters. Thus, the failure to cite more than this one letter supposedly shows that there were independent letters at a stage earlier than our textual evidence.

Textual criticism as usually employed in New Testament studies does not know any evidence of multiple Philippian letters, since all of the manuscripts in which the letter appears have only the one Philippian letter. It is also important to note that the earliest Pauline nonfragmentary manuscript, $\mathfrak{P}$46 (ca. 200), includes a single Philippians. While one might hypothesize that the significant textual changes took place before this time, this is difficult to prove because of our limited external textual evidence before this time. More to the point here is that, if a different hypothesis on the content of the original letters is used, the letter to the Laodiceans is seen to be citing at least two, if not three, of these letters; thus the theory not only fails to prove what it claims but supports the integrity hypothesis by attesting to early knowledge of most parts of Philippians.

h. In 2:25-30, it seems to have been a long time since Epaphroditus was away, but in 4:18 it seems that he recently arrived. This would be consistent with a view that 4:10-20 was part of the first letter and 2:25-30 part of a later letter (this does not fit well with the two-letter hypothesis, however).

This theory works only with a view that sees three or more letters; it may not even be a clear argument for such a position, however, since 4:18 with its supposed recent arrival of Epaphroditus hardly supports such a hypothesis.

---

26. P. Sellew, "Laodiceans and the Philippians Fragments Hypothesis," *Harvard Theological Review* 87 (1994): 17-28.

i. Polycarp (70–156) refers to "letters" of Paul (*To the Philippians* 3.2). In this hypothesis, Polycarp, as an early writer, had clear knowledge of several letters to the Philippians and conveys that information.

In another reading of Polycarp, however, it is not clear that this is what Polycarp is saying. The statement is sufficiently ambiguous that Polycarp may mean multiple letters to the Philippians,[27] or our canonical letter together with letters to other churches, or a single letter of importance indicated by use of the plural form,[28] or the abundant contents of our single letter. Polycarp does not indicate the content of these letters. He may be referring not to letters addressed only to the Philippians but to all of the Pauline letters, since by this time Paul's letters could well have been gathered into a letter collection available to the various Pauline churches.[29]

2. Hypotheses of Composition

Because of the kinds of arguments covered above, several hypotheses are put forward regarding the number of letters that lie behind the single book of Philippians in the New Testament. The multiple-letter hypotheses are numerous. Some suggest up to five letters, but two or three letters are the normal number. Several of the more prominent hypotheses are summarized in table 4.

Recent work in the areas of literary structure and rhetoric attempts either to prove or to disprove the multiple letters of Philippians. Those who utilize the principles of literary and rhetorical analysis argue that Philippians exemplifies literary and rhetorical unity (e.g., consistently mentioned themes or a clear rhetorical structure) that indicate that the letter as we have it was composed as a unified and integral whole.

Studies by Duane Watson, for example, perhaps aid our understanding of particular passages in Philippians,[30] but his work is far from proving that Philippians was originally written as a unity. Such methods encounter two major problems. First, the critical tools being employed may not be appropriate to the task for which they are being used. It is not certain that the principles of literary criticism can and should be applied to letters as they would be to modern literature, and there is sustained and recurring criticism of applying the principles of ancient rhetorical criticism to the epistolary genre, since rhet-

27. F. W. Beare, *A Commentary on the Epistles to the Philippians* (BNTC; London: A&C Black, 1959), 4.
28. Lightfoot, *Philippians*, 138–40; and Williams, *Enemies of the Cross of Christ*, 44.
29. See chapter 6 §4 for my theory on the Pauline letter collection.
30. See D. Watson, "A Rhetorical Analysis of Philippians and Its Implications for the Unity Question," *NovT* 30 (1988): 57–88.

oric was designed with persuasive *oral* discourse in mind (not written letters).[31] Indeed, when comparison is made of other letters in the ancient world, one sees that they are often quite incoherent in shape and structure according to the principles of literary and rhetorical criticism employed. Second, attempts to discover the literary or rhetorical unity may be doing nothing more than establishing the literary and rhetorical competence of the redactor or redactors of the letters, not the original author. Hence, these tools may be able to produce a unified reading of Philippians, but they cannot be used to establish integrity.

In recent criticism, discourse analysis makes a major contribution to the study of the New Testament, and so principles of discourse analysis are employed to analyze the letter to the Philippians. The results, however, are ambiguous. On the one hand, Wolfgang Schenk, utilizing its principles in his commentary on Philippians, confirms his analysis that the letter is a composite.[32] On the other hand, David Alan Black, also utilizing these principles, discovers that it is a unity.[33] This divided opinion is not true of all discourse analysis; for the most part, discourse analysis works from the premise that discourses are cohesive, and the task of the analyst is to show how the text coheres and how it is structured to bring certain ideas into prominence. One cannot begin with the idea of literary unity or disunity and then claim to prove this. All that can be claimed is that the analytical tool provides criteria for judging integrity. But the criteria themselves do not establish integrity; this must be established on other grounds.[34]

Since there is no external textual attestation that many letters were written and sent by Paul to Philippi, there is the question of motivation for bringing the letters together. It is not difficult to imagine that there was a church, possibly at Philippi, that had a keen desire to retain the Pauline letters and would oversee their consolidation into a single letter. But why? First, this consolidation must have occurred extremely early. To some extent, the date of consolidation depends upon when the Pauline letter collection was made. If the collection was made around the turn of the first century, then the consolidation must have occurred between Paul's death and approximately 100, a fairly narrow window of opportunity. But if Paul himself had something to do with the collection of his letters (see chapter 6 §4), it is almost impossible that there was a window of

---

31. S. E. Porter, "Paul of Tarsus and His Letters," in *Handbook of Classical Rhetoric in the Hellenistic Period, 330 B.C.–A.D. 400* (ed. S. E. Porter; Leiden: Brill, 1997), 533–85.

32. W. Schenk, *Die Philipperbriefe des Paulus: Ein Kommentar* (Stuttgart: Kohlhammer, 1984).

33. D. A. Black, "The Discourse Structure of Philippians: A Study in Textlinguistics," *NovT* 37 (1995): 16–49.

34. For an assessment of these issues, see Reed, *Discourse Analysis of Philippians*, esp. 34–122 on method.

opportunity for the consolidation (unless Paul perhaps did it himself, because he wished for the letters to be preserved in this way, in which case we are back to a single Philippian letter).

Second, one must ask what kind of compulsion there was to consolidate the letters. The Pauline corpus as we have it has several examples of multiple letters to various churches—Corinth, Thessalonica, and Colossae (with Philemon)—and to Timothy. The authorship of several of these is questioned, and there is a multiple-letter hypothesis regarding 2 Corinthians as well, but prima facie there is no compelling reason why the letters would have to be united. The church at Philippi, however, may not have known of these multiple letters to other churches. Nevertheless, its members must have known that they had multiple letters, and even if only they knew this, it is still unclear why they would have consolidated them. Third, several opposing factors apparently compete to explain why these letters would have been united. On the one hand, the argument would have to hold that the church at Philippi united the letters out of some sense of reverence for the writings of Paul. This makes perfect sense in light of what is known about reverence for Paul's writings in the early church (2 Pet 3:16)[35] and about the gathering of the Pauline corpus. On the other hand, in order to consolidate the letters, the church would have had to delete certain portions of the apostle's words. We do not know what the original letters included, but it is a virtual certainty that we would not have all of the two or three letters (even aside from the deleted openings and closings). When the individual hypothetical letters are examined for length, they are seen to be shorter in length than any of Paul's other letters to churches. If 4:10–19/20 constitutes a single letter, its only rival is Philemon, a personal letter (but even then it is considerably shorter). This means that the individual letters, at least as they are reconstructed, would be very uncharacteristic of the other Pauline letters. This is either an argument against multiple letters or an argument that some portions of these letters have been excised and now lost. At the least, the openings and closings of the letters, except for one, have been edited out. Furthermore, it can be argued that the editor himself must have been working at cross-purposes. On the one hand, it was considered important to edit the various individual letters into a single whole, yet the editor did his job relatively badly, leaving several telltale signs that this was done (e.g., 3:1 and 3:2, and placement of 4:10–20).

In conclusion, there are good reasons to read Philippians as a single doc-

---

35. Regardless of the date of 2 Peter, it does give testimony—which probably began very early, as evidenced by the number kept by churches—to the regard for the Pauline letters in the early church.

ument, especially as arguments for the multiple-letter hypothesis—as interesting and provocative as they are—remain unproved.

Table 4. Multiple-Letter Hypotheses for Philippians

Two-Letter Hypothesis

	Material	Content
Hypothesis 1	3:2–4:23 (or 4:20)	thanks for the gift
Hypothesis 2	1:1–3:1 (and 4:21–23)	letter sent with Epaphroditus

Three-Letter Hypothesis

	Material	Content
Hypothesis 1	4:10–20	thanks for the gift
	1:1–3:1; 4:2–9, 21–23	letter sent with Epaphroditus
	3:2–4:1	interpolation warning readers
Hypothesis 2	4:10–20	thanks for the gift
	1:1–2:30; 4:21–23	letter sent with Epaphroditus praising him
	3:1–4:9	Paul facing death
Hypothesis 3	1:1–2; 4:10–20	thanks for the gift
	1:3–3:1; 4:4–9, 21–23	letter sent with Epaphroditus
	3:2–4:3	warning regarding Judaizers

D. Opponents, Occasion, and Purpose of Philippians

In this section, three important and interrelated topics are treated together: the opponents Paul is confronting, the occasion, and the purpose of his writing his letter to the Philippians.

Determining the opponents and the occasion of the letter to the Philippians has proved exceedingly difficult.[36] The reasons are the diversity of evidence within the book itself and the lack of knowledge about the situation that warranted the letter's being written. Definitive answers are far from certain; the following survey gives some idea of the options.

36. Williams, *Enemies of the Cross of Christ*, 59–60, notes that J. J. Gunther, *St. Paul's Opponents and Their Background: A Study of Apocalyptic and Jewish Sectarian Teaching* (NovTSup 35; Leiden: Brill, 1973), 2, identified no less than eighteen possible solutions to the identity of these opponents.

1. Evidence for Opponents

There are four main passages to consider in trying to determine the nature of the opponents or problems at Philippi.[37]

a. *Philippians 1:15–18*. In this passage, Paul mentions that the gospel is being preached but not always out of the same good motives. Apparently this refers to some rivalry between Paul and other Christian groups. The question of importance here, however, is whether it refers to a problem in Philippi. Some think that Paul may be opposing a group of Christian missionaries who had a "divine man" theology—as mentioned earlier, a theology in which the man of God was expected to be some sort of miracle worker—and that Paul as a prisoner did not conform to this image.[38] By all accounts, Paul stood opposed to this characterization of a man of God because he endorsed humility, meekness, and suffering (e.g., 1:13–14, 20–24; 3:12–13). Perhaps these opponents questioned whether Paul was a legitimate apostle. There are three problems with this position. First, the language does not make it clear that this was a problem at Philippi. Second, this view has difficulty harmonizing with the other evidence of opponents at Philippi, since the problem in 1:15–18 would seem to indicate an internal church problem, not one with external opponents. Third, "divine man" theology is probably a later development, not one of the first century (see chapter 9 §3C2). It is possible that the preachers with bad motives were part of one of the other groups of opponents (see other options below), but this is only a hypothesis. Paul mentions these preachers in his opening section of the letter, in which he is discussing the general advancement of the gospel despite his own imprisonment (1:12–18). It is therefore unlikely that in 1:15–18 he is referring to specific opponents at Philippi, and certainly not to a situation that threatens the church there.

b. *Philippians 1:27–30*. In this section, Paul admonishes the Philippians to stand firm in the faith and not to be frightened by those who oppose them. Paul goes on to draw a contrast between the opponents' impending destruction and the Philippians' salvation, but affirms that part of their calling has been to suffer. These statements are vague, and it is difficult to

---

37. See G. F. Hawthorne, *Philippians* (rev. R. P. Martin; WBC 43; N.P.: Nelson, 2004), l–lv, for a concise discussion of the passages; cf. V. Koperski, *The Knowledge of Christ Jesus My Lord: The High Christology of Philippians 3:7–11* (Kampen, Netherlands: Kok Pharos, 1996), esp. 113–32.

38. See R. Jewett, "Conflicting Movements in the Early Church as Reflected in Philippians," *NovT* 12 (1970): 362–90.

know whether they are made in reference to theologically based opponents or general adversity in Philippi. That the suffering they are undergoing or can expect to undergo may not be from religious conflict but, rather, from general life in society is perhaps supported by Paul's saying that they are going through the same struggle he had gone through (1:30). The idea here may be that Paul is in prison because of the Roman authorities and it is the Roman authorities who are in some way causing trouble for the Philippians. In this case, the passage would not be a reference to some form of religious opponents, even if Paul's response reflects his own theological position.

c. *Philippians 3:2-4.* Paul here enjoins the Philippians to "beware of the dogs, beware of the evil workers, beware of those who mutilate the flesh" (NRSV). The first two characterizations could be general. In light of 3:3-6, however, where Paul continues on about circumcision (there is an apparent play on the words "mutilation" [κατατομή] and "circumcision" [περιτομή]) and emphasizes his Jewish background, it is likely that 3:2-4 is a characterization of either Jewish or Jewish-Christian opponents. It is generally agreed that Jews did not try to compel Gentiles to be circumcised and conform to their laws, so it is probable that Jewish Christians are in view here. In other words, Paul has in mind opponents similar to those who threatened the Galatians. He uses strong language to characterize these possible Judaizers, but it is noticeably more restrained than what he uses in Galatians (Gal 2:11-3:5, esp. 2:21-3:1); this causes some to doubt the identification.[39] There are several possible responses, however. One is that Paul, in his experience and age, has mellowed in his approach to such problems. A second is that although the opponents are similar, the threat is not seen to be as strong, possibly because the Jewish population in Philippi was at best quite small. These Judaizers could have come from outside Philippi, but in any case, no significant Jewish presence has been discovered at Philippi, making it difficult to believe that significant numbers were involved.

d. *Philippians 3:18-19.* In these verses (cf. also 3:11-16), Paul draws attention to those who live lives as enemies of the cross, whose god is their stomach

39. Ian Elmer, however, states that the language is similar enough (an echo) to identify these two groups as one and the same; *Paul, Jerusalem, and the Judaizers: The Galatian Crisis in Its Broadest Historical Context* (WUNT 2/258; Tübingen: Mohr-Siebeck, 2009), 191-95. See also W. Marxen, *Introduction to the New Testament: An Approach to Its Problems* (trans. G. Buswell; Oxford: Blackwell, 1968), 63-64; and W. Schmithals, *Paul and the Gnostics* (trans. J. E. Steely; Nashville: Abingdon, 1972), 82-83, who also think that the opponents in Philippi and Galatia were the same.

and whose glory is in their shame. Their minds are on earthly things. Paul is apparently addressing those with libertine tendencies, who indulge their appetites in an unhealthy way. The emphasis is perhaps upon gluttony and nudity. Some suggest that this indicates that the opponents in Philippi were some form of protognostics or those with an overrealized eschatology (they believe that the eschaton had already begun), such as were also possibly found at Corinth. Some people who had gnostic tendencies became ascetics, but others took an opposite turn and became overly indulgent.[40] The probable reasoning was that since earthly substance was illusory and hence ultimately did not matter, indulgence was a viable option with no enduring consequences. Similarly, if those to whom Paul refers had an overrealized eschatology, they may well have believed that they had already entered into the eschaton and that therefore their spiritual situation was secure, with the result that they could indulge with impunity. Gordon Fee, however, points out that this group is mentioned nowhere else in the letter than in this tearful description and may better serve as a general description of those Paul has previously told them about, but not present opponents.[41]

From this range of evidence, it is difficult to determine the exact nature of Paul's opponents at Philippi, or even, in fact, whether there was such a group. The evidence of a strong, concerted effort by a definable group to oppose him is certainly lacking. At best, the Philippian Christians appear to have encountered some opposition, possibly by some who wished them to be more "Jewish," but it does not appear that these opponents constituted a major threat at this point, apart from calling for Philippian caution and awareness.

2. Occasion and Purpose

The occasion and purpose of Philippians are closely related to the opponents. In light of the proposals above, describing the occasion and purpose of composition may well involve the following factors.

a. *Paul's assessment.* Paul wished to offer an assessment of his current situation to the church at Philippi, one that had recently demonstrated

---

40. E.g., F. Thielman, *Paul and the Law: A Contextual Approach* (Downers Grove, IL: InterVarsity, 1995), 150–51, who argues that the Philippian opponents were probably gnostic and antinomian.

41. G. D. Fee, *Paul's Letter to the Philippians* (NICNT; Grand Rapids: Eerdmans, 1995), 9, 366–75.

its continued concern and support for his work by giving a helpful gift (4:10–19/20). To this gift, Paul appears to have responded in a way that was fitting for close personal friends (see §2C1b). Furthermore, he wishes to tell them why Epaphroditus and not Timothy is returning to them. It is because of this close friendship and concern that Paul addresses several other issues. By informing the Philippian church of his own suffering yet joyful attitude (1:12–26; 2:24)—expecting release yet desiring the benefits of heaven—Paul is able to teach them the importance of remaining joyful even amid adversity. He commends himself and Christ as examples. He acknowledges that there has been opposition to his ministry in various quarters, some taking advantage of his imprisonment for their own selfish gains, but he is willing to accept this as long as the gospel is preached.[42]

b. *Paul's opponents.* For the most part, Paul is concerned with commending the Philippians for their unity, for their good thinking, and for being a source of joy to him (1:5; 1:19; 2:2; etc.). But he is also aware that other influences may have crept into the church that might threaten their unity and their having the mind of Christ (4:2–3). Here he offers words of warning regarding the opponents. Some research emphasizes the possibility and even likelihood that the situation in Philippi was a complex one that involved several competing interests.[43] One of these appears to have been the influence of Judaizers. They probably were only a small group within Philippi, or a group of outsiders who were arguing that the Philippian Christians needed to participate in Jewish rituals. The influence of this group was not as pronounced or as advanced as it had been in Galatia, and so Paul did not respond as forcefully. The influence of this group of Judaizers may have been aided by the situation in Philippi. As mentioned above, Philippi was a Roman colony, in which Roman law was clearly exercised and where the emperor cult was probably beginning to grow.[44] Even if the Jews did not have special rights as a "recognized religion" (*religio licita*) within the Roman Empire, being a Jew did permit them a certain

---

42. See L. G. Bloomquist, *The Function of Suffering in Philippians* (JSNTSup 78; Sheffield: JSOT Press, 1993).

43. See M. Tellbe, "The Sociological Factors behind Philippians 3.1–11 and the Conflict at Philippi," *JSNT* 55 (1994): 97–121; and B. W. Winter, *Seek the Welfare of the City: Christians as Benefactors and Citizens* (Grand Rapids: Eerdmans, 1994), 81–104. B. J. Oropeza, *Jews, Gentiles, and the Opponents of Paul: The Pauline Letters* (Apostasy in the New Testament Communities 2; Eugene, OR: Wipf & Stock, 2012), 205, states that the persecutors in Philippi should not be considered the same as Paul's opponents in 1:15–18 nor those in Phil 3.

44. See L. M. McDonald and S. E. Porter, *Early Christianity and Its Sacred Literature* (Peabody, MA: Hendrickson, 2000), 80–88, esp. 84.

amount of latitude regarding participation in certain rituals of Roman religion, especially in a world as religiously complex as the Roman one. Gentiles who decided to become followers of Christ, however, would not have had as much latitude and may have found themselves forced to make a decision how to respond to the pressures of pagan religion. This would have raised questions of what it meant to be a "good citizen" of Philippi and of heaven. The Judaizers would have been offering a way to continue being Christians and to resist some of the pressures of pagan worship. To this Paul responds in two ways. First, he informs them that their status as believers is determined by a spiritual or internal transformation, not by outward signs. Second, he reminds them that their citizenship and duty to be good citizens are defined by what is required of them as followers of Christ. His response is formulated in language similar in some ways to that of the Stoics regarding appropriate behavior.

E. Date and Place of Writing of Philippians

As mentioned at the beginning of this chapter, Philippians was written by Paul during an imprisonment. This has a direct influence upon when and where the letter could have been written. A more detailed treatment of the issue of Pauline imprisonment can be found in chapter 2 §3. This section draws attention to issues that relate specifically to Philippians.

If Paul wrote Philippians during an Ephesian imprisonment, he would have written the letter either in 52/53 during his first Ephesian visit or, more likely, somewhere between 53 and 55 during his lengthy two-year stay.[45] If Paul wrote Philippians during his Caesarean imprisonment, he would have written the letter in 57–60. If he wrote it during his Roman imprisonment, he would have written it in 61–62.

According to the discussion of imprisonment in chapter 2 §3, Paul most likely wrote the Prison Epistles during the Roman imprisonment, but several other factors internal to Philippians point in this same direction.

1. Pretorian Guard

In Phil 1:13, Paul mentions the pretorian guard. This was a special detachment of soldiers assigned to the emperor. Since being the emperor of the Roman Empire was a precarious occupation (half of the emperors of the first century

---

45. See Reumann, *Philippians*, 3.

were murdered or died under mysterious circumstances), in part because of the political intrigue in which the emperor had to participate to maintain his status, the emperors maintained a special group of soldiers to try to ensure their protection. It is possible that other cities may have had detachments of the pretorian guard (and it appears that Philippi had such a detachment), especially cities visited frequently by the emperor, but a reference to the pretorian guard would most likely mean the guard in Rome, since it is known for certain that they were there.[46]

2. Those of Caesar's Household

Reference to Caesar's household in 4:22 is often misinterpreted. It probably does not mean that some close to Caesar had become followers of Christ but that some persons within the vast expanse of Caesar's household were followers. They could have included lowly servants and slaves and even individuals higher up. Caesar's household encompassed all those in the employ of Caesar for domestic and administrative duties. It is likely that some of his household were in other cities where Caesar maintained residences, but the largest contingent was in Rome.

3. Historical and Personal Context

Paul was in prison but possibly nearing release (1:7, 19–27; 2:24). His references to a possible release make the most sense in terms of a Roman imprisonment, for he is confident that due process will result in his release and that there is no higher authority to which appeal against accusations can be made.

Though limited, this evidence all points in a similar direction and tends to confirm further a Roman imprisonment for Paul's writing Philippians.

F. Outline of Philippians[47]

A. Opening (1:1–2)
1. Sender (1:1a)

---

46. See S. Bingham, *The Praetorian Guard: A History of Rome's Elite Special Forces* (Waco, TX: Baylor University Press, 2013).

47. Cf. L. Alexander, "Hellenistic Letter-Forms and the Structure of Philippians," *JSNT* 37 (1989): 87–101; and R. Russell, "Pauline Letter Structure in Philippians," *Journal of the Evangelical Theological Society* 25 (1982): 295–306.

2. Addressee (1:1b)
3. Greeting (1:2)
B. Thanksgiving (1:3–11)
  1. Thanksgiving proper (1:3–8)
  2. Prayer/intercession (1:9–11)
C. Body: living Christ's example (1:12–2:30)
  1. Formal opening: advance of the gospel (1:12–18)
  2. Paul's situation (1:19–26)
  3. Living the Christian life worthy of Christ's gospel (1:27–2:18)
  4. Pauline travelogue (2:19–30)
D. Paraenesis (3:1–4:19)
  1. Introduction: repetition as a safeguard (3:1)
  2. Opponents not to be followed (3:2–6)
  3. Summary of Paul's theology (3:7–11)
  4. Striving for perfection (3:12–4:1)
  5. Exhortation to unity and joy and peace in personal relations (4:2–9)
  6. Word of thanks for the Philippians' gift (4:10–19)
E. Closing (4:20–23)
  1. Doxology (4:20)
  2. Greetings (4:21–22)
  3. Grace benediction (4:23)

G. Content of Philippians

Opening (1:1–2)

Paul opens with a short, standard greeting, identifying himself and Timothy as servants of Christ Jesus. He writes to "all the saints in Christ Jesus who are in Philippi" (NRSV), including the overseers and deacons (probably early church offices, though this is disputed by many scholars).[48]

Thanksgiving (1:3–11)

Paul gives thanks for the Philippian believers in all of his prayers because of their partnership in the gospel since the beginning of his ministry. He is confident that God will complete what he started in them. He holds them in his heart, because they have participated with him in his imprisonment and

48. For recent discussion, see Reumann, *Philippians*, 36–39.

defense of the gospel,[49] and he states how he yearns for them with the affection of Christ, and that he desires that they also abound in love more and more with knowledge and all discernment so that they may be ready for the day of Christ.

Body: Formal Opening—Advance of the Gospel (1:12–18)

Paul reassures his readers that his imprisonment has happened for the advancement of the gospel, because of his being able to share the gospel with the entire imperial guard and those imprisoned with him. Not only that, but most of the other believers are much bolder to preach the gospel because of Paul's imprisonment. There are even some who preach Christ out of ulterior motives, such as preaching in order to afflict Paul in his imprisonment, but Paul is satisfied in knowing that, whether out of pretense or truth, Christ is simply being preached.

Body: Paul's Situation (1:19–26)

Paul conveys his confidence in knowing that the Philippians are praying for him and that their prayers along with the help of the Spirit of Jesus Christ will result in his deliverance. He eagerly expects this and knows that Christ will be honored in his body, whether he lives or dies. To live is Christ and to die is gain, he states. He would rather depart from this world and be with Christ, but he will also stay so that he can continue his ministry to them. Considering this, he knows that his deliverance from prison will come and that he can rejoice with them in their progress and joy in the faith.

Body: Living the Christian Life Worthy of Christ's Gospel (1:27–2:18)

Paul continues by stating that their manner of life should be worthy of the gospel of Christ, so that, when Paul sees them or hears of them, they are standing firm in one spirit and striving together for the gospel, not afraid of those who oppose them. In fact, it is to be assumed that those who believe in Christ will also suffer for his sake.

So, Paul says, if they experience any encouragement in Christ, any comfort from love, any participation in the Spirit, any affection and sympathy, he asks them to complete his joy by having the same mindset with one another, having the same love, and being united together. They should not do anything from

49. Mark Keown sees congregational support of evangelism as central to Philippians. See M. J. Keown, *Congregational Evangelism in Philippians: The Centrality of an Appeal for Gospel Proclamation to the Fabric of Philippians* (Milton Keynes: Paternoster, 2008).

competition or empty conceit, but, in humility, they should consider others more important than themselves, looking toward others' interests as much as they look to their own interests. This is the mindset they are to have, the mindset that Christ had. Although he was in the form of God, he did not grasp on to his position of equality with God but made himself nothing, taking the form of a slave in the likeness of humanity. Being found in human likeness, he humbled himself in such a way that he died, and not only did he die but he died on a cross. Because of his humility, God highly exalted him and gave him the name that is above every name, so that everyone would worship and proclaim his name, Jesus Christ the Lord.

So Paul encourages them to continue working out their salvation as they have been with fear and trembling, regardless of whether he is there or not, because God works in them so that they might do what pleases God. They are to do everything without complaining, blameless and innocent like children of God, shining lights in this crooked world. In doing this, Paul would be glad and know that the afflictions he experienced for preaching the gospel were worth the pain.

Body: Pauline Travelogue (2:19–30)

Paul conveys his desire to send Timothy to them, so he can hear from him that they are doing well. Timothy is the best person for them, caring deeply about their well-being. They should know Timothy, how he is like a spiritual son to Paul in the gospel, and as soon as it is feasible, Paul will send him and follow him to Philippi some time afterward. He will also send Epaphroditus, Paul's fellow worker but also their messenger and minister to Paul. He has been wanting to visit for some time as well, especially since he was distressed to hear that they had been distressed, because he himself was ill. He actually was severely ill to the point of death, but God had mercy on him and healed him. God's mercy was also shown to Paul himself—Epaphroditus's death would have meant "sorrow upon sorrow" (NIV) to Paul. That is why Paul is eager to send him to Philippi, so that they may rejoice at seeing him and receive him in the Lord with all joy. They should also honor him, since he risked his life in service for the ministry.

Paraenesis: Introduction—Repetition as a Safeguard (3:1)

As a transition, Paul tells them, "finally" (τὸ λοιπόν),[50] to rejoice in the Lord. He does not mind repeating the same things, since it works as a safeguard for

---

50. See §2C1c on the meaning of this two-word Greek phrase as a transition.

them as well. This opens the paraenetic section in which he puts forth a series of commands in light of what has already been said.

Paraenesis: Opponents Not to Be Followed (3:2–6)

Paul warns the Philippians believers to watch out for the dogs, the evildoers, those who mutilate (the flesh). He uses strong language in order to underscore the severity of what these opponents are doing against the gospel. But he says that "we are the circumcision," those who worship by the Spirit of God and put no confidence in the flesh ("flesh" here may be a subtle, or not so subtle, reference to circumcision). Yet Paul declares that he has many reasons for having fleshly confidence and proceeds to list them: circumcised on the eighth day as prescribed by the law, of Israel, of the tribe of Benjamin, and a speaker of Hebrew. Regarding the law, he was a Pharisee; regarding zeal, he was so zealous he persecuted the church; and regarding righteousness, he was blameless.

Paraenesis: Summary of Paul's Theology (3:7–11)

But if these things were a gain to him, Paul says that he counts them as a loss in order that he might know Christ Jesus his Lord. Not only does he count these seeming gains to be a loss, they are excrement, in order that he would gain Christ and obtain a righteousness not from the law but through faith in Christ. The ultimate gain is to know him and the power of his resurrection and to share in his sufferings, doing anything to attain the resurrection from the dead.

Paraenesis: Striving for Perfection (3:12–4:1)

All this, Paul says, has not been attained by him yet, but he presses on in order to make it all his own, because Christ Jesus made him his own. He admits it is not yet his own, but one thing he does is to leave the past behind and strive toward what is ahead. He presses on toward the prize of the upward call of Christ Jesus. Those who are mature should have this mindset as well, and if, in any of this, they think differently, Paul says that God will reveal it to them.

Paul requests them to imitate him and to look to those who follow this example, because many live as enemies of the cross of Christ. These people end up in destruction and worship their appetites; their glory is their shame, with their minds set on earthly things. In contrast, Paul identifies himself and the Philippians as citizens of heaven, awaiting the Savior to transform them. Keeping all of this in mind, Paul exhorts them to stand firm in the Lord.

Paraenesis: Exhortation to Unity and Joy and Peace in Personal Relations (4:2–9)

A substantial dissension between two significant women in the Philippian congregation, Euodia and Syntyche, happened to reach Paul's ears. He addresses them and tells them to "agree in the Lord," invoking the help of Paul's true companion,[51] who was to help these women who have labored in the gospel with Paul, Clement, and the rest of Paul's companions.

The rest of this section contains various exhortations for the Philippians. He tells them to rejoice in the Lord continually, and that their gentleness should be made known to all. Since the Lord is at hand, they should not be anxious about anything, but by prayer should make their needs known to God. Then God's peace, which transcends human understanding, will protect their hearts and minds in Christ Jesus. Finally, they are to think about things that are true, honorable, just, pure, lovely, commendable, and excellent, anything worthy of praise. They are to practice whatever they learned or saw in him, so the peace of God would be with them.

Paraenesis: Word of Thanks for the Philippians' Gift (4:10–19)

Speaking of rejoicing, Paul states his joy in their concern for him, even in spite of not being able to do anything about it at the time. But he wants to let them know that his need is not really a need, because he has learned to be content in whatever situation he is in, whether hungry or full. He is able to do all things through Christ who strengthens him.

But even though Paul is content, it was kind of them to recognize his trouble. He reminds them of what they already knew—that when Paul started his gospel ministry, they were the first ones to partner with him. They even partnered with him in giving (and receiving, since they received from Paul in other ways) when he was in Thessalonica, providing for whatever needs he had. He reminds them that it is not the gift itself that matters to Paul, but the blessings that the Philippians receive from their generous work. Paul has everything he needs, as they had sent supplies with Epaphroditus. And he says that God will in turn supply their needs according to his abundant riches.

---

51. The identity of this true companion is debated by interpreters. Theories are proposed that it might be Timothy, possibly Epaphroditus, or even an unknown wife of Paul; see the discussion of options in G. W. Hansen, *The Letter to the Philippians* (PNTC; Grand Rapids: Eerdmans, 2009), 284–85. It may be, however, that Paul is addressing the Philippians as a singular companion to depict their unity in bringing peace to their conflict.

Closing (4:20–23)

In all of this, Paul gives glory to God the Father. In closing, Paul asks them to greet every saint in Christ Jesus, and says that those with him greet them. In addition, all of the saints greet them, including those of Caesar's household.[52] He ends with a benediction that the grace of the Lord Jesus Christ may be with them.

3. Colossians

On his second missionary journey, Paul was in the area of the cities of Derbe and Lystra (Acts 16:1–6) and traveled to various cities in the area (16:4). During this time, he apparently either sent emissaries to Colossae or made a short visit to the city himself unrecorded in Acts. Whether Paul ever visited Colossae we do not know, but this letter to the Christians there has played a significant role in understanding Pauline thought. This letter is often linked to Philemon, discussed immediately after. In this section, I first discuss the city of Colossae and then consider authorship, imprisonment and date, and the opponents, occasion, and purpose, before presenting an outline and its content.

A. City of Colossae

Colossae was the least important city to which any of Paul's letters is addressed.[53] The city was located in the Lycus Valley in the western part of the Roman province of Asia, near the more important cities of Laodicea and Hierapolis (Col 2:1; 4:3, 15–16), in the region of ancient Phrygia, and was known for its cold-water supply, which fed various surrounding cities. It was near the Meander River, of which the Lycus River is a tributary, approximately a hundred miles east of Ephesus.

Herodotus mentions Colossae as a "great city of Phrygia" (*Histories* 7.30.1 LCL), though he is inaccurate in his description of its location; this reference attests to its antiquity and early greatness. Xenophon, too, says that it was

---

52. This does not necessarily mean those of Caesar's immediate family but could refer to any one of his servants or those associated with him. See Hansen, *Philippians*, 331.

53. See C. J. Hemer, *The Letters to the Seven Churches of Asia in Their Local Setting* (JSNT-Sup 11; Sheffield: JSOT Press, 1986), 178–86; J. B. Lightfoot, *St. Paul's Epistles to the Colossians and to Philemon* (London: Macmillan, 1875), 1–72, with references to the ancient sources; and C. Arnold, "Colossae," *ABD* 1.1089–90.

populous, wealthy, and large (*Anabasis* 1.21.6). The city suffered varied political fortunes under the Seleucids, however, until the Romans had the entire region given to them in 133 BC. Commentaries frequently include comments about a period of decline for Colossae in the first century BC, and Strabo refers to it as a small town (*Geography* 12.8.13). This decline is true but may not be the entire story. According to Peter O'Brien, on the basis of inscriptional evidence, Colossae continued to exist well into the first century. It was in the middle of an area given to wool production and was very well known for a very fine quality of dark red dyed wool, called Colossian or in Latin *colossinus* (Strabo, *Geography* 12.8.16; Pliny, *Natural History* 21.51).[54] A major difficulty in gaining knowledge about Colossae is the site's never having been excavated, although there are rumors that such excavation is imminent.

Laodicea, a more recently founded city, was located near Colossae. Laodicea had been founded under the Seleucid king Antiochus II in 261 BC and was named after his wife, Laodice. It was the center of the judicial circuit, had a Roman cohort stationed there, and was the center of the financial and banking industries. In contrast to the modest financial wealth of Colossae, it is reported that after a particularly bad earthquake in 60/61 (Pliny, *Natural History* 5.105; according to Strabo, Laodicea and its environs were known to have numerous earthquakes) Laodicea was sufficiently wealthy to be able to afford rebuilding itself with its own money (it is unknown whether or how Colossae was affected by this earthquake). Hierapolis, or "holy city," located a few miles northwest of Colossae, was also a Seleucid city, founded either in 281–261 BC or 197–160 BC. It was known for its hot mineral springs.

The Jewish settlement at Colossae probably originated sometime in the early second century BC when Babylonian Jews were brought into the area (according to Josephus, *Jewish Antiquities* 12.147–53), although it is possible some Jews settled there a little earlier. These Babylonian Jewish settlers may well have originally been sent as military troops, the terms of service being no taxes for ten years and the right to live under their own laws. There was a tradition (2 Macc 8:20) that these Diaspora Jews were particularly good fighters. On the basis of accounts that record a dispute in 62/61 BC about the temple tax (the Roman governor Flaccus tried to prevent the sending of the temple tax, but he was removed from office for this; see Cicero, *Pro Flacco* 28.68) and about whether money could be sent from one region to another, scholars try to estimate the number of Jews in the area. The debates over the temple tax indicate that a large number of Jews, possibly as many as 11,000, lived in the Laodicea and Hierapolis area.

54. P. T. O'Brien, *Colossians, Philemon* (WBC 44; Waco, TX: Word, 1982), xxvi–xxvii.

It is difficult to determine the origin of the Christian population of Colossae. There are two major alternatives. The first is that those from the surrounding area were responsible for bringing the gospel to Colossae. Acts 2:10 says that Phrygians were in Jerusalem on the day of Pentecost; they may have been responsible for bringing Christianity to the area upon their return home. The second alternative is that the city was evangelized by Paul but perhaps not directly, even though he evangelized elsewhere in Phrygia-Galatia (Col 2:1)—and hence may have visited the city—but by one of his fellow missionaries, such as Epaphras (1:7; 4:12-13), probably at the time of Paul's stay in Ephesus during his second missionary journey (Acts 19:10). In either case, it appears that the area had been evangelized by Christians within twenty-five years of Christ's death. The church may have turned away from Christianity for a while, quite possibly because of the problems addressed in the letter (see also 2 Tim 1:15), but it appears to have remained faithful for at least a few years after the letter was written.[55]

B. Authorship of Colossians

Many critical scholars now reject Pauline authorship of Colossians, but the percentage is probably not lopsided in favor of pseudonymity. The first serious doubts about Pauline authorship of the letter were raised by the German scholar Theodor Mayerhoff in 1838, and they were more rigorously pursued by Ferdinand Christian Baur and his followers.[56] The debate concerning authorship has been lively and ongoing ever since, and, along with discussion of the Colossian opponents, is one of two major critical issues regarding Colossians.[57] I will present the arguments against Pauline authorship first, before

55. See Lightfoot, *Colossians*, 41-72, on the Colossian church.
56. See D. Guthrie, *New Testament Introduction* (4th ed.; Downers Grove, IL: InterVarsity, 1990), 572-77, for discussion. See Baur, *Paul the Apostle of Jesus Christ*, 2.1-44, where he also considers Ephesians.
57. See R. DeMaris, *The Colossian Controversy: Wisdom in Dispute at Colossae* (JSNTSup 96; Sheffield: JSOT Press, 1994), 11-12, for a summary of the discussion of authorship. Two important studies arguing against authenticity are W. Bujard, *Stilanalytische Untersuchungen zum Kolosserbrief: Als Beitrag zur Methodik von Sprachvergleichen* (Studien zur Umwelt des Neuen Testaments 11; Göttingen: Vandenhoeck & Ruprecht, 1973), although his method appears now to look relatively primitive; and G. E. Cannon, *The Use of Traditional Materials in Colossians* (Macon, GA: Mercer University Press, 1983). The standard commentaries discuss these issues: see, e.g., E. Lohse, *Colossians and Philemon* (Hermeneia; Philadelphia: Fortress, 1971), 84-91; M. Barth and H. Blanke, *Colossians* (AB 34B; New York: Doubleday, 1994), 114-26; J. L. Sumney, *Colossians: A Commentary* (NTL; Louisville: Westminster John Knox, 2008),

presenting the arguments for Pauline authorship—the latter of which I find much more convincing.

1. Arguments against Pauline Authorship

The major arguments against Pauline authorship revolve around the issues of vocabulary, style, and theology.[58] These are the usual considerations in discussions of authorship of the Pauline letters.

a. *Vocabulary*. Scholars who argue against Pauline authorship frequently draw attention to the absence of many of the favorite Pauline words and expressions, such as "salvation," "righteousness," and "justification." Colossians contains thirty-four words found nowhere else in the New Testament (so-called *hapax legomena*), such as the words translated "visible" (τὸ ὁρατόν; 1:16) and "the record" (τὸ χειρόγραφον; 2:14). More than this, Colossians also contains a number of unusual expressions not used by Paul elsewhere in his writings, such as "the blood of his cross" (τὸ αἷμα τοῦ σταυροῦ αὐτοῦ; 1:20), "evil deeds" (τὰ ἔργα τὰ πονηρά; 1:21), "the forgiveness of sins" (ἡ ἄφεσις τῶν ἁμαρτιῶν; 1:14), and "the fullness of deity" (τὸ πλήρωμα τῆς θεότητος; 2:9) (all above NRSV renderings).

b. *Style*. Many scholars draw attention to the rough Greek style of Colossians, wording uncharacteristically less refined and polished than the sentences of the main letters of Paul. For example, 1:9–12 and 1:24–27 constitute one sentence each in the Greek text, what some would argue are overly long and convoluted sentences. Another element of the letter's style that often incites comment is the redundancy found in such phrases as "praying . . . asking" (1:9), "wisdom and understanding" (1:9), "endurance and patience" (1:11), "securely established and steadfast" (1:23), "teach and admonish" (3:16), and "psalms, hymns, and spiritual songs" (3:16). A further characteristic of the style of Colossians is the linking of several modifying phrases (phrases using modifying words in the Greek genitive case). Some of these phrases end up forming chains of expressions whose sense is difficult to understand. Some of these include "all the riches of the fullness of knowledge" (2:2) and "of the faith of the work of God" (2:12) (renderings my own).

1–21; and D. J. Moo, *The Letters to the Colossians and to Philemon* (PNTC; Grand Rapids: Eerdmans, 2008), 25–59.

58. A bibliography of interpreters who hold either view can be seen in Moo, *Colossians and Philemon*, 29n5.

c. *Theology.* The major arguments against Pauline authorship concern theology. The general tenor of such arguments is that the theology of Colossians is developed to a sufficient degree to indicate non-Pauline authorship. The arguments take several forms. One is that there are a number of theological arguments that cannot be found in the other Pauline letters. For example, in 1:24, Paul depicts himself as in some way a vicarious sufferer on behalf of Christ, by some means filling up what is lacking in Christ's afflictions. In light of the emphasis upon justification apart from works in the major Pauline letters, especially Galatians and Romans, the notion that there may be something that Christ has not accomplished that Paul can in some way fulfill comes as a fairly radical departure. Furthermore, the major letters depict the fulfillment of the Christian life as in process or still not complete, but in Colossians, it is argued, that sense of urgency or constraint is missing. In Colossians, the end is seen as already present (1:28), a form of realized eschatology. There is none of the apocalyptic urgency of the earlier authentic letters, with their apocalyptic woes or discouragement regarding human behavior. Instead, God has already delivered believers from the realm of darkness (1:13), so that they are buried and raised with Christ (2:12–13), and the estranged are now reconciled (1:22). Hope is not something looked forward to (as in Rom 8:24–25), but is already stored up in the heavenly realms as a symbol of assurance and confidence (Col 1:5). Lastly, imagery regarding the church is more developed. In 1 Cor 12:12–27, Christ is equated with the body of believers, with the emphasis upon the unity within the church body; in Colossians, the church is the body of Christ of which he is its head as a cosmic, universal figure (1:15–20, 24). The church has expanded from a local body of believers to a universal spiritual entity that is part of Christ's universal reconciliation. Church order has developed with this body imagery. The use of the word often translated "minister" or "servant" (διάκονος; 1:7, 23, 25; 4:7; elsewhere sometimes "deacon") differs from its use in the main letters. In Colossians, it seems to relate closer to a particular vocation in the church, as in 1 Tim 3:8, 12 and 4:6 (but cf. Rom 16:1 and Phil 1:1, where it may indicate a vocation).

On the basis of this evidence, those who dispute Pauline authorship of Colossians usually argue for pseudonymous authorship.[59] The salutation of 1:1 indi-

59. See, e.g., M. C. Kiley, *Colossians as Pseudepigraphy* (BS 4; Sheffield: JSOT Press, 1984); and O. Leppä, *The Making of Colossians: A Study on the Formation and Purpose of a Deutero-Pauline Letter* (Publications of the Finnish Exegetical Society 86; Göttingen: Vandenhoeck & Ruprecht, 2003).

cates the possibility of dual authorship by Paul and Timothy, and it is known that Paul used a scribe on several occasions (Rom 16:22; Gal 6:11), but this solution does not commend itself to those who dispute Pauline authorship. Most of Paul's letters, especially other letters attributed to Paul and Timothy (such as Galatians), have some sort of joint attribution, but the style and subject matter of Colossians are still thought to be sufficiently different from the undisputed letters. The issue of the use of a scribe in the ancient world is a very difficult one. Even though the scribes Paul used for Galatians and Romans were probably different from the scribe he used for Colossians, the distinctive Pauline voice comes through well enough in those major letters that those who dispute Pauline authorship of Colossians note that this same voice is not to be found in Colossians. The result of such analysis is that a later date for composition, by some writer who pseudonymously represents himself as Paul, must be posited, probably sometime in the last quarter of the first century.

2. Arguments for Pauline Authorship

In spite of these rather skeptical comments, however, there are still many valid arguments for Pauline authorship. In assessing the issue of authorship, one must be careful not to be misled by some of the evidence and argumentation. For example, Edwin Freed claims that the view of baptism is very different in 2:11–12, where baptism and circumcision are equated (or at least seem to be equated), from elsewhere in Paul's letters, such as Rom 6.[60] According to Freed, circumcision is a "meaningless Jewish rite" for Paul! First of all, however, Paul is not quite so negative about circumcision. To be sure, circumcision has no redemptive value for Paul, but the word itself is used in several different ways, sometimes in a metaphorical sense, as in Rom 2:28–29, where circumcision of the heart is positive. Second, Freed must admit that there is some correlation between Col 2:11, regarding circumcision without hands, and Rom 2:29, and between Col 2:13–14 and Rom 6:3–5, both speaking of baptism as participating in new life. This kind of argumentation does not clarify the issue of authorship.

When more substantial arguments are considered, the case for non-Pauline authorship of Colossians is less clear, and in fact a very plausible and convincing case can be made for authenticity. There are four lines of evidence to consider: external evidence, word statistics, lexicography and grammar, and theology (especially the so-called Colossian hymn).

60. E. D. Freed, *The New Testament: A Critical Introduction* (Belmont, CA: Wadsworth, 1991), 305–6.

a. *External evidence.* The claim for Pauline authorship is supported by various kinds of external evidence.[61] Several important church fathers, such as Ignatius (*To the Ephesians* 2; *To the Magnesians* 2; *To the Philadelphians* 4; *To the Smyrnaeans* 1.2; 12; *To the Trallians* 5.2), Irenaeus (*Against Heresies* 3.14.1), Tertullian (*Prescription against Heretics* 7), and Clement of Alexandria (*Stromata* 1.1), and the Muratorian Fragment, endorse Pauline authorship of Colossians, and none of them entertain any doubts about this attribution. The connection of Colossians with Philemon must also be considered, since the links between the two are very strong. Both contain Timothy's name with Paul's in the salutation (Col 1:1; Phlm 1), and greetings are sent from some of the same people in both letters, including Aristarchus, Mark, Epaphras, Luke, and Demas (Col 4:10–14; Phlm 23–24; only Jesus/Justus is excluded in Philemon). In Phlm 2, Archippus is called a "fellow soldier"; in Col 4:17, he is directed to fulfill his ministry. In Col 4:9, Onesimus, the slave of Philemon, is mentioned as being sent with Tychicus. The lines of connection between Colossians and Philemon are so strong that if Colossians is not authentically Pauline, there was a distinct effort to deceive the early church into accepting it as Pauline (see chapter 6 §3).

b. *Word statistics.* Word statistics are not always clear, and one must be careful in drawing conclusions from them. For example, Galatians has thirty-one unique words, roughly the same number as Colossians, but this causes no one to raise any doubts as to whether Galatians was written by Paul. No doubt the reason for this is that Baur and many after him use Galatians and Romans (along with 1–2 Corinthians) as the basis against which the other letters are compared, when the entire corpus should be used as the body for comparison. More to the point, even the counting of supposedly unique words is difficult. For example, ἀνταναπληρόω ("fill up") in Col 1:24 is often cited as a unique occurrence in Colossians, but προσαναπληρόω in 2 Cor 9:12 is the same basic verb with a different prefix (they are cognates). Similarly, ἀποκαταλλάσσω ("reconcile") in Col 1:20 and 1:22 is also cited as a unique occurrence, but καταλλάσσω in Rom 5:10 and three times in 2 Cor 5:18–20 is the same verb with one less prefix (they too are cognates). As most recent work with vocabulary statistics indicates, this is not a firm criterion for disputing authorship.[62]

61. See J. Moffatt, *An Introduction to the Literature of the New Testament* (3rd ed.; Edinburgh: T&T Clark, 1918), 154.
62. For more linguistically informed authorship studies, see M. B. O'Donnell, "Linguistic Fingerprints or Style by Numbers? The Use of Statistics in the Discussion of Authorship of New

c. *Lexicography and grammar.* It is often noted that the author of Colossians uses a different word for "reconcile" (ἀποκαταλλάσσω) than Paul uses in Rom 5:10 and 2 Cor 5:19 (καταλλάσσω). Freed goes so far as to claim that this makes a "slight difference in the concept of reconciliation," but he does not say what that difference is.[63] The form in the Romans and Corinthian passages is not prefixed with a preposition as it is in Colossians. The words are in separate entries in a standard lexicon, but they clearly overlap in form and in sense.[64] Not too much should be made of these differences. It may well be that the style has been adapted to suit the subject matter, with twelve of the thirty-four new vocabulary items in Colossians appearing in possible descriptions of or responses to opponents (e.g., 1:10–20; 2:16–23) or in distinctively liturgical style (e.g., 1:15–20).

d. *Theology.* The so-called hymn of Col 1:15–20 raises interesting questions regarding authorship. This passage arouses discussion in three areas: authorship, origin, and use.[65] Many scholars believe that this hymn was written by someone other than the author of the letter to the Colossians and that it became part of the liturgy of the early church and was included here by the author because it was thought appropriate. Other scholars, however, are not convinced that such is the case. Some grant that it may have been written by the author, quite likely Paul, on another occasion than the composition of the letter, but they note that nothing prohibits the author of such a passage as 1 Cor 13 from having written this passage as well. Some who posit that the hymn was written independently of the letter suggest a form of Semitic precursor, while others suggest a Greek original. All these attempts to characterize the hymn, however, have the same problem: the supposed hymn, as it appears in Colossians, cannot be convincingly shown to reflect known forms of either Semitic or Greek

Testament Documents," in *Linguistics and the New Testament: Critical Junctures* (ed. S. E. Porter and D. A. Carson; JSNTSup 163; Sheffield: Sheffield Academic, 1999), 206–62. See also A. W. Pitts, "Style and Pseudonymity in Pauline Scholarship: A Register Based Configuration," in *Paul and Pseudepigraphy* (ed. S. E. Porter and G. P. Fewster; PAST 8; Leiden: Brill, 2013), 113–52.

63. Freed, *New Testament*, 306.

64. See S. E. Porter, *Καταλλάσσω in Ancient Greek Literature, with Reference to the Pauline Writings* (Estudios de Filología Neotestamentaria 5; Córdoba: Ediciones El Almendro, 1994), 172–85.

65. See Sanders, *New Testament Christological Hymns*, 75–87; Fowl, *Story of Christ*, 103–54; Porter, *Καταλλάσσω*, 163–69; C. E. Arnold, *The Colossian Syncretism: The Interface between Christianity and Folk Belief at Colossae* (WUNT 2/77; Tübingen: Mohr-Siebeck, 1995), 246–51; and M. E. Gordley, *The Colossian Hymn in Context: An Exegesis in Light of Jewish and Greco-Roman Hymnic and Epistolary Conventions* (WUNT 2/228; Tübingen: Mohr-Siebeck, 2007), esp. 170–269.

poetry. Indeed, it is highly difficult to outline this passage as a hymn, even when the two relative pronouns in 1:15 and 1:18 ("who") are used as markers of hymnic structure (but cf. 1:13 as well).[66] Furthermore, it is missing any type of rhythm or meter, which was characteristic of hymns in that period.[67] Various reconstructions divide this passage into two, three, or four stanzas, with interpolations posited at significant points. Some suggest that a form of either Semitic wisdom Christology or Greek-based protognostic theology rests behind the hymn (the gnostic theory has fallen on hard times lately—see below). In both cases, Christ is seen as the creator of all things (1:16), with three different prepositions (in [ἐν], through [διά], and to/for [εἰς]) used to describe his creative function. Christ is depicted in the hymn as the firstborn of all creation (1:15), which is variously interpreted as first in a temporal sequence (e.g., Prov 8:22 regarding Wisdom) or as first in rank or priority (Ps 89:27). This is admittedly a very high Christology, but it probably should not be seen as having its origins in either wisdom theology or protognostic thought.[68] Gnosticism did not develop the idea of the heavenly redeemer figure until later, probably under the influence of Christianity. What is said here of Christ goes well beyond the subordinate role given to Wisdom in wisdom literature. This is seen in Christ's being recognized by language that elsewhere is reserved for God in his function as creator and sustainer of the universe. Even more, the hymn goes on to depict Christ as the head of the church on the basis of his resurrection (Col 1:18). All the fullness of God is said to dwell in Jesus. If this is protognostic language, the author is usurping it for his own purposes, because he goes on to say that complete reconciliation of all things is through Christ, meaning his death (cf. 1:23). This passage causes a dilemma for those who argue against Pauline authorship. If the passage is either non-Pauline or at least not written by the author of this book, then its non-Pauline characteristics cannot be used as evidence for the non-Pauline authorship of the book. If it was part of an earlier liturgical or creedal statement used by the church, then the argument of the overly developed theology is dissipated. For if the passage

66. See E. Schweizer, *The Letter to the Colossians* (trans. A. Chester; Minneapolis: Augsburg, 1976), 55–60, whose analysis has been very influential.

67. Sumney, *Colossians*, 60–61.

68. Sanders, *New Testament Christological Hymns*, 79–80. There is the possibility of origins in Mithraism, a syncretistic cult based upon worship of the sun. Mithraism had conceptual and theological similarities with Christianity (e.g., a heavenly mediator) and thrived in the Roman Empire. It was not, however, particularly strong in Asia Minor. See A. S. Geden, ed., *Select Passages Illustrating Mithraism* (London: SPCK, 1925), for comparison. See also chapter 3 §2.

existed earlier (and it is difficult to say how much earlier), it must have been early enough to be formalized and passed down.

Philosophers of the Greco-Roman world depicted various organizations by means of the analogy of the body (e.g., Maximus of Tyre, *Orations* 15.4–5).[69] Regarding the church as the body of Christ, there is no doubt that Colossians seems to have a more developed understanding of this metaphor or analogy than other letters commonly accepted as Paul's. One question to be asked is whether a plausible line of connection can be created from the acknowledged authentic Pauline use of this imagery to the imagery in Colossians. If it appears that the development is too far removed or cannot be accounted for on this basis, we must ask how the early church was led to believe that such a stretched and strained metaphor could have come from Paul. The church's depiction as the body of Christ is a common Pauline metaphor (Rom 12:4–5; 1 Cor 12:12–30; Gal 3:28). The metaphor is essentially the same in Colossians; what is new is that now Christ is the head of the church in the analogy of the body (Col 1:18, 24). This lies along a very plausible conceptual (though not necessarily temporal) trajectory: it began with the church depicted as a body (Rom 12:4–5), then this body was equated with Christ's body (1 Cor 12:12–27), and finally this body was given a head, Christ (Col 1:15–20). Indeed, it would have been surprising if the analogy had not been developed in this way. Since the first two stages are found in writings acknowledged as authentically Pauline, it is plausible that the third is authentically Pauline as well.[70]

e. *Conclusions.* Colossians is either Pauline or non-Pauline in authorship. Since the letter purports to be by Paul, non-Pauline authorship would mean that the letter is pseudonymous (see chapter 6 §2). To claim Pauline authorship raises the issues of the role played by the coauthor, in this case Timothy, and the possible role of a scribe. It is in fact argued again that Timothy may have been the actual author of the letter, possibly writing somewhat independently of Paul.[71] Since none of these theories can be

---

69. See A. J. Malherbe, *Moral Exhortation: A Greco-Roman Sourcebook* (LEC; Philadelphia: Westminster, 1986), for examples of this and other texts.

70. Cf. S. Grindheim, "A Deutero-Pauline Mystery? Ecclesiology in Colossians and Ephesians," in *Paul and Pseudepigraphy* (ed. S. E. Porter and G. P. Fewster; PAST 8; Leiden: Brill, 2013), 173–95, who argues that the theology contained in both Colossians and Ephesians can be seen to reflect expected developments of Paul's "earlier" motifs in his undisputed letters, seen as the "continued work of the apostle's fertile and creative mind" (195). Cf. G. P. Fewster, "Hermeneutical Issues in Canonical Pseudepigrapha: The Head/Body Motif in the Pauline Corpus as a Test Case," in *Paul and Pseudepigraphy*, 89–112.

71. J. D. G. Dunn, *The Epistles to the Colossians and to Philemon* (NIGTC; Grand Rapids:

quantified in any meaningful way, it is very difficult to factor this scribal or coauthorship hypothesis into the equation. On the basis of the other evidence cited above, however, even though there are some recognizable differences in Colossians from the other Pauline letters, a plausible case for Pauline authorship remains the best explanation of authorship.

C. *Paul's Imprisonment and Date of Colossians*

Colossians is one of the four letters often referred to as the Prison Epistles (along with Philippians, Philemon, and Ephesians). Ephesus, Caesarea, and Corinth are suggested as possible places of authorship, but the traditional view of the Roman origin of the letter still commands the greatest degree of probability and scholarly support.[72] This means that Colossians would have been written during Paul's Roman imprisonment in approximately 61–62 (see chapter 2 §2E3).

D. *Opponents, Occasion, and Purpose of Colossians*

Trying to determine the occasion that elicited Colossians—the second most important critical issue regarding the letter, after authorship—arouses significant discussion but leads to no scholarly consensus. One of the difficulties is the issue of authorship. If the letter is non-Pauline and thus probably written at the end of the first century, if not later, it is even more difficult to establish the situation to which it is addressed, since little can be known of the actual author, situation, or audience.[73] Consequently, the discussion below assumes Pauline authorship. Those who hold to non-Pauline pseudepigraphal authorship have a range of options available and little grounds for agreement or proof.

1. Opponents

There are six important scholarly views about the opponents whom Paul addresses in his letter to the Colossians.

Eerdmans, 1996), 35–39, who admits, however, that his view may be very close to forms of scribal or Pauline authorship.

72. See the discussion in Moo, *Colossians and Philemon*, 41–46.

73. This has not stopped scholars from speculating, however. See H. Koester, *Introduction to the New Testament* (2 vols.; FFNT; Philadelphia: Fortress, 1982), 2.261–67. Much of the argument, however, is not concerned with authorship.

a. Morna Hooker argues against the traditional criteria used in most discussions of the opponents, noting that nowhere is there a formal exposition of any heresy that the author disputes.[74] So far as her reading is concerned, the only comments made in the letter argue against the readers' conformity to the beliefs and practices of their Jewish and their pagan neighbors. Hooker chooses to stress the positive statements that Paul makes rather than the negative. One of her complaints against most historical reconstructions of the situation behind the New Testament is that there is a circular reasoning at play, in which a heresy is posited and then this heresy is read out of the evidence.

   Hooker's approach is a welcome one in many ways, not least because it brings to mind many of the pitfalls and implied assumptions of historical reconstruction. Most scholars do not respond positively to the challenge that her work presents, however. The familiar evidence in Colossians dealing with the opponents includes the following. (i) Colossians appears to be confronting some form of philosophy (2:8) based upon tradition (2:8) and designed to impart knowledge or wisdom (2:23). (ii) Some of the characteristic beliefs of these opponents are endorsement of some kind of entrance into a realm of further knowledge or understanding (2:18), an entrance that might require a form or procedure of worship involving humility and harsh treatment of the body (2:23). What is worshiped is somehow connected with what are perceived to be the fundamental or basic principles of the universe, or with angelic beings (2:8, 20). (iii) Paul appears to be quoting, or at the least paraphrasing, some of his opponents' own language, including such phrases as "all the fullness/the whole fulness" (1:19; 2:9), "self-abasement and worship of angels" (2:18), and "do not handle, do not taste, do not touch" (2:21) (all quotations NRSV).

b. In light of this evidence,[75] one of the most popular and enduring positions regarding the Colossian opponents is that this is a form of Gnosticism. Lightfoot, for example, proposes that Paul was responding to a form of Jewish Gnosticism.[76] According to Lightfoot, there were elements of Judaism that Paul was opposing (such as Sabbath rules and dietary restrictions), but they were gnostic in nature, including an emphasis upon an

---

74. M. D. Hooker, "Were There False Teachers in Colossae?" in *Christ and Spirit in the New Testament* (ed. B. Lindars and S. S. Smalley; Cambridge: Cambridge University Press, 1973), 315–31.

75. See DeMaris, *Colossian Controversy*, 18–40.

76. Lightfoot, *Colossians*, 73–113. See R. Yates, "Colossians and Gnosis," *JSNT* 27 (1986): 49–68; and M. Goulder, "Colossians and Barbelo," *NTS* 41 (1995): 601–19, who argues for Jewish-Christian Gnosticism.

intellectual elite who took pride in wisdom, cosmological speculation (accounting for the "fullness" language), asceticism, mysteries, and various regulations that followed the calendar. Günther Bornkamm refines this by proposing a syncretistic gnostic Judaism with pagan elements, which came to be identified with Essene Judaism.[77] This theory combines elements of Judaism with Gnosticism and various other Eastern pagan cults. Lightfoot's position dominated thought for seventy-five years after he put it forward, but there are two major problems with it. First, it is unclear that Essene Judaism was in fact gnostic, and there is considerable doubt about how much Gnosticism is found in the first century. This objection jeopardizes all gnostic understandings of the Colossian problem. Second, some of the distinctive features of Essene Judaism, such as ritual washings, are not mentioned at all in Colossians.

Martin Dibelius emphasizes the gnostic elements further in terms of a mystery religion, citing the use of the word for "entering into [mysteries]" (ἐμβατεύω) (2:18) as meaning initiates' entrance into the sanctuary to consult the oracle on completion of a rite, and the "basic principles" (στοιχεῖα) (2:20; NRSV: "elemental spirits") as meaning the powers to whom the worshipers were devoted.[78] Dibelius's analysis draws attention to some important terminology, but one of the problems with pagan mystery cults is that they were highly secretive. Various forms of often syncretistic mystery religions flourished in the empire, including Mithraism, but only the initiates were allowed in to experience the mysteries (see chapter 3 §2C). This secrecy makes it very difficult to establish any sort of systematic understanding of their beliefs or practices, and it must have been an obstacle even for Paul to obtain enough knowledge to argue against them.

c. In light of the discovery of the Dead Sea Scrolls, Stanislav Lyonnet proposes the existence of a syncretistic Judaism that combined beliefs of the Essenes, perhaps as represented at Qumran, with various other Jewish beliefs.[79] This theory sees supposedly gnostic characteristics paralleled in

77. G. Bornkamm, "The Heresy of Colossians," in *Conflict at Colossae: A Problem in the Interpretation of Early Christianity Illustrated by Selected Modern Studies* (ed. F. O. Francis and W. A. Meeks; rev. ed.; SBLSBS 4; Missoula, MT: Scholars Press, 1975), 123–45.

78. M. Dibelius, "The Isis Initiation in Apuleius and Related Initiatory Rites," in *Conflict at Colossae: A Problem in the Interpretation of Early Christianity Illustrated by Selected Modern Studies* (ed. F. O. Francis and W. A. Meeks; rev. ed.; SBLSBS 4; Missoula, MT: Scholars Press, 1975), 61–121.

79. S. Lyonnet, "Paul's Adversaries in Colossae," in *Conflict at Colossae: A Problem in the Interpretation of Early Christianity Illustrated by Selected Modern Studies* (ed. F. O. Francis and W. A. Meeks; rev. ed.; SBLSBS 4; Missoula, MT: Scholars Press, 1975), 147–61.

other Greek thinking, and such important concepts as "elemental spirits," "worship of angels," and entrance into the mysteries are all reinterpreted. The problem with this solution is the challenge to find where syncretistic Jewish belief of this sort existed, apart from a reconstruction of the Colossian situation.

d. Jewish mysticism is also seen to be the origin of the Colossian problem. Fred Francis proposes an ascetic and mystical kind of Judaism, similar to apocalyptic Judaism. According to this position, the opponents advocated observance of a number of practices (such as dietary restrictions, calendar observance, and circumcision [2:11]) to prepare the person for a mystical vision and journey with angels to worship God. This has become a very popular position, and it is significantly bolstered by recent work on the apocalyptic dimensions of the contemporary Judaism.[80] The major problem with this position is the interpretation of the Greek phrasing. For example, the phrase "worship of angels" is taken as indicating worship alongside angels, which is not the most likely interpretation of the phrase, especially in light of the study of extrabiblical texts.[81]

e. Some form of Hellenistic philosophy is cited by a number of more recent scholars as the most likely explanation of the Colossian opposition. For example, Eduard Schweizer contends that the statements concerning eating, the ascetic statements, and the issue of the "basic" or "fundamental principles" do not indicate a Jewish element but, rather, the concerns of Greco-Roman philosophical circles. Neo-Pythagorean teaching dealt with these kinds of issues; according to it, humanity strives through various ascetic practices to escape this lower realm of existence. More recently, Troy Martin argues that Hooker is correct that Colossian Christians are responding to the beliefs and practices of their neighbors, which include elements of Cynic philosophy. Important features are asceticism, bodily humiliation, criticism of others, viewing oneself as an inhabitant of the cosmos, and the human will.[82] The emphasis upon Hellenistic elements

80. F. O. Francis, "Humility and Angelic Worship in Col. 2:18," in *Conflict at Colossae: A Problem in the Interpretation of Early Christianity Illustrated by Selected Modern Studies* (ed. F. O. Francis and W. A. Meeks; rev. ed.; SBLSBS 4; Missoula, MT: Scholars Press, 1975), 163–95; T. J. Sappington, *Revelation and Redemption at Colossae* (JSNTSup 53; Sheffield: JSOT Press, 1991); and C. Stettler, "The Opponents at Colossae," in *Paul and His Opponents* (ed. S. E. Porter; PAST 2; Leiden: Brill, 2005), 169–200.

81. See C. Rowland, "Apocalyptic Visions and the Exaltation of Christ in the Letter to the Colossians," *JSNT* 19 (1983): 73–83, for references.

82. Schweizer, *Letter to the Colossians*, 127–33; and T. W. Martin, *By Philosophy and Empty*

is a useful redress of the imbalance of previous scholarly emphasis upon Jewish elements, but one must question whether this provides the best interpretation of the factors involved. There is no doubt that early Christianity came into contact with various Hellenistic philosophies, but it is unproven that either of the two suggested above had a strong influence upon the Colossian Christians.

f. The final proposal, that the Colossian opponents were syncretistic, takes various forms. For example, Roger DeMaris, emphasizing 2:8 and 2:16–23, especially 2:16–19, as the polemical core of essential texts requiring interpretation, argues that there is a "distinctive blend of popular Middle Platonic, Jewish, and Christian elements that cohere around the pursuit of wisdom."[83] In his focus upon these passages, DeMaris's study is like the others noted above, even though he contends that his analysis recognizes the diversity of evidence. Middle Platonism was the later, mystical expansion of Plato's thought, and its elements include the order of the cosmic elements (2:8, 20), the asceticism that liberates the investigative mind (2:18, 23), and the intermediary figures (2:18). A recognizable weakness of such a hypothesis is in finding a group that actually held to such beliefs, apart from the Colossians. Clinton Arnold argues for a similar syncretistic solution, invoking local evidence to characterize the philosophy. Distinguishing between polemic (2:4–8, 16–23) and theology (1:15–20; 2:9–15) and drawing upon a wide array of inscriptional and papyrological evidence, Arnold concludes that "the beliefs and practices of the opponents at Colossae best cohere around the category of what might loosely be called folk religion."[84] This theory has the advantage of comprehensiveness but the disadvantage that it cannot be proved either true or false. Virtually every feature of this syncretistic belief can be found in a parallel text of some sort and, by definition, can be included within the structure of the set of syncretistic beliefs.

Despite these various proposals, no theory commands widespread consent. The range of the evidence is diverse and highly suggestive, but not definitive. Despite this, we still can gain some idea of how Paul responds to his opponents.

Deceit: Colossians as Response to a Cynic Critique (JSNTSup 118; Sheffield: Sheffield Academic, 1996), esp. 106–13.

83. DeMaris, *Colossian Controversy*, 17.

84. Arnold, *Colossian Syncretism*, 5. Arnold may, however, misrepresent DeMaris as taking a philosophical position, when it is better described as syncretistic. Cf. also Moo, *Colossians and Philemon*, 58–59.

2. Paul's Response

Paul's response to the opponents as found in Colossians, whoever or whatever they were, takes a three-pronged approach: Christology, apostolic teaching and tradition, and the importance of Christian freedom.[85]

a. *Christology.* Paul relies upon a high and developed Christology in Colossians (problems that this raises for authorship are discussed above). The opponents are seen as threatening this supremacy of Christ, who is the head of the church (2:19). Instead, Christ is depicted in Colossians as taking a cosmic and universal role as creator (1:15-17) and reconciler of both heaven and earth (1:19-23). While some of the opponents may have created the role of intermediaries, and even placed Christ in that role, for Paul there is no role for intermediaries, and even Christ is not to be seen in this position, for it is in him and only in him that the fullness of divinity dwells (1:19; 2:9). The consequences for this preeminence of Christ are seen in his position of authority over all creation, including the cosmic forces (1:18; 2:10). Nevertheless, Paul, along with his view of the exalted Christ, sees this position of exaltation predicated upon the humanity of Christ. This includes the reality of the incarnation (1:22; 2:9, 11-12) and redemption's being on the basis of the cross, where Christ's blood was shed (1:20) and suffering occurred (1:24).

b. *Apostolic tradition and teaching.* In Colossians, Paul opposes the traditions and teachings of the opponents with the apostolic tradition. Repeating a theme that he also emphasizes in Galatians (1:16-17), Paul makes clear that the tradition that he is conveying is antithetical to human tradition (Col 2:8, 22). The Colossians learned from Epaphras of God's grace (1:7) and heard the gospel preached (1:5), which they accepted by faith in Christ Jesus (1:4). Paul admonishes them to continue to walk in this tradition, which they have received (2:6), and to bear fruit and grow in it (1:6).

c. *Christian freedom.* On a more practical level, Paul opposes what is being taught at Colossae because it impinges upon Christian freedom. The imposition of regulations by the opponents constitutes a threat to Christian freedom (2:8), since the Colossians were called to live Christian lives without these false regulations and restrictions (2:22). Rather than enlightening them, which can only come from Christ's power (1:12; 3:1-3), in which they have participated in Christ's work of conquering demonic forces (2:20),

---

85. See R. P. Martin, *New Testament Foundations: A Guide for Christian Students* (2 vols.; 2nd ed.; Grand Rapids: Eerdmans, 1986), 2.214-16.

these false regulations impose darkness upon them (2:17). Their old nature has died to self, and they now have a new nature from Christ (2:11–13; 3:9–12). Christ, as head of the church, has transformed all of their previous relations and standards of behavior (3:5–11 on the earthly passions, and 3:18–4:1 on social relations in the Christian household). They are now one body (3:15), joined together by Christian love and peace (3:14–15).

It is difficult to say what the exact situation was at Colossae. It seems to have been related to competition from some form or forms of religious belief—quite possibly with ties to Judaism or some other group with tendencies toward, or interest in, mysteries—which threatened to substitute such religious practices for belief and worship of Christ. Paul seems to be concerned not only to exalt the position of Christ but to ensure that there is no belief or practice in the Colossian church that could in any way displace the rightful role of Christ.

E. Outline of Colossians

A. Opening (1:1–2)
  1. Sender (1:1)
  2. Addressee (1:2a)
  3. Greeting (1:2b)
B. Thanksgiving (1:3–12)
  1. Thanksgiving proper (1:3–8)
  2. Intercession (1:9–12)
C. Body: the superiority of Christ (1:13–2:15)
  1. Formal opening: deliverance and redemption through Christ (1:13–14)
  2. Christ, the Supreme Being (1:15–23)
  3. The work of Paul for Christ (1:24–2:5)
  4. Christ Jesus as Lord (2:6–15)
D. Paraenesis (2:16–4:9)
  1. Do not submit to false regulations (2:16–23)
  2. Rules for living a holy life (3:1–17)
  3. The Christian household (3:18–4:1)
  4. Christian behavior as seen by others (4:2–6)
  5. Travelogue of Tychicus (4:7–9)
E. Closing (4:10–18)
  1. Greetings (4:10–17)
  2. Benediction (4:18)

F. Content of Colossians

Opening (1:1–2)

Paul begins this letter by identifying himself as an apostle of Christ Jesus by the will of God, along with Timothy their brother. He writes to those in Colossae who are saints and faithful brothers and sisters in Christ. He concludes the opening with "grace to you and peace from God our Father."

Thanksgiving (1:3–12)

Paul tells them that he always thanks God when he prays for them, as he hears of the faith they have in Christ Jesus and the love they have for all the saints, because of the hope laid up for them in heaven (cf. 1 Cor 13:13; 1 Thess 1:3). They have already heard of this in the word of truth, the gospel, which is spreading all over the world. It was taught to them by Epaphras, Paul's beloved coworker in the gospel and a faithful minister of Christ. Since Paul heard from Epaphras about their love in the Spirit, he has not ceased to pray for them, that they would have knowledge of God's will in all spiritual wisdom and understanding so that they would live in a way that is worthy of the Lord, pleasing to him in every way and bearing fruit and increasing in his knowledge. Paul also prays that they may be strengthened with all power by God's glorious might, to have endurance and patience in joy, as they give thanks to the Father who has qualified them to share in the inheritance of the saints.

Body: Deliverance and Redemption through Christ (1:13–14)

Paul seamlessly transitions from thanksgiving to discuss the benefits of being in Christ, as he states that they have been rescued from the domain of darkness and transferred to the kingdom of God's beloved Son, in whom they have redemption and the forgiveness of sins.

Body: Christ, the Supreme Being (1:15–23)

Speaking of Christ, Paul states that Christ is the image (εἰκών) of the invisible God, the firstborn (πρωτότοκος) of all creation. Paul does not mean that Christ is simply an image of God but that he is a visible manifestation of the invisible God. He also does not mean that Christ is chronologically the firstborn, but uses the word πρωτότοκος to communicate Christ's preeminence over all creation.[86] He explains this by stating that all things were created through Christ; whether in heaven, under heaven, visible or invisible, kingdoms, powers, rulers, or anything else, all things were created by him and for him. He is before all things, and in him all things hold together. He is the head of the body, which is the church. He is the beginning, the firstborn (πρωτότοκος) of the dead, and he is preeminent in everything. It is in Christ that the fullness of God dwells, and through him he has reconciled all things to himself, making peace through his blood on the cross.

Speaking of reconciliation, Paul reminds his readers that they had at one time been alienated from God, having a hostile mind and evil deeds, but they were reconciled through Christ's death in his body so that he would present them holy and blameless before God, as they continue in the faith, stable and committed, not wavering in the hope of the gospel for which Paul became a minister.

Body: The Work of Paul for Christ (1:24–2:5)

Without directly mentioning it, Paul states that he rejoices in his afflictions (referring implicitly to his imprisonment) for their benefit, and in filling up in his flesh what is lacking in Christ's afflictions for the sake of his body, which is the church. This church is that of which Paul became a minister, according to the stewardship of God that was given to him, so that the word of God would be fully known. The word of God was a mystery for a long time, but it has now been revealed to his saints, the great mystery of Christ in them. Paul's proclamation is Christ, warning and teaching everyone so that they would be mature in Christ. This is why Paul struggles and works so hard with the strength that God gives him.

Paul wants the Colossians to know that the struggle that he has for them, as well as for the Laodiceans and even for those he has not yet met in person, has been great. His struggle is for them to be deeply encouraged, being knitted together in love, so that they would confidently know God's mystery, which is Christ. In him are all the treasures of wisdom and knowledge. Paul simply tells them this so that they would not be deluded by anyone with seductive arguments. He may not be there in person, but his heart is there, and he wants to see them in their firmness of faith.

---

86. Cf. N. Turner, *Grammatical Insights into the New Testament* (Edinburgh: T&T Clark, 1965), 122–25; and F. J. Matera, *New Testament Christology* (Louisville: Westminster John Knox, 1999), 141–42.

Body: Christ Jesus as Lord (2:6–15)

In light of his desire to see them established in Christ, Paul tells his Colossian readers to walk in Christ just as they received him, rooted and built up in him, established in the faith as they have been taught. They are to watch out so they are not captivated by the various philosophies and empty falsehoods that are based on human tradition and basic principles of the world rather than on Christ. It is Christ who contains the fullness of deity in bodily form, and they have been filled with him who has all authority. Not only that, but they were circumcised in him, not with a physical circumcision but with a spiritual one, when buried in baptism with him and raised with him as well through the powerful work of God. They were once dead in trespasses but God made them alive together with him, forgiving them of those trespasses, cancelling the record of debt, and nailing them to the cross.

Paraenesis: Do Not Submit to False Regulations (2:16–23)

In light of God's work in them, Paul commands them not to allow anyone to judge them regarding food and drink, or special days or Sabbaths, since these things are a shadow of the things to come, but the substance of these things is Christ. They are not to be disqualified by asceticism, worship of angels, focusing on visions, or being puffed up without reason. Those who participate in these things are disconnected from the head, Christ, from whom the entire body gets its nourishment and growth. So if they have died to these elemental things, Paul asks them, why do they still submit to these human regulations, like "do not handle," "do not taste," or "do not touch." These things look like they have value but really have only an appearance of wisdom in promoting self-made religion and asceticism.

Paraenesis: Rules for Living a Holy Life (3:1–17)

Paul encourages the Colossians, then, that if they have been raised with Christ (first-class conditional; assumes the protasis to be true for the sake of argument),[87] they are to seek the heavenly things where Christ is. They are to set their minds on the heavenly things rather than earthly things, because they have died and their life is hidden in Christ and will appear when Christ appears.

In setting their minds on heavenly things, they are to kill the earthly

---

87. Cf. S. E. Porter, *Idioms of the Greek New Testament* (2nd ed.; Biblical Languages: Greek 2; Sheffield: Sheffield Academic, 1994), 255–59.

things in them, things like sexual immorality, impurity, lusts, evil desires, covetousness, and idolatry, because these are the reasons why God's wrath is coming. Their past lives were characterized by these things, but they are to put away such things as anger, wrath, malice, slander, and profanity from their mouths. They are not to lie to one another, which is the old self, but to put on the new self in the image of Christ. There is no distinction here among people, but Christ is all and in all.

Rather than exhibit the above qualities, as God's chosen ones, holy and loved by God, they are to put on such things as compassion, kindness, humility, meekness, and patience, bearing with each other in love and forgiving each other if there is any complaint. The example of forgiveness is God, who has forgiven them, so they too should forgive one another. They are to put on love, the overarching characteristic of all of these things, which binds everything together in harmony. They are to let the peace of Christ rule in their hearts, and the word of Christ dwell in them abundantly, as they teach and admonish each other in wisdom, by singing psalms, hymns, and spiritual songs, with thankfulness in their hearts. Whatever they do, they are to do in the name of the Lord Jesus, with a thankful attitude toward God.

Paraenesis: The Christian Household (3:18–4:1)

One of several *Haustafeln* (household codes for behavior, but literally "house table"; cf. Eph 5:22–6:4; 1 Pet 2:18–3:7) in the New Testament, Paul gives instructions for how various members of the household should behave. He tells wives to submit to their husbands as is fitting in the Lord. Husbands are likewise to love their wives, rather than be harsh with them. Children are to be obedient to their parents, since this pleases the Lord. Parents are to refrain from provoking their children, since they may become discouraged. Slaves are to obey their masters in everything, not simply when they are being watched but sincerely, as if God were watching them. They are to do everything with all their heart as if to the Lord and not for other people, knowing that their reward comes from God and that wrongdoers will face judgment for their actions. Finally, masters are to treat their slaves fairly and justly, knowing that they are ultimately accountable to their own master.

Paraenesis: Christian Behavior as Seen by Others (4:2–6)

Paul addresses the Colossian believers in general by telling them to continue faithfully in prayer and by asking them to pray for him and to pray that God would allow more opportunities for declaring the mystery of the gospel, the reason why he was imprisoned at the time he was writing to them. He asks for prayer to make it clear how he should speak. He also commands them to walk in wisdom toward outsiders and to make the best use of their time. Their speech is to be seasoned with salt, so that they will know how to answer everyone.

Paraenesis: Travelogue of Tychicus (4:7–9)

Paul tells them that Tychicus will inform them (when he comes) all about Paul's activity. He assures them that Tychicus is a faithful brother and fellow servant of the Lord. Paul sends him to encourage them about himself and those with him, and tells them he will also send Onesimus, a faithful and beloved brother who is one of them. They will tell the Colossians of everything that has happened there.

Closing (4:10–18)

Paul ends with various greetings to them from his coworkers: Aristarchus, who has been in prison with Paul; Mark, Barnabas's cousin, who, if he comes, should be welcomed by them; and Jesus, also called Justus. These are men of the circumcision who have comforted Paul, but others also send greetings. Epaphras, who is one of them, a servant of Christ Jesus, greets them. He prays with a burden for them that they would stand mature and fully assured in all the will of God, and Paul testifies that he worked hard for them and those in Laodicea and Hierapolis. Luke, the physician, as well as Demas, greets them too. Paul then asks for greetings to be sent to the brothers in Laodicea and to the sister Nympha, including those in her house church.

Paul instructs them to exchange letters with Laodicea—they had a letter written to them as well—after they have read their letter in the assembly. This instruction is probably an indication that Paul's letters were read publicly at this time (cf. 2 Pet 3:15–16). The last instruction is that they are to tell Archippus to fulfill the ministry that he received from the Lord. Paul ends the letter with the statement that he himself writes (the ending) with his own hand. He tells them to remember his chains, and that grace will be with them.

4. Philemon

Philemon is by far the shortest of the Pauline letters. In several ways, as will be noted below, it is uncharacteristic of the Pauline corpus. Instead of causing problems, however, this helps to endear the letter to readers and also helps it to endure and even avoid some of the controversy that attends other Pauline letters. Nevertheless, within the space of only twenty-five verses, it manages to raise a number of highly provocative and even contemporaneous issues. I examine authorship, date and place of composition, and then occasion and purpose, before presenting an outline and its content.

A. Authorship of Philemon

The letter to Philemon, despite some characteristics noted below, is a personal letter, one of few such not only in the Pauline corpus but also in the New Testament. Apart probably from the Pastoral Epistles (see chapter 12), only Philemon and 3 John in the New Testament appear to be written as personal letters. This is confirmed by its placement at the end of the group of personal letters, following the church letters, in the Pauline canon (see chapter 6 §4). The form of the letter seems to be that of a letter from the apostle to a person or persons about a personal matter, rather than about a matter of concern to a local church. This is not to say that the matters raised in the letter do not have and have not had implications for the church, especially regarding the issues of authority and slavery. But this letter follows very closely the form of a letter of commendation or petition, which was widely used in the ancient world.

In a letter of commendation, the author commended another person, often in conjunction with some sort of petition or request. This is exactly what Paul seems to be doing in this letter.[88] His commendation concerns the escaped or runaway slave Onesimus, and Paul, in an indirect way, makes fairly specific petitions of Onesimus's owner, Philemon. As Werner Georg Kümmel states regarding authorship of Philemon: "Only tendenz-criticism could doubt the authenticity of this letter, which was already included in Marcion's authoritative writings. The letter, which of all Paul's letters stands closest in form to ancient private letters, displays in its personal features the signs of a genuine true-to-life quality."[89]

While Philemon appears to be a personal letter, and the content is the discussion of a personal matter, the form of the letter does not entirely support this analysis. This is seen in two ways. First, the letter is said to be from Paul and Timothy. This follows the form of all the other Prison Epistles except

---

88. See N. Petersen, *Rediscovering Paul: Philemon and the Sociology of Paul's Narrative World* (Philadelphia: Fortress, 1985).

89. Kümmel, *Introduction*, 349-50. Nevertheless, Baur did doubt it; see *Paul the Apostle of Jesus Christ*, 2.80-84.

Ephesians (which has no joint attribution) and reflects the general Pauline epistolary convention that a letter comes from Paul and a cosender, often Timothy, his traveling companion and fellow missionary. Second, the letter is addressed not just to Philemon but to Philemon, Apphia, Archippus, and the church that meets in "your" (singular) house. The letter begins with the plural address, but the rest of the letter continues in the second-person singular "you." This will be discussed further below, when alternative reconstructions regarding Philemon are introduced. But it appears, and will be the view taken here, that the letter was addressed primarily to Philemon, but with the idea that others in the church at Colossae, in particular Apphia and Archippus, would be interested in how Philemon responded to the apostle's letter.

As mentioned in chapter 5 §1, the average papyrus letter in the ancient Greco-Roman world, of which Egypt was representative, would have been somewhere around 275 words in length; but the letter to Philemon is around 335 words, hence slightly longer than the usual personal letter. The letter is surprisingly similar in form to that of the ancient Greco-Roman letter as well. As noted in chapter 5 §3, the typical Pauline letter has a five-part structure—opening, thanksgiving, body, paraenesis, and closing—an expansion of the typical three-part structure of the Greco-Roman letter. Philemon, however, departs from this structure in that it does not have a paraenetic section—although some may see the request for Philemon to receive Onesimus back to be paraenesis. However, since the purpose of the entire letter is this request, it is preferable to see this as part of the body rather than paraenesis. Since the paraenesis appears to have been one of the distinctives of the Pauline letter, at least insofar as he developed this into a major section of his letters, perhaps its absence is not surprising in a personal letter, especially one that conforms so closely to the ancient Greco-Roman form. These letters often had a prayer of thanksgiving to the gods at the close of the greeting or at the beginning of the body (depending upon how one analyses the letter form). The only other Pauline letter that follows Philemon's form is 2 Timothy.

B. Date and Place of Composition of Philemon

The letter to Philemon has a close connection to Colossians, and so, to some extent, its dating depends upon this connection. As mentioned in the discussion of Colossians above, of the six companions of Paul who send greetings in Colossians (Col 4:10–14), five of these (Jesus/Justus is missing) send greetings to Philemon (Phlm 23–24). Onesimus is referred to as one of the Colossians in Col 4:9.

The letter was written during Paul's imprisonment (Phlm 23), in either Rome, Ephesus, Caesarea, or Corinth, with Rome being the most likely (see chapter 2 §§2, 3, for where I place this letter in the context of Paul's imprisonments). It was probably sent by means of Tychicus (Col 4:7), who took the letter to Colossae, along with Onesimus, who was returning to Philemon.[90] If the Roman imprisonment is the correct one, then the letter was probably written in 61–62, with Paul's attitude possibly indicating that it was near the end of this time.

C. Occasion and Purpose of Philemon

The occasion and purpose of the letter to Philemon are usually closely tied together, but here the two will be separated for the sake of clarity of discussion.

1. Occasion

There are two major views regarding the occasion of the letter to Philemon (and a few other views as well, probably not worth mentioning here).

a. *The traditional view.* The traditional view is that Philemon was a member of the Colossian church.[91] Apparently he was converted under Paul (Phlm 9), though it is not known how or when this took place. Philemon had a slave named Onesimus, who had either fled from his master's control, possibly taking money or valuables, or simply not returned when he had been sent on a task for his master or, in one version, went to seek Paul to mediate a dispute between Philemon and himself. Onesimus intention-

90. Moo, *Colossians and Philemon*, 363.

91. For a good representation of the traditional view, see F. F. Bruce, *Paul: Apostle of the Heart Set Free* (Grand Rapids: Eerdmans, 1977), 393–406; cf. also B. M. Rapske, "The Prisoner Paul in the Eyes of Onesimus," *NTS* 37 (1991): 187–203; C. S. Wansink, *Chained in Christ: The Experience and Rhetoric of Paul's Imprisonments* (JSNTSup 130; Sheffield: Sheffield Academic, 1996), 175–99; J. A. Fitzmyer, *The Letter to Philemon* (AB 34C; New York: Doubleday, 2000), 17–23; and Moo, *Colossians and Philemon*, 364–69; among many others. On slavery and its use in the New Testament, see D. B. Martin, *Slavery as Salvation: The Metaphor of Slavery in Pauline Christianity* (New Haven: Yale University Press, 1990); M. J. Harris, *Slave of Christ: A New Testament Metaphor for Total Devotion to Christ* (Downers Grove, IL: InterVarsity, 1999); J. Byron, *Slavery Metaphors in Early Judaism and Pauline Christianity* (WUNT 162; Tübingen: Mohr-Siebeck, 2003); Byron, *Recent Research on Paul and Slavery* (Recent Research in Biblical Studies 3; Sheffield: Sheffield Phoenix, 2008), esp. 116–37; and J. A. Harrill, *Slaves in the New Testament: Literary, Social, and Moral Dimensions* (Minneapolis: Fortress, 2006).

ally or unintentionally came into contact with Paul, probably in Rome. If Onesimus had been on a trip for his master or had gone specifically to find Paul, it may well have taken him directly to where Paul was; this would obviate the difficulty of the distance between Colossae and Paul's place of imprisonment. Indeed, the trip may have taken Onesimus to Rome itself, if he had been a particularly well-trusted slave, possibly even sent to minister to Paul (though not so likely if he were seeking Paul on his own). Nevertheless, even if he had fled from Colossae, a thousand miles from Rome, he could have made the trip in five weeks, so this is not an insuperable difficulty for the Roman imprisonment hypothesis. We do not specifically know how Onesimus came into contact with Paul. He may have stumbled onto him by accident, or perhaps he was pointed in Paul's direction by someone Onesimus knew or had met, or he knew where Paul was and intentionally sought him out. Onesimus may even have known Paul from when they had both been in Asia. In any event, Onesimus had apparently become a Christian through Paul (Phlm 10) and had served him for a short while. Now he is being returned to his master, Philemon, accompanied by this letter, the letter to Philemon.

b. *The Knox hypothesis.* John Knox has an alternative view of the historical occasion of Philemon and its consequences.[92] His theory is that Philemon was the overseer of churches in the region of Colossae and Laodicea. Archippus—not Philemon—who lived in Colossae and in whose house the church met, owned the slave Onesimus, who was sent to Paul. Paul was sending Onesimus back, but by returning him by means of Philemon, with this letter, to Laodicea (for Knox, this is the lost Laodicean letter). Paul did not know the owner (Col 4:16) and requested that Onesimus be released for Christian service. The two letters, Colossians and what we call Philemon, were to be read out at Colossae when Philemon and Onesimus arrived. Archippus's ministry (Col 4:17) was the task of receiving back his slave. In the early second century, a letter of Ignatius (*To the Ephesians* 1.3; cf. 2.2) refers to an Onesimus as bishop, and this Onesimus, according to Knox, was responsible for gathering the Pauline letters. This accounts for why this letter was kept.

The Knox hypothesis raises several interesting issues and attempts to solve them, but most scholars reject this theory for several good reasons:[93]

---

92. J. Knox, *Philemon among the Letters of Paul* (rev. ed.; London: Collins, 1960); original edition published in 1935.

93. For thorough discussion of these issues, see B. W. R. Pearson, *Corresponding Sense: Paul, Dialectic, and Gadamer* (Biblical Interpretation Series 58; Leiden: Brill, 2001), 46–92.

First, Archippus is the third addressee in the letter, making it unlikely that he was its intended primary recipient. Second, the "church in your house" most likely refers to Philemon's house, as he is mentioned first, not to Archippus's. Third, Archippus's "task" of Col 4:17 is probably more than simply the matter of receiving his slave, since this would be a very obscure reference at best. It might also imply that Paul did know that Archippus was the slave's owner. Fourth, Paul seems to know the slave's owner, as Phlm 19 makes clear. Fifth, the text is not explicit that Onesimus was a runaway slave, but this is probably a more likely scenario.[94] Sixth, it is difficult to believe that this is the letter to the Laodiceans (Col 4:16) and that this was the letter to be read out. The statement in Colossians seems to imply an exchange of equal types of letters, but the letter to Philemon is out of balance in almost every way with Colossians.

2. Purpose of Philemon

The purpose of Philemon appears relatively straightforward.[95] Paul requests that his friend, whom he converted, receive his slave Onesimus back. Philemon must recognize, however, that the situation has changed. Onesimus is no longer to be treated as a slave but, rather, as a fellow servant of Christ and Philemon's partner in the spread of the gospel.[96]

Several important features show how Paul attempts to effect this change in relationship.[97] For example, Paul tries to maintain two levels of status in relation to Philemon. On the one hand, he plays on his own hardship by depicting himself as a prisoner (1, 10) and an old man (10; the word for "old man" may mean simply "elder"). On the other hand, he maintains the position of being at least Philemon's equal (17) and an apostle (22; understanding this as invocation of his apostolic presence). In depicting Philemon and Onesimus, Paul uses the language of family and social relations; for example,

94. See J. G. Nordling, "Onesimus Fugitivus: A Defense of the Runaway Slave Hypothesis in Philemon," *JSNT* 41 (1991): 97–119; contra S. C. Winter, "Paul's Letter to Philemon," *NTS* 33 (1987): 1–15; and Wansink, *Chained in Christ*, 174–99.

95. However, for a survey of various interpretations of this letter, see D. F. Tolmie, "Tendencies in the Research on the Letter to Philemon since 1980," in *Philemon in Perspective: Interpreting a Pauline Letter* (ed. D. F. Tolmie; Berlin: de Gruyter, 2010), 1–28; and Moo, *Colossians and Philemon*, 366–69.

96. One interpreter argues that the relationship between Philemon and Onesimus is not between master and slave, but as brothers. See A. D. Callahan, *Embassy of Onesimus: The Letter of Paul to Philemon* (New Testament in Context; Valley Forge, PA: Trinity, 1997). This, however, is an unlikely situation, as it is clear that slavery is involved.

97. See Petersen, *Rediscovering Paul*, 89–199.

Onesimus is his son (10) and his very heart (12), and is Philemon's brother (16). A second feature is that Paul, through indirect means, makes it clear that he expects Philemon to treat Onesimus as an equal as well. Paul recognizes that Onesimus has done wrong, probably in stealing from Philemon but also possibly having run off, but he also provides a means for him to be forgiven. Paul, playing upon Onesimus's name, which is cognate with the word for "useless," states that in Onesimus's new condition of being a follower of Christ, he is a "useful" person both to Paul and to Philemon. At the beginning of the letter, Paul commends Philemon because he has heard of his faith and his love for all of the saints (5, 7). Paul appeals to Philemon's love as the basis for his treatment of Onesimus as an equal in Christ. He points out that Onesimus had served in Philemon's stead while Paul was in prison. He does not describe what he expects Philemon to do, but at the least he counts on him to welcome Onesimus as he would welcome Paul himself (17). And if there is a debt owed—and here we see Paul tighten the screws—he instructs Philemon to charge it to Paul's account, but remembering that Philemon owes his Christian life itself to Paul, a difficult debt ever to repay (18). As a final gesture to guarantee compliance, Paul instructs Philemon to prepare a guestroom for Paul (22).

On the one hand, Paul is complying with the law, which required him to return a slave. Harboring a slave would have incurred punishment equivalent to the loss of income the owner could have gained per day from the work of the slave.[98] On the other hand, Paul is apparently instigating a subtle yet significant change in the social system, at least insofar as Christian treatment of slaves is concerned. As F. F. Bruce observes: "What this letter does is to bring us into an atmosphere in which the institution [of slavery] could only wilt and die. When Onesimus is sent to his master 'no longer as a slave, but as a dear brother,' formal emancipation would be but a matter of expediency, the technical confirmation of the new relationship that had already come into being."[99] For Paul to call for widespread manumission of slaves, however, would have incurred the wrath of the Roman government and an oppression of Christians that could well have proved fatal to the cause. As Ralph Martin rightly says: "It is sometimes alleged that since the New Testament never explicitly condemns slavery it is defective at a crucial point. But

---

98. See C. F. D. Moule, *The Epistles to the Colossians and to Philemon* (Cambridge Greek Testament Commentary; Cambridge: Cambridge University Press, 1957), 34–37, who cites a very instructive papyrus (P.Par. 10), which asks for help regarding return of a slave.

99. Bruce, *Paul*, 401. Cf. J. M. G. Barclay, "Paul, Philemon, and the Dilemma of Christian Slave-Ownership," *NTS* 37 (1991): 161–86.

part of the answer to this is that Paul does not advocate a social philosophy which countenances revolution and violence. Given the social structures of the Roman Empire of Paul's day, slavery could have been overthrown only by violent means; and the apostle will be no party to class hatred or violent methods (cf. Rom 12:17–21)."[100]

D. Outline of Philemon

  A. Opening (1–3)
    1. Sender (1a)
    2. Addressee (1b–2)
    3. Greeting (3)
  B. Thanksgiving (4–7)
  C. Body: commendatory or petitionary letter (8–22)
    1. Formal opening: Paul's request (8–14)
    2. Basis for the request (15–21)
    3. Pauline presence (22)
(D. Paraenesis—none)
  E. Closing (23–25)
    1. Greetings (23–24)
    2. Benediction (25)

E. Content of Philemon

Opening (1–3)

Paul introduces himself as a prisoner of Christ Jesus and his partner Timothy their brother. He writes to Philemon, their fellow beloved worker, as well as Apphia, Archippus, and members of the church in Philemon's house. Paul ends the opening with his conventional "grace to you and peace from God our Father and the Lord Jesus Christ."

Thanksgiving (4–7)

Paul always thanks God for Philemon when he remembers him in his prayers, because he hears of his love and faith toward the Lord Jesus and all of the

---

100. Martin, *Foundations*, 2.313.

saints. He prays for him, praying that the sharing of his faith would be effective for the full knowledge of every good thing that is in them for the sake of Christ. He reiterates that evidence of Philemon's love has been very encouraging to him because of the effect it has had in refreshing the saints.

Body: Paul's Request (8–14)

Paul states that, although he is bold enough to make this a command, he appeals to Philemon on the basis of love, as an old man (or elder) and prisoner for Christ, on behalf of Onesimus. He became a father to Onesimus during his imprisonment, and while Onesimus was previously "useless" to Philemon (a play on words involving Onesimus's name), he has now become useful to Paul. He sends Onesimus, his very heart, back to Philemon, although he could have kept and used him in service during his imprisonment. But Paul prefers not to make this decision without Philemon's consent, so that Philemon will not be compelled to do what he asks.

Body: Basis for Request (15–21)

Perhaps Onesimus left Philemon for a wrong motive, but God used the circumstance to bring Onesimus to Paul so that he would repent and be sent back as a brother. So Paul asks Philemon, if he considers Paul a partner in the gospel, to receive Onesimus back, and, if there is any debt or payment to be received, Paul will pay him back.[101] Paul writes this in his own hand to further authenticate this request and promise for remuneration. He guarantees he will repay it, but reminds Philemon that he, in turn, owes Paul his very life. He eagerly awaits some benefit from Philemon and asks for his heart to be refreshed in Christ.

Body: Pauline Presence (22)

Paul adds that he plans on passing through and visiting Philemon upon release from his imprisonment, so Philemon is to prepare a place for him; he knows that Philemon has been praying for his release.

---

101. This is probably Paul's way of asking Philemon to release Onesimus from the bonds of slavery and treat him as a true brother in the Lord; see G. F. Wessels, "The Letter to Philemon in the Context of Slavery in Early Christianity," in *Philemon in Perspective: Interpreting a Pauline Letter* (ed. D. F. Tolmie; Berlin: de Gruyter, 2010), 149–68.

Closing (23–25)

In closing, Paul mentions the greetings of Epaphras, his fellow prisoner, as well as Mark, Aristarchus, Demas, and Luke. He wishes the grace of the Lord Jesus Christ to be with him.

5. Ephesians

Ephesians was called the "quintessence of Paulinism" by F. F. Bruce.[102] By this Bruce means that it contains the concentrated essence of genuine Pauline teaching; other scholars take the view that Ephesians may well give the essence of Paul, but an essence written later by a close follower and disciple of the great apostle. This is only one of several critical questions about this book that continues to excite widespread critical interest. In this section, I first discuss the city of Ephesus and then authorship and date of composition, the relation of Colossians and Ephesians, and the origin, purpose, occasion, and destination, before finishing with an outline and its content.

A. City of Ephesus

According to Acts, Paul visited the city of Ephesus—the once beautiful and important city to which the letter is addressed—on at least two occasions, once for a short time near the end of his second missionary journey (18:19–21) and the other for two years and three months at the beginning of his third missionary journey (Acts 19). By this time, Ephesus was already an important and impressive Greco-Roman city enjoying the height of its economic and political, as well as religious, success.[103] Habitation in the area dates back to

102. Bruce, *Paul*, 424, following A. S. Peake, "The Quintessence of Paulinism: A Lecture," *Bulletin of the John Rylands University Library* 4 (1917–18): 5–31.

103. On the city of Ephesus, among many sources see Hemer, *Letters to the Seven Churches*, 35–56; C. E. Arnold, *Ephesians: Power and Magic. The Concept of Power in Ephesians in Light of Its Historical Setting* (SNTSMS 63; Cambridge: Cambridge University Press, 1989), 13–29; G. H. R. Horsley, "The Inscriptions of Ephesos and the New Testament," *NovT* 34 (1992): 105–68; R. E. Oster Jr., "Ephesus," *ABD* 2.542–49; H. Koester, ed., *Ephesos: Metropolis of Asia: An Interdisciplinary Approach to Its Archaeology, Religion, and Culture* (Valley Forge, PA: Trinity, 1995); P. Trebilco, "Asia," in *The Book of Acts in Its Graeco-Roman Setting* (ed. D. W. J. Gill and C. Gempf; BAFCS 2; Grand Rapids: Eerdmans, 1994), 291–362, esp. 302–57; and Trebilco, *The Early Christians in Ephesus from Paul to Ignatius* (WUNT 166; Tübingen: Mohr-Siebeck, 2004), esp. 11–51. Cf. also P. Scherrer, *Ephesus: The New Guide* (trans. L. Bier

the second millennium BC, and the city's history is divided into four distinguishable periods: Ionian, Greek, Greco-Roman, and Byzantine and later Byzantine. The third period, during which Paul evangelized the city, dates from when the Greek ruler Lysimachus (ca. 280 BC) moved the city from lower land to a location between two hills and built an extensive wall around the city. The city of Ephesus was a generally prosperous and influential city for the next roughly five hundred years—although it constantly had to fight the problem of an important harbor that was threatened by the inflow of silt. Today, the site of ancient Greco-Roman Ephesus is several miles from the Mediterranean sea, because of the buildup of silt that finally marked the end of the influence of Ephesus.

Ephesus was strategically located where the Cayster River entered the Mediterranean and positioned to become a center of influence and importance. Ephesus came under the control of Rome in 133 BC, when Attalos III turned his kingdom over to them. Roman Ephesus was at the center of turmoil for its first one hundred years, including revolting against Rome and being visited by Antony and Cleopatra. Ephesus's importance for the Romans was recognized by Caesar Augustus, who granted the city its freedom and established it as the capital of Asia. This was a logical decision, as Ephesus stood at the center of important trade routes by sea and land. Because of its excellent harbor (when the silt was under control through dredging), Ephesus became a major port of call for ships traveling in all directions, including those heading to and from the Aegean Sea and Bosporus in the north, to and from Palestine in the east, to and from Egypt in the south, and to and from the west. Ephesus was also the terminus for two major trade routes leading to the Euphrates Valley and Persia, one heading north and the other south across Asia Minor (its status is indicated by Roman milestones being calculated from Ephesus along these routes). As a result, Ephesus grew during Roman times to become the third largest city of the empire, with an estimated population of around 200,000–250,000 (behind only Rome and Alexandria in population). This population probably included a Jewish contingent, although direct evidence is lacking. The result of Ephesus's strategic location and resources (especially the harbor) was significant trade and commerce that led to major wealth. This then led to numerous major building projects.

When Paul visited Ephesus, during which time he probably wrote 1 Corinthians (as well as possibly some other letters) and may (though unlikely) have

and G. M. Luxon; Turkey: Zero, 2000); E. Akurgal, *Ancient Civilizations and Ruins of Turkey* (trans. J. Whybrow; 10th ed.; Istanbul: NET, 2007), 142–71, 354–60; and J. Murphy-O'Connor, *St. Paul's Ephesus: Texts and Archaeology* (Wilmington, DE: Glazier, 2008).

been in prison (see chapter 2 §2E3), Roman Ephesus was also an important religious center. There were a variety of religious cults and their related temples (e.g., Hestia, Serapis, and Zeus and the Mother goddess, as well as documentation for worship of many others), with the major one being the Temple of Artemis. Though worshiped elsewhere, the Ephesian Artemisian of the Greco-Roman period (it was at least the fourth temple to her in Ephesus) was one of the seven wonders of the ancient world and the largest Greek temple built in ancient times. Artemis was seen as a goddess of health and well-being, but her cult exercised influence in a wide variety of civic, cultural, and other ways. As a result, a lucrative devotion and business grew up around her worship. This resulted in a fervent defense of her cult by Ephesians, as well as protection of the industry that went along with it. Much superstition was attached to Ephesian religion, including the so-called seven Ephesian letters, used to ward off evil and perform other feats. The theater was another marvelous structure, seating an estimated 20,000–25,000 people in an arena designed for both civic and entertainment purposes. The original theater was built in the early third century BC and then went through various renovations during the first century. There were also a number of other buildings that one would expect in a major Roman city, such as marketplaces (agoras), baths, gymnasiums, and some beautiful private homes (whose remains are now on display).

B. Authorship and Date of Composition of Ephesians

The issue of the authorship and date of Ephesians is highly complex, and one that divides critical scholars.[104] As with authorship of Colossians, there is a fairly even divide among scholars regarding the authenticity of Ephesians, as Harold Hoehner shows in his extensive study of critical opinion on Ephesians.[105] In the current debate, three major views are argued: (1) the traditional view, which maintains Pauline authorship; (2) the pseudonymous view, which maintains that Paul did not write Ephesians; and (3) various mediating positions, which posit the influence of a colleague, such as Luke. The discussion of authorship will raise many other related issues of content that are important to discuss as well. Unlike previous discussions, I begin here with argument *for*

---

104. Since before the time of Baur, there have been a number of skeptics. See Baur, *Paul the Apostle of Jesus Christ*, 2.1–44, who also discusses Colossians. See also Kümmel, *Introduction*, 357–58, who shows the history of discussion from the eighteenth century, including issues raised regarding the style of Ephesians by Erasmus.

105. H. W. Hoehner, *Ephesians: An Exegetical Commentary* (Grand Rapids: Baker, 2002), 2–61, esp. 6–20.

Pauline authorship, before considering the arguments against it and a mediating view. Nevertheless, I still find the traditional view the most convincing.

1. Pauline Authorship

The traditional view is that the apostle Paul was the author of Ephesians. Many scholars still maintain that the letter was originally sent to the church at Ephesus by Paul;[106] the destination of the letter, however, does not have a necessary bearing upon the issue of authorship. Scholars with such diverse opinions as Donald Guthrie and Michael Goulder argue for Pauline authorship of the letter. There are at least five reasons in defense of Pauline authorship.[107]

a. *The epistle's self-claims.* The author of this letter clearly claims to be Paul, with his apostolic authority (1:1; 3:1). The other Prison Epistles are said to be coauthored with Timothy, but Ephesians (like Romans, even though a scribe was involved; Rom 16:22) has the singular claim of having been written only by Paul. This claim to authorship is reinforced by regular use of the first-person singular ("I, me") throughout the letter (Eph 1:15–16; 3:3–4, 7, 13–15; 4:1, 17–18; 6:19, 21–22). One would expect this to be the case if the letter were written by Paul; if it is not by Paul, either directly or indirectly, the issue of pseudonymity is introduced (see chapter 6 §2).

b. *External evidence.* It appears that Ephesians was written before the turn of the first century and was in widespread circulation by the mid-second century. The letter is clearly cited by Clement (*1 Clement* 64 [citing Eph 1:3–4]; 46.6 [4:4–6]; 36.2 [4:18]; 59.3 [1:18]), who wrote around 96, as well as by the *Didache* (4.10–11), Ignatius (*To Polycarp* 1.2; 5.1; *To the Smyrnaeans* 1.1; *To the Ephesians* 1.1; 10.3), Polycarp (*To the Philippians* 1.3; 12.1), and the *Shepherd of Hermas* (*Mandate* 3.1.4; *Similitude* 9.13.17).[108] The Muratorian Fragment, line 51, also lists the letter. On the basis of this external evidence, one might be able to date Ephesians to 80–95 but still

---

106. Hoehner, *Ephesians*, 2–6.

107. See Guthrie, *New Testament Introduction*, 509–28; and M. D. Goulder, "The Visionaries of Laodicea," *JSNT* 43 (1991): 15–39. An instructive opposition of positions is found in two essays: J. N. Sanders, "The Case for the Pauline Authorship" and D. E. Nineham, "The Case against the Pauline Authorship," both in *Studies in Ephesians* (ed. F. L. Cross; London: Mowbray, 1956), 9–20 and 21–35.

108. See Moffatt, *Introduction*, 394; cf. T. K. Abbott, *A Critical and Exegetical Commentary on the Epistles to the Ephesians and to the Colossians* (ICC; Edinburgh: T&T Clark, 1897), ix–xiii; and S. E. Fowl, *Ephesians: A Commentary* (NTL; Louisville: Westminster John Knox, 2012), 9. See also Hoehner, *Ephesians*, 2–6.

not require Pauline authorship. Another factor to consider is the apparent assumption in the letter that the temple in Jerusalem is still standing (hence before 70). When the author speaks of the reconciling activity of Christ as destroying the dividing wall (2:14), he is probably referring to the wall of the temple dividing the holy of holies from the outer areas and, to make the analogy understandable, assumes that this wall is standing.[109] Taking the dividing wall metaphorically as some other division between Jew and Gentile is possible, but not likely in light of the context, which seems to place the scene in Jerusalem around the death of Jesus, and hence during the lifetime of Paul.

c. *Letter form.* The letter itself follows the standard outline of a Pauline letter, with the five major sections: opening (1:1–2), thanksgiving (1:3–23), body (2:1–3:21), paraenesis (4:1–6:20), and closing (6:21–24). Indeed, in some ways it forms the archetypal Pauline letter, showing a balance of proportion not found in others.

d. *Language.* Differences of style in Ephesians have been noted since the time of Erasmus, but there are also several typical Pauline characteristics in the language of Ephesians. These include the vocabulary, which for the most part is more in harmony with the language used in Paul's earlier letters than any other of the letters falling into this later period (see below). The author makes use of paradoxical antitheses (6:15, regarding shodding feet with the gospel; and 6:20, with an ambassador in chains), typical of the main Pauline letters, and relies upon citation of the Old Testament, typical only of the main Pauline letters, in particular Romans.[110] Not only does he cite the Old Testament (4:8–11, citing Ps 68:18); he makes use of Old Testament imagery (Eph 1:22; 2:13, 17; 4:25; 5:2; 6:1–3). A number of objections are raised to other features of the language of Ephesians. The most important of these is the use of strings of modifying phrases. Opponents of Pauline authorship frequently cite numerous examples in Ephesians where modifying phrases, often using words in the genitive case, are strung together, arguably without a clear sense of modification (e.g., 1:18, literally: "the riches of the glory of his inheritance"), as we saw above in Colossians. In his insightful work on the opponents in Ephesians (which he takes to be the letter to the Laodiceans), Goulder points out two things. First, in Paul's letters, including his main letters, one of his common techniques is to cite his opponents' claims but gloss them with his own rebuttal (e.g.,

109. See M. Barth, *Ephesians* (AB 34; 2 vols.; Garden City, NY: Doubleday, 1974), 1.283–87.
110. On use of the Old Testament, see T. Moritz, *A Profound Mystery: The Use of the Old Testament in Ephesians* (NovTSup 85; Leiden: Brill, 1996).

1 Cor 2:6–7; 2 Cor 3:1–3, 7; 4:4). Second, when Paul responds, he often does so by stating what he believes has been accomplished in Christ. Thus a mammoth single sentence such as Eph 1:3–14 makes good sense of its repeated use of "in Christ" phrasing when opponents with a subordinate view of Christ are concerned (see also 3:16–17). As Goulder says: "Once one is aware of this tendency, the loose trailing on of clauses and genitival phrases is seen to be no more un-Pauline in Ephesians than in 2 Cor 4.4. The denial of Pauline authorship is the consequence of the widespread temptation to substitute counting for thinking."[111]

e. *Theology.* There are numerous theological similarities between Ephesians and the other Pauline letters. Included among these are references to God as glorious (1:17), powerful (1:10–20), merciful (2:4–10), and predestining (1:5–14). Christ is seen to have a high and exalted position, witnessed not only by the repeated use of "in Christ" language discussed in chapter 4 §2B (e.g., 1:3, 10, 11) but also by the function he is given of reconciling humanity to God and humans to each other by means of the cross (2:13–16). Christ is also the one who triumphs over all other powers (1:21–22). The Holy Spirit serves as an agent of revelation (2:18; 3:5) and as a unifying force in the Christian community (4:3; 5:18). The church has been brought together or reconciled by Christ so that Jew and Gentile form one new creation (2:13–16). Men and women are to be mutually submissive to each other (5:21).

These arguments provide very convincing reasons for affirming the Pauline authorship of the letter to the Ephesians. There are a number of individual elements within the letter, but overall the arguments point toward Pauline authenticity.

2. Non-Pauline Authorship

A significant number of scholars, however, do indeed deny that Paul wrote Ephesians, even if over the last hundred years or so the numbers are roughly equal for and against Pauline authorship.[112] According to this view, any references to Paul as writer must be taken as pseudonymous references and not historically precise. Three major reasons are offered for the pseudonymous authorial position.[113]

---

111. Goulder, "Visionaries of Laodicea," 21.
112. See the extensive discussion in Hoehner, *Ephesians*, 6–20.
113. See A. T. Lincoln, *Ephesians* (WBC 42; Dallas: Word, 1990), lix–lxxiii.

a. *Point of view.* The point of view in Ephesians seems to reflect a period later than that of the life and ministry of Paul. This is seen in two ways. First, Paul is treated with a high amount of dignity unbefitting his writing the letter himself (3:1–13) but more in keeping with a later follower or disciple of Paul writing with reverence and respect for the former apostle to the Gentiles, as if he were still speaking to the Christian community. Second, and in keeping with the first, the letter seems to refer to the apostles as if they were a closed group (2:20; 3:5). If Paul were one of the apostles, it is unlikely that he would refer to the group as a separate and distinct foundational group that the current church had been constructed upon (cf. 1 Cor 12:28, where the closer integration of apostles with others in the church reflects the tone of 1 Corinthians).

b. *Language and style.* There are forty *hapax legomena*, or words not found elsewhere in the New Testament (fifty-one words are not found in the undisputed letters of Paul), including the words translated "tossed to and fro" (κλυδωνίζομαι; 4:14) and "lost all sensitivity" (ἀπαλγέω; 4:19). Other words found in other letters are used in a new sense, such as "mystery" (μυστήριον; 5:32), "plan" or "commission" (οἰκονομία; e.g., 1:10; 3:2, 9), and "fullness" (πλήρωμα; 1:23). Many see the language of Ephesians reflecting the language not of the early Pauline letters but of the Apostolic Fathers, indicating a date in the late second century.[114] When words that are Pauline are found in Ephesians, it is not uncommon to find that they have been compounded or that they are strung together in large phrases and expressions (1:3–14, 15–23; 2:1–10)—often highly repetitious ones such as "great love with which he loved us" (2:4) or "holy and blameless" (1:4). Colossians and Ephesians are quite similar in arrangement and subject matter (see below), and, by the traditional chronology and views of authorship, they must have been composed at very close to the same time. They are sufficiently different in their language and style, however, to raise questions. Some might posit the greater involvement of a scribe or secretary in composition, but this would mean that the secretary had sacrificed Paul's language for that of another.

c. *Theology.* In Ephesians, certain doctrines seem to have either faded from prominence or been replaced by other doctrines. For example, to some it appears that the stress on the death of Christ and the theology of the cross has faded from view in Ephesians. The cross is directly mentioned

114. See C. L. Mitton, *The Epistle to the Ephesians: Its Authorship, Origin, and Purpose* (Oxford: Clarendon, 1951), 111–58; cf. 279–315, where Mitton finds that Ephesians draws heavily upon the other Pauline letters in its wording, as well as upon 1 Peter.

only at Eph 2:16, and Christ's death only at 1:7 and 5:2, 25. While the earlier Pauline letters seem to reflect a futuristic eschatology (1 Thess 4:13–17; 2 Thess 2), Ephesians seems to reflect a realized eschatology in which believers are already seated in the heavens with Christ (2:6), although there is a current battle with evil powers (2:2; 6:12). Concerning marriage, it appears that the author of Ephesians is making concessions regarding the strong position exemplified in 1 Cor 7, which has a firm but egalitarian posture. Ephesians 5:22–33 is said to alter that stance, however, by imposing a subordinationist position on women and moving the discussion away from considerations of actual life to a spiritualized sense in which husband-wife relations are related to Christ and the church. The church, instead of being built on Jesus Christ (cf. 1 Cor 3:11), is now seen to be built on the "apostles and prophets" (Eph 2:20) and is the replacement of Israel, an idea hinted at in the main Pauline letters only possibly in Gal 6:16.

In spite of this recognizably strong evidence, there are two major problems with the view that Ephesians is not by Paul. First, the evidence tends to be negative (e.g., regarding language and style)—finding problems with the traditional view but not concerned to explain the evidence at hand. For example, most would argue for a date of 80–90 if the letter is not by Paul, even though some of the evidence used to establish non-Pauline authorship claims that the language dates to the late second century. Contradictory negative arguments do not combine to form a positive argument regarding pseudepigraphal authorship. Second, there are the historical and theological problems, as with all pseudonymous-letter theories. Since the letter is clearly attributed to Paul, it means that some later writer who was not Paul used the apostle's name. This raises important issues regarding the nature of the Pauline corpus (see chapter 6 §3).[115] Another issue is that the letter contains exhortations for its readers to speak truthfully (e.g., 4:25), yet lies about its author being Paul without any moral justification.[116] Nevertheless, many scholars still maintain that Ephesians was written as a letter for the Pauline churches of Asia Minor after the apostle had died, since he had left followers, possibly a school, who perpetuated his tradition through written letters.

---

115. I examine some of the implications in S. E. Porter, "The Implications of New Testament Pseudonymy for a Doctrine of Scripture," in *Interdisciplinary Perspectives on the Authority of Scripture: Historical, Biblical, and Theoretical Perspectives* (ed. C. R. Bovell; Eugene, OR: Pickwick, 2011), 236–56.

116. F. Thielman, *Ephesians* (BECNT; Grand Rapids: Baker, 2010), 5.

3. Mediating View

For some scholars, the faceoff between those for and against Pauline authorship demands a third perspective. The mediating position, represented by
Ralph Martin, recognizes the weight of the evidence for Pauline authorship.[117]
He notes the kinds of similarities in language and thought mentioned above,
as well as the external evidence. But he also recognizes that there are persistent difficulties and problems in accepting the letter as Pauline, in the
same sense that other letters are accepted as Pauline, such as Philippians.
The solution he proposes is that the teaching, while authentically Pauline
and originating with the apostle, has been compiled and published by a
faithful follower. This person must have been someone familiar with Paul's
thinking, one who could be entrusted to represent what Paul had to say, but
could adapt it to the situation being addressed. For Martin, the logical choice
of writer is Luke. In support of such a hypothesis, of the words found in
Ephesians but not in Paul's main letters, twenty-five are found in Luke–Acts,
and ten of these are found nowhere else in the New Testament; in addition,
some phrasing seems Lukan. Further support is found in parallels between
Ephesians and Paul's meeting with the Ephesian elders recorded in Acts
20:17–38—for example, the discussion regarding the Holy Spirit (Acts 20:23,
28; Eph 3:5; 4:3–4).

If Martin is correct and Luke was the actual "writer" of Ephesians, that
is, the one who took Paul's thinking and applied it to the situation at Ephesus and committed this to writing, several difficulties are overcome. First,
this would account for stylistic differences between Ephesians and the major
Pauline Epistles. It would even account for Ephesians often being seen as
not a personal letter, since only Tychicus is personally greeted at the end of
the letter (6:21). Second, the portrayal of Paul's apostleship as unique and
authoritative (3:1–13) would make sense if the writer or compiler of the letter
were someone such as Luke, a longtime traveling companion and follower
of the great apostle. Third, such a view of authorship would make sense of
some of the modifications in thought from other letters, such as the waning
of expectation regarding the parousia (3:20–21) or the view of the church as
a new creation, with racial boundaries abolished (especially if the writer were
a Gentile such as Luke).

Martin's idea has much to commend it, but it also encounters two sets of
difficulties. One concerns particular items of his comparisons. For example,
C. L. Mitton raises the discrepancy that Acts apparently does not know of

---

117. Martin, *Foundations*, 2.230–33.

Paul's letters, while Ephesians—supposedly written by Luke—knows of Acts 20.[118] The second set of difficulties concerns what constitutes evidence and how the hypothesis can be proved true or false. On the one hand, similarities between Ephesians and the Lukan writings become evidence for Luke's involvement because Ephesians is already seen to be under Luke's influence. On the other hand, anything that does not conform to Paul's style or thinking can be attributed to Luke as well. It is difficult to know what would constitute proof that Luke—or almost any other writer—was (or was not) involved in the writing process. Furthermore, so little is known about the traveling companions of Paul, including Luke, that it is difficult to attribute such writing activities to them or know the nature of any involvement by them.

In conclusion, the critical issues above—especially the Lukan hypothesis and the negative, rather than positive, evidence regarding non-Pauline authorship—are highly problematic and difficult to prove. As noted above, they may raise questions about the authenticity of Ephesians, but they do not make a positive alternative argument. Since the arguments for Pauline authorship at least address the major problems, authentic Pauline authorship remains, to my mind, the most reasonable and persuasive choice among the alternatives.

C. Relation of Colossians and Ephesians

The complex relation of Colossians to Ephesians—already noted above—is important regardless of the view one takes of authorship.[119] For those who hold to Pauline authorship (the position taken here), it indicates composition of the letters at a similar point in Paul's ministry—while being held prisoner, probably in Rome. It suggests that Paul wrote one of the letters, probably Colossians, first, and then used some of the same ideas, and occasionally even the same wording, when writing Ephesians. A comparison of Colossians and Ephesians may suggest something similar for those who hold to the mediating view of Pauline authorship, according to which the writer—whether he was Luke or someone else is unimportant at this stage—likely used Colossians in some way as a template for his composition. For those who hold to non-Pauline authorship of Ephesians, the picture may well have been similar, except that there was an interval between the writing of Colossians by Paul—if in fact

---

118. C. L. Mitton, *Ephesians* (NCB; Grand Rapids: Eerdmans, 1973), 17. Mitton's minimal level of knowledge of Paul's letters in Acts may well be questioned. See S. E. Porter, *How We Got the New Testament: Text, Transmission, Translation* (ASBT; Grand Rapids: Baker, 2013), 113-14.

119. See Hoehner, *Ephesians* 20-25.

it was by Paul—and its use by someone to create a letter to a fellow church in Asia (or at least one that purports to be to this church). The purpose of this section is not to argue for a particular view of Ephesians' relation to Colossians but, rather, to present the similarities so that they can be appreciated in studying the two letters.[120]

It is estimated that 34 percent of the words of Colossians reappear in Ephesians. Or if the movement was the other way, 26.5 percent of Ephesians appears in Colossians.[121] Despite this significant amount of overlap, very few extended passages are paralleled. The one important exception is Col 4:7–8 and Eph 6:21–22, which have extended verbal agreement of twenty-nine words. In all other parallel passages, five to seven words at most are the same from one letter to another. Perhaps more noticeable than the verbal parallels, however, are similarities not only in the epistolary form but also in the topics. These are set out in table 5. One must be careful with such a chart, however. As Andrew Lincoln points out, there are also a number of differences in content. And certain organizational features (e.g., the opening) regularly appear in set places in the Pauline letters, thus minimizing some of the similarities of these two letters.[122]

Table 5. Colossians and Ephesians: Parallel of Outline and Content

	Colossians	Ephesians
opening	1:1–2	1:1–2
thanksgiving, intercessory prayer	1:3–14	1:3–14, 15–23
readers' alienation but now reconciliation	1:21–23	2:11–22
Paul as a suffering apostle and minister of mystery	1:24–29	3:1–13
head-body relation	2:19	4:15–16
old and new person	3:5–17	4:17–5:20
household code	3:18–4:1	5:21–6:9
exhortation to prayer	4:2–4	6:18–20
Tychicus commended	4:7–9	6:21–22
benediction	4:18	6:23–24

120. I argue, however, in a previous article that the Pauline usage of reconciliation language in both letters points to Pauline authorship; cf. S. E. Porter and K. D. Clarke, "Canonical-Critical Perspective and the Relationship of Colossians and Ephesians," *Biblica* 78 (1997): 57–86.

121. See Lincoln, *Ephesians*, xlviii. An excellent synopsis of the two biblical books is provided in Moffatt, *Introduction*, 375–81.

122. See Lincoln, *Ephesians*, xlix.

D. *Origin, Purpose, Occasion, and Destination of Ephesians*

Determination of the origin of Ephesians directly depends upon one's view of authorship. If the letter is by Paul or a close associate, such as Luke, it originated during his imprisonment in either Rome, Ephesus, Caesarea, or Corinth, with Rome being the most likely (see chapter 2 §2E3). If the letter is non-Pauline, it is impossible to determine the origin or destination of the letter.

The destination, purpose, and occasion of the letter are closely interconnected. These will be treated together in light of the difficulty with the opening of the letter. There is serious debate regarding the destination of the letter in 1:1 because all of the best and earliest manuscripts ($\mathfrak{P}$46, Sinaiticus [א 01], and Vaticanus [B 03], among others) lack the words "in Ephesus." If the words "in Ephesus" are taken out, as they almost assuredly should be, the Greek phrasing is not only awkward but unparalleled,[123] indicating that at some time there must have been some city or destination listed in the manuscript. Unfortunately, the manuscript tradition lists no city but Ephesus. Origen, the church father, attempting to explain the opening without a destination, speculated that the opening "the saints who are" refers to those called into existence by God, who is Being himself. Others try to explicate "the saints who are" and the "faithful" as Jewish and Gentile Christians respectively. None of these proposals proves satisfactory. Other solutions are more enlightening.[124]

1. Letter to the Ephesians

For those who maintain Pauline authorship of the letter, some might still maintain that it was originally addressed to the church at Ephesus, even if it was addressed to other churches as well. This position recognizes that, despite the dispute over the destination of the letter, Ephesus is nevertheless the only one recorded in the textual tradition, including the church fathers.[125] For example, Peter O'Brien notes, while the manuscript evidence points to not having

---

123. See F. Blass and A. Debrunner, *A Greek Grammar of the New Testament and Other Early Christian Literature* (trans. R. W. Funk; Chicago: University of Chicago Press, 1961), §413(3).

124. See E. Best, "Recipients and Title of the Letter to the Ephesians: Why and When the Designation 'Ephesians'?" *Aufstieg und Niedergang der römischen Welt* 2.25.4 (1987): 3247–79; Lincoln, *Ephesians*, 1–4; and D. A. Carson and D. J. Moo, *An Introduction to the New Testament* (2nd ed.; Grand Rapids: Zondervan, 2005 [1992]), 488–91.

125. See F. J. A. Hort, *Prolegomena to St. Paul's Epistles to the Romans and the Ephesians* (London: Macmillan, 1895), 86–98.

"in Ephesus" in the original reading, that so many later manuscripts contain those words may indicate that the letter ended up in Ephesus in one away or another.[126]

This view of Ephesus as the destination still encounters several objections, especially if Paul is the author of the letter. The letter gives the idea that the author does not know the congregation (1:15; 3:2–3; 4:21), even though Paul spent several years ministering in Ephesus (see Acts 19). Furthermore, as mentioned, there are no personal references in the letter, apart from the mention of Tychicus (and this is a commendation), and no apparent firsthand knowledge of the situation in Ephesus. The letter appears to be addressed to Gentiles, but there probably were also Jewish Christians in Ephesus. This evidence seems to indicate either that Paul was addressing only one faction of the congregation or that the traditional destination is not accurate and must be reassessed.

2. Circular Letter

The lack of an explicit destination in the inscription leads to the circular-letter position. The view that the letter is a circular letter can take at least two forms.[127] Some argue that the letter is authentically Pauline but was not addressed to only one church; in other words, it was a circular letter, quite possibly taken by Tychicus at the same time he carried to Colossae the letters to the Colossians and Philemon. This would account for the blank in the early manuscripts, since it was left to the reader of the letter in a given city to fill in the name of that city; for the lack of formal greetings and the more distant tone; and, in the view of certain scholars, for the letter's assemblage of some of Paul's essential thoughts. Later, possibly because a copy of the letter remained in Ephesus, the letter became associated with that city. One problem with the circular-letter hypothesis is that besides the place of destination, "Ephesus," the word "in" is missing from the earliest manuscripts. One might expect the inclusion of this word to indicate where to insert the destination (i.e., "in . . .").

Others argue that the letter was a circular letter that is not authentically Pauline. Written in the spirit of an authentic Pauline letter, it was designed to disseminate his message to a number of churches in Asia. This view has similarities to Edgar J. Goodspeed's hypothesis regarding the origin of the Pauline letter corpus (see §5D5 below and chapter 6 §4).

126. P. T. O'Brien, *The Letter to the Ephesians* (PNTC; Grand Rapids: Eerdmans, 1999), 48–49.

127. See, e.g., D. A. Hagner, *The New Testament: A Historical and Theological Introduction* (Grand Rapids: Baker, 2012), 588–89; cf. 600.

3. Safeguard Letter against the Colossian Heresy

The view that Ephesians was written against the Colossian heresy, and tied to the circular-letter hypothesis, argues that the letter was not written to the Ephesians alone but, rather, to the larger surrounding community of Christians in Asia to provide a safeguard against the spread of the heresy (see §3D1 above). This theory would explain why the letter uses or reveals dependence upon Colossians, since it was designed to provide a more general statement that a large number of churches could read with profit. According to this view, Tychicus probably carried this letter as well and set it in circulation when he arrived in the area.

4. Letter to the Laodiceans

Colossians 4:16 states that, after the letter to the Colossians has been read, it was apparently to be exchanged with a letter to the Laodiceans so that the latter can be read to the Colossian church. There have been many attempts to locate the letter to the Laodiceans, but several hypotheses aside, no letter has been found (a fourth-century Latin letter, cited in §2C1g above, is certainly not that letter).[128] Goulder argues that Ephesians must be the letter to the Laodiceans, if it is authentic (which he believes it is), for several reasons: the associating of the Colossians with the Laodiceans (Col 2:1), the linkage between the two letters, problems about the identification of the addressee, and Marcion's purported attribution of Ephesians to a Laodicean origin (Tertullian, *Against Marcion* 5.17.1; note also that there is a Marcionite prologue for a letter to the Laodiceans but not one for Ephesians).[129]

The evidence cited plausibly points in the direction of the Laodicean letter, but such attribution is still not in the manuscript tradition. Goulder argues that, when the Laodicean community became anti-Pauline (Rev 3:14–22), the original letter was destroyed but a copy survived at Ephesus; the ancient evidence, so he believes, commends this view.

5. Ephesians and the Pauline Corpus

A final view links the occasion of Ephesians with the formation of the Pauline corpus. E. J. Goodspeed proposes that the Pauline letters were gathered together around the turn of the first century, after waning in importance since

128. See J. K. Elliott, *The Apocryphal New Testament* (Oxford: Clarendon, 1993), 543–46.
129. Goulder, "Visionaries of Laodicea," 16n1.

the death of the apostle. Interest in Paul's writings revived, and the letter we know now as Ephesians was written as a cover letter for this collection.[130] In Goodspeed's view, a devoted follower of Paul, writing it for those unfamiliar with Paul's writings, used the opportunity to summarize what he thought was important and enduring in Paul's thought. The collection of the Pauline letters would have circulated to various churches, with the addressee conceivably being changed according to the church in receipt of it.

The problems with this view are several. Since recent rethinking about the formation of the Pauline letter collection does not recognize a time when Paul's letters were under a threat of being forgotten, this theory is less plausible than ever. The major problem is that there is no trace that Ephesians was ever at the head of any collection of the Pauline corpus. One would expect to find some collection in which this order of assemblage is reflected, but no set of manuscripts or manuscript list shows this. There are also further difficulties. How do we explain the reference to Tychicus if he were not involved in the letter's dissemination? And why was Colossians, of all letters, chosen as the letter to imitate in Ephesians, especially when Romans has traditionally been seen to serve the function of introducing the major Pauline teachings?

6. Summary

The occasion for Ephesians is, in many ways, one of the most difficult to determine because of the several and varied factors mentioned above. It is clear that the letter was addressed to a Gentile church (2:11; 3:1), quite possibly under some form of threat from a group of Judaizers, Jewish Christians who were arguing for the continued practice of the law (2:11). Paul's response was to assert that the Jewish practices had been abolished (2:15) and that both Jew and Gentile are on equal footing with God (2:13–16), since salvation is by grace through faith (2:8), thus creating one unified church (5:18–21). Goulder argues that there was a problem with Jewish visionaries promoting an apocalyptic Jewish-Christian theology that compromised the position and preeminence of Christ.[131] One does not need to go as far as Goulder, however, to appreciate the situation that the letter addresses, one that Paul encountered elsewhere in his missionary endeavor (e.g., Galatians).

---

130. E. J. Goodspeed, *New Solutions of New Testament Problems* (Chicago: University of Chicago Press, 1927), chaps. 1–2. See chapter 6 §3 above.

131. Goulder, "Visionaries of Laodicea," esp. 37–39.

E. Outline of Ephesians[132]

A. Opening (1:1–2)
  1. Sender (1:1a)
  2. Addressee (1:1b)
  3. Greeting (1:2)
B. Thanksgiving (1:3–23)
  1. Thanksgiving proper (1:3–14)
  2. Intercession (1:15–23)
C. Body: unity in Christ (2:1–3:21)
  1. Salvation by grace to do good works (2:1–10)
  2. Incorporation of Gentiles into one Christian faith (2:11–22)
  3. Paul as minister of the mystery (3:1–13)
  4. Concluding prayer and doxology (3:14–21)
D. Paraenesis (4:1–6:20)
  1. Living a worthy life (4:1–6)
  2. Responding to God's grace (4:7–16)
  3. Living the Christian life (4:17–5:20)
  4. Submission in household relationships (5:21–6:9)
  5. Being strong in the Lord (6:10–17)
  6. Praying in the Spirit (6:18–20)
E. Closing (6:21–24)
  1. Tychicus (6:21–22)
  2. Benedictions (6:23–24)

F. Content of Ephesians

Opening (1:1–2)

Paul introduces himself in this letter opening as an apostle of Christ Jesus by the will of God. As in Romans, he does not list anyone else as a cowriter here. He writes to the saints and the faithful in Christ Jesus (the earliest manuscripts do not contain "in Ephesus," so this is probably not original; see discussion above). The exact identity of Paul's audience in this letter is a matter of scholarly debate, and Ephesians may very well be a general letter to various churches in the area. In any case, he ends the opening with his standard "grace to you and peace from God our Father and the Lord Jesus Christ."

132. See Lincoln, *Ephesians*, xliii.

Thanksgiving (1:3–23)

Paul begins this section with a word of blessing to God, who has blessed them with every spiritual blessing in the heavenly places. They have been chosen and predestined before the foundation of the world to be holy and blameless, to receive adoption as children of God, and to have redemption through Christ's blood, which is the forgiveness of sins by the abundance of his grace. God has made known to them the mystery of his will, which he set forth in Christ. In him, they received an inheritance, having been predestined according to his own purpose and according to his will. This is so that they, as the first to hope in Christ, might exist for his glory. It is in Christ that they also receive the seal of the Holy Spirit, which occurred when they heard the word of truth, the gospel. This seal guarantees them of their inheritance until they receive it.

For this reason, Paul says, he does not stop giving thanks for them in his prayers because of their faith in Jesus and their love for the saints. He prays that they would receive a spirit of wisdom and revelation in the knowledge of Christ and that they would know the hope to which they were called. He prays that they would also know the riches of his glorious inheritance, the immeasurable greatness of his power toward believers, and the power that raised Christ from the dead. Not only did that power raise Christ, but it set him as head over all things and established him as head of the church, which is his body.

Body: Salvation by Grace to Do Good Works (2:1–10)

The Ephesian Christians used to be dead in their sins, in which they used to live according to the ways of the world, following the spirit that results in disobedience. They used to live according to the passions of their flesh, doing whatever they desired as children of wrath. But God, who is rich in mercy, because of his immense love for them, made them alive with Christ and raised them up with Christ. Their salvation has come by grace through faith as a gift from God, not by works so that no one would have grounds to boast. They are God's handiwork, created for good works that God had prepared in advance for them to do.

Body: Incorporation of Gentiles into One Christian Faith (2:11–22)

Paul wants the Ephesians to remember that, as Gentiles, called the "uncircumcision" by those who call themselves the "circumcision," they were once separated from Christ, strangers to the covenant and outcasts of Israel. But because of Christ Jesus, those who were once far away are brought near through his blood, since Christ is their peace, breaking down the dividing wall between Jew and Gentile, so that there is no longer hostility but reconciliation. Through Christ, they have access to one Spirit and no longer are strangers and aliens but fellow citizens of God's household. The foundation of the house was built by the apostles and prophets, with Christ as the cornerstone, upon whom the whole structure of the building is held together as a holy temple in the Lord.

Body: Paul as Minister of the Mystery (3:1–13)

So because of there being peace between Jew and Gentile, Paul is a prisoner for Christ on their behalf, because of the stewardship he received from God to proclaim the mystery of the gospel. This mystery is that the Gentiles have been made fellow heirs of the promise in Christ Jesus, and they get to participate as members of the same body.

Paul states that he was made a minster according to God's grace, given to him by God's power. He admits that, while he is the least of the saints (probably in reference to his former life as a persecutor of Christians; cf. 1 Cor 15:9), he was given the task to preach the incomprehensible riches of Christ to the Gentiles. All of this was according to God's purpose, which has been realized in Christ Jesus, in whom they have boldness and confidence. So they are not to be discouraged because of his suffering, because it is their glory.

Body: Concluding Prayer and Doxology (3:14–21)

Thus, Paul prays to God that, according to the riches of his glory, he would grant them strength through his Spirit in their inner being and that Christ would dwell in them so that, having love as their foundation, they would be able to comprehend the depth of the love of Christ, and that they would be filled with the fullness of God. Paul then bursts into doxology: to him who is able to do far more than they could even imagine be glory in the church and Christ Jesus throughout all generations forever.

Paraenesis: Living a Worthy Life (4:1–6)

To begin the paraenetic section, Paul again reminds the Ephesians of his imprisonment and urges them to walk in a manner worthy of the calling that they have received, with all humility, gentleness, and patience, bearing with each other in love, and being eager to maintain the unity of the Spirit in peace.

This unity is required, because there is one body and one Spirit, as they were called to the one hope. There is one Lord, one faith, one baptism, and one God and Father.

Paraenesis: Responding to God's Grace (4:7–16)

But, he says, grace has been given to each one of them according to the measure of Christ's gift. Paul quotes from Ps 68:18, which implies the descent and ascent of Christ from the grave, in order to discuss Christ's gifts. These gifts include apostles, prophets, evangelists, shepherds, and teachers, given in order to equip the saints for the work of the ministry and to build up the body of Christ until they reach full maturity, which is the unity of faith and knowledge of Christ. This maturity works to prevent them from being tossed around by the waves and being swayed by the various teachings of crafty and cunning people. Instead of being easily swayed, they are to grow into maturity, speaking the truth in love, with Christ as the head. The rest of the body, which is connected to the head, when it works properly, grows and builds itself up in love.

Paraenesis: Living the Christian Life (4:17–5:20)

In working toward maturity, then, Paul tells the Ephesians that they are no longer to live like the Gentiles do. They were futile in their minds and darkened in their understanding, alienated from the life of God because of their ignorance. They were callous and hardened, giving in to sensuality, greed, and impurity. But Paul says that is not how they learned about Christ, assuming that they have learned about him. They were instead to put off their old self, in their corrupt and deceitful ways, and put on their new self by being renewed in the spirit of their minds and made in the likeness of God in true righteousness and holiness.

So putting away falsehood, Paul tells them to speak truth, since they are members of one another. It is permissible to be angry, yet without sinning and without letting it last for too long, so that the devil does not take the opportunity to tempt them to sin in their anger. The thief is no longer to steal, but to work an honest job so that he might be able to share what he has earned. They are to prohibit corrupting talk but promote only talk that builds up and is fitting for the occasion. They are also not to grieve the Holy Spirit, since he is the one who has sealed up their inheritance until the day of redemption. They are to put away all kinds of bitterness, wrath, anger, clamor, slander, and malice; instead, they are to be kind to each other, tenderhearted, and forgiving one another, just as God forgave them in Christ.

Having God's forgiveness of them in mind, they are to be imitators of God, as his beloved children. They are to walk in love, just as Christ loved them by sacrificing himself for them. They would do this by refraining from sexual immorality, impurity, and covetousness; they should not even be associated with any of these things. There should be no profane talk or crude joking, since these do not fit with the type of people they are called to be, but instead they should be filled with thanksgiving. Paul warns them that it is certain that no one who is sexually immoral or impure or covetous (an idolater) will receive their inheritance in the kingdom of Christ. They are to watch out for empty words, because it is these sorts of things that lead to the wrath of God. They are not to partake in darkness, but to discern what pleases God and even to expose that darkness, since whatever is exposed by light becomes visible. Paul quotes from an unknown source:[133] "Arise, O sleeper, and arise from the dead, and Christ will shine on you."

They are, then, to watch carefully how they walk, avoiding foolishness and understanding the will of the Lord. They are not to get drunk with wine (a likely reference to the cult of Dionysus),[134] which is debauchery, but instead they are to be filled with the Spirit. This can be done by addressing one another in psalms, hymns, and spiritual songs, singing and making melody to the Lord, and always giving thanks for all things.

Paraenesis: Submission in Household Relationships (5:21–6:9)

One other way in which they may be filled with the Spirit is through submission to one another, which Paul expands in this next section. As one of several *Haustafeln* (household codes of behavior, but literally "house table"; cf. Col 3:18–4:1; 1 Pet 2:18–3:7) in the New Testament, Paul gives basic instructions for the functioning of the household, beginning with the injunction to submit to one another out of reverence for Christ. Wives are to submit to their husbands, as the church submits to Christ. Husbands are to love their wives, in turn, as Christ loved the church. They are to love their wives as they love themselves. Paul refers to the Genesis account, where a man leaves his parents to join with

---

133. See Hoehner, *Ephesians*, 686–88, who states that while there may be some similarity to Old Testament passages like Isa 26:19; 60:1; or Jonah 1:6, the Greek does not resemble these passages too closely.

134. Cf. S. E. Porter, "Ephesians 5.18–19 and Its Dionysian Background," in *Testimony and Interpretation: Early Christology in Its Judeo-Hellenistic Milieu: Studies in Honour of Petr Pokorný* (ed. J. Mrázek and J. Roskovec; JSNTSup 272; London: T&T Clark, 2004), 68–80; and C. A. Evans, "Ephesians 5:18–19 and Religious Intoxication in the World of Paul," in *Paul's World* (ed. S. E. Porter; PAST 4; Leiden: Brill, 2008), 181–200.

his wife, and this mystery concerns Christ and the church, which corresponds to husband and wife.

Children are to obey their parents in everything, and Paul refers back to the Decalogue, for children are to honor their father and mother, the first commandment with a promise. Parents, on the other hand, are not to provoke their children to anger but, instead, to bring them up in the discipline and knowledge of the Lord.

Slaves are to obey their masters with fear and trembling with a sincere heart, not just performing well when they are being watched but working as for God. Paul commands masters to treat their slaves well, without threatening them, since they also have a Master in heaven.

Paraenesis: Being Strong in the Lord (6:10–17)

In the final series of commands, Paul tells the Ephesians to be strong in the Lord, using the analogy of armor. They are to put on this armor so that they might be able to fight against the schemes of the devil. Their battle is not a physical battle but a spiritual one, and they are to prepare themselves respectively. The armor consists of the belt of truth, the breastplate of righteousness, the shoes of the gospel of peace, the shield of faith, the helmet of salvation, and the sword of the Spirit, which is the word of God. There are different interpretations of this armor, but the point that Paul makes here, without being too restrictive in reference to the exact pieces, is that believers are to prepare and be ready for spiritual battle.

Paraenesis: Praying in the Spirit (6:18–20)

With this armor, they are to continue praying in the Spirit. Paul asks for prayer regarding his words, so that he would speak boldly to proclaim the mystery of the gospel. It is for this gospel that he is an ambassador in chains.

Closing (6:21–24)

Paul is confident of his readers' concern for him, so he informs them that Tychicus, who is the carrier of this letter, will let them know how Paul is doing. He wishes them peace and love with faith from God the Father. He ends with the benediction, grace to all who love the Lord with an incorruptible love.

Sources for Further Study

Commentaries

Philippians

Beare, F. W. *A Commentary on the Epistle to the Philippians*. BNTC. London: A&C
    Black, 1959.

Bockmuehl, M. *The Epistle to the Philippians*. BCNT. Peabody, MA: Hendrickson, 1998.

Collange, J.-F. *The Epistle of Saint Paul to the Philippians*. Translated by A. W. Heath-
    cote. London: Epworth, 1979.

Fee, G. D. *Paul's Letter to the Philippians*. NICNT. Grand Rapids: Eerdmans, 1995.

Hansen, G. W. *The Letter to the Philippians*. PNTC. Grand Rapids: Eerdmans, 2009.

Hawthorne, G. F. *Philippians*. Revised by R. P. Martin. WBC 43. N.P.: Nelson, 2004.

Lightfoot, J. B. *St. Paul's Epistle to the Philippians*. London: Macmillan, 1891.

Martin, R. P. *Philippians*. NCB. Grand Rapids: Eerdmans, 1976.

O'Brien, P. T. *The Epistle to the Philippians*. NIGTC. Grand Rapids: Eerdmans, 1991.

Reumann, J. *Philippians*. Anchor Yale Bible 33B. New Haven: Yale University Press,
    2008.

Silva, M. *Philippians*. BECNT. 2nd ed. Grand Rapids: Baker, 2005.

Colossians and Philemon

Abbott, T. K. *A Critical and Exegetical Commentary on the Epistles to the Ephesians
    and to the Colossians*. ICC. Edinburgh: T&T Clark, 1897.

Barth, M., and H. Blanke. *Colossians*. AB 34B. New York: Doubleday, 1994.

Bruce, F. F. *The Epistles to the Colossians, to Philemon, and to the Ephesians*. NICNT.
    Grand Rapids: Eerdmans, 1984.

Callahan, A. D. *Embassy of Onesimus: The Letter of Paul to Philemon*. Valley Forge,
    PA: Trinity, 1997.

Dunn, J. D. G. *The Epistles to the Colossians and to Philemon*. NIGTC. Grand Rapids:
    Eerdmans, 1996.

Fitzmyer, J. A. *The Letter to Philemon*. AB 34C. New York: Doubleday, 2000.

Harris, M. J. *Colossians and Philemon*. Exegetical Guide to the Greek New Testament.
    Grand Rapids: Eerdmans, 1991.

Lightfoot, J. B. *St. Paul's Epistles to the Colossians and to Philemon*. London: Mac-
    millan, 1875.

Lohse, E. *Colossians and Philemon*. Hermeneia. Philadelphia: Fortress, 1971.

Moo, D. J. *The Letters to the Colossians and to Philemon*. PNTC. Grand Rapids: Eerd-
    mans, 2008.

Moule, C. F. D. *The Epistles to the Colossians and to Philemon*. Cambridge Greek Testament Commentary. Cambridge: Cambridge University Press, 1957.

O'Brien, P. T. *Colossians, Philemon*. WBC 44. Waco, TX: Word, 1982.

Pokorný, P. *Colossians: A Commentary*. Translated by S. S. Schatzmann. Peabody, MA: Hendrickson, 1991.

Schweizer, E. *The Letter to the Colossians: A Commentary*. Translated by A. Chester. Minneapolis: Augsburg, 1976.

Sumney, J. L. *Colossians: A Commentary*. NTL. Louisville: Westminster John Knox, 2008.

Wright, N. T. *Colossians and Philemon*. TNTC. Grand Rapids: Eerdmans, 1986.

Ephesians

Abbott, T. K. *A Critical and Exegetical Commentary on the Epistles to the Ephesians and to the Colossians*. ICC. Edinburgh: T&T Clark, 1897.

Barth, M. *Ephesians*. 2 vols. AB 34–34A. Garden City, NY: Doubleday, 1974.

Bruce, F. F. *The Epistles to the Colossians, to Philemon, and to the Ephesians*. NICNT. Grand Rapids: Eerdmans, 1984.

Fowl, S. E. *Ephesians: A Commentary*. NTL. Louisville: Westminster John Knox, 2012.

Hoehner, H. W. *Ephesians: An Exegetical Commentary*. Grand Rapids: Baker, 2002.

Kitchen, M. *Ephesians*. London: Routledge, 1994.

Lincoln, A. T. *Ephesians*. WBC 42. Dallas: Word, 1990.

Mitton, C. L. *Ephesians*. NCB. Grand Rapids: Eerdmans, 1973.

O'Brien, P. T. *The Letter to the Ephesians*. PNTC. Grand Rapids: Eerdmans, 1999.

Robinson, J. A. *St. Paul's Epistle to the Ephesians*. 2nd ed. London: Macmillan, 1904.

Schnackenburg, R. *The Epistle to the Ephesians: A Commentary*. Translated by H. Heron. Edinburgh: T&T Clark, 1991.

Thielman, F. *Ephesians*. BECNT. Grand Rapids: Baker, 2010.

Monographs and Books

Arnold, C. E. *The Colossian Syncretism: The Interface between Christianity and Folk Belief at Colossae*. WUNT 2/77. Tübingen: Mohr-Siebeck, 1995.

———. *Ephesians: Power and Magic. The Concept of Power in Ephesians in Light of Its Historical Setting*. SNTSMS 63. Cambridge: Cambridge University Press, 1989.

Bloomquist, L. G. *The Function of Suffering in Philippians*. JSNTSup 78. Sheffield: JSOT Press, 1993.

Byron, J. *Recent Research on Paul and Slavery*. RRPS 3. Sheffield: Sheffield Phoenix, 2008.

————. *Slavery Metaphors in Early Judaism and Pauline Christianity.* WUNT 162. Tübingen: Mohr-Siebeck, 2003.

Cross, F. L., ed. *Studies in Ephesians.* London: Mowbray, 1956.

DeMaris, R. *The Colossian Controversy: Wisdom in Dispute at Colossae.* JSNTSup 96. Sheffield: JSOT Press, 1994.

Elmer, I. J. *Paul, Jerusalem, and the Judaizers: The Galatian Crisis in Its Broadest Historical Context.* WUNT 2/258. Tübingen: Mohr-Siebeck, 2009.

Fowl, S. *The Story of Christ in the Ethics of Paul: An Analysis of the Function of the Hymnic Material in the Pauline Corpus.* JSNTSup 36. Sheffield: JSOT Press, 1990.

Francis, F. O., and W. A. Meeks, eds. *Conflict at Colossae: A Problem in the Interpretation of Early Christianity Illustrated by Selected Modern Studies.* Rev. ed. SBLSBS 4. Missoula, MT: Scholars Press, 1975.

Gordley, M. E. *The Colossian Hymn in Context: An Exegesis in Light of Jewish and Greco-Roman Hymnic and Epistolary Conventions.* WUNT 2/228. Tübingen: Mohr-Siebeck, 2007.

————. *Teaching through Song in Antiquity: Didactic Hymnody among Greeks, Romans, Jews, and Christians.* WUNT 2/302. Tübingen: Mohr-Siebeck, 2011.

Harrill, J. A. *Slaves in the New Testament: Literary, Social, and Moral Dimensions.* Minneapolis: Fortress, 2006.

Harris, M. J. *Slave of Christ: A New Testament Metaphor for Total Devotion to Christ.* Downers Grove, IL: InterVarsity, 1999.

Hemer, C. J. *The Letters to the Seven Churches of Asia in Their Local Setting.* JSNTSup 11. Sheffield: JSOT Press, 1986.

Hort, F. J. A. *Prolegomena to St. Paul's Epistles to the Romans and the Ephesians.* London: Macmillan, 1895.

Keown, M. J. *Congregational Evangelism in Philippians: The Centrality of an Appeal for Gospel Proclamation to the Fabric of Philippians.* Milton Keynes: Paternoster, 2008.

Kiley, M. *Colossians and Pseudepigraphy.* BS 4. Sheffield: JSOT Press, 1986.

Knox, J. *Philemon among the Letters of Paul.* Rev. ed. London: Collins, 1960 (1935).

Koester, H., ed. *Ephesos: Metropolis of Asia: An Interdisciplinary Approach to Its Archaeology, Religion, and Culture.* Valley Forge, PA: Trinity, 1995.

Koperski, V. *The Knowledge of Christ Jesus My Lord: The High Christology of Philippians 3:7–11.* Kampen, Netherlands: Kok Pharos, 1996.

Leppä, O. *The Making of Colossians: A Study on the Formation and Purpose of a Deutero-Pauline Letter.* Publications of the Finnish Exegetical Society 86. Göttingen: Vandenhoeck & Ruprecht, 2003.

Martin, D. B. *Slavery as Salvation: The Metaphor of Slavery in Pauline Christianity.* New Haven: Yale University Press, 1990.

Martin, R. P. *Carmen Christi: Philippians 2:5–11 in Recent Interpretation and in the Setting of Early Christian Worship.* Rev. ed. Grand Rapids: Eerdmans, 1983.

Martin, T. W. *By Philosophy and Empty Deceit: Colossians as Response to a Cynic Critique.* JSNTSup 118. Sheffield: Sheffield Academic, 1996.

Mitton, C. L. *The Epistle to the Ephesians: Its Authorship, Origin, and Purpose.* Oxford: Clarendon, 1951.

Moritz, T. *A Profound Mystery: The Use of the Old Testament in Ephesians.* NovTSup 85. Leiden: Brill, 1996.

Pearson, B. W. R. *Corresponding Sense: Paul, Dialectic, and Gadamer.* Biblical Interpretation Series 58. Leiden: Brill, 2001.

Peterman, G. W. *Paul's Gift from Philippi: Conventions of Gift Exchange and Christian Giving.* SNTSMS 92. Cambridge: Cambridge University Press, 1997.

Petersen, N. *Rediscovering Paul: Philemon and the Sociology of Paul's Narrative World.* Philadelphia: Fortress, 1985.

Porter, S. E., and G. P. Fewster, eds. *Paul and Pseudepigraphy.* PAST 8. Leiden: Brill, 2013.

Reed, J. T. *A Discourse Analysis of Philippians: Method and Rhetoric in the Debate over Literary Integrity.* JSNTSup 136. Sheffield: Sheffield Academic, 1997.

Sanders, J. T. *The New Testament Christological Hymns: Their Historical Religious Background.* SNTSMS 15. Cambridge: Cambridge University Press, 1971.

Sappington, T. J. *Revelation and Redemption at Colossae.* JSNTSup 53. Sheffield: JSOT Press, 1991.

Thielman, F. *Paul and the Law: A Contextual Approach.* Downers Grove, IL: InterVarsity, 1995.

Tolmie, D. F., ed. *Philemon in Perspective: Interpreting a Pauline Letter.* Berlin: de Gruyter, 2010.

Trebilco, P. *The Early Christians in Ephesus from Paul to Ignatius.* WUNT 166. Tübingen: Mohr-Siebeck, 2004.

Wansink, C. S. *Chained in Christ: The Experience and Rhetoric of Paul's Imprisonments.* JSNTSup 130. Sheffield: Sheffield Academic, 1996.

Williams, D. K. *Enemies of the Cross of Christ: The Terminology of the Cross and Conflict in Philippians.* JSNTSup 223. Sheffield: Sheffield Academic, 2002.

12

Pastoral Epistles: 1–2 Timothy, Titus

1. Introduction

"Although these letters purport to be written by Paul . . . most scholars believe they are post-Pauline—even later than Colossians, Ephesians, and 2 Thessalonians."[1] The Pauline origin of the Pastoral Epistles was apparently not disputed from their earliest attestation until the late eighteenth century,[2] but today the broad consensus among many if not most critical scholars is that the Pastoral Epistles were not written by Paul but, rather, by some later followers of Paul using his name. In fact, in some critical circles, the question of whether Paul wrote the Pastoral Epistles is not even a topic for discussion, as the conclusion is beyond doubt (he did not).[3] Hence they claim that these letters are pseudonymous. This scenario raises a number of very intriguing and difficult questions for discussion, since there are a number of factors that must be taken into account (see chapter 6 §§2, 3). In this chapter, I first discuss the nature of the Pastoral Epistles as personal letters addressed to Timothy and Titus, before turning to the critical difficulties regarding their epistolary form; their style, content, and theology; how they fit the Pauline chronology; their use in the

---

1. E. D. Freed, *The New Testament: A Critical Introduction* (Belmont, CA: Wadsworth, 1991), 440.

2. J. van Nes, "The Problem of the Pastoral Epistles: An Important Hypothesis Reconsidered," in *Paul and Pseudepigraphy* (ed. S. E. Porter and G. P. Fewster; PAST 8; Leiden: Brill, 2013), 153–69, esp. 153 and n. 1; see also L. T. Johnson, *The First and Second Letters to Timothy* (AB 35A; New York: Doubleday, 2001), 20–54; and P. H. Towner, *The Letters to Timothy and Titus* (NICNT; Grand Rapids: Eerdmans, 2006), 4–6.

3. A well-known German scholar told me that this is the case in Germany. As an example, see O. Wischmeyer, ed., *Paul: Life, Setting, Work, Letters* (trans. H. S. Heron with rev. by D. T. Roth; London: T&T Clark, 2012), 309, 321–28, where the Pastorals are called trito-Pauline.

early church; and then various solutions to the issue of their authorship, before presenting outlines of the letters and their individual contents.

2. Timothy and Titus

One of the clear things about the Pastorals is that they appear to be written as if they are personal letters addressed to single individuals.[4] The personal nature of the letters, however, is widely disputed; most scholars consider them to be church or community documents (in line with comments in the Muratorian Fragment, which commends them, though along with Philemon, for their instruction on church discipline). This communal or ecclesial dimension is not readily apparent, however, from the way the letters present themselves. As a result, it was not until the early eighteenth century that 1-2 Timothy and Titus were first referred to as the Pastoral or Shepherd Letters (implying an ecclesial function),[5] apparently appearing to most until that time (and many afterward) to be personal letters, even if they address issues of interest within a larger church or pastoral setting. A few recent scholars argue that this terminology should be abandoned, in favor of something less determinative.[6]

A number of personal characteristics are worth noting. For example, Timothy is a very important minor character in the New Testament. The son of a Jewish mother named Eunice and a Greek father (Acts 16:1-2) with an unknown name, he was an associate of Paul (17:14-15; 18:5; 19:22) and is at least given credit for coauthorship in the New Testament by being included in the salutation of a number of Paul's letters (1-2 Thessalonians, 2 Corinthians, Philippians, Philemon, and Colossians). Indeed, he is mentioned in all but three of the traditional Pauline letters (Galatians, Ephesians, and Titus). In the Pastoral Epistles, he is shown remaining at Ephesus at the time of Paul's supposed release from his (first Roman?) imprisonment (1 Tim 1:2-3) and is still there when Paul is back in prison in 2 Tim 1:18 (cf. 4:9-18). He did important missionary work at Thessalonica (1 Thess 3:2) and Corinth (1 Cor 4:17),

---

4. Some, however, contend that these are not personal letters because of the other individuals named at the end of the letters and the absence of a good-health wish; e.g., R. F. Collins, *I & II Timothy and Titus* (NTL; Louisville: Westminster John Knox, 2002), 7. But that the letters address other issues does not mean that they must be discounted as personal letters; this seems to be an overly restrictive position to take.

5. W. G. Kümmel, *Introduction to the New Testament* (trans. H. C. Kee; 17th ed.; Nashville: Abingdon, 1975), 367.

6. See, e.g., Towner, *Letters to Timothy and Titus*, 88-89; contra D. A. Hagner, *The New Testament: A Historical and Theological Introduction* (Grand Rapids: Baker, 2012), 634-35.

although he appears to have had a timid personality, such that he may have been easily intimidated by others at Corinth and Ephesus.[7]

Less is known about Titus, who is mentioned twelve times in the New Testament. He was a Greek and remained uncircumcised (Gal 2:3). He apparently had a bolder personality than Timothy and consequently undertook several difficult tasks for Paul, especially at Corinth (2 Cor 7:6-7, 13-15; 8:6; 12:18), including taking the "severe letter" and 2 Corinthians to the church there and reporting to Paul when the crisis apparently was over. Titus was—according to the book with his name—left at Crete by Paul (Titus 1:5) and then rejoined Paul at Nicopolis (3:12); at the end of Paul's life he was in Dalmatia, right across from Rome (2 Tim 4:10).[8]

It is entirely appropriate that the Pastoral Epistles—whether authentically Pauline or pseudonymous (to be discussed further below)—are called personal letters and are addressed to these historical figures involved in various ways in the ministry and mission of the historical Paul.

3. Critical Difficulties

Even if the Pastoral Epistles are rightly called personal letters because of their ostensive addressees, many remaining critical difficulties are raised, critical difficulties that are said to point away from their being authentically Pauline. The four major critical difficulties regarding the Pastoral Epistles concern the epistolary form; style, content, and theology; Pauline chronology; and use of these letters in the early church.[9]

A. Epistolary Form of the Pastoral Epistles

The Pastoral Epistles purport to be addressed to individuals. But it is often argued that the letters are in fact community or church letters, like virtually all of the other Pauline letters (the apparent exception being Philemon). One reason for this position is the amount of material in the letters concerned

---

7. On Timothy, see F. F. Bruce, *The Pauline Circle* (Grand Rapids: Eerdmans, 1985), 29-34.
8. On Titus, see Bruce, *The Pauline Circle*, 58-65.
9. See S. E. Porter, "Pauline Authorship and the Pastoral Epistles: Implications for Canon," *BBR* 5 (1995): 107-13; M. Davies, *The Pastoral Epistles* (NTG; Sheffield: Sheffield Academic, 1996); W. D. Mounce, *Pastoral Epistles* (WBC 46; Dallas: Word, 2000), lxxxiii-cxxx; Johnson, *First and Second Letters*, 55-90; and Hagner, *New Testament*, 615-22, for treatment of the issues involved. Cf. chapter 6 §2.

with such things as the faith or Christian belief, the administration of the church—including its officers and those who serve in it—and social issues that the early church confronted, such as the responsibility for widows. Another reason is that the personal elements, typical of Paul's personal letters, supposedly recede into the background as church interests emerge. But which personal letters provide suitable examples for comparison? Philemon, addressed to Philemon, Apphia, Archippus, and the church? Some would say that Philemon is the only authentic personal letter in the Pauline corpus, while others would question whether even Philemon is a genuine personal letter. If this is the case, it is difficult to categorically deny, on the basis of aberrant epistolary form, that the Pastoral Epistles are personal letters, since there is only one or no authentic Pauline personal letter for true comparison.

According to Martin Dibelius and Hans Conzelmann, 2 Timothy best fits the picture of the Pauline personal letter, because the personal element is "strongly emphasized." Titus holds an intermediate position, since addressing instructions to a person where there is not an established church order is at least understandable. First Timothy, however, "affords the most difficulties. For here, personal elements fade into the background."[10] But how does one determine this fading of the personal elements in 1 Timothy? Subject matter alone is not a sufficient criterion, since it does not compromise the integrity of a personal letter to discuss matters that affect those other than the primary person(s) involved (as the nonliterary papyri amply attest—e.g., when one writes to another about a third party or about an external subject, such as one's donkey). There would need to be some formal characteristic in the language of the letter to establish this fading of the personal. But there is no instance in 1 Timothy, for example, of second-person plural verb forms, only second-person singular, and no instance of second-person plural pronouns, only second-person singular, apart from the formulaic closing in 6:21.[11] So far as formal criteria are concerned, it is not clear how one could establish the features of personal address in 1 Timothy more clearly.

This criterion of epistolary form does not seem to indicate anything other than that they are personal letters, and nothing that would call into question Pauline authorship.

10. M. Dibelius and H. Conzelmann, *The Pastoral Epistles* (Hermeneia; Philadelphia: Fortress, 1972), 11.

11. J. T. Reed, "To Timothy or Not: A Discourse Analysis of 1 Timothy," in *Biblical Greek Language and Linguistics: Open Questions in Current Research* (ed. S. E. Porter and D. A. Carson; JSNTSup 80; Sheffield: JSOT Press, 1993), 90–118 at 106.

B. Style, Content, and Theology of the Pastoral Epistles

The question regarding style, content, and theology is whether differences in content from the other Pauline letters can be explained by the nature of the letters, or whether they point to non-Pauline authorship. Debate regarding style falls essentially into two areas: vocabulary and style proper. Numerous statistical studies show how un-Pauline the vocabulary and style of the Pastorals are on the basis of a high number of singular occurrences of certain terms (*hapax legomena*), varying word or word-class frequencies, and more regular and less varied sentence structure. Likewise, a number of studies counter these claims by showing flaws in the calculations regarding vocabulary and arrangement; by configuring the vocabulary items counted in different ways in relation to the other Pauline letters, the rest of the New Testament, and other bodies of literature; and by arguing that differences of context and subject matter require modified word choice and sentence structure.[12] Despite all of the effort expended upon these studies, two unresolved issues remain.

The first is the size of the appropriate sample for study. In Kenneth Neumann's discussion of the issue, he includes a survey of the numbers proposed for comparative study. These range from 85 to 3,500 words in recent studies, and as high as 10,000 words in earlier studies. What is evident is that there is no agreed-upon number of words for a sample. Thus, Neumann apparently, almost arbitrarily, decides that 750 words will be his sample size, not on the basis of a reasoned argument but only so that the Pauline letters can be included. Even so, Titus, with its 659 words, is still too small for inclusion in his own study by this criterion.

The second consideration regarding style is what exactly is being determined and how significant the findings must be before one can decide that a letter is or is not Pauline. The methods used to determine authorship are almost as varied as the scholars doing the calculations, with very little control on what criteria are being used and what would count as an adequate test of

---

12. See K. J. Neumann, *The Authenticity of the Pauline Epistles in the Light of Stylostatistical Analysis* (SBLDS 120; Atlanta: Scholars Press, 1990), esp. 23–114, for a survey of research and a bibliography; and A. Kenny, *A Stylometric Study of the New Testament* (Oxford: Clarendon, 1986), esp. 80–100. On methodological issues, see M. B. O'Donnell, "Linguistic Fingerprints or Style by Numbers? The Use of Statistics in the Discussion of Authorship of New Testament Documents," in *Linguistics and the New Testament: Critical Junctures* (ed. S. E. Porter and D. A. Carson; JSNTSup 163; Sheffield; Sheffield Academic, 1999), 206–62; Mounce, *Pastoral Epistles*, xcix–cxviii; and A. W. Pitts, "Style and Pseudonymity in Pauline Scholarship: A Register Based Configuration," in *Paul and Pseudepigraphy* (ed. S. E. Porter and G. P. Fewster; PAST 8; Leiden: Brill, 2013), 113–52.

the method. Furthermore, aside from the appearance of scientific accuracy, one must still interpret the results. What does it mean that one of the early church fathers' writings satisfies certain statistical tests and is placed close to the authentic Pauline letters, whereas one of the disputed Pauline letters is further away? What does it mean that one of the supposedly authentic Pauline letters is further away than a disputed letter? In other words, how much variety is tolerable in the statistical outcome before one questions authorship? This has not been determined.[13]

These two major difficulties make it extremely difficult to use statistics to determine non-Pauline authorship of the Pastoral Epistles.

Formalization of church order is often mentioned as a criterion for authorship.[14] In many scholars' minds, the Pastoral Epistles appear to be referring to an established church structure. This structure has formal offices (elders, overseers/bishops, deacons), with people who occupy these positions having authority over the other members of the community. The charisma of the Spirit, according to this view, has been curtailed and has been replaced by an orderly succession through the laying on of hands. Furthermore, the church finds itself responding to a form of thinking (1 Tim 6:20) that advocates asceticism and a kind of legalism (1 Tim 1:7; 4:3, 8; Titus 3:9) in the context of a realized eschatology (2 Tim 2:17-18). This is all seen to reflect an "early catholicism," typical of what appears in writings of the second century and later, especially those influenced by Gnosticism.[15] In order to back up this theory, however, one must successfully deal with several issues. The first is how to explain that Phil 1:1 uses the terms "bishops/overseers" and "deacons,"[16] singling them out in the very order in which they appear in 1 Tim 3. They are not defined in Philippians, but they probably reflect an early form of institutional

13. See B. M. Metzger, "A Reconsideration of Certain Arguments against the Pauline Authorship of the Pastoral Epistles," *Expository Times* 70 (1957-58): 94.

14. See, e.g., J. D. G. Dunn, *Unity and Diversity in the New Testament* (Philadelphia: Westminster, 1977), 341-45; and Kümmel, *Introduction*, 378-82.

15. "Early catholicism" is the increased institutionalization of the church in the light of fading hope of the return of Christ, resulting in the faith taking on fixed forms. See Dunn, *Unity and Diversity*, 341-66, following E. Käsemann, "An Apologia for Primitive Christian Eschatology," in *Essays on New Testament Themes* (trans. W. J. Montague; Philadelphia: Fortress, 1964), 169-95; and Hagner, *New Testament*, 605-13. But cf. I. H. Marshall, "'Early Catholicism' in the New Testament," in *New Dimensions in New Testament Study* (ed. R. N. Longenecker and M. C. Tenney; Grand Rapids: Zondervan, 1974), 217-31, for a competing view.

16. F. Young, *The Theology of the Pastoral Letters* (NTT; Cambridge: Cambridge University Press, 1994), 107. Cf. W. Schenk, *Die Philipperbriefe des Paulus: Ein Kommentar* (Stuttgart: Kohlhammer, 1984), 78-82, who takes these references as a later interpolation. The textual evidence cannot be made to show this.

structure already present in the Pauline churches. (Incidentally, the author of
Luke–Acts may know something of this in Acts 14:23, which refers to elders
being appointed in the Pauline churches.) The second issue concerns the form
of opposition being confronted in the Pastoral Epistles. The tendency is to
place the opponents in the second century, but there is still some question
whether any of the practices or apparent beliefs mentioned in the Pastorals
are totally unfamiliar to the authentic Pauline letters (e.g., 1 Cor 7:1; 8:1–3;
15:17–19; Gal 4:8–10; cf. also Col 2:20–22).[17] The issue of church order, rather
than pointing to non-Pauline authorship, seems consistent with developments
within early Christianity.

Regarding the theology of the Pastoral Epistles, certain terminology that
occurs in the undisputed Pauline writings is supposedly used in different and
incompatible ways. Thus the concept of faith, which, in the undisputed Pauline
letters, seems to be a subjective or obedient response to God, takes on the more
objective sense of a common body of belief or virtue, or even Christianity itself
(1 Tim 1:2, 5, 14, 19; 2:7, 15; 3:9; 4:1, 6, 12; 5:8, 12; 6:10, 11, 12, 21; 2 Tim 1:5; 2:22; 3:8,
10; Titus 1:4, 13; 2:2; 3:15). This tradition is to be received, protected, and passed
on.[18] Righteousness, which, in the undisputed Pauline letters, signifies the state
of being in right relation with God, seems to take on the more neutral and
objective sense of justice in the Pastoral Epistles (1 Tim 6:11; 2 Tim 2:22; 4:8;
Titus 1:8). Love, which is a key virtue in the authentic Pauline writings, is seen
as one virtue among others in the Pastoral Epistles, often side by side with faith
(1 Tim 1:14; 2:15; 4:12; 6:11; 2 Tim 1:7, 13; 2:22; 3:10; Titus 2:2). The Pauline phrase
"in Christ" (ἐν Χριστῷ), which is variously interpreted but seems to indicate
some sort of relation in which believers find themselves within the sphere of
Christ's control, seems to have taken on a more technical sense of "existence
within the Christian community" in the Pastoral Epistles (1 Tim 1:14; 2 Tim
1:2, 9, 13; 2:1, 10; 3:12, 15). In the Pastoral Epistles, God is called Savior in six of
the eight times that such phrasing appears in the New Testament (1 Tim 1:1;
2:3; 4:10; Titus 1:3; 2:10; 3:4; cf. Phil 3:20; Eph 5:23). In the Pastoral Epistles the
conscience of members of the community is either good and pure or soiled
and seared, rather than strong or weak (e.g., 1 Tim 1:5, 19; 3:9; 4:2; 2 Tim 1:3;
Titus 1:15), just as teaching is now either healthy or sick, rather than holy or
unholy (1 Tim 1:10; 4:6; 2 Tim 4:3; Titus 1:9; 2:1, 7). A few ideas are unique to the
Pastoral Epistles and are often related to the use of unique words or phrases.
An example would be "the saying is sure" (e.g., 1 Tim 1:15; 3:1; 4:9; 2 Tim 2:11;

17. L. T. Johnson, *The Writings of the New Testament: An Interpretation* (Philadelphia:
Fortress, 1986), 384.

18. This, too, is often seen as a reflection of "early catholicism."

Titus 3:8), for which there is no true parallel in the undisputed Pauline letters.[19] And 1 Tim 1:13, which says that Paul was shown mercy by God because of his previous ignorance and unbelief, may reflect non-Pauline thought. Including these, ideas unique to the Pastoral Epistles are admittedly few.

Nevertheless, there are some perceivable theological differences, at least in their context of usage, within the Pastoral Epistles, when compared with the undisputed Pauline letters. In other words, some ideas in the undisputed Pauline letters are developed in the Pastoral Epistles. The nature of this development, however, is not altogether clear. Is it complementary development, and hence still possibly Pauline, or is it contradictory, and hence possibly non-Pauline?[20] Complementary development does not necessarily indicate non-Pauline authorship, but may only illustrate plausible conceptual connection between previous and subsequent thought—and might well be found, even expected, in an author writing over the course of several decades. The latter kind of development, contradiction, would be necessary to establish with any degree of certainty the distinctiveness of the Pastoral Epistles, but would also raise the further question of how and why these writings were incorporated into the canon if they were in contradiction with established Pauline belief and thought. One would require clear instances of explicit contradiction to make a defensible case for non-Pauline authorship, but it is questionable whether any such contradictory theological stance has been identified.

None of these three criteria, style, content, or theology, provides a firm or indisputable basis for questioning the authenticity of the Pastoral Epistles.

C. Pauline Chronology

The third major issue concerns how these letters fit in with the Pauline chronology as established in Acts and the other Pauline letters. If there were a number of so-called Prison Epistles written during an imprisonment in Rome, such as the one recorded in Acts 28:29-31, then where do the Pastorals fit in? This is made more acute by 2 Tim 1:17 apparently indicating that it was written from Rome. Most scholars consider it highly unlikely that it was written from Rome during the same imprisonment. This suggests a second Roman imprisonment,

---

19. As G. W. Knight III admits; *The Faithful Sayings in the Pastoral Letters* (Amsterdam: Kok, 1968; repr. Grand Rapids: Baker, 1979), 1.

20. Cf. P. Pokorný, *Colossians: A Commentary* (trans. S. S. Schatzmann; Peabody, MA: Hendrickson, 1991), 6–7 and table 2, who notes that the theology of the Pastoral Epistles is a relatively logical development from Paul's authentic writings and only appears so divergent when compared with other supposedly deutero-Pauline writings, such as Colossians and Ephesians.

for which there is no other attestation. A further difficulty is that although Paul states his intention in Rom 15:24, 28 to visit Rome on the way to Spain, the Pastoral Epistles have him traveling in the eastern Mediterranean. First Timothy is apparently written from Macedonia (1 Tim 1:3), the book of Titus to Crete, where there is apparently an established Pauline church (Titus 1:5), and 2 Timothy from imprisonment in Rome (2 Tim 1:16–17). It is not apparent how these fit together. Nevertheless, Paul was in, or had every intention of going to, Macedonia several times during his travels, as his undisputed letters state (1 Cor 16:5; 2 Cor 1:16; 2:13; 7:5; Phil 4:15).

There is no other record of Paul's visiting Crete, apart from his brief stop at Fair Havens on his way to Rome (Acts 27), but Titus 1:5 may not be saying that Paul actually left Titus there, only that he left him to his task, Paul being elsewhere,[21] and he was imprisoned several times, again according to his undisputed letters (2 Cor 6:5; 11:23; Phlm 1, 9). The result is that 1 Timothy and Titus could be placed within the Pauline letter chronology. Does 2 Tim 4:16, with its reference to a "first" or "earlier" defense, imply a previous imprisonment, as some argue, or only a previous defense, which the language could well mean? Since we do not know all of Paul's travels from the letters (the key example is Paul's so-called tearful visit to Corinth from Ephesus in the middle of his correspondence with them; see chapter 9 §2C), there is the possibility that he made a significant trip to Macedonia.[22]

Neither Paul's letters nor Acts gives a complete chronology of Paul's life and travels; hence, it is impossible to solve the chronological issues in the Pastoral Epistles. However, nothing in the chronological issues themselves necessarily calls the authenticity of the Pastoral Epistles into question (see the various chronological reconstructions in §4 below).

D. Use of the Pastoral Epistles in Early Church

Most scholars consider the external evidence of use of the Pastorals in the early church to be weak and therefore to point to later, non-Pauline authorship. The most common arguments are that evidence of use of the Pastorals by Ignatius (ca. 35–107) and Polycarp (80–155) is inconclusive at best and perhaps indicates

21. Paul's absence may well clarify why Paul has to explain why he left Titus to his task, since, if he had actually left him, it is plausible to think that he would have told him why at that time. See Johnson, *Writings of the New Testament*, 383.
22. These issues are discussed in S. E. Porter, "Pauline Chronology and the Question of Pseudonymity of the Pastoral Epistles," in *Paul and Pseudepigraphy* (ed. S. E. Porter and G. P. Fewster; PAST 8; Leiden: Brill, 2013), 65–88.

instead that the Pastorals used these church fathers, that Marcion (mid-second century) does not include them in his canon, and that the early and important papyrus text of the Pauline letters, 𝔓46 (ca. 200), does not include them.[23] This evidence warrants consideration in the attempt to arrive at an estimation of authorship. For the most part, however, this purportedly negative evidence is at best ambiguous, while other important evidence is slighted.[24] For example, evidence of the literary dependence of Ignatius and Polycarp upon the Pastorals is stronger than often thought. According to Newport White, there appear to be at least five clear instances in Ignatius, and three in Polycarp, of literary dependence on the Pastoral Epistles.[25] Marcion does not include the Pastorals, but Tertullian in *Against Marcion* 5.21 states that he is surprised "that he [Marcion] rejected the two epistles to Timothy and the one to Titus" (*Ante-Nicene Fathers* 3.473). Tertullian's statement may be apologetic and not in fact prove that Marcion rejected them. But as Werner Georg Kümmel points out, Marcion's failure to include them does not mean that these letters were not in existence.[26] The lack of the Pastorals in 𝔓46, while important to note, cannot prove that they were not in existence, since there are several possible explanations for this lack. These include the scribe's difficulty in calculating how many pages of the papyrus codex were left (it is incomplete at both beginning and end); further adjustments the scribe may have made in writing the letters when he realized he was possibly running out of room, because he wanted to fit them in (the scribe already shows an increase from twenty-six to thirty-two lines per page; the scribe could also have added pages to the codex if needed); and our lack of knowledge regarding the purpose of this particular papyrus collection of writings. Not only are the Pastorals missing from 𝔓46; it breaks off in 1 Thessalonians and lacks the rest of 1 Thessalonians, 2 Thessalonians, and Philemon as well. Two other fragmentary papyri, however, are dated to approximately the same time as 𝔓46: 𝔓32, a fragment of Titus (1:11–15; 2:3–8), and 𝔓87, a fragment of Philemon (13–15, 24–25).[27] There also seems to be a lit-

23. See Dibelius and Conzelmann, *Pastoral Epistles*, 1–2, for this line of argument.

24. Cf. B. Weiss, *A Manual of Introduction to the New Testament* (trans. A. J. K. Davidson; 2 vols.; London: Hodder & Stoughton, 1887), 1.201–6.

25. See Ignatius, *To the Magnesians* 8 (Titus 1:14; 3:9), 2 (2 Tim 1:5, 12; 1:10; 2:5; 4:5), 3 (2 Tim 2:12), 4 (1 Tim 6:1, 2), and 6 (2 Tim 2:4), plus other possible instances; and Polycarp, *To the Philippians* 4 (1 Tim 6:7, 10), 9 (2 Tim 4:10), and 12 (1 Tim 2:2; 4:15), plus other references. These are cited in N. J. D. White, "The First and Second Epistles to Timothy and the Epistle to Titus," in *Expositor's Greek Testament* (ed. W. R. Nicoll; 5 vols.; London: Hodder & Stoughton, 1897), 4.56–202 at 77–79.

26. Kümmel, *Introduction*, 370.

27. See D. Trobisch, *Paul's Letter Collection: Tracing the Origins* (Minneapolis: Fortress, 1994), 16, for information on 𝔓46 and the above.

erary relationship between the Pastoral Epistles and *1 Clement* (ca. 96).[28] Some see the Pastorals as dependent upon *1 Clement*, but a trajectory beginning with the Pastorals is also a possibility, if not a likelihood.

The supposed weak external attestation of the Pastoral Epistles is far from conclusive; in fact, there is early evidence of their existence.

This brief conspectus provides a summary of the major arguments made in discussing the authorship of the Pastoral Epistles. So far, the evidence, though widely promoted as indicating non-Pauline authorship of the Pastoral Epistles, fails to provide a convincing argument against the traditional view. Nevertheless, this evidence must be taken into account in arriving at a conclusion regarding their authenticity, as will be done below in discussing various solutions.

4. Proposed Solutions to the Problems of the Pastoral Epistles

With so many problems raised by the Pastoral Epistles, it is not surprising to find a number of solutions as well. I will recount four of them, each with at least some major proponents.

A. Pseudonymity and the Pastoral Epistles

In light of the supposedly manifest difficulties raised above, it is suggested and maintained by a number of scholars that the Pastoral Epistles are pseudepigrapha.[29] This position argues that the letters were written after Paul's death, quite possibly in the second century, in response to some form of threat to the Pauline churches, and that they were written to express what Paul himself would have said if he were addressing these issues. It must also follow from this view that the events and personal references in the Pastoral Epistles, including the very personal references in 2 Tim 4 (esp. 4:6–14 and 4:19–21) and

28. See *1 Clement* 2 (Titus 3:1; cf. also *1 Clement* 34 and 2 Tim 2:21; 3:17), 7 (1 Tim 2:3, 4), 29 (1 Tim 2:8), 32 (Titus 3:5–7), 37 (1 Tim 1:18; cf. 2 Tim 2:3, 4; 2 Cor 10:3), 45 (2 Tim 1:3; cf. 1 Tim 3:9), and 55 (2 Tim 2:1), among others. See White, "First and Second Epistles," 4.76–77; cf. J. B. Lightfoot, *The Apostolic Fathers* (2 vols.; 1889–90; repr. Peabody, MA: Hendrickson, 1989), 1/2.19, 104, 113, 138, 180.

29. Besides commentaries, see L. R. Donelson, *Pseudepigraphy and Ethical Argument in the Pastoral Epistles* (HUT 22; Tübingen: Mohr-Siebeck, 1986); and R. F. Collins, *Letters That Paul Did Not Write: The Epistle to the Hebrews and the Pauline Pseudepigrapha* (Wilmington, DE: Glazier, 1988), 88–131.

the mention of Rome, were artificially created by the author or authors of these letters to enhance the likelihood that the letter would be accepted as Paul's. If so, whoever did this would have been creating a literary deception.[30] On the other hand, if pseudonymy were a common convention of the early church (as has been argued, incorrectly I believe), then such references would have been unnecessary and served no legitimate purpose. This raises the question why it would have been necessary to write pseudepigrapha at all. The position that the Pastoral Epistles are pseudepigrapha helps explain the apparent contradiction that advice regarding behavior and church order were given to Timothy, a very close companion of Paul, although he would apparently have known Paul's thinking on such issues, since he was a traveling companion and coauthor of so many letters. If the letters are pseudepigraphal, then the writers borrowed the name of Timothy, but they needed to have this redundant information declared to Timothy as if for the first time so that they could explicitly state it for their contemporary church situation. They hoped that ascribing Paul's name to the letter would ensure its acceptance and compel its obedience.

B. *Fragmentary Hypothesis of the Pastoral Epistles*

The fragmentary hypothesis, proposed earlier in the last century by P. N. Harrison and later followed by others, claims that certain sections within the Pastoral Epistles are authentic.[31] Harrison performs several analyses upon the letters, later revising his first findings. The major authentic sections Harrison discerns are the following: Titus 3:12–15; 2 Tim 1:16–18; 3:10–11; 4:1, 2a, 5b–8, 9–15, 20, 21a, 22b and the ascription "Paul." A variation on this hypothesis is that another person in a Pauline church produced this literature and, in so do-

30. See Davies, *Pastoral Epistles*, 105–18, esp. 113–17, who raises the question of the ethical dilemma in pseudepigraphy and its possible implications for the canon. See further S. E. Porter, "The Implications of New Testament Pseudonymy for a Doctrine of Scripture," in *Interdisciplinary Perspectives on the Authority of Scripture: Historical, Biblical, and Theoretical Perspectives* (ed. C. R. Bovell; Eugene, OR: Pickwick, 2011), 236–56.

31. P. N. Harrison, *The Problem of the Pastoral Epistles* (Oxford: Oxford University Press, 1921); cf. also R. Falconer, *The Pastoral Epistles* (Oxford: Clarendon, 1937), 1–30. Some similarities to this view are to be found in J. D. Miller, *The Pastoral Letters as Composite Documents* (SNTSMS 93; Cambridge: Cambridge University Press, 1997); and I. H. Marshall with P. H. Towner, *A Critical and Exegetical Commentary on the Pastoral Epistles* (ICC; Edinburgh: T&T Clark, 1999), 85–92, who argues for a real letter behind 2 Timothy and use of authentic material by a later writer, perhaps Timothy or Titus, a view Marshall calls "allonymity." Despite his attempts to escape the issue of deception, Marshall cannot help but introduce it. See also Towner, *Timothy and Titus*, 86–88, who remains agnostic.

ing, also shared something of what happened to Paul with his readers: people in Asia turned against him, others abandoned him while he was in prison, and he died in Rome full of faith. In other words, authentic traces of Paul in the Pastorals may not mean that Paul necessarily wrote them; instead, they tell a true story, and there was no other reason to include these authentic details. The conclusion of such a hypothesis is that the Pastorals are Pauline in a strictly limited sense, with the latter form of the hypothesis virtually indistinguishable from the pseudepigraphal hypothesis (see above).

One noticeable shortcoming of the traditional fragmentary hypothesis is that it still does not explain the origin of 1 Timothy, since there are no purportedly authentic fragments found in it; neither does it explain the necessity of three letters rather than a single one. How and why were these particular fragments determined to be authentic, other than that they tend to be those concerned with personal matters? One might contend that there is no reason for these portions to be passed on unless they are authentic and that there was no reason to fabricate them, because they did not otherwise significantly add to the message of the book. Precisely because these are such ordinary bits of information, no one can find an occasion for which they might be created for the church of a later generation.

All of these contentions, however, seem to work from the assumption that the letters are inauthentic, and they try to find an explanation of the fragments instead of starting from the letters and determining the fragments from that direction. In any event, this view of authorship recognizes the problem with the personal elements if the letters are not Pauline, but it does not then adequately explain the rest of the letters. It seems highly unlikely that elaborate letters concerning a number of issues were constructed around such personal matters, certainly when the personal matters do not suggest the subjects of the rest of the letters. When these particular fragments of personal information are examined more closely, however, it is surprising to find that such fine judgments are made by scholars regarding several quite ordinary pieces of information. In this case, a bad job has been done of creating plausible letters around the preserved fragments of authentically Pauline material. To claim that the author incorporates authentic Pauline tradition into his letters in order to clarify the tradition is a more plausible explanation why so little material is preserved, but it does not address the question why the letters were written in the first place, since the message of the letters purportedly suits a later stage in the development of the church rather than the context of the authentic Pauline letters and Acts. The concerns of the letters themselves are more comfortable in a subsequent generation when faith was waning, Christ had not returned, and the temptation to leave the church was greater.

The use of vocabulary statistics from second-century writers, one of the foundations of Harrison's argument, is also called into question.[32] It is further argued that the words used within the Pastoral Epistles, contrary to Harrison's claim, do indeed suit their purported historical circumstances.[33] Furthermore, it is argued from a linguistic analysis of the letters, including various cohesive devices, boundary markers, and semantic chains, that there is enough coherence in each of these letters to warrant literary unity.[34] One still wonders, then, about the validity of the fragmentary hypothesis if the only basis for it is the similarities of the fragments with authentic Pauline material.

C. Amanuensis in the Pastoral Epistles

It is an undeniable fact, as Randolph Richards clearly shows, that the use of scribes was widespread in the ancient world.[35] As was discussed in chapter 5 §4, these scribes or amanuenses performed a wide range of functions, from taking straight dictation to serving a creative role similar to that of modern personal assistants given responsibility for composing letters sent under their bosses' names. It is also known that Paul used scribes, as is seen in Rom 16:22 (which refers to Tertius); 1 Cor 16:21 (where he states that he writes in his own hand); Gal 6:11–16 (where Paul apparently takes up the writing instrument himself); and 2 Thess 3:17 (where Paul writes his own greetings). A recurring problem in Pauline studies is the role that the Pauline scribe played in the composition of his letters. The view of most scholars is that Paul probably allowed for only a limited amount of scribal creativity, since there is an overwhelming consistency of presentation in his major letters in both content and style. There is the possibility that he tended to use the same scribe (perhaps Timothy's role should be given larger credit?), but it is thought more likely that he used different scribes but his rhetorical skills dominated the correspondence. Such a scenario allows for the possibility that, on another occasion, a scribe was given the opportunity to write a letter on Paul's behalf with a degree of freedom not previously given.[36] It is suggested that such a writer would likely be

32. See, among others, D. Guthrie, *The Pastoral Epistles* (2nd ed.; TNTC; Grand Rapids: Eerdmans, 1990), 224–36; cf. van Nes, "Problem."

33. Mounce, *Pastoral Epistles*, civ–cix.

34. R. Van Neste, *Cohesion and Structure in the Pastoral Epistles* (JSNTSup 280; London: T&T Clark, 2004).

35. See E. R. Richards, *The Secretary in the Letters of Paul* (WUNT 2/42; Tübingen: Mohr-Siebeck, 1991).

36. Mounce, *Pastoral Epistles*, cxxix; and Towner, *Timothy and Titus*, 86–88.

Luke, the reputed author of Luke–Acts and possibly the traveling companion of Paul.[37] He is referred to in 2 Tim 4:11 as the only one left with Paul and could be considered one of Paul's most enduring companions. In support of this hypothesis are certain similarities in vocabulary between Luke–Acts and the Pastoral Epistles.

There are also some difficulties with this position, however, since the Pastorals actually share more words in common with the other Pauline letters than with the Lukan writings. Furthermore, if the Lukan hypothesis is to explain authorship of the Pastorals and Ephesians, one would expect them to have significant similarities. It is argued, however, that the Pastoral Epistles have important similarities to Paul's speech to the Ephesian elders (Acts 20:17–38),[38] a passage often thought to resemble the style of Ephesians, but the evidence does not clearly point to common authorship of the Pastorals and the letter to the Ephesians. One final factor to consider is that, in the other Pauline letters, it is explicit that Paul used an amanuensis, either by direct name or implication of a statement about his writing with his own hand. In each of the Pastoral Epistles, however, no such statement or implication exists.

D. Pauline Authenticity of the Pastoral Epistles

There is continued support among a small group of English-language scholars for the authenticity of the Pastoral Epistles.[39] There are, I believe, many good reasons for their holding to this position. I begin with the chronological question, before turning to the textual evidence.

---

37. See J. N. D. Kelly, *A Commentary on the Pastoral Epistles* (BNTC; London: A&C Black, 1963), 21–27, who describes a possible scribe; C. F. D. Moule, "The Problem of the Pastoral Epistles: A Reappraisal," *Bulletin of the John Rylands University Library* 47 (1965): 430–52, who argues that Luke composed the letters during Paul's lifetime; F. J. Badcock, *The Pauline Epistles and the Epistle to the Hebrews in Their Historical Setting* (London: SPCK, 1937), esp. 114–33, who argues for the possibility of Luke using Paul's notes after Paul's death, so that the letters are authentically Pauline (he also argues that 2 Timothy is composed of two letters); and S. G. Wilson, *Luke and the Pastoral Epistles* (London: SPCK, 1979), who argues for composition by the "Luke" who wrote Luke–Acts but was not a companion of Paul (he does not apparently know the work of Badcock).

38. See W. Lock, *A Critical and Exegetical Commentary on the Pastoral Epistles (I & II Timothy and Titus)* (ICC; Edinburgh: T&T Clark, 1924), xxiv–xxv.

39. These include, among some others, G. W. Knight III, *The Pastoral Epistles* (NIGTC; Grand Rapids: Eerdmans, 1992), 21–52; Mounce, *Pastoral Epistles*, xlvi–lxix; and Johnson, *First and Second Letters*, 91–99.

1. Chronology

If the Pastoral Epistles are authentic, then the letters must be located some-where within the Pauline chronology.[40] If they are inauthentic, as noted above, then the letters were written from anytime soon after Paul's death to well into the second century—without a clear means of determining when (or by whom or from where). The two Pauline solutions are worth weighing.

    a. *Paul's life after Acts 28:31.* The most common solution to the problem of au-thorship by those who hold to authenticity of the Pastoral Epistles suggests that the story of Paul's life does not end with the account found in Acts and that he composed the letters after his release from a first Roman im-prisonment.[41] Some reason for optimism for his release is found in both Acts and the Pauline letters themselves, as well as in extrabiblical writings (e.g., Eusebius, *Ecclesiastical History* 2.22.2-8; Muratorian Fragment, lines 38-39). Acts makes it clear throughout that the Roman authorities had no legitimate complaint against Christians, including Paul, and that the Jews were mainly responsible for the troubles, as recognized by such Roman officials as Gallio. In Phil 1:25-26; 2:14; and Phlm 22, Paul himself seems optimistic that his release is imminent. Philemon 22 also suggests that Paul will be traveling east from Rome (if he was imprisoned in Rome, as I suggest that he was) to Colossae. If Paul did eventually suffer mar-tyrdom under Nero, this could have occurred at the earliest in 64. If the chronology of Acts for Paul's missionary journeys is accurate and the Acts imprisonment occurred somewhere around 61-62, then two more years must be accounted for. Eusebius (*Ecclesiastical History* 2.22.2-8) speaks of two imprisonments of Paul, stating that, in the interim, he traveled to the various places recorded in the Pastoral Epistles. It is possible, of course, that Eusebius obtained this information from the Pastorals and created his own scenario, but it is at least as likely that, if he had known another scenario, he would have presented it. There is thus a reasonable basis for the hypothesis of two Roman imprisonments, with a span of approxi-mately two years for Paul to carry out the traveling and correspondence suggested by the Pastoral Epistles, especially 1 Timothy and Titus.

    b. *Paul's life before Acts 28:31.* Another scenario based upon Paul's life as found in Acts is suggested.[42] The personal references are fewer in 1 Tim-

---

40. See Porter, "Pauline Chronology," 67-87, for the various positions.
41. For a summary of this position, see Knight, *Pastoral Epistles*, 21-45.
42. See J. A. T. Robinson, *Redating the New Testament* (London: SCM Press, 1976),

othy, but on the basis of 1 Tim 1:3, which states that Timothy was urged to stay on at Ephesus when Paul was heading toward Macedonia, John A. T. Robinson, Luke Timothy Johnson, and Bo Reicke posit that 1 Timothy was written on the third missionary journey, perhaps from Corinth after Paul had left Ephesus and traveled through Macedonia into Achaia. Jakob van Bruggen, however, argues that during Paul's stay in Ephesus recorded in Acts 19:9 (which is to be divided into two periods, separated by a period of travel), while he was away from Ephesus for a period, he wrote to Timothy. Van Bruggen also believes that Paul wrote the letter to Titus during this same period. On the basis that Titus had left Corinth (he is not mentioned in the greetings of Rom 16) and had been sent off to Crete to deal with the church there (Titus 1:5), Robinson and Reicke suggest that Titus was written after Paul left Ephesus and traveled to Macedonia and Achaia (Acts 20:1–3), after he had written Romans but before going through Macedonia on his way to Jerusalem. The similarities in the names mentioned in 2 Timothy and Colossians and Philemon, together with the sense of desperation, compel Robinson and Reicke to argue that 2 Timothy was written during Paul's imprisonment in Caesarea, where his future was still in doubt, after an assassination attempt against him in Jerusalem. Van Bruggen and Johnson claim that 2 Timothy, along with the other Prison Epistles (which were written earlier), was written during Paul's first and only Roman imprisonment. As mentioned in chapter 2 §2, most scholars do not accept these types of reconstructions, but it is unwise, and probably unfair, to be too dogmatic on either view of the chronology of the Pauline letters, since this solution does provide a plausible account of how Paul's letters can be integrated into the Acts chronology.

2. Internal Evidence

The following gives a brief summary of the evidence often marshaled in discussion of the authorship of the Pastoral Epistles. There are some inherent dangers in this approach—that is, discussing all three of the letters together—since it runs the risk of blurring their distinctives.[43] Still, if they are pseudonymous,

---

esp. 67–85; J. van Bruggen, *Die geschichtliche Einordnung der Pastoralbriefe* (Wuppertal: Brockhaus, 1981); Johnson, *First and Second Letters*, 65–68, 135–37, 319–20; and B. Reicke, *Re-examining Paul's Letters: The History of the Pauline Correspondence* (ed. D. P. Moessner and I. Reicke; Harrisburg, PA: Trinity, 2001). See also M. Prior, *Paul the Letter-Writer and the Second Letter to Timothy* (JSNTSup 23; Sheffield: JSOT Press, 1989).

43. J. L. Sumney, "Studying Paul's Opponents: Advances and Challenges," in *Paul and His Opponents* (ed. S. E. Porter; PAST 2; Leiden: Brill, 2005), 7–58, esp. 39–44, notes that most

they were probably written by the same person over a short amount of time,[44] and the similarities seem to be close enough to warrant viewing them together at least in this discussion.

a. Opponents

Two kinds of evidence are often marshaled regarding the opponents in these letters: Jewish elements and gnostic or protognostic elements. The Jewish elements include the claim by the opponents to be teachers of the law (1 Tim 1:7), disputes over the law (Titus 3:9), and the reference to those of the circumcision (1:10). The opponents were concerned with various fables and genealogies (1 Tim 1:4; Titus 1:14; 3:9), perhaps connected to Genesis (1 Tim 2:13-14), and were ascetics (1 Tim 2:15?; 4:3; 5:23), but they were not Judaizers, at least of the kind that Paul had to combat earlier in his ministry. The gnostic or protognostic elements of this group are indicated by some of the same evidence of Jewish elements: attention to fables and genealogies (1 Tim 1:4; Titus 1:14; 3:9), concern for knowledge (1 Tim 6:20), and a view of the world as evil (1 Tim 4:4). On the contrary, Paul puts forward a view of God as "one" (2:5), the creator (4:3-4), and the savior (1:1; 2:3; Titus 1:3; 2:10; 3:4). The only mediator between God and the world is Christ (1 Tim 2:5). The letters dispute that the readers have already experienced the resurrection (2 Tim 2:17-18), as they seem to have been promoting.

When could such a mix of these two kinds of elements have arisen in the early church? Two major solutions are usually put forth. One is that the opponents were second-century gnostics who believed in access to the heavenly realm through emanations and ascetic practice.[45] The major problem with this position is that our knowledge of Gnosticism is incomplete. It is now commonly recognized that fully developed Gnosticism did not emerge until the second century at the earliest, even though many of the elements of Gnosticism have their roots in Hellenistic and even classical philosophy and in Jewish apocalyptic thought. This makes it difficult to establish a clear beginning point for gnostic influence, as distinct from protognostic influence. A further difficulty is that, from what we do know, the emanations were never called genealogies, a link that some have thought necessary in order to find this

---

interpreters lump the Pastorals together for identifying the opponents. But some note that even though the author may be the same for all three, their respective situational contexts may be different and may warrant identifying different opponents; see, e.g., Kelly, *Pastoral Epistles*, 10-11.

44. Collins, *I & II Timothy and Titus*, 9.

45. See, e.g., Kümmel, *Introduction*, 378-79.

important gnostic doctrine in the Pastorals. One would have fully expected a more sharply defined criticism of such a movement, were it really behind these letters. Besides, this position does not explain the Jewish elements apparently present.

A second proposal—perhaps as likely as any other—is that the author has sensed in several of these churches a movement with a set of beliefs very similar to those opposed at Colossae.[46] Perhaps it represents a syncretistic form of Judaism with some ascetic and legalistic elements peculiar to its beliefs. In conjunction with this, there may have been problems of church organization—posited by some as reflecting early catholicism—or concerning widows, including the question of egalitarianism (equal status) for various groups of women.[47] This movement does not constitute the kind or degree of threat that some other sets of opponents would, so the author responds in more general terms, reaffirming essential belief regarding God and Christ—comments that could have been directed to any belief system that was highly syncretistic.

b. Theology

There is no denying that many elements of the theology of the Pastorals are consonant with the theology found in the main Pauline letters.[48] These include the affirmations that God's mercy was revealed in Jesus Christ (1 Tim 1:12–17; Titus 3:3–7) and that salvation depends upon God's grace (2 Tim 1:9; Titus 3:5) through faith in Christ (1 Tim 1:16), who is the redeemer, ransomer, and justifier for sinners (1 Tim 2:5–6; Titus 3:7). Eternal life is the goal of the Christian life, but there is a sense in which something of the joy of that existence is experienced now (1 Tim 6:12; cf. 2 Tim 1:1; Titus 1:2; 3:7). Besides the more formally theological elements, a number of moral issues are also addressed, such as "second" marriages (1 Tim 3:2, 12; 5:9), slaves (6:1), and the state (2:1–4).

In addition to these elements of commonality, however, a number of elements strike many, if not most, scholars as representing differences from established Pauline theology. First, several major concepts are not found in the

---

46. Knight, *Pastoral Epistles*, 12.

47. See C. K. Barrett, "Pauline Controversies in the Post-Pauline Period," *NTS* 20 (1973–74): 229–45; E. Käsemann, "Paul and Early Catholicism," in *New Testament Questions of Today* (trans. W. F. Bunge; Philadelphia: Fortress, 1969), 236–51; and H. Koester, *Introduction to the New Testament* (2 vols.; Philadelphia: Fortress, 1982), 2.300–305. Cf. B. Holmberg, *Paul and Power: The Structure of Authority in the Primitive Church as Reflected in the Pauline Epistles* (Philadelphia: Fortress, 1978).

48. See P. H. Towner, *The Goal of Our Instruction: The Structure of Theology and Ethics in the Pastoral Epistles* (JSNTSup 34; Sheffield: JSOT Press, 1989), for a thorough discussion.

Pastoral Epistles. For example, it is often said that the notion of faith as a "justifying principle" is missing in the Pastorals, and that instead faith has taken on the idea of a body of belief, that is, "orthodoxy" (1 Tim 3:9; 4:1; Titus 1:13; 2 Tim 4:7). Faith as the justifying principle is, however, represented in 1 Tim 1:4, 16 and Titus 3:8. The kind of semantic expansion found in the Pastorals is perfectly legitimate to find within one author, especially one who wrote over a number of years. Also, Jesus as "Son" is not found in the Pastorals. This is true, but it is likewise not found in Philippians and Philemon and only once in 2 Corinthians; so perhaps this is not a legitimate criterion.

Second, some scholars state that certain terms are used radically differently in the Pastorals than in the other Pauline letters. An example of this is the concept of love, which is said not to be as key a virtue in the Pastorals as it is, for instance, in Rom 5:5, which speaks of the love of God being poured out in our hearts. But the importance of love, for Paul, as a cardinal virtue in motivating God's action is perhaps not as central and in need of repetition as some argue. In addition, in 1 Tim 1:5, the author says at the outset of the letter that love from a pure heart is the goal of their instruction, an idea that is not totally foreign to the authentic Paul. Others argue that "in Christ" is synonymous with what it means to be a Christian in the Pastorals, not with the mystical union of believers to Christ as in the authentic Pauline letters. But the sense of mystical union is overdrawn in discussing "in Christ" language in Paul (see chapter 4 §2B), and besides, there is the use of similar language in the Pastorals, for example in 2 Tim 1:13, which says that faith and love are "in Christ Jesus."

A third supposed theological difference concerns the way doctrine and orthodoxy themselves are viewed in the Pastoral Epistles. According to some scholars, what distinguishes the Pastorals is the treatment of Christian doctrine as something entrusted to believers (1 Tim 6:20) that is to be handed on (2 Tim 1:13–14; 2:2; 3:14); that is, it takes on the status of tradition, consistent with a later date of writing. The only problem with such an analysis (and it is not to be denied that there is this sense of Christian doctrine as something to be handed on to subsequent believers) is that a similar idea is found in the other Pauline letters, such as 1 Cor 15:1–3, where Paul says that he has passed on to the Corinthians what he himself first received. Not only are the concepts traditional; so is the means of formulation: Paul cites what is perhaps early church tradition already formulated in a memorable creedal statement (15:3–8).

c. Language and Style

It is argued that a number of words and phrases, many of them prominent, are not found in the other Pauline letters but are found in the Pastorals. It is true that a number of crucial terms appear to be unique to the Pastorals. Examples include words often translated "to be healthy" or "sound" (ὑγιαίνω; 1 Tim 1:10; 6:3; 2 Tim 1:13; 4:3; Titus 1:9, 13; 2:1, 2), "self-controlled" (ἐγκρατής; Titus 1:8), and "piousness" or "godliness" (εὐσέβεια; 2 Tim 3:5; Titus 1:1).[49]

As mentioned in chapter 6 §3, the questions that this evidence raises are these: How different must the results of a stylistic and lexicographical analysis be before serious doubt is thrown on the idea of two works sharing a common author? And how divergent must such results be before it becomes implausible to entertain works as authentically Pauline?[50] At the end of the day, the results are mixed for the Pastoral Epistles. Romans has the same percentage of unique words as do 2 Timothy and Titus, yet it is hardly doubted that Romans is Pauline.[51] In light of the small corpus available and the uncertainty of the results of such tests, it is perhaps better not to rely upon them as the deciding factor, especially when other explanations are available for the deviance, such as the occasion and audience (that is, whether the letters are personal or to churches), the role of an amanuensis, or the possibility of a trusted compatriot as author (such as Luke).

A further consideration regarding statistical analysis is whether the proper framework for analysis is being used. In a sophisticated study that promises to open up new avenues of discussion of the question of pseudepigraphal authorship, Andrew Pitts utilizes register theory from systemic functional linguistics to examine the question of pseudonymy in the Pauline letters.[52] He creates what he calls a register profile of Paul's letters, which includes examination of register variation, semantic clustering, style and vocabulary, and grammar. This is an attempt to get beyond the simple counting of individual features (such as particular words) and take into account contextual variation. The result is that he finds that variation in the context—which he defines using recent work in sociolinguistics that analyzes contextual variation for individual authors—can account for register variation. This suggests that the range of difference within the Pauline corpus, including the Pastoral Epistles, can, on the basis of comparative studies, be accounted for within the range of variation within a single author.

---

49. Cf. the analysis of language and style in J. D. Quinn and W. C. Wacker, *The First and Second Letters to Timothy: A New Translation with Notes and Commentary* (Eerdmans Critical Commentary; Grand Rapids: Eerdmans, 2000), 4–6.

50. The example of Hebrews is not germane here, since the book is formally anonymous and there is a long history of discussion of authorship in the early church regarding it, discussion not to be found regarding the Pastoral Epistles.

51. See Knight, *Pastoral Epistles*, 40–45; cf. Guthrie, *Pastoral Epistles*, 224–40.

52. Pitts, "Style and Pseudonymity," esp. 130–52.

3. Pauline Authorship

The authorship issue of the Pastoral Epistles is no doubt a complex one, and it is often either ignored or a source of division among various critical scholarly groups. In this final major section, I wish to discuss the issues in light of the considerations above.

As with Colossians and Ephesians, there are only two real conclusions regarding authorship of the Pastoral Epistles: pseudonymous or authentic Pauline authorship. The pseudonymous explanation must answer a number of questions, including the following: (1) Why are there three letters and not one or two? The point here is that similarities among the three letters indicate common authorship at probably roughly the same time, and the question is why three letters would have been necessary to accomplish what one well-constructed letter could do. It is unlikely that there were several pseudepigraphers, one following another, at various times and in various locales. (2) Why are there so many personal details, especially in 2 Timothy? If the personal details are included to try to convince the reader of Pauline authorship, is there not the issue of deception to face? That is, was the early church deceived into believing that these letters were by Paul, and was the pseudepigrapher inconspicuously trying to convince readers that the letter was actually written by Paul when it was not? This also raises the question whether 1 Timothy, with its personal style and features, should be seen as plausibly Pauline.[53] The answer to this last question may well be affirmative, at least in many scholars' minds.

If the author of the Pastoral Epistles was Paul, several difficulties are resolved. First, the opponents are consistent with those found in other Pauline letters, such as Colossians, so there is no need to speculate on a hypothetical scenario sometime in the second century or even later. Authentic Pauline authorship allows the Pastorals to be read as they appear, that is, not as fiction but as real correspondence. It is difficult to account for the long personal sections unless they reveal a genuine set of circumstances; otherwise one has great difficulty accounting for the references to Hymenaeus and Alexander in 1 Tim 1:20. If the pre–Acts 28:31 suggestion is not accepted about integrating the Pastoral Epistles into the Acts chronology (most do not accept it, despite its tantalizing merits), then one must date Paul's release from Roman impris-

---

53. James Aageson concludes in the opposite direction, that 2 Timothy, because of affinities with Philippians, might be authentically Pauline, while 1 Timothy and Titus are not, according to a trajectory that he develops; *Paul, the Pastoral Epistles, and the Early Church* (Library of Pauline Studies; Peabody, MA: Hendrickson, 2008), 86–89.

onment sometime around 62. First Timothy would have been written from Macedonia to Ephesus, understandable in light of the church at Philippi and its support of Paul (1 Tim 1:3), although it is possible that Paul went first to Spain and then to Macedonia. In any event, he could have then gone to Crete (his reference in Titus 1:5 does not require his having gone there) after spending the winter in Nicopolis (Titus 3:12), but this is not known for sure. Paul was then arrested and taken to Rome, or arrested in Rome, probably after going to Troas (2 Tim 4:13), Miletus (4:20), and Corinth, and imprisoned a second time in Rome, where he died under Nero's persecution, beginning in 64/65.

5. Outlines of the Pastoral Epistles

1 Timothy
  A. Opening (1:1–2)
   1. Sender (1:1)
   2. Addressee (1:2a)
   3. Greeting (1:2b)
  (B. Thanksgiving—none)
  C. Body: behaving as a leader in God's church (1:3–4:16)
   1. Formal opening: refuting the false teachers (1:3–11)
   2. Paul's faithfulness to his calling (1:12–20)
   3. Instructions for orderly behavior and church governance (2:1–3:16)
   4. Timothy's role in the church (4:1–16)
  D. Paraenesis (5:1–6:19)
   1. Household duties (5:1–6:2)
   2. The return to false doctrine and godliness (6:3–10)
   3. Pursue what is righteous, etc. (6:11–19)
  E. Closing (6:20–21)
   1. Closing words to Timothy (6:20–21a)
   2. Grace benediction (6:21b)

2 Timothy
  A. Opening (1:1–2)
   1. Sender (1:1)
   2. Addressee (1:2a)
   3. Greeting (1:2b)
  B. Thanksgiving (1:3–5)
  C. Body: serving Christ (1:6–4:18)
   1. Formal opening: God gives a spirit of power (1:6–14)

2. Some have not been faithful (1:15–18)
3. Endurance is for long-term service (2:1–13)
4. False teaching is to be resisted (2:14–26)
5. Eschatological climax (3:1–9)
6. Apostolic charge (3:10–4:18)
(D. Paraenesis—none)
E. Closing (4:19–22)
   1. Greetings (4:19–21)
   2. Benediction (4:22)

Titus
A. Opening (1:1–4)
   1. Sender (1:1–3)
   2. Addressee (1:4a)
   3. Greeting (1:4b)
(B. Thanksgiving—none)
C. Body: leading the church (1:5–16)
   1. Qualifications for elders (1:5–9)
   2. Response to false teachers (1:10–16)
D. Paraenesis (2:1–3:14)
   1. Teaching sound doctrine (2:1–15)
   2. Living under rulers, authorities, and others (3:1–7)
   3. Avoiding divisiveness (3:8–11)
   4. Personal comments (3:12–14)
E. Closing (3:15)
   1. Greetings (3:15a)
   2. Grace benediction (3:15b)

6. Content of the Pastoral Epistles

First Timothy

Opening (1 Tim 1:1–2)

Paul opens the letter by identifying himself as an apostle of Jesus Christ by the command of God and Christ Jesus. He writes to Timothy, whom he calls his "true child in the faith" (New American Standard Bible). The opening ends with a variation of Paul's standard opening, "grace, mercy, and peace from God the Father and Christ Jesus our Lord."

Body: Formal Opening: Refuting the False Teachers (1 Tim 1:3–11)

Paul does not include a thanksgiving section in this letter, which may denote some type of urgency, as seen in the first comments after the opening or possibly a level of familiarity with his recipient. He begins instead by urging Timothy to remain at Ephesus, so that he can instruct certain people not to teach any different doctrine, or any myths or endless genealogies, which have nothing to do with being stewards of their faith. The main goal of their teaching is love from a pure heart, a good conscience, and a sincere faith. Paul states that certain people have strayed from these basic fundamentals by speculating about such empty things. He states that the law is good, but for those who practice all sorts of disobedient and ungodly acts.

Body: Paul's Faithfulness to His Calling (1 Tim 1:12–20)

Paul gives thanks to God for saving a sinner such as he, as he used to persecute the church. He has been judged faithful in spite of his former life, receiving mercy from God. In fact, the maxim that Jesus Christ came to save sinners is true, and Paul identifies himself as the foremost sinner. But he was shown mercy so that Jesus Christ would show his perfect patience as an example for those who believe in him. Prompted by the subject matter, Paul bursts into a brief doxology: to the king of ages, immortal, invisible, the only God, be honor and glory forever and ever!

Paul continues his warning to Timothy and states that he entrusts him to continue fighting the good fight, as previous prophecies have confirmed about him. Unfortunately, some have deserted their faith by ignoring their conscience, such as Hymenaeus and Alexander; Paul has handed them over to Satan so that they would learn not to blaspheme.

Body: Instructions for Orderly Behavior and Church Governance (1 Tim 2:1–3:16)

First of all, Paul instructs Timothy that prayer should be made for all people, including kings and those in similar positions, that they would lead peaceful and ordered lives and be godly and dignified in all respects. This type of prayer is good, as God wants all to be saved and to come to a knowledge of the truth, based upon there being one God, and one mediator, Jesus Christ, who gave himself as a ransom for all.

In view of this, Paul states that men should pray in every place with their hands raised and women should wear respectable clothing that reflects modesty and godliness. A woman is to learn in an orderly and appropriate way, not teaching or having undue authority over a man but learning with propriety. Paul refers to the Genesis account of Adam and Eve to make his point regarding propriety and states that she will be saved through engaging in the normal activities of life, such as sexual relations with her husband (which is the referent of childbearing), in faith, love, and holiness (cf. 1 Tim 4:3).[54]

Paul moves to the topic of offices in the church, beginning with the office of overseer/bishop. Those who desire this office desire a noble task, and they must exhibit such characteristics as being above reproach, faithful to their spouse, sober-minded, respectable, hospitable, able to teach, not a drunkard, not violent but gentle, not argumentative, and not a lover of money, but good managers of their own household. They must not be recent converts, in case of pride, and must have a good reputation in the community.

Likewise, the office of deacon requires that a person be dignified, not duplicitous, not addicted to much alcohol, and not greedy. They must have a clean conscience in their faith and should be tested first. Those who are women should also exercise similar qualities, and all deacons should be faithful to their own spouse, managing their own households well.

Paul writes of the purpose of this letter that, although he plans on visiting Timothy soon, in case his plan gets delayed, Paul wants to instruct Timothy on proper conduct within the Christian community. Paul ends this section with a hymnic passage addressed to Christ, who was manifest in flesh, justified in spirit, seen by angels, preached among nations, believed in the world, and raised in glory.

Body: Timothy's Role in the Church (1 Tim 4:1–16)

Paul warns Timothy of some who will depart from the faith, just as the Spirit says will happen in the later times, by devoting themselves to deceitful spirits and the teachings of demons. These teachings include forbidding marriage and promoting abstinence from foods. God created all things, and they are to partake in these things with thanksgiving to God.

Timothy is to be a good servant of Christ by dismissing irreverent, silly myths; instead he is to train himself for godliness. Just as physical training is of

54. Cf. S. E. Porter, "What Does It Mean to Be 'Saved by Childbirth' (1 Timothy 2.15)?" *JSNT* 49 (1993): 87–102; and "Reframing Social Justice in the Pauline Letters," in *The Bible and Social Justice: Old Testament and New Testament Foundations for the Church's Urgent Call* (ed. C. L. Westfall and B. R. Dyer; McMaster New Testament Studies; Eugene, OR: Wipf & Stock, 2015), 125–51.

some value, spiritual training has much more, since it holds promise for this life and also for the life to come. They toil and strive for the hope that is in Christ Jesus. Timothy is not to allow his youth to be a stumbling block, but he is to set an example in speech, conduct, love, faith, and purity. He is to devote himself to the public reading of Scripture, not neglecting his gift but persisting in teaching.

Paraenesis: Household Duties (1 Tim 5:1–6:2)

Paul continues to instruct Timothy on church conduct in this section. He states that older men should not be rebuked but encouraged like fathers, younger men like brothers, older women like mothers, and younger women like sisters. Regarding widows, those who have no family should be honored, but those who have family should receive care from them. Those who do not provide for their own family members have gone so far as to deny their faith and are worse than an unbeliever. Nevertheless, a widow can be enrolled if she is at least sixty years old (this is telling of a woman's financial need in ancient times) and if she has been a faithful spouse with a good reputation. They are not to enroll younger widows, who may fall away from Christ and abandon their faith. Paul would rather have younger widows remarry, bear children, and manage their own households.

Regarding elders, Paul says that those who rule well should be considered for "double honor," especially those involved in preaching and teaching. He cites Deut 25:4 in making his case, using the metaphor of oxen. Elders should not be accused, except if two or three witnesses testify. Timothy is not to let sin persist, nor be hasty in laying on hands (commissioning or ordaining someone to ministry). As a personal aside, Paul encourages Timothy to drink a little wine to help with his stomach problems.

Those who are slaves are to be an example by honoring their masters. Those with masters who are fellow believers are not to do their work any less well and take advantage of their masters, but to work even harder because they are brothers.

Paraenesis: The Return to False Doctrine and Godliness (1 Tim 6:3–10)

Paul returns to the subject of false doctrine and tells Timothy that those who do not agree with the words of Jesus Christ are puffed up with conceit and understand nothing. These people have unhealthy cravings for controversy and arguments about words, which produces all sorts of negative effects, like envy, dissension, slander, and suspicion. They think that godliness is a means for gain, which is true if by gain one refers to godliness with contentment. But those who desire to obtain wealth fall into a temptation and trap, which results in ruin and destruction for many people. Paul states that the love of money is the root of all types of evil, and it is because of this greed that some have left the faith.

Paraenesis: Pursue What Is Righteous, etc. (1 Tim 6:11–19)

Paul addresses Timothy as a man of God and exhorts him to flee these evil things; instead, he is to pursue righteousness, godliness, faith, love, perseverance, and gentleness. He is to fight the good fight of the faith and to take hold of the eternal life about which he preaches. Paul states that the rich should be instructed not to be proud or to hope in their riches, but to hope in God, who provides everything they need. They are to be rich in good works, to be generous, and to store up treasures in this way.

Closing (1 Tim 6:20–21)

Paul's final words of this letter include the dictum to Timothy to guard the deposit entrusted to him and, again, to avoid irreverent babble, since it causes some to depart from the faith. The letter ends with a short "grace be with you [plural]."

Second Timothy

Opening (2 Tim 1:1–2)

Paul's second letter to Timothy begins by identifying himself as an apostle of Christ Jesus by the will of God according to the promise in Christ. He writes to Timothy, whom he calls his beloved child. The salutation is similar to 1 Timothy.

Thanksgiving (2 Tim 1:3–5)

Paul gives thanks for Timothy as he constantly thinks of him in his prayers. As he remembers the heartache that Timothy went through, he longs to see him so that he would be filled with joy. He knows of his sincere faith, a faith that he inherited from his grandmother Lois and his mother Eunice. He is confident that the same faith lives on in Timothy.

Body: Formal Opening: God Gives a Spirit of Power (2 Tim 1:6–14)

Because of this, he encourages Timothy that God has given him a spirit, not of fear, but of power, love, and self-control. Because of this power, Timothy should not be ashamed of the testimony about the Lord nor ashamed of Paul the prisoner. He is instead to share in suffering for the gospel, relying on the power of God, because God saved and called them to this holy calling. Paul suffers because Christ Jesus abolished death and brought life and immortality through the gospel. He looks forward to the day and will guard what has been entrusted to him; Timothy is to do likewise.

Body: Some Have Not Been Faithful (2 Tim 1:15–18)

Timothy knows this already, but Paul tells him that those in Asia turned away from him, including Phygelus and Hermogenes. On a brighter note, Onesiphorus's household often refreshed Paul, and he even went out looking for Paul when he visited Rome. Timothy knows the type of service Onesiphorus gave when he was in Ephesus.

Body: Endurance Is for Long-term Service (2 Tim 2:1–13)

Paul commands Timothy to be strengthened by God's grace and to entrust the gospel to other faithful people who can teach. Using three consecutive metaphors, Paul tells Timothy to be a good soldier, athlete, and farmer for Christ. The point of the gospel is Jesus Christ, and Paul continues to endure because of this gospel and so that the elect may obtain the salvation that is in Christ.

Body: False teaching Is to Be Resisted (2 Tim 2:14–26)

As he wrote in his first letter, Paul tells Timothy to teach his people not to argue about mere words, which only ruins people. He is to present himself to God as an approved worker, not ashamed, rightly handling the word of truth. He is to avoid irreverent babble, which leads to ungodliness as it did with Hymenaeus and Philetus. They have swerved from the truth and have believed that the resurrection already happened, affecting others along with them. Using a metaphor of a house containing honorable and dishonorable items, Paul tells Timothy to cleanse his house of dishonorable things (people) so that he would be ready to serve the master of that house.

Timothy is to flee youthful passions and instead to pursue righteousness, faith, love, and peace. He is not to be involved in foolish controversies that lead to arguments, but to be kind with everyone, teaching with patience and correcting with gentleness. He hopes that God will grant repentance to these dissenters.

Body: Eschatological Climax (2 Tim 3:1–9)

Paul warns Timothy of the difficulty of the last days. People will be lovers of self, lovers of money, proud, arrogant, abusive, disobedient, ungrateful, unholy, and all kinds of ungodly characteristics, having the appearance of godliness without any of its power. Timothy is simply to avoid such people. They will do such things like creep into households and take advantage of vulnerable women. Just as Jannes and Jambres opposed Moses, he says, they also oppose God in the same manner. But Paul assures him that they will not get very far in their rebellion.

Body: Apostolic Charge (2 Tim 3:10–4:18)

In contrast with these people Paul just described, Timothy is different; he followed the example of Paul in his teaching, life-purpose, faith, patience, love, and perseverance. He followed the persecutions that happened to him in Antioch, Iconium, and Lystra, and notes that all who aspire to live a godly life in Christ Jesus will in fact be persecuted. Evil people will continue to do what they do, but Timothy is to continue in what he has learned. Ever since he was young, he has been acquainted with the sacred writings, which make him wise for salvation, as all Scripture is God-breathed and effective for teaching, rebuking, correcting, and training in righteousness, in order to equip for every good work.

Paul charges Timothy to preach the word, in season and out of season. The time will come when people want only to hear things that please them, but he is to be sober-minded, endure suffering, and fulfill his ministry. Paul looks at his own ministry and sees that his time is coming to an end, and he can say that he has fought the good fight and has finished the race. He leaves himself as an example for Timothy to follow.

In reflecting on the time he has left, Paul wants Timothy to visit him soon. Many have left him. Demas fell in love with the world and deserted Paul. Crescens went to Galatia. Titus went to Dalmatia. Only Luke is with him. He tells Timothy also to bring Mark with him, because of his usefulness. He sent Tychicus to Ephesus. Paul remembers that he left his cloak with Carpus in Troas, and asks Timothy to bring it with him, as well as the books and of course the parchments. Paul recalls the misdeeds of Alexander the coppersmith against Paul and hopes God will exact justice in that situation. In fact, Timothy should be careful of him as well, because he opposed their message. Paul recalls that, at his first or previous defense, no one came to his aid, but he does not hold that against any of them because the Lord was with him. He anticipates that the Lord will rescue him from all evil and bring him into his heavenly kingdom.

Closing (2 Tim 4:19–22)

Paul's closing words include greetings to Prisca (Priscilla) and Aquila and to the household of Onesiphorus. He lets Timothy know the status of Erastus, who remained at Corinth, and Trophimus, who was left ill at Miletus. He requests again for Timothy to visit him before winter. Eubulus, Pudens, Linus, and Claudia, along with all the other believers, send greetings to Timothy.

Titus

Opening (Titus 1:1–4)

Paul identifies himself in this letter as a servant of God and an apostle of Jesus Christ, with an extended statement about the eternal life that has been promised by God and manifested through Paul's preaching ministry. He writes to Titus, his "true child in the common faith." He concludes his opening with the standard words "grace and peace from God the Father and Christ Jesus our Savior."

Body: Leading the Church (Titus 1:5–16)

Paul tells Titus that he left him in Crete so that he would organize what was going on there and appoint elders in each town. He told him what sort of elders should be appointed: those who are above reproach, are faithful to their spouse, have believing children, and are not accused of debauchery or insubordination. Other characteristics that an overseer should have include not being arrogant, quick-tempered, a drunkard, violent, or greedy, but being one who is hospitable, a lover of good, self-controlled, upright, holy, and disciplined. They should be those who have a firm faith, so they can teach others and rebuke those who contradict sound doctrine.

This is important because many are insubordinate, especially those of the circumcision party. They, in fact, are upsetting whole families and should be stopped. They should be rebuked sharply, so that they would be sound in the faith and not devote themselves to false teachings.

Paraenesis: Teaching Sound Doctrine (Titus 2:1–15)

Titus, on the other hand, is to teach in line with sound doctrine. Older men are to be sober-minded, dignified, self-controlled, and sound in faith, love, and perseverance. Older women are to exhibit similar behavior and not to slander or be addicted to alcohol. They are to teach the younger women to be godly as well. Likewise, younger men are to be taught to be self-controlled. In all his teaching, he is to lead by example, showing them a model of good works. Paul adds instructions for slaves to be submissive to their masters in their work.

The grace of God has appeared, Paul declares, which brings salvation to all people, training them to denounce ungodliness and to live upright lives and to anticipate the appearing of Jesus Christ. Titus is to exhort and rebuke with all authority on these matters, letting no one disregard him.

Paraenesis: Living under Rulers, Authorities, and Others (Titus 3:1–7)

Titus is to remind the Cretans to be submissive toward rulers and other authorities, to be obedient and ready for every good work, to speak evil of no one, to avoid quarrels, to be gentle, and to be courteous toward everyone. They were once disobedient and slaves to various passions, but when the goodness and kindness of God appeared, they were saved. This was not because of anything they did or deserved but by his own mercy and the washing and regeneration of the Holy Spirit. They were justified by his grace, becoming heirs according to the hope of eternal life.

Paraenesis: Avoiding Divisiveness (Titus 3:8–11)

Paul instructs Titus to focus on these things, so that believers in God would devote themselves to good works, which are profitable. Foolish controversies about the law, on the other hand, are not profitable and in fact are worthless. Those who cause dissension are to get two warnings, and then they are to be tolerated no longer.

Paraenesis: Personal Comments (Titus 3:12–14)

Paul informs Titus that he is sending Artemas or Tychicus to him, at which point he asks for him to meet him in Nicopolis, where he plans to spend the winter. He also requests that Titus quickly send Zenas the lawyer and Apollos, so that they have no lack of help. Finally, Titus is to instruct Christian people to devote themselves to good works so they can help in urgent cases.

Closing (Titus 3:15)

Paul closes with greetings from those with him (not naming any specific names), with a request to greet those with Titus in the faith. Paul ends with the wish, "grace be with you all."

Sources for Further Study

Commentaries

Collins, R. F. *I & II Timothy and Titus.* NTL. Louisville: Westminster John Knox, 2002.

Dibelius, M., and H. Conzelmann. *The Pastoral Epistles.* Hermeneia. Philadelphia: Fortress, 1972.

Fee, G. D. *1 and 2 Timothy, Titus.* New International Biblical Commentary. Peabody, MA: Hendrickson, 1988.

Guthrie, D. *The Pastoral Epistles.* Rev. ed. TNTC. Grand Rapids: Eerdmans, 1990.

Hanson, A. T. *The Pastoral Epistles.* NCB. Grand Rapids: Eerdmans, 1982.

Johnson, L. T. *The First and Second Letters to Timothy.* AB 35A. New York: Doubleday, 2001.

Kelly, J. N. D. *A Commentary on the Pastoral Epistles.* BNTC. Peabody, MA: Hendrickson, 1963.

Knight, G. W., III. *The Pastoral Epistles.* NIGTC. Grand Rapids: Eerdmans, 1992.

Lock, W. *A Critical and Exegetical Commentary on the Pastoral Epistles (1 and II Timothy and Titus).* ICC. Edinburgh: T&T Clark, 1924.

Marshall, I. H., with P. H. Towner. *A Critical and Exegetical Commentary on the Pastoral Epistles.* ICC. Edinburgh: T&T Clark, 1999.

Mounce, W. D. *Pastoral Epistles.* WBC 46. Dallas: Word, 2000.

Parry, R. St. *The Pastoral Epistles.* Cambridge: Cambridge University Press, 1920.

Quinn, J. D. *The Letter to Titus.* AB 35. New York: Doubleday, 1990.

Quinn, J. D., and W. C. Wacker. *The First and Second Letters to Timothy: A New Translation with Notes and Commentary.* Eerdmans Critical Commentary. Grand Rapids: Eerdmans, 2000.

Simpson, E. K. *The Pastoral Epistles.* London: Tyndale, 1954.

Towner, P. H. *The Letters to Timothy and Titus.* NICNT. Grand Rapids: Eerdmans, 2006.

Monographs and Books

Aageson, J. W. *Paul, the Pastoral Epistles, and the Early Church*. Library of Pauline Studies. Peabody, MA: Hendrickson, 2008.

Bruce, F. F. *The Pauline Circle*. Grand Rapids: Eerdmans, 1985.

Davies, M. *The Pastoral Epistles*. NTG. Sheffield: Sheffield Academic, 1996.

Donelson, L. R. *Pseudepigraphy and Ethical Argument in the Pastoral Epistles*. HUT 22. Tübingen: Mohr-Siebeck, 1986.

Harrison, P. N. *The Problem of the Pastoral Epistles*. Oxford: Oxford University Press, 1921.

Knight, G. W., III. *The Faithful Sayings in the Pastoral Letters*. Amsterdam: Kok, 1968. Reprinted Grand Rapids: Baker, 1979.

Miller, J. D. *The Pastoral Letters as Composite Documents*. SNTSMS 93. Cambridge: Cambridge University Press, 1997.

Porter, S. E., and G. P. Fewster, eds. *Paul and Pseudepigraphy*. PAST 8. Leiden: Brill, 2013.

Prior, M. *Paul the Letter-Writer and the Second Letter to Timothy*. JSNTSup 23. Sheffield: JSOT Press, 1989.

Towner, P. H. *The Goal of Our Instruction: The Structure of Theology and Ethics in the Pastoral Epistles*. JSNTSup 34. Sheffield: JSOT Press, 1989.

Van Neste, R. *Cohesion and Structure in the Pastoral Epistles*. JSNTSup 280. London: T&T Clark, 2004.

Wilson, S. G. *Luke and the Pastoral Epistles*. London: SPCK, 1979.

Conclusion

We have now reached the conclusion of this introduction to the life, thought, and letters of the apostle Paul. However, we are far from completing and exhausting a study of this significant figure, the contours of his variegated thought, and the thirteen letters within the New Testament canon that he wrote. As I have attempted to indicate throughout this volume and at various specific points, such study would not even exhaust many more volumes, most of them larger than this one. Nevertheless, this volume will have served its purpose adequately if it has offered to the reader a suitable introduction to Paul, with the hope and encouragement that readers now have foundational knowledge sufficient to provide the basis and trajectory of their own further thought—whether this thought takes up topics of their own interest or is encouraged by other factors.

As a means of concluding this volume, let me offer some summative statements that place the various topics within a larger overall context. This volume begins with a discussion of Paul the person. In doing so, I attempt to build a discussion of Paul's thought and letters upon the person of Paul himself—as difficult a task as that is. Because of the limited nature of the evidence, we can only speculate about a number of the physical features and some of the material realia that attend the apostle Paul. However, despite the lack of evidence, we are confident of a few facts about the man who still occupies a major place within Christian history. He was one of the earliest writers, if not the earliest writer, of any book in the New Testament; he had a missionary ministry to Gentiles (even though he himself was a Jew, educated under one of the leading teachers of the day); and he was one of the church's greatest theologians. Even though he was less than prepossessing in appearance (on the basis of our limited accounts), he received a better-than-average education, first in Tarsus and then in Jerusalem. He also benefited from being a Roman citizen, a fact noted in the book of Acts but not in his own letters. Even though he lived as a citizen within the Roman Empire, he took a moderate view toward its institutions, in which he realized that divine institutions replaced the Roman ones. Paul made his living as a craftsman within this world, enabling him to travel widely to proclaim his Christian message. He was born and reared as a faithful Jew, but was then dramatically converted—and "conversion" is probably the right word to describe what happened to Paul on the Damascus road as suggested in his letters and more graphically described in the book of Acts. This conversion transformed the trained Pharisee, who had probably at one time skeptically observed and even heard Jesus teach, into a force to be reckoned with within the early church and its evangelistic outreach. Even the brief description above (and more so in this entire volume), as is evident to those who have studied the life of Paul, draws upon the book of Acts as a reliable guide to understanding Paul. I believe that this is legitimate. In any case, this is the man Paul who forms the center of the exposition that this volume contains.

Once I establish the person of Paul, I examine other important elements of the Pauline tradition. These topics of necessity must be selective rather than exhaustive. The topics that are specifically treated in this volume comprise the remainder of the first part of the book. These topics are the chronology of Paul's mission and ministry; the background to Paul's thought; a summary of major themes found in Paul's letters; a discussion of the Pauline letter form; and, especially important for contemporary critical discussion, consideration of the role of pseudonymity in the formation of the Pauline canon. I begin with Pauline chronology in order to provide a convenient framework in which to place the remainder of the discussion of Paul, in particular the treatment of his individual letters. The chronology concentrates upon Paul's conversion, his three missionary journeys, and his trip to Rome and Roman imprisonment. I attempt to offer a plausible reconstruction of the ministry of Paul drawing upon the book of Acts and his letters. One of the features of this reconstruction that offers intriguing insights is the placement of some of the letters that traditionally either fall outside of the usual recognized Pauline canon (that is, beyond the usual seven letters) or revolve around the number of Paul's Roman imprisonments. There are a number of issues regarding placing such letters as the Pastoral Epistles within the Pauline chronology that raise intriguing questions. In conjunction with this chronological reconstruction is the question of Paul's imprisonments. We know that Paul was a prisoner on several occasions, although we are not entirely sure where those imprisonments occurred when he wrote some of his letters. I attempt to show that the Roman imprisonment theory probably best accounts for the evidence.

Within the constant fluctuations in New Testament scholarship regarding the attempt to understand and appreciate its Jewish and its Hellenistic background, and the interaction between the two, I offer a brief discussion of the formative influences on Paul's thought. A number of features of Paul and his writings can be traced directly to Greco-Roman influence, such as his use of the Greek language, his use of the ancient letter form, and some of his thought and philosophy. There are of course Jewish elements as well. These include the influence of the Jewish Scriptures, the appearance of Jewish thought-forms, and the role of the synagogue. Other influences could be discussed, but these constitute some of the most important as forming a backdrop for discussion of the individual letters. They also provide a useful cultural platform for discussion of Paul's thought. I refrain from labeling this discussion a Pauline theology, but instead approach it as a way of breaking down the major contours of Paul's ideas. I divide them into two. These include his fundamental beliefs and his developed beliefs. Paul has fundamental, even assumed, beliefs regarding God, Jesus Christ, the Holy Spirit, grace, and faith. Some of his developed beliefs concern such subjects as justification, the law and its relation to God's work in Christ, reconciliation, sanctification or holiness, salvation, the triumph of God, the gospel, the church, and Jesus's death and resurrection. I realize, as I admit in the chapter, that there are so many other topics that are worth discussing within Paul's thought—and perhaps here there is more that could be said than in any other of the sections of the book. I realize that the depth of Paul's thought has continued to challenge and excite the imaginations of scholars. This is no less true of this era in Pauline thought than it has been in earlier eras—in fact, there is much interesting discussion currently being undertaken in Pauline studies to develop further not only these ideas but some new ones that I may well need to return to in subsequent scholarly venues. Nevertheless, this chapter is designed to provide at least a basic ideational framework upon which to hang the major concepts to be found within Paul's thought as one turns to treatment of his individual letters.

The forms of these individual letters constitute the subject matter of a discussion in its own right. There was a well-established tradition of letter writing within the ancient world, and Paul was one of its most important practitioners. We have abundant evidence of the letter-writing conventions of the ancient world on the basis of numerous examples found in the documentary remains of ancient Hellenistic Egyptian sites. Ancient letters had both designated and defined functions and recognizable forms. Paul was not content simply to adopt the letter form of the Greco-Roman world but developed it in significant ways that enhanced the function of his letters. This occurred in relation to all of the parts of the ancient letter. He not only adapted the standard parts for his own purposes but also developed in new ways other parts of the letter into the Pauline letter form that we now recognize. When we examine the Pauline letters more closely, we also note that Paul was part of a missionary endeavor that involved more than simply himself. This is reflected in his letters, which raises questions regarding the role of an amanuensis in his writings. We know from specific references that Paul used an amanuensis, but the pertinent question is the level of involvement of these amanuenses or even his purported coauthors in the letter-writing process. In conjunction with discussion of the role of the amanuensis is that of pseudonymity. Pseudonymity has been one of the most important topics of recent discussion of Paul's letters. In some scholars' minds, these questions have already been solved, to the point that for them the consensus beyond need for debate is that Paul wrote only some of the letters attributed to him, usually a group of seven (Romans, 1 and 2 Corinthians, Galatians, Philippians, 1 Thessalonians, and Philemon). I, however, am not convinced by these claims for several reasons that I lay out in the chapter. In some ways, I have taken on the harder task of arguing for inclusion of all thirteen canonical letters as authentically Pauline. I recognize that this poses some critical problems, but I also believe that it solves a number of critical, theological, and canonical issues. As a result, I offer a reconstruction of the formation of the Pauline canon, in which I discuss the various views by which it is thought that the Pauline canon came together, and then argue—against the usual views—that Paul himself had a major role to play in the gathering of his own letter collection. I recognize that this is an adventuresome hypothesis, but I believe that it is one that solves many problems and offers a coherent account of why we have the Pauline letters that we do in the New Testament.

Having concluded discussion of these important yet in some ways secondary issues, I turn to the letters of Paul themselves. I treat the letters in roughly the order that I think they were originally written, while at the same time recognizing some natural groupings (e.g., 1 and 2 Thessalonians, 1 and 2 Corinthians, the Prison Epistles, and the Pastoral Epistles). As a result, I treat Galatians first (rather than treating it along with Romans, due to some other theories of when Galatians was written and how it theologically relates to Romans); then 1 and 2 Thessalonians (probably written in that order); 1 and 2 Corinthians (again, probably in that order, even if they are not the only letters Paul wrote to Corinth); the great letter to the Romans; then the Prison Epistles in the order of Philippians, Colossians, Philemon, and Ephesians; and finally the Pastoral Epistles as a whole. What I have attempted to do is to find a balance among the critical issues and the content of each of the books. As a result, for each book, I provide a discussion of the major critical issues such as authorship, date, occasion and purpose, relation to other letters, and the like; an outline of the letter following an epistolary format; and then a summary of the content of the letter following that outline. Those who have had the occasion to use major commentaries on the Pauline letters or to read major critical New Testament introductions will know that there are many other issues to discuss regarding each of these letters. However, I have tried to provide what I consider to be the major pressing issues that have an impact on the role and placement of the letters within the Pauline canon and/or the content and importance of the teaching of the letters.

The completion of a book of this nature must recognizably leave the author and the readers with mixed thoughts and feelings. Both the author and the readers are aware at every turn that the person, thought, and individual letters of the apostle Paul merit much more comment than a single introduction of this kind can provide. The abundance of continuing Pauline studies are testimony to this fact, and an encouragement to readers to undertake further exploration of topics of interest in other works more specialized and focused upon some of these topics. However, I am optimistic that this volume has provided a sufficient amount of material, with reference to pertinent and meaningful secondary sources, so as to reward the study not just of this volume but of the letters of Paul, with the accompanying desire that the reader will find in this introduction sufficient depth of thought and analysis as to provide a substantial introduction to a corpus of material that still demands the attention of serious readers. The apostle Paul, whether considering his life, his thought, or his letters, continues to offer the attentive reader more than sufficient intellectual and affective content to challenge a new generation of readers. If this volume has served a useful role in this endeavor, then its purpose will have been ably fulfilled.

Index of Modern Authors

INDEX OF MODERN AUTHORS

Index of Ancient Sources

Index of Ancient Sources

JOSEPHUS

Against Apion

2.8	123
2.18	12

Jewish Antiquities

12.147–53	355
13.172	14
14.228–40	19
15.11.5	123
18.13	14

Jewish War

2.308	19
5.2	123
7.132–33	82
7.148–57	82

PHILO

On Dreams

2.250	28

On the Embassy to Gaius

210	12
212	123

On the Life of Abraham

28	28

RABBINIC WRITINGS

Babylonian Talmud
Shabbat

30b	14

Mishnah
'Abot

2.2	24
3.16–17	117
3.19	14
4.14	14
5.21	12

Tosefta
Qiddushin

1.22	24

EARLY CHRISTIAN LITERATURE

Acts of Paul

6	64

Apostolic Constitutions

6.16	159

Barnabas

4.9	229
15.5	229
18.2	229

1 Clement

2	419
5.4	296
5.7	5, 302
7	419
29	419
32	419
32.2	292
33.1	292
34	419
35.4–6	292
36.2	292, 387
37	419
45	419
46.6	387
47.7	292
55	419
59.3	387
61.1	292
64	387

Clement of Alexandria
Stromata

1.1	360
5.3	229

Didache

4.10–11	387

Eusebius
Ecclesiastical History

2.14.6	297
2.22	61
2.22.1–8	44
2.22.2–8	424
6.12.1–6	158

Ignatius
To Polycarp

1.2	387
5.1	387

To the Ephesians

1.1	387
1.3	379
2	360
2.2	379
9	292
10.3	387
19.3	292

To the Magnesians

2	360, 418
3	418
4	418
6	418
6.2	292
8	418
9.1	292

To the Philadelphians

4	360

To the Smyrnaeans

1.1	387
1.2	360
12	360

To the Trallians

5.2	360
9.2	292

Irenaeus
Against Heresies

3.7.2	229
3.14.1	360
5.6.1	213
5.25.1	229

Made in the USA
Columbia, SC
16 January 2024

30553316R00290